ECSCW 2011: Proceedings of the 12th European
Conference on Computer Supported Cooperative
Work, 24-28 Sep   Denmark

T0180803

Susanne Bødker • Niels Olof Bouvin
Wayne Lutters • Volker Wulf • Luigina Ciolfi
Editors

ECSCW 2011: Proceedings of the 12th European Conference on Computer Supported Cooperative Work, 24-28 September 2011, Aarhus, Denmark

 Springer

Editors
Susanne Bødker
Aarhus University
Denmark
bodker@cs.au.dk

Niels Olof Bouvin
Aarhus University
Denmark
n.o.bouvin@cs.au.dk

Wayne Lutters
University of Maryland
U.S.A
lutters@umbc.edu

Volker Wulf
University of Siegen
Germany
volker.wulf@fit.fraunhofer.de

Luigina Ciolfi
University of Limerick
Ireland
luigina.ciolfi@ul.ie

ISBN 978-1-4471-6150-9   ISBN 978-0-85729-913-0 (eBook)
DOI 10.1007/978-0-85729-913-0
Springer London Dordrecht Heidelberg New York

British Library Cataloguing in Publication Data
A catalogue record for this book is available from the British Library

Cover design: Integra Software Services Pvt. Ltd.

Printed on acid-free paper

Springer is part of Springer Science+Business Media (www.springer.com)

Table of Contents

From the Editors

This volume represents the proceedings of ECSCW 2011, the 12th European Conference on Computer Supported Cooperative Work, held in Aarhus Denmark, September 24-28, 2011.

ECSCW 2011 received 85 competitive paper and note submissions. After extensive review, 22 were selected to form the core of the traditional single-track technical programme for the conference. These are supplemented by exciting workshops and masterclasses that cover a broad range of topics and allow for wider and more active participation. These will be published in the on-line supplementary proceedings, together with the expanded selection of demonstrations, videos, and poster abstracts.

The technical program this year focuses on work and the enterprise as well as on the challenges of involving citizens, patients, and others into collaborative settings. The papers embrace new theories, and discuss known ones. They challenge the ways we think about and study work and contribute to the discussions of the blurring boundaries between home and work life. They introduce recent and emergent technologies, and study known social and collaborative technologies, such as wikis and video messages. Classical settings in computer supported cooperative work, such as meetings and standardization are looked upon anew. With contributions from all over the world, the papers in interesting ways help focus on the European perspective in our community.

Many people have worked hard to ensure the success of this conference, and we briefly acknowledge them here: all the authors who submitted high quality papers; all those who contributed through taking part in workshops, masterclasses, demonstrations, and posters; the 83 member global Programme Committee, which dedicated time and energy to reviewing and discussing individual contributions and shaping the programme; the people who helped organise the programme: the workshop and masterclass chairs, the chairs of demos and videos, posters, student volunteers, and various other arrangements. Finally, the student volunteers who provided support throughout the event; and we thank the sponsors and those who offered their support to the conference.

Susanne Bødker, Niels Olof Bouvin,
Wayne Lutters , Volker Wulf and Luigina Ciolfi

ECSCW 2011 Conference Committee

General Chairs
Susanne Bødker, Aarhus University, Denmark
Niels Olof Bouvin, Aarhus University, Denmark

Programme Chairs
Wayne Lutters, University of Maryland Baltimore County, USA
Volker Wulf, University of Siegen, Germany

Workshops and Masterclasses Co-Chairs
Claus Bossen, Aarhus University, Denmark
Tone Bratteteig, University of Oslo, Norway

Demos and Videos Co-Chairs
Martin Brynskov, Aarhus University, Denmark
Frank Allan Hansen, Aarhus University, Denmark

Posters Co-Chairs
Monika Büscher, Lancaster University, UK
Preben Mogensen, Aarhus University, Denmark

Doctoral Colloquium Co-Chairs
Andy Crabtree, University of Nottingham, UK
Marianne Graves Petersen, Aarhus University, Denmark

Treasurer
Olav Bertelsen, Aarhus University, Denmark

Proceedings Chair
Luigina Ciolfi, University of Limerick, Ireland

Student Volunteers Coordinator
Nikolaj Gandrup Borchorst, Aarhus University, Denmark
Matthias Korn, Aarhus University, Denmark

Local organizers
Erik Grönwall, Aarhus University, Denmark
Pär-Ola Zander, Aalborg University, Denmark
Marianne Dammand Iversen, Aarhus University, Denmark

ECSCW 2011 Program Committee

Mark Ackerman, University of Michigan, USA

Alessandra Agostini, Università di Milano-Bicocca, Italy

Antonella De Angeli, University of Trento, Italy

Gabriela Avram, University of Limerick, Ireland

Liam Bannon, University of Limerick, Ireland

Olav Bertelsen, Aarhus University, Denmark

Pernille Bjørn, ITU Copenhagen, Denmark

Jeanette Blomberg, IBM Almaden Research Center, USA

Claus Bossen, Aarhus University, Denmark

Tone Bratteteig, University of Oslo, Norway

Barry Brown, University of California, San Diego, USA

Monika Büscher, Lancaster University, UK

Susanne Bødker, Aarhus University, Denmark

Federico Cabitza, Università di Milano-Bicocca, Italy

John M. Carroll, Pennsylvania State University, USA

Peter Castensen, Alexandra Instituttet, Copenhagen, Denmark

Luigina Ciolfi, University of Limerick, Ireland

Francoise Darses, Conservatoire National des Arts et Métiers, France

Prasun Dewan, University of North Carolina, USA

Monica Divitini, Norwegian University of Science and Technology, Norway

Batya Friedman, University of Washington, USA

Sue Fussel, Cornell University, USA

Víctor M. González, Instituto Tecnológico Autónomo de México (ITAM), México

Antonietta Grasso, Xerox Research Centre Europe Grenoble, France

Tom Gross, Bauhaus-University Weimar, Germany

Christine Halverson, IBM T.J. Watson Research Center, USA

Jörg Haake, Fern University Hagen, Germany

Richard Harper, Microsoft Research Centre Cambridge, UK

Bo Helgeson, Blekinge Institute of Technology, Sweden

Thomas Herrmann, University of Bochum, Germany

Eva Hornecker, University of Strathclyde, UK

Kori Inkpen, Microsoft Research, USA

Giulio Jacucci, Helsinki Institute for Information Technology, Finland

Marina Jirotka, Oxford University Computing Laboratory, UK

Aditya Johri, Virginia Tech, USA

Helena Karasti, University of Oulu, Finland

Wendy Kellogg, IBM T.J. Watson Research Center, USA

Michael Koch, BW-University, Munich, Germany

Timothy Koschmann, Southern Illinois University, USA

Kari Kuutti, University of Oulu, Finland

Hideaki Kuzuoka, University of Tsukuba, Japan

Charlotte Lee, University of Washington, USA

Myriam Lewkowicz, Université de Technologie de Troyes, France

Gloria Mark, University of California, Irvine USA

David W. McDonald, University of Washington, USA

Giorgio De Michelis, Università di Milano-Bicocca, Italy

David Millen, IBM T.J. Watson Research Center, USA

Michael Müller, IBM T.J. Watson Research Center, USA

Keiichi Nakata, University of Reading, UK

Maria Normark, Södertörn University College, Sweden

Jacki O'Neill, Xerox Research Centre Europe Grenoble, France

Gary Olson, University of California, Irvine, USA

Volkmar Pipek, University of Siegen and International Institute for Socio Informatics, Germany

Wolfgang Prinz, Fraunhofer FIT, Germany

Rob Procter, University of Manchester, UK

Dave Randall, Manchester Metropolitan University, UK

Madhu Reddy, Penn State University, USA

Toni Robertson, University of Technology Sydney, Australia

Markus Rohde, University of Siegen and International Institute for Socio-Informatics, Germany

Mark Rouncefield, Lancaster University, UK

Pascal Salembier, Université de Technologie de Troyes, France

Kjeld Schmidt, Copenhagen Business School, Denmark

Carla Simone, Università di Milano-Bicocca, Italy

Cleidson da Souza, IBM Brazil
Gerry Stahl, Drexel University, USA
Gunnar Stevens, University of Siegen, Germany
Lucy Suchman, Lancaster University, UK
Yngve Sundblad, KTH, Sweden
Stephanie Teasley, University of Michigan, USA
Hilda Tellioğlu, Vienna University of Technology, Austria

Michael Twidale, University of Illinois Urbana-Champaign, USA
Ina Wagner, Vienna University of Technology, Austria
Suzanne Weisband, University of Arizona, USA
Jun Zhang, Pitney Bowes Research, USA

Additional Reviewers

Sebastian Behrend, Alexander Boden, Nathan Bos, Eduardo Calvillo Gamez, Luis Castro, Grace De La Flor, Elisa Di Biase, Patrick Tobias Fischer, Blaine Hoffman, Hao Jiang, Benedikt Ley, Elena Pavan, Christian Reuter, Harold Robinson, Simon Smith, Torben Wiedenhoefer, Jiang Yang, Shaoke Zhang, Ann Zimmerman.

Dynamic Self-moderation in a Corporate Wiki to Improve Participation and Contribution Quality

Silviya Dencheva, Christian R. Prause, Wolfgang Prinz
Universität Bonn, Fraunhofer FIT
silviya.dencheva@googlemail.com, christian.prause@fit.fraunhofer.de,
wolfgang.prinz@fit.fraunhofer.de

Abstract. Contribution to a corporate wiki for the purpose of knowledge transfer can be very low because of continuously pressing tasks, a chronic lack of spare time, and motivational reasons. This is a problem because the wiki fails to achieve its purpose of collecting valuable knowledge, and becomes less attractive through this over time. We present a reputation-based system that socially rewards employees for their contributions, and thereby increases their motivation to contribute to the wiki. In a four months trial of productive use with two work groups, we could show that our concept increases the quantity and quality of articles in the repository, leads to higher activity in general, and draws employees to the wiki who had not contributed before.

Introduction

Organizational knowledge comprises highly specialized knowledge, insights and experiences about the organization's field of business. Preservation and continuous sharing of such knowledge among workers is essential in knowledge-intensive businesses. Knowledge management helps to avoid redundant work, to reduce employee training times, and to adapt to changing environments. It saves intellectual capital when employees leave, if they become temporarily unavailable, or if they change to a different position (McAdam and McCreedy, 2000). Dynamic corporate information systems like wikis can be deployed to support knowledge management.

Wikis are easy to use hypertext systems that can be read and modified by its online users through their browsers. The most prominent example of a wiki is probably Wikipedia. Wikipedia has several thousand registered users and an unknown number of anonymous users from all over the world. The users edit existing articles or add completely new texts. Millions of articles in different languages were authored by volunteers in this way (Danowski and Voss, 2004).

Numerous companies, research institutes and private persons rely on wikis to manage their business-related knowledge (Danowski and Voss, 2004; Rohs, 2007). While most CSCW literature is focusing on analyzing user behavior and cooperation in Wikipedia (Antin and Cheshire, 2010; Kittur and Kraut, 2010), our work concentrates on work environments. The *Mobile Knowledge* (MoKnow[1]) and *Context and Attention in Personalized Learning Environments* (CAPLE[2]) work groups at Fraunhofer FIT share a wiki — called the MOKNOWPEDIA — for documentation and knowledge management. Typical topics of articles are news, projects and persons, technical documentation and tutorials, trade fair exhibitions, seminars and workshops, publication planning, processes, interesting links, or IT infrastructure.

However, first experiences with MOKNOWPEDIA showed that participation and contribution was not as active as hoped. In order to improve knowledge exchange in the groups, the articles' quality and quantity needed to be improved. Although resilient numbers are hard to come by for work environments, MOKNOWPEDIA is surely not an exception (see also Hoisl et al. (2007)). Indeed, Kraut et al. (2010) find that success stories like that of Wikipedia are rare. Out of 6000 installations of the MediaWiki software, not even every second one has eight users or more.

A major problem is that users of public and corporate wikis have to make personal efforts and invest their own precious time in creating and improving content that is often far more useful to others than themselves: an article's author already has the knowledge he writes about. To him, the article is of less value because it provides only few benefit. Rational beings like humans will clearly prefer consuming content over producing it. But a wiki with few contents and poor articles fails to support knowledge management as there is nothing to consume. The wiki is not attractive, and the few contributors are further demotivated as they feel that nobody else is contributing. In a closed community, where the number of potential authors is limited and everyone is a specialist with specialist knowledge, a small percentage of volunteers is not enough. Instead, active participation of all is necessary.

We make the following contributions that help to increase contribution quantity (article count and size) and quality (readability and timeliness) in a corporate wiki:

- a concept that motivates personnel by means of reputation,
- an implementation of our concept that amplifies contributing behavior,
- an evaluation based on a four months field-test in productive use,
- a comparison of the three rewarding mechanisms integrated in our solution,
- and we inform the future design of corporate knowledge repositories.

---

[1] http://www.fit.fraunhofer.de/projects/mobiles-wissen_en.html
[2] http://www.fit.fraunhofer.de/services/mobile/caple_en.html

Motivation

This section explains the motivation behind our concept. Starting from a view of the wiki's deployment history, we interviewed users for the problems they see with the wiki, and discuss theoretical backgrounds of the mentioned problems.

History of the MOKNOWPEDIA

A few years ago, MoKnow and CAPLE decided that a new form of managing knowledge was needed. In a dedicated discussion, it was decided to set up the MO-KNOWPEDIA based on the MediaWiki[3] software. One advantage that favored the MOKNOWPEDIA approach was that a free wiki software is cost-saving compared to other commercial software. Furthermore, there is no need for an explicit editorial control. The wiki structure can evolve freely and all kinds of articles are possible. As MediaWiki puts only few restrictions on users and what they write, it provides a work space that enables the vertical and horizontal exchange of knowledge between group leaders and equal colleagues. Additionally, entrance barriers to wiki use are low because users can easily contribute to collaboratively written articles, just by using their browsers. Finally, the success stories of Wikipedia or wikis used by open source software projects clearly voted for the wiki approach. In practice, however, it turned out that MOKNOWPEDIA had some troubles taking off:

Only a few members of the group actively participated in the wiki. Not everybody seemed equally motivated to contribute. There was a higher number of people willing to consume than those willing to produce. "You should write an article about this!" was often heard but rarely done. In the end, the total number of articles remained low; leading to a limited exchange of knowledge through MOKNOWPEDIA. Most information was still conveyed in the old ways like hallway conversations or explicit requests for documentation. Instead, we wanted to achieve that information was provided pro-actively through a central and well-known repository.

Our observations with MOKNOWPEDIA confirm the results in a similar study of knowledge sharing tools and processes by Reichling and Veith (2005).

An investigation into the users' problems

To qualitatively investigate into the reasons for low contribution, we interviewed all members of the work group. We wanted to know why they themselves or someone else was possibly not actively contributing to MOKNOWPEDIA, and what could be changed to improve this situation and motivate them to contribute. Our interviewees reported various problems. Saying that a good tool would be reward enough to use it, many named mostly shortcomings of the wiki as problems:

Every fifth interviewee answered that the wiki's syntax was too complex to use and learn. This stopped them from using it. Also, it was missing a clear structuring. Half of the interviewees mentioned that there should be someone who creates the

---

[3]   http://www.mediawiki.org

structure. Adding own contributions would be much easier then. Some interviewees stated that there were so many other group tools requiring their attention that they could not additionally contribute to MOKNOWPEDIA. Others said that they preferred to have a semantic wiki, instead, because it would help them to better structure the wiki. No opportunity should be left out to promote the wiki, too. A few persons were frustrated because they felt they were the only ones to write and tend to articles in a certain domain. Especially student employees were missing an instructor that regularly reminded them to contribute, or told them to write a certain article. Students were also afraid that they were not competent enough to make professional and quality contributions. Finally, most interviewees stated that they did not have enough time to write articles, although they would really like to do so.

Implications, target group and goals

Although there is truth in many of the users' complaints, we think that the main problem is that they are not motivated sufficiently to try to overcome the hurdles by themselves: The reason that they do not have the time — to learn the wiki syntax, to create a structure, have their attention drawn to other tools, have no one to tell them what to do, felt incompetent, and have other important things to do — is that they do not see enough value for themselves in contributing.

For rational, thinking beings, a clear disproportion exists: Writing articles costs them their own time, in the extreme case even making themselves replaceable, while others profit from easily accessible information. While the group as a whole would profit, every single person is tempted to free ride on the group's achievements. Reducing the extent of this disproportion is key to increasing contribution.

The target group in our study are self-organizing project teams at a research institute with flat hierarchies. Individuals have far-reaching freedom and autonomy in organizing their work. Explicit instruction or punishment are, at most, rare. Intrinsic motivation is valued very much. Staff members are mostly researchers, one third working students, and two executive managers. The vast majority has a computer science background with a few exceptions that still have good computer knowledge. In this environment, we design our solution to the following goals:

- G1: Increase content volume to preserve a broader spectrum of information.
- G2: Improve article quality to make information more easy to grasp.
- G3: Involve deniers to preserve the unique expert knowledge of everyone.
- G4: Keep the cost of operation low.
- G5: Do not force contribution and avoid punishment (self-organizing groups).
- G6: Do not cause destructive phenomena like rat races or bullying.

The reputation model

According to the Oxford Dictionary, *reputation* is what is generally said or believed about the abilities or qualities of somebody or something. A reputation system is a software that determines a means of a user's reputation from his actions. The computed reputation scores can be used to predict future user behavior or be published. A reputation system is a core component in many modern web-based communities, where it serves to promote well-behaving and trust (Jøsang et al., 2005).

In our concept, users earn reputation points by serving their work group with valuable contributions to MOKNOWPEDIA. For example, writing high quality articles earns users a certain amount of reputation points. The users' reputation points are published resulting in appreciation by their peers. This gives users something in exchange for their efforts, and motivates them to systematically collect more points.

Consider the following scenario as a simplified example: Sonny creates a new article in MOKNOWPEDIA. Rico reviews the article with a rating of "average". For his review, Rico receives one point, while Sonny receives ten points for his average-quality article. Later, Gina edits Sonny's article, replacing about one third of the text. The article's ten points are now split proportionally between Sonny (seven points) and Gina (three points). In addition, Rico's review loses timeliness because it applies to a quite different, older revision of the article. Rico only retains 0.7 points for his old review. Gina adds a new review of "good" to the article, giving her an extra point for the review itself. When the voted quality of the article is determined from reviews, Gina's new review weighs more than Rico's old review. Therefore, the average rating of the article is almost "good". Because of its quality, fifteen points (instead of ten) are now distributed among contributors of the article. This leaves Sonny with ten points, Gina with five points plus one for her review, and Rico with 0.7 points. When Rico refreshes his review, he gets the full point again.

In the example, you see that there are two ways for users to collect reputation points: The first one is to provide a quality assessment of an article in form of a rating and a review comment. The quality assessments are used to democratically determine the quality of an article. A fresh review earns the user one point. However, this worth decreases as the review ages due to later changes to the article. The reviewer has to refresh his review to regain the full point. A reviewer cannot have more than one active review per article, but can revise his review at any time. And, to avoid that reviewers are influenced by fear of bad (or expectation of good) consequences for themselves (Elster, 1989), reviews are always submitted anonymously.

The second way to earn reputation points is by contributing to MOKNOWPEDIA articles. The amount of reputation points that are awarded for a contribution to an article depends on three criteria: quality of the article as determined by above democratic review process, importance of the article (e.g. size, page views), and ratio of the contributor's contribution to all contributors' contributions to the article.

While users contribute to articles in the wiki and review them, a reputation system collects information about reputation-relevant interactions between users and MOKNOWPEDIA in the background, gauging the social value of their interactions. The collected reputation data is visualized in three different ways, to make users themselves and other users aware of how much they have done for their group:

- **Levels** — similar to Internet forums, every user is assigned to a level in a hierarchy. Users have to collect a certain amount of points before being promoted to a new level. This mechanism addresses the users' drive for achievement.

- **Ranking** – the total number of points of each user is displayed in a ranking table, with top users at the top of the table. This mechanism motivates users through social comparison and competition.

- **Awards** – once per week the not too seriously meant title "MOKNOWPEDIA Held der Woche" (Hero of the Week) is awarded to the user who contributed most during the week. This mechanism is a chance for newcomers to quickly achieve something. It rewards short-term contribution.

Metrics and calculating reputation

To compute the reputation that is awarded to user u for contributing to articles $a \in A$, CollabReview depends on article importance $w(a)$, quality $q(a)$ and contribution ratios $C(u, a)$ that are determined by an authorship function. With this data, the reputation score s_u of every user u is defined as the average of twice-weighted article quality scores (plus the score obtained from their reviews s_u^r)

$$s_u = \frac{\sum\limits_{a \in A} q(a)w(a)C(u, a)}{|A|} + s_u^r.$$

Article importance depends on two factors: a logarithmic function of article size in characters, and the average number of article views per week. Size is included to represent the fact that larger articles potentially contain more information because they aggregate more contributions. The page view frequency is included to accommodate the fact that the article probably contains more interesting information, and is referenced more often in other articles. It should therefore have a higher weight. Multiplying the two numbers results in an article's estimated importance $w(a)$.

The contribution ratio of a user for an article is determined by his authorship in the article, i.e. it depends on the ratio of characters contributed by that user. A line of text is considered as being contributed by a user, when that user last edited the line. We use an adaptation of the algorithm by Prause (2009): each new revision of an article is compared to several of its probable ancestors. When an optimal candidate has been found, the algorithm determines an author for the newly added or modified lines; unmodified lines will retain their author. If a non-trivial line (e.g. one that contains only whitespace) is found to be a clone of an already existing line, authorship information is copied from there. Otherwise, the creator of the revision is considered as the line's author.

Implementation

This section describes how we implemented our concept in MOKNOWPEDIA. We describe the software architecture and present user interfaces.

Software architecture

The software architecture of MOKNOWPEDIA combines two distinct softwares into one integrated platform: CollabReview and MediaWiki.

MediaWiki is one of the most widely used wiki softwares. It is written in PHP and published free under the GNU General Public License (GPL). MediaWiki is easy to use, but has diverse functionalities and is very customizable (Barrett, 2008). The online encyclopedia Wikipedia is operated by the MediaWiki software.

CollabReview (Prause and Apelt, 2008) is a Java-based web application for reputation management in collaboratively written software source code. With multiple developers engaged in developing software code, responsibility for a specific piece of code is difficult to assign. Nonetheless, responsibility is a major factor in achieving quality and preventing code from being developed carelessly. CollabReview statistically acquires per developer per document accountabilities and enables learning and self-monitoring processes within a development team while maintaining anonymity to a certain degree in order to not endanger team spirit.

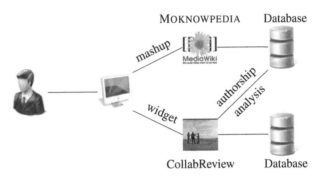

Figure 1. Architecture of the integrated MOKNOWPEDIA platform.

Figure 1 depicts how the MOKNOWPEDIA platform is composed of the subsystems MediaWiki and CollabReview. Users access MOKNOWPEDIA with their browsers. When logging on to MOKNOWPEDIA, a single-sign-on mechanism ensures that a user is automatically logged on to both sub-systems. All interaction of the user with the MOKNOWPEDIA happens through the user interface of MediaWiki. However, the MediaWiki user interface has been extended with widgets that pass through CollabReview functionality (see Section "User interfaces").

Apart from the user interface, some necessary communication happens directly between MediaWiki and CollabReview. In order to compute reputation scores, all articles and their revisions are run through an additional processing step by CollabReview. It analyzes articles for authorship and responsibility information, and stores review and quality data in its own database. Additionally, CollabReview's own user management was removed. CollabReview, directly accesses the MediaWiki user database, instead.

User interfaces

The user interface of MOKNOWPEDIA is a mash-up of the original MediaWiki interface and additional services provided by CollabReview. MediaWiki's menu on the left is augmented with a widget that allows to submit or update a review for the current article. It is visible on every page of MOKNOWPEDIA (see Figure 2).

Figure 2. Review widget in the menu bar, left of a MOKNOWPEDIA article.

When entering a review for an article, a user can select a rating from one of "sehr gut" (very good), "gut" (good), "befriedigend" (satisfactory), "ausreichend" (sufficient), or "mangelhaft" (poor). He can also enter an optional review comment in the text box below. The comment is meant as justification of the rating, and as a hint on how to improve the page. The submit button ("Senden") will enter the review into the database, and is send to the authors of the article via email. Below the button, there are three indicators: the stars represent the average quality rating as determined by the users' reviews, the gauge in the middle shows the article's importance level, and the traffic light shows how up-to-date the user's review is. In this case, the review is outdated and should be refreshed. The link at the bottom of the widget ("Alle Bewertungen") lets users view all reviews for the article without revealing reviewer names (see Figure 3).

A screenshot of the starting page of MOKNOWPEDIA can be seen in Figure 3. Users typically arrive at this page first when opening MOKNOWPEDIA. Two more widgets are embedded in the article text: the left one is presenting the reputation ranking list of users. The user with the most reputation points has 100%, all other

Figure 3. Main page with ranking and hero of the week; review widget shows reviews of article.

users' scores are given as percental value of the top contributor. The right widget shows who has achieved the most points in this week so far, and how many points he has. This is the Hero of the Week aspirant. Any other user that surpasses the aspirant will automatically become the aspirant himself. As long as no user has made at least one point, there is no aspirant.

Once a week, right before the weekly group meeting, the current aspirant becomes the Hero of the Week. The new hero is automatically announced via email on the group's mailing list. Additionally, he receives a chocolate bar during the meeting. After this, the aspirants are reset, so that for the next week everybody has the same chance of being the aspirant and becoming Hero of the Week.

Figure 4 displays a cutout of the MOKNOWPEDIA's user page. This page lists all members of the work group and links to personal introductory pages. Every user entry uses a MediaWiki template to standardize the presentation form. The template has been extended to include a widget that will show each user's reputation level.

Evaluation

We evaluated our concept in a field-test that would last for several months. This section describes the approach, reports our findings, and interprets results.

Approach and threats to validity

The evaluation serves the purpose to find out, if enhanced MOKNOWPEDIA satisfies our six goals. However, the focus of our evaluation is explorative, and on qualitative data and human aspects. We obtained a good impression of the impact of the

Figure 4. Cutout of MOKNOWPEDIA's user overview article and individual user reputation levels.

reputation mechanisms on a personal level, albeit at the cost of only having a small number of probands and limited statistical significance. At start and end of the evaluation, the work group had 18 and 16 members, respectively. Due to fluctuation in personnel, only 15 employees were able to participate for the full evaluation period.

Before making our modifications to MOKNOWPEDIA, we interviewed all members of our work groups and had them fill out questionnaires. This was to capture the initial spectrum of opinions as a base line. A second round of interviews was executed after the evaluation phase. The results of both interviews could then be compared. Yet we did not tell probands that we would interview them twice. A possible social desirability bias would then be in effect during both interviews and cancel itself out. Additionally, the time between the two interviews is probably too long for probands to remember earlier answers.

The evaluation phase itself — between the two interviews — ran for four months. During this time, we recorded any incidents and observations regarding the modified MOKNOWPEDIA. In addition to the interviews, we collected actual usage data, and compared it to data of the four months right before the evaluation. Although the evaluation phase of about four months of productive use is long, our results might still be influenced by seasonal events like holidays.

Socio-technical systems are highly complex due to the involved human beings that tend to be unpredictable. Changing only a minor factor in the environment or the people themselves, could lead to very different results. For example, if the work groups were not built on friendly cooperation and intrinsic motivation, if the environment were more competitive, or if the majority were not computer scientists, then results might have been different. Also, when the evaluation started, the MOKNOWPEDIA was about two years old. Usage behavior had had its time to establish and stabilize, with several attempts to improve contribution. Yet we cannot fully preclude that the change in behavior we observed during the evaluation, is not due to some other effect.

Usage statistics

By analyzing the data in databases and server logs, we compare the four months before the review extensions were added to the four months of the evaluation period. Start of the evaluation period was February 18th, 2010.

The number of new article revisions raised from 320 to 517, which is an increase of about 62%. As the four pre-evaluation months span Christmas time, we also compared our evaluation phase to the same period in 2009. Here we found 363 new revisions, which still means an increase by 42%. The average number of characters per article in MOKNOWPEDIA grew from 5324 to 6134.

In addition to an increased number of contributions, we also counted an increased number of viewed articles. MediaWiki counted 176 page views in the four months before the evaluation phase, and 258 views during the evaluation. This is an increment of 47%. The number of page views is lower than that of changes because MediaWiki does not count page views that recur in a short period. We attribute this increment to advertising effects of the MOKNOWPEDIA extensions.

Finally, we wanted to know if users used the review tool actively. After the evaluation phase, we counted 237 reviews in the database. 155 reviews (more than half of all reviews) additionally contained sensible comments. In total, these reviews were submitted by 16 different users. Only one user who had participated for the evaluation's full duration had not submitted a single review.

Even after the evaluation phase is over, MOKNOWPEDIA's review facilities keep being used, and new reviews are being added continuously.

Results from pre- and post-evaluation interviews

Before and after the evaluation period, the users were interviewed with questionnaires. The next two sub-sections discuss the results of the interviews to evaluate

1. if contents improved, and if the reviewing extensions were accepted,

2. and to gather future design recommendations.

Quantitative feedback: effects on MOKNOWPEDIA and acceptance

The pre- and post-test questionnaires contained twelve statements to which users should express their degree of agreement on a Likert scale: "fully agree", "agree", "neutral", "disagree", "absolutely disagree". Items 1 to 8 concerned the effect that reviewing extensions had on the Wiki contents. The remaining four items related to the reviewing extensions themselves. Detailed agreement is presented in Figure 5.

Assigning one ("absolutely disagree") to five points ("fully agree") to each user's agreement, an average agreement score is computed. The average agreement of first and second interview can then be compared to see how agreement has

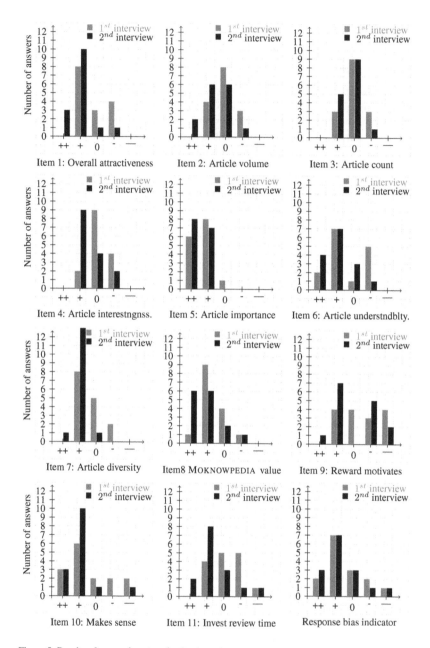

Figure 5. Results of pre- and post-evaluation interview.

#	Statement	Pts.	Chng.
1	MOKNOWPEDIA is generally attractive	4.0	+0.73
2	The articles in the wiki are substantial	3.6	+0.53
3	The total number of articles is satisfactory	3.3	+0.27
4	The articles are interesting to read	3.5	+0.60
5	The wiki contains important and useful information	4.5	+0.20
6	Article core information is comprehensible and easy to find	3.9	+0.53
7	The treated topics are diverse	4.0	+0.60
8	It is worth using MOKNOWPEDIA	4.1	+0.47
9	A reward motivates me to use the wiki more actively	3.0	+0.47
10	A mechanism to rate the quality of articles is valuable	3.9	+0.53
11	It makes sense to invest time in reviewing and commenting	3.6	+0.80

Table I. User agreement to items in post-test questionnaire.

changed. The texts of the different statements, translated into English, and the associated agreement scores — absolute and relative change between first and second interview — are liste in Table I. The answers substantiate that MOKNOWPEDIA and its contents improved during the evaluation. In the second interview, users disagreed with the positive statements about MOKNOWPEDIA in only seven cases, as compared to 22 before. Many users that were previously undecided, later agreed to positive statements.

Four statements regard the reviewing extensions themselves (see Table I). Before the test, there were several users that were not sure of whether rewards would motivate them (Item 9). Through the test, these users changed to agreement. Also, the number scepticists decreased so that afterwards a slight majority was in favor of the reviewing extensions. However, this statement is still the one with most objection. Similarly, most users initially did not think that they would invest time in writing reviews (Item 11). This has clearly changed towards acceptance: the number of agreeing users grew from four to ten, and disagreeing users decreased from six to two. Although the majority of users agreed from the start that reviewing would makes sense, after the test even more agreed (Item 10).

We wanted to know, if the acceptance of the reviewing system was especially high among profiteers. But we found only weak correlations (Spearman rank) between the Items 9 to 11, and the user's position in the ranking list. The strongest correlation we found was $r_{Item11} = 0.25$ for Item 11 ($r_{Item9} = 0.14$, $r_{Item10} = -0.06$): Profiteers might be more willing to do reviewing work than others. Yet none of the correlations is significant due to the size of the test set. It could be that there is no relation between profiting from the review extensions and advocating them.

The last depicted item was mixed into the statements as an indicator of a possibly changing response bias. It was intentionally formulated diffuse (*The integration of a reward system into the wiki is interesting.*). The intention was that it could reveal a bias towards giving more positive feedback in the second interview. We observed only a small change in feedback behavior (3.7 points, +0.2), so it seems that there is few social desirability bias, thus supporting that observed improvements in the other items are real.

Qualitative feedback: future design recommendations

In the second interview, there were three additional statements about the rewarding mechanisms. All three rewarding mechanisms were not perceived as very effective at motivating users. On the average, they were all weakly rejected. The ranking list was perceived as most effective (2.9 points), followed by the Hero of the Week (2.7 points), and finally the level hierarchy (2.6 points).

The questionnaire invited users to provide further remarks of what had or would have motivated them, what they had liked or disliked, and if it changed their behavior. In the following, we provide the major design recommendations:

A few users said that they would not feel motivated by the rewards in any way. Instead, they answered it would have required much larger rewards, or coercion. They had a distrust against the reviewing system, and considered reviewing articles as distracting and a waste of time that they could rather spend on writing articles. Some users bore concern that the extensions could be manipulated, and be attacked systematically to harm targeted people.

Positive remarks were that the design was pleasant, the integration fitted well into the existing MOKNOWPEDIA. It was simple to access, and easy to use and understand. The comments were regarded as very useful because they motivated and helped with improving articles. Users felt that the reviews made them read and tend to more articles. Reviews also gave them a feeling of trust. But also the anonymity of writing reviews was appreciated. Several users valued that they could see their own activity, or compare it to the others' activity. Some users noted a positive fun factor in the rewarding mechanisms, which they regarded as entertaining.

One user testified that the rewards had motivated him to start contributing to MOKNOWPEDIA. Others browsed more vigilantly to be able to give reviews, or wrote articles more carefully. A major contributor, however, said that he had reduced his contributions to give others a chance. A couple of users felt appealed by the rewards and answered that it had changed their behavior, but noted that the motivation was not sustainable, and could not withstand other pressing tasks. The lack of time was given as the major reason for not contributing to articles as well as not reviewing. A few users told us that they would not care for the rewards and, in fact, were using the wiki because they were convinced by it, but they also said that the rewards made them think more about the wiki.

Wishes for future improvements were to harden MOKNOWPEDIA against manipulation, to provide a user with hints how to earn his next points, a way to immediately respond to reviews, and to have computer-generated initial quality assessments. The value of rewards should be increased (e.g. an additional day off), and getting a certain amount of reputation points per week should be compulsory. Even punishment like paying money into a thank-you box was proposed. Another wish was to have user groups so that teams could compete against each other.

Observations during evaluation phase

This section describes observations that either we ourselves or designated confederates made during the evaluation phase. It is a collection of episodes that clarify the reception of MOKNOWPEDIA in the work group.

Curiosity   Trudy had missed the meeting in which the MOKNOWPEDIA extensions were introduced. She was curious and went to her colleagues to ask them how she could try the extensions. As the extensions were already installed in MOKNOW-PEDIA, she could start using them without problems.

Missing comment   Gina goes to one of the administrators of MOKNOWPEDIA and complains that somebody gave her article a bad review rating without writing a comment. The administrators themselves could not do anything about it, but after this incident we updated MOKNOWPEDIA to allow rejecting of seemingly unjustified reviews. Yet there were no further incidents like this one.

First activity   Lou, who was registered in MOKNOWPEDIA but had never written an article before, started to regularly write and review articles. Within one week, he made it from zero points to the fifth position in the rankings. He announced that the extensions motivated him to start contributing to MOKNOWPEDIA.

Frustration   During the evaluation, Izzy became Hero of the Week several times in a row. This frustrated other users. They complained that there must have been something wrong with MOKNOWPEDIA. As a consequence of this, Izzy deliberately chose to contribute less to give others a chance to earn the title, too.

Playful competition   Incited by the fact that a colleague had overtaken him in the rankings, Larry went to several colleagues, asking them for hints on how he could quickly gather some more points. They gave him the advice that an easy way to get some points was to write reviews. Within a few hours, Larry reviewed dozens of articles until he had again overtaken said colleague. For the next weeks, he kept an eye on the rankings, watching to remain ahead of that colleague. Although he reviewed articles primarily to get the points, his reviews were fair and contained valuable review comments.

Anti-hero   Caitlin had been a minor contributor, only contributing what she had explicitly been requested to. She never submitted a review and for a long time none of her articles had received a review, leaving her with zero points. She was proud of being the last one in the reputation ranking with zero points. One day, however, she received a number of points; not because she had done something recently, but because one of her older articles had received a good review. So she came to our office and asked if she could rate her own articles down to get her old position back. We told her that she then would get points for the reviews, what she did not like.

Unique positions — even if not directly associated with a positive merit — have a certain attraction to users.

Improvement   Through a review comment, Martin was adverted to the template that is recommended for creating user profiles. He had not used the template before, so he asked his colleagues about the profile and had them help him to change his profile page. Feedback from the reviews was helpful to him and for improving article quality.

Manipulation   To quickly gain a considerable amount of points and become Hero of the Week, Stan hacked the MOKNOWPEDIA by writing a script that rated all articles "good". Although he immediately received lots of points, he still did not win the title because the articles' authors received more points than him. Additionally, hundreds of emails for the reviews were sent within seconds. The incident shows that — given enough incentive — attacks against the system become probable. We removed all reviews that were created through the attack and negotiated that no one would attempt such an attack anymore.

Teasing   From his office, Rico saw Sonny at the end of the hallway, he laughed and jokingly called: "Hey Sonny, I rated your last meeting minutes 'poor'!" Yet a few minutes later Rico changed the review to a better and more appropriate rating. The users used MOKNOWPEDIA to tease each other, leading to a form of viral advertising.

Interpretation of results

The users expressed the wish to have more time to make their contributions and reviews, or even want to be forced by their managers. With our concept, we take a different approach. We think that if users have enough motivation to contribute, then they themselves will find the time to do so. Although purely intrinsic motivation would be preferable, our concept has some extrinsically motivating effects that lead to the desired effects.

Earlier in this paper, we defined six goals that we want to achieve with our concept. Our first goal (G1) is to increase the volume of contents in MOKNOWPEDIA. The evaluation shows that we have reached this goal: Users feel that the number of articles increased. We measured an increase in content size, too. The same holds true for quality, where users think that interestingness and understandability increased. Additionally, reviews provide confidence in article content, further adding to their quality (G2). MOKNOWPEDIA became more attractive through this.

With our extensions, we were able to draw more users to MOKNOWPEDIA. Except for very few users that denied the review concept outright (one of them was a quite active contributor of articles), there was no user that did not at least contribute some reviews. At least one user admitted to have started contributing because of the rewarding system. Although we were not able to achieve active contribution by everyone without exceptions, our concept can be considered successful at drawing additional users to MOKNOWPEDIA (G3).

The additional cost of operation of our extensions is negligible. All that is needed is a little more computing power, and a small reward for the Hero of the Week (G4). By its design, our reputation mechanism does not prescribe users what to do; in our implementation, no one is forced to comply and there is no threat or punishment involved (G5). Similarly, we did not record any events that would suggest the existence of undesirable phenomena like rat races, or bullying (G6). Instead, we observed that the reputation system was perceived as fun.

We acknowledge that all six goals are closely related to the subjective value of reputation for the individual. The more reputation is worth, the more efforts will users invest to attain a high reputation (Jøsang et al., 2005). For example, by relying on coercion or higher rewards, and thereby giving up on goals G4 or G5, the value of reputation can be increased. This will lead to greater successes in goals G1, G2 and G3, but at the cost of risking destructive effects (G6).

Related Work

In social media and the Internet, *quality* is often interchangeably used with trust and credibility. Reputation systems are central to these communities (Jøsang et al., 2005; Resnick et al., 2000). Ordinary wiki software like MediaWiki offers no integrated reputation system. However, the demand for such systems has pushed researchers and practitioners alike to research and develop extensions. Freely available extensions for the MediaWiki software are, for instance, *Review*[4], which lets logged in users decide if an article is ready to be printed, or *AjaxRatingScript*[5], where quality ratings from different users are collected and averaged. This approach is quite similar to how we determine article quality, except that it does not consider ageing of reviews.

Wiki extensions that compute reputations for authors are much fewer. The social rewarding extension of Hoisl et al. (2007) is similar to our approach. They determine a score for every author in order to recompense users investing their time and effort contributing to the wiki. However, their approach differs from ours in the way how reputation is computed. They do not make a distinction between article quality and article importance. Also, they calculate responsibility for articles from size differences and passed time instead of considering the authorship of the article's text. Next, they rely on only one social reward: displaying reputation in a ranking list. In their concept, reviewing is not a valued contribution. However, as they have automatic means of assessing article quality, it is not so important for them, too. Hoisl et al. did not test their tool with users, and do not provide experience or evaluation data.

Adler et al. (2008) present a system that computes trust values for articles of the

---

[4]   http://www.mediawiki.org/wiki/Extension:Review
[5]   http://www.mediawiki.org/wiki/Extension:AjaxRatingScript

online encyclopedia Wikipedia. Readers can use WIKITRUST to identify words that are deemed trustworthy or not trustworthy, respectively. The higher an author's reputation, the higher is the predicted quality of his contributions. Consequently, such content should remain unchanged for a longer time. They predict the imminence of deletion of a word in the next revision of an article by means of recall and precision. Yet WIKITRUST does not publish the reputation scores it computes. It does not want to change contributor behavior but rather help readers to trust in content.

In their study, Holtzblatt et al. (2010) similarly report that the cost of contributing to articles is an important impeding factor to wiki contribution. They conclude that social incentives are worth exploring in corporate environments.

Muller et al. (2009) argue in their paper on metrics for enterprise social software "Social media applications should record and analyze the activities of information-consumers, ... to understand what information and knowledge is proving to be valuable to employees ...". We believe that our approach provides a valuable contribution towards that direction. Our evaluation demonstrates that participation in our wiki was increased both from contributors as well as commentators and evaluators due to the provision of statistical data about user activities.

Farzan et al. (2008) use social incentives (levels and ranking list) to motivate contributions to a corporate social network. They find that social rewards can effectively increase contribution and that different kinds of incentives are needed to motivate different people. A major recommendation from their study is, however, that points should decay. The hero of the week is a similar mechanism in MO-KNOWPEDIA. Yet we found no indication that points should generally decay over time; at least not in wikis.

Conclusion

We implemented an extension to MOKNOWPEDIA that lets users review, comment on and rate articles. For each article, every user can provide exactly one review, so that potentially there is a set of reviews for the article. While the review comment is plain text that helps authors with how to improve their article, the review ratings are aggregated to obtain an average quality assessment. This helps users identify high and low quality articles. In this context, quality can be defined as the readability, understandability and information payload of an article. However, in all comparable solutions it is normally up to the community to define their notion of quality.

We extend the basic concept of reviewing tools by adding the CollabReview reputation system that tracks and reconstructs how much individual users do for the wiki. In order to calculate personal reputation scores, the reputation system determines who has contributed to what articles, how important these articles are, and what the quality of the articles is. Authors that have contributed much to high quality articles will have a high reputation score, while authors that have made only few or low quality contributions will have low reputation scores. Additionally, we also regard the users' reviews as valuable contributions to articles that earns the reviewers a few more reputation points.

The idea is that if authors are given something in exchange for high reputation scores, then they will — to further raise their reputation score — try to contribute high quality articles, increase the quality of existing low quality articles, or provide hints for improvement. For the MOKNOWPEDIA, three different social rewarding mechanisms are simultaneously fueled by the reputation scores: a ranking list, a Hero of the Week award, and a level hierarchy. Of these three, the ranking list seems to be the most effective rewarding mechanism.

After installing the reputation system extension in MOKNOWPEDIA, we evaluated its use for several months with two work groups. The goal of the evaluation we conducted was to gather first experiences with such a system. The focus was on qualitative feedback from observations in the field and interviews with users. However, we also collected some hard usage numbers.

All in all, the evaluation results are promising. Not only have the employees accessed the wiki more often, but they have also read more articles, and made more contributions. The quality and quantity of the articles in MOKNOWPEDIA increased. Most users accepted our extensions and enjoyed using them. Some users even made their first contributions because of our system. The trial allayed our initial fear that the system might be misused as a tool for bullying, or be confronted with total rejection.

Besides showing the overall good success of our concept, we inform the design of similar future systems with the findings from our evaluation. The usage observations provide a vivid picture of the social processes. These are complemented by improvement hints gathered through the final interviews.

Acknowledgments

This paper is based on Dencheva (2010). The research was supported by the Hydra (IST-2005-034891) and BRIDGE (project number 261817) EU projects.

References

Adler, B. T., K. Chatterjee, L. de Alfaro, M. Faella, I. Pye, and V. Raman (2008): 'Assigning Trust to Wikipedia Content'. In: *International Symposium on Wikis (WikiSym)*.

Antin, J. and C. Cheshire (2010): 'Readers Are Not Free-riders: Reading as a Form of Participation on Wikipedia'. In: *Proceedings of the 2010 ACM Conference on Computer Supported Cooperative Work (CSCW)*. New York, NY, USA, pp. 127–130, ACM.

Barrett, D. J. (2008): *MediaWiki*. USA: O'Reilly Media.

Danowski, P. and J. Voss (2004): 'Bibliothek, Information und Dokumentation in der Wikipedia'. *Information, Wissenschaft und Praxis*, vol. 55, no. 8.

Dencheva, S. (2010): 'Entwicklung und Evaluation einer soziotechnischen Komponente zur dynamischen Selbstmoderation in einem Firmeninformationssystem'. Diplomarbeit, Fraunhofer FIT, Universität Bonn.

Elster, J. (1989): *The cement of society: A study of social order.* Cambridge University Press.

Farzan, R., J. M. DiMicco, D. R. Millen, C. Dugan, W. Geyer, and E. A. Brownholtz (2008): 'Results from Deploying a Participation Incentive Mechanism within the Enterprise'. In: *26th Annual SIGCHI Conference on Human Factors in Computing Systems.* New York, NY, USA, pp. 563–572, ACM.

Hoisl, B., W. Aigner, and S. Miksch (2007): 'Social Rewarding in Wiki Systems — Motivating the Community'. In: *Online Communities and Social Computing.* Berlin Heidelberg New York, p. 362–371, Springer.

Holtzblatt, L. J., L. E. Damianos, and D. Weiss (2010): 'Factors Impeding Wiki Use in the Enterprise: a Case Study'. In: *28th International Conference Extended Abstracts on Human Factors in Computing Systems.* New York, NY, USA, pp. 4661–4676, ACM.

Jøsang, A., R. Ismail, and C. Boyd (2005): 'A survey of trust and reputation systems for online service provision'. *Decision Support Systems,* vol. 43, no. 2, pp. 618–644.

Kittur, A. and R. E. Kraut (2010): 'Beyond Wikipedia: Coordination and Conflict in Online Production Groups'. In: *Proceedings of the 2010 ACM Conference on Computer Supported Cooperative Work (CSCW).* New York, NY, USA, pp. 215–224, ACM.

Kraut, R., M. L. Maher, J. Olson, T. W. Malone, P. Pirolli, and J. C. Thomas (2010): 'Scientific Foundations: A Case for Technology-Mediated Social-Participation Theory'. *Computer,* vol. 43, no. 11, pp. 22–28.

McAdam, R. and S. McCreedy (2000): 'A critique of knowledge management: using a social constructionist model'. *New Technology, Work and Employment,* vol. 15, no. 2, pp. 155–168.

Muller, M. J., J. Freyne, C. Dugan, D. R. Millen, and J. Thom-Santelli (2009): 'Return On Contribution (ROC): A Metric for Enterprise Social Software'. In: I. Wagner, H. Tellioğlu, E. Balka, C. Simone, and L. Ciolfi (eds.): *Proceedings of the 11th European Conference on Computer-Supported Cooperative Work (ECSCW).* pp. 143–150, Springer London.

Prause, C. R. (2009): 'Maintaining Fine-Grained Code Metadata Regardless of Moving, Copying and Merging'. In: *Proceedings of the IEEE International Working Conference on Source Code Analysis and Manipulation.* Los Alamitos, CA, USA, pp. 109–118, IEEE Computer Society.

Prause, C. R. and S. Apelt (2008): 'An approach for continuous inspection of source code'. In: *Proceedings of the 6th international workshop on software quality.* Leipzig, Germany, pp. 17–22, ACM New York, NY, USA.

Reichling, T. and M. Veith (2005): 'Expertise Sharing in a Heterogeneous Organizational Environment'. In: H. Gellersen, K. Schmidt, M. Beaudouin-Lafon, and W. Mackay (eds.): *Proceedings of the Ninth European Conference on Computer-Supported Cooperative Work (ECSCW).* pp. 325–345, Springer-Verlag.

Resnick, P., K. Kuwabara, R. Zeckhauser, and E. Friedman (2000): 'Reputation systems'. *Communications of the ACM,* vol. 43, no. 12, pp. 45–48.

Rohs, M. (2007): 'Qualitative Forschung auf dem Wiki Way'. *Technologie verändert die Bildungsforschung,* vol. 2, no. 4, pp. 1–17.

Digital Traces of Interest: Deriving Interest Relationships from Social Media Interactions

Michal Jacovi[*], Ido Guy[*], Inbal Ronen[*], Adam Perer[**], Erel Uziel[*], and Michael Maslenko[*]

[*]IBM Research, Haifa, Israel, [**]IBM Research, Cambridge, USA

[*]{jacovi, ido, inbal, erelu, mmichael}@il.ibm.com, [**]adam.perer@us.ibm.com

Abstract. Facebook and Twitter have changed the way we consume information, allowing the people we follow to become our "social filters" and determine the content of our information stream. The capability to discover the individuals a user is most interested in following has therefore become an important aspect of the struggle against information overflow. We argue that the people users are most interested in following are not necessarily those with whom they are most familiar. We compare these two types of social relationships – interest and familiarity – inside IBM. We suggest inferring interest relationships from users' public interactions on four enterprise social media applications. We study these interest relationships through an offline analysis as well as an extensive user study, in which we combine people-based and content-based evaluations. The paper reports a rich set of results, comparing various sources for implicit interest indications; distinguishing between content-related activities and status or network updates, showing that the former are of more interest; and highlighting that the interest relationships include very interesting individuals that are not among the most familiar ones, and can therefore play an important role in social stream filtering, especially for content-related activities.

Introduction

In the era of information overflow, feed readers have emerged as a means to aggregate syndicated web content such as news headlines, blogs, or podcasts, in a single location for easy viewing (Bergamaschi et al., 2009; Aizenbud-Reshef,

21

Guy, & Jacovi, 2009; Samper et al., 2008). Emerging applications such as Facebook and Twitter[1] allow users to get updates from the set of people they are connected to or follow. By providing streams of news based on people, these applications have essentially become "social feed readers" that allow users to stay up-to-date through their friends or the people they follow, who serve as "social filters" (Zhao & Rosson, 2009). We refer to applications that provide news streams based on lists of people chosen by the user as *social stream applications*.

As part of the Facebook social network site (SNS), the Facebook News Feed is based on the user's set of Facebook friends – a familiarity relationship. While familiarity is probably a good indication of being interested in a person, it is not an ideal source for populating the list of people from whom the user gets news. On the one hand, not all connected people are necessarily an interesting source of news: some friending invitations are accepted for mere politeness and with no intension for a close follow-up; other connections may be with people the user anyway meets frequently and does not need to follow online. On the other hand, users may be interested in individuals who are not their friends and to whom they do not feel comfortable enough to send an invitation that needs to be reciprocated.

As opposed to Facebook, Twitter and many other social stream applications (e.g[2]., FriendFeed or Google Buzz on the web; Yammer or Chatter for the enterprise) apply an asymmetric model that allows users to follow other individuals without the need for reciprocation. When applying jump-start techniques to help new users populate the list of people they follow, these applications still typically rely on symmetric familiarity-based social network information. This information typically originates from email or instant messaging applications, reflecting the people with whom the user communicates; or from SNSs that reflect reciprocated connections. These jump-start techniques usually require that users give their passwords for accessing the third-party services, which may pose privacy issues. Moreover, communication information might be considered sensitive by users.

In this paper, we propose a novel approach for identifying the people who are of potential interest to the user. We mine social network information that reflects interest from public data sources, including commenting on another person's blog, reading someone's publicly shared file, following a person's micro-blog, or tagging another individual. We argue that mining and aggregating these interest relationships can be useful in different applications and, in particular, help improve the population process of people-following lists in social stream applications.

The mining of social network information has been previously studied. These studies have focused on mining familiarity relationships (Gilbert and Karahalios, 2009; Guy et al., CHI'08; Matsuo et al. 2006) or similarity relationships (Guy et al., 2010; Xiao et al., 2001) on the web and within enterprises. Familiarity rela-

---

[1] www.facebook.com, www.twitter.com

[2] www.friendfeed.com, www.google.com/buzz, www.yammer.com, www.salesforce.com/chatter

tionships are based on indications that two individuals know each other, e.g., an explicit connection on an SNS, or a tight collaboration on a wiki page. Similarity relationships are based on similar behaviors and activities of people who may actually be strangers, such as using the same tags, or commenting on the same blog posts. Having addressed mining of different sources for implicit people relationships, we came to realize that some of the sources imply a third type of relationship – **interest** – reflecting curiosity or care about another individual. Interest is different from both familiarity and similarity, as it reflects a directional type of link, while familiarity and similarity are symmetric in their nature. A possible theory connecting all three relationship types can be stated as follows: when two people are similar and one of them becomes aware of this similarity, s/he may become interested in the other person. If the other is also aware and interested, the two may become familiar. However, as both similarity and familiarity do not necessarily imply interest, there is value in distinguishing interest relationships from them. To the best of our knowledge, this is the first work to suggest such a distinction in people-to-people relationships.

There are several reasons for exploring "interest relationships", both on the web and behind the firewall. Such exploration may help point out the more interesting people in a community or a division; it may be used for identifying influence or reputation, or designing diffusion algorithms over networks; and it may facilitate attention management by allowing users to focus on news coming from the people they are most interested in, when stressed for time. In this paper, we focus on the latter scenario, inside the enterprise.

We provide an extensive evaluation of the interest relationships. First, we measure their directionality by examining how many of the people users are interested in are also interested in them. We then compare the interest relationships harvested from different sources to understand the richness of available information. We also compare the interest relationships to familiarity, which is typically used for jump-starting the list of people to follow. Familiarity is used here as a baseline that has been previously studied more thoroughly (Gilbert and Karahalios, 2009; Guy et al., CHI'08). Our main evaluation is based on a user study that combines a direct evaluation of people (rating lists of people as well as individuals) with an evaluation of content produced by these people (rating news items within an enterprise social stream application). As far as we know, this is the first study to combine both types of evaluations, for this purpose. We believe it is important to apply both evaluations, to verify that the people that seem to be more interesting indeed produce more interesting content (news items, in our case).

Our results indicate that the four sources for interest relationships provide a very different list of people than the user's top familiar people. While this list is noisier, it also contains individuals that are more interesting than the most familiar ones. Providing news based on this list can be useful, especially when hybridized with the familiarity list, and most prominently for news items that refer to other pieces of content, like wikis or blogs.

The structure of this paper is as follows: we open with related work. The evaluation section presents our data sources and research method, and then reports the results of an offline analysis as well as a user study. Our discussion summarizes and raises ideas for future research. We end with a conclusions section.

Related Work

Micro-blogging and Twitter

Micro-blogging is one of the key examples of social stream applications, allowing users to write short messages, often referred to as "status updates", describing their activities and opinions, or pointing at interesting content. Twitter is the leading micro-blogging service with over 100 million users worldwide writing real-time updates through "tweets" of up to 140 characters. Ever since its emergence in 2006, there have been numerous studies on Twitter in particular and micro-blogging in general (Huberman, Romero, & Wu, 2009; Java et al., 2007; Kwak et al., 2010; Naaman, Boase, & Lai, 2010). Twitter has also been studied as a source for recommendations, such as of interesting URLs (Chen et al., 2010) or of news stories within RSS feeds (Phelan, McCarthy, & Smyth, 2009). Several studies have examined enterprise micro-blogging, highlighting its value for enhancing information sharing, supporting information seeking, building a common ground, and sustaining a feeling of connectedness among colleagues (Ehrlich & Shami, 2010; Zhang et al., 2010; Zhao & Rosson, 2009).

From our perspective, the most interesting feature of Twitter is the option to follow other users. Following a person is an explicit indication of interest. As following does not need to be reciprocated, the Twitter network is asymmetric, in contrast to most leading SNSs. Kwak et al. (2010) find that Twitter indeed poses a low level of reciprocity: 77.9% of the user-user relationships are non-reciprocal. Zhao & Rosson (2009) argue that Twitter serves as a "people-based RSS feed", where users are able to get trustworthy and useful information from people they know personally. They also point out that often, the followed individuals are selected because they share similar interests with the subscriber, concerning either social hobbies or their professions. Bernstein & Chi (2010) interview Twitter users and point at three factors that drive satisfaction from reading individual tweets: topic relevance, tie strength (referring to the intensity of both familiarity and interest, without explicit distinction between them), and serendipity. In this work, we offer the distinction between familiarity and interest relationships, inspect the differences between the respective networks, and leverage both to yield a better list of people to follow.

Facebook News Feed and Social Aggregators

While the Twitter stream contains solely status updates, the stream we examine contains other enterprise social media activities, such as posting or commenting on blog entries, editing wikis, joining communities, and creating bookmarks. Due to its heterogeneity, this stream is more similar to one of the most prominent features of Facebook – the News Feed (Sanghvi, 2006) – whose introduction in 2006 marked a major change on the site (Lampe, Ellison, & Steinfield, 2008). The News Feed occupies the central part of each user's Facebook homepage, showing friends' recent activities, including, apart from status updates, such other activities as group joining, page "liking", profile changing, photo sharing, application adding, and more. As opposed to Twitter, Facebook applies a symmetric model where the only people shown in the News Feed by default are the users' friends, to whom they are reciprocally connected. Research on the Facebook News Feed is sparser than studies about Twitter, and focuses mainly on privacy issues (Boyd, 2008; Hoadley, Xu, Lee, & Rosson, 2010) and diffusion models (Sun et al., 2009).

Perhaps most similar to the stream inspected in this work are the streams created by social aggregators that consolidate friends' updates across various social media sites. FriendFeed (Gupta et al. 2009) is one of the most prominent examples of such aggregators, collating activities across many popular social media services, such as blogging systems, micro-blogging services, social bookmarking services, and many others. Similarly to Twitter, users can choose whom to follow within FriendFeed without the need for reciprocation. Current literature on FriendFeed is very sparse. Celi et al. (2010) provide a descriptive analysis of the social interactions taking place. They also perform a cluster analysis of the Italian FriendFeed network that yields a distinction between weak and highly-dedicated users. Garg et al. (2009) examine the evolution of the FriendFeed network and find that membership period, proximity within the network, and subscription to common services are all factors that affect the formation of new relationships.

Relationship Type Distinction

In this work, we distinguish between two types of social relationships: familiarity and interest. A few studies have also made the distinction between different relationship types. The most prominent example is probably the comparison between familiarity and similarity relationships in the context of recommender systems, such as for movies (Bonhard et al., 2006) or social software items (Guy et al. 2009). A few studies have suggested enhancing regular collaborative filtering, which is based on similarity between users and their tastes, with direct familiarity relationships, such as the ones articulated in SNSs (Groh & Ehmig, 2007; Lerman, 2007; Sinha & Swearingen, 2001). Hinds el al. (2000) discuss the effects of both familiarity and similarity in the context of selecting team members, while Cosley, Ludford, & Terveen (2003) compare demographic similarity with interest-based similarity in terms of affecting interaction and cooperation while performing an online task. Hogg et al. (2008) argue that supporting multiple relationship types, such as friend, fan, or colleague, can enhance the significance of the network created within an SNS. They demonstrate this through Essembly, an online political SNS that allows users to engage in content creation, voting, and discussion. Essembly semantically distinguishes between three relationship types: friends, ideological allies, and nemeses. None of these works has distinguished between familiarity and interest relationships. In this work, we directly compare the effectiveness of the familiarity and interest networks for providing newsworthy items.

Evaluation

Evaluation Settings

Our research is conducted inside IBM, a large, global IT organization that acknowledges the importance of social media, both for communication with its customers and for internal collaboration and knowledge sharing (Hibbard, 2010). To extract social network information from the rich set of enterprise social media inside IBM, we use SONAR, our social aggregation platform that harvests relationships between people from over 15 organizational sources. SONAR can be configured to aggregate specific sets of relationships and create weighted lists of people related to a user based on those relationship sets. Guy et al. (CHI'08) provide a detailed description of the aggregation and weighting algorithms.

As new enterprise social applications continue to emerge, the number of data sources and relationships aggregated by SONAR has increased (Guy et al., 2010). In previous works, SONAR classified relationships into two categories – familiarity and similarity. In this paper, we identify four relationships that are likely to imply a third category – interest in a person. These relationships are: 1) following a person's tweets within an enterprise microblogging application (Ehrlich & Shami, 2010), an explicit expression of interest; 2) tagging a person within a people-tagging application (Farrell & Lau, 2006), possibly implying the wish to speedily find the person in future searches, and indicating some knowledge about the person; 3) reading someone's file[3] in a file-sharing system (Shami, Muller, & Millen, 2011), which suggests the user found that person's content of interest (reading more files of the same person indicates more interest); and 4) commenting on a person's blog post within a blogging system (Huh et al., 2007), indicating the user read the blog and felt strongly enough about the content to comment on it (more comments on a person's blog indicate a stronger interest). For each of the

---

[3] As we are referring to an enterprise application, most shared files are documents or presentations, hence we refer to file downloading as "file reading"

four relationships, SONAR is used for extracting the ranked list of people the user is interested in.

We observe that these four interest relationships can be classified into two categories: 1) **person-interest** – following a person's tweets and tagging a person reflect interest in a person as a self, and 2) **content-interest** – reading a file and commenting on a blog post reflect interest in content created by the person. Apart from investigating each of the relationships separately, we define an aggregated interest list (I), retrieved by combining the four relationships above.

We use SONAR to harvest familiar people into a familiarity list (F), based on 24 different relationships that indicate familiarity, such as being explicitly connected on a social network site, being connected via the organizational chart, co-editing a wiki page, co-authorship of patents and papers, and other relationships (Guy et al., 2009). Previous research has indicated that aggregating familiarity relationships this way effectively produces a list of people the user knows well.

In our analysis, we examine lists I and F above, as well as a hybrid list ($I+F$). This list combines people from I and F by ranking the people that appear in both lists according to the sum of their ranks in the individual lists, and then alternating between the lists for those that appear only in one of them, according to their rank. As a result, this list gives priority to people who appear in both I and F over those who appear in just one of them.

For the last phase of our study, we use an enterprise social stream aggregator that displays an activity stream of recent public news items that took place across the organization's social media applications. The news items can originate from various sources, including: (1) profiles (status updates, additions to social network, people tagging); (2) wikis (creating and editing a public wiki); (3) blogs (creating, editing, or commenting on a blog); (4) files (creating, editing, commenting, or recommending a public file); and more. Our evaluation examines the recommendation of news items to the user, originating from different lists of people that the user may be interested in.

Research Method

The initial, offline part of our study aims to quantitatively examine the lists of people originating from the different interest relationships. We start by focusing on each separate source of interest information and studying its directionality: i.e., the match between the list of people a person is interested in, and the list of people who are interested in that person. Next, we compare the lists returned from the four interest sources to each other to examine their diversity. Finally, we compare the lists returned by the four sources to the list of familiar people, which has been extensively studied in previous papers. As social stream applications typically rely on familiarity relationships for providing news, we regard that list as a relevant baseline and seek to validate the hypothesis that the lists produced by interest relationships are indeed different from the familiarity list.

The greater part of our study is based on a personalized online survey sent as a link via email to selected participants. The survey consists of two phases: in the first phase, participants rate their direct interest in other people. In the second phase, they rate their interest in news items produced by those people. This unique combination allows us to evaluate both the direct interest in people as well as the interest in the news items they produce. We also examine the correlation between the two phases, testing whether people chosen as interesting indeed produce more interesting items.

The first phase, for rating people directly, includes two sub-phases of its own: in the first sub-phase (1a), participants are asked to rate their interest in different people **lists**, generated according to the relationships and aggregates, as described above. Each list includes 10 people. Since comparing and rating lists of people may be a complex task, we introduce a second sub-phase (1b), in which participants select individual people whom they find most interesting. We conjecture that the combination of the people list rating with individual people selection would allow us to receive a good overall picture of how interesting the people in each list are. We next describe all phases in detail.

As our goal is to identify and compare interest relationships from different sources, we focus on users who make use of at least two of the four single interest sources described above and who have at least 10 people in both their I list and F list. This ensures that participants have enough data to generate comparable lists of people and items for both phases of the survey. We identified and invited 470 such users to participate.

In phase 1a, participants are presented with up to seven lists of 10 people each. The lists are generated according to the four interest relationships described above: 1) micro-blogging following, 2) blog commenting, 3) file reading, and 4) people tagging, as well as the aggregates 5) I, 6) F, and 7) $I+F$. Each list includes the top 10 people and is not labeled according to its relationships to avoid bias. Lists that include less than 10 people are not shown (these are only lists based on a single relationship, as the selection of participants ensures at least 10 people in the aggregate lists). Thus, each participant rates between three and seven lists. In practice, the average number of lists rated by a participant was 4.89 (stdev: 1.02, median: 5).

Participants are asked to rate each list according to how much the people in the list represent a set of people from whom they would like to get news items. Rating is based on a 5-point Likert scale, ranging from "Does not represent a list of people I am interested in" to "Very much represents a list of people I am interested in". Additionally, participants are asked to indicate the best list out of those presented. Figure 1 shows a screenshot of this part of the survey.

Vijay Nehry	Natalie Olmos	Samantha Daryn	Jasmine Haj	Minh Li
Ted Amado	Lucille Suarez	EdEl Amon	Minh Li	Amar Sriva
Suzanne Miles	Ling Shin	Denn	Ling Shin	Gardner Raynes
Steve Williams	Jasmine Haj	Suzanne Miles	Simone Dray	Frank Adams
Simone Dray	Steve Williams	Dan Misawa	Ted Amado	Steve Williams
Samantha Daryn	Heather R	Charlie Hamilton	Gardner Raynes	Dennis Michaels
Ron Espinosa	Gardner Raynes	Steve Williams	Dennis Michaels	Ling Shin
Pierre Dumont	Suzanne Miles	Betty Zechman	Lucille Suarez	Ted Amado
Natalie Olmos	Minh Li	Amar Sriva	Amar Sriva	Betty Zachman
Minh Li	Frank Adams	Pierre Dumont	Betty Zachman	Pierre Dumont

Figure 1. Online survey, phase 1a

In phase 1b, participants are presented with a combined list of all the people that appeared in the previous lists and are asked to select exactly five people from whom they would most like to get news items.

In phase 2, participants are asked to rate a set of news items which are generated in the following way: For each of the three aggregate lists (I, F, and $I+F$), we extract from the social stream aggregator the 25 latest news items that relate to at least one person on that list. We then randomly choose eight items out of the 25 items and mix all chosen items while removing duplicates, resulting in a list of at most 8x3=24 items. By selecting eight items at random out of 25, rather than simply the most recent eight, we aim to increase the diversity of news items, both over time and with regards to the corresponding people and sources.

> **Lucille Suarez** edited the wiki page How to contribute to OpenSocial in the Social Computing Standards and Open Source wiki.
> 5 days ago
> O Very interesting O Interesting O Not interesting O Already know
>
> Comment:

Figure 2. Sample news item in phase 2 of the survey

Figure 2 shows a sample news item. Each item includes an icon indicating the source it originates from, a descriptive text (e.g. "P1 commented on the blog post X" or "P2 tagged P3 with 'hci'", where Pi are people names, linking to their profile pages, and X is a blog post title, linking to its page). Below each news item is an indication of the time it was posted, e.g., "2 hours ago". Participants are asked to evaluate each item as "Very Interesting", "Interesting", "Not Interesting", or "Already Know". They can also leave a comment next to each item. At the end of the survey there is another opportunity to leave a general comment.

Results – Offline Analysis

Asymmetry of Interest Relationships

The first analysis compared the directionality of the four interest relationships, examining the match between the list of people a person is interested in, and the list of people who are interested in that person using the Match@10[4] measure. The results are presented in Table I.

Table I: Examination of the directionality of the sources

	Micro-blogging	People tagging	Blog commenting	File reading
Match@10	4.75	0.42	1.09	0.51

For the micro-blogging system, 118 users with at least 10 people in both their 'following' and 'followed' lists were identified. The average Match@10 for these users is 4.75, indicating that almost half of the relationships are reciprocated.

The other relationships show far lower reciprocation. Blog commenting (with 282 users having at least 10 people in both their 'comment to' and 'comment by' lists) has about one matching person (1.09). File sharing (with 335 users) and people tagging (138 users) have even lower matches, around 0.5.

The reciprocation of these relationships is not inherent in the system, although it is sometimes encouraged. When people comment on a blog post, a link to their blog is automatically attached to their comment, encouraging the blog owner to visit and potentially comment. Following people on Twitter is visible to all, and an email message actually notifies the user about new followers, explicitly encouraging reciprocation, even if just out of courtesy. People-tagging and file-sharing require a higher level of involvement – you actually need to know something about a person to tag them; similarly, you actually need to have an interesting file to share so the other person can read it. These requirements may explain why these sources are the least reciprocated.

Overall, Table I shows that the four interest relationships pose a great deal of directionality – people you express an interest in do not necessarily express an interest in you, and the other way around. This shows us that these relationships may be different from the symmetric relationships that have been previously examined, raising a motivation to study them further.

Comparing the Interest Relationships

Next, we compared the interest direction (people the user is interested in) in each of the four relationships to one another, in an attempt to understand the resemblance between them and the richness of information that can be harvested from them. For each pair of relationships, we identified the users who have at least 10 people in both relationships, and calculated the average Match@10. The results are shown in the bottom three rows of Table II.

The results show that the four relationships are very different, having less than one match, on average, out of the top 10 people they return. This tells us that har-

---

[4] Match@k – considers the percentage of overlapping people between the top k items in two lists (we used k=10). The match@k measure captures the similarity between the lists. It reflects how well one list can approximate the other (Guy et al. CSCW'08).

vesting the four relationships would yield different information, and that aggregating them would create a richer set of interesting people. In our user study, we examined the aggregates of the relationships as well as each one on its own.

Table II: Match@10 between interest relationships

	Tweet following	Tagging	Blog commenting	File reading
Familiarity	1.10	1.65	0.57	0.65
Tweet following		0.12	0.44	0.71
Tagging			0.30	0.40
Blog commenting				0.26

Comparing Interest Relationships to Familiarity

As familiarity is commonly used as a seed list for following people, we refer to it as a baseline and compared the interest direction of all four relationships with familiarity. The results are shown in the first row of Table II above.

Tagging people has the highest average match with familiarity (1.65), with tweet following the next highest match (1.10). File reading and blog commenting have lower match rates (0.65 and 0.57, respectively). These results reflect our suggested classification of interest relationships: people-interest relationships have higher overlap with familiarity than content-interest relationships, as one may have expected.

Comparing the familiarity list (F) to the aggregation of the four interest relationships results (I) in a Match@10 of 1.49. All in all, the match between the interest relationships and familiarity is quite low; indicating that harvesting the interest relationships may enrich the set of people to follow.

Results – Online Survey

Exactly 200 people agreed to be participants and completed phase 1 of the survey; 192 completed both phases. These 192 originated from 23 countries, spanning the organization's different divisions: 35% were from the Sales Division, 27% were from Software, 16% from Headquarters, 15% from Services, 2% from Systems, 2% from Research, and 3% from others.

Comparing Lists of Interesting People

In Phase 1a of the online survey, participants were asked to rate up to seven lists of 10 people and select the best list. Table III shows a summary of the results. The first row shows the number of times each type of list was presented. The three aggregates were presented to all 200 users; the lists originating from individual relationships were presented when relevant (i.e., when containing at least 10 people). The second row shows the percentage of times a list was selected as the best list, relative to the number of times it was presented. List *I,* an aggregation of all interest sources, has a statistically significant lower percentage of best votes than list F (7.78% vs. 32.34% with p=1.25E-07 in a one-tailed paired t-test). The hybrid list *(I+F)* is perceived best (most interesting) even more times than the *F* list. Among the individual sources (listed on the right side of the table), the list based on file reading has the highest rate of best votes (13.89%), followed by people tagging (11.11%). Interestingly, these are the two lists for which more participants had data (108 and 135, respectively) – apparently they are indeed more interesting and attract more users.

Table III: Selecting interesting lists of people

	I	F	I+F	micro-blogging	People Tagging	Blogs	Files
# appearances	200	200	200	60	135	74	108
Best list selection %	7.78%	32.34%	37.72%	6.67%	11.11%	4.05%	13.89%
Average score	3.14	3.57	3.81	3.18	2.98	2.88	3.10
% rated 1	6.50%	7.00%	2.50%	8.33%	10.37%	9.46%	9.26%
% rated 2	23.50%	14.00%	12.00%	15.00%	24.44%	31.08%	24.07%
% rated 3	34.00%	22.00%	17.50%	36.67%	32.59%	28.38%	25.00%
% rated 4	22.00%	29.00%	38.50%	30.00%	22.22%	24.32%	30.56%
% rated 5	14.00%	28.00%	29.50%	10.00%	10.37%	6.76%	11.11%

The bottom part of Table III refers to the 1-5 ratings. As in the case of the best votes, the *I* list yields the lowest average rating of the three aggregates, while the average score of *I+F* is higher than that of *F*. The distribution of scores can be seen in the last five rows of the table, where we see that *I+F* not only has the best average, but in fact obtains the highest number of 4 and 5 ratings (most interesting). This is encouraging and hints that there is value in harvesting the interest relationships for composing lists for people following applications. The bottom of the table visualizes the comparison between the sources, and especially the individual sources, showing that reading files and following micro-blogs typically create more interesting lists, whereas blogs seem to yield less interesting lists.

Selecting Interesting Individuals

Phase 1b of the study presented the participants with the same set of people they saw in phase 1a, but this time in a single list out of which they were asked to select five individual people who are of most interest.

Table IV: Selecting interesting individuals

	I	F	I+F
# of appearances	2000	2000	2000
# selected from group	424	329	565
relative percent	21.20%	16.45%	28.25%

The results, depicted in Table IV, are quite different from phase 1a. The *I* list yields more interesting individuals than the *F* list, despite being rated lower as a whole list in phase 1a (difference is statistically significant, $p=1.88E-05$ in a one-tailed paired t-test). The aggregated list $I+F$ yields even more selected individuals. This tells us that while the F list, as a whole, is more interesting on average, the very interesting individuals are actually in the I list. This may be explained by the fact that in addition to the most interesting people, I also contains less interesting people, some of them unfamiliar to the user, who are considered "noise" when examined as part of a whole list.

An interesting discussion is raised here, about the tension between receiving the most interesting news along with noise, versus missing out on the most interesting news, but getting less noise. One participant wrote a related comment: *"An interesting dilemma is that there are those who are of interest for my day job, whilst others are inspirational or of interest for skill expansion!"* Another wrote: *"I think I would always want direct reports to be included in my feed. [However] if you removed them, and then presented the list, things may be more interesting."* It seems that hybridization combines the benefits of both I and F, being rated highest as a whole list as well as containing the most top-five individuals.

Comparing Interesting Items

In phase 2 of the study, users were presented with actual news items, associated with people in the I, F, and $I+F$ lists. 192 people completed this part of the survey. As a whole, they were presented with 3629 news items, and were asked to rate them as "very interesting", "interesting", "not interesting", or "already know". In our analysis, we merge the responses of "very interesting" and "interesting" under "all interesting". Figure 3 summarizes the distribution of item ratings coming from the three lists.

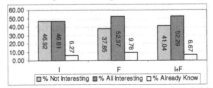

Figure 3. Interest rate comparison of all 3629 items

The F list has an advantage over the I list in this case: it has more items rated interesting and less of its items are considered "noise" (not interesting). These findings are statistically significant ($p=9.13E-06$ in a one-tailed unpaired t-test). The percentage of items rated interesting in $I+F$ is very similar to F. F has the higher percentage of already-known items, but also the lowest percentage of non-interesting items. The I list evidently helps lower the expectedness of news, while at the same time increasing the noise. One participant commented: *"Some of these people I work with on a daily basis at the same location, so although I am very interested in their activities, my need to follow them on social software is minimal."*

In order to examine the correlation between participants' ratings in phases 1 and 2, we examined whether the people selected among the top five most interesting individuals in phase 1b indeed yielded more interesting news items as rated in phase 2. Table V shows this comparison over all 192 participants who completed both phases. Individuals selected among the top five in phase 1 yielded 57.8% all interesting items vs. 35.4% non-

Table V. Interest rate in phase 2 items by people selection in phase 1b

	All Interest	Not Interest	Known
top-5 ppl	57.8%	35.4%	6.8%
others	47.2%	46.5%	6.3%

interesting ones, while individuals who were not selected among the top five, yielded items rated 47.2% all interesting vs. 46.5% non-interesting. These differences are statistically significant ($p=1.7E-10$ in a one-tailed unpaired t-test) and indicate that participants' selection of top-five individuals indeed reflects higher likelihood that the news items they produce are interesting. While the I list contains more top-five individuals who yield more interesting news items, the overall rating of its news items is slightly lower than those of the F list, which has fewer top-five individuals. This reinforces our suspicion that alongside the highly interesting individuals, the I list contains more non-interesting individuals who ultimately overshadow the high rating of news items yielded by the top-five individuals.

Studying the various sources

The analysis discussed above examined an aggregation of all sources of news. However, it turns out that items originating from different types of sources are very different in the interest level they yield. We next examine several different sources of news items to better understand these differences.

The source that provides the most interesting news is the file-sharing application. 311 items originated from it, notifying of file creations and edits. Figure 4 shows that in this case, the I list has a slightly higher percentage of

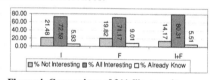

Figure 4. Comparison of 311 file news items

interesting items than F. The $I+F$ list outperforms both the I and F lists, with over 80% of interesting items. It even has less already-known items than the I list. The F list has the highest percentage of already-known items – 9%.

Wikis turn out to be another source for relatively interesting items. 282 items originated from wikis, notifying of wiki creation and editing. Their rates are shown in Figure 5. Here, I outperforms F by an even more no-

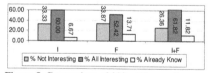

Figure 5. Comparison of 282 wiki news items

ticeable gap, while $I+F$ is slightly better than I. The I list has substantially less already-known items than the F and $I+F$ lists.

Blogs are another example of a source that produces mostly interesting items – 57% out of 270 blog updates were rated as interesting or very interesting. The figures of the I, F, and $I+F$ lists are very similar for blog updates with a slight advantage of I over F (58.82% vs. 57.14% items rated interesting; 57.52% for $I+F$.)

Next, we examine the 518 status updates (Figure 6). The general interest rate for these items is around 54%, which is lower than files, wikis, and blogs. F outperforms I here, both in the percentage of interesting items,

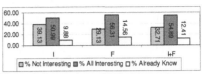

Figure 6. Comparison of 518 status updates

and in the noise level. $I+F$ yields similar ratings to F, but does not outperform it.

Network addition news items and updates about related people adding or being added as friends, are examples of items of less general interest (Figure 7). One participant commented: *"NEVER NEVER NEVER*

Figure 7. Comparison of 401 network additions

show me someone else's network additions! This is useless." Indeed, the interest rates for these types of news items are the lowest. F again performs better than I here, with both more interesting items and less noise. $I+F$ performs quite similarly to F.

Another source of less general interest is people tagging. As can be seen in Figure 8, while the F list contains an even rate of interesting vs. not-interesting items, the I list contains mostly non-interesting items.

It seems that item types of less

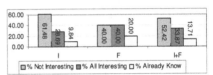

Figure 8. Comparison of 232 people tagging items

general interest have a better interest rate when coming from familiar people (the F list). This may be explained by the fact that even if the item's content is not interesting, one still gains something when learning about familiar people. All in all, it seems that the variance of interest among the sources feeding the news feed is large and deserves dedicated research.

Inspecting these results, we observe that the news sources can be categorized into three categories: (1) **content-related activities**, such as activities related to files, wikis, and blogs; (2) **micro-blogging** messages, such as status updates; and (3) **network activity**, such as people tagging and friend addition. The general interest in each category is quite different. News concerning content generated the most interest: from about 57% for blogs to nearly 75% for files. Status updates generate slightly less interest, with about 54% of the news items rated interesting. Network activities are far less interesting, with around 34% general interest in people tagging and only 25% interest in network additions.

Even more interestingly, for the content-related sources, the I list produces slightly better results than the F list (as in files, wikis, and blogs). For status updates, F outperforms I, while for network activities the gap slightly grows. Thus, the I list is especially productive for the most interesting news types, the content-related activities. This is a substantial outcome when considering which news items should ultimately be on the user's news feed.

Consistently across almost all news item types, F yields more already-known items, while I yields more noise. In many of the cases, the hybridization combines both advantages – it has less known items than F and less noise than I, often also leading to a slightly higher percentage of interesting items. Several participants commented that they wished to get hybrid news from both close colleagues and people outside their organization circle. One wrote "*I like a mix of people, with a few from different organizations and geographies … I specifically don't want only people in my own organization*," while another stated "*Most interested either up my management chain or outside my organization, for strategic networking*".

Discussion, Limitations, and Future Work

The previous section provides diverse analysis of the interest relationships. First, we show that interest relationships are indeed often asymmetric – the people you are interested in are not necessarily interested in you. This is reflected in a very low level of symmetry across all interest relationships, apart from following people on micro-blogging, for which reciprocity is explicitly encouraged. In this work, we focus on one direction of the interest relationships – the people a user is interested in. Comparing the lists of people that are returned from four public sources reveals that the overlap is low, as each brings a rather different list of people. As a result, aggregating them produces a richer picture of one's "network of interest". The overlap with familiarity is generally low, indicating that the people you are most interested in are not necessarily the ones you are most familiar with. This overlap also reflects the distinction suggested for the interest relationships: person-interest relationships (following and tagging) have a higher overlap with familiarity than content-interest sources (file reading and blog commenting).

Our online survey focuses on comparing the interest list with the familiarity list and a hybridization of the two. The people-based evaluation (phase 1) indicates that the interest list consists of a few very interesting people (who are often selected among the top five most interesting) but also some "noise" – people who are not interesting at all (and may not even be familiar to the user). Hence, when evaluating lists of people, most users would prefer the more "solid" familiarity list; however when picking the top interesting individuals, more would come from the interest list. The hybrid $I+F$ list is found to be the best performing list in all aspects of this phase: it has the highest average rating, marked best most times, and its individuals are most often among the top five. These results indicate that mining interest relationships and combining them with familiarity can enhance automatic inference of the people who are of the most interest to the user.

The news item evaluation (phase 2) shows that the F and $I+F$ lists produce very similar percentage of interesting items (slightly over 52%). $I+F$ produces less already-known items, while F produces less noise (non-interesting items). The I list produces the least interesting items (about 47%) and has the most noise (also about 47%). These results point at the tension between getting the most interesting items that span beyond your close network, but with some noise; and getting a more solid list of interesting yet more expected items, and missing out on the most interesting ones. Users of social stream applications should be allowed to choose between these two options. Hybridization offers a way to mitigate the noise while maintaining the non-expectedness level. In this work, we examined one specific hybridization method. Further techniques for hybridization and their potential to improve the results should be examined in future research.

Breaking down the results by item type reveals that interest diversity across types is high: while content-related activities are very interesting (e.g., files yield 75% interesting items), network-related activities are mostly not (e.g., additions to network yield only 25% interesting items). Status updates are in-between with slightly over 50% of interest. In terms of the comparison between I and F, the I list yields better results for the content-related activities (files, wikis, blogs), while F substantially outperforms I for status updates and network-related activities.

Some of the comments we received help understand these differences. One participant wrote *"Someone else's network additions is of no interest to me ... unless it is someone I know well, and even then mainly for gossip,"* and another commented *"I'm only interested in updates on tagging if it's one of my close colleagues who has been tagged or used the tag."* On the other hand, items that relate to other content are interesting beyond a user's close social circle and in general are considered more interesting news. It can also be that for content-related activities, people have other channels (like face-to-face meetings or email) to get the updates from their close colleagues; hence the results for the F list are lower than for the other lists for these item types. In any case, these findings indicate that the I list has the most substantial effect on the category of most interesting news.

Following a person on an enterprise micro-blogging system is the most explicit expression of interest, analogous to a connection on an SNS for familiarity relationships. One might assume that having micro-blogging as one of the sources in the I aggregation has the strongest influence on its performance. However, inspecting the results for the 108 participants who do not use the micro-blogging application and do not have it as a source, reveals that ratings of items from their I list are not lower than for the entire population. This tells us that a good interest list can be composed even if there is no explicit following information.

Our survey respondents are not a representative sample of the organization's employees, but rather avid users of our enterprise social media, for whom interest lists can be produced. While this is not an optimal choice, trying to identify a representative sample would result in too little data for most participants, as social media is still not prevalent enough. However, we believe that the potential population who can benefit from automatic mining of their interest network will grow in the years to come, as social media becomes more popular in organizations, and as web users get used to exposing more information in public. File reading within an enterprise file-sharing application (Shami, Muller, & Millen, 2011) is an example of a new public source of information, which exposes very valuable data about people's interests. In most of our results, file reading is indicated to be the most effective interest indicator, even if by a small margin, over the other three.

We compare an initial set of aggregated interest relationships (four overall) with a well-established aggregation of familiarity relationships (24 overall). While this combination of familiarity relationships has been shown effective in producing a list of people the user knows, we show that for producing a list of people the user is interested in, the four interest sources are important. Combining both lists can be beneficial in yielding a final list that is diverse and contains very interesting people outside the close workgroup of the user. As enterprise social media becomes more popular, new sources for mining interest may become available. Aggregating a richer set of interest relationships can reduce noise and ultimately make the interest network even more representative.

Claypool, et al. (2001) discuss *implicit interest indicators* in items, such as movies or web pages. Such indicators include clicking, viewing, or searching for the item. In this work, we essentially propose *implicit interest indicators* in **people**. These indicators are based on public data, such as commenting on a blog, tagging, or following. Our future plans include the investigation of private implicit interest indicators, such as viewing a person's profile or searching for the person. Such private indicators, however, involve sensitive data that might raise privacy issues.

Other future directions include exploring harvesting of interest relationships outside the enterprise, where the variety of social media applications and thus potential sources for mining interest relationships is larger. The interest relationships we examined in this work have counterparts on the web (following, commenting, reading, tagging), while the potential richness of sources further grows outside the firewall (e.g., "liking" another person's content as on Facebook). Finally, we plan to inspect more scenarios for leveraging the interest relationships. For example, collaborative filtering, the most popular technique for recommender systems, recommends items, such as movies or books, based on the preferences of similar people. Executing collaborative filtering based on interest relationships can potentially further boost its performance.

Conclusions

Social stream applications rely mainly on familiarity relationships to filter news items or jump-start the list of people from whom users get news. In this work, we suggest mining a new type of social relationships – interest. Interest relationships reflect directional curiosity or care about another individual and are more asymmetric in nature than previously studied familiarity or similarity relationships.

Our evaluation examines four sources for mining interest relationships inside a large global enterprise, showing each source to yield a rather different set of individuals. The aggregated interest network is found to be very different from the familiarity network. In spite of being based on solely four relationships, the interest network is found to include very interesting people beyond the user's closest workgroup (in parallel with some noise). Hybridizing this network with the familiarity network can be highly valuable in producing interesting and diverse news items for users of social stream applications.

References

1. Aizenbud-Reshef, N., Guy, I., and Jacovi, M. 2009. Collaborative feed reading in a community. *Proc. GROUP '09*, 277-280.

2. Bergamaschi, S., Guerra, F., Orsini, M., Sartori, C., and Vincini, M. 2009. Relevant News: a semantic news feed aggregator. *Proc. Italian Semantic Web Workshop 2007*.

3. Bernstein, M., Kairam, S., Suh, B., Hong, L., and Chi, E.H. 2010. A torrent of tweets: managing information overload in online social streams. *Workshop on Microblogging, CHI '10*.

4. Bonhard, P., Harries, C., McCarthy, J., & Sasse, M. A. 2006. Accounting for taste: using profile similarity to improve recommender systems. *Proc. CHI' 06*, 1057-1066.

5. Boyd, D. 2008. Facebook's privacy trainwreck: exposure, invasion, and social convergence. *Convergence* 14 (1).

6. Celi, F., Di Lascio, F.M.L., Magnani, M., Pacelli, B., and Rossi, L. 2010. Social network data and practices: the case of Friendfeed. *Advances in Social computing*, 346-353.

7. Chen, J., Nairn, R., Nelson, L., Bernstein, M., and Chi, E.H. 2010. Short and tweet: experiments on recommending content from information streams. *Proc. CHI '10*, 1185-1194.

8. Claypool, M., Le, P., Wased, M., & Brown, D. 2001. Implicit Interest Indicators. Proc. IUI '01, 33–40.

9. Cosley, D., Ludford, P., and Terveen, L. 2003. Studying the effect of similarity in online task-focused interactions. *Proc. Group '03*, 321-329.

10. Ehrlich, K. and Shami, N.S. 2010. Microblogging inside and outside the workplace. *Proc. ICWSM '10*.

11. Farrell, S., & Lau T. 2006. Fringe Contacts: People Tagging for the Enterprise. *Workshop on Collaborative Web Tagging*, WWW' 06.

12. Garg, S., Gupta, T., Carlsson, N., and Mahanti, A. 2009. Evolution of an online social aggregation network: an empirical study. *Proc. IMC '09*, 315-321.\

13. Gilbert, E. and Karahalios, K. 2009. Predicting tie strength with social media. *Proc. CHI '09*, 211-220.

14. Groh, G., and Ehmig, C. 2007. Recommendations in Taste Related Domains: Collaborative Filtering vs. Social Filtering. *Proc. GROUP'07*, 127-136.

15. Gupta, T., Garg, S., Carlsson, N., Mahanti, A., and Arlitt, M. 2009. Characterization of Friendfeed: A web based social aggregation service. *Proc. ICWSM '09*.

16. Guy, I., Jacovi, M., Meshulam, N., Ronen, I., Shahar, E. Public vs. private: comparing public social network information with email. *Proc. CSCW '08,* 393-402.

17. Guy, I., Jacovi, M., Perer, A., Ronen, I., and Uziel, E. 2010. Same Places, Same Things, Same People? Mining User Similarity on Social Media. *Proc. CSCW '10*, 41-50.

18. Guy, I., Jacovi, M., Shahar, E., Meshulam, N., Soroka, V., & Farrell, S. 2008. Harvesting with SONAR: the value of aggregating social network information. *Proc. CHI'08*, 1017-1026.

19. Guy, I., Zwerdling, N., Carmel, D., Ronen, I., Uziel, E., Yogev, S., and Ofek-Koifman S. 2009. Personalized Recommendation of Social Software Items based on Social Relationships. *Proc. RecSys '09*, 53-60.

20. Hibbard, C. 2010. How IBM Uses Social Media to Spur Employee Innovation. Social Media Examiner online Magazine (Feb. 2010). http://www.socialmediaexaminer.com/how-ibm-uses-social-media-to-spur-employee-innovation/

21. Hinds, P. J., Carley, K. M., Krackhardt, D., & Wholey, D. 2000. Choosing work group members: Balancing similarity, competence, and familiarity. *OBHDP 81 (2)*, 226–251.

22. Hoadley, C.M., Xu, H., Lee, J.J, Rosson, M.B. 2010. Privacy as information access and illusory control: The case of the Facebook News Feed privacy outcry. *Electronic Commerce Research and Applications 9, 1 (Jan. 2010)*, 50-60.

23. Hogg, T., Wilkinson, D., Szabo, G, and Brzozowski M. J. 2008. Multiple relationship types in online communities and social networks. *Proc. AAAI Symposium on Social Information Processing.*

24. Huberman, B., Romero, D., and Wu, F. 2009. Social networks that matter: Twitter under the microscope. *First Monday* 14, 1 (Jan. 2009).

25. Huh, J., Jones, L., Erickson, T., Kellogg, W. A., Bel-lamy, R. K., and Thomas, J. C. 2007. BlogCentral: the role of internal blogs at work. *Proc. CHI '07*, 2447-2452.

26. Java, A., Song, X., Finin, T., and Tseng, B. 2007. Why we twitter: understanding microblogging usage and communities. *Proc. WebKDD '07*, 56-65.

27. Kwak, H., Lee, C., Park, H., and Moon, S. 2010. What is Twitter, a social network or a news media? *Proc. WWW '10*, 591-600.

28. Lampe, C., Ellison, N. B., and Steinfield, C. 2008. Changes in use and perception of Facebook. *Proc. CSCW '08*, 721-730.

29. Lerman, K. 2007. Social networks and social information filtering on Digg. *Proc. ICWSM'07.*

30. Matsuo, Y., Hamasaki, M. et al. Spinning multiple social networks for semantic Web. *Proc. AAAI '06* (2006).

31. Naaman, M., Boase, J., and Lai, C. 2010. Is it really about me?: message content in social awareness streams. *Proc. CSCW '10*, 189-192.

32. Phelan, O., McCarthy, K., and Smyth, B. 2009. Using twitter to recommend real-time topical news. *Proc. RecSys '09*, 385-388.

33. Samper, J. J., Castillo, P. A., Araujo, L., Merelo, J. J., Cordón, í., and Tricas, F. 2008. NectaRSS, an intelligent RSS feed reader. *J. Netw. Comput. Appl.* 31, 4 (Nov. 2008), 793-806.

34. Sanghvi, R. (2006, September 5). Facebook Gets a Facelift. Retrieved January 17, 2010, from http://blog.facebook.com/blog.php?post=2207967130

35. Shami, S.N., Muller, M.J., and Millen, D.R. 2011. Browse and discover.: social file sharing in the enterprise. *Proc. CSCW '11.*

36. Sun, E., Rosenn, I., Marlow, C., Lento, T. 2009. Gesundheit! Modeling contagion through Facebook News Feed. *Proc. ICWSM '09.*

37. Xiao, J., Zhang, Y., Jia, X., & Li, T. 2001. Measuring similarity of interests for clustering web-users. *Proc. ADC'01*, 107-114.

38. Zhang, J., Qu, Y., Cody, J., and Wu, Y. 2010. A case study of micro-blogging in the enterprise: use, value, and related issues. *Proc. CHI '10*, 123-132.

39. Zhao, D. and Rosson, M. 2009. How and why people Twitter: the role that micro-blogging plays in informal communication at work. *Proc. GROUP '09*, 243-252

Studying the Adoption of Mail2Tag: an Enterprise2.0 Tool for Sharing

Les Nelson, Gregorio Convertino, Ed H. Chi and Rowan Nairn
Palo Alto Research Center, Inc.
*Email: lesnelson@acm.org, convertino@parc.com, ed.h.chi@gmail.com,
rnairn@gmail.com*

Abstract. The Mail2Tag system leverages existing practices around enterprise email to move relevant information out from individual inboxes. With Mail2Tag users share information by emailing content to a special email address, such as CC to sometag@share.company.com, where 'sometag' can be any keyword. The system then adaptively redistributes the information based on profiles inferred from prior user activity in the system. In this way no changes to the email client are required for users to participate in the system and information is routed based on individual need, while the amount of information noise is reduced. We study the Mail2Tag system and its 20-month deployment in an organization as a lens to understand how to measure the adoption for this type of tool for sharing. We assess adoption via quantitative and qualitative measures and identify key factors that facilitate or constrain adoption. Our findings suggest that perceived usefulness is a key facilitator and that people are drawn to different levels of use depending on their social role in the organization. Each level of use is a valuable contribution in itself and should be accounted for when assessing adoption.

Introduction

Enterprise social software borrows heavily from its consumer counterpart. This may be seen in a number of ways: in the terms of Web2.0 [26] and Enterprise2.0 [24] developments, the suite of tools such as wikis, blogs, microblogs, and actual work practices such as collective generation of content, folksonomies, tagging of content, and commentaries. The interest in adopting Web2.0 the enterprise often manifests itself as a bottom up, "grassroots" introduction of technology and practices into organizations. However, an implicit expectation of Enterprise2.0 is the viral grofigurewth and enormous collective action and constructions that might be possible, but this expectation is not easy to meet (e.g., [4, 10]).

We developed and deployed Mail2Tag, an enterprise social software system for organizational information sharing. The design of the system builds on the ever-present use of email as a fundamental mechanism for sharing. By enabling knowledge workers to use freeform tags as addresses in an email, it leverages existing email practices to promote bottom-up folksonomy-based organization of the knowledge shared without the need to install any special email client. Studying the deployment, we wondered: How successful was Mail2Tag in being adopted? What criteria and comparisons should be used to evaluate its success?

Based on two years of Mail2Tag deployment, we have found that answering these questions is actually quite difficult. The first issue is that an organization's management often expects 100% adoption. Their comparison point is often the popularity of email, which is expected to be pervasive and attended to by all users [34, 9]. Email is now essential and adopted for a wide variety of purposes [9]. However, not all tools fit into work practices as pervasively as email. Second, the related literature shows that many volunteer-based contribution systems based on Web2.0 technology have similar contribution adoption rates, and in the range of 2-15% adoption rate (e.g., [4, 10, 13, 32, 38]). Ironically, this is consistent with power law adoption curves from consumer sites, where the minority (10-20%) of the users contributes the majority (80-90%) of the content (e.g. [1, 21]). With Mail2Tag we found adoption rates equivalent or slightly better than the current best cases [10, 32]: e.g., 17% of the employees contributed some content and 46% accessed some content at least once. Thus we ask if these best cases of 10-20% contribution rates in organizations are to be considered success stories.

In this paper, we use the Mail2Tag system and its deployment in an organization to understand how to measure the successful adoption of enterprise collaboration systems. Our approach is as follows:

- First, we describe our system's usage data, including production contribution as well as reading or 'lurking' behaviors to show the different levels of engagement. We show that the adoption story for different users leads to a stratification from readers to leaders [30].
- Second, we conducted an adoption survey with users across various degrees and forms of system use and measured the impact of perceived usefulness, ease of use, and social influence on system use. We present our findings about what predicted adoption in our study.
- Third, assuming that there is a natural division of labor in the organization, one would expect the functionality of an information sharing system to appeal to specific roles. We show how the brokerage in the sharing network correlates with use of the system. That is, the way features of the

system fit into workers' practices matters a great deal in the kind and level of adoption that we can expect by different individuals.

We discuss the related literature on adoption and then briefly describe the Mail2Tag system. A detailed system description is beyond the scope of this paper, which focuses on the adoption issues (see [25] for more system information). Next we describe a 20-month deployment and detail the analysis of multiple measures of system use during the deployment. We conclude with implications for adoption of information sharing tools in organizations.

Related Work

Adoption data of Web2.0 and Enterprise2.0

We report here findings about adoption for Web2.0 tools in the consumer domain and for similar Enterprise2.0 tools [24, 4].

Numerous success stories of adoption for Web2.0 tools have emerged in the consumer space. By significantly lowering the costs for users to share content and collaborate [26], several of these tools have succeeded in recruiting very large populations of users from the public Web. Evident successes include tools such as wikis (e.g., Wikipedia is edited by 300,000 users monthly), sites for sharing videos, photos or bookmarks (e.g. YouTube.com has 2 billion views daily), blogs and forums (e.g., Yahoo Answers has 15 million visitors daily), social networking sites (e.g., Facebook has 500 million users), and microblogs (e.g., Twitter has 190 million unique visitors monthly).

Organizations and researchers are now exploring how similar successes can be replicated in the context of organizations. A key question is *whether the processes that drive adoption in organizations are the same as in the consumer space.* Multiple researchers have described the participation rates for Web2.0 tools with power law or Pareto distributions (e.g., [1]). This distribution exhibits a narrow head and a long tail: that is, a minority of the users, or power users (the narrow head), generates the majority of the contributions; the majority of the users (the long tail) generates the minority of the contributions. This trend in the contribution rate is consistent across several Web2.0 communities: Wikipedia editors [21], Usenet discussions [36], and social tagging systems [15]. A first challenge for Enterprise2.0's success is to create the conditions so that the system is sustainable over time. A second challenge is to make sure that the tools reduce costs or increase benefits to a sufficient extent so that a critical mass of users is led to "inhabit" the head of the distribution.

While there is hope that Enterprise2.0 will replicate consumer space adoption, results suggest that Web2.0 tools recently deployed in organization are affected by low contribution rates. The rates range between about 2-15% and vary widely by factors such as the specific tool, the organization and its size, and culture. The overall rates of contribution reported for corporate blogs in large companies such as IBM [10, 14] and Microsoft [11] is about 3%. Similarly, about 2-4% of the IBM workforce visited the Beehive social networking site monthly, while about 15% of the workforce had registered over two years [32, 13]. Brzozowski and collaborators [4] found that the participation rates in social media at HP varied widely depending on the country (10% in UK vs. 1.9% in Japan and Mexico), job function, group, and the manager's activity in the system. For example, among HP employees, the discussion forums were more popular than blogs and wikis (10 and 28 times more popular, respectively) [4]. Other statistics about corporate wikis from MITRE [19], IBM [2], and Microsoft [17] suggest that while many employees report that they used wikis, very few are those who actually contribute.

Studies of adoption: key factors

Pioneering case studies of adoption of collaborative systems in organization were conducted on electronic calendars [12], Lotus Notes [27], and email [23]. Ehrlich [12] and Grudin [16] found that a key limit to adoption of electronic calendars in an organization is the disparity between those who do the work and those who get the benefit. In her study of Lotus Notes, Orlikowski [27] observed that organizational factors (e.g., policies and procedures) and individual factors (e.g. impact on individual productivity) are likely to "shape the adoption and early use" of collaborative systems. Studying email when it was still new for organizations, Markus [23] observed that the adoption and use of a new medium is affected by social factors of sponsorship, socialization, and social control.

Palen and Grudin [28] reviewed prior work on adoption and drew two general points. First, while there is consensus that upper management advocacy is a key top-down facilitator, prior success cases suggest that the bottom-up factors of having evangelists and peer pressure are equally important for adoption. For electronic calendar the peer pressure was channeled by the interface and by being integrated with email, as this reminded non-users of the use by others and benefits they might be missing. A similar condition was sought in the design of Mail2Tag.

A second general point proposed by Palen and Grudin [28] is that the term adoption has been used with different meanings in different research communities. For researchers of Management Information Sciences (MIS), who have an organizational focus, 'adopt' means 'acquire' or 'decide to use', at the level of the organization. Differently, for Human-Computer Interaction (HCI) researchers, who have a user-centered focus, 'adopt' means 'begin to use', at the level of the user. The Management Information System (MIS) perspective, which is closer to a managerial view, has tended to use more the term in the sense of acceptance, which assumes lack of choice (see Technology Acceptance Model (TAM), Davis [8]). For these researchers it would be possible to say a system was adopted or accepted even when there was little usage. In contrast, for HCI researchers adoption, which in this case assumes presence of choice, implies that it was deliberately used at the user level. This discrepancy of meaning will gradually disappear as the theoretical models proposed in the context of MIS research are applied to study the actual usage. The results on adoptions presented in this paper, together with a few recent studies [7], are initial research efforts testing these theoretical models.

While HCI researchers have focused on usability and user choice, MIS researchers have found repeatedly that perceived usefulness is an even stronger predictor of use for systems. Davis [8] conducted two studies on the acceptance of technology. One of these pertained to the use of email and a file editor at a large IBM laboratory in Canada. In both studies, he found that perceived usefulness was a better predictor of system use than perceived ease of use.

MIS researchers have proposed revised or competing models to TAM that better predict acceptance and usage. Venkatesh et al. [33] developed the Unified Theory of Acceptance and Use of Technology (UTAUT) model. UTAUT considers four key factors of performance expectancy, effort expectancy, social influences, and facilitating conditions, as potential predictors of intention to use and actual use [33]. The first two factors correspond to the factors of perceived usefulness and perceived ease of use considered in the earlier TAM model [8]. Using data from two organizations Venkatesh et al. showed that performance expectancy continued to be the strongest predictor and that UTAUT outperformed eight existing adoption models [33].

In a few more recent studies, researchers have started examining the distinctive characteristics of the Enterprise2.0 deployments and identifying factors that may be limiting contribution rates on tools such as corporate blogs and wikis. These factors include high costs for contributing and maintaining content [19, 17], time [20] or attention [38], the large amount of irrelevant or outdated content [20, 17], or the limited relevance of the content for business goals [20], or other factors such as not knowing how to get started [20, 10], not wanting to share unfinished work or disclose potentially sensitive information [19]. Viewing Enterprise2.0 as a new domain, researchers are now experimenting with ways for facilitating adoption. For example, Blog Muse [10] increased the adoption rates compared to regular blogs. Our study and deployment are part of this ongoing effort.

Finally, studies have pointed to factors inherent to structures of the social network within organizations, which may affect (or be affected by) the use of tools for knowledge sharing. Knowledge sharing is effective and productive when there are proper network conditions and roles [3]. At the level of cohesive groups (or sub-network intragroup [6]), some advantages for the workers are obtained by bridging with like-minded people. There are advantages for some workers to bridge across expansive groups, or sub-networks [6]. Burt [5] proposes that, although bridging incurs extra costs in the short term, the people who bridge structural holes have a long-term advantage of exposure to greater diversity of information and know-how. The brokers have opportunities to discover greater amounts of useful, productive knowledge. Thus having the right proportion of active brokers is functional to the productivity of workers in an organization [5, 29]. Information brokers represent a special class of users to be accounted for when reporting on the adoption of a knowledge sharing system.

Studies of participation and motivation

Several HCI researchers have also focused on the factors that affect participation or the motivations to participate. This new research, however, has not been connected yet with the prior work on adoption. Preece and Shneiderman [30] have studied the how users can move between different degrees of participations, from reader to leader, in an online community. Zhang [39] defines ten design principles that take into account people's motivations for usage based on known psychological, cognitive, social, and emotional sources of motivation. Lampe et al. [22] describe an empirical study of participation in a social website designed for sharing user-generated content. They found that participation was predicted by social motivations such as the desire to make connections. It was predicted by the value that individuals derive from providing informative content but not by social interaction. Moreover, the main barrier to participation was motivational and not due to usability, even though users had initially anticipated that it would be.

The Mail2Tag System

While email remains the channel of choice in the enterprise, keeping email interesting and relevant, reducing the amount of information noise, and enabling efficient reuse are growing challenges in knowledge work organizations. The system investigated in this research, Mail2Tag, was designed to address these challenges. In Mail2Tag the user can share by simply sending an email message with the content to be shared, and addressing the message to one or more topic-specific keywords. For example, one might use the address, bizdev@share.X.com, for referring to information related to the topic of "business development" (see Figure 2, top left). Thus, the content of that email is 'tagged' by the keyword 'bizdev'. Any mail may have multiple tags attached to it in this manner in the 'To' or 'CC' fields of an email using any client. Any keyword can be used on-the-fly, as in a social tagging system.

Mail2Tag works as an independent mail server running inside the corporate network (e.g., a host called share.X.com, where X is the company's domain name). A brief overview of the system follows:

- Workers send email messages with 1 or more tag addresses (tag@share.company.com) in the TO or CC fields of the message and, generally, also email addresses of colleagues who may be interested.
- This causes the Mail2Tag mail server to selectively receive theses topic-related email messages, parse the address fields, and sets up subscriptions between the tags, the message content, and the people involved. The content posted into the system can be anything expressible as an email message, including attachments.
- Then, these published messages can be searched, viewed, and edited via a web2.0 interface (Figure 1, bottom). The interface gives different views of the posted content and is available within the company network only (at http://share.company.com). The system allows sharing across the entire company or within groups that an administrator can easily create upon demand. The interface support functions to add more tags or people to an existing message or to reply to it via the web browser rather than via email.
- Digests of recent activities are periodically sent to users (Fig. 1, top right). The frequency is based on their preferences and their activity in the system.
- The workers who send or receive a message are implicitly subscribed to the message's tags by the system as they send or receive a tagged email message. They can also explicitly subscribe or unsubscribe to topical tags or specific messages (as for a discussion thread) via the web interface.

Thus the system augments existing practice of sharing information via email by allowing a tag address in a message. While enabling easy publishing and re-finding of this information, the system does not induce people to send additional emails other than those that they are already sharing and the periodic digests that the system sends (the user can regulate the frequency of these digests).

The different features leave traces of activity in the system logs that are the primary focus of this paper. Features that describe content consumption, or 'reading', include clicks on the website, feed requests of recent change, and receiving a tagged email. Features for contributing (or content production) include emailing content into the system, add tags in a form field directly on the website, and using the 'social' website features such as thanking, commenting, administering, and editing shared content. These features produce a range of activity for which logs are collected for measuring adoption.

Mail2Tag Deployment and Setting

Mail2Tag was deployed for 20 months in a research center with about 300 employees. Staff includes scientists, engineers, managers, support staff and administrators, and a temporary population of about 20-30 interns per summer.

There are three tiers of management in the company: executive, labs, and area or team levels. Each area or team has 4 to 17 people, and each lab has 4 to 8 areas or teams. Almost all employees are located within a single three-floor building. There are two hardware labs located on the ground floor, two software labs groups on the middle floor, and business and operations teams on the third floor. Mail2Tag was introduced, promoted, and administered by one area or team in a software lab (we refer to them here as the "first adopters"). The system became available for limited use in December 2008 by a small team of users. Invitations for general use were announced in June 2009 and a second release of the system with interface changes and rebranding of the server to its permanent name, share.X.com occurred in August 2009. The technology was announced via word of mouth and presentations at lab meetings (one for each lab or business groups).

Figure 1 (Top). A contribution is sent to the system via email (left). Digests are received from the system in email (right). (Bottom) A web interface gives organization-wide access to posted content (see also [25]

Measures of Adoption

We used both quantitative and qualitative measures to examine people's engagement with Mail2Tag, based on activity log data, survey response data, and direct feedback from interviews with users. Using these data, we applied a number of analytical methods to assess adoption from different perspectives.

Basic statistics of use: We logged postings of tagged emails and web site use. People have unique corporate email addresses. Accesses to the web site are made from computers with traceable unique IP addresses associated with the owner of that computer. Figures 2 and 3 show basic statistics for posting and clicking data, which reveal the production and consumption behaviors of users in the system.

Growth of the Mail2Tag social graph over time: The posts and clicks form a set of relationships between people (those producing the time-stamped, tagged content and those consuming that content by receiving a tagged email or clicking on the web page produced by an email). These form a directed graph with one-way connections of producers of information to consumers of that information (Figure 4, left, where the nodes represent aggregation of activity at the area / team level). Consistent with prior research on social capital of teams [31, 18], we mostly aggregate data at the area or team level, as this grouping is very cohesive in terms of physical location of people, their topics of interest, and work assignment. We may examine the growth of this graph over time to get a view of diffusion of adoption of Mail2Tag across the company.

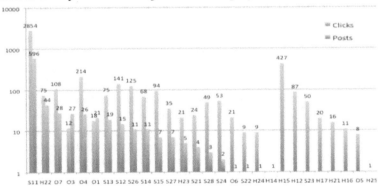

Figure 2. Frequencies of posts (production) and clicks (consumption) by team (x-axis)

Using the graph that reconstructs the information flow via Mail2Tag (Figure 4, left), we can calculate the centrality of the nodes in that graph. We used the NetworkX open source network analysis package (http://networkx.lanl.gov) to compute betweenness, degree, and closeness centrality. NetworkX defines the betweenness of a node as the fraction of all shortest paths that pass through that node; degree of a node as the fraction of nodes it is connected to; and closeness of a node is the reciprocal average distance to all other nodes.

Survey of Technology Acceptance and Comparison to Actual Use: We used the UTAUT survey [33], an established MIS questionnaire to measure the adoption of systems in organizations and key known predictors. Here we apply it in the context of Human-Computer Interaction research. The survey provided us with self-reported measures such as Behavioral Intent (to use Mail2Tag) and possible predictors of adoption such as usefulness and ease of use of Mail2Tag.

We also gave the participants a small survey for feedback on specific system features. That is, combining the UTAUT and this small survey we evaluated both the adoption of the entire system ("I would find the system useful in my job") as well as at the use of specific features, such as the posting or browsing functions.

We sent the survey to 111 people, who represent about 47% of the active workforce at the time of the survey. This was a stratified sample composed by four strata, at four levels of activity (as measured by global use scores described below). Forty-five of the workers in this sample responded to the survey (i.e., 41%), including sets of employees from each of the four classes:

- Frequent users (5>score>14): 11 respondents.
- Occasional users (2>score=>5): 11 respondents.
- Rare users (0>score=>2): 13 respondents.
- Non-users (score=0): 8 respondents.

Use Scores: We collected both behavioral (or actual) and self-reported (or perceived) measures of use. For the behavioral measures of use, we computed an ad hoc measure based on the adoption of the multiple features of the system. That is, we count the levels of diversity of people's usage of the system features. This measure allows for calculating a use score that is a more fine-grained and *quantitative* understanding of 'reader to leader' behavior. Reading features include clicks on the website, RSS feed requests, and receiving a tagged email. Production features include creating tags, using tags, and using the 'social' website features of thanking, commenting, and administrative features of the website. We scored people's participation by looking at log data across the seven reading and production features, scoring 0 for non-use of a feature, 1 for below median use of a feature, and 2 for above median use. Summing across the feature set results in scores ranging from 0 to 14 (Figure 6).

Also, as our self-reported (or perceived) measures of use we considered: the Behavioral Intention (BI) score obtained from the UTAUT survey (i.e., based on ratings of questions such as "I intend to use the system in the next 12 months") and monthly use reported in response to the question "How many times have you used share.X.com per month (on average)?" (a survey question that we added).

Observation and interviews of exemplary use-cases: Finally, through observation and 20 interviews with users we also examined different usage scenarios of Mail2Tag that people worked into their current work practices.

Results on Adoption

The measures above allow analysis of adoption from different viewpoints.

Basic Overall Use Statistics: Posts and Clicks

We identified 295 workers who could have accessed system over 20 months based on logs and the company organization chart. Among these 295 workers, we find that 137 people have clicked on the web site at least once (46%) and 49 have posted some content via email (17%, 920 messages with 579 tags). 9% of the workers contributed 3 or more posts, which is the median level of individual use.

Aggregating the data at the area or team level, Figure 2 above shows the post and click data sorted by decreasing level of production, side by side with the consumption. The data is shown using a log scale, reflecting the power law nature of contribution. Toward the right of the figure we see groups of people consuming content, but not posting themselves. These readers might be considered 'lurkers'.

Figure 3 shows the results about adoption by feature. We find that the most prevalent feature used were those for information consumption: Clicks on the web site, receiving a tagged email. 46% of all people clicked on a piece of content in Mail2Tag at least once. About production features, 17% of people posted content at least once. Other features such as the social web features are below 10% use. Overall, the adoption rates of the Mail2Tag system appear equivalent or slightly better than other cases of similar systems deployed in organizations [10, 32].

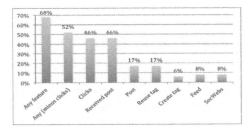

Figure 3. Percentage use by feature is shown for the 295 employees.

Growth of the Social Graph over Time

We also analyzed the activities of posting and clicking through a social graph to visualize underlying social patterns. This is a directed graph connecting those who produce information with those who consume it. Figure 4 (right chart) illustrates the accumulated exchanges over the 20-months deployment.

Three observations emerge from this graph (Figure 4). First, we observe some cluster of nodes illustrating groups with greater sharing activity amongst themselves than with others. See the blue and green nodes indicating the two hardware labs, on the first floor. This clustering effect is obtained using a minimum crossing graph layout algorithm, which computes shortest distance optimization (www.graphviz.org). Second, we notice that the labs that have connections throughout the network, as the two software labs in yellow and orange, tend to get pulled in different directions and become intermixed with other labs. Third, the management and operations teams take a central role among the labs as shown by the central position of the gray nodes in the graph.

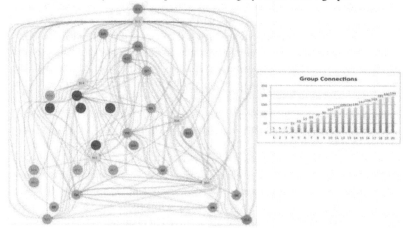

Figure 4. (Left) The post and click data forms a directed graph of inter-group connections observed over 20 months. Colors indicate teams belonging to one of the four labs, with management teams (e.g., Marketing, Human Resources) shown in grey. (Right) Cumulative frequencies of exchanges between teams over the 20 months of deployment is shown.

The rate of growth of directed connections between groups is given in the inset graph of Figure 4. We see a slow start typical of social system use, with a steady rate of group connections formed through efforts to promote the technology.

This graph also gives us a way to quantify the reader or lurker activity as a percentage of the network connection activity. Each arc in Figure 4 is created by one or more posts or clicks. If we separate the post and click contributions, we can see those arcs produced only by click behavior (i.e., one group clicking on the posting made by another group). We observed a monthly average of 3.2% of the arcs in the network are created by clicks or pure reader activity (with SD=2,1% and range 0-7.7%). If we count the total number of arcs touched by click activity monthly, the average is 12.7% (SD=4.3% and range 5.9-23.8%).

We look further into network activity by considering centrality measures of the graph. After a 20-month period we observe a flattening out of degree and closeness centrality across the groups, indicating formation of different hubs of activity. The primary brokerage may be seen in the betweenness centrality, with 'first adopter' departments (S11 and H22) dominating this measure, but decreasingly so over time as the other groups gain in betweenness (Figure 5).

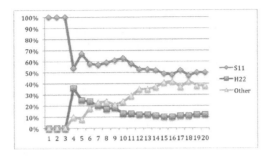

Figure 5. Betweenness centrality of early adopter teams (S11, H22) decreases as others increase.

Survey of Technology Acceptance

We measured adoption using two subjective measures, namely frequency of monthly use and behavioral intention (BI) to use Mail2Tag in the next 12 months, and two objective measures, namely feature use score and a score of use that excluded clicking actions (Table 2, rightmost columns). Monthly use correlated significantly with behavioral measures (Global use: r=.55, p<.001, Use [no clicks]: r=.60, p<.001). This supports the concurrent validity of these adoption measures. Table 1 shows the distribution of employees by level of use (Global use score). The score ranges from 0 (non-use) to greater levels of use, as more features of the system are adopted and added into an individual's use score.

Freq	97	64	53	20	12	18	9	5	5	6	1	2	2	2	1
Score	0	1	2	3	4	5	6	7	8	9	10	11	12	13	14

Table 1. Employee distribution by Global use score. (N=295) based on uses of system features.

The UTAUT questionnaire [33] measured four potential predictors of adoption:
- Performance Expectancy (PE) (see Perceived Usefulness in [8])
- Effort Expectancy (EE) (see Perceived Ease of Use in [8])
- Social Influence (SI) (e.g., influence from colleagues or management)
- Facilitating Conditions (FC) (e.g., required knowledge, assistance)

The questionnaire measured intended use or Behavioral Intent (BI), with three questions, and we added a new question to measure actual monthly use.

We run a factor analysis with the responses to questions measuring the four potential predictors (PE, EE, SI, FC) and the intended use (BI). We used the factor analysis to verify that the questions loaded sufficiently on each factor, see [8, 33]. We extracted a single score for each factor, while ensuring that the questions with higher loading on that factor had higher impact on the score. As shown by Cronbach's alpha values in Table 2 (second column), the reliability analysis confirmed that the clusters of questions that measured each of the four potential predictors and intended use (BI) were well inter-correlated.

To establish if any of these four factors were good predictors of use, we run correlation and regression analyses. As shown by the Pearson correlation values in Table 2 (PE' row), Performance Expectancy (PE), was the only factor that significantly correlates with and predicts intended (BI) and actual use (Monthly use, Global use, Use (no clicks)). Table 3 shows the results of the linear regression analysis.

About Effort Expectancy (EE), or perceived ease of use, while the ratings for this factor were higher (average score: 4.9, sd: 1.08) than for Performance Expectancy (PE), or perceived usefulness (average score: 3.6, sd: 1.18), its correlation with adoption was lower than between PE and adoption (Table 2). Similarly, the regression analysis did not exhibit a significant effect of this factor as for PE.

In the regression analysis, multiple alternative methods were used to select the predictors in the model (stepwise, backward, forward selection). All methods led to the same results: PE was the significant predictor and the other three variables were excluded. Among the response variables, BI and global use showed highest R-values for the model and monthly-use lowest (Table 3). While EE and SI have some correlation with some responses (0.4-0.5, Table 2) they do not reach significance as predictors in the regression.

Overall, these results are consistent with prior TAM findings [8, 22, 33].

	Alpha	PE	EE	SI	FC	BI	Month ly use	Global use	Use (no clicks)
		Predictors of use				**Self-reported or behaviors of use**			
PE (Perf. Exp.)	0.86		.59**	.52**	0.21	**.83****	**.37***	**.40****	**.33***
EE (Effo. Exp.)	0.90			.44**	.51**	.46**	0.18	**0.30***	0.19
SI (Soc. Influ.)	0.73				0.16	.51**	0.04	0.18	0.12
FC (Fac. Cond.)	0.52					0.15	0.11	0.06	0.13
BI (Beha. Inte.)	0.97						0.25	**0.39***	**0.33***
Monthly use								**.55****	**.60****
Global use									**.97****

Table 2. Pearson correlation. The r values marked with ** or * indicate correlations that are significant at the p<0.01 or p<0.05 levels, respectively (2-tailed test).

	BI		Monthly		Global use		Use (no clicks)	
	R-sq.	Beta	R-sq.	Beta	R-sq.	Beta	R-sq.	Beta
PE	0.69	**0.83*****	0.10	**0.32***	0.16	**0.40****	0.11	**0.33***

Table 3. Linear regression: Performance Expectancy (PE) was the only significant predictor. Beta values marked with ***, ** or * indicate correlations that are significant at the p<0.001, p<0.01 or p<0.05 levels, respectively.

The data did not violate assumptions of independence for regression analysis for any of the models run. The potential problem of multicollinearity among the predictors was ruled out based on several diagnostics: the values for Variance Inflation Factor, VIF<2.0 (i.e., smaller than 4), tolerance >.6 (i.e. bigger than .01), and Condition Index<2.7 (i.e., smaller than 15).

Adoption for Users with Different Social Roles

We find that knowledge workers who are more central in the network or who act as brokers are also those who show the greatest diversity in their use of Mail2Tag. This seems consistent with prior findings [5, 3]. Focusing on the users only, we analyzed the association of adoption measures with network metrics (closure, betweenness, and degree centrality), which characterized the positions of the users in the Mail2Tag social network. We found that betweenness had the strongest association with global use (betweenness: r=.75, p<.001) while betweenness and degree centrality had stronger association with intended future use (betweenness: r=.54, p<.001, and centrality: r=.48, p<.005). The survey-based score of Behavioral Intention (BI, which correlates with actual use, Table 2) correlated the highest with betweennes (r=.55, p<.001), which is an indicator of brokerage role. Both this role and the usage scores are affected the by job roles: 20% of top-25 scoring users are managers (score greater than 6, see Figure 6), while they compose only 10% of the total workers with access. Overall this shows the importance of being in a brokerage position, which is strongly associated with actual use and intent to use (BI from survey). Also, this role is related the user's job function (20% of top-25 users are managers).

Adoption at the Level of Specific Functions

In addition to measuring overall system adoption, we also collected data about the use of (or willingness to use) specific features of the system, such as posting a new message or replying to a prior message into the system (production) and interacting with the web interface (consumption). This allowed us to analyze more in detail the actual use or perceived need for specific functions of Mail2Tag.

On the feature of posting a message, we collected responses from 41 participants, of which 54% had not used it, and 12% and 34% had used it once or more times, respectively. Most reported using this feature for informing colleagues about useful information. Some reported sharing on generic topics, such as "conference announcements and article pointers" or "news-type items", while others preferred sharing on specific topics (e.g., "robotics" or "ethnography"). Among non-users, several emphasized that knowing if information is or will be relevant to other's would be critical for them to start contributing. They indicated that recommendations or clear visibility of others' interests would motivate them to post. Some reported being unaware of the feature and a few noted that the presence of enough colleagues already in the system is another motivator.

Among the participants surveyed, about 18% had used the feature of replying to a tagged message. The motivations for using this feature were very similar to those of posting, namely, for sharing or informing. Differently, however, non-users seemed more apt to use this reply feature compared to initiating a thread themselves ("I probably would do this by default, if I had gotten emails this way."). Similarly, some non-users emphasized the need for providing relevant-enough content and reducing the current noise for them to start using the feature.

Regarding consumption, we asked participants about the use of the web interface feature. Among participants surveyed 11% and 46% had used it one or several times, respectively. The main reasons for visiting were monitoring and discovering information that was being shared in the organization. Several non-users of the website reported that they were not aware of it ("I didn't know that the web interface exists. I only occasionally received emails from the systems"), while others non-users did not feel the need for it since they had already enough sources of information. However, several non-users pointed, again, to the importance of having highly relevant information on the site for them to visit.

Mail2Tag Use Cases

Finally, use cases of people adapting Mail2Tag to their needs also informs us about adoption. We highlight two cases of unique appropriation of Mail2Tag.

First, several hardware teams have used the system for idea management. One 'grassroots' leader (an early adopter in a hardware group) introduced the system to those departments as a means for "documenting a business need or problem in 1-3 lines of free text, browsing through the recorded problems and get inspired (or tell a colleague), and searching (full text/tags) to see if one of your solutions fits a need out there". This 'problem matching' is an example of a unique appropriation for sharing within and across groups. It takes advantage of Mail2Tag's ability to serve ad hoc and transient group formation, that change as interests evolve.

Second, a group of employees who also speak German used Mail2Tag for an informal sharing in German. Content about events in the home country and issues relating to the expatriate experience are posted, usually in the foreign language. Other people not involved with that group would occasionally 'stumble upon' the foreign text and ask about it with curiosity. This use illustrates coexistence without interference among separate interest groups.

Discussion

Case studies have pointed to relevant factors facilitating or hindering adoption of new systems in organizations. Palen and Grudin [28] remind us that management's sponsorship is a key top-down factor. However, for discretionary systems, versatile functionality and ease of use combined with adequate infrastructure, integration with email, and peer pressure have led to success. Brzozowski [4] found that peer pressure and feedback are good facilitators for workers' adoption of Enterprise2.0 systems. Extending these findings, our results from the 2-year deployment of Mail2Tag suggest that 'grassroots' systems for sharing may have their own adoption patterns in organizations.

We found that, even if our Enterprise2.0 system was discretionary and volunteer-based, its *perceived usefulness* was the key predictor of actual use, rather than its perceived ease of use or formal management's sponsorship. Related to the effect of perceived usefulness, is also our finding that the social role in the organization is likely to affect if the worker will see this type of system as useful and usable.

Taking Mail2Tag as an example, if we design a tool that is specifically attractive to brokers of information, then those are the people who will gravitate to it, and that could likely set a bound on the people who will be vigorous contributors. Brokers feel that it is part of their job to disseminate such information. We designed Mail2Tag as an organization-wide information-sharing tool. As a result, the functionality of our information sharing system appealed to brokers more than others. There is a complex relationship between the sanctioned job role individuals have in the organization (e.g., managers) and their actual social role in the network (e.g., brokers). In our deployment this relationship appeared to be at the heart of adoption. An implication for future deployments of Enterprise2.0 systems that support specific functions for the organization (e.g., sharing, awareness, or coordination) is that the adoption process could be scaffolded more effectively if the system is targeted to workers who hold *'relevant' roles*.

We find lurkers matter when assessing adoption. Readers (or 'lurkers') accounted for about ~12% of activity recorded in Mail2Tag (see similar results about Enterprise2.0 [13] and online communities [30]). Our findings suggest that in an organization there are distinct audiences for, or groups drawn to, the system who will exhibit different levels of participation. These observations raise questions.

How much effort does it take for going to the next level of participation and what is the process for allowing others to step up? Mail2Tag has a unique approach for bringing people into its network: via email (see also [28]). The contributors at lowest level of use (score = 1, Figure 6) made their first contact with the system by either receiving a tagged email or visiting the web site (e.g. via a intranet search). 22% of all the employees with access to the system are in this first level (64 users, Figure 6). Most users interact with the system via email. Then, it is the email digest received that draws some of the users over to the web site, which has the other features that can be used. Designing this *ladder of involvement* may be very important for leading 'readers' to become 'leaders' [30].

How many brokers can realistically participate in the system? This is a management issue for the adoption process. The proportion among all the job roles that have information sharing as a critical function will set the participation level. One of our goals in Mail2Tag was leveraging the popularity of email use, but also helping 'un-silo' email for more effective information routing and reuse in the organization. We find it is mainly brokers (as identified by 'official' job role or individual predisposition to promote 'grassroots' sharing) who carry this forward by using our variant of email practice.

Finally, what are the goals a system is meant to address as use evolves? Mail2Tag was originally designed for 'information sharing'. However, we observed that while sharing is much talked about and an 'obvious' organizational objective, for knowledge workers it is a means rather than an end. In fact, we saw several bursts of activities in Mail2Tag when sharing, as-means, found a good match with specific ends or goals of groups of users: e.g. idea management or cultural groups with distinct interest. Thus, a system invokes a wider audience when it can be appropriated for a wider range of goals; e.g., as in the uses of 'plain-old-email'. We note that such flexibility may also imply that reappropriation will contribute to information overload (e.g., as with keeping up with email). Past an initial phase when the priority is to evoke adoption, systems may need to transition into a later phase when the priority becomes limiting information overload. For this reason we designed adaptive digests, tracking interests in topics and tuning delivery.

We measure adoption by the numbers for use, the network structures elicited in an organization (for sharing), and accounting for the contribution from all users in relation to their organizational roles. Mail2Tag has made inroads in these areas but has room to grow. We would like to see more users involved in brokerage between groups. This will rely on awareness of features as it applies to daily routine. And that relies on promoting the end goals for brokerage as in idea management and the facilitating of community interest groups.

Conclusion

We developed and deployed Mail2Tag, an enterprise social software system for information sharing. We use its 2-year deployment as a lens to understand how to measure the adoption of an organizational sharing system. In response to the current need for common methods to compare adoption of systems across deployments [35], we provided an operationalization of how adoption occurs in one organization, what factors can affect it, and what measures can help us assess it. We presented a suite of measures: quantifying the role of lurkers; measuring the social graph over time both in reach and network structure (centrality);

explicitly checking for acceptance, as well as identifying criteria for extending participation; pursuing the acceptance of features; and combining the above with qualitative results about reasons for using the technology.

Our results suggest that 'grassroots' systems for sharing, such as Mail2Tag, may have their own adoption patterns in organizations. We find that perceived usefulness is a key facilitator and that users are drawn to different level of contribution depending on their roles in the organization. The functionality of our system seemed to appeal to one class of worker more than others; namely, brokers. We also find that lurkers matter when assessing adoption, since they account for a good deal of the activities recorded in the system.

References

1.   Adamic, L. A., Zhang, J., Bakshy, E., and Ackerman, M. S. (2008). Knowledge sharing and yahoo answers: everyone knows something. Proc. WWW'08, 665-674.

2.   Arazy, O., Gellatly, I., Soobaek J., Patterson, R., (2010). Wiki deployment in corporate settings. In Technology and Society Magazine, IEEE, 28(2) (2009), 57-64.

3.   Bouzdine T. and Bourakova-Lorgnier M. The Role of Social Capital within Business Networks: Analysis of Structural and Relational Arguments. In Proc. of OKLC, April 2004.

4.   Brzozowski, M. J., Sandholm, T., and Hogg, T. (2009). Effects of feedback and peer pressure on contributions to enterprise social media. Proc. GROUP '09. 61-70.

5.   Burt, R.S. (2004). Structural holes and good ideas. Am. J. of Sociology, 110 (2). 349-399.

6.   Cummings, J. N. (2004). Work groups, structural diversity, and knowledge sharing in a global organization. Management Science, 50(3), 352–364.

7.   Dapper G. User acceptance of Enterprise 2.0. (2007) A case study at an internationally operating private bank. Twente Student Conference on IT, Enschede, 2007

8.   Davis, F.D., 1989. Perceived usefulness, perceived ease of use, and user acceptance of information technology. MIS Quarterly 13 (3), 319–342.

9.   Ducheneaut, N., Bellotti, V. (2001). E-mail as habitat: an exploration of embedded personal information management. Interactions, 8(5), 30-3.

10. Dugan, C., Geyer, W., and Millen, D. R. (2010). Lessons learned from blog muse: audience-based inspiration for bloggers. In Proc. of CHI 2010. ACM, New York, NY, 1965-1974.

11. Efimova, L. and Grudin, J. (2007). Crossing Boundaries: A Case Study of Employee Blogging. In Proc. HICSS 2007. IEEE Computer Society, W DC, 86.

12. Ehrlich, S. F. (1987). Strategies for encouraging successful adoption of office communication systems. ACM Trans. Inf. Syst. 5, 4 (Oct. 1987), 340-357.

13. Farzan R., DiMicco JM, Brownholtz B. (2010) Mobilizing Lurkers with a Targeted Task. Proc. of ICWSM '10. May 2010.

14. Geyer W., Dugan C. (2010). Inspired by the Audience A Topic Suggestion System for Blog Writers and Readers. In Proc. of ACM CSCW 2010.

15. Golder S. and Huberman B. A. (2006). Usage patterns of collaborative tagging systems. Jour. of Information Science, 32(2): 198–208,

16. Grudin, J. (1988): Why CSCW applications fail: Problems in the design and evaluation of organizational interfaces. Proc. of CSCW'88, 85-93. ACM. Extended vers. In Office: Technology and People, 4(3), 245-264.

17. Grudin, J. and Poole, E. S. (2010). Wikis at work: success factors and challenges for sustainability of enterprise Wikis. In Proc. WikiSym '10. ACM, NY, 1-8.

18. Hansen, Morten T. (1999). The search-transfer problem: the role of weak ties in sharing knowledge across organization subunits. Adm. Science Quart. 44 82-111

19. Holtzblatt, L. J., Damianos, L. E., and Weiss, D. 2010. Factors impeding Wiki use in the enterprise: a case study. In Proc. of CHI 2010. ACM, NY, 4661-4676.

20. Jackson, A., Yates, J., Orlikowski, W. Corporate Blogging: Building community through persistent digital talk. In Proc. of HICSS'07, IEEE Press.

21. Kittur, A., Chi, E., Pendleton, B. A., Suh, B., & Mytkowicz, T. (2007). Power of the few vs. wisdom of the crowd: Wikipedia and the rise of the bourgeoisie. Alt.CHI, 2007.

22. Lampe, C., Wash, R., Velasquez, A., Ozkaya, E. (2010), Motivations to participate in online communities, In Proc. of CHI 2010, pp. 1927-1936.

23. Markus, M. L. Electronic mail as the medium of managerial choice. Org. Sci., 5(4), 502-527.

24. McAfee, A. Enterprise 2.0: New collaborative tools for your organization's toughest challenges. Harvard Business Press,.Boston, MA. 2009

25. Nelson, L., Convertino, G., Nairn, R., Chi, E. H., Mail2Tag: information sharing through augmenting email practices with implicit tag-based categorization, to appear in Proc. of The 2011 International Conference on Collaboration Technologies and Systems (CTS 2011), 2011.

26. O'reilly, T., (2007). What is Web 2.0: Design Patterns and Business Models for the Next Generation of Software. Communications & Strategies, 1, p. 17.

27. Orlikowski, W. J. (1992). Learning from Notes: organizational issues in groupware implementation. In Proc. of CSCW 1992. ACM, New York, NY, 362-369.

28. Palen, L. and Grudin, J. 2003. Discretionary adoption of group support software: lessons from calendar applications. In Implementing Collaboration Technologies in industry: Case Examples and Lessons Learned, Munkvold, Ed. Springer-V., London, 159-179.

29. Pirolli, P. (2009). An elementary social information foraging model. In Proc. of CHI'09.

30. Preece J. and Shneiderman, B. (2009) The reader to leader framework: Motivating technology-Mediated social participation. AIS Trans. on HCI, 1(1), 13-32

31. Rosenthal, Elizabeth A. (1996). Social Networks and Team Performance. Dissertation. University of Chicago, Graduate School of Business.

32. Steinfield, C., DiMicco, J. M., Ellison, N. B., and Lampe, C. (2009). Bowling online: social networking and social capital within the organization. In Proc. of C&T '09. ACM, NY, 245-254.

33. Venkatesh, V., Morris, M. G., Davis, G. B., & Davis, F. D., User acceptance of information technology: Toward a unified view, (2003). MIS Quarterly, 27(3), 425-478.

34. Whittaker, S. and Sidner, C. (1996). Email Overload: Exploring Personal Information Management of Email. Proc. CHI'96, 276-283.

35. Whittaker, S., Terveen, L., and Nardi, B. A. 2000. Let's stop pushing the envelope and start addressing it: a reference task agenda for HCI. HCI. 15, 2 75-106.

36. Whittaker, S., Terveen, L., Hill, W., and Cherny, L. (1998). The dynamics of mass interaction. In Proc. of CSCW '98. ACM, NY, 257-264.

37. Wilkinson D. M. Strong regularities in online peer production. In Proc. of the 9th ACM conf. on Electronic commerce (EC'08), NY, USA, 2008. ACM. 302–309.

38. Yardi S., Golder S. A., and Brzozowski M. J.. (2009) Blogging at work and the corporate attention economy. In Proc. of CHI '09. 2071-2080.

39. Zhang P. (2008) Motivational affordances: Fundamental reasons for ICT design and use, Comm. ACM, 51(11).

Challenges and Opportunities for Collaborative Technologies for Home Care Work

Lars Rune Christensen[1] and Erik Grönvall[2]

[1]Technologies in Practice Group, IT-University of Copenhagen
[2]Department of Computer Science, Aarhus University
Lrc@itu.dk, Gronvall@cs.au.dk

Abstract. This article offers an exploration of home care work and the design of computational devices in support of such work. We present findings from a field study and four participatory design workshops. Themes emerging from the findings suggest that home care work may be highly cooperative in nature and requires substantial articulation work among the actors, such as family members and care workers engaged in providing care for older adults. Although they provide home care for older adults in cooperation, family members and care workers harbour diverging attitudes and values towards their joint efforts. The themes emerging are used to elicit a number of design implications and to promote some illustrative design concepts for new devices in support of cooperative home care work.

Introduction

Asia and Europe may be singled out as the two regions where a significant number of countries face severe population ageing in the near future. In these regions within twenty years many countries will face a situation where the largest population cohort will be those over 65 and the average age will be approaching 50. Most of the developed world (with the notable exception of the United States) now has sub-replacement fertility levels, and population growth now depends largely on immigration together with population momentum that arises from previous large generations now enjoying longer life expectancy (Gesano et al. 2009).

An aging population means that the health care sector becomes under increased pressure and it becomes a growing concern how to for example support elderly people in a manner that allows them to continue a quasi-independent lifestyle in their own homes rather than moving to some sort of institutional care - allowing the elderly people to stay longer in their own home makes sense seen from the elderly persons point of view as well as from the point of view of the economy of the welfare state (Gesano et al. 2009).[1]

This paper is concerned with an understanding of home care work and the design of associated technologies that may enable older adults to stay longer in their own homes for the benefit of the elderly as well as society at large. More precisely, an attempt is made to achieve a better understanding of how family members and care workers in concert contribute to the care of older adults living in their own homes and how this cooperative home care work may be supported with new information technology.

Family members and care workers in distinct yet complementary ways contribute to the care of older adults. That is, there is something akin to a division of labour in place where the relatives handle one type of tasks and the professional caregivers handle another set of tasks. In this manner the role of the relatives as caregivers for older adults is partly constituted as complementary to the role of the professional caregivers, and vice versa. The different roles or positions of family members and care workers in relation to taking care of older adults make for pronounced differences in the attitudes and values that they may harbour in regard to taking care of older adults. We hold that such issues are worth considering, as they may have ramifications for the design of new information technology. By considering these issues a greater understanding of how to design for the diverse ensemble of actors taking care of older adults might be reached.

The paper is based on ethnographic fieldwork (including interviews) as well as a series of design workshops - the main setting for the fieldwork where the home of the elderly persons receiving home care.

We will proceed in the following manner: First we will discuss related work and the methods of the study. Secondly, we will describe how family members and care workers are part of the care of older adults. Third, we will explore the values and attitudes of family members and care workers respectively. Finally, we will discuss design implications and describe two concrete design concepts.

---

[1] Institutional care of older adults is in general significantly more resource demanding than home care.

Related work

A wide range of publications exists in relation to home-care, coordination of care and the role of the different actors involved (e.g. the elderly person, family members and professional caregivers) as well as the role technology can take in a home-care scenario. For example, Mynatt (Mynatt et al. 2001) propose that part of the solution to the challenge of supporting 'aging in place', is to promote awareness among family members of senior adults' day-to-day activities through information technology i.e. 'digital family portraits'. Consolvo et al (Consolvo et al. 2004) discusses the care network and how to support it. The article introduces an augmented picture frame inspired by Mynatt et al (Mynatt et al. 2001). Through miniature sensors and machine learning the frame can be updated with information to be used locally by the care network. Wittenberg-Lyles et al. (Wittenberg-Lyles et al. 2010) discuss how video technology can be used to include family caregivers in staff meetings at a Hospice. This work includes another setting, but points out how beneficial a dialogue is for both private and professional caregivers. Another article, Abowd et al. (Abowd et al. 2006), discusses how automated systems can be used to support the elderly and the care network. The article mentions e.g. 'Monitoring' as a key issue with elder care and care networks. Morris et al. (Morris et al. 2003) puts the focus on the elderly person and how to support an everyday life through different sensors and sensor data. This idea is also shared by e.g. Le et al. (Le et al. 2007). Demiris (Demiris 2009) discuss shared decision making where older adults gets involved in their healthcare planning. The article points out the benefits of the inclusion, but also identifies challenges when for example an older patient for different reasons has problems to participate as an equal partner in the decision process. Petrakou (2008) provides an ethnographic account of the use of a paper binder for communication between family members and care workers in relation to home care work while Rook (1987) is concerned with the emotional health of caregivers.

This paper, then, relates to both general studies of home care work (Kahn 1993; Lindley et al. 2008; Petrakou 2007; Rook 1987) as well as literature with an explicit focus on the design of technology to support elderly in the home setting (Abowd et al. 2006; Mynatt et al. 2001; Rowan and Mynatt 2005).

In relation to other ethnographic accounts of home care work this paper makes a contribution as it takes a special interest in not only the division of labour between family members and professional caregivers as they perform home care work but also the diverging values and attitudes held by the various participants. For example, whereas a number of previous studies have focused solely on the practices of the care workers (Petrakou 2007), the interest here is as indicated to explore how family members and care workers actively and in cooperation engage in the practicalities of taking care of older adults (an interest partly shared with e.g. (Rook 1987; Spitze and Gallant 2004)).

In regard to the literature focused on the design of technology to support the elderly in the home setting this paper diverges from other papers on the subject as it aims to support *articulation work* among the network of actors that support the elderly, rather than support e.g. *awareness practices* (Mynatt et al. 2001; Rowan and Mynatt 2005) or monitoring of the elderly (Abowd et al. 2006) or the collection of senor data (Morris et al. 2003).

Methods

This paper is based on ethnographic fieldwork as well as participatory design work carried out in the course of five months in relation to home care work. That is, the authors participated in home care work observing and following home care workers as well as family members of the elderly people. The main setting for the fieldwork was the homes of the elderly recipients of home care. As part of the fieldwork, twelve semi-structured interviews where held with fourteen people (5 men, 9 women, aged 30-75) seven where family members of the elderly and seven where home care workers.

Subsequent to the fieldwork, four participatory design workshop where held, one with three family members of the elderly, another with five care workers, and finally two joint workshop with three family members and five care workers were held. Each participatory design workshop lasted between three and four hours.

Cooperative home care work

As indicated above, according to Mynatt (Mynatt et al. 2001) part of the solution to the challenge of supporting 'aging in place', is to promote awareness among family members of senior adults' day-to-day activities. The concrete suggestion that Mynatt and associates make is to provide peace of mind through 'digital family portraits' that may provide qualitative visualizations of an adult's daily life. They designed a family household object, that is, a digital portrait frame populated with iconic imagery that summarize the last 28 days of the elderly person, with the aim of providing a means for the family to remain aware of the day-to-day activities of a distant elderly relative. Although this approach may be part of the solution, there are a number of practices which awareness support alone does not address. Obviously, it does not support the ongoing communication between family members and care workers regarding the coordination of care tasks. There is far more to taking care of an elderly person, from a family member's (as well as a care worker's) point of view, than simply being aware of how she is doing by looking at for instance icons appearing on a picture frame.

Many family members are far more than mere spectators to the lives of their elderly kin. More to the point, there is a *de facto* division of labour between professional caregivers and family members. Where the professionals, simply put, handle what may be dubbed ordinary tasks (e.g. personal care and food preparation, and etc) and the family members handle what is beyond the job description of the professionals, what is deemed extraordinary (e.g. social events and light maintenance). That is, the role of the relatives as caregivers for older adults are partly constituted as complementary to the role of the professional caregivers, and *vice versa*. We will now turn to describe this state of affairs through the example of the case of Elisabeth.

The case of Elisabeth

Elisabeth is 92 years old when we meet her. She uses a wheelchair due to partial paralysis in her left side - the effects of a stroke she suffered some ten years ago. Due to her physical condition she requires comprehensive care, day and night, including help with getting dressed, getting a bath and generally getting around. She lives alone in her own home in a senior residential area. She has regular as well as 'on call' support from caregivers employed by the municipality. That is, a team of home care workers provide Elisabeth with round the clock care. This ads up to seven daily visits, including one in the morning (getting breakfast and getting dressed), one in the evening (getting to bed), four in between (mostly meals and brief fluid intake visits) and finally a visit in the middle of the night (check up and shifting Elisabeth's sleeping position). In this manner the home care providers take care of many of the basic necessities of Elisabeth's life, including clothing, bathing, cooking, medicine, cleaning, and so on. However, there are a number of tasks that the professional caregivers employed by Elisabeth's municipality do not perform as it is not part of their job description. As a matter of principle, the local caregivers, for example, do not perform tasks perceived as directly related to participation in social events such as Christmas or birthdays. Consequently, when Elisabeth is invited to social events such as a birthday party, it is her daughter Ann who lives some 100 km away who prepares her wardrobe, irons the clothes etc. Furthermore, on the day of such an event Ann or another family member has to remind the local caregivers to dress Elisabeth in the clothes prepared for the event, otherwise they may easily forget to do so. Elisabeth does not remember such things herself.

Furthermore, Elisabeth usually spends Christmas Eve at Ann's house, some 100 km away in the city. She has done so for the past 10 years. Such a trip involves family members organizing transportation in a special wheelchair friendly taxi-bus. It also involves notifying the municipal caregivers, so Elisabeth can receive professional care as she travels out of her own municipality and spends the holidays at her daughter's house. The latter notification is handled by Elisabeth's home municipality, her daughter merely has to call them up on the phone to make sure that they have been notified and that they are coming on the right dates.

In addition, Elisabeth's local caregivers do not handle maintenance work (again, this is not part of their job description). Included in the category of maintenance work is for example the replacement of a broken light bulb. Consequently, if a light bulb needs to be replaced, this requires the help of friends or relatives - since Elisabeth is not physically able to perform such a task herself (she is confined to a wheelchair after all). Elisabeth used to call the local electrician and have him send an apprentice over to replace the bulb. However, she cannot manage to perform this kind of phone calls any more, and may simply sit in the dark until a family member or a friend discovers that the bulb is broken and replaces it for her. In this manner the daughter for instance is involved in the care of Elisabeth if not on a daily basis then on a weekly basis.

In addition to task performance per se (e.g. ironing and replacing light bulbs) family members also assist the elderly person in her contact with the professional caregivers. That is, the family members play an active role in the coordination of the care of the elderly person. For example, Elisabeth had out-clinic cataract surgery on both eyes recently and in connection with this procedure, her daughter Ann arranged the wheelchair friendly transportation back and forth between the clinic and the home. That is, Ann made the arrangements with a local cab company. After the surgery a nurse gave Elisabeth some eye drops and told her to administer them two times a day for two weeks. However, Elisabeth frequently forgets to take her medicine and consequently Ann had to make sure that the professional caregivers who frequented Elisabeth's home received and understood this message. Ann called them and gave them instructions regarding the eye drops, as she does not herself visit her mother every day. Note how the performance of surgery on an elderly person and the subsequent related care required the involvement of not only professionals but family members as well.

In regard to Elisabeth's own efforts we may say that she does everything that she can. However due to her physical condition this is more or less limited to making gestures such as offering cookies and the opportunity for visitors to brew their own coffee in her kitchen. That is, Elisabeth is very dependent on the help that she receives.

We may say that family members and care workers collaborate and have different roles in relation to taking care of older adults. Family members, typically sons and daughters, take care of their older adults whereas care workers provide care in a professional capacity i.e. as part of their occupation. That is, family members typically care for just the one aging mother or father, whereas a professional home care provider may tend to as many as ten different elderly individuals in the course of a week (this number easily quadruples during the course of a year). Furthermore, family members may provide care in accord with varying obligations elsewhere, whereas the team of homes care providers provides care for older adults every day.

As indicated above, there is a *de facto* division of labour between professional caregivers and family members (and not only in the case of Elisabeth). Where the professionals, simply put, handle what may be dubbed ordinary tasks (e.g. personal care and food preparation, and etc) and the family members handle what is beyond the job description of the professionals, what is deemed extraordinary (e.g. social events and light maintenance). Strauss' point is that 'in any division of labour' there is articulation work - indeed that is part of what we have described in the case concerning Elisabeth. Recall, for example, how Ann had to call the caregivers in regard to the eye drops and the wardrobe for the birthday. How do we support such articulation work involving professional caregivers and family members (as well as the older adults themselves)?

What does articulation work entail? In the words of Strauss, articulation work is a kind of supra-type work in any division of labour, done by the various actors concerning the meshing and integration of interdependent cooperative work tasks (Strauss 1985, p.8).

At this juncture we may note that the concept of articulation work has been used extensively within CSCW. A series of focused, in-depth field studies have been undertaken with the specific purpose of investigating how the distributed activities of cooperative work arrangements are articulated and, in particular, how prescribed artifacts are devised, appropriated and used for these purposes (e.g. Bardram and Bossen 2005; Carstensen and Sørensen 1996; Schmidt and Bannon 1992; Schmidt and Simone 1996). Below we will consider articulation work in the context of home care work.

At present articulation work involving family members and care workers is mainly handled through the exchange of written messages placed in a paper binder as well as the *ad hoc* use of telephones. Such a binder is for example situated in the kitchen of Elisabeth. The binder includes the nursing and care plan, specifications for medicine intake, food and liquid intake forms, as well as sheets of blank paper to write messages on. The idea is that this binder should facilitate the exchange of messages in the context of the collaboration between care workers and family members (see also e.g. (Petrakou 2007; Rook 1987)). That is, the envisioned purpose of the binder is to facilitate the coordination of cooperative home care work. However, in our experience especially care workers find the binder cumbersome to use. They are hard pressed to find the time to read and write messages in the binder, and family members find it unreassuring that there is no way of telling whether a message have been read by the care workers or not. The present form of the binder may be said to fall somewhat short of its objective and there is certainly scope for improvement (we shall return to this below).

On the face of it, it seems as if all we designers have to do is to computer support articulation work in home care work by e.g. changing and improving the binder with information technology. This is precisely part of what we shall suggest. However, before we do so we shall attempt to deepen our understanding of the actors involved in providing home care. Concretely, we shall consider the values and attitudes that they hold in relation to home care work.

Values and attitudes

In this section, we shall explore the attitudes of family members and professional care workers towards taking care of older adults. We hold that these attitudes are worth considering, as they may have ramifications for the design concept. That is, by considering these issues, a greater understanding of how to design for the diverse ensemble of actors may be reached.

On the attitudes of family members

We will now turn to consider the attitudes of family members towards taking care of their aging relatives.

Generally speaking, family members are emotionally invested in the care of their aging relatives. That is, they are emotionally invested in the tasks that they themselves perform as well as the tasks performed by others most notably the care workers. This state of affairs may come as no great surprise, although we could ask what sort of description we are giving when we say of someone that he or she is emotional or emotionally invested? According to Ryle (Ryle 1949), being emotional is to *react* in some vaguely describable, thought easily recognizable, ways whenever certain junctures or circumstances arise. We may say that family members are emotionally invested in the care of their elderly in the sense that they are frequently e.g. glad, distraught or flustered when faced with the various circumstances pertaining to the care of their loved ones. We shall now turn to a few examples of this.

During an interview, the son of an elderly woman reports with joy how a treasured care worker handles the care of his mother with great consideration and attention to detail:

"Joanne [the care worker] is very considerate. In the morning, she always remembers to put two lumps of sugar and lots of milk in my mother's coffee - just as she likes it. And for her weekly walk, my mother is dressed in her beige dress and her black shoes – Joanna makes sure of that. She is a gem, that Joanne!"

Note how a great deal of joy and praise seems to be derived from the fact that the elderly woman receives her coffee in a certain way or is dressed in a particular manner before she leaves the home for a weekly walk. Of course most people would welcome this level of attention to detail in the care of older adults. However, not everybody would react upon witnessing it as next of kin often does i.e. with joy and even elation. However, as we shall see other parts of the emotional spectrum are also at play.

In addition to joyous feelings, family members may be in a fluster or state of uneasy confusion in regard to the care that their elderly relative receives. For example, the daughter of an elderly man states that:

"My father is suffering from dementia, so he cannot really tell us much of anything about the care that he receives. I can for example ask him if he had his visits [i.e. from the care workers] and he will tell me 'no'. He will tell me that nobody has been there all day ... When I talk to the manager [of the care workers] he says that of course my father has had his three visits that day. My father probably just forgot."

In a similar vein a family member reports that there is no telling when an elderly relative last had a shower in the sense that nobody seems to be able to fully account for that. That is, neither the elderly person nor the many different care workers who frequent the home seem to have a firm sense of it. Conflicting reports or vague assertions may leave the family members in a fluster. Sometimes such uneasy confusion may give way to agitated frustration and even outright anger, as we shall see next.

Family members may express anger or become frustrated especially with what is perceived as an inability to change the manner in which care workers perform their tasks. In the words of the daughter of an elderly woman:

"My mother does not drink enough water and this makes her dehydrate. They [the care workers] have to sit with my mother when she is served something to drink otherwise she forgets to drink it. However, more often than not they don't. I have told the manager this again and again - but nothing changes. This is serious ... one evening my mother isn't answering her phone and I drive up there to find her on the floor dehydrated. I had to call an ambulance."

In our experience, it is common when family members describe their dealings with care workers and their managers that frustration, flustering and even anger colour their narratives. Especially what is perceived as an inability to get the message through, to change the manner in which care workers perform their tasks, seems to lead to a state of agitated frustration. Perhaps this is not surprising considering the heavy emotional investment that family member may have in the care of their elderly relatives.

The strong emotional investment in the care of e.g. an aging mother or father makes for less than perfect 'peace of mind'. We found that worry, uneasiness, concern and distress are, more or less pronounced, part of what it means to be a caring and involved relative. Is my mother in good health? Has she eaten today? Is my father in good spirits, does he get out of the house or is he just sitting there all alone? In addition, joy and elation may be pronounced when things are in perfect order. We are so lucky that mom is so well cared for! What a great job they are doing!

Of course not every individual family member is heavily emotionally invested in the care and wellbeing of their aging relatives. Just as there are those who are engaged, there are those that are not. Indeed some family members are quite passive and have disengaged themselves from the care of their elderly family members on an emotional as well as a practical level for various reasons that we shall not get into here.

On the attitudes of care workers

We will now turn to consider the values and attitudes of care workers towards providing care for older adults.

Burnout stemming from emotional stress is a significant liability for workers in service industries (Ashforth and Humphrey 1993; Rafaeli and Sutton 1989), especially those employed in care giving professions (Kahn 1993). Care workers are often forced to manage their emotions when dealing with clients and family members. In this process they may adopt what could be described as a detached stance or attitude towards their professional work in order to safeguard their own emotional health. As such their engagement with elderly persons, compared to that of family members, is of a different nature. We may say, then, that care workers attempt *not* to become as emotionally invested as family members in the care of older adults. We shall now turn to a few examples of this.

Care workers may detach themselves from what they regard as undesirable emotional involvement by contrasting their own role with that of the family members. For example, an experienced care worker states that:

"You cannot allow yourself to get involved as if it where your own family – you have to learn to keep a certain distance."

The care worker continues and emphasise that:

"You are not some sort of spare son or daughter and you should not act like one."

As mentioned above, care workers may strive to detach or distance themselves from the emotional pressures of everyday care work. The rationale for this, according to one care worker, is that the job would become intolerable if she had to worry constantly about the wellbeing of all her many aging clients.

Care workers describe it as especially challenging and emotionally taxing to provide care for mentally unstable clients. That is, caring for elderly persons that suffer from depression with associated pronounced apathy is experienced as especially taxing. In contrast, providing intimate personal care such as washing the private parts of a client or dealing with blood, vomit, feces or urine is not regarded as demanding and being squeamish about it is portrayed as unprofessional. The care workers see it as part of their job to set aside any personal qualms in the performance of such tasks. As one care worker express it:

"You don't have to like it [e.g. washing the private parts of a client], you just have to do it."

Turning to interactions with family members, these may also be experienced as emotionally taxing the care workers. Recall that family members may be highly emotionally invested in the care of their elderly relatives and consequently easily distraught, flustered or even angry when faced with the various circumstances pertaining to the care of their loved ones. This can at times make for highly charged interactions between care workers and family members.

Another source of tension between care workers and family members is when the relatives of the elderly person treat the care workers as something akin to servants. According to several care workers some relatives may mistake the care workers for domestic help. A care worker reports how some family members are under the impression that its is the care worker's duty to for example clear the table and do the dishes after a family dinner. Contrary to this (mis)conception several care workers emphasise that they are there to provide care and services for the elderly person rather than for the relatives of the elderly person. The care workers are generally keen to avoid being labelled or treated as 'servants' and prefer to be regarded as simply care workers.

Although it seems that care workers strive to adopt a detached attitude towards taking care of older adults, we find that this attitude is not completely dominating and of course it varies across the many relationships that the care workers enter into during the course of their work life.

Design implications

The findings outlined above can be used to draw a number of implications regarding how computer technologies might be designed to support the network of actors taking care of older adults. The main challenge is to support their articulation work in a manner that pays heed of the heterogeneous nature of the network of actors, including the division of labour and the range of attitudes towards care work that we have described.

Although as already indicated, the purpose of this paper is to support the network of actors caring for older adults, rather than older adults *per se*, it is important to remain sensitive to the issue that some elderly may feel that their personal autonomy and dignity is compromised by being e.g. the object of communication between family member and care workers.

Seen from the family members' point of view it is important to have a secure and reliable means of communicating with those care workers that frequent the home of the elderly. It is important to feel confident that the individual care worker in fact receives a message as intended. This is related to the high level of emotional investment many family members have in the care of their elderly relatives. Furthermore, family members seem to prefer receiving messages at all times, at home or at work, concerning the wellbeing of their aging relative. Again, this preference may be seen as connected to the strong emotional investment that family members may have in the care and wellbeing of their aging relatives. Indications are that good reliable exchange of messages may provide some measure of peace of mind for family members.

Care workers seem to prefer unobtrusive communication when engaging with family members. That is, seen form the care workers' point of view receiving messages from what may be emotional family members at all hours of the day is something to be avoided or at least curbed. Messages may well have to wait until there is time and energy to deal with them. This preference could be seen as connected to the emotionally detached stance or attitude that care workers may strive for in order to safeguard their own emotional health.

Design concepts

We will now present and discuss two designs in an attempt to address the challenges described above to support cooperative home care work. As mentioned, a number of participatory design workshops were held with the authors as well as three family members and five care workers. The large number of ideas generated in these workshops were evaluated against the design implications, before a smaller selection of the ideas were refined. Two of the resulting designs are presented here as a means of illustrating some of our findings and highlighting the questions that they raise. Neither of the two designs is meant to supplant existing technology practices based on e.g. telephones. The designs provide complementary exchange of messages, while attempting to take into consideration the division of labour, the attitudes and the preferences of the diverse ensemble of actors described above.

We may note that the designs do share similar backgrounds and findings with many of the articles mentioned above in the 'related work' section. However, our designs are not pro-active ubiquitous or smart home systems. Furthermore, our designs do not try to empower the elderly people themselves, as this is most often not possible due to their frail condition. Instead, we aim to empower the care network surrounding the elderly person. Hence, our technology is primarily intended for the care network, and not for the elderly person him/herself. Our designs stands out by not providing automated data gathering that can provide data input in 'the background'. As proposed by Rogers (Rogers 2006), our designs support proactive people rather than proactive systems.

Our two designs support active collaboration and communication through the designs, rather than introducing an automated sensor system that provides data that can be discussed among care network members. Our work supports creation of data in place, by humans and through interaction between humans. This communication is supported by our described prototypes. Being rather open-ended designs, our prototypes open up for emergent, non-foreseen situations and use. Our systems do not offer monitoring of the elderly, they do not offer a safety alarm or other health status events that can be monitored, but rather facilitate the human-to-human communication (articulation work) within the care-network through technology (our prototypes).

The two design concepts currently undergo evaluation together with all members of the care network.

Augmented binder

As described above in the context of the case of Elisabeth, one intention with the (original) paper binder is to facilitate the exchange of messages and provide written information in the context of collaboration between care workers and family members. However, especially care workers find the binder cumbersome to use in its present form and are hard pressed to find the time to read and write messages in it, and the family members find it unreassuring that there is no way of telling whether a message has been read by its intended recipient or not. In its original form, there is no need to actually open the binder at each visit e.g. by the care workers, nor is there a way to signal for new information. One has to read through the whole binder to ensure that no new data is available. Indeed, our studies have shown a very diverse and sparse use of the binder in its current form. The Augmented binder design attempts to address these issues.

In the proposed augmented binder (see figure 1), messages are written with the Anoto pen and paper (Anoto 2011). The Anoto digital pen is a combination of ordinary ink pen and a digital camera (as well as supporting hardware) designed to digitally record everything written with the pen. The pen works by recognizing a special non-repeating dot pattern that is printed on the paper. The non-repeating nature of the pattern means that the pen is able to determine which page is being written on, and where on the page the pen is. The main purpose of the Anoto pen and paper is to capture and digitize what the actors engaged in care work write in the augmented binder. Furthermore, Light Emitting Diodes (LEDs) are incorporated into the binder cover and on the register tabs inside the binder in order to indicate the status of messages, and a network connection is available for propagation of information to the actors. The Anoto system has previously been used in other care and therapeutic contexts. One such example is the system Abaris that supports collaborative decision making in the care of children with autism (Kientz et al. 2006). Augmented binder is a tool for collaboration and information exchange including a range of different professional and non-professional care providers, in contradiction to Abaris that focus on different professional actors.

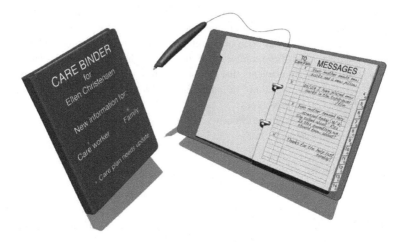

Figure 1. The augmented binder employs a pen for the digital capture of messages, and provide notifications of new messages employing RFID technology.

The Augmented binder is composed by three layers: (1) A physical layer (i.e. the written notes on paper), (2) a logical layer (e.g. indicators when new information is available) and finally, (3) a networked layer that support mirroring of the physical layer (the written notes) to a server for documentation and traceability as well as distribution and propagation of the logical level (e.g. status updates). As such, the network layer propagates the locally created and available functionality (layer 1 and 2) to the actors. We shall now turn to describe a use scenario in an effort to cast some light on the workings of the proposed design.

Imagine that a care worker, Sarah, comes into the kitchen where the Augmented binder is located. The Augmented binder identifies Sarah's RFID[2] badge as she enters the kitchen and signals through the LEDs on its cover that new information is now available for her i.e. the 'care-worker'. Notified by the LED light, Sarah goes to the binder, opens it up and immediately she can see where new information has been entered or updated as this is indicated on the register tabs. Once read, Sarah can close the binder or write a reply. In comparison, looking at the old binder Sarah cannot perceive when new, updated information of relevance has been entered for her to read.

Furthermore, we may note that when closing a page where new text is written for the current user, the text is logically tagged as 'read' and does not turn on the indicator LED's again for the same care worker. However, through the personal

---

[2] RFID is an acronym for Radio Frequency Identification and denotes any identification system in which electronic devices occur that use radio waves fields to communicate with identification units fastened to objects.

RFID tags another care worker will still receive information about what for him or her is new and unread messages in the binder.

In the same way as Sarah received a message from a family member (also equipped with a RFID tag), she can write a message to a family member (or e.g. a colleague on the night shift) to report something relevant, e.g. the need to buy new clothes for the client or inform about a shift in the clients mood. The message is tagged with the destination, in this case: 'family'. The LED on the binder's' front cover indicating a new message for the family members will be turned on the next time a family member (and his or her RFID tag) gets close to the binder. That new messages are available or that they have been read is status events that also can be forwarded to a user via the Internet. This mechanism allows the different actors to write and address messages to each other, with a notification when the different messages have been read.

Furthermore, in the binder there are sheets with boxes to check - one for each day. A checked box indicates that 'all is well' at the time the box was checked. At each visit the care worker is prompted to open the binder and assess the elderly person's situation and check any of the free boxes with the Anoto pen according to the clients status. This action, together with the RFID tag will indicate when a care worker was attending the elderly person and if all was well. If the care worker does not check the box, this results in one of three outcomes: (1) all is not OK and someone must act upon this (this can also be documented as text in the binder), (2) the person forgot or did not care to check the box and hence someone will remind the person about this and (3) no-one has visited the referred person which of course also should initiate an activity.

All information written in the binder is made available in digital form (through the use of the Anoto pen) and hence supports the documentation activity related to each referred person. Today, this is handled by some of the care workers at their office, at specific scheduled 'documentation time slots'. Here the use of a smart paper system will combine the two separate, parallel documentation activities into one and hence make the use of the binder more attractive for the care workers, since it removes redundant, time consuming and not directly care related tasks. A part from propagation of documentation data to an administrative system, only status notifications and not the messages themselves propagate to for example next of kin. The binder is intended for local use, to discuss and elaborate on issues related to the care of the older adult *in situ*. Augmented Binder supports local collaboration with the elderly person in focus, extending the original binders functionality while still being mainly a local tool for information exchange and documentation.

PressToTalk

We will now describe a design concept, called PressToTalk, for on-location exchange of voice messages between family members and care workers.

The concept PressToTalk breaks with the written form of both the original binder and the augmented binder as it relies exclusively on the exchange of voice messages. It is designed for placement in the hallway of the home of the elderly person - for everyone to pass entering or leaving. In regard to the design of the device we may initially note that it is an assembly of several units that may be combined and recombined according to the demands of the situation. Central is an indispensable base unit[3] for the play back of messages, the reminder of the units can be described as each hosting a large push button made to initiate the recording of messages for pre-defined distinct groups of actors such as 'family members' or 'care workers'. These latter units may be attached freely to the base and each other (see figure 2). In addition to these units the system includes a number of active RFID tags to be distributed among the users of the system for (unique) identification and access control. We shall now turn to describe a use scenario in an effort to cast some light on the workings of the proposed design.

Consider a PressToTalk device, placed in the home of an elderly person named Elisabeth, comprised of a base unit with a button hosting a 'play' symbol, and two auxiliary units with 'record' symbols where one is labelled 'Family' and another 'Care Worker'. Now imagine that a care worker presses the record button on the unit labelled 'Family' and records a message for family members: "*Elisabeth does not drink enough water and this makes her dehydrate*". Subsequently, when a family member enters the home an RFID reader on the base unit identify an RFID badge carried by the individual relative of the elderly person and notify that there are 'new' messages. That is, the device makes a soft sound and the LCD display lights up with an indication that there is a new message for family members to playback. The LCD display is necessary in order to indicate the intended recipient in the event that more RFID badges are present in the vicinity of the device. Upon being notified, the family members may press the playback button on the base unit and hear the message. Subsequently, the family member can press the record button on the unit labelled 'Care Worker' and record a message for the care workers: "*please observe that you have to sit with my mother when she is served something to drink otherwise she forgets to drink it - perhaps you could have a soft drink yourself, she likes the company*". This voice message may then be played back by a care worker that enters the home, etc. This is very simple and fast in use: just press a button in the hallway, state your message, and be on your

---

[3] The base unit hosts a microphone, a recording device, a loudspeaker, and a radio frequency identification (RFID) reader, a small LCD display and a push button with a 'play' symbol.

way. Subsequently, when the intended recipient enters the home, the messages may be played back at the recipient's leisure.

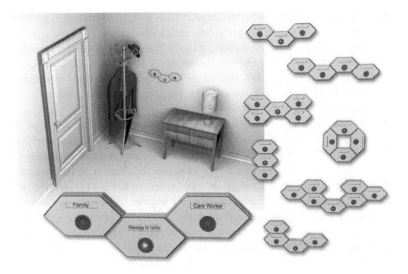

Figure 2. The PressToTalk device is placed in the hallway of the home. It is an assembly of several units (minimum one playback unit and 1-to-many recorder-units, one per user (category)) that may be combined and recombined according to the demands of the situation. The physical shapes as such are irrelevant for the functionality but allow for aesthetical considerations and make the system more adaptable and therefore more easily enters in hallways with little space, 'bending' around a picture or a coat hanger for example.

In the scenario above only two units for the recording of messages for two groups of actors, namely 'Family' and 'Care Worker' respectively, were envisioned as attached to the base unit. However, the design is open in the sense that in a future scenario more units for the recording of messages for additional groups of actors such as for example 'volunteers' and 'home care nurses' may be added if needed. This is the rationale for making the design modular. Furthermore, note that successful delivery of messages is virtually guaranteed. Unless you are hard of hearing, there is no avoiding receiving a message as the intended recipients trigger the audio indication that there are new messages for playback immediately upon entering the hallway of the home (assuming that the actors do carry their RFID badges as stipulated). If not taken into consideration, the 'new message' notification will play every time the user enters the hallway until the 'play messages' functionality is activated. This addresses the need for a reliable means of message delivery as sought after by family members and care workers alike.

In addition, note that the actors can only record messages in the home of the elderly person. Of course it would be tempting to provide the opportunity to remotely place messages over a network, but this functionality was disregarded, as especially the care workers were concerned that it could lead to an inflation of the amount of messages. The care workers prefer to mainly interact with family members that frequent the home on a regular basis and the restriction to limit the recording to the local setting must also been seen in this light.

Furthermore, only someone carrying an RFID badge may actually gain access to recorded messages, this provides a measure of privacy not included in the binder were anyone could flip the pages and read a message. Only family members can play back messages intended for family members, and only care workers can play back those for care workers.

In addition to the part of the system immediately visible in the home of the elderly person, there is a backend server connected to the device with a network connection that allows the system to e.g. send notifications to family members via email or phone text when there are new messages for them or in the event that messages have been played back by the care workers. This service was envisioned in order to accommodate family members' preference for being in contact and receiving messages continuously. This service of remote notification is not envisioned as being used by the care workers as they tend to find such services intruding and overwhelming as mentioned above.

Finally, although the system is mainly targeted for the group of actors taking care of older adults, older adults themselves may actually use the system to create reminders to the people visiting them (and to themselves). This may be of use considering that some senior citizens may be challenged when it comes to remembering.

Conclusion and perspectives

This article has explored home care work with the aim of understanding how this might be supported with computer technology. Findings suggest that home care work may be highly cooperative in nature and require substantial coordination or articulation work among the actors, such as family members and care workers, engaged in providing care for older adults. Although they jointly provide home care for older adults, family members and care workers harbour diverse attitudes towards their joint efforts. Family members may be highly emotionally invested in the care of their aging relatives. In comparison, care workers may adopt what could be described as an emotionally detached stance or attitude towards their professional work in order to safeguard their own emotional health.

The impression of these differences in attitudes and values are further reinforced by the fact that family members seem to prefer receiving messages at all times, at home or at work, concerning the wellbeing of their aging relative, whereas care workers regard receiving messages from what may be emotional family members at all hours of the day as something to be avoided or at least curbed.

Two design concepts were presented. The designs are centred on supporting articulation work i.e. the exchange of messages for the coordination of cooperative home care work. The first concept, namely the 'augmented binder', relies on the augmentation of an existing paper binder for the exchange of written messages between family members and care workers. The second concept, namely PressToTalk, breaks with the written form as it relies solely on the exchange of voice messages. The design concepts are presented as a means of illustrating some of our findings and highlighting the questions that they raise.

The challenge for CSCW emerging from this study is related not only to the fact that home care work is highly cooperative in nature but also to the fact that it is carried out by a work ensemble comprised of professional actors (the care workers) as well as non-professional ones (the family members). How can we with information technology reduce the cost and increase the reliability of this distributed process of coordinating and integrating of cooperative home care work while remaining sensitive to the highly diverse sensibilities, values and attitudes of the actors? The designs above offer our preliminary suggestion.

Acknowledgements

We would like to sincerely thank the elderly people and their families, Frederiksbjerg Lokalcentre and their personnel as well as the consortium User Driven Healthcare Innovation and the Danish Ministry of Science, Technology and Innovation for making this project possible. Lastly, we would like to thank all our colleagues for inspiration and feedback not least Morten Kyng, Rikke Aarhus, Simon Bo Larsen and Margit Kristensen.

References

Abowd, G.D., G.R. Hayes, J.A. Kientz, L. Mamykina, E.D. Mynatt. 2006. Challenges and Opportunities for Collaboration Technologies for Chronic Care Management. *The Human-Computer Interaction Consortium (HCIC 2006). Fraser, Colorado, USA, 2006.*

Anoto. 2011. Anoto Group AB, Traktorvägen 11, Box 4106, SE 227 22 Lund, Viewed April 26th 2011, http://www.anoto.com

Ashforth, B.E., R.H. Humphrey. 1993. Emotional Labor in Service Roles: The Influence of Identity. *The Academy of Management Review* 18(1) 88-115.

Bardram, J.E., C.A. Bossen. 2005. A web of coordinative artifacts: collaborative work at a hospital ward. *In Proceedings of the 2005 international ACM SIGGROUP Conference on Supporting Group Work (Sanibel Island, Florida, USA, November 06 - 09, 2005).* ACM Press, NY, Sanibel Island, Florida, USA.

Carstensen, P., C. Sørensen. 1996. From the Social to the Systematic: Mechanisms supporting coordination in design. *Computer Supported Cooperative Work. The Journal of Collaborative Computing* 5(4) 1996.

Consolvo, S., P. Roessler, B. Shelton, A. LaMarca, B. Schilit, S. Bly. 2004. Technology for care networks of elders. *IEEE Pervasive Computing* 22-29.

Demiris, G. 2009. Independence and shared decision making: The role of smart home technology in empowering older adults *Engineering in Medicine and Biology Society, 2009. EMBC 2009. Annual International Conference of the IEEE*, 6432-6436.

Gesano, G., F. Heins, A. Naldini. 2009. Regional Challenges in the perspective of 2010, Regional desparities and future challenges. ISMERI Europa.

Kahn, W.A. 1993. Caring for the caregivers: Patterns of organizational caregiving. *Administrative Science Quaterly*. 38 539-563.

Kientz, J.A., G.R. Hayes, G.D. Abowd, R.E. Grinter. 2006. From the war room to the living room: decision support for home-based therapy teams *Proceedings of the 2006 20th anniversary conference on Computer supported cooperative work*. ACM, Banff, Alberta, Canada, 209-218.

Le, X.H.B., M. Di Mascolo, A. Gouin, N. Noury. 2007. Health Smart Home - Towards an assistant tool for automatic assessment of the dependence of elders. *Engineering in Medicine and Biology Society, 2007. EMBS 2007. 29th Annual International Conference of the IEEE* 3806 - 3809.

Lindley, S., R. Harper, A. Sellen. 2008. Designing for Elders: Exploring the Complexity of Relationships in Later Life *In Proceedings of the 22nd BCS conference on Human Computer Interaction (HCI 2008)*, 77-86.

Morris, M., J. Lundell, E. Dishman, B. Needham. 2003. New Perspectives on Ubiquitous Computing from Ethnographic Study of Elders with Cognitive Decline *UbiComp 2003: Ubiquitous Computing*. Springer Berlin / Heidelberg, 227-242.

Mynatt, E.D., J. Rowan, S. Craighill, A. Jacobs. 2001. Digital family portraits: supporting peace of mind for extended family members *Proceedings of the SIGCHI conference on Human factors in computing systems*. ACM, Seattle, Washington, United States.

Petrakou, A. 2007. Exploring cooperation through a binder: A context for IT tools in elderly care at home. L. Bannon, I. Wagner, C. Gutwin, R. Harper, K. Schmidt, eds. *ECSCW'07: The Tenth European Conference on Computer Supported Cooperative Work, 24-28 September 2007, Limerick, Ireland*, 271-290.

Rafaeli, A., R.I. Sutton. 1989. The expression of emotion in organizational life. . L.L. Cummings, B.M. Staw, eds. *Research in organizational behavior*. JAI Press, Greenwich, CT, 1-42.

Rogers, Y. 2006. Moving on from weiser's vision of calm computing: Engaging ubicomp experiences. P. Dourish, A. Friday, eds. *UbiComp 2006: Ubiquitous Computing*. Springer Berlin / Heidelberg, 404-421.

Rook, K.S. 1987. Reciprocity of social exchange and social satisfaction among older women. *Journal of Personality and Social Psychology* 51(1) 145-154.

Rowan, J., E.D. Mynatt. 2005. Digital family portrait field trial: Support for aging in place *In Proc. CHI '05*. ACM, 521-530.

Ryle, G. 1949. *The Concept of Mind*. Hutchinson, London.

Schmidt, K., L. Bannon. 1992. Taking CSCW Seriously: Supporting Articulation Work. *Computer Supported Cooperative Work (CSCW). An International Journal*. 1(1-2) 7-40.

Schmidt, K., C. Simone. 1996. Coordination mechanisms: Towards a conceptual foundation of CSCW systems design. *Computer Supported Cooperative Work: The Journal of Collaborative Computing* 5(2-3) 155-200.

Spitze, G., M.P. Gallant. 2004. The bitter with the sweet: Older adults' strategies for handling ambivalence in relations with their adult children. *Research on Aging* 26(4) 387-412.

Strauss, A. 1985. Work and the division of labor. *The Sociological Quarterly* 26(1) 1-19.

Wittenberg-Lyles, E., D.P. Oliver, G. Demiris, P. Baldwin. 2010. The ACTive Intervention in Hospice Interdisciplinary Team Meetings: Exploring Family Caregiver and Hospice Team Communication. *Journal of Computer-Mediated Communication* 15(3) 465-481.

The Use of Narratives in Medical Work: A Field Study of Physician-Patient Consultations

Troels Mønsted[1], Madhu C. Reddy[2] and Jørgen P. Bansler[1]

[1] University of Copenhagen, Denmark, [2] The Pennsylvania State University, USA

monsted@diku.dk, mreddy@ist.psu.edu, bansler@diku.dk

Abstract. Medical reasoning involves more than just summarizing clinical data and guidelines. Illness trajectories of chronic patients are often long, complex and full of uncertain information that requires interpretation. Understanding the complex interrelations is an important aspect of medical reasoning that displays narrative rather than scientific characteristics. While the qualities of the medical record as a repository of information or as a coordinative tool are well known, the role it plays in the unfolding of narratives in medical reasoning is less discussed. This paper examines this issue through a case study of patient consultations that take place as part of a distributed treatment of chronic heart patients. We found that the record, even though fragmented and to some extent incomplete, enables the physician to construct an *ad hoc narrative.* During the actual consultation, physicians and patients unfold a more detailed narrative, which we refer to as the *re-emplotted narrative,* that includes additional information and entails a collaborative exploration of uncertainties. While this may point to some inadequacies of the medical record as a supportive tool for the process of unfolding narrative, we suggest that is it in fact a crucial component of the medical reasoning activity that must be considered in design of supportive systems.

Introduction

Patient consultations are highly collaborative activities where the patients tell their story and describe their complaint, and the physician seeks to make sense of the patients' problem in medical terms and come up with a treatment plan. While the conventional view on medical diagnosis and decision making puts general scientific rules and knowledge at the forefront, patient consultations require much more than rule following and formal decision making, because the generalized knowledge of medical science must somehow be connected with the unique experience of the individual patient (Waymack 2009). Referring to Berg (1992), Kane and Luz (2009) argue that:

"(...) a physician, in transforming a patient's problem into a solvable problem, does not simply combine some cognitive items together, such as historical and examination data, but actively articulates an array of heterogeneous elements within the transformation." (Kane and Luz, 2009:358)

According to Montgomery (2006), medical practice cannot be characterized purely as science or a technical skill, but as:

"(...) the ability to work out how general rules – scientific principles, clinical guidelines – apply to the particular patient" (Montgomery, 2006 :5).

Rather than considering medical practice to be a science, it can be characterized as *medical reasoning* - an instance of practical reasoning, or in Aristotle's words, phronesis. Through medical reasoning, information is put together with conditional certainty (Hunter, 1996; Montgomery, 2006)

The narrative aspect of medical reasoning is mirrored in the primary tool for storing and conveying clinical information, the medical records. These documents have a strong narrative aspect because narratives supply a workable medium for representing knowledge that is time- and context-dependent – and often uncertain or ambiguous as well. They are created to organize, record and capture practical experience. Medical records are therefore far from a straightforward presentation of clinical data. As argued by Berg and Bowker (1997), a medical record embodies multiple, intertwined representations of the patient. These representations do not fully mirror the body of the patient, nor determine them. Instead they argue that the medical record:

"(...) mediates the relations that it organizes, the bodies that are configured through it" (Berg and Bowker, 1997:514).

Likewise Fitzpatrick (2004) depicts medical records, not as passive information repositories, defined as the archival record, but as the *working record*, defined as:

"a set of complexly interrelated clinician-centred documents that are locally evolved, maintained and used to support delivery of care (...)" (Fitzpatrick, 2004:291).

While researchers have studied how physicians through social behavior such as *mindfulness*, i.e. non-judgmental moment-to-moment awareness can assist the unfolding of narratives (Conelly, 2005), much less has been reported on how the diverse clinical and narrative information stored and conveyed by medical records, is used in practice. This is however highly relevant for design of electronic patient records.

As argued by some (Arminen and Poikus, 2009; Hartswood et al, 2003), the design of medical systems is often based on flawed or overly simplified assumptions about the nature of clinical practices creating a mismatch between the presupposed and the actual use of a given system. Often technical solutions are posed as answers to inherently socio-technical problems (Hartswood et al, 2003). One common misconception, as argued by Paoletti (2009) is that information is *out there* to be used and processed in a linear diagnostic process, rather than being narrative information that require interpretation.

The study presented here examines the use and role of medical records in the collaborative unfolding of narratives at patient consultations. We examine this in the context of patient consultations taking place as part of the distributed treatment of chronic heart patients in Denmark. In this study, we are interested in developing a more detailed picture of how records are brought in play and how different kinds of content, clinical evidence and narrative information, affect the medical reasoning taking place.

The paper is structured as follows: In the following section, we elaborate on the concept of narratives in healthcare and related research on medical records. Next, we present our field study of consultations of chronic heart patients at a local hospital. We finally discuss how and to what extend the record support the narrative component of medical reasoning at patient consultations.

Background

Narratives in Clinical Practice

"Despite all the prohibitions against 'anecdotal knowledge' in medicine, case narration is the principal means of thinking and remembering – of knowing – in medicine. The interpretive reasoning required to understand signs and symptoms and to reach a diagnosis is represented in all its situated and circumstantial uncertainty in narrative." (Montgomery, 2006:46).

The notion of narratives is increasingly recognized as an influential concept in helping us understand reasoning processes, interaction and information sharing in healthcare settings. The concept has been applied at multiple levels of analysis. Recently, Hayes et al (in press) applied *narrative networks* as an alternative analytical lens to traditional workflow diagrams, to foreground how interrelating *narrative fragments* of many multiple stakeholders constitute a network that goes beyond the view of the individual healthcare practitioner. Some studies have investigated the role, conditions for, and significance of *patient stories* and *storytelling* in medical practice from a patient perspective (e.g. Kleinman, 1988; Brody, 2003) while others have studied the role of narratives from the perspective of doctors (Hunter, 1991; Atkinson, 1995). In this paper focus on the body of literature concerning the role narratives play in medical reasoning.

The attention towards narratives is partly motivated by the challenging task it is for healthcare professionals to deal with and comprehend long *illness trajectories* that, following the definition of Strauss et al (1997) refers to:

"(…) not only to the physiological unfolding of a patient's disease, but to the total *organization of work* done over that course, plus the *impact* on those involved with that work and its organization." (Strauss et al, 1997:8).

It is increasingly recognized that medical reasoning, without disregarding the scientific foundation of medicine, also has a strong interpretative, hermeneutic component (Lock, 1990). While healthcare professionals as argued by Mol (2002) configure their own experience of a given patient, and therefore see slightly different bodies and diseases, they still must position themselves in relation to a past and an anticipated future (Mattingly, 1998). An important question therefore is how healthcare practitioners make sense of a patient's illness trajectory.

Based extensively on the pioneering work of Weick (1995), several studies have portrayed the role of sensemaking in healthcare, focusing on patients' sensemaking of interactions with nurses (Hargle et al, 2009) and social and collaborative aspects among healthcare professionals (Albolino, 2007; Paul and Reddy, 2010).

As argued by Lock (1990), the concept of narratives embraces the diverse components of medical reasoning (Lock, 1990).

"I will claim that narrative is a fundamental language event which allows the explanatory discourse of science and the meaningful discourse of human relations to be grafted onto it" (Lock, 1990:42)

According to Feldman et al. (2004) narrative form is not necessarily a neutral and fully inclusive story. Rather they define narratives as:

"(…) a sequence of events, experiences, or actions with a plot that ties together different parts into a meaningful whole" and "(…) the narrative includes, excludes, and emphasizes, the storyteller not only illustrates his or her version of the action but also provides an interpretation or evaluative commentary on the subject" (Feldman et al, 2004:148).

The central, unifying structure of narratives is the *plot*. In contrast with the mere chronological account of events provided by *stories*, a narrator imposes a causal or moral structure to a sequence of events organized by the plot (Hydén, 1997, Hobbs, 2003). This configuration process, referred to as *emplotment*, is by Mattingly (1994) described as marshalling the relation of events to transform from mere sequence to causality. While emplotment can be an individual activity it often involves collaboration in healthcare settings. Brody (2002) have portrayed patients as active and important participants in the joint construction of narratives, and according to Mattingly (1998) a narrative is often made through the combined efforts of all players, with the therapist in charge.

The Role of Records in Clinical Practice

Medical records are often thought of as a document containing all patient related information within an institution. They were initially introduced as educational tools, consisting of loosely structured descriptions of particular cases, authored retrospectively using a free-from narrative style (Siegler, 2010). The medical record has since evolved to be a highly formalized and structured document used actively in patient care. However, the medical record is far more than a single repository of information. As argued by Berg and Bowker (1997), the record consists of multiple bodies and is constituted by:

"(...) all written, typed, or electronically stored traces of any aspect of patient treatment that has official status within the hospital system and is in principle stored for a period of time (at least equal to the patient's stay in the hospital" (Berg and Bowker, 1997:515).

This fragmentation of the medical record may be a product of increased complexity and a tendency towards distributing treatments across multiple, specialized healthcare providers, typically referred to as *shared care* (Pritchard and Hughes, 1995) or *integrated care* (Kodner and Spreeuwenberg, 2002). One strategy to meet an increased demand for collaboration across professional and organizational boundaries is to improve design of Electronic Medical Records (EMR). Winthereik and Vikkelsø (2005) argued that EMRs are important change agents that can help satisfy a growing interest in organizing care along the specific patient cases, rather than along organizational boundaries.

According to Berg (1999) medical records fulfill two important roles: They both accumulate information, and coordinate activities. The coordinative role of EMRs has been of major interest in CSCW research. Østerlund (2002) studied how records are used to convey information within and across organizational boundaries. Reddy et al (2001) studied the EMR as a *Common Information Space* that serves as an important resource of coordination among heterogeneous, physically co-located actors because of its ability to de- and re-contextualize information. Munkvold and Ellingsen (2007) have studied the benefits and limitations of Common Information Spaces to form links between the disconnected trajectories of different organizations along the overall illness trajectory of a patient.

While medical records fulfill a crucial role as coordinative artifacts, they also fulfill another – and just as important – role as "tools to think with". In other words, they act as artifacts that underpin the process of medical reasoning and facilitate the exercise of clinical judgment. Østerlund (2008) argued that records are important tools by doctors and nurses in their sensemaking activities. Some studies suggest that the medical record may in fact be a poor resource for answers to the often very complex questions of physicians in their local practices (Gorman, 1995). Furthermore, these highly complex EMRs may draw physicians' attention away from the patient and therefore, hinder their engagement with the patient. However, relatively few studies address how medical records are used in medical consultations and how this complex information infrastructure supports medical reasoning and unfolding of narratives.

While the narrative content of medical records have been portrayed in some detail (e.g. Tange et al, 1997), much less have been reported on how the narrative aspect of medical reasoning is facilitated or mediated by technology.

Research Site

To inquire into the role of the medical record in medical reasoning during patient consultations, we studied a particular type of consultation, *the medical follow-up* of patients with implanted ICD device. An ICD (*Implantable Cardioverter Defibrillator*) is a programmable electric impulse generator. The ICD constantly monitors the heart and intervenes when it detects a pre-specified rhythmic abnormality, either by pacing the heart or by delivering an electric shock. ICD therapy is typically combined with medical therapy, often consisting of a cocktail of different drugs.

Due to a high degree of professional specialization, the care of ICD patients is distributed across multiple healthcare providers; consequently, the illness trajectory crosses several professional as well as organizational boundaries. Thus, ICD care in our study involves at least two hospitals, a general practitioner, additional home care, a rehabilitation unit, and other specialists. ICD care is therefore constituted by a number of independent but somewhat interdependent practices.

The main aspects of ICD care are provided by two hospital units. The responsibility for implantation and monitoring of ICD devices is carried out by one of the five national *ICD Centers,* located at major teaching hospitals in Denmark. In this unit, staff (physicians, laboratory technicians and nurses) specialized in electrophysiology, are responsible for ICD implantation and for monitoring the technical functioning of the device, the latter referred to as *device follow-ups*. These are either conducted as consultations or by a remote monitoring system, where the patients receive feedback while at their home.

The *local hospitals* are responsible for the rest of the patient's medical treatment. This is assessed at regular medical follow-ups, where the patient's progress is assessed and the treatment adjusted accordingly. Local hospitals are distributed widely across the country.

Methods

We used multiple methods to develop a rich picture of the use of records medical reasoning at patient consultations. The study involved a combination of observations, interviews, document and system studies and design workshops, conducted over a period of approximately 12 months. The observations were conducted over a two-day period where one researcher shadowed a physician conducting patient consultations. As part of the observations, the researcher conducted several informal interviews with the physician focusing on specific aspects of his practice, documents, and systems. We also examined the documents and the systems by conducting video-recorded walkthroughs in situ and by collecting and analyzing five full sets of progress notes from the medical records of ICD patients. The five design workshops, each lasting 2-3 hours, involved five physicians, representing two hospitals involved in ICD care, and five designers and researchers. The overall purpose of the workshops was to explore current practices and to develop concepts and prototypes for improving support of distributed ICD care. One central activity at these workshops was discussion and mapping of the current work practices and the information systems in use.

All consultations were audio- and video-recorded and were fully transcribed. All data have subsequently been categorized and analyzed through open coding and axial coding (Strauss and Corbin, 1998).

Participants

This paper focuses on medical follow-ups conducted at the local hospitals. The main participant in the study is a physician who we observed while he was conducting medical follow-ups. The physician is a trained cardiologist and is one of the leading specialists in ICD care at this particular hospital.

The patients involved in the study all suffer from chronic, severe heart arrhythmia. Approximately half of the patients have an implanted ICD device, while the others either have been or are considered potential ICD candidates. The group includes young patients in their thirties as well as middle-age and elderly patients. Their physical as well and mental capabilities varied from being severely impaired to being relatively well-functioning. Furthermore, some of the patients suffered from other chronic conditions, such as diabetes or COPD (Chronic Obstructive Pulmonary Disease). Although some of the patients attended the consultation individually, most brought a relative and/or a translator.

Tools

At the patient consultations, the physician has a broad selection of paper and IT-based information systems at his disposal. The backbone of the information infrastructure at the local hospital is a paper-based patient record, a cross-departmental folder, used by all wards at the local hospital in which the patient is treated. The patient record can therefore grow to become a substantially sized document. The first section of the record containing the *progress notes* is particularly important to the physician. As we will later elaborate, the progress notes contain the narrative parts of a medical record, as opposed to other sections containing more quantitative clinical data. The progress notes are comments dictated by all healthcare professionals who interact with the patient. The notes summarize findings and decisions made at each event. In some cases, the progress notes also contain more substantial information, e.g. about the course of events in the patient's illness trajectory.

The physician also has a large number of IT-systems and dedicated databases at his disposal. During consultations, the physician will have approximately ten systems running on his computer. The most important systems are:

- *HjerterPlus* - an IT-based local, dedicated heart record.
- *Opus Notat*, - a system used to manage progress notes.
- *Labka* - a system that stores results from laboratory examinations.
- *EPM* - a system intended to provide a centralized list of medicine prescribed to a patient.
- *www.icddata.dk* - an online repository of ICD information containing information from the device follow-ups at the ICD.

Physician-Patient Consultations

Medical follow-ups take place at regular intervals, depending on the condition of the patient and the stage of the treatment. The purpose is to assess the patient's condition and progress and to adjust the medication accordingly. If the medical treatment is assessed to be optimal and the patient is in a stable condition, the consultations at the local hospital are discontinued and the patient is referred to follow-ups at his/her general practitioner. Under normal circumstances, 15 minutes is allocated for each consultation, the physician's preparation included. During our observations, the schedule was however frequently adjusted, either because of cancellations or extended consultations.

Before calling the patient to his office, the physician at the local hospital would usually prepare for the consultation by reading the medical record as well as any other information located in the IT systems. This was done to get an overview of the patient's current condition, illness trajectory and to identify important issues to address during the consultation.

Before the consultation, the physician prepared by quickly reading the progress notes in the paper record and the online record of ICD information, www.icddata.dk. The patient, a male, had a biventricular ICD implanted in 2004. He does not suffer from ischemic heart disease. In 2008, the patient was admitted with a severely impaired condition. Treatment with beta-blockers was commenced in an attempt to improve his condition, but this was made difficult due to the patient's hypertension. The patient' EF value was 10 the last time it was measured. The physician furthermore found a medicine list in the record. Finally, the physician learned that the patient hadn't recently received ICD therapies.

The record provided the physician with a general overview of the history of significant events in the illness trajectory. Also, more specifically, it pointed out the treatment with beta-blockers as an area of concern that he should attend to during the consultation. During his preparation, the physician would usually take short notes on a printout of the scheduled consultations. This annotated printout came to represent his summary of the patient's illness trajectory.

When prepared, the physician calls the patient to his office. During our observations, the physician most often initiated the consultation by first highlighting his understanding of the patient's condition and then asking a set of routine questions.

The physician initially told the patient that he had read his record and medicine list, and that he could see that the patient had been very ill, but also that his condition had improved. He then commented that the patient didn't have shortness of breath from walking to his office. The patient confirmed this and furthermore told the physician, that he can walk around effortlessly, unless the weather is cold. The physician also asked and received confirmation that the patient did not experience chest pains. Finally the physician told the patient that he could tell from the record that the medicine the patient was taking was working well.

The questions asked by the physician are important for his assessment of the patient's condition. As part of this routine, the physician also measures the patient's blood pressure and pulse and on some occasions conducts other forms of physical examinations. After these initial steps, consultations can proceed in a variety of ways. Often, the physician's questions will unveil symptoms or conditions that need further examination. On other occasions, they trigger the patient to tell the physician about his own experience or concerns.

During the conversation, the patient told the physician that the beta-blockers caused strong side effects. He stated that he experienced fatigue and troubled bowel movements from the particular beta-blocker he was taking, drug A. He furthermore expressed strong concerns that his body couldn't tolerate all this medicine. Because of the patient's discomfort, the physician suggested replacing drug A with another beta-blocker, to which the patient reluctantly agreed. The physician first suggested drug B. The patient, however, recalled that he had already previously tried this drug and that it too had strong side effects. This pattern repeated when the physician suggested drug C, although the patient said that it had been a long time since he had tried this drug. The physician suggested that he try it once more, because his body might have adjusted to the new situation. After some consideration, the patient agreed to try drug C again.

As is often the case during consultations, the patient pointed out a relevant issue – what particular drug to use – that needs to be addressed. Furthermore he provided the physician with information that was highly relevant for physician's medical reasoning, namely that the medication adjustment attempts were not only affected by his physical problems but also by his experiences with the side effects. The patient also provided the physician with a historical account of the types of drugs that had taken previously. In this case, this information and discussion lead to a more informed decision of re-prescribing one of the previously attempted drugs.

Towards the end of a consultation, the physician and the patient agree on the outcome of the consultation, e.g. new treatment initiatives or other examinations that the patient might need. The physician gives the patient prescription for medications and lab work and schedules the next consultation. As the last part of the routine, the physician will dictate a progress note that a secretary will later enter in the medical record. These progress notes cover a brief description of the patient's condition, provide detailed list of prescribed medicine and diagnostic codes. The progress notes also often point to uncertainties or aspects of the patient's treatment that the physician wants future caregivers to examine when seeing the patient.

Findings

During the medical follow-up, clinical evidence played an important role: the physician's decision to advise the patient to recommence treatment with beta-blockers was partially based on clinical guidelines. This scientific foundation was central to his argument to the patient in one consultation where he advised a patient to disregard his anxiety and take a prescribed type of medicine in spite of strong side effects:

> "All research show that it is the medicine that causes people to live longer and prevent them from being admitted to a hospital again" (Physician)

In other consultations, we observed the use of the *echocardiogram* – an examination that among other things is used to determine the EF value (*ejection fraction* or popularly the *pump function*) of a heart. According to the physician, the echocardiogram is *"the keyword in all our algorithms"*. It is used to indicate if the patient is an ICD candidate, and to assess the progress of the treatment. If the patient during the consultation is diagnosed with hypertension, the patient will usually be advised to begin treatment with antihypertensive medicaments. This medical treatment will be adjusted until the physician assesses the patient to be *optimally treated*, which means that the dosage reaches a level defined on the basis of clinical evidence and particularities of the patient.

The decision to prescribe the beta-blocker, drug C, described in the section above displayed certain narrative characteristics. The outcome of the consultation was not only a product of compilation of clinical facts but also involved assessment and interpretation of causality in clinical information that is equivocal or not recorded in full detail, social and contextual factors and the experience of the patient. An important prerequisite for this kind of medical reasoning is that the physician, building on insight in both the patient's clinical condition and the patient's experiences, is able to configure relevant elements of the patient's illness trajectory into a meaningful narrative.

Due to the chronic condition of ICD patients, and the fact that patients with chronic heart arrhythmia often suffer from other chronic illnesses, the medical records often contain large number of pages. The same is true for the other systems where patient data are registered. The challenge for the physician during the consultations is to identify relevant elements of the patient's illness trajectory and through emplotment construct a narrative that explains relevant causal relations. This narrative is highly context dependent and we refer to it as the *ad hoc narrative*.

In the following sections, we highlight how the ad hoc narrative emerges within the medical follow-up. First, we examine how narratives reside in the medical record, and then demonstrate how the narrative is unfolded during consultations.

Narratives in the Medical Record

The multiple documents and systems that constitute the medical record used during medical follow-ups reveal the complex nature of medical reasoning. Due to the scientific component of medical work, a substantial amount of the information stored in the record can be characterized as clinical evidence. The paper record will for instance often contain a printed echocardiogram and extensive medicine lists, while adjacent IT systems such Labka and www.icddata.dk, respectively, contain results from laboratory tests and highly condensed information, primarily numeric, describing the functioning of the ICD device.

The progress notes in the paper records, one of the more prominent components in use at the medical follow-up, displays more narrative properties. Since progress notes are dictated after every contact with the patient, they can vary greatly in format and content depending on the author and particular issue dealt with during the consultation.

Some progress notes contain very concise data on the patient's current condition and state of the treatment. This type of progress notes report on a narrow set of issues concerning the particular consultation:

As of today, patient attended a consultation with a nurse in the heart failure clinic.
The patient's son took part in the consultation.
See HjerterPlus under standard forms.
Blood pressure 120/60. Weight 65,9 kg NYHA 1.
Pt is in a good state of health.
Plan: Cres Caps. Odric 2mg x 1 vesper.
Ct. other medicine unchanged.
Pt. have appointed with physician at 8/10 09.
Pt. gives consent to the above mentioned.

However, some progress notes have a more narrative character and reveal fragments of the patient's past illness trajectory, particular findings that influence the treatment plan, and uncertainties that must be taken into consideration. These progress notes, therefore, not only provide the reader with clinical facts, but also provide parts of the context surrounding the medical reasoning performed at a particular consultation.

> Pt was admitted with incompensation for 6 months ago, presumably with secondary to paroxysmal atrial fibrillation.

> EF was 25% and there was light mitral insufficiency and severe pulmonary hypertension. KAG was attempted, but could not be accomplished due to severe calcification of a. femoralis. It has been decided to complete the medical treatment alone. Pt has tolerated the treatment well under NYHA class 1-2, no chest pain or syncopes. Blood samples not abnormal. Blood pressure 140/60, pulse 75 beats per minutes.

> (This was followed by a comprehensive medicine list)

A progress note like this one positions specific events in the patient's illness trajectory and explains the causal relationships and interdependencies among particular parts of the patient's treatment. In isolation, the example, presented above, only provides the physician with a description of a minor fragment of the patient's illness trajectory. When combined with other similar progress notes, the physician is however able to construct a timeline of events and interdependencies, which is why the progress notes can be important resource for the physician. They are used in unfolding of ad hoc narratives.

A less common but interesting subcategory of progress notes is referred to by the physicians as *summaries*. Summaries are rich accounts that contain a substantial description of the patient's illness trajectory. A summary is often produced in response to certain events that require the responsible professional to develop detailed insights into the patient's illness trajectory. For instance, summaries are written when the patient is (re-)admitted, referred to other healthcare providers or, more broadly, in situations in which significant decisions have to be made. One common feature of summaries is that they provide a relatively comprehensive description of the patient's condition, the illness trajectory, and contextual information. Although the content and format may vary they provide information on allergies, past events, cardiological risk factors, current condition, other medical conditions, medicine, social situation, objective findings and the author's conclusion.

All progress notes including summaries are entered into the medical record as part of or immediately after a triggering event. Consequently, at the medical follow-up, the physician dictated the progress notes immediately after the consultation. The narrative content of progress notes in general and summaries in particular are a textual representations of ad hoc narratives unfolded during medical reasoning processes, e.g. at patient consultations. We refer to them as *textual narratives*. Though the content of textual narratives is framed by a particular event, they are often important resources for medical reasoning at other patient consultations.

Unfolding the Narrative

The main objective of a patient consultation is to adjust aspects of the treatment to improve the patient's condition. A significant aspect of this is the physician's attempts to make sense of the patient's current condition and identify relevant aspects of the past illness trajectory – which we refer to as *unfolding the ad hoc narrative*. During our study we observed that this emplotment process happened in two stages: Prior to the consultation the physician constructed a *proto-narrative* – a narrative based solely on information found in the medical record, either clinical data or textual narratives. During the consultation the proto-narrative was corrected or refined through physician-patient interaction – what we refer to as *re-emplotment*. An important resource during re-emplotment was the *patient's narrative* – the patient's own configuration of significant events and experiences from his/hers illness trajectory. In the following two sections we elaborate on these two observations.

The Proto-narrative

Before a consultation, the physician began to read the progress notes in the medical record, and explained to the researcher:

> "We have a nineteen hundred pages record here [presumably an ironic exaggeration]. I can't remember that I've seen him before. Okay. There is a note from December where we have summarized a bit. December 08, more than a year ago. There is also a very good summary if we go back to March 08." (Physician)

During his preparations, the paper record, and in particular the progress notes are important resources for the physician. According to the physician, he will usually first look through the most recent progress notes in search of a summary, since it will provide him with a relatively thorough overview. Summaries are, however, often not available or too old to provide information on more recent developments. In those situations, the physician instead has to construct the proto-narrative from the often more fragmented short progress notes based on previous consultations and hospital admissions. Depending on the particular situation, he may also use one or more of the dedicated IT systems or databases. In this way, he is able to construct an overview of the more significant events in the patient's illness trajectory. When constructing the proto-narrative, the physician configures a plausible narrative from often incomplete, ambiguous, and even contradictory information from multiple sources. In this process, the physician seeks to find answers to questions such as 'what happened, when, how and why?' He furthermore identifies significant events and makes decisions on which information to include, exclude, stress, or subordinate. Finally, he arranges events in a certain order that implies a particular causality.

The physician stated that he would prefer to have this proto-narrative prior to the actual consultation. However, he can also construct it while the patient is present. In the following example, the physician constructed and articulated the proto-narrative to the patient at the beginning of a consultation:

"I will just summarize what we know about you, so you can correct it if we have gotten some of the facts wrong. It is a long story. Blood clot in the heart in 2002, where a "balloon treatment" was attempted. Blood clot again in 2005, where a new "balloon treatment" was attempted, but it didn't really succeed. Then you had a bypass operation. Then came a blood clot in the head. Then a new coronary angiography in 2006. Then we know that you have decreased pump function in the heart, which is why you got this ICD device. You were admitted in 2008 where we made a new coronary arteriography of the carotid artery. Nothing has changed here. This [implicitly the observed consultation] is only about the medical treatment of the heart. I can see that you have talked to (name of other physician at the cardiology ward at the local hospital) recently. Three or four weeks ago?" (Physician)

By combining information from multiple sources (i.e. several progress notes), the physician actively constructed a proto-narrative with a clear plot. The purpose was to organize, make sense of and explain causalities in the available data on the recent developments in the patient's condition and treatment. In this case, the physician identified relevant but incomplete information, namely the patient's recent and apparently non-routine consultation with a cardiologist at the same ward at the local hospital. However, the purpose and outcome of the consultation was not described in the record.

The Re-emplotted Narrative

The consultation often begins with the proto-narrative because the physician usually initiates the conversation by explaining the account he has just constructed to the patient. The ensuing conversation leads to an elaboration of issues raised in the proto-narrative based on the *patient's narrative*. Continuing the example above, the patient provided additional information about the outcome of the recent consultation:

The patient explained that drug A was changed into drug B at the recent consultation, although he hadn't yet commenced this treatment, because the medicine is incredibly expensive. The physician asked whether or not he had applied for an economic subsidy. The patient confirmed that this application was in progress. The physician then informed the patient that he would get the subsidy retroactively, so, he could initiate the treatment immediately. The patient was unaware of this.

In other situations, the patient's narrative brings up issues not described in the proto-narrative, e.g. personal concerns and questions or conditions and clinical facts that initially were left out by the physician.

In one consultation, a patient expressed concerns over the dosage of one of the drugs he was taking, drug A, an antihypertensive medicament. The patient stated that, *"as far as I understand, it should not be so high"*. After the physician had clarified that the patient referred to a measure of his blood viscosity and not the dosage of the drug, the patient stated that he believed it to be *"three point something"*. According to the physician, this measure should preferably be between 2 and 3. He therefore examined the latest blood tests using the Labka system and found that this number was in fact 4.1, which under normal circumstances would require adjustment of the medicine. The patient stated that the medicine was not adjusted at a recent consultation with a nurse, and he did not believe that she had taken this into consideration. Since neither of the systems available at the office provided information on this consultation, the physician had to leave the consultation, to procure the nurse's record, which is a separate document. When he returned approximately five minutes later, he had clarified that the responsible nurse was in fact aware of the high blood viscosity, and that the medicine had been adjusted accordingly. They did, never the less, agree on a slight adjustment to the medicine.

In this situation, the re-emplotted narrative included perspectives from the medical record and the patient's knowledge and concerns. It also came to include perspectives, rationalities and causal explanations of healthcare professionals, who were not present or directly represented through any parts of the medical record. The patient's narrative thus pointed out areas of concern that required elaboration.

During the consultations, we observed that the re-emplotted narratives provided the physician with relevant information that initially had been missing in the proto-narrative. The consultations also involved a collaborative exploration of information that was inaccurate or missing. This narrative re-emplotment is therefore not only about filling out information gaps but involves a set of interactions where parts of the story are further explored, specified and reshaped. This adds a layer of social interaction to the medical reasoning activity.

After all medical follow-ups, the physician dictates a new progress note that is later be transcribed by a secretary and placed in the medical record. Apart from a medicine list, a set of diagnostic codes, and information about the decisions made at the medical follow-up, this progress note contains a brief summary of the physician's view of the patient's illness trajectory. In this way a textual narrative is created on the foundation of the ad hoc narrative unfolded during the consultation. This textual narrative may potentially become a resource for unfolding ad hoc narratives at future consultations.

Discussion: The record as supportive tool for unfolding of narratives

Our studies of medical follow-ups show that while clinical facts and guidelines play a crucial role for the outcome of consultations, many decisions rest upon a far more complex process of medical reasoning. For instance, medicine prescriptions are highly influenced by clinical guidelines for chronic heart patient care, but involve other considerations as well, e.g. contextual factors such as other health related conditions as well as observations and interpretations from other healthcare professionals. A prerequisite for medical reasoning is, therefore, that the physician not only has access to clinical facts, but also that he is able construct a plausible account of events and establish causal relations regarding the patient's illness trajectory. This is what we refer to as the *ad hoc narrative*, which is compiled through a partly collaborative process.

As described in the previous section, the process of unfolding narratives is a convoluted and sometimes difficult activity for the physician. During his preparations prior to a consultation, the physician explained it to the researcher in this way:

> "I guess you can see, that when I am trying to get the overview here... This one only goes back to 2007, so it really isn't that long. I need to get an overview of the patient and I could start from one end, but I can't stand that. The original progress notes goes from 2007 to 2009. That's 70 pages. Then we changed to a new system, and then the record goes on with another 23 pages. That's 93 pages, right. Then it would be nice with a short summary." (Physician)

To produce a proto-narrative, the physician must in a matter of minutes look at several documents and systems, select a small subset of information from a large, fragmented body of patient data and position these in the overall illness trajectory to form a narrative of a patient's chronic heart condition. Considering the complexity of this practice, the medical record and in particular the progress notes serve remarkably well as conveyors of information.

Our study did, however, also reveal some significant limitations. The proto-narratives produced by the physician prior to the consultation rarely proved a fully comprehensive account. Often, clinical data from the local hospital and other healthcare providers were left out and some of the included information proved to be out of date. Furthermore, narrative information such as the assessments of other healthcare providers and the patient's own knowledge, experience and anxiety were often not detailed. One explanation for the medical record's apparent inadequacies as a supportive tool for the unfolding of narratives may be that the medical follow-ups were situated in a distributed and somewhat fragmented practice.

The healthcare providers involved in ICD therapy use and maintain a broad array of documents and systems that are not well integrated. In this context, very little information migrates across platforms and even less across organizational boundaries. The backbone of the local hospital's information infrastructure is the paper-based medical record. Although some information from adjacent systems can appear in the paper record, either as printouts placed in the folder or in progress notes, patient information is fragmented into multiple systems and documents. At the medical follow-ups, physicians may use up to ten documents or systems to gather important information. Gaining an overview of this variety of information in a short period of time is in itself a cumbersome task. Furthermore, similar sets of documents and systems with much of the same information may be maintained by other healthcare providers e.g. the ICD Center.

As shown by figure 1, only a few systems are designed to support coordination and convey information across the organizational boundary: The computer system 'Opus Notat' is primarily used to manage local progress notes, although it also enables the user to access progress notes from other hospitals. The online database 'www.icddata.dk' contains subsets of information from the device follow-up that can be accessed by physicians at the local hospital. However, this information is highly specialized, and will often require extensive background knowledge correctly interpret. Finally, the medicine database 'EPM' is intended to constitute centralized, single list of medicine prescribed to the patient. The system is however relatively time consuming to use, which is why it is not updated regularly. Therefore, the information contained in EPM is likely to be incomplete.

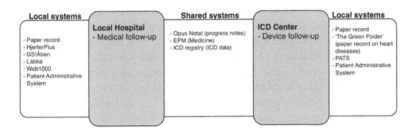

Figure 1. Fragmentation of the medical record

The current medical record in distributed ICD care is relatively fragmented, with patient information distributed across a number of poorly integrated systems. Therefore, the medical record provides healthcare providers with data that is potentially incomplete. It also functions poorly in supporting coordination across organizational boundaries. This is a generally recognized as a risk in healthcare, since lack of coordination can lead to organizational fragmentation and lack of continuity of care (Cebul et al, 2008). While the ad hoc narrative can to some extent be viewed as a symptom of the limitations of the medical record, it should also be considered to be a necessary and even desirable component of medical reasoning. The collaborative unfolding of the ad hoc narrative often adds information such as updated medicine lists. However, our study suggests that the process of unfolding the ad hoc narrative does more than just provide the physician with missing information. It also often provides a more appropriate plot of the patient's condition. This *emplotment* process is only partially supported by the medical record. The record provides the physician with information about the patient's illness trajectory and may provide cues to what is uncertain or untold. However, the complexity and fragmentation of the record makes it difficult to gain full insight into the patient's condition within the relatively limited time span of a medical follow-up without the collaborative unfolding of the ad hoc narrative.

Conclusion

The narrative component of medical reasoning permeates the activities, the interaction, and the medical record used in patient consultations. In this study, we focused on medical follow-ups taking place as part of a distributed treatment of chronically ill heart patients with an implanted ICD device. The goal of these consultations is to assess the condition and progress of the patient, and adjust the medical treatment accordingly. Due to the long illness trajectories, the fact that ICD patients often suffer from multiple chronic conditions and the distributed and somewhat fragmented nature of ICD care, a crucial task for the physician is to construct a plausible account the patient's current condition as well as past events that may influence the outcome of the consultation. This process involves more than merely accumulating clinical facts. To ensure continuity of care, the physician must make sense of incomplete information, contextual factors, assessments from other healthcare providers, the outcome of recent events and not least the patient's own experiences and concerns. A prerequisite for medical reasoning at such patient consultations is, therefore, to unfold an ad hoc narrative.

We found that the ad hoc narrative was typically unfolded in two stages: First, the physician would construct the *proto-narrative* based on information found in the medical record. The medical record supports this process relatively well, although it's substantial size and fragmented nature makes it virtually impossible for the physician to gain full insight in the patient's illness trajectory. As a result, the proto-narrative is often incorrect or imprecise. During the consultation the *re-emplotted narrative* is unfolded through interaction between the physician and the patient. Beside of including information that was either overlooked by or unavailable to the physician when unfolding the proto-narrative, unfolding the re-emplotted narrative is a way to construct a plot that is more appropriate for the particular consultation.

Acknowledgments

We thank physicians and patients at the local hospital, for allowing us to observe and interview them. We also thank all other researchers affiliated to the Co-constructing IT and Healthcare (CITH) project, who have participated at workshops or otherwise contributed to this study.

References

Albolino, S., Cook, R., and O'Connor, M. (2007): 'Sensemaking, safety, and cooperative work in the intensive care unit', *Cognition, Technology & Work*, vol. 9, no. 3, pp. 131-137.
Arminen, I. and Poikus, P. (2009): 'Diagnostic Reasoning in the Use of Travel Management System', *Computer Supported Cooperative Work*. Vol. 18, no. 2, pp. 251-276.

Atkinson, P. (1995): *Medical Talk and Medical Work*. SAGE Publications, London.

Berg, M. (1992): 'The Construction of Medical Disposals', *Medical Sociology and Medical Problem Solving in Clinical Practice. Sociology of Health and Illness*, vol. 14, no. 2, pp. 151-180.

Berg, M. and Bowker, G., C. (1997): 'The Multiple Bodies of the Medical Record: Toward a Sociology of an Artifact', *The Sociological Quarterly*, vol. 38, no. 3, pp. 513-537.

Berg, M. (1999): 'Accumulating and Coordinating: Occasions for Information Technologies in Medical Work', *Computer Supported Cooperative Work*, vol. 8, no. 4, pp. 373-401.

Brody, H. (2002): '"My Story Is Broken; Can You Help Me Fix It?" Medical Ethics and the Joint Construction of Narrative', In K. W. M. Fulford, D. L. Dickenson, and T. H. Murray (eds.): *Healthcare Ethics and Human Values: An Introductory Text with Readings and Case Studies*, Blackwell Publishers Ltd, Malden, Massachusetts, 2002, pp. 133-140.

Brody, H. (2003): *Stories of Sickness*. Oxford University Press, New York.

Cebul, R. D., Rebitzer, J. B., and Votruba, M. E. (2008): 'Organizational fragmentation and care quality in the U.S. healthcare system', *Journal of Economic Perspectives*, vol. 22, no. 4, pp. 93-113.

Conelly, J. E. (2005): 'Narrative Possibilities. Using Mindfulness in clinical practice', *Perspectives in Biolology and Medicine*, vol. 48, no. 1, pp. 84-94.

Feldman, M. S., Sköldberg, K., Brown, R. N., and Horner, D. (2004): 'Making Sense of Stories: A Rhetorical Approach to Narrative Analysis', *Journal of Public Administration Research and Theory Journal of Public Administration Research and Theory*, vol. 14, no. 2, pp. 147-170.

Fitzpatrick, G. (2004): 'Integrated care and the working record', *Health Informatics Journal*, vol. 10, no. 4, pp. 291-304.

Hargle, O., Brataas, H., and Thorsnes, S. (2009): 'Cancer patients' sensemaking of conversations with canser nurses in outpatient clinics', *Australian Journal of Advanced Nursing*, vol. 26, no. 3, pp. 70-78.

Hartswood, M., Procter, R., Rouncefield, M., and Slack, R. (2003): 'Making a Case in Medical Work: Implications for the Electronic Medical Record', *Computer Supported Cooperative Work*, vol. 12, no. 3, pp. 241-266.

Hayes, G. R., Lee, C. P., and Dourish, P. (In Press): 'Organizational routines, innovation and flexibility: the application of narrative networks to dynamic workflow', *International Journal of Medical Informatics*.

Hobbs, P. (2003): 'The Use of Evidentiality in Physician's Progress Notes', *Discourse Studies*, vol. 5, no. 4, pp. 451-478.

Hunter, K. M. (1991): *Doctors' Stories: The Narrative Structure of Medical Knowledge*, Princeton University Press, Princeton, New Jersey.

Hunter, K. M. (1996): 'Narrative, Literature, and the Clinical Exercise of Practical Reason', *The Journal of Medicine and Philosophy*, vol. 21, no. 3, pp. 303-320.

Hydén, L.-C. (1997): 'Illness and narrative', *Sociology of Health and Illnes*'. Vol. 19, no. 1, pp. 48-69.Kane, B. and Luz, S. (2009): 'Achieving Diagnosis by Consensus', *Computer Supported Cooperative Work*, vol. 18, no. 4, pp. 357-392.

Kleinman, A. (1988): *The Illness Narratives. Suffering, Healing & the Human Condition*, Basic Books.

Kodner, D. L. and Spreeuwenberg, C. (2002): 'Integrated care: meaning, logic, applications, and implications - a discussion paper', *International Journal of Integrated Care*, vol. 12, no. 2, pp. 791-806.

Lock, J. D. (1990): 'Some Aspects of Medical Hermeneutics: The Role of Dialectic and Narrative', *Theoretical Medicine*, vol. 11, pp. 41-49.

Mattingly, C. (1994): 'The Concept of Therapeutic 'Emplotment'', *Social Science & Medicine*, vol. 38, no. 6, pp. 811-822.

Mattingly, C. (1998): *Healing Dramas and Clinical Plots: The Narrative Structure of Experience*, Cambridge University Press, Cambridge.

Munkvold, G. and Ellingsen, G. (2007): 'Common Information Spaces along the illness trajectories of chronic patients, *Proc ECSCW 2007*, pp. 291-310.

Mol, A. (2002): *The Body Multiple: Ontology in Medical Practice*, The Duke University Press, Durham and Londong.

Montgomery, K. (2006): *How Doctors Think. Clinical Judgment and the Practice of Medicine*, Oxford University Press, New York.

Paoletti, I. (2009): 'Communication and Diagnostic Work in Medical Emergency Calls in Italy', *Computer Supported Cooperative Work*, vol. 18, no. 2-3, pp. 229-250.

Paul, S. A. and Reddy, M. C. (2010): 'Understanding Together: Sensemaking in Collaborative Information Seeking', *Proc. CSCW 2010*, pp. 321-330.

Pritchard, P. and Hughes, J. (1995): Shared Care: The future imperative?, The Royal Society of Medicine Press.

Reddy, M. C., Dourish, P., and Pratt, W. (2001): 'Coordinating Heterogeneous Work: Information and Representation in Medical Care', *Proc. ECSCW 2001*, pp. 239-258.

Siegler, E. L. (2010): 'The Evolving Medical Record', *Annals of Internal Medicine*, vol. 153, pp. 671-677.

Strauss, A. L., Fagerhaugh, S., Suczek, B., and Wiener, C. (1997): *Social Organization of Medical Work*, Transaction Publishers, New Brunswick, New Jersey

Strauss, A. and Corbin, J. (1998): *Basics of Qualitative Research: Techniques and Procedures for Developing Grounded Theory*, Sage Publications, Inc.

Tange, H. J., Hasmana, A., Robbéb, P. F. d. V., and Schoutenc, H. C. (1997): 'Medical Narratives in Electronic Medical Records', *International Journal of Medical Informatics*, vol. 46, no. 1, pp. 7-29.

Winthereik, B. R. and Vikkelsø, S. (2005): 'ICT and Integrated Care: Some Dilemmas of Standardising Inter-Organisational Communication'. *Computer Supported Cooperative Work*, vol. 14, no. 1, pp. 43-67.

Østerlund, C. S. (2002): *Documenting Dreams: Patient-Centered Records versus Practice-Centered Records*, Sloan School of Management (Organization Studies Group). PhD dissertation.

Østerlund, C. S. (2008): 'Documents in Place: Demarcating Places for Collaboration in Healthcare Settings', *Computer Supported Cooperative Work*, vol. 17, no. 2-3, pp. 195-225.

Weick, K. E. 1995 Sensemaking in Organizations. Sage Publications.

Waymack, M.H. (2009): 'Yearning for Certainty and the Critique of Medicine as ''Science''', *Theoretical Medical Bioethics*, vol. 30, pp. 215-229.

The Pendulum of Standardization

Torbjørg Meum[1], Eric Monteiro[2] and Gunnar Ellingsen[3]

[1,3] Department of Telemedicine and E-Health, University of Tromsø
[2] Department of Computer and Information Science, Norwegian University of Science and Technology
torbjorg.meum@uit.no, *eric.monteiro@idi.ntnu.no* , *gunnar.ellingsen@hn-ikt.no*

Abstract. Cooperation and collaboration are generally an inherent part of everyday practice, and particularly among nurses. However, the technologies that support these practices are still inadequate. In this study, we present and discuss the use of classifications in nursing practice, and highlight the collective re-construction of classifications that emerge over time. Specifically, we study how the negotiation between global classifications and local practice takes place with long-term use, and depict this dynamic interaction as a pendulum movement. Furthermore, we characterize this standardization as a collective re-construction grounded in everyday practice. This paper contributes *to* the body of research on this topic by doing the following: (i) characterizing the process of standardization as a pendulum movement; (ii) drawing out theoretical perspectives for standardization as a collective, emerging accomplishment; (iii) stating the practical implications of our perspective. Finally, we compare the local adjustment (local classifications) discussed in this study with social classifications (social tagging), and suggest how social classification may lead to increased flexibility in the use of classifications.

Introduction

Continuity of care is the "Holy Grail" of hospital information systems. Although such care has been widely discussed, it is difficult to carry out. Standardization is a key objective of the strategy for electronic cooperation in the health care sector in Norway. This strategy considers electronic interaction to be crucial for ensuring the free flow of information necessary to achieve the vision of continuity of care (Norwegian Ministry of Social Affairs and Health 2008, p. 72). In line with this strategy, standardization and the use of classifications have been introduced on a large scale in Norwegian hospitals. Standardization efforts have also been discussed in the CSCW community, and standardized categories are considered to be mechanisms of interaction, in the sense that they reduce the complexity of articulating cooperative work (Schmidt et al. 1992). An extensive amount of work practice studies illustrate some of the challenges of the role, use and impact of standardized categories embedded in collaborative technologies (Hanseth et al. 2001; Ellingsen et al. 2007). It is by now well established in such studies that standardization involves a negotiation between the "global" and the "local" (Timmermans et al. 1997), and that there are implicated trade-offs and dilemmas (Bowker et al. 2000). However, there is scant evidence on exactly how these negotiated standards get constructed, i.e., the time-dependent dynamics. In our study, we focus on this negotiation process by describing the process as a pendulum movement between global standards and local classifications.

Our empirical material draws on a longitudinal and ethnographically inspired case study of the implementation and use of electronic care plans and nursing classifications in a psychogeriatric ward at the University Hospital of North Norway. The work at the ward is highly interdisciplinary, and nurses play a key role in observing and monitoring patients' needs, as well as assessing the patients' cognitive abilities to self-care. Taking care of the patients is a collective task, and requires cooperation among nurses and other health care professionals. Specifically, we ask the following research question: *How are classifications used in nursing practice, and what are the consequences when they are applied in local practice?* Our analytical approach is aimed at investigating the long-term use of classification and how this change process is handled in practice. We contribute by (i) characterizing the process of standardization as a pendulum; (ii) drawing out theoretical perspectives for standardization as a collective, emerging accomplishment; and (iii) stating the practical implications of our perspective.

The structure of the paper is as follows. The paper is organized in the following way First, we start with a brief theoretical description of both standardization in general, and standardization efforts in nursing practice. Second, we describe our methodological approach, followed by a chronological case describing the different phases of implementation and the use of nursing classifications. Third, we offer a discussion section, which investigates the collective negotiation process that takes place over time, and where new categories emerge as a result of collegial collaboration. Finally, we conclude the paper by conceptualizing social classifications in relation to healthcare, as well as the practical and theoretical implications to CSCW systems design.

Theory

Standardization

Globalization and an increased reliance on large- scale information technology have involved an ongoing transformation of modern organization and everyday life. In this transformation, standards remain the sine-qua-non in virtually all fields of information technology. Previous research has mainly considered standards as being technical artefacts, which are part of programming languages, communication protocols and exchange formats (Schmidt et al. 1998). Traditionally, there has been a technocratic, top-down approach to standardization as an objective, absolute and static state (Ure et al. 2009). The increased complexity and scope of standardization in our "networked" world requires a conceptualization that is typically broader than past research has indicated, and involves investigation from various streams. While previous studies mostly focused on standards as being a technological development, recent studies have focus on the social shaping of technology, and consider standards to be the backbone of a socio-technical network (Hanseth et al. 2001). Fomin, Keil and Lyytinen (2003) have provided a framework for analyzing standardization as a process of design, sensemaking and negotiation. Similar studies emphasize standardization as a dynamic interaction in a socio-technical network (Hanseth et al. 2001), where a standard represents agreed upon rules for the production of the (textual or material) objects required (Bowker et al. 2000). A key feature is the dynamic interaction between both human and non-human actors in the network. Consequently, standardization is not just a technical issue, but a negotiation between technical artefacts, humans, work practice, procedures and so on. Scholars from this tradition aim at achieving more flexibility in the standardization process, to make it adaptable across diverse practice (Timmermans et al. 1997; Bowker et al. 2000; Hanseth et al. 2001).

Other studies have also emphasized the need for more flexibility in the standardization process. Hinrich, Pipek and Wulf (2005) developed the concept of "context crabbing" to assign contextual information in the form of metadata. A similar study by Simone and Sarini (2001) focused on the importance of classification schemes for intra- and intergroup collaboration. They distinguished between exogenous and endogenous classification schemes as a framework for analyzing the complexity inherent to the situated, distributed and evolving nature of collaboration, when such classification schemes are taken into account.

Collaboration and interaction are inherent properties of most work practices in hospitals, where information and knowledge need to be shared across time and space. Moreover, standardization is embedded in efforts to improve efficiency and quality in health care (Timmermans et al. 1997; Ellingsen et al. 2007). Based on these perspectives, it is particularly interesting to study a special kind of standardization, such as standardization of nursing.

Standardization of nurses' work

Standardization in nursing is considered to be a powerful movement, and has been an ongoing process over the last two decades. National strategies for the implementation of Electronic Patient Records (EPR) in Norway consider standardization to be a means for improving quality, increasing effectiveness and achieve cost-saving through the use of information and computer technology. In the nursing community, special attention has been directed at the use of terminologies, decision support and knowledge-based nursing. Terminologies in nursing are developed to create a common language with uniform definitions that reflect nursing practice, and consider the use of classifications as a means for improving nursing documentation within and between various health care professions (NNO 2009). Health care data must serve multiple and diverse purposes, like providing day-to-day documentation of care processes, facilitating management of care, identifying best practice, triggering of clinical guidelines and facilitating communication within the health care team (Moen et al. 1999). Consequently, a number of various nursing classifications have been developed and are widely used. An increased importance of sharing clinical data among health care providers, increased focus on patients' outcomes, and the introduction of the EPR has increased the need for a well- developed language to represent nursing judgments. The application of formal models to nursing terms has aimed at developing complete and comprehensive terminology in which the phenomena are presented in a clear and non-redundant fashion (Moen et al. 1999). However, some researchers are skeptical to the oversimplified reduction of knowledge embedded in nursing practice, which are typically used in the formal classification schemes (Benner 2004). Patricia Benner questions the flattening of nursing care, and suggests that we must find alternative ways of valuing the unclassified:

> "The classifications of nursing intervention can make nursing more visible and traceable in the medical record. However, categories belie the logic of caring practices, nursing knowledge, and skill that cannot be reduced to techniques or discrete interventions. Nurses are required to trade one form of visibility to another." (Benner 2004, p. 427)

Bowker and Star express the same skepticism to make the invisible work visible by using classifications:

> "As the layers of complexity involved in its architecture reveal, however, a light shining in the dark illuminates certain areas of nursing work but may cast shadows elsewhere." (Bowker et al. 2000, p. 254)

These scholars highlight the trade-off between pre-defined categories and the cases that do not fit into formal classification systems. Similar studies have emphasized both the enabling and constraining characteristics of classifications (Orlikowski 1994), as well as the tension between interoperability and local usability (Ure et al. 2009). On the one hand, formal terminologies enable shared meaning and comparability across different contexts. On the other hand, their use restricts activity that does not conform to the types recognized in the category systems. The enabling factor is dependent on the degree to which it facilitates their actions outweighs the difficulties created by its restrictions (Orlikowski 1994). Accordingly, the use of international classifications in nursing is not only a translation of concepts to local practice, but a process of negotiation and transformation (Carlile 2004).

Despite these challenges, nursing classifications have been nationally and internationally adopted, and there is an ongoing struggle to integrate the classifications as part of electronic nursing documentation, and to facilitate the use of nursing care plans. The uses of both classifications and care plans are closely related to each other, since classifications are often used to describe the steps of the nursing process. This is a well-known method for nursing, and consists of five phases: assessing, diagnosing, planning, implementing and evaluating. The nursing process is the basis for the use of care plans for documenting nursing. Still, as some researchers have suggested, the implementation of care plans has been slow due to the lack of a uniform and unambiguous system (Bjorvell et al. 2002). The implementation process and the use of new technology has thus generated new expectations for the use of electronic care plans as a support for information sharing and collaboration. Although some researchers fear that the use of care plans will lead to "cookbook medicine," Timmerman and Berg (1997) also elaborate on how the use of "protocol allows more complex and detailed treatment plans to become possible. Once implemented, the protocol can articulate activities and events over time and space – staff members can delegate coordinating tasks to it, transforming the nature of their work." (Timmermans et al. 1997, p. 296). Furthermore, they emphasize, "how standards manage the tensions among transforming work practices while simultaneously being grounded in those practices". Similar studies by Bowker and Star (2000) illustrate how standardized applications are an attempt to regularize the movement of information from one context to another, and how shared objects arise in the tension between locales as an ongoing relationship between different social worlds (ibid. p.292). From these perspectives, the tension between standardized care plans and local practice can be viewed as a dynamic process of naturalization. These perspectives also illustrate how standards entail new opportunities at the same time as they are challenges in a process of change.

Standardization as an ongoing change process over time

Previous studies have shown how the implementation of new technology in complex, dynamic organizations has led to a re-configuration of work processes (Hanseth et al. 2001; Ellingsen et al. 2007). Key issues in these studies have been the re-construction of standards in situated action and how working infrastructures transform both the new infrastructure and the local practice. Bowker and Star (2000) have nicely illustrated how the use of classifications leads to a trade-off between visibility and comparability. On the one hand, nursing classifications have to be constructed broadly enough to support numerous users in diverse contexts, and at the same time be sufficiently narrow to make sense for the individual nurse in local practice. Balancing the tension between different viewpoints across various contexts, and at the same time having both local and shared meaning, is a balance of translation, integration and local configuration.

All of the above-mentioned studies have discussed the tension between global and local standards, but have paid less attention to how such negotiation developed over time. In contrast, our study focuses on standardization as a temporal process that evolves in daily practice. Furthermore, we look at the dynamic interaction that evolves as a process of change. According to Orlikowski and Hoffman (1997), change management is more of an ongoing improvisation than a staged event. They have further recognized three different types of change: anticipated, emergent, and opportunity-based. Our study is especially interested in the emergent- and opportunity-based change. These types of changes are characterized by spontaneous interaction with the new technology over time, and in response to unexpected opportunities. This model has a more optimistic attitude toward change than traditional models that consider change to be a planned event where the main goal is to regain stability as soon as possible.

One example of opportunity-based change is the gradual development of Folksonomies (i.e., user-generated metadata or tags). The origin of this "grassroots" categorization comes from social web communities, where users started to tag content on websites. It is part of a new generation of tools for the retrieval, deployment, representation, and production of information, commonly termed Web 2.0. (Peters 2009). In contrast to formal, predefined classification systems that are relatively static, folksonomies are highly flexible and dynamic. Firstly, there is a mutual dependency between the development of collaborative information services (tags), the production of user-generated content, and the increased usage of folksonomies. Secondly, users create their own tags instead of pre-defined classifications, and thereby allow users to implement their own terminology for indexing and representing content (ibib.2009 p.3). Despite the fact that there are high expectations for the use of collaborative tagging, there are also challenges, such as potential ambiguity in the meaning of tags (Halpin et al. 2007). However, an increased use of web technology for sharing information and knowledge has gradually developed the method, and has led to increasing attention and expectations beyond the internet community, such as in science and knowledge management. Yet various academic communities consider the use of folksonomies to be a useful supplement to formal, expert-created classifications. The use of a core ontology combined with folksonomies has emerged as an approach for managing the difficulty of replicating the role of local knowledge and communication in large-scale, multidisciplinary and distributed collaboration (Ure et al. 2009, p. 423). Such bottom-up strategies are the compromise between the hierarchical meta-model and folksonomies, and they support the distribution of information to those persons who are actually doing the work (Hepsø et al. 2009, p. 444)

Methodology

Our field study focused on everyday information sharing between nurses and social workers in a psycho-geriatric ward at the University Hospital of North Norway. Patients who are admitted to the ward are 65 years or older, and their hospitalization lasts for an average of six to eight weeks. The psychogeriatric ward is an in-patient ward with 14 beds, and provides treatment and care to patients who suffer from psychiatric disorders like dementia, anxiousness, and depression. The work at the ward is highly interdisciplinary and nurses are believed to play a key role in observing and monitoring patients' needs, as well as assessing the patients' cognitive abilities for self-care. The clinical staff comprises physicians, psychologists, nurses, social workers, occupational therapists, physiotherapists, and unskilled personnel.

The empirical data was collected and analyzed following the interpretive tradition of field study in information systems (Klein et al. 1999). The study was guided by this data collection to point out the aspects that were prominent in the standardization process. It has been an iterating process where we have focused on standardization in general, and then considered different aspects of information sharing.

The primary methods of data collection were interviews and participant observation. Between 2008 and 2010, the first author carried out 200 hours of observation of the work practices of nurses and social workers to gain insight into the historical, social, and local context of information work at the ward. The first author was also given access to the EPR system during the observation study. This provided important contextual information on how they actually performed the electronic documentation. To gain additional insight into the information work, 13 semi-structured interviews and 6 open-ended interviews were carried out, which lasted from half an hour to an hour and a half. The first author also had regular meetings with key personnel at the ward during the last two years, participated in various projects at the ward and has had access to different kinds of internal documentation. All of the interviews were taped and transcribed. Along with the field notes, the transcribed interviews constituted the basis for analysis where data have been systematized in relation to key elements of the situation of inquiry.

The process of data collection and analysis has gone back and forth between fieldwork, case description, and the use of related literature to gain new theoretical insights. It has been a process in which our understanding has been constructed through the empirical data that has been analyzed in relation to theories discussed in the previous section. This has provided a new understanding, and has generated further data collection. This iterative process continued until a theoretical saturation point was reached, meaning that further data collection no longer was significant for the interpretation of empirical data.

Case

Background and motivation

Information work is an essential part of clinical work practice in hospitals, and is strongly embedded in everyday work practice. Traditionally, clinical information has been documented and stored in the paper-based patient records. Over the past decade, clinical information has been gradually digitized and become part of the EPR. In accordance with national strategies for seamless integration between clinical systems, laboratory systems and administrative systems, the University Hospital of North Norway changed to a new, modular-based EPR system in 2003. As part of the implementation of the new EPR system, the hospital also decided to introduce a nursing module, which was available in the system. During 2005, the electronic nursing module was implemented in all departments at the hospital, and the Department of Special Psychiatry was one of the pilot departments. During the implementation period, a local project team was established that was in charge of preparing the nursing module, training end-users and coordinating activities between the local sub-project and the central project at the hospital's other departments.

The nursing module has been developed by the vendor, in close cooperation with its users, and has been widely used in Norwegian hospitals since 2003. It has been developed in accordance with professional and health policy guidelines for documentation in the EPR, and facilitates the use of the nursing process as recommended by the national and international nursing community. The use of care plans has a pivotal position, and the nursing module facilitates a flexible use of such plans, and provides multiple approaches for composing a care plan. One approach is to use a standardized language, and international classifications have been translated into Norwegian and made available in the system. However, the use of classifications is just one option. It is also possible to use a free-text language instead of, or in combination with, classifications, in order to describe the various steps in the care plan. The individual user, or hospital ward, may decide himself/herself if he/she wants to use a standardized language in the nursing plan. Another approach is to use "Standard plans/guidance plans" that can be made available in the system. Using this option allows the user to fetch a "Standard plan" in the nursing module, and choose among pre-defined diagnoses and interventions that are developed by each hospital in relation to specific illness trajectories. This is also a functionality that is optional, and it is one that each hospital may choose to use as a support in facilitating the use of the care plan.

The use of classifications and standard plans have been adopted on a large scale in many Norwegian hospitals, in accordance with the implementation of an electronic care plan module. However, the University Hospital of North Norway has chosen a mixed strategy. While the Department of Special Psychiatry has adopted international classifications, the other departments at the hospital have decided to use free text to describe diagnoses and interventions in the care plan. The psycho-geriatric ward, which was one of the pilot wards during the implementation, has particularly aimed at using a standardized language to describe nursing practice. Both during and after the implementation, a key person from the project team was also employed at the ward and completed several internal projects which focused on highlighting care plans as a key player in the nursing documentation.

In this study, we have focused on the implementation and use of nursing classification at the psycho-geriatric ward. In the further case description, we will illustrate the generation, implementation and adoption of nursing classification as an episodic, punctuated process of change that evolved over time. To illustrate this, we have divided the process into four phases that illuminate the development from free-text documentation into a collective adjustment of international classifications as well as the cyclic variation between the different phases over a certain period of time.

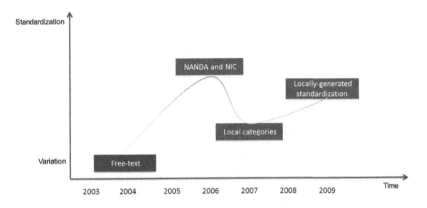

Figure 1. The phases in the local standardization process.

Phase 1. Free-text documentation (Before 2005)

Information sharing in the traditional, paper-based patient record was characterized by a chronological, sequential report of each shift, where the use of narratives, as well as an unstructured language, was prominent. Usually, the individual nurse or social worker wrote a report that reflected what had happened during the shift. There was great variation in the reports. Sometimes they were detailed narratives, yet in other cases short messages, including "The patient has been restless", "The patient has slept well". In accordance with professional guidelines for the documentation of nursing, a care plan was generally created for each patient on admission, but it was not updated or used in daily work practice. Some nurses also found it time consuming and demanding to use a care plan. Moreover, both nurses and unskilled staff were employed at the ward, and therefore had varied knowledge and experience about the use of care plans. Consequently, the content and language of the earlier paper-based reports were depended on the knowledge and skills of the individual health care workers to document nursing assessments and reflections. Two of the nurses expressed it this way:

"A care plan was often composed when the patient was admitted, but when we turn over the pages in the Kardex, it was forgotten."

"You might as well have written it in sand. It was only work you created for yourself, no one used it."

The above quotes illustrate some of the attitudes about paper-based documentation. Moreover, paper-based documentation was widely characterized as incomplete, inaccurate, and subjective, and with the use of a local jargon in the language used in the reports. In addition, they were largely dependent on oral communication for exchanging information about patients. Consequently, the staff was highly motivated to adopt the new electronic system as a step toward improving the quality of nursing documentation.

Phase 2. Mandatory use of NANDA and NIC (2005 – 2006)

As we have already indicated, the psychogeriatric ward decided to adopt a standardized language for describing nursing practice. As a strategy for the implementation of the electronic nursing module, it was decided that using classifications was mandatory. The main motivation was to provide a language for describing both planned and performed care in their daily work practices. Key users at the ward assume that mandatory use would give nurses and social workers a chance to become familiar with the classifications, as well as how they could be used in daily practice. Mandatory use was supposed to give the users a qualified choice and provide a better language for describing patient problems and planned interventions. Moreover, the care plan was emphasized as being a key player in the daily documentation and exchange of information between nursing staff.

The implementation of the nursing module involved a major change process. First, staff had to learn to use the new electronic system. Second, they had to become familiar with a new language for describing nursing practice. The electronic nursing module is an integrated part of the EPR system, and has been developed to support the nurses' daily reporting routine, as well as a structured nursing care plan that supports assessment, planning, implementation and evaluation of nursing care.

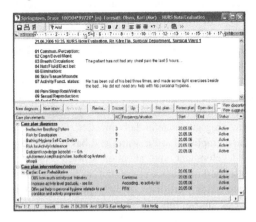

Figure 1. Screenshot of the nursing plan, where the lower part of the note contains the care plan, and the upper part shows the evaluation of the given care according to the plan. The yellow field indicates the nursing diagnoses, and the blue field indicates the nursing interventions.

The nursing module contains two separate parts that are interdependent. The lower part of the screen contains the care plan, which represents nursing diagnoses and interventions. The term nursing diagnosis has become an internationally used concept for identifying the specific nursing needs of the individual patient. These are needs that provide a focus for the planning and implementation of nursing care. At the core of the nursing plan are the international classification systems of the North American Nursing Diagnosis Association (NANDA) and the Nursing Intervention Classification (NIC) (NANDAInternational 2007; Bulechek et al. 2008). Both NANDA and NIC classifications are supported by research, and facilitate continuity of care across settings. The vendor of the EPR system, in cooperation with the Norwegian nursing community, has translated these classifications to Norwegian, and made them available as part of the nursing module. By clicking on the menu item "New diagnosis" in the action bar in the care plan, the system provides a new search window where the classifications are listed, and enables the user to search and select a NANDA diagnoses, in order to make it available in the care plan. The same procedure is used to create an intervention, where the NIC classifications are available in the system. While the care plan represents the planning and implementation of nursing care, the upper part of the document represents evaluation of the nursing care provided in relation to the care plan. When a care plan has been composed on behalf of a patient, it is attached to the following nursing notes as part of the daily report. Consequently, the nursing note usually written for each shift is merely an evaluation of nursing care according to the plan, as a report on any deviation from the plan. The report section of the nursing note is based on free text documentation, but it is structured by function areas to facilitate the link between the care plan and daily report. Nursing diagnoses and interventions in the care plan are linked to a function area that is indicated by a number in the plan, which reflects the structure of the report section.

The use of the nursing module required new knowledge and skills, and education and guidance was a priority during the implementation period. First, users were offered an introductory course to ensure that everyone had a basic knowledge of classifications and usage of the new system. Second, six key users were trained on providing guidance in daily practice. Finally, a key person in the project team was also employed at the ward, and has been a support and driving force for further development and attention toward nursing documentation. Despite some skeptics and reluctance at the start, experiences during the first year showed that the care plans were used in daily practice and that classifications were used extensively. During this period, nursing documentation had become a central part of the interaction among the staff, as is illustrated in the below quote:

"It is great to use the care plan as a basis for discussing the individual patient." (Nurse)

Gradually, classifications became embedded in local practice and were used as a support in daily documentation, professional meetings and discussions.

Phase 3. Releasing the use of local categories (2006 – 2007)

The continuous focus on classifications and care plans involved an increased awareness of the language used in nursing documentation. Consequently, the ward gradually developed increased knowledge of classifications while they also experienced limitations and shortcomings in the use of classifications. When they experienced difficulties in finding adequate classifications, the project nurse started asking: *"What would you have written if you could use your own words?"* In cooperation with each other, they began to gradually develop their own terms to compensate for shortcomings in the system. They used NANDA and NIC as a support, but if they did not find appropriate terms, they started to choose their own concepts, as illustrated in the quote below.

"I think it is okay to work with classifications because it is easier to change something that already exists than to reinvent the wheel. If I find a classification that does not completely fit the situation of the patient, it is still easy to use the classification as a starting point. Instead of 'Self Care Deficit, Eating', I can write 'Self Care Deficit, All Function Areas'."(Nurse)

In this way, the use of local concepts was gradually unleashed to compensate for limitations in NANDA and NIC, in order to combine several classifications, and to facilitate the coherence between nursing diagnoses and interventions in the care plan. For example, frequently used classifications are "Risk for falls" and "Impaired Physical Mobility". If used separately, these terms represent two different NANDA diagnoses. However, some nurses prefer to link several terms into one nursing diagnosis, such as "Impaired Physical Mobility with Risk for falls". In these cases, they have become familiar with two different NANDA terms and combine them to form a local diagnosis. One problem with NANDA is that the terms are fragmented. Firstly, patients often have many different problems that are related to each other. In many cases, it would therefore be appropriate to relate to the symptoms and causes of nursing diagnosis. Secondly, many patients do have several problems, and the care plan may consequently be very long and complex if the information is fragmented. As a result, through experience and discussions, it has become common to link different problems with one nursing diagnosis.

In order to establish a nursing diagnoses, specification is recommended in relation to a PES-format, i.e., defining the problem or health state, aetiology or related factors, and associated signs and symptoms (Gordon 1998). For example, "Anxiety" is a commonly used NANDA diagnosis, but requires a more specific definition. They need to specify the symptoms related to anxiety, and aetiology or probable factors causing or maintaining the condition. Entering this information in the care plan requires intensive mouse clicking in various windows, dialogue boxes and menus in the application, and some nurses find it easier to just add the entire entry as a local diagnosis.

The adjustments of local concepts have gradually taken place in relation to both NANDA and NIC. Since these are two different classification systems, they have developed local concepts that facilitate the overview of the care plan. Some NIC concepts are often used, but in many cases, they have become accustomed to relating interventions to a nursing diagnosis.

"In making a link between problem and intervention in the care plan, we have become accustomed to writing, for example, intervention related to anxiety. Similarly, there is a NIC classification called wound care. A corresponding NANDA diagnosis is "Impaired Skin Integrity". We are more accustomed to using the term "wound" and think it fits better in relation to the NIC classification."

In this way, global concepts have been adjusted to local needs. This adaptation was the result of collaboration with colleagues when they sat together and wrote care plans, and in discussions and meetings.

Phase 4. Gradual development of local classifications (2007 -)

Gradually, key users experienced an increasing use of local concepts, and also found a resemblance between NANDA and local concepts. In order to further explore this progress, an internal evaluation was carried out during the spring of 2008. Two nurses along with the first author were responsible for carrying out the evaluation. Reports from the EPR system formed the basis of the evaluation that included a) the incidence of NANDA diagnoses and locally developed diagnoses, and (b) whether the local diagnosis could be mapped onto a NANDA diagnosis. The study addresses the incidence of NANDA during the first period (April 2005/March 2006) and the second period (2007). The findings indicated a clear decline in the use of NANDA diagnoses. To further identify the concepts that were used instead of NANDA, a mapping between free-text concepts and NANDA was carried out. Terms from the local diagnoses were compared with terms in NANDA and characterized as "Same", "Similar", "Broader", "Narrower" or "No Match". This mapping implied that NANDA diagnoses and local diagnoses mapped onto NANDA constituted 95.5% of all the nursing diagnoses documented in 2007, a strikingly high coverage (see, Meum et al. 2010). Firstly, the evaluation showed that international classifications like NANDA and NIC had been embedded into the local language used at the ward. Secondly, it also showed that several mouse clickings were required to search for NANDA and many found it easier to just write the same diagnosis as free-text. Thirdly, it confirmed the shortcomings of NANDA. For example, nursing diagnoses related to emotion, aggression and euphoria, and the adverse effects of medication and problems related to allergy are lacking in NANDA. Accordingly, the attention was directed at the progress of a professional language.

In accordance with the increased awareness of the written documentation, interaction patterns at the ward also changed. Making the care plan a key player in information exchange among the staff has also caused that the care plan has been given a central role in the handover process and in meeting. In this context, the electronic care plan was visually projected onto a wall screen and enabled a collective reading and information seeking. Gradually, local concepts emerged, which is illustrated in the quote below.

"One day I said to my colleague – we should write down all these local terms that are 'buzzing around'. So we sat down and created a local list of terms that we often use instead of NANDA."(Nurse)

This list was first written down on paper, but then an inventive nurse suggested making the list available as a "Standard plan" in the nursing module.

Figure 2. Screenshot of the electronic care plan and local concepts

Using this functionality in the nursing module made it easy to click on the menu item "standard plan" and then choose from local concepts. Since then, the local list has become a supplement to NANDA to attend to local needs.

Discussion

In accordance with the internal goals and motivations for adopting a standardized language, this case study illustrates a successful outcome. The psychogeriatric ward extensively use NANDA and NIC, and the nurses have acquired skills in using the system, gained an increased awareness on the use of language, and promoted the use of care plans as a major factor in information sharing at the ward. However, if we study the implementation process more closely, we see that unintended changes have also occurred. As anticipated changes have taken place, even opportunity- based and emergent changes have arisen (Orlikowski et al. 1997). These changes have not happened on a stable basis, but have been part of an ongoing process, and we illustrate this as a pendulum that moves back and forth over time. In the subsequent analysis, we will elaborate on some of these changes, including a) the gap between global classifications and local categories, and b) the collaborative creation of social classifications.

Bridging the gap between global classifications and local categories

As mentioned above, the use of classification has had a major impact on nursing language used by the ward. This progress has been influenced by several factors, not just the use of NANDA and NIC per se. A cyclic variation between global classifications, local routines, skills and the technical system have shaped the local information infrastructure. This has been an ongoing process, where increased knowledge about classifications has involved increased opportunities to improvisation. In accordance with the change model described by Orlikowski and

Hoffman (1997), many changes made during the ongoing process cannot all be anticipated ahead of time. Some changes occur as intended, while other changes occur spontaneously out of local innovation. Furthermore, the change process may also entail new opportunities in response to unexpected events, or breakdowns (Orlikowski et al. 1997). Just consider how nurses *changed* NANDA diagnoses to establish a link between diagnosis and intervention in the care plan. This shows how the use of classification has involved new opportunities, and how nurses "tinkering" with the classifications to generate coherence in the care plan. According to Timmerman and Berg (1997), this "tinkering" with standards is a kind of leeway for adjusting standards to unforeseen events, and a prerequisite for the standards to function (Timmermans et al. 1997). Similarly, Bowker and Star (2000) emphasize how the classifications have been naturalized to suit local practice. The quote below illustrates how nurses change and naturalize classification on the basis of local needs:

We have a pragmatic attitude to the use of NANDA. We use what works, and delete or modify classifications that don't fit. (Nurse)

Although NANDA is designed to support nursing practice, it also has limitations. The North American Nursing Association developed NANDA in the 1970's. It is research based, and in recent years has been internationally used in the nursing community on a widespread basis. Currently, 206 nursing diagnoses are available in the classification system, and every two years they are updated through a comprehensive review process. Consequently, many of the terms used in the system are well known in the nursing community. Bowker and Star (2000) describe this as a naturalization of categories. *"The more at home you are in a community of practice, the more you forget the strange and contingent nature of its categories seen from outside"* (Bowker et al. 2000, p. 294). A diagnosis such as "Anxiety" is an example of NANDA diagnoses that is widely utilized in local practice, as well as in the nursing community. However, NANDA is supposed to be used across geographical, cultural and disciplinary boundaries, and it covers the patient's trajectory from the "cradle to grave". Accordingly, the concept of anxiety may have a different meaning for nurses working in a psychiatric department than for those working in surgical department. In order to be useful in local practice, the classification has to be specified in accordance with the current clinical situation. Thus, in the local practice at the ward, nurses have become accustomed to adding, for example, "related to depression". The nursing community also recommends this and shows how broad terms are made to fit different contexts. However, this level of granularity entails some tension and trade-offs. On the one hand, they must be precise enough to be useful in the situation at hand and at the same time broad enough to provide a shared understanding across boundaries. This may lead to a simplification of practice, and a sorting out of gradations of nursing knowledge (Benner 2004). Just consider how they use the NANDA diagnosis "Sensory/Perceptual Alterations". As with all diagnoses in NANDA, this has a label, a definition, defining characteristics, and related factors.

DISTURBED SENSORY PERCEPTION
(Specify: Visual, Auditory, Kinesthetic,
Gustatory, Tactile, Olfactory)
(1978, 1980, 1996)

Definition *Change in the amount or patterning of incoming stimuli accompanied by a diminished, exaggerated, distorted, or impaired response to such stimuli*

Defining Characteristics

• Change in behavior pattern	• Hallucinations
• Change in problem-solving abilities	• Impaired communication
	• Irritability
• Change in sensory acuity	• Poor concentration
• Change in usual response to stimuli	• Restlessness
• Disorientation	• Sensory distortions

Related Factors

Altered sensory integration	Electrolyte imbalance
Altered sensory reception	Excessive environmental stimuli
Altered sensory transmission	Insufficient environmental stimuli
Biochemical imbalance	Psychological stress

Figure 4. Guide to nursing diagnoses developed by NANDA International.

Although this diagnosis may be useful in some contexts, it does not make sense in local practice:

"I cannot stand to use this diagnosis, it sounds strange and does not fit what I want to express." (Nurse)

The above quote illustrates a general attitude to this particular diagnosis among the staff at the ward. First, they found the sound of the classification to be strange and it to be difficult to translate the classification to everyday language. Second, the classification is comprehensive and covers a wide range of problems related to nursing care. Consequently, they did not use it, and have instead developed local categories like "Impaired vision" and "Impaired hearing". The way they have made local categories available as a list in the nursing module is an achievement of neutralization and co-construction of NANDA and NIC, and a way of managing the tension between divergent viewpoints (global and situated). Thus, how has this process of "artful standardization" occurred? How are local classifications created, maintained and made sense of? These questions are particularly interesting since many of the local categories are the same or similar to NANDA. This was not planned in advance, and the alteration had not been possible without the knowledge of NANDA and NIC.

Collective development of local categories over time

The development of the local concept at the ward has been an ongoing, emerging process, and has many similarities with folksonomies (social tagging, social classification). The dynamic and structure of folksonomies are characterized by frequency of tagging, the information value of tags, and a feedback cycle between the elements involved in the process (users, tags, resources). This process relies on human knowledge where semantic structure and folksonomies might emerge from the aggregate behavior of individual users (Halpin et al. 2007). Consequently, the system is self-evolving, self-maintaining and flexible. As with folksonomies, the local concepts have emerged through a bottom up process based on collegial collaboration. However, this collaboration has been grounded in face-to-face interaction among the staff in the process of formalizing the electronic nursing documentation.

The process of formalizing the language used in clinical nursing has not been a static state, but a dynamic ongoing process. The change process has involved new knowledge, which in turn has provided new opportunities that constantly have to be adjusted to practice. An increased focus on specifying nursing diagnoses and interventions requires knowledge, both formal and implicit know-how gained from clinical experience. Moreover, staff have to make sense of the information and translate it into written documentation in the care plan. Previously, they were more dependent on oral information sharing. They could say, for example: "You must be careful because he falls over easily, this must be followed up." In the electronic system, they must first specify the problem, such as searching for the NANDA diagnosis "Risk to fall" and then specifying aetiology and symptoms, as well as intervention to prevent falls. This information was previously more or less in the mind of the individual nurse, but the new care plan requires that they share information in a more formal and precise way. Describing this process requires both knowledge and skills. Such clinical problems are an important part of everyday work practice, where knowledge and language are constantly evolving. While NANDA and NIC are static concepts, clinical knowledge is in constant movement where reaching consensus about nursing diagnoses and intervention is a collective process, as indicated in the quotes below:

"We have certainly been more confident in using classifications, but still we discuss the meaning of diagnoses and give feedback to each other." (Nurse)

"I often look at the care plan of other patients who have the same problem, to decide what terms to use." (Nurse)

The need to formalize and discuss clinical knowledge has also been part of internal meetings and handover processes. The nursing care plan has become an important actor in this context, as a structure and guide for professional reflection. For example, a nurse may give an oral presentation of a clinical situation. At the same time, the care plan is displayed on the wall using a projector and enables collective information seeking. Together, they try to describe what the problem is and what intervention to initiate. Usually, they first search between NANDA and NIC, but if they do not find a classification that quite fits the clinical situation, they discuss other options. Just consider how they did not like the sound of the NANDA classification "Sensory/Perceptual Alterations". By discussing the clinical situation in question, everyone contributes to a common assessment, where new concepts are reviewed, and they often come up with a consensus. In this way, local classifications emerge as a result of the professional development of the language used in local practice. This process shows how the gap between the static classifications of NANDA/NIC and the dynamic interaction in the situated practice is managed.

This is not an argument against the use of NANDA and NIC, but rather demonstrates that there are limitations that must be confronted. Instead of distinguishing between formal and informal classifications, we must look at how these constitute each other. The development of local classifications is considered to be successful at the ward. However, in the electronic system, they are handled as free-text and require the use of workarounds. This implies that we need new technologies to support this artful standardization.

Conclusion

We have presented here an innovative deployment of nursing classification. Much of this so-called "artful standardization" can be attributed to engaged leadership, as well as skills and competence achieved in everyday practice during long-term use. First, we have illustrated how they collectively reconstructed the use of classification to manage the gap between global classifications and local practice. Second, we have showed how the re-construction of classifications has emerged over time, and describe this change process as a pendulum movement that moves back and forth. We have emphasized this pendulum movement, since the long-term use of classifications has not been well described in the literature. We have further compared the emergence of local classifications as they have collectively evolved as a supplement to formal classification. The way in which the local classifications have been used in the electronic system can be considered to be a workaround. However, we suggest that this innovative use of classification highlights local knowledge and supports a shared meaning among nurses in everyday practice. Global and local classifications used in combination both constitute each other and support professional development. Finally, we argue that we need a more bottom-up approach to standardization and believe that local classifications (folksonomies) may be a useful supplement to formal classifications, and a contribution to system design.

References

Benner, P. (2004): "Designing formal classification systems to better articulate knowledge, skills, and meanings in nursing practice." *Am J Crit Care* 13(5)Sep: 426-430.

Bjorvell, C., R. Wredling, et al. (2002): "Long-term increase in quality of nursing documentation: effects of a comprehensive intervention." *Scand J Caring Sci* 16(1)Mar: 34-42.

Bowker, G. and S. Star (2000): *Sorting things out: classification and its consequences*. Cambrigde, The MIT Press. Cambrigde, MA.

Bulechek, G., H. Batcher, et al. (2008): *Nursing Intervention Classification*. Mosby Elsevier, St.Lous.

Carlile, P. R. (2004): "Transferring, translating, and transforming: An integrative framework for managing knowledge across boundaries." *Organization Science* 15(5) 555-568.

Ellingsen, G., E. Monteiro, et al. (2007): "Standardisation of work: co-constructed practice." *The Information Society* 23(5) 309 - 326.

Gordon, M. (1998): "Nursing nomenclature and classification system development." *Online Journal of Issues in Nursing* 30.

Halpin, H., V. Robu, et al. (2007): The complex dynamics of collaborative tagging. WWW2007, Canada, ACM.

Hanseth, O. and N. Lundberg (2001): "Designing Work Oriented Infrastructures." *Computer Supported Cooperative Work (CSCW)* 10(3 - 4) 347 - 372.

Hepsø, V., E. Monteiro, et al. (2009): "Ecologies of e-Infrastructures." *Journal of the AIS* 10(5) 430-446.

Hinrichs, J., V. Pipek, et al. (2005): Context grabbing: assigning metadata in large document collections. ECSCW 2005, Springer.

International, N. (2007): *Nursing Diagnosis: Definition & Classification*. NANDA International, Philadelphia.

Klein, H. and M. D. Myers (1999): "A set of principles for conducting and evaluating interpretive field studies in information system." *MIS Quarterly* 23(1) 67 - 94.

Meum, T., G. Wangensteen, et al. (2010): "Standardization--the iron cage of nurses' work?" *Stud Health Technol Inform* 157, 85-90.

Moen, A., S. B. Henry, et al. (1999): "Representing nursing judgements in the electronic health record." *J Adv Nurs* 30(4)Oct: 990-997.

NNO (2009): NNO Strategy 2009 -2013. eHealth - Everybody's responsiblity and in everyone's interest. Norwegian Nurses Organisation.

Norwegian Ministry of Social Affairs and Health (2008): Samspill 2.0. Nasjonal strategi for elektronisk samhandling i helse- og omsorgssektoren 2008 - 2013. Nasjonal streategi.

Orlikowski, W. and D. Hoffman. (1997). "An Imporvisational Model for Change Managment: The Case of Groupware Technologies." 1997, from http://ccs.mit.edu/papers/CCSWP191/CCSWP191.html.

Orlikowski, W. J. (1994): "Categories: concept, content, and context." *Computer Supported Cooperative Work (CSCW)* 3(1) 73-78.

Peters, I. (2009): *Folksonomies: Indexing and Retrieval in the Web 2.0*. KG Saur Verlag Gmbh & Co, Berlin.

Schmidt, K. and L. Bannon (1992): "Taking CSCW seriously." *Computer Supported Cooperative Work (CSCW)* 1(1)7-40.

Schmidt, S. and R. Werle (1998): *Coordinating technology: studies in the international standardization of telecommunications*. The MIT Press, Cambridge, MA.

Simone, C. and M. Sarini (2001): Adaptability of Classification schemes in Cooperation: what does it mean? ECSCW01, Kluwer Academic Publishers, Bonn, Germany.

Timmermans, S. and M. Berg (1997): "Standardization in action: Achieving local universality through medical protocols." *Social studies of science* 27(2) 273-305.

Ure, J., R. Procter, et al. (2009): "The Development of Data Infrastructures for eHealth: A Socio-Technical Perspective." *Journal of the Association for Information Systems* 10(5) 415 - 429.

MyReDiary: Co-Designing for Collaborative Articulation in Physical Rehabilitation

Naveen Bagalkot and Tomas Sokoler
IT-University of Copenhagen
nlba@itu.dk, sokoler@itu.dk

Abstract. In this paper we present our exploration of co-designing for supporting a collaborative articulation of rehabilitation process. Based on our reading of key CSCW literature, we describe three facets of a collaboratively articulated rehab process: Interdependence, Distributed Process, and Interoperability. We highlight Magic-Mirror-Spiral, the design ideal guiding the co-designing of MyReDiary that is aimed to support the three facets as an example in this regard. We offer the conceptual understanding of Collaborative Articulation, the Magic-Mirror-Spiral and MyReDiary as a *'compositional whole'*: an example manifestation providing an enhanced conceptual understanding that is built around our experiences of designing for collaborative articulation in specific design situations.

Introduction

Most of the developed world is facing a demographic challenge, of providing better welfare for an increasing population of senior citizens. A white paper from the Danish Government (2004) states how a successful rehabilitation of senior citizens is central in facing this demographic challenge. It defines a successful rehabilitation as follows:

"A goal-oriented, cooperative process involving a member of the public, his/her relatives, and professionals over a certain period of time. The aim of this process is to ensure that the person in question, who has, or is at risk of having, seriously diminished physical, mental and social functions, can achieve independence and a meaningful life. Rehabilitation takes account of the person's situation as a whole and the decisions he or she must make, and comprises coordinated, coherent, and knowledge- based measures."

Simultaneously in the recent years, the field of physiotherapy is increasingly calling the attention of the therapists for a more holistic view on the nature of human body and its relation to the world. For instance, Nicholls & Gibson (2010) for e.g.) stress that successful physiotherapy requires the therapists to develop a more holistic view that includes the everyday situation of the citizen undergoing rehabilitation. Furthermore the practice and theory of physiotherapy is increasingly realizing the importance of actively engaging the citizens in their rehabilitation process (Whitepaper, 2004), collaboratively articulating the rehabilitation process with their therapists and other caregivers (for e.g., McClain, 2005).

We read these initiatives as a broad call for promoting a 'continuous and coherent' rehabilitation process as experienced by the physiotherapists and the senior citizens. In our recent work (Bagalkot et al, 2010) we argued that there are four aspects central in answering this call: self-monitoring for the senior citizens while exercising, a more collaborative articulation of the rehab process, an integration of rehabilitation with other everyday activities, and an inclusion of friends and family in the rehabilitation process. Following up, in this paper we discuss our early experiences in designing digital technology for collaborative articulation of senior citizens' rehabilitation process post a hip replacement surgery. In particular, we highlight our co-design process that shaped the *compositional whole,* consisting of collaborative articulation as the concept, Magic-Mirror-Spiral as the design ideal, and MyReDiary as the designed artifact, together pointing to specific possibilities of designing for senior citizens to collaboratively articulate the rehab process with their therapists.

Firstly, informed by some foundational perspectives within Computer Supported Cooperative Work (CSCW), we summarize three facets of a collaborative articulated rehabilitation process: Interdependence, Distributed Process, and Interoperability. To guide our design for supporting the three facets of collaborative articulation, we present the 'Magic-Mirror-Spiral', a design ideal that guides our co-design exploration. We then present the designed artifact, 'MyReDiary': a personal device for the senior citizens that is aimed to act as a tool for collaboration by supporting the three facets. Further we describe in detail our early exploration of the design space offered by the Magic-Mirror-Spiral in collaboration with the therapists and senior citizens that lead to the formulation of MyReDiary. We then reflect on the co-design exploration highlighting how MyReDiary supports the three facets, thereby facilitating the collaborative articulation of the rehabilitation process.

Concept: Collaborative Articulation of the rehabilitation process

Physical rehabilitation can be seen as a process of constant negotiation between the senior citizens undergoing the therapy, their therapists, and other caregivers. While recent works in designing digital technology for rehabilitation (Sokoler et al, 2006; 2007; Björgvinsson & Hillgren, 2004; Hillgren & Linde, 2006, for e.g.) have addressed the need to support the collaborative articulation of rehabilitation process, yet there is need for a detailed discourse to be developed; as is developed in supporting the collaborative processes of other healthcare settings (Pratt et al, 2004; Andersen et al, 2010; for e.g.). We move towards setting up such a discourse by articulating Collaborative Articulation as a conceptual construct informed by CSCW literature, and which will further inform the design of digital technology for successful rehabilitation.

To being with, we look towards the field of CSCW that has an already established way of approaching the support of articulation work in the setting of cooperative and collaborative work. Schmidt & Bannon (1992) argue that the central focus of CSCW initiatives should be to support the articulation work that is distributed, with different actors depending on each other to make sense and achieve the work. Further Simone et al (1999) stress interoperability of the shared objects as central in collaboratively articulating work. Based on these readings and our understanding of current practices in rehabilitation, we highlight three facets of a collaboratively articulated rehabilitation process:

- Interdependence
- Distributed Nature of the Rehabilitation Process
- Interoperability

Interdependence

The success of a rehabilitation process requires the perspective that it is a collaborative effort between experts of different kinds: the physiotherapists as the experts on the bio-mechanical processes of human body, and the senior citizens as experts of their own everyday life situations, for instance. The physiotherapists have to consider each individual's holistic situation for suggesting an exercise program. The senior citizens contribute to this process by expressing their aspirations of achieving everyday activities, thereby providing a richer picture of their situation.

Distributed Nature of the Rehabilitation Process

The rehabilitation process starts at the rehab clinic with the therapists meeting the senior citizens and suggesting an exercise program based on the situation. They further suggest the senior citizens to exercise at home in between the periodic visits to the clinic. During these periodic visits, the therapists measure if there has been any progress based on how the citizens perform the exercises. Hence the rehabilitation process moves from the rehab clinic to homes and back, with the therapists and senior citizens part of it in different times and locations.

Interoperability

Further the therapists and the senior citizens have to arrive at a common framework to make sense of the rehabilitation process. The therapists have to articulate their suggestions in the everyday language of the senior citizens and in turn, the senior citizens have to make efforts to understand the technical terms of physiotherapy. As they move ahead in this process, ideally they reach to a common understanding of each other's actions and articulations, thereby leading to a more successful process.

These three facets form our understanding of 'Collaborative Articulation' of the rehabilitation process. This understanding gives us the conceptual foundation informing our exploration of, if, and how, digital technology can be designed to support collaborative articulation, paving way for a more successful rehabilitation process.

The Design Ideal: The Magic-Mirror-Spiral

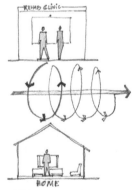

Figure 1: The Magic-Mirror-Spiral: new rehabilitation process that moves back and forth between Rehab clinic and home

The particular situation of our exploration was the physical rehabilitation of senior citizens after a hip-replacement surgery. Currently the senior citizens after the surgery undergo a six-week therapy, during which, the senior citizens visit the clinic twice a week to perform the exercises under the supervision of the therapists. Additionally, the senior citizens are recommended to exercise at home. However the therapists don't have much information on how the senior citizens managed to do these exercises, and the senior citizens don't have much clearer instructions during exercising at home.

This situation of isolated exercise practices led us to explore the possibilities that are opened up by movement of the exercise data from the rehab center to home, and back. When the Collaborative Articulation concept met the above particular situations we formulated the *design ideal*: Magic-Mirror-Spiral[1]. Magic-Mirror-Spiral drives the design exploration with its perspective of changing the current rehabilitation processes to preferred ones, allowing for more successful collaborative articulation between the therapists and the senior citizens.

The spiral starts off at the rehab center, by video recording the exercises the senior citizen performs under the supervision of their therapist. The senior citizen takes home this video and uses it as the 'reference' exercise to monitor self while exercising at home. During this the system tracks the body movements, and overlays it on the instructional video, thus giving the senior citizen a self-referential video for exercising. The senior citizen takes back this home video to the center to discuss the progress in detail with the therapist (see figure 1).

As a Design Ideal, the Magic-Mirror-Spiral points to desirable future situations that we foresee the present situation could advance to. Specifically, we foresee how by engaging in the Magic-Mirror-Spiral may support the interdependent, distributed and interoperable facets, thereby enabling the senior citizens and the therapists to collaboratively articulate their rehab process. The recording, self-monitoring, and sharing of the exercise data between the center and the home is central in supporting the three facets. Below we present our designed artifact: MyReDiary that is guided by, and exemplifies, the possibilities opened up by the Magic-Mirror-Spiral.

Designed Artifact: MyReDiary

MyReDiary is a personal device of the senior citizens that is designed for supporting the three facets of a collaboratively articulated rehabilitation process. We envision it, as a tool for collaboration, and a personal device moving back-and-forth the rehab clinic and the home (see figure 2), in addition to a self-reflection tool.

It consists of a touch pad with a webcam and Internet connectivity. The first session of the senior citizens with the therapists is recorded in the device. This becomes the reference exercise for the senior citizen at home. They can plug the device to their television and exercise, which is again recorded as video snippets. Further, the senior citizens can make notes in the form of audio and pictures, thereby preparing for their next meeting with the therapists. A set of body sensors

---

[1] For more information on the relation between concept, design ideal and designed artifact, please refer to Bagalkot et al (2011).

measure the muscle activities while the senior citizens are exercising at home. This sensor data is presented along with the related exercise videos, and is aimed towards the therapists who need to look at quantitative data.

In summary,

- It is a personal device of the senior citizen containing her rehabilitation data, thereby invoking a *sense of ownership* of rehab data and the process.
- It provides facilities for video recording and audio-note-making thereby giving an opportunity for the citizen to display and share her everyday exercise practice with her therapist, *providing a language* for the senior citizens to do so.
- It provides corresponding quantitative sensor data meeting the language of the therapists.
- And when the therapist and the patient meet, they can enter this data through *different 'handles'*: the sensor data, the videos or the notes

With these features, MyReDiary supports the interdependent, distributed and interoperable facets of the collaboratively articulated rehab process. We envision that as the senior citizens and the therapists move ahead in the Magic-Mirror-Spiral, some citizens may learn how to relate the quantitative data with the videos of their exercises, and the therapists may engage with the videos.

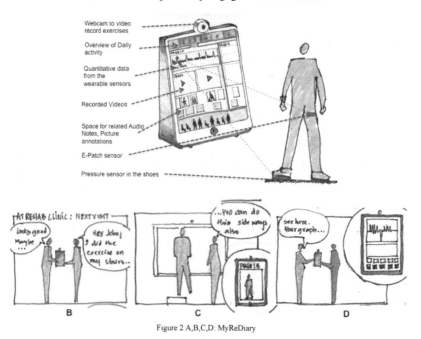

Figure 2 A,B,C,D: MyReDiary

Co-exploring the Magic-Mirror-Spiral

Our exploration of the Magic-Mirror-Spiral follows the research-through-design methodology (Stolterman & Wiberg, 2010; Zimmerman et al, 2007, Bagalkot et al, 2011), a process that is driven forward by engaging in an interplay between the conceptual construct and designing for a particular situation leading to the creation of designed artifact. As central to this process, we used early design sketches as evocative artifacts to evoke participation of the therapists and some senior citizens in the explorations, which unfolded in the local rehab center, and the living rooms of the senior citizens.

Figure 3: Sketching and Co-exploring Magic-Mirror-Spiral, at rehab clinic, home and back.

From our initial discussion with the therapists, we concluded that the vertical body position, balance of weight on feet, and knowledge about hip muscle activity are the three 'key' things the therapists want to monitor during the exercise process. We sketched some basics sketches (figure 3A) of a 'balance board' with pressure sensors measuring the weight balance, a belt with an accelerometer for vertical position, a counter for counting the number of exercises, all connected to a laptop with a webcam which video recorded the exercises, and displayed the sensor information over the video in real time. This immediate feedback enables the senior citizens to monitor their exercise while they are exercising.

The First cycle of the Magic-Mirror-Spiral

We explored the enactment of first cycle as indicated by the Magic-Mirror-Spiral: recording at rehab clinic, exercising at home, and discussing the home exercises at the rehab clinic back again.

Recording the exercises at rehab clinic

We first took the sketches to the rehab clinic, where we demonstrated how the hardware-sketches work to the therapists. The therapists then grouped up and discussed how best they can enact the possibilities of these sketches, finalizing an exercise scheme of four exercises including a stepping exercise. They introduced the sketches to a senior citizen, undergoing rehab for hip-replacement, by demonstrating how they work. The citizen then performed the four types of exercises, which were video recorded by the laptop (figure 3B).

Exercising at Home

Following week, we took these recorded exercises to the home of the senior citizen where we first showed her what she did at the rehab clinic. We discussed how these videos from the rehab clinic could be useful at home, with the senior citizen and the therapists. We then asked the senior citizen to exercise using the sketches for monitoring her performance (figure 3C). These home exercises were video recorded with the webcam in a laptop.

Back at the rehab clinic

We made a series of 8 cards from the videos of the exercises from the rehab clinic and home. Each card had the title of the exercise along with select key-frames of the video. We asked the therapists at the rehab clinic to envision a scenario where the citizen will bring these cards to discuss how the exercises happened at home. We then set-up a discussion table with a TV screen connected to the laptop (figure 3D). Each card was connected to the video, and a team-member would pull up the video on the TV monitor when a particular card was picked up for discussion, employing the Wizard-of-Oz method.

We then summarized the three-part exploration in an extended discussion with the citizen and the therapists.

Early Reflections

Reflecting on this initial exploration of the first cycle of the MagicMirror spiral, we found out that:

- While the therapists were actively involved in exploring the sketches and setting up the exercises for the citizen in the first round, they were not so impressed by the amount of time it would take to go through the home videos of the citizens. The therapists rather found the sensor data to be more useful than the video material. The sensor data was more close to their expert language and they could relate to that closer than the video.
- However, the citizen expressed that the video from the rehab clinic would help her in reflecting on her progress. She was not comfortable with the overlap of exercise videos from the rehab clinic over the live video while exercising, and suggested that she would rather look at the videos from clinic separately for reflection on her progress.
- The citizen stated that recording her exercises at home to show it to the therapists would mean that she has to commit herself to the practice.

This would mean an external motivation for her to be engaged in the process: a "whip" in her terms.

From these initial reflections, we realized that the self-monitoring of exercises at home gives way to reflection and an awareness of ones progress in the ongoing process. Simultaneously sharing of this recorded data with the therapists gives the senior citizens a 'language' to discuss their experiences from home. While the therapists have an established 'language', based on bodily measurements, to talk to the citizens, the citizens did not have concrete tools to talk to the therapists about their embodied experiences in everyday life beyond the rehab clinic.

The central takeaway from the exploration was the fact that the recorded data simultaneously plays two different roles:

- Supporting self-reflection and increased awareness for senior citizens by providing opportunities for *self-monitoring* while exercising at home.
- Enhancing the *collaborative articulation* of the senior citizens' rehab process with their therapists by giving them concrete language to share their exercise practices at home.

This simultaneous facilitation supports the two aspects to be entangled narratives of the same rehabilitation process, and calls for a shift in focus: *from designing isolated tools for rehabilitation* to *taking account of possibilities for collaboration.*

This realization of the need for a shift led us to the designing of MyReDiary. As described above, MyReDiary aims to support the three facets of collaborative articulation of a rehabilitation process. Below we describe the first electronic sketch of MyReDiary and the early experiences of the senior citizens trying it out.

Sketching and Experiencing MyReDiary

Based on this early feedback, we sketched an interface that visualized both the sensor data and corresponding video data. We supported this with information about how active the senior citizens were on each day at home to provide a brief overview for the therapists (figure 4A). Along with this electronic sketch, we drew up some possible scenarios of use and took them back to the rehab clinic.

As with the previous explorations, the therapists took ownership of the exploration, scripting the trials. They had chosen four senior citizens for this exploration, and asked each one of them to try out the sketch that recorded their exercises through sensors and video. Further they asked one of them to act out his first day at the rehab clinic after surgery (Figure 4B). After this, the recorded video and sensor data was shown to the citizen and therapist. They followed this with a general discussion of the sketch and the scenarios (Figure 4C).

Figure 4: Sketching and Co-Designing MyReDiary

Reflections

Reflecting on the co-designing of MyReDiary we can see how it supports the three facets:

Interdependence

MyReDiary provided opportunities for the senior citizens to record the exercises and therapist suggestions at the clinic and bring them to home for reflection. Further they can record the exercises at home and bring them to the therapists, thereby brining a richer picture of everyday situations of exercising at home. This movement of exercise data supports a two-way consultation between the two experts.

Distributed Process

MyReDiary obviously facilitated the movement of the exercise data from clinic to home and back. Further the recording of the exercise and self-monitored data makes it available for access for getting an overview of the process and articulate further steps.

Interoperability

The more important thing MyReDiary does is to provide a language for the senior citizens to express their situation with the therapists. As we realized the senior citizens do not have an established language similar to the therapists. MyReDiary enables the citizens to record and annotate the everyday situations at home by videos, audio notes and pictures. Simultaneously it overlaps the quantitative data from the sensors over this data thereby providing different entry points into the shared data.

Thereby, MyReDiary holds the possibility of supporting the three facets of a collaboratively articulated rehabilitation process.

Compositional Whole

Looking back, we started with a conceptual understanding of collaborative articulation and its three facets. When this met the particular design situation, we formulated the Magic-Mirror-Spiral design ideal, which drove us to explore possible and desirable future states supporting collaborative articulation. This exploration of the conceptual understanding in the particular design situation led us to the design of MyReDiary, which as described above becomes one of the instantiation of designing for the three facets of collaborative articulation. As argued by our recent work (Bagalkot et al 2011) this cycle of interplay forms a *compositional whole* constituting the conceptual understanding of collaborative articulation, the Magic-Mirror-Spiral design ideal, and the designed MyReDiary artifact.

Concluding Remarks

Recent work in designing for collaborative articulation (Björgvinsson & Hillgren, 2004; Hillgren & Linde, 2006) has been exploring the recording of instructions by the therapists in the form of video as a language that citizens understand, on one side. On another, works have explored the design of digital technology to support patients to record their activities outside clinic to share them with their therapists (Sokoler et al, 2006; 2007). The *compositional whole* presented here, with its interrelated constituents, is our contribution to advance these recent and ongoing efforts: it as an example manifestation of designing for collaborative articulation in specific design situation. Further we enhanced the concept of collaborative articulation by reflecting on our experiences in engaging with the design process and demonstrating how digital technology can be designed to support the three facets of a collaboratively articulated rehabilitation process.

Future Work

The work presented in this paper is work-in-progress. However, one of the challenges to address in future is that of the issue of ownership of data. While MyReDiary is envisioned to give ownership of data with the citizens, it may undercut the current 'ownership' patterns. This calls for exploring ways to provide opportunities for the therapists and the citizens to *negotiate* the means of sharing and owning the data. In future we plan to explore if and how MyReDiary be designed as a boundary object along with its current form of a personal device.

Acknowledgments

We thank the therapists and the senior citizens from the Gentofte Commune for being integral co-explorers in this pilot project funded by the *Danish Enterprise and Construction Authority*. We further thank the four anonymous reviewers for their insightful and informative comments.

References

Andersen, T. et al., 2010. Designing for collaborative interpretation in telemonitoring: Reintroducing patients as diagnostic agents. *International Journal of Medical Informatics*. http://www.ijmijournal.com/article/S1386-5056(10)00171-1/abstract

Bagalkot, N., et al., 2010. Facilitating Continuity: Exploring the Role of Digital Technology in Physical Rehabilitation. In *Proc. Of NordiCHI 2010*. ACM, USA

Bagalkot, N., Sokoler, T., 2011, MagicMirror: Towards Enhancing Collaborative Rehabilitation Practices, To appear In *Proc. Of CSCW* 2011.

Bagalkot, N., et al., 2011 (forthcoming). Magic-Mirror-Spiral: Looking into the role of 'design ideal' in interaction design research projects. Accepted for publication in *Proc. Of Nordes* 2011, Helsinki, Finland, May 29-31.

Björgvinsson, E. & Hillgren, P.-A., 2004. On the spot experiments within healthcare. In *Proc. of PDC 04*. USA: ACM, p. 93–101.

Hillgren, P. A. & Linde, P., 2006. Collaborative articulation in healthcare settings: towards increased visibility, negotiation and mutual understanding. In *Proc. of NordiCHI '06*. USA: ACM

McClain, C., 2005, Collaborative Rehabilitation Goal Setting, *Topics in Stroke Rehabilitation*, Volume 12, Issue 4.

National whitepaper on rehabilitation 2004, http://www.marselisborgcentret.dk/fileadmin/filer/hvidbog/hvidbog.pdf.

Nicholls, D.A. & Gibson, B.E., 2010. The body and physiotherapy. *Physiotherapy Theory and Practice*, 26(8), pp.497-509.

Pratt, W. et al., 2004. Incorporating ideas from computer-supported cooperative work. *Journal of Biomedical Informatics*, 37(2), pp.128-137.

Schmidt, K. & Bannon, L., 1992. Taking CSCW seriously. *Computer Supported Cooperative Work*, 1(1-2), pp.7-40.

Simone, C., Mark, G. & Giubbilei, D., 1999. Interoperability as a means of articulation work. In *ACM SIGSOFT Software Engineering Notes*. New York, NY, USA: ACM, pp. 39–48.

Sokoler, T. et al., 2006. The CARE Concept: Holding on to augmentable paper during post surgery rehabilitation. In *2006 Pervasive Health Conference and Workshops*. Innsbruck, Austria, pp. 1-4.

Sokoler, T., et al., 2007. Explicit interaction for surgical rehabilitation. In Proc. of *TEI'07* ACM, USA.

Stolterman, E. & Wiberg, M., 2010. Concept-Driven Interaction Design Research. *Human – Computer Interaction*, 25(2), pp.95-118.

Zimmerman, J., et al., 2007. Research through design as a method for interaction design research in HCI. In *Proc. Of CHI'07*. ACM, USA, 493-502.

Relation work: Creating socio-technical connections in global engineering

Pernille Bjørn and Lars Rune Christensen
IT University of Copenhagen, Denmark
Email: (pbra,lrc)@itu.dk

Abstract. In this article the notion of *relation work* will be put forward to describe efforts of connecting people and artefacts in a multitude of ways as part of facilitating global interaction and coordination in an engineering firm. Relation work can be seen as a parallel to the concept of *articulation work*. Articulation work describes efforts of coordination necessary in cooperative work, but, arguably, focuses mainly on task-specific aspects of cooperative work. As a supplement, the concept of relation work focuses on the fundamental relational aspect of cooperative work. Relation work forms the fundamental activities of creating socio-technical connections between people and artefacts during collaborative activities required to create and enact the human and electronic network and engage with articulation work in cooperative engagements. The concept of relation work is applied within an ethnographic study of War Room meetings in a Global engineering firm. It is argued that relation work is a perquisite for other activities such as articulation work. Relation work is described in a number of dimensions, including connecting people with people, people with artefacts, and artefacts with other artefacts.

Introduction

Engineering a cement factory is a highly complex collaborative engagement between approximately 300 geographically dispersed engineers, whose work over a two-year period is highly dependent. Specifically, the work entails numerous dependencies between tasks and sub-tasks, such as ensuring that the internal design of equipment fits the overall external design of buildings, or that the factory exterior fits the local landscape of the factory—one factory has approximately 6000 tasks and sub-tasks that must be coordinated. We have had the pleasure of ethnographically investigating how engineers from a large global firm coordinated the work of engineering cement factories. In this paper we focus on one of the key coordinative activities, namely the execution of the so-called War Room meetings between engineers located in Denmark and India.

The concept of the War Room has been investigated previously in CSCW research. However, whereas the War Room in these studies referred to physical spatial arrangements, as in dedicated project rooms where participants are brought together for a short, concentrated period of time spent working on a particular project (e.g. Covi et al., 1998; Mark, 2001; Teasley et al., 2000), the War Room concept we investigate focuses on War Room *meetings*. The War Room meeting is an invention of the engineering company that is based on lean principles. Lean principles in question focus on the process and in particular of the interfaces between individual yet tightly coupled tasks. They form weekly 15-30 minute globally distributed meetings where select participants located in Denmark and India "meet" to identify key challenges and tasks that require particular attention. Thus, previous War Room studies differ from ours in terms of time (all time vs. weekly for 15-30 minutes), overall purpose (continues synchronous collaboration vs. coordinates activity), and geography (collocated vs. geographically distributed). However, similarities also exist. Our War Room meetings took place in particular dedicated rooms (located in India and Denmark), and used large wall-mounted posters to guide coordinative activity.

When we first began investigating the War Room meeting as a coordinative activity, we were looking at how the articulation work (Schmidt and Bannon, 1992; Strauss, 1985) was performed between the globally distributed participants, and, in particular, how the key coordinative artefact (the War Room poster) supported the articulation work required to make the collaboration function. However, during this study we found another type of work that was fundamental to the execution of articulation work, which we present in this article as *relation work*. Relation work forms the fundamental activities of creating socio-technical connections between people and artefacts required to create and enact human and electronic networks and handle articulation work in cooperative engagements. Relation work becomes particularly evident in collaborative engagements with a high degree of discontinuities, as is typical of global collaborations (Bjørn and Ngwenyama, 2010); but, we suggest that relation work might also be relevant in ordinary collocated collaboration.

We will proceed by introducing the theoretical framework of collaboration, articulation work, and relation work, followed by a presentation of the empirical case and methodology. Then we present the analysis, where we show relation work first as connecting people to people, second people to artefacts, and third as connecting artefacts to artefacts. Next we discuss our empirical observations and connect them to previous work, and finally we conclude by connecting relation work to larger debates within CSCW.

Theoretical Framework

It is widely agreed within CSCW that collaboration can analytically be divided into work and articulation work, where articulation work is all of the extra activities required when two or more individuals have to collaborate to get a particular task done (Schmidt and Bannon, 1992). Articulation work is all the of tasks required to coordinate a particular task, including scheduling, recovering from errors, and assembling resources (Gerson and Star, 1986). In this way, articulation work implies an overhead cost of extra work in labour, resources, and time, and the justification for this extra work is that one participant alone is not able to accomplish the whole task without interdependent engagements with others (Schmidt & Bannon 1992). If we look at the case of the engineers, it is quite obvious that one engineer cannot accomplish the total work involved in engineering a cement factory; thus collaboration, and, consequently, articulation work, is required. Previous work in CSCW has focused on different strategies for handling the effort involved in articulation work, and key concepts are awareness and coordinative artefacts. Next we will introduce awareness and coordinative artefacts as they have been found in collocated settings. Following that we will reflect on how remote spatial arrangements might affect these strategies, which leads to the introduction of our concept of *relation work*.

Awareness and collocation

CSCW research over the last two decades has highlighted the rich and subtle interaction that collocation affords. Importantly, the concept of *awareness* practices has sprung from this research. The idea of awareness, at least in CSCW, originally emerged in a number of work place studies, including Heath and Luff (1992; , 1996) of Line Control Rooms on the London Underground as well as the studies of air traffic control work by the Lancaster group (Harper and Hughes, 1993; Harper et al., 1989a; Harper et al., 1989b). In these studies, it was noted how collaborative activity in complex organizational environments rests on the individuals' abilities to create awareness through bodily conduct while engaged in their respective activities. That is, it was described how actors produce awareness by rendering a feature of their conduct or a feature in the environment *selectively* available to collocated others. In the course of their work performance, actors may find that the activity in which they are engaged becomes potentially relevant for others within the domain, and yet their colleagues are seemingly involved in something else. In such circumstances, an actor may modulate an activity (e.g., speak louder, stare in an obvious manner, or overtly move an object about) to enable others to gain awareness of some matter at hand, without demanding that anybody should respond.

Much production of awareness through bodily conduct relies on collocation, and previous studies of collocated War Rooms found that the proximity of the spatial arrangement allowed the team members to overhear each other, and by informally monitoring each others' activities, they also volunteered advice (Teasley et al., 2000). In Teasley et al.'s study, the success of the War Room was that the participants were ready at hand, and these authors did speculate whether it would be possible to create a similar War Room setting remotely (Teasley et al., 2000). In addition to the subtle "awareness" practices that Heath et al. (2002) describe, collocation also allows for frequent and informal conversation. For example, it may be the case that during the conversation "at the water cooler," "in the lunch room," or "in the hallway," important work-related exchanges are triggered even though that conversation was not the original intent of the trip there. Furthermore, it is most often possible to tell if someone is available for a conversation from cues such as open doors, knowledge of local schedules, habits, and practices. In addition, voice mail and e-mail are more likely to be answered by someone you do know well from sharing the same location (Herbsleb et al., 2000, p.320). These findings suggest that collocation may foster awareness and communication that plays a crucial role in the coordination of cooperative work.

Coordinative artefacts

Coordinative artefacts support the aligning, scheduling, and integrating of interdependent activities in collaborative settings. Coordinative mechanisms are particular types of coordinative artefacts consisting of a protocol reducing efforts of articulation by being embedded within the artefact (Schmidt and Simone, 1996). If we identify the key artefact of the War Room meetings in our case of the engineers, it is clearly the *War Room poster*. The War Room poster is a large, brown paper wall-mounted in either Denmark or India. The poster is a coordinative artefact illustrating the plan, as well as all the dependencies between the activities of engineering the cement factory, divided into weeks and milestones. For each week there are connected lists of tasks that must be conducted, and the War Room meetings establish whether tasks are finished according to plan, or whether the plan has to be adjusted. There are strict protocols for how the War Room poster is to be used. If a participant during a meeting brings up an issue (a task which have not been done, a piece of information lacking to complete a task etc), the facilitator will create a yellow sticker writing three types of information: The issue, name of the responsible person to handled the issue, and the date. The yellow sticker will be placed on the War Room poster at the following week, where the responsible person should report back. In this way, the War Room poster does embed a particular protocol for use, and, as such, it can be labeled a coordination mechanism. Because the poster itself is a tangible object created by physical paper, the War Room poster is a local object, used, however, in a global setting. Investigating the shared artefacts in a collocated War Room, Covi et al. found that the shared visual displays supported the work by making intangible work visible and editable via representations (Covi et al., 1998, p. 58). In this way, it was the tangible characteristic of the shared display which was essential in that study. Prior studies of how groups use electronic or physical scheduling also found that the size, location, and physical qualities of material tangible tools engender certain essential group processes, which current digital coordination tools fail to support (Whittaker and Schwarz, 1999). Likewise, the War Room poster in our case supports coordination by making the intangible plan visibly available in certain ways essential for the execution of the War Room meeting, which is not possible with the current digital schedule. Still the lack of digitalization also creates new challenges for the use of the War Room posters, due to the geographical dislocation of the participants.

Spatial arrangements

Distance matters (Olson and Olson, 2000), and in contrast to the rich potential for interaction afforded by collocation, there are convincing accounts that the frequency of communication drops off sharply with the physical separation of co-workers. Allen (1977), in a study of engineering organizations, reported that the frequency of communication (including, for example, phone calls and emails) among engineers decreased with distance. He even noted that when engineers' offices were more than 30 meters apart, the frequency of communication dropped to nearly the same low level as people with offices separated by many miles. Kraut and associates (Kraut et al., 1990) found similar results in their study of scientific research collaboration. That is, they found that the rate at which scientists collaborated was a function of physical distance between offices, and that this effect was even more powerful than that of same-discipline scientists tending to collaborate. It seems that close physical proximity led to frequent conversations, during which common interests were discovered and acted upon.

These findings are particularly pertinent for globally distributed work practices. The global distribution of cooperative work tasks creates a number of specific challenges: spatial, temporal, and cultural each embedding discontinuities, which must be negotiated and re-negotiated over time (Bjørn, 2003). The geographical distribution of cooperative work across different parts of the world accentuates and highlights the challenges of cross-site collaboration and intercultural interaction and communication (Herbsleb et al., 2000). These observations concerning cooperation and geographical distance highlight the importance of understanding the dependencies among globally distributed work tasks and the efforts made to manage or articulate these interdependencies.

In a case study of an engineering organization spread across several sites, Herbsleb and Grinter (1999) investigated how the organization used a number of mechanisms, including plans, processes, and specifications, to coordinate the cross-site work. However, each mechanism was vulnerable to imperfect foresight and unexpected events, and substantial communication was necessary to coordinate activities and renegotiate commitments. The difficulties of knowing who to contact about what, of initiating contact, and of communicating effectively across sites led to a number of serious coordination problems. Among these problems were unrecognized conflicts, the assumptions made at different sites, and incorrect interpretation of communications. The most frequent consequence of cross-site problems was delays in the resolution of work issues where more than one site was involved. So, for example, if a part of the design needs to be changed, or if someone needs a better understanding of how some part of the product works, people at more than one site may need to be involved in information exchange, negotiation, and so on, in order to find a solution. Such issues arise very frequently in globally distributed work and are often resolved through articulation work.

Relation work

Awareness activities and the use of coordinative artefacts are essential for handing the collaborative engagements between mutually dependent actors. However, as explained above, spatial arrangements where the participants are geographically distributed create particular discontinuities, challenging the performance of articulation work (i.e., the specifics of putting together tasks, task sequences, task clusters – even aligning larger units such as lines of work and subprojects – in the service of the connected work flow) (Strauss 1988, p.164). If we are to understand how the articulation work becomes challenged, we have to think about what is missing in the geographically distributed setup. *What got lost when we took away the local spatial arrangement supporting awareness and the use of coordinative artefacts*? Here it is important to notice that we do not claim that it is impossible to support awareness and coordination in geographical dispersed settings, what we investigate is how the geographical distribution impacted the organization, structure, and execution of the War Room meetings we have empirically observed. We speculate that what we lose is the fundamental networks connecting people and artefacts into one cooperative engagement. A network, which in the collocated setting was framed by the physical walls of the dedicated project room (Covi et al., 1998). We lost the unique and complicated interplay of human and electronic networks (Mark, 2001, p. 6). In such a situation, articulation work activities are highly constrained and require much more effort to be handled. However, is all of the work that is required really articulation work – or is it another type of work? What is the work that geographically dispersed participants have to engage with besides articulation work? What is the work involved when geographically dispersed participants actively "connect" themselves, creating while enacting the socio-technical network that is fundamental for collaboration to emerge? We label this work that is fundamental for articulation work *relation work.*

Nardi et al. (2002) bring forward the concept of netWORK as the work individuals engage in when creating, maintaining, and activating their assemblages of people who come together to collaborate for a short or long period. People do not come together in friction free interaction smoothly mediated by technology, a "great deal of human communicative work is involved in bringing people together to make collaboration possible (Nardi et al., 2002, p. 209). While we agree that netWORK is essential, we also found netWORK activities were of a different nature than the relation work we saw in our empirical case. There is an important link between relation work and netWORK activities, however were netWORK concerns individuals intensional networks, relation work emerge in synchronous collaborative activities. *The concept of relation work denotes the fundamental activities of creating socio-technical connections between people and artefacts during collaborative activities, enabling, for example, actors in a global collaborative setting to engage each other in activities such as articulation work.* Articulation work cannot be handled in the same way in global environments as in collocated environments. The strategies of awareness and coordination mechanisms cannot be applied *a priori* to the global setting. Actors must create and connect the foundational network of globally distributed people and artefacts in a multitude of ways. That is, actors in a global setting have to achieve the connections that are more or less taken for granted in a single-site environment. Only with these relations in place may other activities, such as articulation work, move forward.

Relation work thus entails an overhead in work essential for geographically distributed collaboration, and the justification for this extra work is similar to that of articulation work. That is, when collaborating in a globally distributed manner, one must engage in the extra activities of relation work in situations where the distribution of actors does not *a priori* establish the network of connections between people, artefacts, and activities. What we suggest is a distinction between, on the one hand, *articulation work,* referring to "the specifics of putting together tasks, task sequences, task clusters – even aligning larger units such as lines of work and subprojects – in the service of work flow" (Strauss, 1988, p.164) and, on the other hand, *relation work,* understood as the fundamental efforts of achieving the very basic human and non-human relations that are a prerequisite for multi-site work such as, for example, global interaction and coordination.

At minimum, relation work is the relational aspect of articulation work, but it can be argued that it is a complementary concept. In articulation work, communication is done to achieve an agreement as to who does what, where, and when, whereas relation work is done to achieve the right configuration of a network of people and things at a certain point in time for the purpose of facilitating multi-site cooperation.

Methodology and Empirical Case

Investigating how engineers managed to coordinate their work when engineering cement factories on a global scale, we initiated an ethnographic workplace study (Randall et al., 2007) in January 2010, which is ongoing. The main focus of the study is to understand how engineers collaborate globally, including the use of various artefacts, engagement in activities, and, in particular, the execution of the War Room meetings. A combination of observation and interviews was used. We interviewed War Room meeting participants (facilitators, project managers, and engineers) in both Copenhagen and Chennai (19 individuals in total). We also observed approximately 11 occasions of War Room meetings (between 4-5 meetings pr occasion), 9 meetings from Chennai and the majority of meetings from Copenhagen. Being based in Copenhagen, we made two field trips to the Chennai location, first in February 2010, and again in November 2010.

Global Engineering and the War Room concept

The engineering firm that provided us with our fieldwork setting is a supplier of cement and mineral factories all over the world. The company has more than 10,000 employees worldwide and has a local presence in more than 40 countries. The main locations for their engineering efforts are Copenhagen (Denmark) and Chennai (India). Most projects—including the one that we studied—required the joint efforts of both of these engineering departments. Approximately 300 engineering specialists from both Copenhagen and Chennai were involved. In order to coordinate their interdependent cooperative work tasks, the engineers used a series of coordinative artefacts, not least of which included conventional time schedules and ATLAS[1] charts. A cement project is initiated when a client places an order for a cement factory to be designed, built, and erected in, for example, Africa or Asia. The clients are large global actors with several cement or minerals factories all over the world. The engineers design while arranging for the factory to be erected in the location picked by the client within a particular time frame: normally 24 months.

The War Room meeting is a particular coordination activity within the company forming short weekly meetings between the global participants, guided

---

[1] ATLAS is the information systems used to plan.

by the War Room poster and facilitated by the War Room facilitator. A War Room is:

> "a way to manage projects, improve communication and foster collaboration across the different team members and functions involved in projects. A War Room serves to make communication and visibility of key project information more effective across all functions involved in the work. The War Room is our way of applying key lean principles such as visual coordination, teaming up around the task, ensuring information flow and introducing the Plan-do-check-adjust cycle within an order-execution project team. War Rooms have a specific flow of information and guidelines for use." (Engineering company description)

War Room meetings support the management and coordination of all the tasks and dependencies involved when engineering a cement factory, focusing on making links between tasks visibly available for the participants, creating commitments to deadlines and deliverables. The War Room meetings are thus designed to keep track of the progress of the individual work, which is part of the shared tasks while identifying outstanding issues. War Room meetings are a series of meetings taking place in joined global locations where local physical rooms complete with coordinative artifacts and video conferencing technology make up highly structured environments for coordinative practices aimed at handling the integration of globally distributed work tasks within engineering.

The meetings entail a tightly scheduled series of short (10 – 15 minute) sessions, each focused on a particular part of the project, such as, for example, pyrotechnical aspects of the project or structural engineering. Each session has a facilitator who organizes and orchestrates the interaction. In a War Room session, the focus is on outstanding issues and challenges, making sure that someone is assigned responsibility for each issue. Each issue is noted on a yellow sticker and then displayed on the War Room poster, connecting the issue to particular time schedules and notes organized according to project. In each weekly meeting, the facilitator asks whether an issue from last week has been resolved or not. Unresolved issues are carried on to the next week.

Relation Work in Global Engineering

Globally distributed participants may have several strategies for making global connections possible through relation work, creating and enacting the social-technical networks required for global collaboration. This includes creating connections between locations, people, artefacts—so that they all perform as one socio-technical network supporting the activity of War Room meetings. Next we will describe the relation work involved in creating these socio-technical networks required for executing the War Room meetings.

Connecting locations

Every War Room meeting is initiated by making a video conference call from Chennai to Copenhagen, or *vice versa*. This video/audio link is the backbone of the connection between the two locations. Making the call is most often an unproblematic and trivial task. However, in the two episodes that we shall consider next, making the connection and keeping the connection becomes laborious, as a "technical breakdown" occurs. What we would like to highlight from the episode described below is the relation work put into making the connection for the video conference call, rather than the somewhat trivial temporary breakdown of technology.

It is quiet in the War Room in Chennai as the War Room facilitator initiates the meeting's video conference call to Copenhagen. However, the call to Copenhagen goes unanswered – nobody is picking up. This is highly unusual. Repeated attempts are made, and about 10 minutes pass with no video connection to Copenhagen. The frustration in the room becomes palpable as time passes. The War Room schedule is tight, with only 10 to 15 minutes available for each meeting, and five War Room meetings are planned as a continuous set of activities. People start arriving for the second War Room meeting planned for that day. The facilitator does his best and starts performing a thorough check of the equipment in the room, including the laptop, the camera, and the Internet connection, in order to determine if there is a technical glitch. He finds all of the equipment in working order and still nobody is answering his scheduled call to Copenhagen.

Subsequently the facilitator receives a text message on his mobile phone; it is Copenhagen reporting that the laptop in Copenhagen – the other node in the video conference call – is in the midst of installing an automatic update to its operating system and hence cannot connect for some time. The engineers in Copenhagen are indicating that they are doing everything they can to connect. Over the course of the next 45 minutes, a host of options are considered for making the connection, including replacing the incapacitated computer in Copenhagen, or simply using ordinary telephones. In the end, and through the use of many text messages, they decide to wait for the computer in Copenhagen to finish its update. Finally, the laptop in Copenhagen is able to receive the call, Copenhagen comes online, and the War Room sessions can commence. By this time, the schedule for the subsequent War Room meetings had been completely reworked.

As indicated above, what is of interest here is the efforts put into making the global connection—efforts that become highly visible as a consequence of the breakdown of technology—efforts centered on making the connection or repairing it. These efforts include inspecting the computers, checking the Internet connections, and making sure the camera is operational, as well as the use of mobile phones to connect and resolve the technical impasse.

Arguably this work, this *relation work*, would not have been necessary had this project not been a multi-site engagement. That is, in a single-site environment, all of the effort put into making a connection between two computers for the purpose of a video conference call would have been completely redundant. There would have been no need for it, and, in this sense, the relation work described above is particular to multi-site interactions such as global collaboration. The argument is not that relation work is unique to multi-site environments, but that multi-site environments require a lot more of it than in a single-site environment, and in many cases these essential efforts are invisible, only appearing when the technology breaks down. All the connections that we may take for granted in a collocated environment have to be created in a global one when we connect local locations into the socio-technical network of global collaboration.

Figure 2. Efforts to connect Chennai to Copenhagen are initially without success, and substantial (relation) work is required to make the connection.

Connecting people

Experienced War Room facilitators know their colleagues in the other location and are able to initiate the War Room meeting by addressing each other by name—for example, "Good afternoon, Ganesh," or "Good morning, Nicolai." This short sentence is more than a simple greeting. It also reflects knowledge about the time of day in the other location and knowledge of who the colleagues are, not simply as "Indian colleague" or "Danish colleague," but as real people with real first names. This knowledge prevents a stereotypical understanding of the "the others" (as the Indian or Danish colleague) and instead puts focus on the person and the relationship between the participants as colleagues of a joint global organization. After observing several War Room meetings during this study, it became clear that this relationship was based on mutual respect between participants, which made it easier for the experienced facilitators to guide and keep the War Room meeting on track—it helped ensure all participants were listening, not interrupting, and answering questions essential for the success of the War Room meeting.

When we observed the less-experienced War Room facilitators (i.e., those who did not know people from the other location by name), particularly when the facilitator did not have direct technical knowledge of the particular area of concern, the meetings clearly took a different form. Here participants—both in Denmark and in India—were noisy, and the facilitator had to ask several times for answers to the questions. In one meeting observed from the Danish location, the Indian participants kept talking about a particular issue, ignoring the Danish facilitator until a more experienced facilitator, also at the Danish location, interrupted them by tapping his finger on the microphone, asking whether they were paying attention. Although this behavior could have been interpreted as rude, it was considered "OK" because of the mutual respect between the geographically distributed participants—respect that was based on their knowledge of each other.

The work that goes into establishing the connections between people, as in mutual respect and knowledge of each others' names, time zones, etc., is part of the fundamental work of making the War Room meeting function; thus we label this relation work. What we see here is that relation work is not only something that must be addressed during the War Room meetings, but it comprises foundation work outside of the meetings. The relation work of establishing connections between people thus involves the work where the participants welcome each other, showing respect by addressing each other as people and not as anonymous "others".[2]

Relation work may be about establishing rapport, i.e., an equal, respectful relationship, and it includes acknowledging the participation of all people present at the meeting. In addition to common courtesy, asking who is present is necessary with regards to practical issues of communication. In many cases, some actors present in one of the offices hosting the War Room meeting may not be visually available to the actors in the opposite War Room because of the location of the cameras. As may be seen in Figure 3, the camera in Chennai is located on the lid of the laptop and is providing a limited field of view to the actors in Copenhagen. For example, people arriving and leaving though the door of the room in Chennai are not visible in the video feed sent to Copenhagen. In a similar

---

[2] One dimension of relation work may be establishing rapport; this dimension of relation work may also take place at social gatherings, such as dinner parties or small talk in the lunchroom. A manager of GlobalEngineering informed us that one of the benefits of flying Danes to meet their Indian colleagues, or vice versa, is that this creates the opportunity for people to engage in small talk and "get to know one another" in a relaxed and informal manner, face-to-face. According to the manager, the friendships or rapport created (through relation work) at social gatherings may later be translated into a smoother working relationship, where people are more attentive and responsive to one another's predicaments and needs.

manner, the camera on the table in Copenhagen only shows the actors in Chennai a portion of the room at any one time. This arrangement makes another type of relation work essential for the global interaction in a War Room setting, namely identifying the actors who are present by repeatedly asking, "Who is present?" The inability to see exactly who is present in the War Room meeting is particular to this kind of global, multi-site interaction, and it fosters repeated relation work. By comparison, the same kind of relation work is hardly necessary in a collocated meeting, as all of the participants can usually see each other.

This kind of relation work is common to the globally distributed War Room meetings. In contrast, actors in collocated meetings would probably not engage in relation work of this kind, as making out who is speaking is relatively effortless when actors are collocated. In other words, in a multi-site environment, the relation work associated with making out "who is there" or "who is speaking" cannot be taken for granted, as it may be in a single-site environment. This observation implies that although relation work is common to both single-site and multi-site work, it is far more pronounced and visible in the latter. This distinction is related to the fact that, at the very least, the actors' opportunity to perceive their globally distributed collaborators is hampered and limited. For example, sight is obstructed or limited by the video feeds, the sound of other voices is blurred or transformed, smell is not conveyed at all, and, importantly, movement and physical interaction is restricted to one location of the War Room meeting. These limitations are obvious but nevertheless pertinent to global interaction.

Figure 3. Several of the engineers present in Chennai are not visible to their colleagues in Copenhagen.

Connecting artefacts

When GlobalEngineering gets a contract for a cement factory, they create a plan that includes milestones, deliverables, tasks, and their dependencies. This plan is created using the IT system ATLAS. All pertinent information is gathered in this plan, which is available to all relevant participants at all sites. However, this plan is "hidden" within the IT-system, and it is all too easy for participants to focus exclusively on their own detailed tasks and deadlines rather than on how their tasks are connected to other tasks, and thus hindering awareness of their role in an interdependent relationship. A key role of the War Room meeting is to make each participant aware of the interdependence of the various tasks within the plan. The philosophy is that by highlighting the dependencies people will become committed to finishing their tasks on time, or even ahead of time. This assumption is supported by prior research arguing that publicly accessible representations is key for sense-making processes (Larsson, 2003) and that shared physical scheduling tools are preferable to be used in critical projects (Whittaker and Schwarz, 1999). The central artefact for this work is the War Room poster, also referred to as the "brown paper." The poster is a visual representation of the ATLAS plan in that all milestones from the plan are added to the poster as pink stickers. Each week the War Room facilitator prints the deliverables for that particular week and monitors which tasks have been marked as "done" (green), "still ongoing – but soon late" (yellow), or "late" (red) within the ATLAS system. The facilitator brings the print-outs to the War Room meeting and tapes the paper lists to the poster.

During the War Room meeting the facilitator asks about all of the out-standing deliverables that he/she identified by examining the print-outs prior to the meeting. The facilitator also asks the participants present whether there are other issues they need to address. Each issue of concern raised "gets a yellow sticker," meaning the facilitator takes a sticker and writes down the issue and the name of the person responsible for addressing the issue. The rule is that you can only write the names of people present; thus, if the person who is supposed to be addressing the issue is not at the meeting, the facilitator will write down the name of someone who is present, who will then follow up with the person responsible for addressing the issue. At the top of the note, the facilitator will write the date, then the task, and at the bottom, the responsible person. For example, a sticker might read: "Tom must contact Jim about MG-drawings (mil)." The facilitator then places the yellow sticker on the War Room poster under next week's War Room meeting, which means that the facilitator will ask about the issue at the next meeting to see if it has been resolved. It is essential that there are no discussions during the War Room meetings, only follow up on outstanding issues. Discussions should be taking place outside the War Room meetings and only the results should be put forward.

The War Room poster is the central coordinative artefact between the engineers in GlobalEngineering when coordinating the dependencies between tasks. The results of the meetings—i.e., the outstanding issues that were identified—are only captured by the yellow stickers. Having the yellow stickers as tangible objects is part of creating a tangible "feeling" of the plan; you can see and touch the outstanding issues. However, because of the materiality of the stickers and the fact that the poster is a local device, if the participant responsible for the task is at the opposite location, there is a risk that the commitment created during the meeting will disappear after the connection is closed. We observed this phenomenon during a meeting where the War Room poster was geographically located in India, but the issue identified was assigned to a member of the Danish project management team. This meant that the War Room poster was only visually available while the Internet connection was active, although the quality was bad, making it impossible for the Danish participant to examine the yellow stickers on the poster behind the Indian facilitator. Being fully aware of this limitation, the Indian facilitator read the content of the poster aloud, making this information audibly available for the Danish participants. The War Room meeting participants identified the issue and wrote the Danish participant down as being responsible for solving the task for next week. The following week the Indian facilitator read the yellow sticker aloud and asked the Danish participant about the issue, who then admitted he forgot. All the work of making the plan tangibly available becomes problematic when the poster is local and the team of participants is global. The engineers tried different approaches to solving this issue, for example, making a mirror wall in Denmark of the War Room poster in India, which was essentially a wall with yellow stickers, and they ended up creating an electronic document with a table listing the yellow notes. They can share the table electronically, but the tangibility aspect disappears. What we see here is an example of the relation work in a global interaction that goes into connecting people to artefacts (making them audibly available over geographical distance) and connecting artefact to artefact (connecting the mirror wall to the distant War Room poster, or creating the table of yellow stickers). Without this relation work—bringing local artefacts into the global collaborative space—the articulation work required to handle the complex interdependent tasks of engineering a cement factory would not be supported by the War Room concept.

Figure 4. The engineer in Copenhagen is performing *relation work* (making the poster audibly available) in order to connect his colleagues in Chennai to the poster on the wall in Copenhagen.

Relation Work as a Prerequisite for Articulation Work

The sociology of Anselm Strauss has proven especially useful for looking at cooperative work, as is testified by the wide use of his concepts, especially that of articulation work, within the CSCW community (e.g. Bardram and Bossen, 2005; Schmidt and Bannon, 1992; Schmidt and Simone, 1996). To better understand the efforts put into achieving the connections between globally distributed actors, we took articulation work as a starting point. However, we found that although lots of articulation work was done when the engineers collaborated across geographical distance, another other type of work was also being done. We propose the concept of *relation work* as an elaboration of the task-specific aspects of articulation work and argue that it may even be a complementary concept. Relation work, as we understand it, involves the work needed to create and enact the socio-technical networks that are a prerequisite for other collaborative engagement, for example, the performance of articulation work. The concept of articulation work as proposed by Strauss "refers to the specifics of putting together tasks, task sequences, tasks clusters – even aligning larger units such as lines of work and subprojects – in the service of work flow" (Strauss, 1988, p. 164). Strauss posits the concept of articulation work as part of a theory of action that stresses the ongoing efforts of actors to accomplish their tasks and goals in interaction with other actors. In opposition to a means-end view of action, where a linear process between start and end points is assumed, Strauss argues that the complexity within which action takes place, and the contingencies that most often arise, require an actor to continuously adjust and readjust his or her actions. Hence, action in its practice is a continuous readjustment of envisioned courses of action rather than a straight line from start to end strung out by rules or norms. When we move to considering several cooperating actors in a global setting, the process of continuous readjustment is further complicated by the fact that actors occupy different geographical positions and have different stances, cultures, and attitudes. Therefore, making first-order relations in a global setting is, in practice, an achievement: actors need to connect on a physical, cultural, and social network across multiple-sites in order to cooperate. This work of connecting the network of actors and artefacts is what we dub *relation work.*

Relation work, as we see it, is concerned with the achievement of the right network of people and artefacts across multiple sites and can be seen as the relational aspect of a multi-site work trajectory. The challenge of relation work arises from the fact that, in practice, a global setting is just an abstract space, that is, several localities have to be combined and connected in order to make up the global arena. Furthermore, not only actors but also things and information must be connected, and the establishment of the right combination of people, things, and information is hence an achievement that cannot be (and in practice is not) taken for granted. Efforts of relation work will most often be aimed at making global interactions as smooth as possible (or just possible, in the first place). Factors such as, for example, efficiency (having short and to-the-point meetings), accountability (that agreements are kept), technological dependency (that the technology connecting multiple settings is reliable), and the atmosphere of the meetings (e.g., having a laugh) may all be influential criteria and have to be balanced between the various connections of work and flows of things and information involved.

Actors may have several strategies for making global connections possible through relation work, including connecting people with people, people with things, and things with other things. However, the strategies of awareness (Heath et al., 2002) and coordinative mechanisms (Schmidt and Simone, 1996) are not straightforward in the global situation. For the participants in the War Room meetings to become aware of each others' presence, relation work must be done in order to know who is there (in the local "other room") and who they are (as in names, respect, and knowledge, which ensure they refrain from stereotyping). Refraining from stereotyping and knowing the remote partners has a clear impact on the War Room meetings (as we saw when the facilitator knew the remote partner's name), thus prior netWORK activities seem to benefit the relation work between people. NetWORK as in the deliberate, carefully executed, hidden work constituted by participants' remembering and communicating (Nardi et al., 2002) outside the actual War Room meetings.

Gestures and facial expression are not by themselves visibly available (as we saw when the experienced facilitator tapped on the microphone to make the participants in the other location aware of what was going on) for all participants in the War Room meetings. Instead they require the relation work of locating oneself in front of the camera and still taking into account the quality of the digital signal. The technical infrastructure also requires relation work to ensure the connection between the locations, and if the technical connection breaks (during one of the observation we witnessed how a participant stumbled over the electrical cord attached to the wall socket, entirely disrupting the digital connection in the middle of a War Room meeting), it requires relation work yet again to re-create the connection. Thus, we argue that to bring awareness into the geographically distributed setting of War Room meeting as a strategy for handling articulation work, relation work is a prerequisite.

For the participants in the War Room meeting to be able to use the War Room posters as the coordination mechanism it is designed to be, we found several issues that had to be overcome through relation work due to the geographical dispersion of the participants and artefacts. The War Room poster as an artefact is only available in the global collaborative space as long as the connection is up and running. The second the technical infrastructure is gone, the poster becomes local. In our study we saw how the locality of the poster was experienced as problematic, and how the engineers tried to solve the issue by creating the mirror wall of the distant posters, or by creating the electronic table of yellow notes. Each of these strategies aimed to make the War Room poster into a persistent global coordination mechanism that survived after the meetings and was available outside of the technical connection. However, this work requires the relation work of connecting artefacts with artefacts, again a prerequisite for handling the articulation work during the War Room meetings.

Relation work as a concept is highly linked with invisible work (Suchman, 1995), since it also disappears from sight as long as someone is attending the issues. Relation work only becomes visible when it causes a breakdown, when nobody is attending the work. We suggest that breakdowns caused by the lack of relation work can come in many different shapes and might be linked to key issues such as communication breakdowns, mistrust, uneven coordination, misunderstandings, etc.

Relation work forms the fundamental activities of creating socio-technical connections between people and artefacts during collaborative activities required to create and enact the human and electronic network and engage with articulation work in cooperative engagements.

Conclusion and Perspectives

The introduction of War Room meetings as strategy for handling the coordination of task dependencies when engineering cement factories has significantly reduced the time required to complete projects. Whereas before the introduction of the concept GlobalEngineering took 52 weeks to settle the engineering part of the factory, the War Room meetings reduced the time to 15 weeks. When we ask GlobalEngineering why the War Room concept was such a huge success, they responded that it was about eliminating the air pockets in the plan through committing people to solving their tasks as quickly as possible, which is achieved by making the interdependencies visually available and tangible within the War Room poster. The success makes this case particularly interesting to investigate because if we can learn what kind of work goes into handling the War Room meetings, we can begin to identify areas that could be improved and then start to address these areas from a design perspective for collaborative technologies. One obvious challenge is the locally placed War Room poster, which required relation work by the participants as in when reading aloud the content of the poster locally making it globally available. We are currently collaborating with GlobalEngineering about finding new ways to share the poster globally. In our study we found that an essential part of the work that goes into making the War Room function is relation work, and new designs of collaborative technologies supporting this type of global activities should start here.

Relation work was a prerequisite for other activities such as articulation work, and may be described as the activities of creating socio-technical networks comprised of people and artefacts facilitating cooperative interaction and coordination in a globally distributed setting. Relation work is particularly evident in geographically distributed work, which is also why this became the unit of analysis in this paper. However, it is quite possible that relation work might be a more general matter also relevant for collocated collaboration (this suggestion, of course, requires further investigation). We suggest that relation work is a prerequisite for all types of collaboration but is less troublesome in collocated settings compared to global settings. We see relation work as a key area of interest for the design of new types of collaborative technologies supporting global interaction.

Acknowledgements

Thanks to Carina Rohrbach, who collected parts of the empirical data, and to GIRI, the Global Interaction Research Initiative at the IT-University of Copenhagen (global-interaction.org), who financially supported this research.

References

Allen, T. J. (1977): *Managing the Flow of Technology*. Cambridge, Mass.: MIT Press.

Bardram, J. E., and Bossen, C. A. (2005): A web of coordinative artifacts: collaborative work at a hospital ward., *In Proceedings of the 2005 international ACM SIGGROUP Conference on Supporting Group Work (Sanibel Island, Florida, USA, November 06 - 09, 2005)*. Sanibel Island, Florida, USA: ACM Press, NY.

Bjørn, P. (2003): Re-Negotiating Protocols: A way to Integrate Groupware in Collaborative Learning Settings. Paper presented at the *ECIS, New Paradigms in Organizations, Markets and Society, Proceedings of the 11th European Conference on Information System*, Napoli 19-21 June.

Bjørn, P., and Ngwenyama, O. (2010): Technology Alignment: A New Area in Virtual Team Research. *IEEE Transactions on Professional Communication 53*(4).

Covi, L., Olson, J., Rocco, E., Miller, W., and Allie, P. (1998): A Room of Your Own: What Do We Learn about Support of Teamwork from Assessing Teams in Dedicated Project Rooms? In *Cooperative Buildings: Integrating Information, Organization, and Architecture* (Vol. 1370, pp. 53-65): Springer Berlin / Heidelberg.

Gerson, E. M., and Star, S. L. (1986): Analyzing due process in the workplace. *ACM Transactions on Office Information Systems, 4*(3), pp. 257-270.

Harper, R. H. R., and Hughes, J. A. (1993): What a f-ing system! send 'em all to the same place and then expect us to stop them hitting: Making technology work in air traffic control. In G. Button (Ed.), *Technology in Working Order: Studies of work, interaction, and technology* (pp. 127-144): Routlege.

Harper, R. H. R., Hughes, J. A., and Shapiro, D. Z. (1989a): Working in harmony: An examination of computer technology in air traffic control., *Proceedings of the First European Conference on Computer Supported Cooperative Work, Gatwick, London, 13–15 September, 1989* (pp. 73–86). Gatwick.

Harper, R. R., Hughes, J. A., and Shapiro, D. Z. (1989b): *The Functionality of Flight Strips in ATC Work. The report for the Civil Aviation Authority*: Lancaster Sociotechnics Group, Department of Sociology, Lancaster University. .

Heath, C., and Luff, P. (1992): Collaboration and control: Crisis mangement and multimedia technology in London Underground control rooms. *Computer Supported Cooperative Work (CSCW) An International Journal, 1*(1-2), pp. 69-94.

Heath, C., Svensson, M. S., Hindmarsh, J., Luff, P., and Lehn, D. (2002): Configuring Awarness. *Computer Supported Cooperative Work, 11*, pp. 317-347.

Heath, C. C., and Luff, P. (1996): Convergent activities: Line control and passenger information on the London Underground. In Y. Engeström and D. Middleton (Eds.), *Cognition and Communication at Work*. (pp. 96 - 129). Cambridge: Cambridge University Press.

Herbsleb, D., and Grinter, R. E. (1999): Splitting the Organization and Integrating the Code: Conway's Law Revisited., *Int'l Conf. Software Eng* (pp. 85-95).

Herbsleb, J. D., Mockus, A., Finholt, T. A., and Grinter, R. E. (2000): Distance, Dependencies, and Delay in a Global Collaboration, *CSCW 2000*. Philadelphia, P.A.

Kraut, R. E., Egido, C., and Galegher, J. (1990): Patterns of Contact and Communication in Scientific Research Collaboration. In J. Galegher, K. R.E. and C. Egido (Eds.), *Intellectual Teamwork: Social Foundations of Cooperative Work*. Hillsdale, New Jersey: Lawrence Erlbaum.

Larsson, A. (2003): Making sense of collaboration: The challenge of thinking together in global design teams, *GROUP* (pp. 153-160). Sanible Island, Florida: ACM.

Mark, G. (2001): Extreme Collaboration. *Communications of the ACM.*

Nardi, B., Whittaker, S., and Schwarz, H. (2002): NetWORKers and their activity in intensional networks. *Computer Supported Cooperative Work (CSCW): An International Journal, 11*, pp. 205-242.

Olson, G. M., and Olson, J. S. (2000): Distance Matters. *Human-Computer Interaction, 15*, pp. 139-178.

Randall, D., Harper, R., and Rouncefield, M. (2007): *Fieldwork for design: Theory and practice*. London: Springer.

Schmidt, K., and Bannon, L. (1992): Taking CSCW Seriously: Supporting Articulation Work. *Computer Supported Cooperative Work (CSCW). An International Journal., 1*(1-2), pp. 7-40.

Schmidt, K., and Simone, C. (1996): Coordination mechanisms: Towards a conceptual foundation of CSCW systems design. *Computer Supported Cooperative Work: The Journal of Collaborative Computing, 5*(2-3), pp. 155-200.

Strauss, A. (1985): Work and the division of labor. *The Sociological Quarterly, 26*(1), pp. 1-19.

Strauss, A. (1988): The Articulation of Project Work: An Organizational Process. *The Sociological Quarterly, 29*(2), pp. 163-178.

Suchman, L. (1995): Making Work Visible. *Communications of the ACM, 38*(9), pp. 56-64.

Teasley, S., Cowi, L., Krishnan, M. S., and Olson, J. S. (2000): How does radical collocation help a team succeed?, *Proceedings of the 2000 ACM conference on Computer supported cooperative work*. Philadelphia, Pennsylvania, United States: ACM.

Whittaker, S., and Schwarz, H. (1999): Meetings of the board: The impact of scheduling medium on long term group coordination in software development. *Computer Supported Cooperative Work (CSCW): An International Journal, 8*(3), pp. 175-205.

Discriminating Divergent/Convergent Phases of Meeting Using Non-Verbal Speech Patterns

Junko Ichino
University of Electro-Communications
ichino@is.uec.ac.jp

Abstract. The goal of this paper is to focus on non-verbal speech information during meeting and see if this information contains cues enabling the discrimination of meeting phases—divergent and convergent phases using decision trees. Group task experiments were conducted using a modified 20Q. The recorded speech was analyzed to identify various utterance pattern features—utterance frequency, length of utterance, turn-taking pattern frequency, etc. Discrimination trials were conducted on groups of friends, groups of strangers, and on both groups together using these features, and discrimination accuracy rates were obtained of 77.3%, 85.2% and 77.3%, respectively, in open tests. These results are quite good, considering that they are based on non-verbal speech information alone. Among the features relating to utterance patterns used in this work, we found that silence frequency and quasi-overlapping frequency were especially effective for discrimination. Our results did not find that group friendliness or task difficulty information contributed to effective discrimination of the meeting phases.

Introduction

There are typically two most basic phases, a *divergent phase* and a *convergent phase* in idea generation meetings or problem solving meetings that are the focus on this study. In a divergent phase, issues and ideas are brought to light. In a convergent phase, the issues and ideas are sorted and classified, and solutions are considered and prioritized (Guilford, 1983; Levine et al., 2004). It is important to keep these two phases, which we call *meeting phases* in this paper, separate in these kinds of meetings, since such meetings often contain a mix of divergent and convergent activities. At the scene of meeting, a person who plays a role of facilitator in the meeting has to skillfully organize people who attempt to reach a consensus in spite of divergent phase or people who try to encourage discussion among members in spite of convergent phase. He or she also needs to determine the appropriate point at which a meeting transitions from the divergent phase to the conversion phase, and vice versa (Hori, 2004). However, there is less case of controlling meeting phases properly in actual meeting. Of course, one can hire a facilitator or moderator, but these kinds of specialists are in high demand and costly. Meeting support systems of the future must therefore be capable of effective facilitation.

Many researchers have explored methods to introduce their system into idea generation meetings or problem solving meetings. *ShrEdit* work (McGuffin and Olson, 1991) showed how intermixed the two phases of the meeting are, and illustrated how the tools was used to support both. However, a host of other support tools after *ShrEdit* have been developed that support either divergence or convergence—for example *AIDE* (Nishimoto et al., 1999) and *Inspiration* (Inspiration Software Inc.) provide support for divergent phase while *Colab* (Stefik et al., 1987) and *Gungen* (Munemori et al., 1994) support convergent phase—and the function of the two kinds of systems have very different features. And some of our own previous work aimed at supporting both phases in a meeting showed that certain features are only useful during one of the phases (Ichino et al., 2009). These studies suggest that a meeting support system can cover a whole meeting, not only one part of it, if each of these functions or systems which help only one phase of meeting is integrated into one supporting environment. We therefore propose that it is important to understand how to discriminate meeting phases in real time, so that a system can switch from the function or legacy system which supports one phase of meeting to the function or legacy system which supports another phase, and can present information on a current phase to facilitators and moderators.

The goal of this paper is to focus on speech information during meeting and see if this information contains cues enabling the discrimination of meeting phases. Our work is dedicated to implementing such a system as described above, with the ultimate goal of promoting collaborative work in groups. This is of course where the automatic methods would in turn be the most useful. As a step one in a series of investigations that would need to be carried out for the automatic methods to be ultimately validated, here we will ignore real-time considerations in this paper.

It is well known that in human-to-human communication, non-verbal information plays a major role alongside verbal information in expressing the intent of the speaker (Mahl, 1956). If one observes the dialog of actual meetings, it is apparent that meeting phases are not just manifested by the verbal content or the context, but by conversational tempo, rhythm, pauses before and after speech, turn-taking, and a host of other subtle expressive changes in the conversation. In other words, the information enabling one to discriminate meeting phases is often manifested in the form of non-verbal speech information. Non-verbal speech information we will analyze in this paper include length of utterance, switching pauses between speakers, turn-taking pattern frequency, and other utterance patterns. In order to link these utterance patterns and meeting phases, we will develop a decision tree supervised learning approach for discriminating divergent versus convergent phases of meetings.

Related work

Computer scientists have been analyzing how meetings and discussions are structured and investigating how this information might be shared and stored for years. Progress has been made in structuring and visualizing statements and descriptive content (e.g., Amitani et al., 2005) and in managing argument design intent and design rationale for the development of software design (e.g., Conklin et al., 1988). In these studies, conversation is modeled and structured as an aspect of knowledge based on verbal speech information, then communication is supported based on the model. Due to the technological challenge of analyzing conversational structures in real time, this approach has not been applied to the real-time support of meetings. It has also become apparent that, for correctly understanding the meaning of speech and actions in natural human-to-human communication, it is not enough to just to understand verbal information and other symbolic messages. Non-verbal information is equally important.

Based on this fundamental insight, there has been an upsurge in recent research across a number of different fields exploring the relationship between human dialog communication and non-verbal speech information. In the areas of CSCW and groupware, a number of studies have been done to implement computer-based real-time support for meetings using mostly non-verbal speech information. For example, DiMicco et al. (2007) and Ichino et al. (2009) have proposed schemes that detect the speech time of participants, then present a visualization of the results on a shared display. Another approach called Conversation Clock uses variations in speech energy or volume to display the interaction history of participants as social cues on a table display (Bergstrom et al., 2007). Meeting Mediator is another scheme that seeks to enhance group collaboration patterns by dividing meetings into brainstorming and problem-solving phases, then visualizing group dynamics using speech features (speaking length and speaking energy) and physical movement (Kim et al., 2008; Olguin et al., 2009). The goal of most of these systems is to exploit group dynamics feedback to enhance group satisfaction and performance (Smith et al., 1959), and to develop ways of measuring group dynamics using speech and providing persuasive feedback.

And this approach is not just confined to CSCW and groupware. Studies of non-verbal information in dialog have been applied in discourse analysis, social psychology, Japanese language education, and other areas as well. Osuga et al. developed a scheme for discriminating whether a speaker would yield his turn or continue speaking based on decision tree learning using dialog prosodic features (basic frequency (F0), power, duration, etc.) alone (Ohsuga et al., 2006). Nagaoka et al. (2003) compared cooperative dialog with non-cooperative dialog, and found that in the former, speakers tend to observe the same temporal speech patterns (duration and switching pauses) and backchannel responses. A number of different researches including Wrede et al. (2003) and Cetin et al. (2006) analyzed the prosodic information in human-human dialogs, and found that the prosody and overlapping speech of speakers were closely related to dialog hotspots. Most of these conversational studies have involved just two people (dialogs), but recently we have seen a growing number of studies involving multi-party conversations. For example, Chang et al. analyzed how frequently participants chimed in and prosodic features of poster session conversations, and found that with this information alone, they could predict the points in the presentation that were most interesting and most concerned the listeners (Chang et al., 2008). Bono et al. (2004) also studied multi-party conversations at a poster exhibit presentation, and discovered they could estimate the interest of the listeners from their interaction behavior: standing position, sojourn time, gazing distribution, and the like.

All this work demonstrates the importance of non-verbal information, and the effectiveness of non-verbal speech information for supporting dialog. Yet none of this research analyzing dialog speech has focused on discriminating divergent and convergent phases of meetings. It is generally thought that the discrimination of meeting phases calls for human judgment based on an assortment of different information: knowledge of conversational context and background, shared beliefs of the group members, gestures and eye-gaze information, and so on. Implementing a system that could support such discrimination functionality would require very advanced processing capability. Not to mention the fact that background knowledge and shared belief are highly speaker and task dependent, and would therefore be very difficult to generalize. In this regard, non-verbal speech information would certainly offer a significant advantage, for non-verbal information can be readily input and processed right on the spot, and thus could be used to implement a wide range of different systems.

Divergent and convergent phase meeting experiments

Experimental Design and Hypotheses

Focusing on divergent and convergent phases of meetings, our goal was to see if there were any clear discernable differences in the non-verbal speech information among group members between the two phases.

Non-verbal speech information is broadly classified into two categories: acoustic phonetic attributes such as volume, pitch, speed, accent, and so on, and temporal patterns such as pauses and utterance timing (Daibo, 1998). In a previous study by one of the authors involving brainstorming and problem-solving meeting experiments (Ichino et al., 2009), different temporal utterance patterns were observed for divergent and convergent phases of meetings. In this work, therefore, we will focus on the latter utterance patterns.

H1. Utterance pattern information will contribute to discriminate the divergent and convergent phases of meetings.

In actual real-world meetings, sometimes all the members will know one another such as a typical office meetings, and sometimes the participants will be meeting one another for the first time such as a meeting with new clients. We know that the way people converse varies considerably in terms of eye-contact, posture, whispering, doing things at the same time, and so on, depending on whether they know the other people or not (Nakai, 2006). In terms of the utterance patterns we are interested in, we speculate that meeting with friends or strangers would be manifested in various differences: for example, we would expect the speech tempo to be somewhat faster if the group members are on friendly terms and the timing and pauses when starting to speak might be different between meeting with friends and meeting with strangers. Assuming significant differences between meeting with friends as opposed to strangers, the structural approach we describe in the later section of dividing the groups using a classifier (decision tree) should provide a good way of judging, and here we assess the potential utility of this approach.

H2. There will be some differences between meeting with friends and strangers in utterance pattern information of each meeting phase.

In addition, the difficulty of issues to be solved in real meetings also varies widely. This suggests that the difficulty of the issue could affect the behavior and the performance of the group members (Wilson et al., 2004). Compared to simpler problems, if issues are harder to deal with, members would have to think about them longer, which presumably would prolong the discussion and have other effects on utterance patterns. Just as we observed earlier regarding friendliness of group members, here again we will test whether using a classifier to divide the meetings in terms of task difficulty works well or not.

H3. There will be some differences between task difficulties in utterance pattern information of each meeting phase.

The experimental factors outlined above are summarized in Table I: two meeting phases X two levels of group friendliness X two task difficulties. We analyzed the group friendliness as between-subjects factors and the meeting phase and task difficulty as a within-subject factor. We conducted the Twenty Questions experimental sessions simulating how real meetings deal with above experimental factors, and extracted non-verbal speech information.

Factor	Code	Level	
		1	2
Meeting phase	P	Divergent (P_d)	Convergent (P_c)
Group friendliness	G	Friend (G_f)	Stranger (G_s)
Task difficulty	T	Easy (T_e)	Hard (T_h)

Table I. Experimental factors.

Tasks

To create a simulating situation in which divergent and convergent phases might occur naturally in a meeting environment, we conducted a series of meeting experiments based on a modified version of the game Twenty Questions that involved groups of four participants.

In the traditional game of Twenty Questions (20Q), one player is chosen to be the Answerer, and that person chooses a subject but does not reveal this to the others. The other players than take turns by asking up to 20 questions that can be answered either 'yes' or 'no' to guess the subject. It have been regarded that it is difficult to control the difficulty of the task (Tailor et al., 1952), but in 20Q, the difficulty of the task can be manipulated by altering the obscurity of the word that the others have to guess.

For the purposes of our experiments, we modified 20Q by dividing it into two parts—first half and second half of the game—so that both divergent and convergent meeting phases would emerge in the game. Note that this modification of 20Q is the same as that used by Wilson (2004) and Kim et al. (2008; 2009) in their studies assessing two meeting phases of brainstorming and problem-solving. The first half of the game corresponds to the divergent brainstorming phase, while the second half corresponds to the problem-solving convergent phase. Answers are considered and given by the group. In the divergent phase in the first half of the game, the Answerer provides the group with a set of ten yes/no condition pairs (Figure 1). The group then brainstorms to come up with the greatest number of items satisfying the ten conditions. Then in the convergence phase in the second half of the game, the group tries to name the object that the Answerer has in mind by asking up to ten questions in addition to the ten conditions provided in the first phase. The group strategizes and discusses with the goal of coming up with the correct answer with the fewest number of questions. The group asks the Answerer yes/no questions, and the Answerer responds with a simple yes or no.

The difficulty of the task can be readily manipulated by varying how hard it is to recall the answers. Here we used "number of Google hits" as a rough indicator of difficulty, and extracted multiple terms at random assuming these terms with relatively few hits would be harder and terms with many hits would be easier to recall. Finally, each term was selected after two experimenters conferred and agreed.

Subjects

We recruited 40 male and female subjects ranging in age from 20 to 40 years old from the general public. Twenty of the subjects already knew each other. The subjects were arranged into ten groups of four subjects each, five groups were composed of friends (G_f) and the other five groups were made up of strangers (G_s). Each group consisted of two men and two women to maintain a gender balance. The experiment took approximately two hours, and the subjects were paid for their participation.

Experimental Setup

Each experiment involved a group of four who worked together in solving problems. The four participants sat at a rectangular table, two across from each other (Figure 2). During the experiment, each of the subjects wore a headset microphone (Shure SM10A-CN). Each participant was also provided with a pen and was encouraged to jot information down on post-it notes that were provided. Each session was recorded using a video camera placed at an angle where it could capture all movement, and all speech and non-verbal sounds from the subjects were recorded.

Experimental Procedure

Before starting the experiments, we explained the rules of the game to groups of subjects and had them play one practice game. Then after a short break, the groups started working on the games. There were ten test groups, five made up of friends (G_f) and the remaining five consisting of strangers (G_s). Each group had two hours, enough time for two to three games (not counting the practice game). In order to counterbalance the task difficulty order effect, the ten groups are divided into two sets. One set did the experiments in the order $T_e \to T_h$ ($\to T_e$), while the other set did the experiments in the opposite order $T_h \to T_e$ ($\to T_h$).

As we observed earlier in the tasks subsection, each game was divided into two parts: the first half of the game was the divergent phase for brainstorming (P_d) and the second half of the game was the convergent phase for problem solving (P_c). The divergent phase time was fixed at eight minutes. For the convergent phase, groups are given ten minutes at the beginning of a game, but if they got the correct answer before the ten minutes was up, the game was ended. If a group could not figure out the correct answer within ten minutes, the game is extended up to 15 minutes. Group members could direct questions to the Answerer at any time during the convergent phase. While the experiment was in progress, subjects were free to jot down any potential answers conceived by the group, any potential questions conceived by the group, or any answers provided by the Answerer in response to questions on a sticky note.

Questions	Answers
1 Is it something flammable?	Yes
2 Is it bigger than a sofa?	No
3 Was it born in Asia?	Yes
4 Is it something that can be worn?	No
5 Does it float?	Yes
6 Is it something shared by a family?	No
7 Is it some kind of tool?	Yes
8 Is it used in entertainment?	No
9 Does it make noise?	Yes
10 Is it generally used outside?	No

Figure 1. Typical set of ten yes/no question-and-answer pairs distributed in the divergent phase of Twenty-Questions.

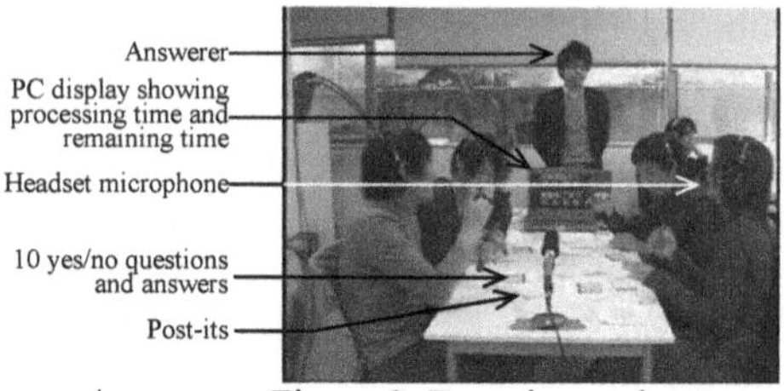

Figure 2. Experimental setup.

Method of analysis

In this work, we developed a procedure of discriminating the divergent phase from the convergent phase of meetings based on utterance pattern-related information using statistical decision tree learning. We then compared groups of friends versus strangers, then further subdivided those groups to deal with easy versus hard tasks, to assess the ability of these different parameters to discriminate divergent versus convergent phases.

Audio Data

For audio data, we used the conversational speech recorded for a total of 22 games in the meeting experiments described in the previous section. We analyzed only the conversation among 4 group members while they participated in the 20Q game sessions. The conversation with the Answerer, which means the members' questions to the Answerer and the Answerer's responses, were excluded in the analysis.

Units of Analysis

Various units have been proposed for analyzing utterances (Bono et al., 2007). With the idea of constructing a real-time meeting support system, here we adopted the inter-pausal unit (IPU) as an objectively definable silence bound unit, and following (Koiso et al., 1998) we define an IPU as a sequence of speech bounded by silence longer than 100 ms. After semi-automatically deriving silence intervals based on speech volume, we verify and correct the results manually, and divide into IPUs.

Utterance Pattern Features

There are five utterance pattern features used for discrimination in the work. Here the (a) *utterance frequency* is the number of utterances (i.e., number of IPUs) per minute of elapsed phase time; (b) *ratio of overlap speech time (%)* is the proportion of time (%) member m speaks when another member is speaking (IPU) during total elapsed phase time; (c) *length of utterance* is the average time length of each IPU (ms) spoken by member m during a phase; (d) *switching pause* is the average interval (ms) during a phase for member m to begin speaking after another member has finished speaking (IPU) (if a speaker begins speaking before the previous speaker has finished, that is not included); and (e) *frequency of different types speaker transition* is the number of transitions to another speaker when member m is speaking during total elapsed phase time (min). In terms of contiguous IPUs, here we follow (Horiuchi et al., 1997; Koiso et al., 2000) in defining the types of transitions between speakers' utterances based on the speaker of each IPU and the temporal relationship into the five categories shown in Table II.

Silence	After the previous IPU by m or other member is finished, member m begin the next IPU after a long pause exceeding 1,700 ms.
Continuation	After the previous IPU by member m is finished, member m starts the next IPU after a pause of less than 1,700 ms.
Switching	After the previous IPU by some member other than m is finished, member m starts the next IPU after a pause of less than 1,700 ms.
Quasi-overlap	Just before (less than 200 ms) the previous IPU by a member other than m is finished, member m starts the next IPU.
Overlap	During the previous IPU by some member other than m, member m starts the next IPU and both IPUs continue simultaneously for longer then 200 ms (including cases where the two IPUs are not contiguous).

Table II. Types of speaker transitions.

Discrimination Results and Analysis

Samples and Discrimination Method

Using features from all subjects extracted from a total of 176 speakers participating in 44 phases of 22 games of 20Q (see Table III) conducted in the meeting experiments described above, we carried out experiments to see if we could discriminate the divergent and convergent phases of meetings.

We employed statistical decision tree learning to discriminate the meeting phases. A decision tree is a tool for helping you to choose between several courses of action. It provides a structure within which you can lay out options and investigates the possible outcomes of choosing those options. A general measure for evaluating of decision tree learning is the discrimination accuracy of the decision trees. We created decision trees for closed data (closed test) and open data (open test). The "closed test" is used to conduct evaluations using a dataset that was used to construct the decision tree, while the "open test" is used to

Group friendliness	Task difficulty	Meeting phase	Number of phases (groups) assumed for meeting experiment	Number of phases (groups) classified by arbiters	Number of peoples per group	Number of samples
Total			44	44		176
Friends (G$_f$)			22	22		88
	Easy (T$_e$)		12	12		48
		Divergent (P$_d$)	6	6	* 4 =	24
		Convergent (P$_c$)	6	6	* 4 =	24
	Hard (T$_h$)		10	10		40
		Divergent (P$_d$)	5	7	* 4 =	28
		Convergent (P$_c$)	5	3	* 4 =	12
Strangers (G$_s$)			22	20		88
	Easy (T$_e$)		12	10		48
		Divergent (P$_d$)	6	7	* 4 =	28
		Convergent (P$_c$)	6	5	* 4 =	20
	Hard (T$_h$)		10	10		40
		Divergent (P$_d$)	5	9	* 4 =	36
		Convergent (P$_c$)	5	1	* 4 =	4

Table III. Number of samples used in discrimination experiment.

conduct evaluations using a dataset that was not used to create the tree. We used decision tree learning not only for its discrimination accuracy but also because we required a simple way to explain the discrimination results. We used C4.5 for the learning tree algorithm (Quinlan, 1992).

Supervised data is required to conduct discrimination experiments using decision tree learning. In the meeting experiment described in the previous section, we assume that the brainstorming task in the first half of the meeting corresponds to the divergent phase while the problem-solving task in the latter half of the meeting corresponds to the convergent phase. Three raters were used to determine which phase the brainstorming and problem-solving tasks actually belonged to. First, we asked the raters to independently classify 44 tasks as either *divergent* or *convergent* while they watched a video with sound of all the groups in action. The raters were instructed to make their decisions based on the criteria that the "divergent phase is when all sorts of possibilities are explored through free association to ideas" while the "convergent phase is when opinions are consolidated to achieve tangible results" (Hori, 2004). The arbiters were next asked to make a final decision as to which tasks were divergent and which were convergent based on majority rule. As a result, all 22 of the brainstorming tasks from the first phase were classified as *divergent*. Of the 22 problem-solving tasks from the second phase, 15 were classified as *convergent* while 7 were classified as *divergent*. These convergent or divergent results as determined by the arbiters was added to the data of the four subjects who conducted the tasks, and this was used as the supervisory data. Table III summarizes the number of samples used in the experiments.

Verifying Appropriateness of Task Difficulty Settings

After the meeting experiments were completed, we analyzed the task performance of the groups during the second half of the game to verify the appropriateness of task difficulty settings. Performance was measured using three criteria: (1) the number of questions the group asked the Answerer (number of questions), (2) whether the group had enough time to get the correct answer (answer time), and (3) the proportion of groups that figured out the Answerer's term within the time limit (15 minutes) (accuracy rate). Figure 3 shows means and standard errors for the three performance criteria. A two-way ANOVA (analysis of variance) based on 2 (group friendliness G: $G_f \cdot G_s$) X 2 (task difficulty T: $T_e \cdot T_h$) revealed that the task difficulty T main effect was significant for all three criteria. Compared to hard tasks (T_h), easy tasks (T_e) were found to require (1) fewer questions (T_e: 2.1 question vs. T_h: 4.8 questions, F (1,18) =6.707, p = .019), (2) shorter answer periods (T_e: 4.2 minutes vs. T_h: 9.7 minutes, F (1,18) = 5.488, p = .031), and yielded (3) higher accuracy rates (T_e: 91.7% vs. T_h: 50.0%, F(1,18) = 5.272, p = .034). Moreover, it was found that group friendliness G main effect and interaction G X T were not significant for all three criteria. These results show that the task difficulty and the task performance during second half of the game were proportionate, thus indicating that the task difficulty was set more or less correctly.

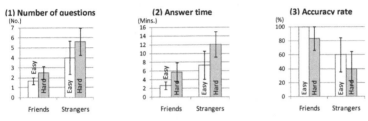

Figure 3. Task performance in the latter half of the game. Groups were made up either *friends* (G_f) or *strangers* (G_s), and given tasks that were either *easy* (T_e) or *hard* (T_h).

Results

First we present discrimination results using data for all subjects and discrimination results based on data for groups of friends and groups of strangers. Next we present discrimination results for groups of friends and strangers, further broken out in terms of task difficulty.

Discrimination results: data for all subjects and classified according to friend versus stranger

Table IV shows the divergent (P_d) / convergent (P_c) discrimination results based on decision trees constructed for each condition. The first tier shows the decision tree results for all subjects data, the second tier shows the results for just the subjects who are friends (G_f), and the fifth tier shows the decision tree results for the subjects who are strangers (G_s) data. One can see that in the closed test, the discrimination rate results are over 90% for all subjects and for strangers (G_s),

	Group friendliness	Task difficulty	Closed test	Open test
All subjects			92.0%	77.3%
	Friends (G_f)		84.1%	77.3%
		Easy (G_f X T_e)	85.4%	75.0%
		Hard (G_f X T_h)	92.5%	70.0%
	Strangers (G_s)		92.0%	85.2%
		Easy (G_s X T_e)	89.6%	62.5%
		Hard (G_s X T_h)	97.5%	95.0%

Table IV. Divergent (P_d) / convergent (P_c) discrimination rates.

which is approximately 8 points higher than the results for friends (G_f). Yet in the open test, the discrimination rate at the highest was 85% for strangers, but hovered below 80% for all subjects and the friends condition (G_f). We examined the 14 misclassified data points in the closed test under the friends condition (G_f), but failed to find any consistent trend.

Figure 4 shows a series of decision trees reflecting the various conditions. Figure 4 (i) shows results of the data for the subjects who are friends (G_f), (ii) shows the results for the subjects who are strangers, and (iii) shows the results based on data for all subjects. For example, leaf P_c1 branching to the left from the highest node reveals that 19 data points were correctly discriminated as convergent (P_c), and of these 1 data point was misclassified as divergent (P_d).

One can see that the friends (G_f) tree in (i) has 3 leaves, 1 discriminated to be divergent (P_d) and the other 2 discriminated to be convergent (P_c). Important features as discrimination factors from the top are (1) silence frequency, and (2) overlap frequency. Among the leaves, the conditions summarizing leaf P_d1 that is discriminated as divergent (P_d) are "low frequency overlap including silence." But at the same time, the leaf discriminated as being convergent (P_c) showing the most data points is P_c1, with 19 points. The condition summarizing this leaf is "absolutely no silence."

Now turning to tree (ii) for strangers (G_s), this tree has 4 leaves: 1 discriminated as divergent (P_d) and 3 discriminated as being convergent (P_c). Important features as discrimination factors from the top are (1) quasi-overlapping frequency, (2) quasi-overlapping frequency, and (3) switching pause. Conditions summarizing leaf P_d2 discriminated as divergent (P_d) are "quasi-overlapping is present, but not too frequently, and switching pauses are prolonged." On the other hand, the leaf discriminated as convergent (P_c) yielding the most data points is P_c3, with 10 points. The condition summarizing this leaf is "absolutely no quasi-overlapping."

Tree (iii) for all subjects has 9 leaves: 4 discriminated as divergent (P_d) and 5 discriminated as being convergent (P_c). Here the important features as discrimination factors from the top are (1) silence frequency, (2) quasi-overlapping frequency, and (3) utterance frequency. The leaf discriminated as being divergent (P_d) with the most data points is P_d4, with 94 points. The conditions summarizing this leaf are "silence and presence of not-too-frequent quasi-overlapping." On the other hand, the leaf discriminated as convergent (P_c)

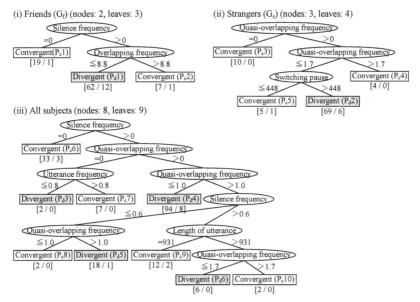

Figure 4. Decision trees generated in the closed test.

having the most data points is P_c6, with 33 points. The condition summarizing this leaf is "absolutely no silence."

It is apparent from the fact that quasi-overlapping frequency is selected as a feature in leaves of the (ii) and (iii) trees that the discrimination is not monotonic. We found from the ANOVA that quasi-overlapping frequency is less significant in the divergent phase (P_d) than in the convergent phase (P_c) (referring to Figure 5, 0.7 times per minute for P_d versus 1.2 times per minute for the P_c. F (1,168) = 6.938, p = .009).

Discrimination results: data classified for easy versus hard tasks

Let us next examine the discrimination results shown in tiers 3-4 and 6-7 in Table IV based on decision trees constructed to further sub classify the friends (G_f) and strangers (G_s) subject data in terms of task difficulty. In the closed test, the discrimination rate results were above 90% for hard tasks (T_h) for groups of both friends (G_f) and strangers (G_s), which was approximately 7-8 points higher than for easy tasks (T_e). In the open test, the discrimination rate increased by about 5 points for easy tasks (T_e) in the case of friends (G_f). Turning to groups of strangers (G_s), the discrimination rate exceeded 90% for hard tasks (T_h), about a 33 point gain over easy tasks (T_e). Examining the misclassified data points for the easy tasks (T_e), it was found that most involved data for groups of subjects that completed their easy task assignment within a relatively short period of time. It could be that these kinds of data features are not suitable for averaging over relatively short periods. Here we would infer that, when tasks are differentiated on the basis on difficulty, since data for one condition is insufficient, (see Table III), a data session that ends after only a short period might have a large impact on the results.

Considerations

Effectiveness of Utterance Pattern Features (H1)

Let us first consider the overall effectiveness of the various features associated with the utterance patterns derived from the discrimination experiment results. The discrimination results presented in Table IV suggest that it is indeed possible to discriminate divergent and convergent phases of meetings without relying on verbal information by using utterance patterns alone. Based on a review of the three decision trees shown in Figure 4 (and other trees for classifying task difficulty that are omitted from the paper), the (e) speaker transition types *silence* and *quasi-overlapping frequency* features noted earlier played an especially significant role in discrimination.

Relationship between meeting phases discriminated by decision trees and observed

A cursory review of decision trees (i), (ii), and (iii) in Figure 4 will reveal that different conversational styles pervade the divergent and convergent phases. In the divergent phase, stretches of speech are comparatively long, and conversation proceeds through turn-taking at moderate intervals. In convergent phases, by contrast we would expect to see a series of comparatively short statements that are strung together. In addition, we conducted a mixed-model analysis of variance (ANOVA) with the random factor of subject group (S) and the fixed factors of meeting phases (P: P_d • P_c), levels of group friendliness (G: G_f • G_s), and degrees of task difficulty (T: T_e • T_h) on the several features presented earlier. The reason we included the subject group factor is to see the subject group effects on analysis. And we found that the features *utterance frequency*; *length of utterance*; *switching pause*; and *frequency of silence, switching, and quasi-overlap* were all significant as meeting phase P main effects. Moreover, we found that compared to convergent phases (P_c), utterances were less frequent; length of utterances was longer; switching pauses were longer; silences were more frequent; and switching and quasi-overlapping were less frequent in divergent phases (P_d) (Figure 5). We also didn't observe a significant main effects of subject group S, group friendliness G, and task difficulty T with the all features. The interaction (P X T X S) was significant with only the feature *frequency of switching*. None of other features and none of other interactions were significant. All of these decision tree learning and ANOVA results are in agreement with our qualitative observations. In watching video of divergent phase sessions, we frequently observed participants carefully explaining vocabulary to share presuppositions and knowledge in conveying new ideas to other members. Then in the convergence phase sessions, we actually observed each member of the group succinctly narrow down to the key points in short phrases without long pauses in between.

Generally, during the divergent phase of problem-solving meetings, members are primarily focused on getting out their thoughts and are more concerned with quantity of ideas than quality. It is a free-wheeling session without anyone being too critical with an emphasis on coming up with ideas. Meanwhile, the convergent phase sessions are quite different. Here the emphasis is on sorting out the ideas raised during the divergent phase, and honing in on one idea (Hori, 2004). This might lead one to expect fewer pauses in divergent phases than in convergent phases, and continuous talking without interruptions. Yet, with the results of our experiments, we found just the opposite. We believe this can be attributed to the instructions and the clear-cut goal we gave the subjects, telling them to work together as a group within time limits during the convergent phase to come up with the correct answer. In ordinary meetings, of course, people are usually under similar time constraints to solve problems and make decisions. The findings presented here should prove useful in understanding typical real-world meetings held under similar circumstances.

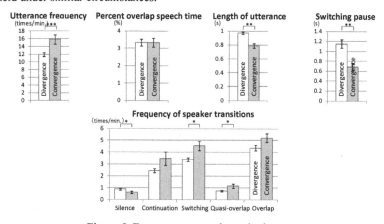

Figure 5. Feature means and standard errors.

Classification Results Based on Group Friendliness (H2)

Next we will consider results of our classification based on group friendliness. We compared the discrimination accuracy of decision trees created for different degrees of group friendliness—i.e., friends versus strangers—against a decision tree based on data for all subjects. First, we compared conditions for friends (G_f) and for all subjects. As one can see in Table IV, the discrimination rate for both under the open test condition is exactly the same at 77.3%. Now when we compare the groups of strangers (G_s) with all subjects, Table IV shows that the discrimination rate for strangers (G_s) is approximately eight points higher than for all subjects (open test). These results are fairly inconclusive, so it would be difficult to effectively discriminate between divergent and convergent phases using decision trees based on different degrees of friendliness. However, the amount of data per condition is very thin, so we cannot be certain.

Here we will consider our earlier inference in the subsection "Experimental Conditions" that utterance patterns would differ if the degree of friendliness of groups differed. First, let us compare the decision trees shown in Figure 4 (i) and (ii) reflecting groups of friends (G_f) and strangers (G_s), respectively. Nodes on the friends (G_f) decision tree were *silence frequency* and *overlapping frequency*, while those on the strangers (G_s) decision tree were *quasi-overlapping frequency* and *switch pauses*, so clearly the features used for discrimination are different. This tells us that our inference was essentially correct. Now, comparing the (i) friends condition (G_f) and (ii) strangers condition (G_s) with the decision tree for (iii) all subjects, it is apparent that both (i) and (ii) are effectively discriminated with few features (number of nodes). This suggests that when using utterance patterns to discriminate meeting phases, the effective utility of using the group friendliness information would not be lost. We need to reassess the effectiveness of classification based on group friendliness using more data and better statistical accuracy.

Generally, real-world human relationships evolve over time starting with a slight acquaintance that grows into full-blown friendship, so it is hard to apply the notion of strangers to a single category. Actually, we must consider a more flexible way of implementing decision trees based on different degrees of friendliness that accommodates phased changes in the degree of friendliness.

We also observed in Figure 3 that, while there was no marked difference in significance, the task performance of subjects who were friends (G_f) was better than that of subjects who were strangers (G_s) ((1) number of questions: 2.7 for G_f vs. 3.9 for G_s, $F(1,18) = 1.345$, $p = .261$; (2) answer time: 4.8 mins. for G_f vs. 8.6 mins. G_s, $F(1,18) = 2.737$, $p = .115$; (3) percentage correct answers: 81.8% for G_f vs. 63.6% for G_s, $F(1,18) = 1.021$, $p = .326$). The findings reported here are consistent with those of Wilson et al. (2004) who conducted a similar 20Q based experiment that divided subjects into groups of friends and strangers.

Classification Results Based on Task Difficulty (H3)

Let us next consider the results of our classification based on task difficulty. We compared the discrimination accuracy of decision trees created for different degrees of task difficulty—i.e., easy versus hard tasks—applied to groups of friends (G_f) and to groups of strangers (G_s) against a decision tree that was not classified for task difficulty. We found that just the hard task condition (G_s X T_h = 95.0% in Table IV) had a discrimination rate ten points higher than the unclassified case (G_s = 85.2% in Table IV) in the open test. For all other conditions (G_f X T_e, G_f X T_h, and G_s X T_e), the discrimination rate was lower than the unclassified case. These results suggest that using decision trees for different degrees of task difficulty may not effectively discriminate between divergent and convergent phases of meetings. Data for one condition is insufficient, so we need to reassess the effectiveness of classification based on task difficulty using more data and better statistical accuracy.

Moreover, in typical meetings, we can assume that the difficulty of topics varies throughout the meeting. As we noted earlier regarding different degrees of group friendliness, here too we must consider a more flexible way of implementing decision trees based on different degrees of task difficulty that accommodates phased changes in the degree of difficulty.

Next, let us consider our hypothesis in the previous subsection that, differences in task difficulty would be reflected in different utterance patterns. Although not included in the paper, we found that comparing easy versus hard tasks for groups of friends (G_f X T_e versus G_f X T_h) based on decision trees, produced different features used for discrimination. But when we compared easy versus hard tasks for groups of strangers (G_s X T_e versus G_s X T_h), both included *quasi-overlapping frequency* nodes. This indicates that this conjecture is not supported.

Now to briefly summarize the above considerations, features associated with utterance patterns do apparently contain information capable of discriminating divergent and convergent phases of meetings. Having this information should prove useful for linking discrimination and control of meeting phases in implementing meeting support systems. However, our experiments did not suggest that dividing up groups in terms of friendliness or task difficulty would serve as an effective approach in discriminating phases of meetings.

Conclusion and future work

In this study, we conducted experiments comparing non-verbal speech information among subjects to see if this information was useful in discriminating divergent and convergent phases of meetings. Using audio recordings of modified Twenty Questions experimental game sessions, we created decision trees using only information relating to utterance patterns—utterance frequency, length of utterance, turn-taking pattern frequency, etc.—then conducted experiments to discriminate divergent and convergent meeting phases using decision tree learning. As a result, the percentage of correct answers for groups of friends was 77.3%, for groups of strangers was 85.2%, and for all subjects was 77.3% (under the open test condition). These findings suggest that, even when verbal information is not used, one can nevertheless achieve fairly accurate discrimination between divergent and convergent phases of meetings from features associated with non-verbal utterance patterns alone. Among the features relating to utterance patterns used in this work, we found that *silence frequency* and *quasi-overlapping frequency* were especially effective for discrimination. Our results did not find that group friendliness or task difficulty information contributed to effective discrimination of the meeting phases, so this calls for further study using more data to achieve more stable discrimination accuracy.

Our results demonstrated that utterance patterns clearly differed between divergent and convergent phases when groups engaged in problem solving within a limited time frame through experimental sessions of Twenty Questions. Choosing an appropriate task for a semi-controlled study like this requires striking a difficult balance between ecological validity of the task, and the level of control required to obtain meaningful answers to our questions. We chose the 20 questions task because a) we believe that it contains most of the relevant elements and patterns of many common tasks (e.g., exchange of information that is not available to everyone), b) has successfully been used in previous studies, which allow us also to compare our results at the same level of validity (Tailor et al., 1952; Wilson et al., 2004), and c) this task allow us to control the level of difficulty in a straightforward way.

However, these results were obtained under conditions ideal for the algorithms to work, namely, a relatively simple task with explicit divergent and convergent phases. Clearly an important next phase is to investigate other tasks. Thorough analysis of the features differentiating divergent and convergent phases of meetings would require more empirical research. It will be necessary to show that divergent and convergent activities can be extracted from more naturalistic meetings, such as the early design phases in software engineering or product design which often contain a mix of divergent and convergent activities.

Building on the work presented here, we would like to perform a more detailed analysis to investigate the generality of using decision trees based on more data. In this work we focused on simple binary discrimination between divergent and convergent phases, but this approach could also be applied to probabilistic behavior, so we would like to add a labeling method and discrimination scheme. Toward implementing a meeting support system, we intend to propose a framework that captures continuous information in real time and implements group interaction control at the discrimination determination stage. We therefore plan to investigate a discrimination method capable of defining features in real time. We would also like to explore other types of the non-verbal information that we didn't touch on in this study—prosodic information such as volume, pitch, velocity, and accent—to assess their potential for discriminating phases of meetings. And by opening the way to other non-verbal cues, such as eye gaze and gesture, this will lead to far better future understanding of the multiple phases of meetings.

Furthermore, we also must investigate whether these methods are language or culture specific. Certainly there are differences in conversational style in different languages. We should make certain the possible influence on the generalizability of the our assumptions and conclusions that meetings can have that encompass people of different cultures, for instance, if people from different countries and cultures really share similar behaviors and patterns in regard to both 'silence frequency' and 'overlapping frequency'.

Acknowledgments

The authors wish to acknowledge that part of this work was supported by a grant-in-aid for scientific research by the Japan Society for the Promotion of Science (JSPS) (No: 19800015).

References

Amitani, S., and Hori, K. (2005): 'A Method and a System for Supporting the Process of Knowledge Creation', *Trans. Information Processing Society of Japan*, vol. 46, no. 1, pp. 89-102.

Bergstrom, T. and Karahalios, K. (2007): 'Conversation Clock: Visualizing audio patterns in co-located groups', *Proc. 40th Hawaii international Conference on System Sciences*, IEEE, 3, pp. 1317-1325.

Bono, M., Suzuki, N., and Katagiri, Y. (2004): 'Conversation: Do Interaction Behaviors Give Clues to Know Your Interest?', *Cognitive studies: bulletin of Jpn. Cognitive Science Society*, vol. 11, no. 3, pp. 214-227.

Bono, M., and Takanashi, K. (2007): 'Methodology for Analyzing Multi-Party Interaction: Overview of Analytic Units of Verbal and Non-Verbal Communication', *J. Jpn. Society for Artificial Intelligence*, vol. 22, no. 6, pp. 838-845.

Cetin, O. and Shriberg, E. (2006): 'Analysis of Overlaps in Meetings by Dialog Factors, Hot spots, Speakers, and Collection Site: Insights for Automatic Speech Recognition', *Proc. Interspeech 2006*, pp. 293-296.

Chang, Z., Takanashi, K., and Kawahara, T. (2008): 'Analysis on Morphological and Prosodic Features of Aizuti and its Correlation to Conversation Mode in Poster Presentations', *Jpn. Society for Artificial Intelligence Technical Report*, SIG-SLUD-A802, pp. 7-13.

Conklin, J., and Begeman, M. L. (1988): 'gIBIS: A Hypertext Tool for Exploratory Policy Discussion', *Proc. CSCW'88*, ACM Press, pp. 140-152.

Daibo, I. (1998): *Gesture and communication medium*. Saiensu-sha, JP.

DiMicco, J. M., Hollenbach, KJ, Pandolfo, A., and Bender,W. (2007): 'The Impact of Increased Awareness while Face-to-Face. Special Issue on Awareness Systems Design', *Human-Computer Interaction*. vol. 22, no. 1.

Guilford, J.P. (1983): 'Transformation: Abilities or functions', *J. Creative Behavior*, 17, pp. 75-86.

Hori, K. (2004): *The ABC of facilitation*. Nikkei Publishing.

Horiuchi, Y., Yoshino, A., Naka, M., et al. (1997): 'The Chiba Map Task Dialogue Corpus Project', *Research reports of Faculty of Technology*, vol. 48, no. 2, Chiba University, pp. 33-60.

Ichino, J., Takeuchi, K. and Isahara, H. (2009): 'Improvement of Member's Concentration during Discussion', *Proc. HCII2009*, LNCS 5617, pp. 59-68.

Inspiration Software Inc.: 'Inspiration', http://www.inspiration.com/.

Kim, T., Chang, A., Holland, L., and Pentland, A. (2008): 'Meeting mediator: Enhancing Group Collaboration using Sociometric Feedback', *Proc. CSCW'08*, ACM Press, pp. 457-466.

Koiso, H., Horiuchi, Y., Tutiya, S., Ichikawa, A., and Den, Y. (1998): 'An analysis of turn-taking and backchannels based on prosodic and syntactic features in Japanese map task dialogs', *Langurage and Speech*, vol. 41, no. 3-4, pp. 295-321.

Koiso, H., and Den, Y. (2000): 'How is the Smooth Transition between Speakers Realized?', *Cognitive studies: bulletin of Jpn. Cognitive Science Society*, vol. 7, no.1, pp. 93-106.

Levine, J.M. and Moreland, R.L. (2004): 'Collaboration: The Social Context of Theory Development', *Personality and Social Psychology Review*, vol. 8, no. 2, pp. 164-172.

Mahl, G. F. (1956): 'Disturbances and silences in the patient's speech in psychotherapy', *J. Abnormal and Social Psychology*, 53, pp. 1-15.

McGuffin, L., and Olson, G. M. (1992): 'ShrEdit: A shared electronic workspace', *CSMIL Technical Report* 45, University of Michigan, Cognitive Science and Machine Intelligence Laboratory.

Munemori, J., Horikiri, I, and Nagasawa, Y. (1994): 'Groupware for New Idea Generation Support System (GUNGEN) and Its Application and Estimation to the Student Experiments of the Distributed and Cooperative KJ Method', *Trans. Information Processing Society of Japan*, vol. 35, no. 1, pp. 143-153.

Nakai, Y. (2006): 'Verbal and non-verbal engagement displays in a Japanese face-to-face conversation between two native speakers and two non-native speakers', *Bulletin of Center for Jpn. Language*, 19, Waseda University, pp. 79-98.

Nagaoka, C., Komori, M., Draguna Raluca Maria, et al. (2003): 'Mutual Congruence of Vocal Behavior in Cooperative Dialogues', *Proc. Human Interface 2003*, Japan, pp. 167-170.

Nishimoto, K., Mase, K., and Nakatsu, R. (1999): 'How an Autonomous Information Retrieval Agent Affects Divergent Thinking by a Group', *J. Jpn. Society for Artificial Intelligence*, vol. 14, no. 1, 58-70.

Ohsuga. T., Horiuchi, Y., Nishida, M., and Ichikawa, A. (2006): 'Prediction of Turn-Taking from Prosody in Spontaneous Dialogue', *Trans. Jpn. Society for Artificial Intelligence*, vol. 21, no. 1, pp. 1-8.

Olguin, D.O., Waber, B.N., Kim, T., et al. (2009): 'Sensible organizations: Technology and methodology for automatically measuring organizational behavior', *IEEE Trans. Syst., Man, Cybern. B, Cybern.*, vol. 39, no. 1, pp. 43-55.

Quinlan, J. R. (1992): *C4.5: Programs for Machine Learning*. Morgan Kaufmann.

Smith, E.E. and Kight, S.S. (1959): 'Effects of Feedback on Insight and Problem-Solving Efficiency in Training Groups', *J. Applied Psychology*, 43, pp. 209-211.

Stefik, M., Foster, G., Bobrow, D. G., Kahn, K., Lanning, S., and Suchman, L. (1987): 'Beyond the chalkboard, Computer support for collaboration and problem solving in meetings', *Comm. ACM*, vol. 30, no. 1, pp. 32-47.

Taylor, D. W., and Faust, W. I. (1952): 'Twenty questions: Efficiency in problem solving as a function of size of group', *J. Experimental Psychology*, 44, 360-368.

Wrede, B and Shriberg, E. Spotting (2003): '"Hot Spots" in Meetings: Human Judgements and Prosodic Cues', *Proc. Eurospeech 2003*, pp. 2805-2808.

Wilson, D.S., Timmel, J. J., and Miller, R.M. (2004): 'Cognitive cooperation: when the going gets tough, think as a group', *Human Nature*, vol. 15, no. 3, pp. 225-250.

"You probably shouldn't give them too much information" – Supporting Citizen-Government Collaboration

Nikolaj Gandrup Borchorst and Susanne Bødker
Department of Computer Science, Aarhus University
ngandrup@cs.au.dk, bodker@cs.au.dk

Abstract. This paper discusses the challenge of supporting digitally mediated citizen-government collaboration in public service provision. With a vantage point in activity theory and the empirical data from three exploratory design cases, we derive a theoretical framework for understanding the way in which citizens share information with government. Through the proposed framework and the notion of Participatory Citizenship, we propose a set of central design challenges to supporting collaboration within this setting. We argue that civil servants and citizens have inherently different foci in the service provision process. Hence, we conclude that the focus of design should not be to support a shared motive for the overall service delivery, but to support a better common understanding of the case process in itself, i.e. the involved actors, their motives, and their mediating artifacts. Moreover, we argue that the aim of technological support for complex collaboration should not be leaner, more rational case processes, but improved citizen involvement in the configuration of service provision and the alignment of actor motives. Lastly, we exemplify how these design challenges can be met by discussing how a concrete exploratory prototype in the form of a web-based timeline addresses collaboration within a complex service provision setting.

Introduction

Technology as a mediator for collaboration in organizations has been explored thoroughly within HCI and CSCW (Schmidt and Bannon, 1992; Grudin, 1994). A natural continuation of this research has been the exploration of collaboration between stakeholders with dissimilar and sometimes contradictive incentives

(Clement and Wagner, 1995; Cohen et al., 2000). Meanwhile, the last decade has seen a remarkable growth in the proliferation of social communities and user contributions on the web. Several studies have explored the nature of these communities (e.g. Bryant et al., 2005) and the positive effects of user contributions in these settings (Marlow et al., 2006). Part of the thrust of New Public Management and e-Government has been a heightened focus on the digitalization of public services and a focus on the citizen as opposed to the bureaucratic institution being the center of attention (Vigoda, 2002). However, very few digitalization efforts have led to the support of fruitful collaboration and empowerment of citizens. The bulk of European digital service solutions still take rationalization of the administration as their primary point of departure and, essentially, let citizens serve themselves when applying for various benefits. As concluded in a report by the European Commission (Osimo, 2008) much can be gained from involving citizens in the provision and development of public services. Nonetheless, this is not an easy task as citizen and government incentives for engaging in such collaboration are very different and vary from setting to setting.

In this paper we explore the challenges of technologically meditated collaboration and citizen contributions in public service provision. With a vantage point in three case studies exploring different collaborative settings, we discuss the notion of *Participatory Citizenship*. We derive three archetypical citizen strategies for sharing information with government and discuss the consequences of these strategies to the support of citizen empowerment in citizen-government interactions. Using the lens of activity theory, we discuss the central challenges to supporting collaborative activities within the sphere of public service provision. Lastly, we exemplify how these design challenges can be met by discussing how a concrete exploratory prototype in the form of a web-based timeline addresses collaboration within a complex service provision setting.

Conceptual Background

This paper defines Participatory Citizenship as *the act of citizens actively engaging in and contributing to the provision of public services in order to improve these services for themselves and other citizens*. The concept creates a link between discussions of active citizenship within the realm of political science (e.g. Westheimer and Kahne, 2004) and the potentials and challenges of user involvement, cf., Participatory Design (Greenbaum and Kyng, 1991). Participatory Citizenship specifically addresses this link within the realm of public service provision. The inspiration for such a focus has come from three exploratory research cases regarding parental leave case processing (Borchorst et al., 2009; Bohøj et al., 2010)), physical citizen service offices, and citizen deliberation through mobile technology (Bohøj et al. 2011). These are introduced more thoroughly below.

The exploratory research cases have led us to a more general focus on what constitutes the collaboration across the boundaries between citizens and government, as well as the challenges of technologically supporting such collaboration.

Substantial ethnographical and sociological research has been done on the subject of social interaction in and between communities (e.g. Lave and Wenger, 1991; Bowker and Star, 1999). Furthermore, technology as a mediator for collaboration between 'groups' has been paid special attention within CSCW (e.g. Bannon and Schmidt, 1991; Grudin, 1994), albeit with a predominant focus on professional organizational settings, rather than our current emphasis. With this focus in mind, Kling's (1991) argument for a stronger consideration of the problematic aspects of cooperation, such as conflict, caution, and control, seems especially pertinent. Compared to studies of workplace settings, citizen-government interaction arguably constitutes an inherently asymmetrical relationship in terms of power and the ability to define the rules for and outcome of the interaction. Consequently, an important point becomes whether the involved parties perceive the interaction in the same way, e.g. as collaborative problem solving, control, compliance with authoritative, legislative procedures, etc.

In the following we introduce activity theory as a theoretical basis for analyzing the dynamics of collaborative activities on the boundaries between citizens and public administration.

Activity Theory

Within CSCW there exists a long tradition for conceptualizing the anatomy of collaborative activity through the perspective of Activity Theory (Bertelsen and Bødker 2001, Bryant et al. 2005, Engeström et al. 1988, Kuutti 1991). We see activity theory as a strong tool for emphasizing the dynamic relationships between organizational activity and individual action from an anti-idealist and anti-individualist perspective (c.f. Star, 1996).

Human activity is carried out through actions with purpose that transforms the *object* from *materials* to outcome. This object is also the target of human expectations and reflections, i.e. the *motive* of the activity. Actions are realized through series of *operations*, each "triggered" by the conditions and structure of the action. Activity is fundamentally marked by dynamics, disturbances, or ruptures, which are often results of more profound tensions and contradictions between activities. Activities are constantly developing as a result of this instability: An activity with a separate motive will at times get subsumed into other activities thereby losing its individual motive. In other instances, clusters of actions turn into separate activities (e.g. Bødker and Grønbæk, 1995).

Human beings develop and accommodate artifacts that mediate their relations with objects (Bødker and Klokmose, 2011). Such artifacts include *tools*, *rules*, and *division of work* and may at the same time support doing the job, and understanding the rules (*secondary artifacts*, c.f. Engeström, 1990). The object towards which the actions are directed, through artifacts, is, on the one hand, ideal and a reflection of the motive of the activity and, on the other hand, a state in the processing of material into an outcome. With this perspective in mind, an artifact may at the same time accommodate and bridge between several interrelated activities (e.g. with different motives but shared or overlapping objects), similar to Star's boundary objects (1989), Robinson's double level language (1991) or Bowers et al.'s formal and informal workflows (1995).

The Hierarchy of Collaborative Activity

We may make analytical distinctions between three levels of collaboration that relate to how participants share motive, object, and orientation toward one another: *co-ordinated*, *co-operative*, and *co-constructive activity* (Engeström, 1987; Engeström et al., 1997; Raeithel, 1996; Bardram, 1998a).

Co-ordinated activity is structured by its common object, while the participants have their own separate mediating artifacts and motive: "*Individuals are gathered together to act upon a common object, but their individual actions are only externally related to each other. They still act as if separate individuals, each according to his individual task*" (Engeström, 1987, p. 333). Within co-operative activity, the object is generally stable and agreed upon by the collaborators, while they do not necessarily share motive and, hence, the artifacts are under negotiation. At the last level, which Raeithel (1996) calls co-construction, the artifacts, as well as the objects, are unstable and the participants take turns producing a communal voice. Engeström et al. (1997) refer to this as reflective communication: "*By reflective communication we mean interactions in which the actors focus on reconceptualizing their own organization and interaction in relation to their shared objects. Both the object and the script are reconceptualized, as is the interaction between the participants.*" (Engeström et al., 1997, p. 373).

Bardram (1998a), elaborates on these levels in order to distinguish between three types of coordination: *communicative*, *instrumental*, and *scripted*. Regarding communicative coordination, he states that "*Coordination of collaboration takes place through communication, including indexical, symbolic, iconic, and conceptual communication*" (ibid., p. 49). Correspondingly, instrumental coordination refers to the way actors coordinate activity through the perceptible actions of other actors through their primary artifacts. Lastly, scripted coordination is made possible when all involved actors share secondary artifacts: "*Such a script for work is embedded in a combination of rules, procedure, protocols, division of work, norms, etc.*" (Bardram, 1998a; p. 51)

In the remainder of the paper, we bring together activity theory and the empirical data from three exploratory design cases, which we present below.

Three Cases

In the following we briefly present the three cases exploring citizen-government collaboration. These cases regard parental leave, citizen service offices, and municipal plans. We draw upon the empirical data from these cases throughout the remainder of the paper.

All three cases involved observations, interviews, and workshops exploring the nature of current collaboration (or lack thereof) combined with a design-oriented exploration of prospective novel patterns of technologically mediated collaboration. Prototypes served as concrete alternatives to current practice, as well as ways of probing the problem area to reveal the anatomy of current and future patterns of cooperation (Bødker and Christiansen, 1997; 2004). Our research approach is grounded in the action-oriented participatory design research tradition, which is strongly influenced by Schön (1983) with respect to reflection in action, as well as micro-sociological thinking, e.g. ethnomethodology and grounded theory, well known in CSCW. All cases were carried out within the eGov+ research project in which we explore the support of novel e-Government services.

Parental Leave

This case study addressed the interaction and collaboration involved in the planning and control of parental leave in a Danish municipality. The planning involves several citizens along with a municipal office and several other stakeholders such as the parents' employers and labor unions. Through a web based timeline artifact the involved actors were supported in communicating and negotiating plans and decisions. We return to a discussion of this timeline in the end of this paper. The iterative development of the timeline prototype was based on observations in municipal offices, and interviews with parents and so-called "mothers' groups". The design process included several design iterations with both paper and software prototypes with groups of citizens and caseworkers. For a thorough discussion of the parental leave case and the design process see Borchorst et al. (2009) and Bohøj et al. (2010).

Citizen Service Offices

The citizen services case took physical citizen service offices as its focal point. Here, we collected data through interviews with citizens and caseworkers, as well as observations and the drawing of heat maps of cooperative activity in the municipal offices. Moreover, we conducted a three-hour workshop with a group of young citizens, age 20-25. With a group of students we developed a number of prototypes suggesting alternatives for citizen-government and citizen-citizen collaboration with a view to citizen empowerment. One example is a tablet device that helped citizens navigate the service provision process by interpreting and helping fill out bureaucratic forms, offering related services according to life situations, and making apparent what other citizens in similar situations had done.

Municipal Plans

The last case explored citizen deliberation in municipal planning through two interconnected prototypes for desktop computers and smartphones respectively. We worked with two primary user groups: citizens and municipal planners. Whereas planners are easily identified, we targeted citizens through two community groups and individual citizens. We conducted in-depth interviews with municipal planners and managers and focus group interviews with the two citizen interest groups. The focus of the case was the different ways for citizens to act and reflect on proposed plans: in-situ, while physically close to the planning object; and ex-situ, when citizens were physically remote from the planning object. The aim was for citizens to engage in continuous reflection in and on action as a collaborative activity with other citizens, hereby creating proposals that municipal workers were better able to process and help turn into concrete changes in the physical environment. For a thorough discussion of the municipal plan case and the design process see Bohøj et al. (2011).

The findings presented in this paper are tied to the investigated empirical contexts. Denmark's renowned welfare model, strong IT infrastructure, and very low corruption levels correspond well with many of the challenges defined by Jaeger and Thompson (2003) as important to to the success e-government services (e.g. accessibility, IT competencies and education). Still, collaboration, democratic responsiveness, and service level uniformity remain challenges to many countries under various types of government. Consequently, albeit cautiously, we would argue for the relevancy of the conclusions brought forward in this paper outside specifically Danish contexts.

Collaboration in Citizen Services

With a foundation in the three exploratory cases, we now turn to a discussion of what we deem to be central challenges to understanding and supporting citizen engagement in digitally mediated citizen-government interactions.

Individual and Organizational Incentives for Collaboration

The distinction between different types of collaborative activity within the current context is especially complex due to the fact that interaction within and with the public sector invariably involves an intricate composition of individual and organizational actors. Several public and private organizations may be involved in the case processes. The many actors involved in parental leave is an example of this. The network of stakeholders involved in the collaborative work is no less complex in countless other citizen services. As expressed by one mother:

> "I think that the biggest difficulty was to figure out where I should send my papers, because I do not have a proper employer. I stopped working before my parental leave and went on unemployment benefits. There were so many instances involved when I was to report all the information. It was very difficult for me to find out how to do that." **Workshop with group of mothers, 28th of May, 2008.**

This complexity renders the concrete configuration of the involved actors' motives and mediating artifacts very hard to unravel for citizens and caseworkers alike. Accordingly, this poses a big challenge to the support of technologically mediated collaboration within these settings.

Collaborators or Representatives?

On the one hand, the intricacies of bureaucratic institutions are often such that numerous municipal employees see and affect any given case process. On the other hand, citizens expect to receive a uniform service regardless of their personal caseworker, as is also the intent of the public administration. However, during the last decade the Danish state has, partly inspired by the thrust of New Public Management, attempted a shift of metaphorical focus towards the citizen, as opposed to the public institutions, being the center of attention. A concrete value in this shift is the idea of citizens' right to meet "a human face" in their interactions with government. Hence, municipal employees walk a fine line between their roles as creative individuals and governmental representatives. This blurring of the motives of the involved actors on both sides of the citizen/caseworker divide severely complicates the actors' ability to understand the nature of the collaboration. While public policy requires for caseworkers to provide a certain service level with a limited amount of resources this may conflict with their own personal definitions of good service, as became apparent in a workshop with parental leave caseworkers:

> "There is a lot of psychology regarding money. [...] People like to have confirmed by a person that they are doing the right thing" **Workshop with caseworkers, 23rd of Jan. 2009.**

The above remark regarded the relation between personal counseling and sending citizens on to explore other information sources, such as online forums. The caseworker was reluctant to encourage citizens to find information from other sources before contacting the municipality, as she thought this was a renunciation of a responsibility of the municipality in a situation where the citizen can be psychologically strained and need to talk to a human being. Consequently, the caseworker preferred counseling every citizen personally, in contrast with the push for cost-effectiveness in the organization.

However, there are also other, somewhat contradictory ways of dealing with responsibility, including that of delegating responsibility to organizations that are trusted for the validity of their legal advice:

"If she [a character in a scenario] is unemployed she has to go to the people who have the information – her employer or her union. If she has no union she's in trouble. [...] If she has no union and no employer she cannot proclaim that she has a good paternity leave agreement!" **Workshop with municipal employees, 28th of Nov. 2008.**

This was supplemented by a middle manager:

"If she is unemployed, she has to see a lawyer about her rights" **Workshop with municipal employees, 28th of Nov. 2008.**

Although the above quotes are examples of the hardliner bureaucratic approach that citizens at times are faced with, the service level provided in the service offices was often of quality that far exceeded official municipal responsibilities. However, this did not necessarily stem from an official service strategy. In one case a citizen asked for EU health cards (often referred to as "blue cards") for all of his family. Counseled by a municipal employee the citizen got a fantastic service, albeit not the one he had expected:

"The caseworker signs the family up for the health cards and returns to the young man: "Can I ask what you all need the cards for?" Young man: "We are going to Turkey on vacation" Caseworker: "The blue card can't be used there and actually it's not of much use anywhere unless one of you has a chronic disease or go abroad for more than three months. What you need is your yellow health card, even though nowadays, you will need insurance for home transport if the worst happens." [...] Caseworker: "[...] you need to think about travel insurance". Young man: "What's a good place for that, you think?" Caseworker: "Well, you need to talk to your insurance company or maybe one of the companies specializing in this. I hear that XX is excellent for price and coverage, but I'm not sure." **Notes from observation in City Hall, 21st of Jan. 2009, 11:40 AM**

The above empirical accounts illustrate the continuum municipal employees have to place themselves within in their interaction with citizens: on the one hand, they act as governmental representatives and are obliged to follow strongly scripted modes of action according to bureaucratic procedure ensuring a swift case process and a uniform level of service: on the other hand, they act as individuals and may creatively choose to adopt more strongly to their personal conception of the situation, i.e. the in situ configuration and alignment of individual needs and motives according to the specific context. This creative space produces a tension between the objectives of the public administration; the collective objective of the citizen and the caseworker oriented towards a common work object; and the respective individual motives of the citizen and the caseworker. The object and artifacts of work are negotiated in situ through the actors' communicative abilities in the reconciliation of their respective motives.

The uncertainty of where governmental actors choose to position themselves within this continuum poses a serious challenge to citizens: Are they creative individuals making self-willed decisions about the level of service, the nature of the collaboration, and the fate of the citizen? Or are they merely governmental representatives executing bureaucratic protocol regarding service models and service quality? In the following, we discuss how this blurring of roles and boundaries challenges collaboration and how it affects the way citizens perceive their own role when interacting with government.

Strategizing on Blurred Boundaries

Arguably, a clear understanding of goals and obligations by the parties involved is a criterion for constructive collaboration in general. Clear boundaries concerning division of work and flow of information are essential to such an understanding. As in the example of a citizen wishing to acquire EU health cards, the majority of citizen services require for citizens to provide certain personal information in order to receive the service that they are entitled to. Another example of this is found within Danish parental leave case processing. Citizens provide information regarding their employer, the nature of their work leading up to the leave period (salary, hours a week), etc. This information is then used by the caseworker to approximate leave circumstances and not least calculate the size of the entitled subsidy. However, as with EU health cards, the information is often also used as a basis for counseling the citizen on his/her options:

> "A young man approaches one of the desks to change his address. He has a wife and some kids. They have moved to a new address and he provides the needed information about family members and the new address. The caseworker swiftly registers the move of the whole family and then looks up: "Actually two people already live at this address at the moment." The young man looks confused: "The ones who are moving out?" They reach to the conclusion that the people registered at the address are the ones who should have moved out. Caseworker: "You need to get in touch with them and ask them to register their move, 'course I assume you still want housing subsidy in the new place?" Young man: "I don't know..." Caseworker: "You have to fill in a new application" Young man: "I thought it would just move with us, since we move to a new flat in the same building" Caseworker: "Well it's a different size flat, isn't it?" The young man leaves with a form for housing subsidy and information about the two people he needs to get in touch with." **Observation, City Hall, 19th of Jan. 2009, 12:37 PM**

The empirical example in several ways corroborates the arguments made in the above sections: Firstly, it exemplifies the caseworkers dual role as counselors and bureaucrats in their relation to the citizen. Secondly, the quote illustrates the complexity of the actors involved in many instances of service provision. In the situation above, two other citizens might end up obstructing the young man in obtaining his housing subsidy. Thirdly, the example underlines how the dual capacity of the municipal employees often confuses citizens. For example, the young citizen might end up receiving a smaller subsidy by providing new information, as required by the caseworker. Hence, citizens may find it hard to define a clear, common objective steering the collaborative activity. In the above case, the employee is in fact oriented towards several simultaneous motives, i.e. controlling and guiding. Some of the actions necessary to reach these two motives overlap and others mesh. However, some actions are conflicting, which forces the caseworkers to continuously prioritize and adjust their actions according to where they position themselves within the continuum between being a collaborator and a governmental representative, in order to resolve the recurring tension created by overlapping motives.

Citizen Approaches to Information Sharing

The caseworkers' continuous adjustments often consign collaborating citizens to a hesitant state. When the governmental employee prioritizes the act of controlling, citizens may inadvertently provide information that worsens their case. Essentially, the problem has to do with understanding the current motives of the involved governmental actor and controlling the flow of information across the boundaries demarcating the collaborative activities. According to how citizens view this complexity, they may adapt very different approaches. Concretely, citizens' willingness to share information can be understood as a continuum comprised by three archetypical approaches: *closing the shutters*, *surrendering*, and *mastering the flow of information*. The approaches used by citizens essentially relate to whether they are able to define the constellation of collaborating actors and their respective motives and artifacts. We elaborate this in the following.

Closing the Shutters

If the collaboration is perceived as inherently adversarial, as discussed by Cohen et al. (2000), the citizen may decide to withhold all information that he/she is not explicitly required to provide by law. This is done in an attempt to avoid weakening one's cause as a product of inadvertently having provided exposing information that might result in a poorer outcome, as in the above example concerning housing subsidy. Typically, this strategy is used by citizens who do not feel they have a clear understanding of the boundaries or the legislation, nor the division of labor in their interaction with the government, as was expressed by one mother:

> "[...] You probably shouldn't give them too much information. What if they tell you: "You know what, then you are not getting any money"? **Workshop with group of mothers, 28th of May, 2008.**

Surrendering

Another approach taken by citizens who do not feel they can comprehend the full complexity of the collaboration is to simply comply to the best of their ability. The citizen lays everything on the table, metaphorically and at times literally, and hopes for the caseworker to favor his/her obligations as a counselor over those of ensuring correct and cost effective case processing. In the citizen service offices we experienced this approach often:

> "Middle-aged woman sits down at the employees' desk. She has brought a large stack of papers, which she hands over. She left her husband and was fired shortly after. She has a bunch of problems and the case seems very complex. She gets daycare subsidy, but the amount is wrong and is based on numbers before she left her husband. She has to pre-pay, but she does not have the money and the amount is bigger than it should be. Municipal employee: "They

have a processing time of 3-4 months." [...] Citizen "It's hard to call so many places! They put you on hold forever! And it's also difficult to figure out the online solutions." The caseworker manages to contact the appropriate public institution directly and apparently settles the problem. Citizen: "Thank you SO much!"'" **Observation, Municipal Office, 29th of Jan. 2009, 2:12PM**

Mastering the Flow of Information

A third archetypical approach is that of citizens 'mastering the game'. They understand their own and the municipal caseworker's role, the objects of work they refer to, and the obligations that adhere to these. They engage in collaboration in order to receive a better service and control the flow of information in such a way that they only provide the exact information needed (and in such a way) that it ensures the best possible service. Moreover, they continuously re-adjust their efforts to fit changing objects of work, available artifacts, and the involved organizational and individual actors.

In the case regarding citizen contributions to municipal plans, we encountered several citizens with intricate knowledge of municipal procedures. One grassroots organization fought to prevent the partitioning of an old camping ground now used as a recreational nature area by the local community. The partitioning of the area for the purposes of building private property would most likely affect the value of the property of several of the associations' members, many of whom had political experience. As a consequence, the association had fought a long and hard battle with the municipality displaying, and making use of, profound insight into bureaucratic procedures and the various latent crystallizations of work practices apparently affecting the process.

At times, citizens display what can almost be perceived as puppeteering of municipal actors, as when one citizen explained how he went about getting his way regarding the aesthetic appearance of renovated old houses in his hometown:

"We had a meeting just prior to the election with the technical chairman at that time. To tell him a little bit about what was going on. [...] We have to make him aware of what they are doing and what the municipality can do. And be careful you don't go too far. We shouldn't tell him EXACTLY what to do, but put pressure on him in such a way that he himself thinks that it's something they need to handle... But we don't provide him with any final solution." **Workshop with citizens, 18th of Jan. 2010.**

The strategies presented above do not only relate to whether citizens understand the motives and artifacts affecting other actors. The approach chosen is also affected by a juxtaposition of effort and gain, i.e. what work goes into understanding the circumstances of the collaborative activities and how does this work measure compared to a prospective gain in the form of a more desirable outcome?

Effort and Gain

As argued by Grudin in his scrutiny of groupware systems, designers of CSCW systems need to carefully consider "*the disparity between who does the work and who gets the benefit*" (Grudin, 1994, p. 96). The tension between contribution and benefit, who sows and who reaps, may change and develop over time. Here, time in itself is an important factor. Certain services are only rarely needed and require relatively little interaction with government (e.g. renewal of various ID cards). In other instances, cases stretch over long periods of time, as in parental leave, or, as described by Bardram (1998b), in cases where citizens act as proxies for ill parents in their prolonged interactions with government. In these instances, citizens' incentives for engaging in collaborative activities with government and investing time in deciphering bureaucratic intricacies increase. Affecting the way in which a public service is provisioned is a convoluted activity and trying to change collaborative activities with governmental actors from one level to another, if possible, (e.g. moving from coordinated to co-operative activity) is a complex and often tiresome affair. Hence, a clear, preferably long-lasting benefit will often be the desideratum for citizens in making the effort needed to understand the anatomy of a given case process and as such acquiring the skills necessary to effect the outcome of their interactions with government, be it understanding the administrative process or appropriating contingent technological tools.

For citizens, the appropriation of such systems put in place to support service provision is comparable to the work of learning the at times opaque bureaucratic rules shaping the interaction. Moreover, these systems may often themselves seem opaque as a result of embedded crystallizations of former work practices and distant political decisions black-boxed to the actors that are affected. This only renders the comprehension of the motives and artifacts driving collaborative activities more difficult to decipher as these have sometimes achieved a tacit status within the governmental organization and, accordingly, within the system.

For example, we learned of a recent self-service solution that turned what used to be a two-page physical form submitted by employers regarding employees' parental leave into a 25-page PDF file of which only four pages were relevant to the processing of the case. This file had to be physically printed and then sorted by the caseworkers. The result of a political decision to improve employers' means of self-service resulted in a significantly increased workload on the caseworkers and, thus, prolonged case processes.

Consequently, a careful consideration of the incentive structures of the involved actors is paramount to understanding and, not least, technologically supporting collaboration in all types of citizen-government interactions.

Perspectives and Design Challenges

In this final section, we summarize the discussion, and relate the arguments made previously to the concrete challenges of designing technology for collaboration in citizen-government interaction. As shown, this collaboration is often of a very complex nature and inherently context-specific. Through our interventions, however, we have been able to establish a number of challenges that seem to apply to citizen-government interaction in a broader sense.

Bridging the Gaps of Collaboration in Participatory Citizenship

The presented empirical examples show that collaboration between citizens and caseworkers and, hence, the notion of Participatory Citizenship has two levels of activity. Accordingly, the actions carried out by citizens as well as caseworkers have dual purposes. One level is that of the specific case or situation that the citizen needs to deal with, be it obtaining a new passport, or receiving parental leave subsidy. Conversely, there exists a second level; learning and reflection. This level is multifarious and potentially encompasses many different activities: improving one's comprehension of the legislation and bureaucratic case processing intricacies so as to act and share information more appropriately in future situations; sharing this knowledge for altruistic purposes; using this knowledge to exercise democratic influence upon the bureaucratic and political system; etc.

A fundamental argument to this analysis is that there exists a double concern for caseworkers, as well as for citizens: providing the individual citizen/couple/family with the service that suits them best, and ensuring a uniform service level complying with legislation. The ultimate motive for citizens is the outcome, e.g. money. The bureaucratic rules and protocols are merely tools (of which the appropriation is time consuming) to achieve this goal. Contrarily, these rules and protocols (which are secondary artifacts to citizens) are the primary for caseworkers. Somewhat cynically put, the parental leave caseworker is essentially not concerned with the amount of money a given citizen receives, as long as this happens according to parental leave legislation, ensuring that the caseworker can defend his or her actions performed in this process. As such, the overall motive of the collaborative activity, and the artifacts used to achieve this, is not agreed upon by the involved actors, creating an inherent tension in citizen-government collaboration within these settings. By this token, citizen-government collaboration may go directly against the Weberian understanding of bureaucracy that is still largely prevalent in today's public institutions. That is, a clear hierarchy; concentration of power among senior officials; formal structures; limited channels of communication; confined openness to innovation; etc. As argued by Vigoda (2002), albeit in a discussion of New Public Management and the notion of citizen responsiveness, these aspects of bureaucracies seem substantially incommensurable with collaborative activities where the citizen can significantly influence the way in which services are provided, i.e. moving towards co-constructive and even co-operative collaboration.

Acknowledging the Tensions in Collaboration

Interaction with government is essentially constituted by actions that citizens wish to limit and is, as such, not a motive in itself. Consequently, supportive technological systems should not increase the work burden of receiving public services, but decrease it. Ironically, this calls for a focus on standardizing citizen-government interactions by moving towards a co-ordinated division of labor. If a clear, common objective ensuring a beneficial alignment of all actor motives were a given this would permit streamlined, effective collaboration through a well-defined division of work and less time spent on the negotiation of the object of work, the common motive, and the artifacts available to achieve this.

Compared to communicative and instrumental actions, scripted actions are very effective as a consequence of the low, or non-existent, need for articulation work. However, the inherent tension between citizen and caseworker motives, which the many empirical examples presented in this paper corroborate, point towards the conclusion that such perfect alignments of actor motives seldom, if ever, exist. Co-ordinated, collaborative activity may be possible within the governmental organization, as the activities here often repeat, and the common motive is often defined from upper levels of the hierarchy, hence, giving the involved actors a chance to develop their knowledge of artifacts over time.

Nevertheless, citizens often engage in interaction with government with a very limited knowledge of the collaborative activity, the rules shaping it, and their possibilities for affecting the activity and the outcome. The first two archetypical strategies to information sharing are salient examples of how citizens somewhat despairingly deal with this knowledge deficit. Neither surrendering, nor closing the shutters are constructive vantage points for fruitful collaboration, and as such do by no means ensure a configuration where all actor needs are accommodated. In fact, the case of citizens surrendering and leaving their fate in the hands of government creates a scenario where object of work and common motive can be exclusively defined by government service models, administrative systems, and latent work practices with no explicit focus on the needs of the single citizen.

Somewhat contrary to basic logic then, the aim for IT systems attempting to support citizen-government collaboration in the provision of more complex services should not be streamlined co-ordinated activity, allowing swift, scripted actions. On the contrary, the aim should be to support co-operative and even co-constructive activity, helping the citizen affect the circumstances of the collaborative activity. This entails a move towards *more* communicative and instrumental actions on behalf of the citizen and certainly also on behalf of the caseworker and other involved governmental actors. Cautioned by the empirical data presented in this paper, it would seem that many of the actions performed by governmental actors are scripted only to the governmental institution, but not to the citizens. Hence, what is perceived as respectively a scripted, communicative or instrumental action differs from actor to actor depending on their knowledge of underlying organizational structures and assumptions. These assumptions do, of course, depend on the complexity of the service in question. Nevertheless, this complexity may seem significantly more manageable to an employee approaching a case grounded in the bureaucratic definition of an isolated service, than it does to a citizen trying to deal with a messy reality. For example, the need to change one's address can be the result of divorce, sudden unemployment, or a variety of other situations resulting in the need of a cluster of services as these are defined and demarcated by the bureaucratic institution.

Returning to the notion of New Public Management and the idea of serving the citizen, this perspective creates an interesting contradiction: A well known deficiency of Weber's iron cage bureaucracy are the negative connotations of the word 'bureaucrats', e.g. employees avoiding individual considerations by hiding behind bureaucratic protocols. Striving for the notion of a human face to the public institution is but one, somewhat vague, approach to addressing this challenge. However, barely any services are carried out in their entirety by single governmental employees. Hence, it is seldom feasible for caseworkers and citizens to share a clear focus, i.e. agree upon the ultimate outcome of the service provision process. Consequently, we suggest that the aim of design for public service provision should not be a common focus on the outcome of the activity as such. On the contrary, design should aim to support a more shared, transparent, and accessible understanding of the case process, i.e. the involved actors and the bureaucratic rules shaping the actions carried out by bureaucratic actors. Such a shared understanding would serve as a critical instrument for collaboration between citizens and caseworkers, by supporting a more equal configuration of the collaboration in the form of a more symmetrical alignment of actor motives within the case process. Such a focus for organizational and technological design would, arguably, be much more feasible than to demand that the focus of all actors involved should be on the overall outcome of the activity.

Addressing Challenges through Design

Within the presented case regarding parental leave, the authors were engaged in a concrete design process addressing the challenges presented in this paper. Concretely, this was approached by way of an exploratory prototype designed to support the planning and applying for parental leave (Figure 1).

The aim of the timeline was to support the handling of a particular case, while helping citizens explore the rules and share their findings and decisions with others in a similar situation. The prototype allowed for interaction and counseling between citizens and caseworkers, while also representing the rules and roles of the municipality, and other actors involved (e.g. the parents' unions). In (Borchorst et al., 2009, Bohøj et al., 2010) we proposed that this prototype could support the sharing of plans and ideas between parental leave takers in general and within their networks of friends and family.

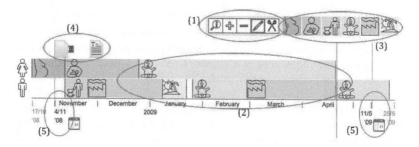

Figure 1. The timeline can be manipulated with the tools in the upper right corner (1). The leave plans for the mother and the father are displayed on the vertical lines (2), upon which the different leave modules can be dragged from the leave time bank (3). Events, such as application documents (4) are indicated by way of different icons. For example, a document can be partially completed, submitted to the municipality etc. Lastly, the citizens can move in time (5) to see the progression of the leave plan, and explore the relations between time and money.

Comparing the timeline and the arguments made in this paper, the prototype can be understood as a concrete exploration of the challenges addressed in this paper: For one, it addresses the citizen strategies to information sharing in complex and changing constellations of actors, as well as the dynamic configuration of boundaries necessary to control changing needs for information sharing across time. Secondly, this support of boundary management and information sharing helps to address the tension between the motives of the collaborating actors, essentially, by rendering these motives more comprehensible to the involved actors. As such, the timeline helps mitigate the discrepancy between these motives, and the artifacts available to achieve these, by functioning as a common tool through which both citizens and caseworkers can each explore their main object; the funding, and the rules respectively. Lastly, it supports a shared understanding of the rules and procedures of the involved actors, while also yielding a shared understanding of the ultimate outcome of the process, parental leave timing and financing.

We propose to see the timeline prototype as a seed for a more general development of technology for citizen service provision. Considering this remedy within the context of "simpler" citizen services such as moving one's address, or receiving EU health cards, it seems necessary to emphasize that such services should not necessarily be understood as simple at face value. As argued, moving one's address, or traveling can account for complex situations in life. Hence, the case process and bureaucratic protocols steering this still need to be rendered clear. As should those of related processes and services, such as housing subsidies along with the possibilities for other private and public actors (e.g. unions, the post office, etc.) enrolled in these interactions.

The Implications of Participatory Citizenship

In the beginning of this paper we defined Participatory Citizenship as the act of citizens actively engaging in and contributing to the provision of public services in order to improve these services for themselves and other citizens. Although it seems there are clear advantages to this kind of citizen empowerment and community knowledge sharing (Bryant, 2005; Marlow et al. 2006), there is a great difference between attempting to support such collaboration within respectively private and public settings. Hence, the notion of Participatory Citizenship raises a number of political, economical, technological, and normative issues.

For one, the resources for supporting an improved level of service through collaboration must still be found in the public administration budget. For private service providers improved service will likely entail more customers, with a resulting increase in profits. However, for public institutions, more customers invariably entail increased expenses. A municipality is not economically rewarded by the state for providing a service of a better quality, sometimes even the contrary. Consequently, some services only exist because all citizens do not take advantage of them. If all citizens were to do so, there would simply not be sufficient administrative resources to maintain the same level of service for all. As such, too attractive, flexible, services may distort a democratically fair distribution of resources, leaving less resourceful citizens behind.

It can, however, be argued that this is already the case. One example corroborating this claim is found in the empirical data from the parental leave case. Here, we learned that most citizens displaying abilities comparable to "mastering the flow of information" i.e. making full use of the complex, but flexible legislation, were more often than not well educated and resourceful. This begs the question of whether design within this field should also be concerned with equal distribution of resources, effectively educating citizens in democratic thoughtfulness. To the authors of this paper it does not seem viable for systems to aim at inhibiting the single citizen's ability to improve his or her personal circumstances by imposing moral values of equal distribution of resources. Contrarily, it seems a much more fruitful approach would be to focus on the notions of bureaucratic transparency and citizen-citizen knowledge sharing as discussed in this paper; supporting citizens in helping themselves and each other, hereby also potentially lessening the administrative burden on the public administration.

Cautioned by this discussion, it seems clear that creating good design within the arena of citizen-government interaction is still an important challenge. As we have shown in this paper, actor motives within the sphere of public service provision are complex and potentially incommensurable. That which is user-friendly, adaptable, and transparent may not necessarily be economically or democratically viable. Hence, the counterbalancing of stakeholder needs is a generic design challenge, which inherently calls for local solutions and hard compromises. There are no quick fixes to this challenge and what stands in the way might very well be complex national legislation, which is not effortlessly commensurable with digital service provision and digitally mediated collaboration.

As a consequence of our concerns in this paper, we would argue that the greatly hyped dynamics of participatory culture on the Internet (Barney, 2000) and Web 2.0 service models (Amazon, Facebook, etc.) are not easily applicable to the sphere of e-Governance and public service provision. Firstly, the web-based discussions of rules, possibilities, etc., currently taking place typically do so detached from public institutions. Because municipalities are concerned with the validity of the information provided within these web-forums, and the degree to which they will be held accountable for that validity, they, hesitate in getting involved. At the same time, it is not obvious whether citizens at large are essentially interested in the discussion of bureaucratic rules. Arguably, only very few citizens will have an incentive to do the work necessary to master the flow of information. Secondly, the mentioned web-forums do not yield access to the state of municipal processes, nor do they reflect the public institutions' underlying rules and procedures. Thirdly, for public institutions to contribute to such forums would entail the considerations of a number of potentially negative implications. It is, however, safe to say that information *will* be shared and collaboration *will* take place – also within the realm of citizen services. The only question remaining is who is left on the sidelines?

Acknowledgements

The authors would like to thank municipal caseworkers, citizens and project group members for their contributions to the case studies. The eGov+ project is financed through the Danish Strategic Research Council.

References

Bannon, L. and Schmidt, K. (1991): 'CSCW, four characters in search of a context', in J.M. Bowers and S.D. Benford (eds.): *Studies in computer supported cooperative work*. North-Holland, Amsterdam, pp. 3-16.

Bardram, J. (1998a): *Collaboration, Coordination, and Computer Support-An Activity Theoretical Approach to the Design of Computer Supported Cooperative Work*, Dissertation Aarhus University.

Bardram, J. (1998b): 'Designing for the dynamics of cooperative work activities'. *Proceedings of the ACM CSCW '98*. ACM Press, New York, NY, pp. 89–98.

Barney, D. (2000): *Prometheus Wired: The Hope for Democracy in the Age of Network Technology*. University of Chicago Press, Chicago.

Bertelsen, O.W. and Bødker, S. (2001): 'Cooperation in massively distributed information spaces.' *ECSCW 2001: Proceedings of the Seventh European Conference on Computer Supported Cooperative Work*. Kluwer, Dordrecht, pp. 1-18.

Bohøj, M., Borchorst, N.G., Bouvin, N., Bødker, S. and Zander, P.-O. (2010): 'Timeline collaboration.' *CHI 2010*, pp. 523-532, ACM Press.

Bohøj, M., Borchorst, N.G., Bødker, S., Korn, M. and Zander, P.-O. (2011): 'Public deliberation in municipal planning: supporting action and reflection with mobile technology,' *ACM Communities and Technologies*, in press.

Borchorst, N.G., Bødker, S. and Zander, P.-O. (2009): ,Participatory citizenship', *ECSCW 2009: Proceedings of the Seventh European Conference on Computer Supported Cooperative Work*, Kluwer, Dordrecht, pp. 1-20.

Bowers, J. Button, G. and Sharrock, W. (1995): 'Workflow from within and without: technology and cooperative work on the print industry shopfloor.' *Proceedings of the fourth conference on European Conference on Computer-Supported Cooperative Work (ECSCW'95)*. Kluwer Dordrecht, pp. 51-66.

Bryant, S. L., Forte, A. and Bruckman, A. (2005): 'Becoming Wikipedian: Transformation of participation in a collaborative online encyclopedia.' *Proceedings of GROUP*, ACM Press, NY, pp. 1-10.

Bowker, G.C. and Star, S.L. (1999): *Sorting Things Out. Classification and its Consequences*, MIT Press, Cambridge MA.

Bødker, S. and Grønbæk, K. (1995): 'Users and Designers in Mutual Activity- an analysis of cooperative activities in systems design,' in Y. Engeström and D. Middleton (Eds.). *Cognition and Communication at Work*, Cambridge University Press, Cambridge UK, pp 130-158.

Bødker, S. and Christiansen, E. (1997): 'Scenarios as springboards in design.,' in Bowker, G., Gasser, L., Star, S.L. and Turner, W. (eds.). *Social science research, technical systems and cooperative work*. Erlbaum, Mahwah NJ, pp. 217-234.

Bødker, S. and Christiansen, E. (2004): 'Designing for ephemerality and prototypicality.' *Proceedings of the 2004 conference on Designing interactive systems: processes, practices, methods, and techniques*, pp. 255 - 260.

Bødker, S. and Klokmose, C.N. (2011): 'The Human-Artifact Model,' accepted for publication in *HCI Journal*.

Clement, A. and Wagner, I. (1995): 'Fragmented exchange: Disarticulation and the need for regionalized communication spaces.' *Proceedings of ECSCW '95*, Kluwer, Amsterdam, pp. 33-49.

Cohen, A.L., Cash, D. and Muller, M.J. (2000): 'Designing to support adversarial collaboration.' *Proceedings of CSCW 2000*, ACM Press, New York, NY, pp. 31-39.

Engeström, Y. (1987): *Learning by Expanding: An activity-theoretical approach to developmental research*, Orienta-Konsultit, Helsinki.

Engeström, Y. (1990): *Learning Working and Imagining. Twelve Studies in Activity Theory*. Orienta-Konsultit, Helsinki.

Engeström, Y., Brown, K., Christopher, L. and Gregory, J. (1997). 'Coordination, Cooperation, and Communication in the courts. 'In Cole, M., Engeström, Y., and Vasquez, O. (Eds.) *Mind, Culture, and Activity*, Cambridge University Press, Cambridge UK, pp. 369–385.

Engeström, Y., Engeström, R. and Saarelma, O. (1988): 'Computerized medical records, production pressure and compartmentalization in the work activity of health center physicians.' *Proceedings of CSCW '88*. ACM, New York, NY, pp. 65-84.

Greenbaum, J. and Kyng, M. (eds.) (1991): *Design at Work: Cooperative Design of Computer Systems*. Erlbaum, Hillsdale, NJ.

Grudin, J. (1994): 'Groupware and social dynamics: eight challenges for developers..' *Communications of the ACM*, 37, 1 pp. 92-105.

Jaeger, P. T. and Thompson, M. (2003): 'E-government around the world: Lessons, challenges, and future directions.' *Government Information Quarterly* 20, pp. 389–394.

Kling, R. (1991): 'Cooperation, coordination and control in computer-supported work.' *Communications of the ACM*. 34 (12), pp. 83-88.

Kuutti, K. (1991): 'The concept of activity as a basic unit of analysis for CSCW research.' *Proceedings of ECSCW'91*. Kluwer, Dordrecht, pp. 249-264.

Lave, J. and Wenger, E. (1991): *Situated Learning: Legitimate Peripheral Participation*. Cambridge University Press, Cambridge UK.

Marlow, C., Naaman, M., Boyd, D. and Davis, M. (2006). HT06, Tagging Paper, Taxonomy, Flickr, Academic Article, ToRead. *Proc. Hypertext '06*, ACM Press, New York, NY, pp 31-40.

Osimo, D. (2008): *Web 2.0 in government: why and how?* Technical Report. JRC, EUR 23358, EC JRC.

Raeithel, A. (1996): 'From coordinatedness to Coordination via Cooperation and Co-construction.' *Workshop on Work and Learning in Transition*, San Diego, January.

Schmidt, K and Bannon, L. (1992): 'Taking CSCW Seriously: Supporting Articulation Work.' *JCSCW*, Vol. 1, Nos. 1-2, 7-40.

Schön, D. (1983): *The Reflective Practitioner. How Professionals Think in Action*. Temple Smith, London.

Robinson, M. (1991): 'Double-level languages and co-operative working.' *AI and Society*, 5(1), pp. 34-60 Springer London.

Star, S.L. (1989): 'The structure of Ill-Structured Solutions: Boundary Objects and Heterogeneous Distributed Problem solving'. *Distributed Artificial Intelligence*, volume II, chapter 3, Morgan Kaufmann, San Francisco, CA, pp. 37–54.

Star, S.L. (1996): 'Working together: symbolic interactionism, activity theory, and information systems.' Engeström, Y. and Middleton D. (Eds.). *Cognition and Communication at Work*, Cambridge University Press, Cambridge UK, pp. 296-318.

Vigoda, E. (2002): 'From responsiveness to collaboration: Governance, citizens, and the next generation of public administration.' *Public Administration Review*, 62(5), pp. 527-540.

Westheimer, J. and Kahne, J. (2004): 'Educating the "Good" Citizen: Political Choices and Pedagogical Goals.' *Political Science and Politics*, pp. 241–247

Theories of cognition in CSCW

Gerry Stahl
The iSchool, Drexel University, Philadelphia, USA
Gerry@GerryStahl.net

Abstract. There are many theories useful for framing CSCW research and they may in principle be irreducible to a single theory. CSCW research explores questions involving numerous distinct—though interacting—phenomena at multiple levels of description. The useful approach may be to clearly distinguish levels such as individual, small-group and community units of analysis, and to differentiate terminology for discussing these different levels. Theory in general has evolved dramatically over the ages, with a trend to extend the unit of cognition beyond the single idea or even the individual mind. Seminal theoretical works influential within CSCW suggest a post-cognitive approach to group cognition as a complement to analyzing cognition of individuals and of communities of practice.

Introduction

There is no one theory for CSCW. Research in CSCW is guided by and contributes to a diverse collection of theories. Even the word *theory* means different things to different CSCW researchers and plays various distinct roles within CSCW work. The reading of the history of theory presented here is itself reflective of one theoretical stance among many held, implicitly or explicitly, by CSCW researchers.

The nature and uses of theory have changed over history and continue to evolve. The theories most relevant to CSCW—in the view developed in this paper—concern the nature of cognition, specifically cognition in cooperating groups. Through history, the analysis of cognition has broadened, from a focus on single concepts (Platonic ideas) or isolated responses to stimulae (behaviorism), to a concern with mental models (cognitivism) and representational artifacts (post-cognitivism). More recent theories encompass cognition distributed across people and tools, situated in contexts, spanning small groups, involved in larger activities and across communities of practice. For CSCW, theory must take into account interaction in online environments, knowledge building in small groups and cognition at multiple units of analysis.

A brief history of theory

CSCW is multi-disciplinary by its nature and because of its origins. Consider the name, *Computer-supported Cooperative Work*: it combines concerns with *computer* technology, *cooperative* social interaction and *work*—very different sorts of scientific domains. CSCW grew out of research in fields like sociology, anthropology, informatics, artificial intelligence, cognitive science and social psychology—domains that are themselves each fundamentally multidisciplinary. Theory in these fields may take the form of predictive mathematical *laws*, like Shannon's (1949) mathematical theory of information or Turing's (1937) theory of computation; of *models* of memory and cognition; or of *conceptions* of group interaction and social practice. They may have very different implications for research: favoring either laboratory experiments that establish statistical regularities or engaged case studies that contribute to an understanding of situated behaviors.

In the European tradition, theory begins with the ancient Greeks—especially Socrates, Plato and Aristotle—and continues through the 2,500-year-long discourse of philosophy. In recent times, theory has veered into unexpected directions as it has morphed into sciences based more on empirical research than on intellectual reflection. For instance, the work of Freud, Darwin and Marx replaced traditional philosophic assumptions about fixed natures of minds, organisms and societies with much more dynamic views. Theory always transcended the opinions of common sense—so-called *folk theories* based on the everyday experience of individuals—to synthesize broader views. But folk theories have also changed over time as they adopt popularized pieces of past theories; thus, a trained ear can hear echoes of previous theories in the assumptions of common-sense perspectives, including in current CSCW research literature.

After the dogmatic centuries of the medieval period, philosophy took some significant turns: the rationalism of Descartes, the empiricism of Hume, the Copernican revolution of Kant, the dialectical development of Hegel, the social situating of Marx, the existential grounding of Heidegger and the linguistic turn of Wittgenstein. These all eventually led to important influences on theory in CSCW and the disciplines that contributed to it.

In particular, empiricism and positivism in philosophy of science culminated in behaviorism in biology and the human sciences. The central metaphor was that of *stimulus* provoking *response*, all objectively observable and unambiguously measurable (as critiqued in Chomsky, 1959). The major theoretical move of the generation before ours was to assert the necessity of taking into account cognitive processes in studying human behavior, from Chomsky's (1969) theories of language based on deep grammar and brain mechanisms to the mental models and internal representations modeled by artificial intelligence programs. Human-computer interaction, the part of computer science dealing with designing for usage, has gone through a similar sequence of behaviorist and cognitivist theories (see Carroll, 2003, for numerous examples). More recently, post-cognitive theories have been influential in CSCW, as will be discussed later.

The unit of analysis

The history of theory can be tracked in terms of the following issue: At what unit of analysis should one study thought (*cognition*)? For Plato (340 BC/1941), in addition to the physical objects in the world, there are concepts that characterize those objects; philosophy is the analysis of such concepts, like *goodness*, *truth*, *beauty* or *justice*. Descartes (1633/1999) argued that if there is thought, then there must be a mind that thinks it, and that philosophy should analyze both the mental objects of the mind and the material objects to which they refer, as well as the relation between them. Following Descartes, rationalism focused on the logical nature of mental reasoning, while empiricism focused on the analysis of observable physical objects. Kant (1787/1999) re-centered this discussion by arguing that the mechanisms of human understanding provided the source of the apparent spatio-temporal nature of observed objects and that critical theory's task was to analyze the mind's structuring categorization efforts. Up to this point in the history of theory, cognition was assumed to be an innate function of the individual human mind.

Hegel (1807/1967) changed that. He traced the logical/historical development of cognition (*Geist*) from the most primary instinct of a living organism through stages of consciousness, self-consciousness and historical consciousness to the most developed trans-national spirit of the times (*Zeitgeist*). To analyze cognition henceforth, it is necessary to follow its biological unfolding through to the ultimate cultural understanding of a society. Figure 1 identifies Hegel's approach to theory as forming the dividing line between philosophies or theories oriented on the individual and those oriented to a larger unit of analysis.

Philosophy after Hegel can be viewed as forming three mainstreams of thought, following the seminal approaches of Marx (critical social theory), Heidegger (existential phenomenology) and Wittgenstein (linguistic analysis). As taken up within CSCW, one can trace how these approaches established expanded units of analysis.

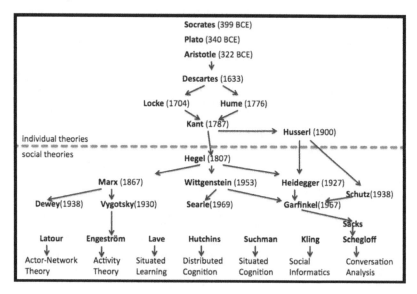

Figure 1. Adapted from (Stahl, 2006, p. 289, Fig 14-1).

Marx (1867) applauded Hegel's recognition of the historical self-generation of mankind and analyzed this historical process in terms of the dialectical co-development of the social relations of production and the forces of production. His analysis took the form of historical, political and economic studies of the world-historical processes by which human labor produces and reproduces social institutions. Here, the study of the human mind and its understanding of its objects becomes focused at the epochal unit of analysis of social movements, class conflicts and transformations of economic systems.

Heidegger (1927/1996) radicalized the Hegelian dialectic between man and nature by starting the analysis of man from the unified experience of *being-in-the-world*. The Cartesian problem of a distinction between an observing mind and an objective world was thereby reversed. Heidegger, instead, had to show how the appearance of isolated minds and an external world could arise through abstraction from the primary experience of being-there, human existence inseparable from the worldly objects that one cares for and that define one's activity. The primordial unit of analysis of cognition is engaged and situated *caring*, the involvement of people in their world.

Wittgenstein (1953) focused increasingly on language as it is used to accomplish things in the world through interpersonal communication. He rejected his own early view (Wittgenstein, 1921/1974), which reduced a rationalist conception of propositional, logical language to a self-contradictory position. Now, linguistic meaning no longer dwelt in the heads of users or the definitions of the words, but in communicational usage. Echoing the *lived world* of phenomenology, Wittgenstein acknowledged the role of the human *form of life*. He also conceptualized language as the playing of *language games*, socially established forms of interaction. The unit of analysis shifted from mental meanings to interpersonal communications in the context of getting something done together.

Marx, Heidegger and Wittgenstein initiated the main forms of post-Kantian, post-Hegelian philosophy and scientific theory (Stahl, 2010c). Kant represents the culmination of the philosophy of mind, in which the human mind is seen as the active constructor of reality out of its confrontation with the objects of nature, which are unknowable except through this imposition of human structuring categories. With Kant—over two hundred years ago—the human mind is still a fixed unit consisting of innate abilities of the individual person, despite how much his philosophy differs from naïve realist folk theories, which accept the world as fundamentally identical with its appearance to the human observer. Hegel overthrows the Kantian view of a fixed nature of mind by showing how the mind has itself been constructed through long sequences of processes. The Hegelian construction of mind can be understood in multiple senses: as the biological development of the brain's abilities as it grows from newborn to mature adult; as the logical development from simple contrast of *being* and *non-being* to the proliferation of all the distinctions of the most sophisticated understanding; or as the historical development from primitive homo sapiens to modern, civilized, technological and cultured person. After Hegel, theory shifted from philosophy to science, to explore the biological, logical and historical processes in more detail and to verify them empirically. Followers of Marx, Heidegger and Wittgenstein adopted approaches to this that can be characterized as *social*, *situated* and *linguistic*. They are all constructivist, following Kant's insight that the structure of known objects is constructed by the knowing mind. However, they all focus on a unit of analysis broader than the isolated individual mind of Descartes.

Seminal theories for CSCW

The social, situated and linguistic theories of Marx, Heidegger and Wittgenstein entered the discourse of CSCW literature with researchers coming from the various scientific traditions that went into forming CSCW as a research domain, including psychology, anthropology, communications, sociology, design studies, computer science and artificial intelligence (e.g., Dourish, 2001; Ehn, 1988; Floyd, 1992; Schön, 1983, Suchman, 1987). Although these fields each introduced various theoretical perspectives, we can see the major philosophic influences largely through several seminal texts: *Mind in Society* (Vygotsky, 1930/1978), *Situated Learning* (Lave & Wenger, 1991), *Lectures on Conversation* (Sacks, 1962/1995) and *Understanding Computers and Cognition* (Winograd & Flores, 1986).

Mind in Society is an edited compilation of Vygotsky's writings from the early 1930s in post-revolutionary Russia, which has been influential in the West since it appeared in English in 1978. Critiquing the prevailing psychology as practiced by behaviorists, Gestaltists and Piaget, Vygotsky did not try to fit psychology superficially into the dogmatic principles of Soviet Marxism, but rather radically rethought the nature of human psychological capabilities from the developmental approach proposed by Hegel and Marx. He showed how human perception, attention, memory, thought, play and learning (the so-called mental faculties) were products of developmental processes—in terms of both maturation of individuals and the social history of cultures. He proposed a dynamic vision of the human mind in society, as opposed to a fixed and isolated function. The Hegelian term, *mediation*, was important for Vygotsky, as it is for CSCW. Even in his early years still talking about stimulus and response, he asked how one stimulus could mediate the memory of, attention toward or word retrieval about another stimulus (Vygotsky, 1930/1978, p. iii). In Hegelian terms, this is a matter of mediating (with the first stimulus) the relation (memory, attention, retrieval) of a subject to an object (the second stimulus). This is central to CSCW because there the work is mediated by technological networking as well as by cooperative interaction, so analysis of cognition has to include the mediating technology and the cooperating partners.

Situated Learning went beyond Vygotsky in expanding the unit of analysis for learning. For Vygotsky and his followers, analysis must include the mediating artifact (tool or word) and the peer or group. For Lave & Wenger, the unit of analysis is a larger community of practice. Adopting the theoretical and analytical centrality of social practices in Marx, they focused on learning as the development of processes and relationships within the community in which individuals participated. Learning was viewed on the model of apprenticeship, in which an individual gradually—and primarily tacitly—adopts the practices that are established within the community in which the individual is becoming a member. Within CSCW, this approach can be seen in the idea that cognition is an aspect of social practices as developed by and engaged in by a community.

Lectures on Conversation laid the cornerstone of Conversation Analysis (CA), which studies the linguistic practices of communities. It was based on the ethnomethodological (Garfinkel, 1967) perspective, grounded in both Wittgenstein's linguistic analysis and Heidegger's (1927/1996) and Husserl's (1936/1989) phenomenological approach. Like Wittgenstein, CA analyzed language at a unit larger than the isolated word or speech act. CA focuses on *adjacency pairs* used in conversation (see Schegloff, 2007 for a systematic presentation based on 40 years of research by the CA community on adjacency-pair structure). An adjacency pair is a sequence of two or three utterances that elicit or respond to each other, such as a question and answer. The significance of the adjacency pair *as a unit of analysis* is that it includes contributions by both people involved in an interaction, and thereby avoids treating speech as an expression of an individual mind. This is analogous to Marx' (1867) focus on the act of commodity exchange between two people as a unit of interaction in contrast to theories that dwell on rational decisions of an individual. What is important in CA is the mode of interaction carried out by the adjacency pair situated in its on-going, sequential discourse context. This should be contrasted with approaches that code isolated utterances based on assumptions about mental models inside the individual mind of the speaker. A CA analysis explicates how a dyad or small group builds upon and solicits each other's contributions, thus providing insight into cooperation patterns. In a sense, the CA unit of analysis is not simply the adjacency pair, which includes multiple speakers, but the linguistic community, which establishes the member methods underlying adjacency-pair practices.

Understanding Computers and Cognition presented a Heideggerian critique of the rationalist foundations of artificial intelligence by a leading AI researcher. The book reviews three theories that endorse contextual analysis: Heidegger's (1927/1996) situated being-in-the-world, Gadamer's (1960/1988) historically grounded conception of interpretation and Maturana's (1987) ecological version of cognition. These theories emphasize the inseparability of the mind from its larger context: human being engaged in the world, interpretation oriented within the horizon of history and the organism bound in a structural coupling with its environment. In contrast, AI software represents mental functions as isolatable units of rational computation, which in principle cannot capture the richness and complexity of situated human cognition and cooperation. The larger, primarily *tacit* (Polanyi, 1966) unit of context cannot be adequately represented in a computer system (Stahl, 2010d). Accordingly, the role of computer software should be to support human interaction and collaboration, rather than to replace or fully model human cognition.

The writings of Vygotsky, Lave & Wenger and Sacks further develop the perspectives of Marx, Heidegger and Wittgenstein that cognition is social, situated and linguistic. Winograd—like others, including Ehn and Dourish—reviews the foundational post-cognitive theories and considers the implications for computer-supported cooperation. But these theories can be—and have been—taken in different directions by CSCW researchers when it comes time to follow their implications for research conceptualizations and methods. These directions can perhaps best be seen in terms of alternative theories of individual, small-group and community cognition in CSCW research.

Theories of individual cognition in CSCW

Many research questions within CSCW involve individual cognition. CSCW research is often treated as a sub-discipline of social-psychological research, oriented to the mind of the individual participant, within group contexts. Such research can follow traditional scientific research paradigms based on pre-Kantian empiricism (Hume) and/or rationalism (Locke). CSCW research often adopts a constructivist approach, based on the Kantian principle that the individual constructs his or her own understanding of reality. Such constructivist theory is cognitivist, in that it involves assumptions about cognitive processes in the mind of the individual underlying their observed behaviors.

Work within CSCW certainly acknowledges the importance of the larger social, historical and cultural context. However, it often treats this context as a set of environmental variables that may influence the outcomes of individual cognition, but are separable from that cognition. In this way, cognition is still treated as a function of an individual mind. This approach may be called *socio-cognitive*. It acknowledges social influences, but tries to isolate the individual mind as a cognitive unit of analysis by controlling for these external influences.

Followers of Vygotsky, by contrast, are considered *socio-cultural*. They recognize that cognition is mediated by cultural factors. Yet, they still generally focus on the individual as the unit of analysis. They investigate how individual cognition is affected by cultural mediations, such as representational artifacts or even by cooperative interactions. Vygotsky himself—who was after all a psychologist—generally discussed the individual subject. For instance, his concept of the zone of proximal development measured an individual's ability when working in a group, not the group's ability as such. Vygotsky was trying to demonstrate that individual cognition was derivative of social or intersubjective experiences of the individual, and so his focus was on the individual rather than explicitly on the social or intersubjective processes in which the individual was involved.

In this sense, much CSCW research investigates individual cognition in settings of cooperation. If one looks closely at most studies—e.g., in social psychology or management—that claim to be about small-group interaction, one finds that they adopt this kind of focus on the individual within a group setting and treat the group interaction as an external influence on the individual.

An example of a theory of individual cognition is psycho-linguistic contribution theory (Clark & Brennan, 1991). This particular paper is often cited in CSCW literature. Although the paper claims to be in the Conversation Analysis tradition, it translates the adjacency-pair structure of grounding shared understanding into the contributions of the individuals. It analyzes the individual contributions as expressions of their mental representations or personal beliefs and treats the resultant *shared understanding* as a matter of similar mental contents or acceptance of pre-conceived beliefs rather than as a negotiated group product of co-constructed meaning making. In a later paper, Clark (1996) tries to unite cognitivism with Conversation Analysis, but he still analyzes the situated, engaged interaction as an exchange of signals between rationally calculating minds, who identify deliberate actions based on "knowledge, beliefs and suppositions they believe they share" (Clark, 1996, p. 12). Interestingly, Clark concludes in favor of recognizing two independent theories with different units of analysis (the individual or the community, but ironically not the small group): "The study of language use must be both a cognitive and a social science" (p. 25).

Theories of community cognition in CSCW

In striking contrast to the steadfast focus on the individual as the unit of analysis is the social-science perspective on social processes. Marx provided a good example of this. Where economists of his day analyzed economic phenomena in terms of rational choices of individual producers and consumers, Marx critiqued the ideology of individualism and analyzed sweeping societal transformations such as urbanization, the formation of the proletariat, the rise of the factory system and the drive of technological innovation. Lave & Wenger (1991) brought this approach to CSCW, showing for instance how an apprenticeship training system reproduces itself as novices are transformed into experts, mentors and masters. Increasing expertise is seen as situated or embedded in this process of the production and reproduction of structures of socially defined knowledge and power.

The theoretical importance of the *situation* in which learning takes place is widely acknowledged in CSCW. Suchman (1987) demonstrated its centrality for human-computer interaction from an anthropological perspective heavily influenced by both Heidegger (via Dreyfus) and Garfinkel, leading to conclusions similar to Winograd's. Suchman and Nardi have helped to establish ethnographic methods—oriented to community phenomena—as relevant to CSCW research. Unfortunately, even perspectives like situated cognition can take a reductive turn: Recent commentaries on situated cognition (Robbins & Aydede, 2009) and distributed cognition (Adams & Aizawa, 2008) frame the issues at the individual level, to the extreme of reducing all cognitive phenomena to neural functions.

Building on Vygotsky and his Russian colleagues, Activity Theory (Engeström, 1987; Engeström, 1999; Kaptelinin & Nardi, 2006) insists on taking an entire activity system as the unit of analysis. In his triangular analysis rubric, Engeström extends Vygotsky's mediation triple of subject, mediator and object to include mediating dimensions from Marx's theory: the division of labor, the rules of social relations and the community of productive forces. Like discourse analysis (Gee, 1992), activity theory is repeatedly looking at small-group interactions but only seeing the larger, societal issues. For instance, when activity theory addresses the study of teams in the most detail in Chapter 6 of (Engeström, 2008), it is mostly concerned with the group's situation in the larger industrial and historic context; rather than analyzing how an analyzed group interactionally builds knowledge it paraphrases how the group deals politically with organizational management issues.

There is something of this avoidance of the small group as the scientific focus in other theories popular in CSCW as well, for instance even in distributed cognition. In defining statements of post-cognitivist theory, Hutchins has indeed explicitly pointed to group-cognitive phenomena:

- "Cognitive processes may be distributed across the members of a social group" (Hollan, Hutchins & Kirsh, 2000, p. 176).
- "The cognitive properties of groups are produced by interaction between structures internal to individuals and structures external to individuals" (Hutchins, 1996, p. 262).
- "The group performing the cognitive task may have cognitive properties that differ from the cognitive properties of any individual" (Hutchins, 1996, p.176).

However, rather than focusing on these group phenomena in detail, he prefers to analyze socio-technical systems and the cognitive role of highly developed artifacts (e.g., airplane cockpits, ship navigation tools). Certainly, these artifacts have encapsulated past cultural knowledge (community cognition), and Hutchins' discussions of this are insightful. But in focusing on what is really the community level—characteristically for a cultural anthropologist—he does not generally analyze the cognitive meaning making of the group itself (but see his analysis of group or organizational learning in Chapter 8 of Hutchins, 1996, for an impressive exception).

Even ethnomethodology (Garfinkel, 1967; 2006) and conversation analysis (Sacks, 1962/1995; Sacks, Schegloff & Jefferson, 1974; Schegloff, 2007) consider themselves social sciences, versions of sociology or communication studies, but not sciences of the small-group unit of analysis. They aim to analyze social practices, defined across a whole society or linguistic community. This may be a quibble over words, for they do in fact define many important processes at the group unit, although they call them *social*. Vygotsky, too, used the term *social* in an ambiguous way when he said that learning takes place socially first and then later individually. *Socially* can refer to two people talking as well as to transformations of whole societies. But for the sake of distinguishing levels of description or units of analysis in CSCW, it seems important to make clear distinctions. Table 1 suggests sets of different terms for referring to phenomena at the individual, small-group and societal levels. The distinction of these three levels is argued for by (Rogoff, 1995), (Dillenbourg et al., 1996), (Stahl, 2006) and others in CSCW and CSCL. We start with these three levels, which seem particularly central to much of CSCW work, although other levels might also usefully be distinguished, such as "collective intelligence" or "collective practices" (Guribye, 2005; Jones, Dirckinck-Holmfeld & Lindström, 2006; Looi et al., 2011). Perhaps consistent usage of such terminological distinctions would lend clarity to the discussion of theories in CSCW.

Table 1. Terminology for phenomena at the individual, small-group and community levels of description. Adapted from (Stahl, 2010a, p. 27, Table 2.1).

Level of description	Individual	Small group	Community
Role	Person / worker / student	Group participant	Community member
Adjective	Personal	Collaborative	Social
Object of analysis	Mind	Discourse	Culture
Unit of analysis	Mental representation	Utterance response pair	Socio-technical activity system, mediating artifacts
Form of knowledge	Subjective	Intersubjective	Cultural
Form of meaning	Interpretation	Shared understanding, joint meaning making, common ground	Domain vocabulary, artifacts, institutions, norms, rules
Learning activity	Learn	Build knowledge	Science
Ways to accomplish cognitive tasks	Skill, behavior	Discourse, group methods, long sequences	Member methods, social practices
Communication	Thought	Interaction	Membership
Mode of construction	Constructed	Co-constructed	Socially constructed
Context of cognitive task	Personal problem	Joint problem space	Problem domain
Context of activity	Environment	Shared space	Society
Mode of Presence	Embodiment	Co-presence	Contemporary
Referential system	Associations	Indexical field	Cultural world
Form of existence (Heidegger)	Being-there (*Dasein*)	Being-with (*Mitsein*), Being-there-together at the shared object	Participation in communities of practice (*Volk*)
Temporal structure	Subjective experiential internal time	Co-constructed shared temporality	Measurable objective time
Theory of cognition	Constructivist	Post-cognitive	Socio-cultural
Science	Cognitive and educational psychology	Group cognition theory	Sociology, anthropology, linguistics
Tacit knowledge	Background knowledge	Common ground	Culture
Thought	Cognition	Group cognition	Practices
Action	Action	Inter-Action	Social praxis

Theories of small-group cognition in CSCW

As suggested above, the CSCW-related literature on small groups and on post-cognitive phenomena provide some nice studies of the pivotal role of small groups, but they rarely account for this level of description theoretically. They are almost always in the final analysis based on either a psychological view of mental processes at the individual level or a sociological view of rules at the community level. They generally lack a foundational conception of small groups as a distinct level of analysis and description. They often confuse analysis at the small-group level and at the societal level, and lack a developed account of the relationships among the individual, small group and community of practice.

It seems obvious that the small-group level should be considered particularly central to CSCW theory, because CSCW is explicitly concerned with supporting cooperative work. There are few other domains in which cooperative work, knowledge building or group cognition necessarily play such a central role. However, CSCW theoreticians have often tried to avoid the implications. We have seen this, for instance, in the case of activity theory—which could profitably be used to investigate group processes—where Engeström (2008) argued against a focus on group cognition because workplace teams tend to come and go quickly, forming changing *knots* of co-workers around ephemeral tasks. This argument echoed the attitude of Schmidt & Bannon (1992) in their programmatic opening article of the inaugural issue of the CSCW journal. In rejecting the use of the term "group" as a defining concept for CSCW, they reduced the theoretical perspective to one focused on individuals "articulating" (i.e., coordinating) their "distributed individual activities" (p. 15). They made this move despite claiming that their concept of "cooperative work" was congruent with Marx' (1867) definition of cooperative work as "multiple individuals working together in a conscious way in the same production process." Marx was analyzing in detail the historic shift of the unit of production from the individual to the group, but Schmidt & Bannon insist on still focusing on the individual. They complain that the units of cooperative workers are not well-formed, clearly defined, persisting groups. But that is beside the point. The theoretical point is that they accomplish work tasks and associated cognitive tasks (including articulation tasks and power struggles) through group interaction processes and that these should be analyzed as such, not simply as sums of individual actions and reactions or as effects of societal forces. In particular, as cooperative work shifts from the manual factory production of Marx's time to knowledge building and other forms of intellectual production in the information age, group cognition phenomena call for analysis at the small-group unit.

There are distinct phenomena and processes at the individual, small-group and community-of-practice levels, and analyses at these different levels of description can reveal different insights. As Grudin (1994) put it,

Computer support has focused on organizations and individuals. Groups are different. Repeated, expensive groupware failures result from not meeting the challenges in design and evaluation that arise from these differences. (p. 93)

If group phenomena are treated seriously as first-class objects of theory, then one can study how small groups engage in cognitive activities such as: interpersonal trains of thought, shared understandings of diagrams, joint task conceptualizations, common references, coordination of work efforts, planning, deducing, designing, describing, problem solving, explaining, defining, generalizing, representing, remembering and reflecting as a group. In CSCW studies of email, wikis, blogs, text chat or discussion forums, for instance, analysis can show group-cognitive accomplishments emerging from the network of meaningful references built up by postings, demonstrating how the group's self-formation and its cognitive accomplishments are enacted in situated interaction. An analytic focus on the group unit of analysis need not imply that groups exist as ontological entities whenever people are observed in proximity or in communication with one another. Of course, effective groups have to constitute themselves as such and they can change dramatically over time. It is not the physical group that is important, but the group processes, which may extend over seconds, days or years. A single momentary exchange of greetings may be a group process of interest to CSCW, as shown by the early conversation analyses of telephone answering on a help phone line (Hopper, 1992).

A theoretical approach that focuses on small-group interaction is that of dialogicality (Linell, 2001; 2009; Mercer, 2000; Wegerif, 2007). Dialogical theory goes back to Bakhtin (1986), a contemporary of Vygotsky. It stresses the linguistic nature of interaction. It also reiterates the idea that a person's identity as an individual arises through the confrontation with ones partners in dialogue—a view that goes back beyond Mead (1934/1962) to Hegel's (1807/1967) master-slave dialectic (Stahl, 2006, p. 333f). The notion of dialogue partners coming from different perspectives and negotiating from these is an important contribution of dialogic inquiry (Wells, 1999). Another key concept is that of a *shared dynamic dialogic space*, within which knowledge building can take place (Kershner et al., 2010). This is similar to the *joint problem space* of (Teasley & Roschelle, 1993), but now developed in an unambiguously post-cognitive manner.

The idea of an interactional *space* for interaction within a small group is central to group-cognition theory (Stahl, 2006) as well. The term *group cognition* was coined to stress the goal of developing a post-cognitive view of cognition as the possible achievement of a small group collaborating so tightly that the process of building knowledge in the group discourse cannot be attributed to any individual or even reduced to a sequence of contributions from individual minds. For instance, the knowledge might emerge through the interaction of linguistic elements, situated within a sequentially unfolding set of constraints defined by the group task, the membership of the group, and other local or cultural influences, as well as due to the mediation of representational artifacts and media used by the group.

The theory of group cognition absorbs many ideas from the theories discussed above, including that of a shared dynamic dialogical space. Despite some scattered case studies by the authors already mentioned and their colleagues, there is not yet much documentation and analysis of empirical instances of effective group cognition. The analysis of group cognition needs not only specially focused methods to track its occurrence, but even prior to that it needs appropriate CSCW technologies and group methods to structure and support groups to effectively build knowledge that can be shown to be a group product not reducible to individual mental representations. The Virtual Math Teams Project was launched to generate a data corpus that would allow for the analysis of group cognition. This project and some analyses by a number of researchers are documented in (Stahl, 2009). Group-cognition theory focuses on the sequential team interaction within case studies of small-group collaboration. This takes place within an interaction *space* or a *world* in the Heideggerian sense, which opens up to allow the production of group-cognitive accomplishments. The interaction that takes place within such a world—whether face-to-face or online—is subject to a variety of constraints, as pictured in Figure 2.

Note that Figure 2 is not intended to be a model of objects and processes. Rather it tries to present some of the complex constraints on the discourse through which group cognition might be achieved. Neither the physical individuals nor their group are represented here as such; the dialogical (Bakhtinian) voices of the individuals enter into the sequential team interaction and respond to it. Over time, the sequential team interaction forms the central shared-dynamic-dialogic space within which the group-cognitive constraints interact. Behind the individual voices that enter into this interaction space are not so much minds containing mental representations, as a fluid background of past experiences and developed resources for action, which surface based on relevance to the interaction. The team discourse is situated in: the shared dialogical context generated by the on-going interaction itself; the culture and history associated with the group's community of practice; and the socio-technical environment including the media of communication. The interaction is goal-oriented toward the task—as given externally but as enacted by the group—and mediated by a variety of kinds of artifacts, including codifications of knowledge products previously generated by the group. These artifacts might end up among the team outcomes, in relation to the guiding task. Of course, other constraints and influences are possible as well, coming for instance from the guidance of a manager or the motivations of a reward system. The point is that one can picture the whole system producing cognitive accomplishments without having to postulate mental representations in individual minds, let alone to reduce the whole system either to rational mental decisions or to regulation by social institutions.

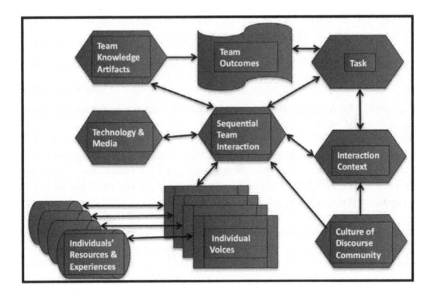

Figure 2. A diagram of constraints on sequential team interaction. From (Stahl, 2010b, p. 256, Figure 1).

The term *constraint* in Figure 2 is chosen to be a neutral term, not implicating a notion of mechanistic causality. While it is clear that the traditional conception of causality is inadequate—stemming back to Aristotle and metaphors of physical mechanics from the everyday world—it is less obvious how to think about the working of the constraints upon group cognition. Folk theory adopts a mechanistic worldview, or even an anthropomorphic view of nature combined with a mechanistic view of causality. Observable behavior of people is taken to be the result of rational decision making in the heads of individuals causing the people to behave as a result of the minds acting as the agency for causing words to be produced and limbs to be moved. But the *linguistic turn* of Wittgenstein (Wittgenstein, 1953) and even more so the recent *practice turn* (Schatzki, Knorr Cetina & Savigny, 2001) have veered radically away from such a view.

Latour (1992) seems to be working toward a post-cognitive notion of causality, perhaps relying heavily on Hegel's notion of mediation. Interestingly, he not only argues against the hegemony of individual minds as agents in the social world, but he also argues against the adequacy of our notion of the *social* (Latour, 2007). History is made neither by rational decisions of individual minds nor by the workings of *society*. Rather, it is the result of concrete, complex networks of mediating actors, including all kinds of artifacts as well as humans. Thus, Latour seems to be advocating an analytic approach that steers clear of both cognitive minds and social institutions to focus on a middle ground. Figure 2 may illustrate the kind of network that he would endorse for picking apart and then reassembling instances of group cognition.

A multiplicity of theories in CSCW

In general, CSCW raises many fundamental questions for traditional theories, oriented as CSCW is to small groups and to online interaction. The accustomed characteristics of the physical world, in which colleagues and interlocutors are embodied and visible to each other, are often missing in CSCW settings, and that brings into question numerous assumptions of folk theories and traditional approaches. The group itself has no identity as a physical body and has no brain to possess its knowledge; it relies on external memories, which differ essentially from personal memories (Donald, 1991). The online world—shared dialogical space—has no location or extension. Team members can come from around the world and do not necessarily share local connections and culture. CSCW involves workers in qualitatively different social relations of production, modes of being in the world or forms of life; even Marx, Heidegger and Wittgenstein's foundational philosophies of post-cognitive theory need to be rethought for virtual groups. Concepts of causality, world, knowledge, cognition, intersubjectivity, interaction and presence need to be reconceptualized for theories in CSCW.

There are many avenues for developing theories in CSCW, as reviewed in this article. Although there are some similarities among these alternatives—often in terms of their critiques of earlier theories—there are strong differences of position and perspective. This is not necessarily a problem. There is a huge assortment of processes taking place in successful CSCW events: at multiple time scales and involving different aspects of interaction. It is possible to raise innumerable research questions, each requiring possibly different methods of investigation at various levels of analysis. It is likely that CSCW requires multiple theories, which are not reducible to one grand unifying theory and which even seem incommensurate with each other. This goes essentially beyond the common notion of *mixed methods*, in which two or more methods of analysis are used to triangulate a single phenomenon from different angles. There are distinct phenomena at different levels of description—and they interact with each other in complex ways in CSCW settings.

CSCW is the study of cooperative work, from a design perspective. Cooperative work often involves large communities, such as a company or a community of practice spread across companies. On the other hand, much of the actual work comes down to tasks done by individuals. But much of the coordination, decision making, articulation, brainstorming, discovery and knowledge building is accomplished by small groups. Community accomplishments are thereby mediated by small groups, which carry out the necessary activities and involve the individuals. Cooperative work involves a tight and complex integration of work at the individual, small-group and community levels. Computer support for cooperative work provides supports at each level and also supports the integration of the activities at the different levels. So CSCW must recognize the levels as distinct and conduct analyses at all levels.

In CSCW, there are many phenomena of interest and they are largely defined by the theories that conceptualize them. So different theories in CSCW can be talking about quite different phenomena (although they may unfortunately be calling them by the same name). In order to avoid confusion and arguments about pseudo-problems, we need to be clear about the theories behind research questions, assumptions, methodologies, analysis tools, findings and claims in the field of CSCW. This article has sketched some of the theoretical landscape underlying CSCW research.

Progress in further developing theories of cognition for CSCW will require careful analysis of case studies and experimental results guided by theoretical perspectives that are clearly enunciated. In many cases, a full understanding of CSCW issues will require distinct analyses at the individual, small-group and community levels of description. These levels will have to be understood as equi-primordial in their mutual interpenetration, rather than being reduced to one of the levels as foundational. Too often, studies still assume (usually unstated) that the small-group processes of CSCW are derivative of individual-cognitive or community-social phenomena, despite the broadly accepted post-cognitive critique of traditional theories of cognition and of assumptions of unified philosophies of science.

References

Adams, F., & Aizawa, K. (2008). *The bounds of cognition.* Malden, MA: Blackwell.

Bakhtin, M. (1986). *Speech genres and other late essays* (V. McGee, Trans.). Austin, TX: University of Texas Press.

Carroll, J. (Ed.). (2003). *HCI models, theories and frameworks: Toward a multidisciplinary science.* San Francisco, CA: Morgan Kaufmann Publishers.

Chomsky, N. (1959). Review of verbal behavior, by B. F. Skinner. *Language. 35*(1), 26-57.

Chomsky, N. (1969). *Aspects of a theory of syntax.* Cambridge, MA: MIT Press.

Clark, H. (1996). *Using language.* Cambridge, UK: Cambridge University Press.

Clark, H., & Brennan, S. (1991). Grounding in communication. In L. Resnick, J. Levine & S. Teasley (Eds.), *Perspectives on socially shared cognition.* (pp. 127-149). Washington, DC: APA.

Descartes, R. (1633/1999). *Discourse on method and meditations on first philosophy.* New York, NY: Hackett.

Dillenbourg, P. (1999). What do you mean by "Collaborative learning"? In P. Dillenbourg (Ed.), *Collaborative learning: Cognitive and computational approaches.* (pp. 1-16). Amsterdam, NL: Pergamon, Elsevier Science.

Dillenbourg, P., Baker, M., Blaye, A., & O'Malley, C. (1996). The evolution of research on collaborative learning. In P. Reimann & H. Spada (Eds.), *Learning in humans and machines: Towards an interdisciplinary learning science.* (pp. 189-211). Oxford, UK: Elsevier.

Donald, M. (1991). *Origins of the modern mind: Three stages in the evolution of culture and cognition.* Cambridge, MA: Harvard University Press.

Dourish, P. (2001). *Where the action is: The foundations of embodied interaction.* Cambridge, MA: MIT Press.

Ehn, P. (1988). *Work-oriented design of computer artifacts.* Stockholm, Sweden: Arbetslivscentrum.

Engeström, Y. (1987). *Learning by expanding: An activity-theoretical approach to developmental research.* Helsinki, Finland: Orienta-Kosultit Oy.

Engeström, Y. (1999). Activity theory and individual and social transformation. In Y. Engeström, R. Miettinen & R.-L. Punamäki (Eds.), *Perspectives on activity theory.* (pp. 19-38). Cambridge, UK: Cambridge University Press.

Engeström, Y. (2008). *From teams to knots.* Cambridge, UK: Cambridge University Press.

Floyd, C. (1992). Software development and reality construction. In C. Floyd, H. Zuellinghoven, R. Budde & R. Keil-Slawik (Eds.), *Software development and reality construction.* (pp. 86-100). Berlin, Germany: Springer Verlag.

Gadamer, H.-G. (1960/1988). *Truth and method.* New York, NY: Crossroads.

Garfinkel, H. (1967). *Studies in ethnomethodology.* Englewood Cliffs, NJ: Prentice-Hall.

Garfinkel, H. (2006). *Seeing sociologically: The routine grounds of social action.* Boulder, CO: Paradigm Publishers.

Gee, J. P. (1992). *The social mind: Language, ideology, and social practice.* New York, NY: Bergin & Garvey.

Grudin, J. (1994). Eight challenges for developers. *Communications of the ACM. 37*(1), 93-105.

Guribye, F. (2005). *Infrastructures for learning: Ethnographic inquiries into the social and technical conditions of education and training.* Unpublished Dissertation, Ph.D., Department of Information Science and Media Studies, University of Bergen. Bergen, Norway.

Hegel, G. W. F. (1807/1967). *Phenomenology of spirit* (J. B. Baillie, Trans.). New York, NY: Harper & Row.

Heidegger, M. (1927/1996). *Being and time: A translation of Sein und Zeit* (J. Stambaugh, Trans.). Albany, NY: SUNY Press.

Hollan, J., Hutchins, E., & Kirsh, D. (2000). Distributed cognition: Toward a new foundation of human-computer interaction research. *ACM Transactions on Computer-Human Interaction. 7*(2), 174-196.

Hopper, R. (1992). *Telephone conversation.* Bloomington, IN: Indiana University Press.

Husserl, E. (1936/1989). The origin of geometry (D. Carr, Trans.). In J. Derrida (Ed.), *Edmund Husserl's origin of geometry: An introduction.* (pp. 157-180). Lincoln, NE: University of Nebraska Press.

Hutchins, E. (1996). *Cognition in the wild.* Cambridge, MA: MIT Press.

Johnson, D. W., & Johnson, R. T. (1989). *Cooperation and competition: Theory and research.* Edina, MN: Interaction Book Company.

Jones, C., Dirckinck-Holmfeld, L., & Lindström, B. (2006). A relational, indirect, meso-level approach to CSCL design in the next decade. *International Journal of Computer-Supported Collaborative Learning. 1*(1), 35-56. Doi: http://dx.doi.org/10.1007/s11412-006-6841-7

Kant, I. (1787/1999). *Critique of pure reason.* Cambridge, UK: Cambridge University Press.

Kaptelinin, V., & Nardi, B. A. (2006). *Acting with technology: Activity theory and interaction design*. Cambridge, Mass.: MIT Press.

Kershner, R., Mercer, N., Warwick, P., & Staarman, J. K. (2010). Can the interactive whiteboard support young children's collaborative communication and thinking in classroom science activities? *International Journal of Computer-Supported Collaborative Learning*. 5(4).

Latour, B. (1992). Where are the missing masses? The sociology of a few mundane artifacts. In W. E. Bijker & J. Law (Eds.), *Shaping technology/building society*. (pp. 225-227). Cambridge, MA: MIT Press.

Latour, B. (2007). *Reassembling the social: An introduction to actor-network-theory*. Cambridge, UK: Cambridge University Press.

Lave, J., & Wenger, E. (1991). *Situated learning: Legitimate peripheral participation*. Cambridge, UK: Cambridge University Press.

Linell, P. (2001). *Approaching dialogue: Talk, interaction and contexts in dialogical perspectives*. New York, NY: Benjamins.

Linell, P. (2009). *Rethinking language, mind, and world dialogically: Interactional and contextual theories of human sense-making*. Charlotte, NC: Information Age Publishing.

Looi, C.-K., So, H.-j., Toh, Y., & Chen, W. (2011). CSCL in classrooms: The Singapore experience of synergizing policy, practice and research. *International Journal of Computer-Supported Collaborative Learning*.

Marx , K. (1867). *Das Kapital: Kritik der politischen Oekonomie* (Vol. I). Hamburg, Germany: Otto Meisner.

Maturana, H. R., & Varela, F. J. (1987). *The tree of knowledge: The biological roots of human understanding*. Boston, MA: Shambhala.

Mead, G. H. (1934/1962). *Mind, self and society*. Chicago, IL: University of Chicago Press.

Mercer, N. (2000). *Words and minds. How we use language to think together*: Routledge.

Plato. (340 BC/1941). *The republic* (F. Cornford, Trans.). London, UK: Oxford University Press.

Polanyi, M. (1966). *The tacit dimension*. Garden City, NY: Doubleday.

Robbins, P., & Aydede, M. (Eds.). (2009). *The Cambridge handbook of situated cognition*. Cambridge, UK: Cambridge University Press.

Rogoff, B. (1995). Sociocultural activity on three planes. In B. Rogoff, J. Wertsch, P. del Rio & A. Alvarez (Eds.), *Sociocultural studies of mind*. (pp. 139-164). Cambridge, UK: Cambridge University Press.

Sacks, H. (1962/1995). *Lectures on conversation*. Oxford, UK: Blackwell.

Sacks, H., Schegloff, E. A., & Jefferson, G. (1974). A simplest systematics for the organization of turn-taking for conversation. *Language*. 50(4), 696-735. Web: www.jstor.org.

Scardamalia, M., & Bereiter, C. (1996). Computer support for knowledge-building communities. In T. Koschmann (Ed.), *CSCL: Theory and practice of an emerging paradigm*. (pp. 249-268). Hillsdale, NJ: Lawrence Erlbaum Associates.

Schatzki, T. R., Knorr Cetina, K., & Savigny, E. v. (Eds.). (2001). *The practice turn in contemporary theory*. New York, NY: Routledge.

Schegloff, E. A. (2007). *Sequence organization in interaction: A primer in conversation analysis*. Cambridge, UK: Cambridge University Press.

Schmidt, K., & Bannon, L. (1992). Taking CSCW seriously: Supporting articulation work. *CSCW*. 1(1), 7-40.

Schön, D. A. (1983). *The reflective practitioner: How professionals think in action*. New York, NY: Basic Books.

Sfard, A. (2008). *Thinking as communicating: Human development, the growth of discourses and mathematizing.* Cambridge, UK: Cambridge University Press.

Shannon, C., & Weaver, W. (1949). *The mathematical theory of communication.* Chicago, IL: University of Illinois Press.

Stahl, G. (2006). *Group cognition: Computer support for building collaborative knowledge.* Cambridge, MA: MIT Press. Web: http://GerryStahl.net/mit/.

Stahl, G. (2009). *Studying virtual math teams.* New York, NY: Springer. Web: http://GerryStahl.net/vmt/book Doi: http://dx.doi.org/10.1007/978-1-4419-0228-3.

Stahl, G. (2010a). Group cognition as a foundation for the new science of learning. In M. S. Khine & I. M. Saleh (Eds.), *New science of learning: Cognition, computers and collaboration in education.* (pp. 23-44). New York, NY: Springer. Web: http://GerryStahl.net/pub/scienceoflearning.pdf.

Stahl, G. (2010b). Guiding group cognition in CSCL. *International Journal of Computer-Supported Collaborative Learning.* 5(3), 255-258. Doi: http://dx.doi.org/10.1007/s11412-010-9091-7.

Stahl, G. (2010c). *Marx and Heidegger.* Philadelphia. PA: Gerry Stahl at Lulu. Web: http://GerryStahl.net/elibrary/marx.

Stahl, G. (2010d). *Tacit and explicit understanding.* Philadelphia, PA: Gerry Stahl at Lulu. Web: http://GerryStahl.net/elibrary/tacit.

Stahl, G., Koschmann, T., & Suthers, D. (2006). Computer-supported collaborative learning: An historical perspective. In R. K. Sawyer (Ed.), *Cambridge handbook of the learning sciences.* (pp. 409-426). Cambridge, UK: Cambridge University Press. Web: http://GerryStahl.net/elibrary/global.

Suchman, L. (1987). *Plans and situated actions: The problem of human-machine communication.* Cambridge, UK: Cambridge University Press.

Teasley, S. D., & Roschelle, J. (1993). Constructing a joint problem space: The computer as a tool for sharing knowledge. In S. P. Lajoie & S. J. Derry (Eds.), *Computers as cognitive tools.* (pp. 229-258). Mahwah, NJ: Lawrence Erlbaum Associates, Inc.

Turing, A. (1937). On computable numbers, with an application to the Entscheidungsproblem. *Proceedings of the London Mathematical Society.* 2(1), 230.

Vygotsky, L. (1930/1978). *Mind in society.* Cambridge, MA: Harvard University Press.

Wegerif, R. (2007). *Dialogic, education and technology: Expanding the space of learning.* New York, NY: Kluwer-Springer.

Wells, G. (1999). *Dialogic inquiry: Towards a socio-cultural practice and theory of education.* Cambridge, UK: Cambridge University Press.

Winograd, T., & Flores, F. (1986). *Understanding computers and cognition: A new foundation of design.* Reading, MA: Addison-Wesley.

Wittgenstein, L. (1921/1974). *Tractatus logico philosophicus.* London, UK: Routledge.

Wittgenstein, L. (1953). *Philosophical investigations.* New York, NY: Macmillan.

Lest we forget

The European field study tradition and the issue of conditions of work in CSCW research

Liam Bannon, Université de Technologie de Troyes, France;
University of Limerick, Ireland; University of Aarhus, Denmark

Kjeld Schmidt, Copenhagen Business School, Denmark

Ina Wagner, Technical University of Vienna, Austria

Abstract. The paper intends to direct attention to the rich and variegated European field study tradition. Focusing on the Francophone ergonomic tradition and especially the German studies of work and working conditions, both based on in-depth field studies in ordinary work settings, the paper attempts to situate these traditions vis-à-vis the research program of CSCW.

It is not a historical accident that ethnographic and other in-depth forms of workplace studies play a dominant role in ECSCW and have come to play an important role in CSCW and HCI at large. Ethnographic studies of cooperative work settings have a central role in CSCW for the simple reason that it is of critical importance for the development of appropriate (and appropriately flexible) coordination technologies to develop a systematic conception of the logics of coordinative practices. And in this regard, the overwhelming challenge is to cope with the enormous variety of work practices. Thus, in the history of CSCW research, a major issue has been to overcome theoretically derived, ideologically postulated, or otherwise preconceived notions about the research phenomenon: cooperative work.

This has involved, first of all, questioning many notions about work, derived from popular management literature, such as the putative advantages of 'group work' or 'team work' and the desirability of more 'cooperation' in the workplace.[1] Notions of 'cooperation' or 'collaboration', understood as unselfish or altruistic behavior or as 'mutual help', were also suggested (often hinging on exhortations of combinations of the word 'shared'), and so was the notion of 'cooperatives' in the sense of communal forms of property (Robinson, 1991). In a rather similar vein, it was sometimes suggested that CSCW be seen as a research area devoted to the 'empowerment' of 'end users' or workers (e.g., Clement, 1990; Agre, 1995). While all of these topics may have some intrinsic interest, basing the field of CSCW on these notions of 'cooperative work' was never widely accepted in CSCW and many of these conceptions were explicitly criticized for lacking in realism and for being intrinsically normative (cf., e.g., Howard, 1987; Bannon and Schmidt, 1989; Kuutti, 1991; Hughes, et al., 1994).

Instead, CSCW, especially in its European instantiation, ECSCW, focused on actually observable cooperative work practices: socially organized work activities that are interdependent in a multitude of ways. Thus, instead of imputing criteria derived from pre-conceived theoretical or evaluative frameworks to actual work practices, CSCW researchers have focused on (or have been encouraged to focus on) identifying and articulating the ordering principles inherent in specific cooperative work practices.

This was expressed with great clarity, in one of the first attempts to delineate the role of field work in CSCW research, namely, in 1994 in a very influential and widely cited paper by John Hughes, Wes Sharrock, Tom Rodden, and others:[2]

'Many of the early writings in CSCW attempted to identify "co-operation" as a distinct, discrete type of activity whereas, and as many studies of the social organisation of work show, matters are much more subtle, and more complicated, than this assumes. [...] The association, for example, of co-operation with synchronously, co-located persons working in a team, tends to ignore the pervasiveness of a variety of interdependencies within work settings which are immensely relevant to CSCW design. In other words, the relevant properties of the social organisation of work do not appear as "readily packaged" within work domains but need to be brought out by an analysis of the ethnographic materials.' (Hughes, et al., 1994, p. 130)

Thus, the authors argued, 'one of the major problems of requirements elicitation, especially as far as the development of CSCW systems is concerned, is the variety of work domains'. Therefore,

'studies of the social organisation of work will need to proceed in a manner which recognises this heterogeneity of domains and develops analytic tools which are capable of exhibiting the relevant scope of this variety. [¶] In significant respects, it is this objective which underpins the use of ethnographic fieldwork and case studies within CSCW as a promising means of design-

---

[1]   Indeed, there was a time when it was suggested that CSCW was committed to a notion of 'cooperative work' defined by being informal, non-hierarchical, relatively autonomous, devoid of competition, etc. (cf., e.g., Sørgaard, 1987).

[2]   This paper, entitled 'Perspectives on the social organization of work', was produced and published as part of a 'deliverable' in the Esprit Basic Research project COMIC (1992-95). The first major European CSCW project, COMIC brought together the bulk of European researchers in the field at the time and has had a profound and lasting impact on the ECSCW field.

ing systems which are more responsive to the needs and the skills of users.' (Hughes, *et al.*, 1994, p. 129)

The conclusion of this is that 'an analytic framework of some generality needs to be developed "from the ground up" as it were, and capable of retaining a sensitivity to the details and the variety of work domains' (Hughes, *et al.*, 1994, pp. 129 f.). In other words, in order to be able to grasp the manifold forms of cooperative work, one should not stipulate specific forms of cooperative work (e.g., 'group work', 'team work', work over 'distance'), a specific moral disposition (e.g., 'team spirit'), or some presumptive 'shared' mental representation (e.g., 'shared understanding', 'shared goal').

For CSCW's research program, with its technological commitments and its focus on computational support of coordinative practices, the requisite 'analytic framework' cannot simply be imported from anthropology, sociology, psychology, business studies, etc., and then applied. The requisite 'analytic framework' must assist in providing answers to the specific questions (to be) raised by CSCW's research program. For the purpose of developing this 'from the ground up' a 'disinterested' focus on actual working practices is essential.

This 'disinterested' approach has proved immensely fruitful. Although a stable 'analytic framework of some generality' or a 'systematic conception of the logics of coordinative practices' is not imminent, this research program has produced a corpus of workplace studies and some essential elements of an analytical framework.

Now, the social, economic, and organizational context of these practices as well as the whole issue of *working conditions* cannot be bracketed out indefinitely.

First, it certainly belongs to the picture of CSCW that there has been explicit socio-political critiques of existing socio-technical regimes (e.g., Wagner and Clement, 1994). It would also be misleading to ignore the strong influence from Participatory Design on CSCW, generally in the form of a noticeable respect for practitioners' skills and competencies and sometimes also articulated as a commitment to certain systems development principles (e.g., 'end-user development', Pipek, *et al.*, 2009). Although it would be fallacious to categorize the major part of current CSCW research as somehow related to the emancipatory aspirations that, at least historically, have motivated the Participatory Design movement, it is nevertheless characteristic of CSCW, especially ECSCW, that there is an obvious overlap in personnel and a cross-fertilization of ideas between CSCW and PD (e.g., the use of ethnography in PD and the use of various techniques of involving practitioners in design considerations in CSCW).[3]

---

[3]   The confluence of CSCW and PD was greatly enhanced as a result of the ACM CSCW'88 Conference, where a number of invited and presented papers were given by members of the Scandinavian PD tradition (Greif and Suchman, 1988).

But most importantly in this context, issues of working conditions, broadly understood, are intrinsically involved in the design-oriented discourse in CSCW. There are, for example, Lucy Suchman's critique of speech-act theory and its application in the design of The Coordinator (1993, 1994), Terry Winograd's response to this critique (1994), and the subsequent series of commentaries (Bannon, 1994, 1995).

However, issues of working conditions are typically only *implicitly* present in design-discourses in CSCW. For example, issues such as control of workload and workers' ability to maintain and develop skills and competencies were and have remained a subordinate theme in the recurrent critique of 'office automation', 'workflow-management systems', 'business process modelling', and so on. Similarly, issues of interruptions, 'mental workload', and stress are implicitly involved in studies of practices of mutual awareness and in related design-oriented studies, but have often not been made a major topic of concern.

At this stage in the evolution of the CSCW field, we believe that the time is ripe for a re-assessment of these background assumptions. An 'analytic framework of some generality' that does not, in some systematic way, address issues of working conditions in existing socio-technical regimes would be so abstract as to be of little actual use in the face of the realities of working life. However, in that regard we are in the fortunate position that a vast and rich array of research traditions has evolved – both in Europe and elsewhere, both in the decades before but also simultaneously with CSCW — that is also based on in-depth field studies of work activities in natural settings. The purpose of this paper is to point to certain of these bodies of literature.

The aim is not to move CSCW's focus away from coordinative practices in cooperative work but simply to say, as it were, that we do not have to start from scratch in building an 'analytic framework of some generality'; that there are blocks, slabs, and beams out there already that we might want to consider.

1. The 'European field study tradition'

In a recent paper on of decision-making in technically complex domains, Emilie Roth and Emily Patterson (2005) make some cogent remarks on the role of 'naturalistic observational studies'. Using two field studies as their cases — a study of the 'function of the current communication technology in railroad dispatching' and a study of communication among operators in a nuclear power plant control room using 'advanced displays' — the authors argue that 'naturalistic observation studies' are essential in that they support the 'discovery phase' of scientific research: 'One of the primary strengths of naturalistic observations is that they support a discovery process' in that they 'serve to draw attention to significant phenomena and suggest new ideas whose validity and generality can then be evaluated through additional studies'. This conception of the role of field studies in technological research is rather similar to the conception outlined by Hughes *et al*. in 1994.

Now, when introducing this concept of 'naturalistic observation studies' Roth and Patterson make an interesting distinction:

> 'Naturalistic observation studies employ a methodology similar in approach to other ethnographically derived methods (e.g., Jordan & Henderson, 1995; Nardi, 1997) and the European field study tradition' (De Keyser, 1990; Heath and Luff, 2000).'

The European field study tradition! What is *that?* The reference to the book by Heath and Luff is of course a gesture at the rich lode of workplace studies in European CSCW research and will be well known to a CSCW audienc. On the other hand, however, the reference to Véronique De Keyser's 'Why field studies?' (1990)[4] is a gesture at a large and rich body of literature that may not be well known to most CSCW researchers. Since it has influenced especially European CSCW research and addresses issues of working life and working practices far more directly than the ethnographic tradition, we consider it relevant for the European CSCW community to know about and consider this legacy.

De Keyser begins her article by sketching the socio-political setting in which the 'European field study tradition' evolved:

> 'For more than thirty years a trend for field studies and work analysis methodologies has been developing in Europe. In order to understand this movement well, it must be placed in its socio-political context. [...] The socio-political situation in Europe, in the 1960s, was characterized by economic prosperity, by the establishment of supra-national European structures and by active social protest. Demands for improved quality of living and better working conditions appeared in industries along with demands for more democratic organizational forms. Safety, working conditions and work organizations would be dominant research themes for the following twenty years.' (p. 305).

In 1962, De Keyser points out, the European Coal and Steel Community (ECSC), the precursor of what has developed into the European Union, launched an international research program on safety in the mining and iron and steel industries:'

> 'This shed crude light on structural factors — absence of coordination, poor communication systems and failures in equipment design — which influenced human reliability. It called for ergonomic systems of which would not only improve work stations but also effect a global revision of organizations.' (ibid.)

De Keyser adds that there, in addition, were movements in the Scandinavian countries and in other parts of Europe that tried, with some success, to promote Industrial Democracy. Again, de Keyser points out, researchers were involved in on-site studies of work practices.

On closer inspection, however, the European field study tradition turns out to be far broader and far more complex than De Keyser's brief remarks suggest. In fact, the European field study tradition is more like a widely ramified web of re-

---

4   The proceedings in which De Keyser's paper was originally published may be difficult to get hold of but it has been republished under a new title (De Keyser, 1992).

search traditions addressing a wide array of social and research problems. Moreover, the web of research traditions is complicated by the influence of different national political and research agendas and, of course, language differences.

In general, however, the first wave of studies was motivated by the need to increase the productivity of European industry after the debacles of the first half of the twentieth century, while at the same time improving working conditions (occupational health, safety). The strong working class movements in Europe after the Second World War influenced these efforts considerably, both directly and indirectly.

The so-called 'socio-technical school' in organizational and workplace studies developed, from the Second World War and well into the 1960s, from similar motivations. Sometimes explicitly related to the Industrial Democracy movement, it grew out of attempts to find work organizations and job designs that would give ordinary workers more autonomy in carrying out and organizing their daily work activities (e.g., Trist and Bamforth, 1951; Engelstad, 1970). Related research attempting to determine the constraints and thus also the degrees of freedom in the design of work organizations undertook carefully conducted, sometimes large-scale and longitudinal, field studies of work organizations in their (presumptively 'causal') relationship to the production technology as represented by existing technical resources and the temporal characteristics and scale of production (cf., e.g., Emery and Trist, 1965; Woodward, 1965).

The early ergonomic field studies, such as those initiated by the ECSC in the early 1960s, developed into and were largely superseded by a second wave, in which the effects of increased mechanization and especially automatic control systems in industry became a key topic of concern. Focal points in these investigations were not only issues of working conditions in highly automated control systems but also and increasingly the issue of the cognitive and organizational requirements of supervisory process control: the skills and strategies involved in decision-making in time- and safety critical work. Field studies of actual work practices, focused on decision-making in technically complex work settings (such as, initially, furnaces and steel plants), have been especially strong in Francophone parts of Europe (see section 2 below). Parallel to this, a related research tradition also largely based on field studies unfolded in the United Kingdom (for a collection of early contributions, cf. Edwards and Lees, 1974). In a very early study, Crossman for example notes:

'Although workers in an automatic plant seem at first sight to be isolated, closer study reveals a surprising amount of inter-communication between individuals operating the machinery: Each member of the team-operators, maintenance men, engineers· and laboratory staff-frequently gives and receives information or instructions about the plant from the others, by word of mouth, in writing and even sometimes by hand signals. It seems that the efficient running of a plant depends a great deal on the effectiveness of these interchanges Therefore, each member of the team must be able to communicate easily with his fellows, understand their points of view and put his own across. In other words, they must exercise *social skills*.' (Crossman, 1960, p. 21)

The European field study tradition is rich and diverse. In fact, it is a family of traditions, and we can only offer a glimpse of it. We focus strictly on field study traditions that focus on working conditions in cooperative work settings, knowing very well that there are other traditions that could also be quite relevant for a CSCW audience in that they, based on naturalistic field work, contribute systematically to the design of large-scale technical systems and technological development.[5]

2. 'Francophone' ergonomics

A distinctive Francophone approach to ergonomics emerged after the Second World War and was given further impetus by the founding of Société d'Ergonomie de Langue Française (SELF) in 1963.

The initial overriding concern was, as already indicated, to enhance the productivity of industry. In contrast to Scientific Management and related traditions in Industrial Psychology and Human Factors, where the emphasis is on adapting the worker to the work and the available technical resources (through conditioning, training, and selection), workers, in the emerging Francophone Ergonomics tradition, 'were seen to be at the centre of work, and, therefore, at the centre of work design' (Laville, 2001, p. 3).

The book *L'analyse du travail* by André Ombredane and Jean-Marie Faverge (1955) is by many considered the initial expression of the specific Francophone approach to 'work analysis'. Other notable pioneers extended this approach, notably Alain Wisner, Jacques Leplat, and Maurice de Montmollin.

In the introduction to the 1955 book, Ombredane noted:

'Two perspectives are to be distinguished when analyzing work: the *What* and the *How*. What is to be done and how do the workers in question do it? On one hand, the perspective of requirements *the task*; and on the other the *operational attitudes and sequences* by means of which the individuals observed *in actual fact* meet these requirements'. (Ombredane and Faverge, 1955, p. 5).

The approach was termed 'work activity analysis', and paid particular attention to field studies of work, to the observed differences between actual and prescribed work, and between task and activity. So there was a strong emphasis on the situated nature of activity, on working procedures and the ways operators carried out

---

5   An obvious example is here the tradition of Cognitive Engineering. Historically, it developed in response to the extraordinary safety issues involved in designing control systems for nuclear power plants, and for many years this research centered on Jens Rasmussen's research group at Risø National Laboratory in Denmark. This research program has developed into an international movement and among leading researchers in this area, in addition to Rasmussen, one should mention Len Goodstein, Morten Lind, Erik Hollnagel, David Woods, and Kim Vicente. (For a historical account of the early years, cf., Vicente, 2001).

their work in specific spatio-temporal settings. In accord with this approach, and in contrast to the US Human Factors tradition, Francophone Ergonomics 'centered on activity analysis that is conducted in real work situations, that is, in a technical and organizational context that includes the production constraints', and in which workers are seen 'as active subjects' in the analysis (Laville, 2001, p. 3).

While this work had a strong focus on actual worker conduct, over time more attention was paid to the operators' reasoning processes and to the influence of the workplace setting. (For brief accounts, cf. Laville, 2001; Neboit, 2006).

In a programmatic paper written decades later, in 1991, Montmollin summarized the basic tenets of the Francophone tradition in ergonomics as follows:

'(1) Operators' actual activities have to be distinguished from the tasks they are requested or supposed to perform; (2) operators working in natural life environments have to be distinguished from anonymous and universal human beings; (3) complex natural life environments have to be distinguished from the [computer] interfaces, as the whole has to be distinguished from one of its parts.' (Montmollin, 1991, p. 95)

De Montmollin then spelled out these three principles as follows:

(1) 'The overwhelming conclusion of all the ergonomic studies of work analysis studies which, in contrast to the normative ones, try to model the natural activities of the operator, is that these activities never conform to the prescribed tasks.' (p. 96 f.)

(2) 'Operators are not to be considered as universal human beings, whose universal characteristics and limits could be discovered and measured from any *homo sapiens* (for instance an undergraduate student), allowing the construction of general "laws". [...] The methodological conclusion of this assumption is that ergonomic analysis and modelling of activities cannot be anything but natural field analysis, in an ecological perspective. Laboratory experiments are considered here as analysis of the experimental situation itself, and nothing else. Experimental situation is almost never real work situation. Therefore, data from laboratory experiments are useful, but in the same way that data concerning the behaviour of monkeys in cages are useful for the explanation of the behaviour of wild monkeys in the wild. There is no industrial environment where workers have to solve the Tower of Hanoi problem eight hours a day, every day, and get paid for it. [...] In the laboratory, complexity has to be avoided to allow for the control of very few independent and dependent variables; in contrast, complexity has to be respected in field work.' (p. 97 f.)

(3) 'Experienced operators are not naive users who have to be convinced to buy or to use a friendly microcomputer; they are people who have to solve problems not directly concerning the interface, but rather, a complex environment, for instance an unusual incident in a chemical process, or a conflict between the planes above an exceptionally overcrowded airport. Natural life environments cannot be reduced to interfaces, even when interfaces are the only windows between the operator and the environment (which is seldom the case). The more complex the environment, the more this ecological approach is relevant.' (p. 99)

The Francophone ergonomic tradition has produced an overwhelming body of field studies, reporting on studies of work in blast furnaces and steel mills, in aircraft cockpits and air traffic control centers, in operating theaters, and so on. (For a collection of key texts, cf. Leplat, 1992, 1993).[6]

---

6   Much of it has been published in the journal *Le Travail Humain* that has been published for close to 75 years and at the annual Francophone ergonomics conference sponsored by SELF. The SELF 2009 con-

As with Anglo-American human factors research, until the early 1990s the Francophone ergonomic research largely focused on individual operators' understandings and activities, but then more explicit concerns with various forms of cooperative work and team work emerged and have become an important thread (De Keyser, 1988; De Keyser and Nyssen, 1993; Samurçay and Rogalski, 1993; Leplat, 1994; Rogalski, 1996). The conference series COOP, located *au principe* in France, has been a site where an mix of Francophone and other European traditions in both ergonomics and CSCW have converged.

In sum, the Francophone tradition of work analysis, with its rich tapestry of field studies, various forms of analysis, and conceptual frameworks, provides a very interesting perspective on forms of work activity and on the more general conditions of work which we believe provide a very useful addition to the corpus of ethnographic studies cited in the main CSCW literature. Any student of CSCW should be aware of this significant body of work, and in the context of the current paper, this work has many insights into more general working conditions.

3. Industrial work and workers' conception of society

The European field study tradition also encompasses a tradition that has been motivated by quite different issues than ergonomic ones. After the Second World War sociologists, especially German sociologists of a Marxist provenance, were concerned with the potential of the industrial working class as a force of socioeconomic change. Simply put, their research was focused around whether the unfolding mechanization and automation of work processes would affect the workers' conception of society and their place in it. Similar questions were pursued in France (Andrieux and Lignon, 1960; Touraine, 1966) but the German research program addressing this issue is characterized by being grounded in meticulous and sophisticated field studies of work procedures and practices.

The idea that workers' conception of society and working class potential for social transformation could be more or less directly based on, and derived from, the nature of work in modern industrial settings is of course, in hindsight, somewhat naive. But the research itself is of impeccable quality.

In the 1950s a group of researchers around Heinrich Popitz and Hans Paul Bahrdt conducted extensive studies of industrial work in the German iron and steel industry, which have been published in the form of two books: *Technique and Industrial Work* (1957a) and *The Worker's Conception of Society* (1957b). Their work had a strong analytical orientation on the one hand, and was based on field studies with a 'phenomenological orientation' on the other, producing de-

---

ference was devoted to *Ergonomie et Organisation du Travail* (Gaillard, Kerguelen, and Thon, 2009). For information, cf. the SELF website (http://www.ergonomie-self.org/).

tailed and concrete microanalyses of cooperative work in industrial settings. Analyzing a broad array of (technically constituted) 'types' of cooperative work, they concluded that 'technical intelligence' was of increasing importance, and they developed a differentiated notion of 'mechanization', identifying two trends: a fixation of work on low levels of skills and collaboration, and the emergence of complex coordination and control work. In their related study of workers' consciousness, which they base on a series of 'topoi', they drew a 'concrete, lively, and compelling' (Beckenbach, 1991) image of the industrial worker in post-war Germany.

Much of German research in this tradition, which culminated in the 1970s and 80s, can be subsumed under the 'automation debate'. A series of key studies has shaped the sociological debate on automation in the 1970s[7]. At the same time work psychologists ('Arbeitswissenschaften'), notably Winfried Hacker and Walter Volpert, developed a conception 'of the workplace conducive to personality development' (Oesterreich and Volpert, 1986, p. 504). One of the most influential studies was a large-scale study of work in the automotive, tool industry, and chemical industries by Horst Kern und Michael Schumann, entitled *Industrial Work and Workers' Consciousness* (1970). Based on a taxonomy defining 'degrees of mechanization', they identify a trend towards a 'polarization' of work (and the qualifications it requires) into certain highly qualified types of work on the one hand, and on the other, low-skilled types of work or 'residual jobs'. Years later the authors reverted to the issue in a critical discussion of the key results of the original study from 1970, under the title *The End of Division of Labor?* (Kern and Schumann, 1984). Studies in the cement, petrochemical and electricity industries performed by Mickler *et al.* (1977) have provided additional and even more detailed empirical evidence of these developments, and have drawn attention to the role of work organization as an intervening factor between production technology and work practice.

Most of these studies cover a large number of workplaces within one industry or branch, or investigate work across branches. Hence, case studies are almost always comparative, allowing us to arrive at a better understanding of the conditions that shape work, as well as observe variations of work practices. The group around Popitz worked over nine months in the field, carrying out 600 interviews, as well as numerous observational studies of work practices. Kern and Schumann (1970) have performed 20 case studies in nine companies in eight industries. They analyzed documents, conducted expert interviews with managers, union representatives, and semi-structured interviews with workers (altogether 981), and produced 122 qualitative workplace descriptions, as well 32 descriptions of work organizations and industrial plants. Pongratz and Trinczek (2010) single out four characteristics of case studies: context-relatedness; multi-perspectivity – integrat-

---

7   It is important to mention that German industrial sociologists never engaged in the rather simplistic and empirically questionable 'deskilling debate', whose main proponent was Harry Braverman (1974).

ing the experiences and perspectives of different actors; triangulation of methods; and openness of the research design to additional 'context factors' that turn out to be relevant in the course of the empirical work.

German Industrial Sociology always has studied work in the larger context of organization, production technology and societal forces, for instance the *working conditions* as shaped by the social division of labor as well as by the organization of work and technology at the level of the work organization, and the corresponding *work practices* ('Arbeitshandeln') and the *work capacity* (skills but also 'interests') of the individual worker.

Although their descriptions of work practices can be enormously detailed, they were produced in the context of a research project that involved analyzing the data within an elaborate theoretical framework, represented by sets of categories that shaped interviews as well as observational studies. This means that work is not only described as observed, but also evaluated according to a set of criteria that included concepts such as skill level, stress, and margins of disposition (discussed below).

We should mention here that, although the cooperative organization of work is often investigated intensely and in detail in the German tradition, it is generally investigated under the aspect of working conditions, that is, as characteristics of work organization and work setting that in different ways and to a different extent afford and limit the autonomy of individual workers and their ability to develop relationships and collective social resources. The overriding concern, as already noted, was the potential of the German working class — after the Second World War and subsequently under the impact of mechanization and automation — as a force of social change. For example, in their incisive study of the organization of work in the German coal and steel industry, Popitz *et al.* (1957a) found two forms of cooperative work: on one hand *team-cooperation*, that is, a form of cooperative work characterized by absence of tightly coupled interdependencies, although an indirect mutual dependency is constituted by the common task; the possibility of contacts among workers in the course of doing the work, and large margins of disposition. In contrast, Popitz *et al.* identified '*gefügeartige*' cooperative work, that is, cooperative work constituted and mediated by technical systems (e.g., a hot-rolling mill in a steel plant) that imposes a strict technical order and tightly coupled work processes. The latter, Popitz *et al.* observed, were characteristic of (at least) the modern iron and coal industry (p. 46).

While, from a CSCW perspective, this lack of interest in cooperative work as a phenomenon in its own right is somewhat problematic, the value of the German studies of work is that they have developed an analytical framework of some generality, which is highly relevant when it comes to designing systems. The tradition focuses primarily on issues of qualification, stress, and margins of disposition – concepts which we now briefly discuss.

Qualification: A distinction is made between the skills needed to perform a particular work practice and the skills an individual has acquired ('Arbeitsvermögen'). A consequence of automation may be that both no longer match, as Littek (1983) shows, using the example of a 'turner' who still has 'his knowledge in his head, the deftness in his fingers', both of which are no longer needed. Some studies of work include detailed observations of work processes. In contrast to many more ethnomethodologically-inspired field studies in CSCW research, these observational studies employ a categorical scheme, based on the 'action regulation theory' developed by German work psychologist Winfried Hacker. Hacker thinks of this theory, which he bases on the work of Vygotskij and Leont'ev, as not just 'a descriptive tool but also a normative guide to efficient and humanized work' — a tool for work design (Hacker, 2003). From the beginning Hacker was motivated by the idea of designing 'mentally demanding work', in contrast to low-skilled repetitive work.

Hacker explains the notion of *action regulation* – a core concept in his approach, as follows:

'The first stage is "action preparation". It includes "orientation to the task" and "redefining the task into a self-set goal" (…). The orientation stage focuses on the conditions under which the goal has to be accomplished, the availability of methods and strategies, and assessing the degrees of freedom to choose different methods. Furthermore, the co-ordination of one's own actions with colleagues is also part of this orientation process. The final phases are "implementation" and "evaluation". The implementation process is guided by continuous feedback on goal accomplishment and is completed with an evaluation of the final outcome in terms of economic task criteria' (Hacker, 2003, p. 108)

Industrial sociologists have used this approach for differentiating between different 'requirement dimensions':

- Sensory-motor skills that are enacted routinely (kinaesthetic cues, 'implicit knowledge');
- Perceptive routines that guide the perception and processing of situational clues, are based on schemata and enacted mostly consciously ('explicit knowledge');
- Intellectual diagnostic and planning skills, with the distinction between empirical-adaptive, systematic-optimizing, strategic-innovative;
- Motivational skills that apply to organizational norms and conditions.

Walter Volpert, another German work psychologist, developed a tool for work analysis (VERA) based on action regulation theory, which was tested by 'nineteen different investigators at 260 workplaces in nine industries' (Oesterreich and Volpert, 1986). Work analysis was carried out in the form of the 'observation interview'.

In the discussion of changing requirements of work, a distinction was made between process-dependent qualifications needed in specific work processes and process-independent ones, such as: habitualization, technical intelligence, and technical sensibility (Popitz, *et al.*, 1957a, b), flexibility, responsibility, as well as what (Asendorf-Krings, Drexel, and Nuber, 1976) term 'reproductive capabilities', which encompasses the ability to recognize aspects of work that are bound to deteriorate the capacity to work and to collectively organize.

Stress: The German word 'Belastungen' captures the whole range of work-related factors that an individual may experience as 'stressful' and that may affect his/her health. Influential, again, was the work of Walter Volpert, who in the tradition of the socio-technical approach investigated the relationship between work and personality, arguing that work with little space for action and decision-making ('margins of disposition') negatively affects a person's physical and psychological well-being and intellectual capacity, and leads to passivity and authoritarian behavior (Volpert, 1985). He defined stress as a subjective reaction, resulting from specific working conditions, a worker's social situation (e.g. competition) and his/her personality. While this approach could be considered 'psychological' and more directed at 'measuring' than at 'observing', others, such as Hoff, Lappe, and Lempert (1982) used very detailed observational data to identify stress-relevant aspects of work, such as: the temporal structure of the work (e.g. repetitive work), the available space for movement; the social relations (the opportunity for informal contact, modes of collaboration); the space for responsibility and control; the level of required skills; and the opportunity to control the stress-relevant working conditions. Moldaschl (1991) added a set of 'contradictory requirements' at work, in particular serious mismatches between work requirements and available resources to this list of stress factors.

Margins of disposition: This is a term that is used in much of the work concerning changing skill requirements at work and has been identified as an indicator of stress at work. Kern and Schumann define this term as follows, arguing that a worker

'has the option of disposition when having the possibility to plan and enact his own work process. There are different possibilities of practicing this design autonomy ('Gestaltungsfreiheit'): in respect to the timing of an intervention, the work techniques and the speed of work; in respect to the quality and quantity of the product; in respect to the physical movement within space' (Kern and Schumann, 1970, vol. I, p. 66).

The margin of disposition is a contested concept but much used in studies of work. Volpert (1974) has argued that conceptually it does not contribute anything new to Hacker's concept of action regulation and, hence, should not be treated as an additional category. Mickler on the other hand uses the term, such as in his description of a NC machine operator:

'technical knowledge and technical sensitivity are demanded, above all during the setting-up of a new series. Since, however, he works only with tested NC programs and may not alter these, he possesses only a comparatively narrow margin of disposition in the shaping of the work processes' (Mickler, 1989, p. 216).

He stresses the importance of looking at the margins of disposition in areas of relatively low skilled work, since it is there that space for movement, the possibility to regulate the speed of work, and so forth, can make a big difference for workers.

What stands out in the German tradition is not so much their normative or their 'sociological' or 'psychological' orientation but its dedication to studying work in ways that may help improve working conditions, hence arriving at work practices that may be less stressful for workers and provide them with the possibility to not only utilize but expand their skills. These concepts are not necessarily imposed dogmatically, although they have a strong theoretical grounding and are in many cases also politically motivated. They are grounded in meticulous fieldwork that seeks to understand actual work practices (and the larger context of organization, production technology and societal forces), hence not simply 'imposed' but derived from observational and interview data and developed over time.

Finally, German studies of work is design-oriented but the focus is less on the design of technologies but on the design of work and organizations. Typical of this orientation are the attempts at generalizing findings, looking for trends that might be taken up – contradicted or promoted - by the unions, such as the notion of 'new production concepts'. Many studies include union representatives and discuss consequences on the strategic level. A good example of this interest is the ambitious German program of 'humanization of work' that sought to support the development of new 'humane' technologies and models of work, with a strong participation of union representatives at all levels.

4. Conclusion

What can the CSCW research field take from the European field work traditions? First of all, of course, the tradition provides an enormous and enormously rich corpus of naturalistic studies of ordinary cooperative work settings. As a foundation for the comparative analysis, which is an essential part of building an 'analytical framework' 'from the ground up', this is of great value.

Secondly, the family of European field work traditions provides an array of investigative techniques that may supplement observation, interview, and video analysis: protocol analysis of reasoning in natural work settings, 'autoconfrontation', studies of skilled work in simulated environments (e.g., training simulators), and so on.

Thirdly, it provides valuable contributions to the much needed framing of CSCW's empirical work. CSCW's focus is not just any kind of 'socially organized activity' but *ordinary cooperative work*: work in hospitals and factories, administrative agencies and research laboratories, software engineering bureaus and lawyers' offices, and so on. This means that issues of working conditions, issues of workload and stress, of dependability and safety, of the debilitating effect of monotonously repetitive work without scope for learning, of professional autonomy in making decisions — are, if not essential or ubiquitous, then *surely typical*. Or to put it differently, these issues are *regular features of working life in contemporary society*. Therefore, issues of working conditions and related issues of dependability, complexity, stress, monotony, etc. are issues analysts and designers of coordination technologies, if their studies aim at any degree of realism and worldly relevance, *invariably* will come across and have to cope with. And when analysts and designers do come across such issues in addressing the specificity of actual work practices, they would do well to draw upon the outstanding scholarly work of generations of sociologists, psychologists, and engineers that has addressed these more general issues in the European field study traditions and have done so systematically. The point is not that these traditions should, or could, replace ethnographic studies in their critical role in CSCW. The point is rather that these traditions should, and can, enrich and qualify our efforts to develop 'an analytic framework of some generality' 'from the ground up'.

5. Discussion

The aim of this paper has not been to discuss the role of ethnography or fieldwork in general in CSCW. However, it seems appropriate to relate the argument of the present paper to a debate that has gathered some momentum over the last ten or fifteen years (e.g., Anderson, 1997; Button, 2000; Dourish, 2006; Randall, Harper, and Rouncefield, 2007; Crabtree, *et al.*, 2009).

In this debate, the argument is being made that for CSCW and related research areas 'fieldwork is not the point', as Graham Button puts it: 'The point concerns the analytic auspices that are brought to bear, and whether they preserve the practices through which those involved in work interactionally pull it off' (2000, p. 327). He is concerned that

'a number of CSCW practitioners are engaging in studies of work themselves, not just appreciating the studies produced by sociologists. These initiatives are, however, in danger of diluting the initial thrust of sociological studies of work for design purposes because although engaging in fieldwork may be important, it is not enough.' (Button, 2000, p. 328)

More specifically, what in his opinion 'dilutes' this whole field of research is what he calls 'scenic fieldwork' (with a term that probably is not meant to be flattering): 'fieldwork that merely describes and codifies what relevant persons do in the workplace' (p. 319).

'Fieldwork may provide data about the organisation of work and collaboration at work, and about the use of technology at work. However, the telling issue is how that data is [sic] analytically worked.' (Button, 2000, p. 328).

Instead, Button is calling for '*analytic fieldwork*, using data gleaned from fieldwork as material for analysis' to 'explicate' 'what people have to know to do work, and how that knowledge is deployed in the ordering and organisation of work' (pp. 319, 328).

Granted, there may be an issue with fieldwork that produces mere descriptions of observations but it is difficult to tell, for Button does not specify which studies he considers 'scenic'. Anyway, Button's objection deserves to be considered carefully. The fieldworker is not a passive 'data collection' vehicle. The fieldworker produces answers to questions he or she are pursuing. Which questions? Where they come from? How are they related? Or, as Button puts it, how are the data 'analytically worked'?

This is hardly contentious. CSCW has benefitted from contributions from a host of conceptual frameworks: Ethnomethodology, Conversation Analysis, Symbolic Interactionism, Activity Theory, Distributed Cognition, Cognitive Engineering, etc., and they have all, in different ways and with varying success, served as analytical orientations in fieldwork. The problem with these contributions, however, is that they all have been developed for other research programs than CSCW's. Is it not asking too much of these and any other research area or school of thought that it should provide 'analytical auspices' (pp. 336 f.) for fieldwork for CSCW purposes?

What we, in CSCW, are dealing with is not 'action', 'activity', or 'socially organized activities' in all generality but socially organized *interdependent work activities*, *cooperative work*, and our research interests are intimately coupled to our technological commitment. If CSCW is to contribute to the development of appropriately designed coordination technologies, then far more and far more specific 'analytical auspices' are required. Fieldwork, to be productive for CSCW purposes, cannot be conducted under other 'auspices' than those of CSCW's own research program: the 'analytic framework' to be developed 'from the ground up': 'Enter, and you must change' (Schmidt and Bannon, 1992, p. 11).

This brings us back to the research program outlined by Hughes *et al.* in 1994. In order to be able to grasp the manifold forms of cooperative work, it is necessary abstain from stipulating specific forms and features of cooperative work; the required 'analytic framework' is to be built 'from the ground up'. There is no other way. Now, while the research program outlined by Hughes *et al.* in 1994 has been quite productive, it would be foolish to hoist the 'Mission accomplished' banners right now. Conceptual progress has been made, but the 'analytical framework of some generality' is not imminent. Ethnographic and similar forms of investigation will continue to play a significant role in CSCW research. However, the research traditions we point to in this paper (and others too), will have *a* role to play in developing this research program further.

References

Agre, Philip E.: 'From high tech to human tech: Empowerment, measurement, and social studies of computing', *Computer Supported Cooperative Work (CSCW): An International Journal*, vol. 3, no. 2, 1995, pp. 167-195.

Anderson, Robert J.: 'Work, ethnography, and system design', in A. Kent and J. G. Williams (eds.): *The Encyclopedia of Microcomputing*, vol. 20, Marcel Dekker, New York, 1997, pp. 159-183.

Andrieux, Andrée; and Jean Lignon: *L'ouvrier d'aujourdhui*, Librairie Marcel Rivière, Paris, 1960. – Éditions Gonthier, Paris, 1966.

Asendorf-Krings, I.; I. Drexel; and C. Nuber: 'Reproduktionsvermögen und die Interessen von Kapital und Arbeit', in L.-G. Mendius, *et al.*, (ed.): *Betrieb - Arbeitsmarkt - Qualifikation*, Frankfurt, 1976, pp. Betrieb - Arbeitsmarkt - Qualifikation.

Bannon, Liam J.; and Kjeld Schmidt: 'CSCW: Four characters in search of a context', in P. Wilson; J. M. Bowers; and S. D. Benford (eds.): *ECSCW'89: Proceedings of the 1st European Conference on Computer Supported Cooperative Work, 13-15 September 1989, Gatwick, London*, London, 1989, pp. 358-372.

Bannon, Liam J. (ed.) 'A new departure [The Suchman-Winograd debate: Part I]'. [Special theme of] *Computer Supported Cooperative Work (CSCW): An International Journal*, vol. 3, no. 1, 1994, pp. 29-95.

Bannon, Liam J. (ed.) 'Commentaries and a response in the Suchman-Winograd debate [Part II]'. [Special theme of] *Computer Supported Cooperative Work (CSCW): An International Journal*, vol. 3, no. 1, 1995, pp. 29-95.

Beckenbach, Niels: *Industriesoziologie*, De Gruyter, Berlin, 1991.

Braverman, Harry: *Labor and Monopoly Capital: The Degradation of Work in the Twentieth Century*, Monthly Review Press, New York and London, 1974.

Button, Graham: 'The ethnographic tradition and design', *Design Studies*, vol. 21, no. 4, July 2000, pp. 319-332.

Clement, Andrew: 'Cooperative support for computer work: a social perspective on the empowering of end users', in T. Bikson and F. Halasz (eds.): *CSCW'90: Proceedings of the Conference on Computer-Supported Cooperative Work, 7-10 October 1990, Los Angeles, Calif.*, ACM Press, New York, 1990, pp. 223-236.

Crabtree, Andy, *et al.*: 'Ethnography considered harmful', in R. B. Arthur, *et al.* (eds.): *CHI 2009: Proceedings of the 27th international conference on Human factors in computing systems, Boston, Mass., 4-9 April 2009*, ACM Press, New York, 2009, pp. 879-888.

Crossman, E. R. F. W.: *Automation and Skill* (1960). In E. Edwards and F. P. Lees (eds.): *The Human Operator in Process Control*. Taylor & Francis, London, 1974.

De Keyser, Véronique: 'De la contingence et la complexité: l'Évolution des idées dans l'étude des processus continus', *Le Travail humain*, vol. 51, no. 1, 1988, pp. 1-18.

De Keyser, Véronique: 'Why field studies?', in M. G. Helander and M. Nagamachi (eds.): *Human Factors in Design for Manufacturability and Process Planning: Proceedings of The International Ergonomics Association, 9-11 August 1990, Honolulu, Hawaii*, Dept. of Industrial Engineering, State University of New York at Buffalo, Buffalo, New York, 1990, pp. 305-316.

De Keyser, Véronique: 'Why field studies?', in M. G. Helander and M. Nagamachi (eds.): *Design for Manufacturability: A Systems Approach to Concurrent Engineering in Ergonomics*, Taylor & Francis, London and Washington, DC, 1992, pp. 305-316.

De Keyser, Véronique; and Anne-Sophie Nyssen: 'Les erreurs humaines en anesthésie', *Le Travail humain*, vol. 56, no. 2-3, 1993, pp. 243-266.

Dourish, Paul: 'Implications for design', in R. E. Grinter, *et al.* (eds.): *CHI 2006: Proceedings of the SIGCHI Conference on Human Factors in Computing Systems, 22-27 April 2006, Montréal, Québec, Canada*, ACM Press, New York, 2006, pp. 541-550.

Edwards, Elwyn; and Frank P. Lees (eds.): *The Human Operator in Process Control*, Taylor & Francis, London, 1974.

Emery, F. E.; and E. L. Trist: 'The causal texture of organizational environments', *Human Relations*, vol. 18, February 1965, pp. 21-32.

Engelstad, P. H.: 'Socio-technical approach to problems of process control' (*Paper Making Systems and their Control*, London, 1970). In E. Edwards and F. P. Lees: *The Human Operator in Process Control*. Taylor & Francis, London, 1974, pp. 367-385.

Gaillard, Irène; Alain Kerguelen; and Pierre Thon (eds.): *44ème Congrès de la Société d'Ergonomie de Langue Française: Ergonomie et Organisation du Travail, Toulouse les 22, 23, 24 septembre 2009*, Société d'Ergonomie de Langue Française (SELF), 2009. <http://www.ergonomie-self.org/media/media41146.pdf>

Greif, Irene; and Lucy A. Suchman (eds.): *CSCW'88: Proceedings of the Conference on Computer-Supported Cooperative Work, 26-28 September 1988, Portland, Oregon*, ACM Press, New York, 1988.

Hacker, Winfried: 'Action Regulation Theory: A practical tool for the design of modern work processes?', *European Journal of Work and Organizational Psychology*, vol. 12, no. 2, 2003, pp. 105-130.

Heath, Christian C.; and Paul Luff: *Technology in Action*, Cambridge University Press, Cambridge, 2000.

Hoff, Ernst; Lothar Lappe; and Wolfgang Lempert: 'Sozialisationstheoretische Überlegungen zur Analyse von Arbeit, Betrieb und Beruf', *Soziale Welt*, vol. 33, no. 4/4, 1982, pp. 508-531.

Howard, Robert: 'Systems design and social responsibility: The political implications of "Computer-Supported Cooperative Work": A commentary', *Office: Technology and People*, vol. 3, no. 2, 1987.

Hughes, John A., *et al.*: 'Perspectives on the social organisation of work', in J. A. Hughes, *et al.* (eds.): *Field Studies and CSCW*, Computing Department, Lancaster University, Lancaster, UK, October 1994, pp. 129-160. COMIC Deliverable D2.2.
<http://www.comp.lancs.ac.uk/computing/research/soft_eng/comic/>

Kern, Horst; and Michael Schumann: *Industriearbeit und Arbeiterbewußtsein: Eine empirische Untersuchung über den Einfluß der aktuellen technischen Entwicklung auf die industrielle Arbeit und das Arbeiterbewußtsein*, vol. 1-2, Europäische Verlagsanstalt, Frankfurt am Main, 1970.

Kern, Horst; and Michael Schumann: *Das Ende der Arbeitsteilung? Rationalisierung in der industriellen Produktion: Bestandaufnahme, Trendbestimmung*, München, 1984.

Kuutti, Kari: 'The concept of activity as a basic unit of analysis for CSCW research', in L. J. Bannon; M. Robinson; and K. Schmidt (eds.): *ECSCW'91: Proceedings of the Second European Conference on Computer-Supported Cooperative Work, 24–27 September 1991, Amsterdam*, Kluwer Academic Publishers, Dordrecht, 1991, pp. 249-264.

Laville, Antoine: 'Historical landmarks of french ergonomics', in: *Comptes rendus du congrès SELF-ACE 2001: Les transformations du travail, enjeux pour l'ergonomie / Proceedings of the SELF-ACE 2001 Conference: Ergonomics for Changing Work*, vol. 1, 2001, pp. 1-6. <http://www.ergonomie-self.org/content/content30521.html>

Leplat, Jacques (ed.): *L'analyse du travail en psychologie ergonomique: Recueil de textes. Tome 1*, Octarès Éditions, Paris, 1992.

Leplat, Jacques (ed.): *L'analyse du travail en psychologie ergonomique: Recueil de textes. Tome II*, Octarès Éditions, Paris, 1993.

Leplat, Jacques: 'Collective activity in work: some lines of research', *Le Travail humain*, vol. 57, no. 3, 1994, pp. 209-226.

Littek, Wolfgang: 'Arbeitssituation und betriebliche Arbeitsbedingungen', in W. Littek; W. Rammert; and G. n. Wachtler (eds.): *Einführung in die Arbeits- und Industriesoziologie*, Campus Verlag, Frankfurt a. M., 1983, pp. 92-135.

Mickler, Otfried, *et al.*: *Produktion und Qualifikation: Eine empirische Untersuchung zur Entewicklung von Qualifikationsanforderungen in der industriellen Produktion und deren Ursachen*, vol. 1-2, SOFI, Göttingen, 1977.

Mickler, Otfried: 'The introduction and use of CNC in the Federal Republic of Germany', in A. Francis and P. Grootings (eds.): *New Technologies and Work: Capitalist and Socialist Persopectives*, Routledge, London/New York, 1989, pp. 187-226.

Moldaschl, Manfred: *Frauenarbeit oder Facharbeit? Montagerationalisierung in der Elektroindustrie II*, Campus Verlag, Frankfurt, 1991.

Montmollin, Maurice de: 'Analysis and models of operators' activities in complex natural life environments', in J. Rasmussen; H. B. Andersen; and N. O. Bernsen (eds.): *Human-Computer Interaction: Research Directions in Cognitive Science: European Perspectives*, vol. 3, Lawrence Erlbaum, Hove, England, 1991, pp. 95-112.

Neboit, Michel: 'Brève histoire de l'ergonomie', 2006. <http://www.preventica.com/actu-interview-self-juillet06.php>

Oesterreich, Rainer; and Walter Volpert: 'Task analysis for work design on the basis of Action Regulation Theory', *Economic and Industrial Democracy*, vol. 7, 1986, pp. 503-527.

Ombredane, André; and Jean-Marie Faverge: *L'analyse du travail: Facteur d'économie humaine et de productivité*, Presses Universitaires de France, Paris, 1955.

Pipek, Volkmar, *et al.* (eds.): *End-User Development: 2nd International Symposium, IS-EUD 2009, Siegen, Germany, 2-4 March 2009: Proceedings*, Springer, Berlin-Heidelberg, 2009.

Pongratz, H. J.; and R. Trinczek: *Industriesoziologische Fallstudien: Entwicklungspotenziale einer Forschungsstrategie*, edition sigma, Berlin, 2010.

Popitz, Heinrich, *et al.*: *Technik und Industriearbeit: Soziologische Untersuchungen in der Hüttenindustrie*, J. C. B. Mohr, Tübingen, 1957a.

Popitz, Heinrich, *et al.*: *Das Gesellscahftsbild des Arbeiters: Soziologische Untersuchungen in der Hüttenindusrtrie*, J. C. B. Mohr, Tübingen, 1957b.

Randall, David W.; Richard H. R. Harper; and Mark Rouncefield: *Fieldwork for Design: Theory and Practice*, Springer, London, 2007.

Robinson, Mike: 'Double-level languages and co-operative working', *AI & Society*, vol. 5, no. 1, January 1991, pp. 34-60.

Rogalski, Janine: 'Co-operation processes in dynamic environment management: Evolution through training experienced pilots in flying a highly automated aircraft', *Acta Psychologica*, vol. 91, no. 3, April 1996, pp. 273-295.

Roth, Emilie M.; and Emily S. Patterson: 'Using observational study as a tool for discovery: Uncovering cognitive and collaborative demands and adaptive strategies', in H. Montgomery; R. Lipshitz; and B. Brehmer (eds.): *How Professionals Make Decisions*, Lawrence Erlbaum, Mahwah, New Jersey, 2005, pp. 379-493.

Samurçay, Renan; and Janine Rogalski: 'Cooperative work and decision making in emergency management', *Le Travail humain*, vol. 56, no. 1, 1993, pp. 53-77.

Schmidt, Kjeld; and Liam J. Bannon: 'Taking CSCW seriously: Supporting articulation work', *Computer Supported Cooperative Work (CSCW): An International Journal*, vol. 1, no. 1-2, 1992, pp. 7-40.

Sørgaard, Pål: 'A cooperative work perspective on use and development of computer artifacts', in: *10th Information Systems Research Seminar in Scandinavia (IRIS), 10-12 August 1987, Vaskivesi, Finland*, 1987.

Suchman, Lucy A.: 'Do categories have politics? The language/action perspective reconsidered', in G. De Michelis; C. Simone; and K. Schmidt (eds.): *ECSCW'93: Proceedings of the Third European Conference on Computer-Supported Cooperative Work, 13-17 September 1993, Milano, Italy*, Kluwer Academic Publishers, Dordrecht, 1993, pp. 1-14.

Suchman, Lucy A.: 'Do categories have politics? The language/action perspective reconsidered', *Computer Supported Cooperative Work (CSCW): An International Journal*, vol. 2, no. 3, 1994, pp. 177-190.

Touraine, Alain: *La conscience ouvrière*, Éditions du Seuil, Paris, 1966.

Trist, Eric L.; and Kenneth W. Bamforth: 'Some social and psycological consequences of the longwall method of coal-getting: An examination of the psychological situation and defences of a work group in relation to the social structure and technological content of the work system', *Human Relations*, vol. 4, 1951, pp. 3-38.

Vicente, Kim J.: 'Cognitive engineering research at Risø from 1962–1979', in E. Salas (ed.): *Advances in Human Performance and Cognitive Engineering Research*, vol. 1, Elsevier, New York, 2001, pp. 1-57.

Volpert, Walter: *Die 'Humanisierung der Arbeit' und die Arbeitswissenschaft*, Pahl-Rugenstein Verlag, Köln, 1974.

Volpert, Walter: 'Psychologische Aspekte industrieller Arbeit', in W. Georg; L. Kißler; and U. Sattel (eds.): *Arbeit und Wissenschaft: Arbeitswissenschaft?*, Bonn, 1985.

Wagner, Ina; and Andrew Clement (eds.): 'NetWORKing'. [Special theme of] *Computer Supported Cooperative Work (CSCW): An International Journal*, vol. 2, no. 1-2, 1994, pp. 1-130.

Winograd, Terry: 'Categories, disciplines, and social coordination', *Computer Supported Cooperative Work (CSCW): An International Journal*, vol. 2, 1994, pp. 191-194.

Woodward, Joan: *Industrial Organization: Theory and Practice*, Oxford University Press, London, 1965.

Flypad: Designing Trajectories in a Large-Scale Permanent Augmented Reality Installation

Martin Flintham[1], Stuart Reeves[1], Patrick Brundell[1], Tony Glover[1], Steve Benford[1], Duncan Rowland[2], Boriana Koleva[1], Chris Greenhalgh[1], Matt Adams[3], Nick Tandavanitj[3], Ju Row Farr[3]
[1]University of Nottingham, UK; [2]University of Lincoln, UK; [3]Blast Theory, UK
mdf@cs.nott.ac.uk, stuart@tropic.org.uk, {prb,atg,sdb}@cs.nott.ac.uk,
drowland@lincoln.ac.uk, {bnk,cmg}@cs.nott.ac.uk,
{matt,nick,ju}@blasttheory.co.uk

Abstract. A long-term naturalistic study reveals how artists designed, visitors experienced, and curators and technicians maintained a public interactive artwork over a four year period. The work consisted of a collaborative augmented reality game that ran across eleven networked displays (screens and footpads) that were deployed along a winding ramp in a purpose-built gallery. Reflections on design meetings and documentation show how the artists responded to this architectural setting and addressed issues of personalisation, visitor flow, attracting spectators, linking real and virtual, and accessibility. Observations of visitors reveal that while their interactions broadly followed the artists' design, there was far more flexible engagement than originally anticipated, especially within visiting groups, while interviews with curators and technicians reveal how the work was subsequently maintained and ultimately reconfigured. Our findings extend discussions of 'interactional trajectories' within CSCW, affirming the relevance of this concept to describing collaboration in cultural settings, but also suggesting how it needs to be extended to better reflect group interactions at multiple levels of scale.

Introduction

Art galleries, museums and exploratoria have proved to be fertile ground for the development and study of CSCW technologies over recent years, due to both their willingness to experiment with new technologies that might engage visitors with cultural experiences, but also due to the inherently group-oriented nature of visiting. Thus, we have seen a variety of novel technologies deployed within these settings, from group-oriented mobile guides (Aoki et al., 2002; Not et al., 1997) and augmented reality technologies (Koleva et al., 2009) that enhance interpretation by overlaying digital material on physical artefacts; to tangible and tabletop interfaces that promise rapid engagement and learning as well as fluid interaction among groups (Mazalek, 2009); to sensor-based physical interfaces that support full-body interaction and playful or even performative social experiences (Snibbe & Raffle, 2009). In turn, studies of visitor conduct with and around 'interactives' in museums and galleries (Brown et al., 2003; Costello et al., 2005; Heath & vom Lehn, 2002; Hindmarsh et al., 2005; vom Lehn, Heath & Knoblauch, 2001) have revealed new challenges and concepts for CSCW, including the idea of *interactional trajectories* in which one visitor's public conduct shapes that of subsequent visitors (see Hindmarsh et al., 2005; Benford et al., 2009). Others have considered the diversity of these settings, highlighting their cultural (Bell, 2002), information (Nardi & O'Day, 1999) or display (Crabtree & Rodden, 2008; Terrenghi et al., 2009) ecologies.

This paper extends this body of work by reporting a study of an interactive installation called Flypad, an eleven-player augmented reality game that was commissioned for permanent exhibition in a major new public arts centre. Our study charts the development of Flypad over a four year period, from initial inception, to public deployment, to subsequent maintenance, drawing on the perspectives of the artists, visitors, curators and technical staff in order to articulate how a large and complex permanent public experience was designed to operate robustly within a high-throughout setting. As a result, we are able to shed new light on ongoing discussions of public interaction within CSCW.

A brief introduction to Flypad

We begin with a very brief overview of Flypad as an experience. Flypad was commissioned to be part of the permanent collection of The Public, an art gallery housed in a purpose-built building designed by architect Will Alsop (Figure 1, left). The internal form of the building is such that visitors were intended to take an elevator to the top (3rd) floor and then gradually wind their way down a sloping ramp, passing through a series of temporary and permanent exhibitions on the way. Flypad is the largest permanent exhibition, being distributed around a large 2nd floor balustrade overlooking the building's central atrium (Figure 1, right & Figure 2). The work was developed by a team of artists, curators, researchers and technical subcontractors over a four-year period, and opened to the public in August 2009.

Flypad is a collaborative augmented reality game in which up to eleven players at a time engage in mid-air avatar wrestling. Eleven game terminals, one per player, are arranged in groups on three 'blisters' that protrude from three sides of a balustrade (four terminals on the 1st and 2nd blisters, three on the 3rd blister). Each terminal comprises a screen on which a player sees an image of their avatar that is overlaid on a video-view of the atrium beyond to create a see-though augmented reality effect (Figure 3, left). By jumping up and down on the centre of a ruggedised footpad that is placed in front of the screen (Figure 3, right), the player can keep their avatar floating in the air. By treading on the four corners of the footpad, they can steer their avatar laterally in space in order to collide with the avatars of other players. These interactions also steer a motorised video camera that is mounted just below the blister (Figure 2, right) so that the camera follows the movements of the avatar in order to keep it in view (i.e., positioned in the centre of the video view that serves as the backdrop) as it moves. This creates the illusion that the avatar is floating in the atrium beyond the screen.

Figure 1. The Public's signature building (left). On the ramp looking across two blisters (right).

Figure 2. Flypad terminals and Tall Trees from below (left). Looking up at a blister (right).

When two or more avatars collide there is a chance that they will enter a wrestling hold in which case they grip onto one another and then mutate by exchanging body parts. The player awarded points for each hold and mutation that they manage to achieve.

Each player's avatar is generated from a library of pre-defined parts to have a quirky and distinct different visual form (inspired by the traditional costumes and masks of Mexican wrestlers) and physical behaviours in terms of how it floats and moves. As time passes in a player's game, so their avatar appears to become heavier requiring them to work harder by jumping on the footpad in order to keep it airbourne. Eventually, no matter how hard they work, their avatar sinks to the floor and their game is over. Flypad is a rolling experience in the sense that new players can join the game at any time (i.e., there is no synchronised start and end time for all players).

Finally, highlights from live or recent (recorded) games are displayed on the 'Tall Trees' a series of large screens mounted on the tops of tall stands that are located in the central atrium (separate from the players' terminals) in order to engage the attention of passing visitors and so attract them to the experience.

Figure 3. Player's screen showing an avatar with instructions overlaid in-game (left). A handpad (top right) and a footpad (bottom right).

Studying Flypad

Our study of Flypad employed ethnography to produce a rich description of the experience of an interactive artwork 'in the wild', that is within the actual setting of a public gallery. In so doing, we build on a tradition of ethnographic studies of interactives in galleries, museums, exploratoria and similar settings as noted previously. Our study is distinct, however, in charting the evolution of Flypad over a four year period from its initial inception as a proposal through to reflections on its sustainability one year after opening to the public. Both the installation and study were delivered by an interdisciplinary team comprising artists, developers and social scientists (the artists had collaborated with members of the team on previous projects). One developer on the project, who had also been trained in ethnography, documented the initial design process as a participant-observer, while a second, who had not been involved in the wider project, was introduced during the study phase to observe visitors and also interview staff at the Public.

Our study provides three complementary perspectives on Flypad, each drawing on a distinct set of materials:

First, we cover the *artists' perspectives on developing Flypad*, drawing on interviews with artist in our team as well as artists and designers involved in the wider project, design documents and field notes from design meetings and testing sessions (all over a three year period) to articulate the rationale behind its design as it evolved from the initial proposal to the public opening.

Second, we explore the *visitors' perspectives on experiencing Flypad*, drawing on observations and field notes (including four hours of video recordings captured at The Public) to show how groups of visitors actually interacted with and around the installation.

Third, we consider the *curators' perspectives on sustaining Flypad*, drawing on interviews with two key staff at The Public—its Artistic Director and a member of the technical support team—as they describe various aspects of day-to-day maintenance, but also reflect on the longer term reconfiguration of the work based on their own observations of use.

We now consider each of these three perspectives in turn before drawing them together in a subsequent discussion.

Developing Flypad

The artists derived inspiration for Flypad in part from sourced such as Char Davies's work (e.g., Osmose), and the arcade experiences of Dance Dance Revolution. Their rationale for Flypad was set out in detail in their initial proposal to a competitive bidding process which included an animated fly-though of the experience as originally envisaged. The stills from this animation shown in Figure 4 reveal how the overall physical arrangement of Flypad was already in place at this very early stage, showing the footpads and screens arranged in groups at the blisters, steerable cameras mounted on the balustrade, and the Tall Trees in the centre. Flypad's overall design evolved in its detail over subsequent years as the artists addressed several key issues in cooperation with the exhibition's curators.

Figure 4: stills from the original proposal animation showing the core design

Responding to the architectural setting

The relatively detailed, and ultimately quite stable, form of this early design arose, at least in part, from being able to respond to the specific architectural setting of the building. As one of the artists stated at interview "the whole work itself springs from the architectural location". Perhaps the most distinctive feature of this setting is the idea that visitors will ascend a lift to the top floor and descend through the exhibit down the spiralling ramp and past the three blisters. Quoting from The Public's own design brief for the overall exhibition, the ramp structure was conceived of as a "dramatic line", starting high-up and moving down to become increasingly focussed, guiding visitor flow through exhibits. The physical design was influenced by this concept, such as the continuous metal handrail that runs along the ramp, which "mutates" into each exhibit's framework. Flypad is situated on the "Hill Top" section of the ramp, which is an area designed "to encourage visitors to form into 3 groups in each of the blisters regardless of [whether] the visitors know one another". The ramp, being physically quite narrow (accommodating a couple of visitors abreast), was seen as significant, particularly due to the "funnelling" and "clumping" of visitors (as the building designers called it).

Personalisation

The original vision for The Public was that each visitor would receive a highly personalised experience. The initial idea was that visitors would first register some personal details and in return, receive an RFID tag that they could use to identify themself to each new exhibit they encountered and that would also help record their progress around the exhibition. The artist's response to this opportunity was for Flypad to take this evolving 'data body' and somehow use it to create a uniquely personal avatar for each player. However, the networked RFID backbone was eventually dropped by The Public due to cost and time constraints, so that the artists had to instead try and generate avatars from a database of pre-designed parts as noted above. However, the decision to drop the RFID system was to have other ramifications as we explore below.

Managing visitor flow

Based upon projected visitor throughput, The Public provided a strict brief as to target 'dwell times' at each exhibit, requiring a game of Flypad to last for a maximum period of five minutes. The artists responded with a game design that, though the use of increasing gravity, would naturally bring each player's game to an end within this period, no matter how well they played. To complement this, the start of the game involved a quick animated instruction and training sequence designed to rapidly bring the player up to speed. The "rolling" nature of Flypad also encouraged high throughput by not having to wait for multiple players to be in place before starting a game. This concern for throughput extended to the physical design of the footpad, whose low profile and lack of a surrounding guard rail was intended to ensure rapid physical engagement and disengagement and a quick handover between players.

The artists envisaged that the spatially bulging nature of the blisters would accommodate both players and spectators, along with a flow of visitors walking past. In sympathy with this, the physical design of Flypad carefully positioned the footpads and screens so as to accommodate an adequate flow past the terminals, but at the same time offer the potential for spectators to cluster around players. However, at interview, the artists expressed some concern about the "linear" structure of the ramp causing a "clump at the first blister", rather than a reasonably even distribution across all terminals that might best exploit the sense of space and "encourage people to think about the space between [them]". Their proposed solution lay in the use of the envisaged RFID tracking system which might control which terminals could be used next or even direct incoming players to a given terminal, so as to ensure a more even distribution of players around the balustrade. Dropping the RFID system resulted in the final version of Flypad making no attempt to balance the loading of players across terminals.

Attracting spectators

Another key concern that was evident from the outset was supporting spectating. In designing the footpads and gameplay the artists attempted to walk a line between encouraging physical movement that would attract spectators in a way similar to "dance pad machines [with] people stand[ing] behind them practicing the moves", but without being "something where you had to move around so much that you made a spectacle of yourself". This visibility also extended to the motorised cameras; the artists wanted visitors on the atrium floor to be "very conscious of these cameras, and if they are all rotating in space". However, it should be noted that to physically protect them and ease power and cabling issues, the cameras were eventually mounted some distance below the game terminals rather than on top of the rail near the screen as originally envisaged (see Figures 2, right and 4, right for the contrast between the final and proposed positions).

The Tall Trees were more explicitly targeted at spectators, not only for visitors already on the ramp, but also for visitors at the start of the experience, in the words of the artists: "leading their eyes up to the gallery", creating a connection between the ground floor and the other ramp floors. However, the artists commented that there was only "limited [...] awareness that we can play with" before visitors could engage with Flypad, "because [visitors are] not just physically remote, they're temporally quite remote from the experience".

Linking real and the virtual

As the artists described it, Flypad was intended to provide a "seamlessly interlinked" experience of the real and the virtual but at the same time retain "the frisson of difference" between the two, a design concept that also impacted on the physical design of the terminals. The artists' ideal was to have "a screen that's as big as possible, with as small a surround to the screen as possible, on as light an arm or mount as possible, on a glass balustrade". The footpads were employed in order to support this experience, as they represent "interactive devices that don't actually get physically in-between you and the experience". Practically this also meant positioning the footpad and screen so a player's "eye moves from the screen to the atrium around them [... as easily ...] as possible" thus merging of the augmented view and the real view.

Other issues became more apparent during testing. One of these was the nature of interaction via the game's software; that is how the footpads should connect to the movement of avatars and cameras. After various early experiments, the artists and developers homed in on a distinctive approach where the avatars operated relatively autonomously (driven by an underlying rigid-body real-time physics engine), floating, entering holds, and exchanging body parts, with the players 'nudging' them around the space rather than controlling their movements in a fine grained way. By using the footpad, players apply simulated forces to avatars, giving the players a sense of 'pushing' or 'prodding' their avatar in a general direction rather than steering it precisely. Use of the physics engine in this way also means that the flexibly jointed avatars may also 'collide' with one another, or bounce off the (invisible) bounding box of the atrium in a deliberately 'buoyant' way. Avatar limbs attract one another when sufficiently close so that the avatars can easily enter pre-programmed wrestling holds without the players having to control the fine details of positioning, grasping and releasing. Consequently, the connection between movements on the footpads and the movements of the avatars became relatively indirect or 'fuzzy' in feel.

Enabling accessibility

Accessibility is a key concern for public institutions and was raised as a requirement shortly after the initial proposal had been accepted. The primary consequence of this was the design and introduction of the three 'handpads, one per blister, to support access by visitors with limited physical mobility.

Experiencing Flypad

Our discussion thus far has been of the artists' (and also curators' and even architects') views of how a visitor's experience should ideally unfold. In order to see how it actually unfolds, one needs to observe visitors in situ. Our recordings (and subsequent interviews with the curators) suggest that for the most part, visitors were generally able to engage with Flypad and play the game following the artists' overall design. However, we observed in the detail of interaction a greater sense of fluidity, less linearity of experience, and often longer overall dwell times than originally anticipated. We saw frequent dis- and re-engagements and exchanges of footpads between players, especially within groups. The following vignette from our video corpus follows a single group—a family— captured by our ethnographers through an extended engagement with Flypad and is broadly representative of many experiences that we observed[1].

Phase 1—Approaching, engaging and disengaging

A family consisting of an adult man (M), adult woman (W) and two children, a boy (B) and a girl (G), walk down the ramp, approaching the first terminals of Flypad. On the family's approach, B steps straight onto the rightmost terminal, shouts "dad" and

---

[1] Due to space and scope constraints we have chosen to detail intra-group interactions rather than attempting to treat inter-group interactions as well. Nevertheless, we found inter-group interactions to be less 'intimate' (e.g., no direct intervention on occupied footpads by another group) yet remain highly fluid and characteristically 'rolling'. As such our vignette does illuminate to *some* extent more general collaborative interactions.

beckons with his hand. G joins him, and steps directly onto his footpad alongside him so that the two are sharing. M then steps onto the adjacent footpad while W stands watching between the two footpads. Another visitor momentarily steps onto the next footpad along from the family group but then walks away from the group. B pushes G off the footpad at the same time as uttering "get off" (Figure 5, left); in response W points to the now-free game terminal to their left, stating "there's another one there".

W accompanies G to the footpad and begins reading out the on-screen instructions ("step on the booster to...") as G steps on to play. During their play, G and B repeatedly glance across at adjacent screens. Family members then remain on their footpads for around 40s (with W still spectating between M and G). During this time, B exclaims "I can see you" (although it is unclear who this utterance is directed towards). G steps off her pad, and W quickly hits the footpad with one foot (Figure 5, middle) while G gets back on the pad. G then steps off the pad again, and says "look, look" (she appears to be watching her avatar slowly sink to the ground). W intervenes, uttering "boost" and stepping onto the footpad, but is subsequently pushed off by G (Figure 5b). B now says "yes I got someone's leg" and G walks over to stand by him, watching. Just as she does this, W, watching the screen of the 3rd terminal, steps onto the now vacant footpad herself and begins another game (Figure 5, right). G returns and stands by W, who steps aside as G remounts her original footpad.

Figure 5. "get off" (left); intervention (middle); the family of players (right).

This complex series of movements and interactions is revealing in several regards. First, the design of the footpads and their relationship to the screens, appears to encourage approach and immediate, experimental engagement as we see here with B as he steps on the rightmost footpad. We observed similar approaches by other visitors, who often walk or run up to the footpads and jump on them, and only after this seem to begin interaction with the game in earnest. The nature of the physical engagement also reflects this, for instance W uses just one foot to play experimentally with the footpad (Figure 5, middle). Indeed the whole sequence here is notable for the ease with which the family repeatedly engages and disengage with the footpads, including trying to share footpads as we see when W steps onto the semi-occupied footpad before G wards them off.

We also note that this rapid handover of footpads enables participants to sustain one another's engagement with the game, as we saw at the end of this phase when W begins a new game on G's recently-vacated footpad, which G then returns to. However, rapid (re)engagements also enable players to take over from each other mid-game. Sometimes this appears to be opportunistic, taking over a game when someone has moved on (as we will see next in phase 2, B takes over G's game seconds after her departure). The 'fuzzy' nature of interactions with avatars due to the physics engine may also contribute to the ease of handing over an ongoing game as it becomes relatively easy to disengage for a few seconds without losing the game, and for others to take over without having to precisely orient to the current state of play. Taking over other's games is also supported by 'sideways spectating' that is, by being able to glance over at an adjacent terminal while playing the game yourself.

It is interesting to speculate here that the original proposal to use RFID to direct visitors to specific blisters or terminals and provide them with personalised avatars might have inhibited this kind of rapid engagement and handover which relies on being able to quickly step onto a footpad and pick up on someone else's game. We saw how some members of a group, W in this phase, take on the role of assigning players to footpads within their group ("there's another one there").

Phase 2—Overlapping game sequences and the footpad

As we rejoin the action, B's game has now finished and he comes over to G and W, looking over the balustrade into the atrium as G plays. M's game also finishes, and he and W stand back, watching G as she jumps up and down the footpad. W and G walk away from the blister, W says "anybody need the toilet?". At this moment (Figure 6, left), B jumps onto the footpad G has just vacated, mid-game, and begins playing while M turns slightly and watches B. M goes over to the handpad next to B and begins playing; B jumps off the footpad mid-game and joins M. After approximately a minute of play, M steps aside and B uses the handpad as M stands behind B (Figure 6, right).

Overlapping games are common, in which a player's game ends while others' are ongoing, leading the player to begin a new one rather than wait around. Thus, although each game may last only a few minutes, overall player engagement can be quite long due to overlapping sequences of games, particularly where a group is concerned, such as this family. Here we see how B does not wait till G's avatar has hit the floor (precipitated by her departure), but rather, seamlessly takes over the vacated spot (Figure 6, left). B later does the same with M's game on the handpad (which M relinquishes for B—Figure 6, right). We suggest that handing over ongoing games may naturally accommodate different roles for adults and children within a party. Thus, we see how B took over M's handpad as M stood aside, and how in phase 1, W, who often watches, stepped up to fill in gaps in play for G on two occasions (Figure 5).

Figure 6. G playing (leftmost image), then leaving with W, after which B takes over mid-game; B playing on the handpad with M behind (rightmost image).

This overlapping play may be further encouraged by the presence of adjacent footpads at each blister, and also by the presence of the handpad at the end of each blister which offers a player a novel and alternative way of experiencing the game again just before they leave a blister. We found that the design of Flypad, both physically and in terms of game structure, to our surprise, often resulted in the kind of repeated, sequential engagements *within* a single blister (as players moved from terminal to terminal) that we see here in this vignette.

Phase 3—Making sense of the augmentation, and local, not global, spectating

B plays on the hand terminal for a further minute. He then points towards the Tall Trees, saying "there's me". M directs his gaze momentarily along the direction of B's arm, but begins answering a call on his mobile phone. W and G return; W stands to the left of B, and M remains standing some distance behind B on his mobile phone. G watches B playing briefly before jumping back onto the middle footpad. A short time later during play, B utters "you're on the screen… you see". G laughs and, continuing to jump on the pad, says "you've got my leg … I can actually see you". G's game ends as her avatar hits the floor, she gets off the pad and walks over to W, saying "mum can one of us go over there [points towards the atrium floor] so we can see each other?" as B continues to play on the handpad.

Throughout our analysis so far we have seen how, through the careful spacing and placing of the footpads, Flypad supports what might be termed 'local spectating' including multiple transitions from spectating to playing and back again. The closeness of the footpads also allows observation of other players' screens while continuing to play (e.g., see phase 1). This support for spectatorship also helps players make sense of the augment reality by relating avatars to one another. As this sequence shows, B and G appear to make sense of the relationship between their avatars (referring to their avatar's limbs and "seeing" one another in the virtual space). Having identified B's avatar, G verbally highlights the action they have performed collaboratively ("you've got my leg"). G also shows understanding to some extent of the nature of the augmentation, in linking the physical space (the atrium floor) with the augmentation on-screen. Interestingly, the immediacy of the footpads permits the visitors to rapidly engage with the game, without requiring that they fully understand the collaborative or augmented reality aspects of it. Instead this understanding is developed gradually.

Finally, in this phase of the vignette, we see how another spectator-oriented aspect of the design, the Tall Trees, which might be termed 'global spectating', comes into play. While the Tall Trees screens are clearly noticeable as B verbally and physically highlights here, both for the display of his own play, and pointing out that of G's ("you're on the screen"), we note that in this sequence his activity had been displayed on the Tall Trees for some time (74 seconds) before he remarked on it. Further to this, the family group has by this time been present at the first blister for over six minutes. In general, we noted that visitors rarely attended to or referenced the Tall Trees. Thus, while the arrangement of the terminals, coupled with the size of the terminal screens and the space behind and to the side of them seems to support spectating upon the local action, the Tall Trees appear have been far less impactful as a global spectator interface.

Maintaining and reconfiguring Flypad

To get a third perspective on Flypad we interviewed the Artistic Director (AD) responsible for the overall curation of The Public, as well as a member of the technical support team (TS) who had been working directly on the day-to-day maintenance of Flypad. In addition to their distinctive professional perspectives, both had spent considerable time observing Flypad in use and were able to extend our own observations; or in the words of TS "I'm an IT guy but I've been watching what people do!"

Maintaining Flypad

While Flypad was reported as generally stable and could mostly operate with mostly only minimal routine maintenance, it became clear that busy times could be more problematic. For instance, as AD reported to us, "last week or the week before we had about 4000 people in a week so [Flypad] got a pasting and perhaps like anything has been difficult this week". In these situations Flypad "needs constant maintenance". Problems mostly involved physical wear and tear such as broken speakers, video cable problems, and faulty USB connections. These tended to be focused around the game terminals nearer the top of the ramp; as TS related "they do take a lot of hammering, those 4 [terminals in the first blister]". Some variation was mentioned at this first blister: "ironically 2 [terminal number 2 within the first blister] gets the most hammering because they're the first ones [visitors] come down to, and they walk past the first screen and jump on to the second screen". Compounding this are challenges with the physical maintenance of Flypad. Resolving problems may require "total downtime" for the whole exhibit for safety reasons, due to the danger of objects falling to floors below while the terminals are dismantled—especially difficult at busy periods [TS].

Reconfiguring Flypad

Beyond routine maintenance, this team was also involved in the longer-term reconfiguration of Flypad in response to their own observations of use and other changes to the exhibitions housed in the space. They identified two main changes to the exhibit itself and the ecology surrounding the exhibit. Firstly, like ourselves, AD had come to the conclusion that the Tall Trees were not especially effective as a spectator interface for Flypad: "nobody ever used them, nobody looked at them or didn't even realise that they were their [player] representations" [AD]; [TS] made similar comments. In response, the Tall Trees had become screens to display other exhibition work: "we've got two Josh Nimoys [...] now running on it [the Tall Trees]" [TS].

However, this reconfiguration extended beyond the Tall Trees to address the entire trajectory through the experience, arguably the most fundamental feature of its design. As AD reflected, "the thought of going up to the top and coming down is an alien one to people visiting a place like this so going the other way makes much more sense". AD was now encouraging reception to steer some visitors up the ramp so that people would approach Flypad from either end. As well as having an overall aesthetic impetus, AD related that this change had practical dimensions. For instance, in order to avoid confusion, visitors had to be "pushed towards the lift [for the 3rd floor]"; AD notes that in spite of this, the curators "lose so many people when they come out of the lift at the third floor [... visitors] don't really know where to go". A secondary but no less important impetus for AD was the need to alleviate visitor flow when crowded and spread wear and tear across terminals. We note that such reconfiguration would be different were the RFID system implemented, as it would have required reprogramming the Flypad software. On the one hand, this might afford curators greater control over the flow through the exhibit, but would also require dedicated software tools.

Finally, there is an issue for more complete reconfiguration of the exhibition space, and the need to "refresh many of the pieces on the ramp", however Flypad is only reconfigurable to a small degree and so is "a difficult piece to think about because I [AD] can't just put different data in and get a different output in that piece". AD observed that the highly distinctive physical form of Flypad compared to some of the other permanent exhibits would make it far more difficult to change in the long term, meaning that "Blast Theory's piece will be on until frankly it doesn't work anymore [... or] get Blast Theory to come in and think of another way they could use the facilities to engage in a different way" [AD].

Discussion—summary of key findings

We begin our discussion by drawing together our findings from a diverse range of sources to identify key issues and challenges for Flypad as a public installation, before then widening our perspective to consider how our study sheds light on recent discussions of interactional trajectories within HCI at large.

As a public experience, Flypad was successfully delivered, installed and has been in use (and re-use) by many thousands of visitors for over a year in a prominent public arts centre. Observations and interviews with curators suggest that, in broad terms, Flypad appears to be playable by a variety of users, including both children and adults, in the sense that they are able to engage with the work and complete a game; and seems to be generally well appreciated by visitors and support staff. However, our study also reveals that, in the detail, the characteristics of use are somewhat different from those anticipated in the original design. While visitors do often undertake an overall journey along (usually down) the ramp, into engagement with Flypad and through the game as envisaged in the initial design, there is also much greater flexibility surrounding how they engage at any given moment, which manifests itself in two main ways as exhibited by the vignette. First, players may rapidly and repeatedly disengage from and reengage with Flypad, including competing for footpads and also taking over each other's foodpads and ongoing games. Second, players may repeatedly engage and experience multiple games as they progress along the ramp, perhaps while waiting for colleagues to finish or maybe when new opportunities present themselves such as the novelty of trying out a handpad.

Underlying these observations, and of clear interest to CSCW, is the group nature of the visiting experience. Visiting cultural institutions such as galleries and museums is very often a group experience leading to a tendency for groups of visitors to stick together as they progress through the exhibition. This natural gravity between individuals in a group, for example, as parents stand by and observe children, or members of a party wait for someone to finish before moving on, underpins the pattern of multiple and rapid engagement that we have documented. In the same way that Flypad is a rolling game, so the experience of a visiting group is also rolling as they appear to gradually tumble along the ramp, engaging and disengaging with Flypad terminals in an interleaved way as they go. We speculate that this rolling engagement might be similar to a group of visitors moving along a traditional gallery of paintings or sculptures, but with the notable difference that they are also collaborating *through* the terminals (i.e., within the game) as well as *around* them. Indeed, we suggest that the detailed design of Flypad encourages this kind of rolling engagement, and now revisit some of early design decisions that we documented previously to consider how this might be so.

- **Responding to the architectural setting**—the linear and elongated nature of Flypad as it is stretched along a winding ramp and affords multiple points of engagement through eleven discrete terminals distributed around three distinct blisters affords a kind of 'stickiness' to the experience. However, this linear structure also led to some unforeseen maintenance problems as terminals on the first blister suffered greater wear and tear than others.

- **Personalisation**—the original plan to have personalised avatars might have inhibited taking over others' games, while the associated decision to drop the RFID system may have enabled a far more fluid engagement as players could easily engage with any vacant, and sometimes even occupied, terminal.
- **Managing visitor flow**—we suggest that the rolling nature of the experience provides a powerful way of managing variations in visitor flow. While each individual game of Flypad lasts for no more than five minutes, repeated reengagement allows for a much longer overall experience during quiet times. Put another way, having an experience with short but repeated engagements may allow people to socially negotiate or self-regulate flow and throughput through the experience.
- **Attracting spectators**—the physical form and placement of the terminals and footpads appears to have been successful at supporting 'local spectating' while also accommodating a flow of visitors along the ramp. Local spectating also extended to sideways monitoring of adjacent players. In contrast, the explicit use of the Tall Trees as a separate spectator interface appears to have been far less successful at supporting 'global spectating', perhaps due to a fragmentation of views in which there were no obvious connections between the clips they were displaying and specific terminals.
- **Linking real and virtual**—not only did the indirect linking of real and virtual through the use of a physics engine make the game more playable, but it also supported the ability to hand over an ongoing game from one player to another.
- **Enabling accessibility**—finally, the provision of the handpad as an alternative way of interacting further encourages reengagement by the wider population as well as supporting accessibility for those with limited mobility.

Interactional Trajectories

Our final contribution in this paper is to relate our findings to the growing literature on interaction in public settings, and especially to recent work on interactional trajectories. As noted in the introduction, previous studies of museum exhibits (Heath & vom Lehn, 2002), artistic installations (Costello et al., 2005) and more general tangible interfaces (Hornecker & Buur, 2006) have raised the idea that there are 'interactional trajectories' through museum and gallery installations in which one visitor's interactions with an exhibit establish a trajectory for subsequent visitors who, having observed them, subsequently approach the interface and engage with it. This idea is closely related to the notion of 'spectatorship' in which a user's interactions with an interface may be made more or less visible to and legible for others. For example, Reeves et al. (2005) introduce a taxonomy that classifies interfaces according to the extent to which they hide, reveal or even amplify a user's *manipulations* of the interface to observers, compared to the extent to which they hide, reveal or amplify the *effects* of these manipulations. Their classification of various interfaces reveals four broad design strategies that they call: *secretive* (manipulations and subsequent effects both hidden); *expressive* (manipulations and effects both amplified); *magical* (effects revealed but the manipulations that caused them hidden) and *suspenseful* or *intriguing* (manipulations revealed but effects—the payoff from these—remain hidden). These strategies suggest various different ways in which interfaces in public settings might attract, engage or inform observers as part of establishing an interactional trajectory.

Other researchers have pointed out that a consideration of interaction within public (or indeed other collaborative) settings needs to extend beyond an individual interface to instead address an entire ecology of interfaces: Nardi has argued for 'information ecologies' that combine people, practices values and technologies within a local environment (Nardi, 1999); Huang et al introduced 'display ecologies' to explain the evolution of use of a series of large displays in the NASA Mars Exploration Rover (MER) control room; while Crabtree and Rodden analysed the operation of a mixed reality game that combined online players with those on the streets of a city in terms of 'hybrid ecologies' (Crabtree & Rodden, 2008). Specifically within museums, Bell (Bell, 2002) introduced the idea of 'cultural ecologies' that combine liminality (meaning an experience set apart from everyday life), sociality, and engagement. Finally, in a practical demonstration of how such ecologies might be assembled, Fraser et al. describe a museum visiting experience in which groups a visitors explored the grounds of an ancient castle, gathering information such as drawings and rubbings on pieces of paper that were electronically tagged (using RFID) so that they could be used to interact with various public displays inside the museum in order to reveal further information (Fraser et al., 2003).

These notions of interactional trajectories and ecologies have recently been combined into a broader conceptual framework for describing cultural experiences that extend over hybrid ecologies of space, time, roles and interfaces (Benford et al., 2009). This framework proposes that such extended experiences can best be described in terms of journeys whose structures are expressed by the relationships between three fundamental types of trajectory. *Canonical trajectories* are defined by artists and represent intended journeys through the experience. *Participant trajectories* are inscribed by individuals undertaking the experience and diverge from canonical trajectories due to interactivity, but then reconverge due to orchestration. *Historic trajectories* synthesise different accounts of what happened in the past, selecting, filtering and recombining different recorded participant trajectories in order to support reflection after the event. The ways in which participant trajectories interweave with one another, approaching, crossing and diverging express varying possibilities for social encounters and isolation. Moreover, these trajectories must be designed to negotiate key *transitions*, moments when coherence may be at risk, including beginnings, endings, role and interface transitions, traversals between real and virtual worlds, disengaging and reengaging as part of episodic interaction, and negotiating disconnections of other technical limitations.

Interactional trajectories in Flypad

How does our study of Flypad relate to this body of literature? We propose that our findings affirm many of these existing concepts, but also suggest ways in which further research might extend them in the future. First, we have shown how the artists, through the fine details of the design and placement of the terminals, support local spectating and so establish a trajectory of interaction into engagement with individual terminals and hence the game. This engagement of local spectators in Flypad mirrors earlier studies of popular dance games such as Dance Dance Revolution (DDR) and ParaParaParadise, which also use footpads, and support organised and impromptu public performance (Smith, 2006). We have described how the artists deliberately designed the terminals to support 'expressive' interactions in Reeve's terminology. However, we have also revealed the impact of aligning several footpads side-by-side on a blister, leaving sufficient space to accommodate spectators and passersby, mirroring Brignull and Roger's (2003) discussion of the 'Honey Pot' effect in which people socialise around public displays and move from being onlookers to participants and back again.

Flypad supports an especially fluid relationship between spectating and participating. We have described how players watch each other's games whilst playing their own, comparing views, interjecting and even swapping over. Thus, we also see the importance of a kind of 'sideways' spectating between players, reflecting Alan Dix's discussion of feedthrough, feedback and awareness in collaborative interfaces (Dix, 1997).

In its larger structure, Flypad affirms the idea of systematically designing an entire ecology of interfaces. Flypad's ecology includes multiple interfaces (8 footpads, 3 handpads, 11 screens, 11 cameras, and the Tall Trees), each of which consists of further components, and which are distributed around the ramp and carefully integrated into the wider ecology of the surrounding building. Our study highlights the problems that can occur when an ecology of displays is not sufficiently integrated; in the case of Flypad, the Tall Trees are not well integrated with the other displays leading to a 'fragmentation of views across multiple displays' (Gaver et al., 1993). While we would not necessarily argue against large public displays as external spectator interfaces, the experience of Flypad suggests that they require careful integration with the overall display ecology.

Finally, there is a clear sense of there being a larger trajectory through the entire hybrid ecology of Flypad of the kind proposed by Benford and colleagues. The most obvious manifestation of this is the way in which the entire experience is largely defined by the presence of the sloping ramp which shapes a clear and constrained path into and through the experience. We have seen how the artists carefully created an overarching 'canonical trajectory' to follow this path from the very first design iteration, but also how 'participant trajectories' do indeed locally diverge from and reconverge to and from this. We have also described examples of designing key transitional moments, especially stepping onto a footpad and subsequent engagement with the game software.

However, while our study affirms this general approach of thinking in terms of extended trajectories, it also challenges it in several important respects, suggesting productive avenues for further study or technical development.

Group trajectories: perhaps the most notable implication of our study is the significance of groups of visitor and the way in which a rolling group trajectory, emerges from several individual overlapping and interleaved participant trajectories. Our descriptions suggests a sense in which each group as a whole may have its own collective trajectory through the exhibit which emerges from or somehow constrains and shapes the ways in which individual participant trajectories overlap and tend to 'stick' together. In our vignette, for example, we saw that, the group, family trajectory through the exhibit as a whole interacted with each individual trajectory (such as B taking over G's game, or W's repeated requests for the group to move onwards). Current notions of trajectories within the literature do not explicitly express the idea of group trajectories, raising an important question for further research.

Multi-scale trajectories: Our study also reveals the presence of nested and interlocking trajectories at a variety of scales. Trajectories defined in The Public range from building scale (the sequence and ordering of exhibits, the ramp), down to individual interfaces (encounters with Flypad), and then into gameplay. Trajectories at these different scales are designed to be interconnected so as to create a coherent overall experience; however we found in our study occasional divergence between the intended, canonical trajectories and the trajectories participants actually engaged in. For instance, we observed visitors revisiting exhibits and travelling in reverse to the designed trajectory. Further, in the vignette, we saw visitors conduct multiple sequential engagements with different terminals, meaning that several individual game trajectories came to be nested within the overall trajectory of interaction with Flypad as a whole. We therefore propose that further research is needed to articulate how the application of trajectories to the study and design of cultural experiences can take into account the ways in which multiple trajectories at multiple-scales can be interlocked.

Evolving trajectories: Finally, we have seen how trajectories may evolve with use. Our study uncovered how curators at The Public have begun to reconfigure the overall trajectory through Flypad, most notably by encouraging the reversal of the flow of visitors from down to up the sloping ramp. A key role of curators may be to continually shape trajectories through multiple exhibits, especially when exhibits change, to reflect patterns of changing use of their space. Our study has also revealed how trajectories may have varying levels of reconfigurability—for instance, certain aspects of the canonical trajectory may be adapted, such as ramp direction, whereas other parts of the trajectory are more fixed, such as the physical arrangement of elements found in Flypad (e.g., screens, cameras, footpads). The broad question of how trajectories evolve and adapt over time, especially as experiences come and go within a given setting, has not been widely discussed in the literature and so offers a further avenue for future research.

Conclusion

By studying the design, experience, maintenance and reconfiguration of Flypad over a four-year period we have been able to shed new light on the design of large-scale interactive experiences for galleries, museums and other settings. We revealed how the artists responded to the architectural setting of the building and paid particular attention to issues of visitor flow, personalisation, spectating, the integration of real and virtual, and accessibility. Beyond documenting a unique example of designing and maintaining a major artwork, our observations of use show that, in the large, these design strategies were broadly successful. However, engagement was often more fluid than anticipated, with many rapid dis- and re-engagements and the sharing of footpads and ongoing games. Finally, we also revealed the challenges of integrating external spectator interfaces—the Tall Trees—into the overall ecology of the experience. From a more theoretical point of view, our study has affirmed several concepts from the CSCW literature including interactional trajectories, spectatorship and notions of ecology. At the same time we have also argued for further extending these ideas, in particular, for extending current notions of trajectories to better accommodate multiple-scales, evolution over time—and significantly for CSCW—the impact of group visiting.

Acknowledgments

We gratefully acknowledge support of the EPSRC grant 'The Challenge of Widespread Ubiquitous Computing' (EP/F03038X/1) and RCUK for the Horizon project (EP/G065802/1). We also acknowledge the useful comments of reviewers.

References

Aoki, P., Grinter, R., Hurst, A., Szymanski, M., Thornton, J. & Woodruff, A (2002); 'Sotto voce: exploring the interplay of conversation and mobile audio spaces', *Proc. CHI*, pp. 431-438, ACM.

Bell, G. (2002): *Making Sense of Museums*, Intel Labs.

Benford, S., Giannachi, G., Koleva, B. & Rodden, T. (2009): 'From Interaction to Trajectories: Designing Coherent Journeys Through User Experiences', *Proc. CHI*, pp. 709-718, ACM.

Brignull, H. & Rogers, Y. (2003): 'Enticing people to Interact with Large Public Displays in Public Spaces', *Proc. Interact*, pp. 17-24, IOS Press, IFIP.

Brown, B., MacColl, I., Chalmers, M., Galani, A., Randell, C. & Steed, A., (2003): 'Lessons From the Lighthouse: Collaboration in a Shared Mixed Reality System', *Proc. CHI*, pp. 577-584, ACM.

Costello, B., Muller, L., Amitani, S. & Edmonds, E. (2005): 'Understanding the Experience of Interactive Art: Iamascope in Beta_space', *Proc. 2nd Australasian Conference on Interactive entertainment*, Sydney.

Crabtree, A & Rodden, T. (2008): 'Hybrid Ecologies: Understanding Cooperative Interaction in Emerging Physical Digital Environments', *Personal & Ubiquitous Computing*, 12:481-493, Springer.

Dix, A., (1997): 'Challenges for cooperative work on the web: An analytical approach', *Computer Supported Cooperative Work*, 6(2-3):135–156.

Fraser, M., Stanton, D, Ng, K., Benford, S., O'Malley, C., Bowers,J., Taxen, G., Ferris, K., Hindmarsh, J., (2003): 'Assembling history: achieving coherent experiences with diverse technologies', *Proc ECSCW*, Kluwer.

Gaver, W., Sellen, A., Heath, C., & Luff, P., (1993): 'One is not enough: multiple views in a media space', *Proc. CHI*, pp. 335-341, ACM.

Heath, C. & vom Lehn, D. (2002): 'Misconstruing interactivity', *Proc. Interactive Learning in Museums of Art and Design*, Victoria and Albert Museum, 2002.

Hindmarsh, J., Heath, C., vom Lehn, D., & Cleverly, J., (2005): 'Creating assemblies in public environments', *Journal of CSCW*, 14(1):1-41, Kluwer.

Hornecker, E. & Buur, J. (2006): 'Getting a grip on tangible interaction, *Proc. CHI*, pp. 437-446, ACM.

Koleva, B., Egglestone, S., Schnädelbach, H., Glover, K., Greenhalgh, C. & Rodden, T. (2009): 'Supporting the creation of hybrid museum experiences', *Proc. CHI*, pp. 1973-1982, ACM.

Mazalek, A., Winegarden, C., Al-Haddad, T., Robinson, S., & We, C., (2009): 'Architales: physical/digital co-design of an interactive story table', *Proc. TEI*, pp. 241-248, ACM.

Nardi, B. & O'Day, V. (1999): '*Information Ecologies: Using Technology with Heart*', pp. 49-58, MIT Press.

Not, E., Peterelli D., Stock O., Strapparava C., & Zancanaro M., (1997): 'Person-oriented guided visits in a physical museum.', *Proc. ICHIM'97*, Archives and Museum Informatics.

Reeves, S., Benford, S., O'Malley, C. & Fraser, M., (2005): 'Designing the spectator interface', *Proc. CHI*, pp. 741-750, ACM.

Smith, J., (2006): 'Digital Dance Hall: The Fan Culture of Dance Simulation Arcade Games.', *Consuming Music Together*, pp. 193-210, Springer.

Snibbe, S. & Raffle, H., (2009): 'Social Immersive Media Pursuing Best Practices for Multi-user Interactive Camera/projector Exhibits', *Proc. CHI*, pp. 1447-1456, ACM.

Terrenghi, L., Quigley, A. & Dix, A. (2009l): 'A Taxonomy for and Analysis of Multi-Person-Display Ecosystems', *Personal & Ubiquitous Computing*, 13:853-598, Springer.

vom Lehn, D., Heath, C. & Knoblauch, H., (2001): 'Configuring exhibits', *Verbal Art Across Cultures*, pp. 281–297, Gunter Narr Verlag Tubingen.

vom Lehn, D., Hindmarsh, J., Luff, P. & Heath, C. (2007): 'Engaging constable: revealing art with new technology', *Proc. CHI*, pp. 1485-1494, ACM.

Characterizing Deixis over Surfaces to Improve Remote Embodiments

Aaron Genest and Carl Gutwin
University of Saskatchewan
aaron.genest@usask.ca, gutwin@cs.usask.ca

Abstract. Deictic gestures are ubiquitous when people work over tables and whiteboards, but when collaboration occurs across distributed surfaces, the embodiments used to represent other members of the group often fail to convey the details of these gestures. Although both gestures and embodiments have been well studied, there is still little information available to groupware designers about what components and characteristics of deictic gesture are most important for conveying meaning through remote embodiments. To provide this information, we conducted three observational studies in which we recorded and analysed more than 450 deictic gestures. We considered four issues that are important for the design of embodiments on surfaces: what parts of the body are used to produce a deictic gesture, what atomic movements make up deixis, where gestures occur in the space above the surface, and what other characteristics deictic gestures exhibit in addition to pointing. Our observations provide a new design understanding of deictic gestures. We use our results to identify the limitations of current embodiment techniques in supporting deixis, and to propose new hybrid designs that can better represent the range of behavior seen in real-world settings.

Introduction

Distributed tabletop applications often provide user embodiments to facilitate communication and improve awareness among collaborators (Benford et al., 1995). These embodiments improve communication between distributed groups in part by showing gestures made by remote users. These gestures are often deictic – that is, indicatory gestures accompanied by speech patterns such as "this one" or "over there" (Bekker et al., 1995). However, embodiments on tables often fail to fully represent the range of expression that is evident in collocated settings.

Embodiments can take many different forms, but can be classified into *realistic* embodiments such as VideoArms (A. Tang et al., 2007) or DOVE (Ou et al., 2003) and *abstract* embodiments such as telepointers (Hayne et al., 1994). Abstract embodiments have been shown to permit the expression of deixis (e.g., Gutwin and Penner, 2002), but are generally limited to conveying simple points or paths. Realistic embodiments represent hands and arms on the remote table with much greater fidelity (e.g., with video), but only in two dimensions, since the embodiment must be projected onto the table surface. In addition, video-based solutions rely on imperfect image separation techniques, can be limited in resolution, and require greater network bandwidth.

The different limitations of both embodiment approaches mean that distributed surfaces often fail to represent the full richness of deixis that can be seen in co-located work – such as the height of a gesture over the surface, or the difference between lightly touching and pressing hard on the surface. Although there has been a great deal of work done on both embodiments and deictic gesture, there is still little information available about how an embodiment should be designed to maximize the information shown to remote users of tabletop groupware. Embodiments cannot currently be evaluated in terms of their expressiveness because there is no clear characterization of deixis over surfaces, and there are no principles available to tell designers which parts of a deictic gesture are most common, or most important. Such a characterization would help people make informed decisions about embodiment design, and could also inform other questions such as how to best convey gesture information in environments with limited network, display, or computational resources, or how to design command gestures so that they do not collide with natural communication gestures.

To address the lack of a surface-based deixis characterization scheme, we carried out three observational studies in which we recorded and analysed more than 450 gestures. Two laboratory experiments investigated information-sharing tasks over projected maps, and a field study observed discussion and collaboration over maps between park wardens and science students. Our observations provided new insights into four questions that have particular importance for the design and implementation of tabletop embodiments: what parts of the body are involved in deictic gestures, what atomic movements make up a deictic gesture, where the gesture occurs in the space above the table, and what other physical characteristics different types of gestures exhibit.

In this paper, we describe our investigations of these questions, and use our results to analyse the strengths and limitations of realistic and abstract embodiments. From this analysis, we present a set of recommendations for the design of tabletop embodiments, and propose a new set of hybrid visualizations that can better represent the full range of expression and subtlety that is evident in real-world deixis.

Previous Work

Gestures and deixis are a key component of collocated communication (McNeill, 1992), and representing gestures for remote collaborators is an important groupware design factor (Gutwin & Greenberg, 2000). There are two foundations to our work: understanding the role of deixis in communication, and developing systems that successfully represent deixis with an appropriate level of fidelity.

Understanding Deixis

Although there are several studies that examine the use of gestures in a variety of communication contexts (e.g., Clark, 2003; Hindmarsh et al., 2000), research that describes gestures in surface-based collaborations is less common. General research into deixis in communication contexts, such as the work of Bekker et al. (1995), has found that gestures are used as a communication medium in face-to-face meetings almost as frequently as words. Bekker identified four categories of gestures, one of which was deixis (described as a "point" gesture). Other studies have identified the presence of understandable deixis as critical to smooth collaboration (Hindmarsh & Heath, 2000). One important result of deixis research is an understanding of how to evaluate deictic communication: the success rate of conversational grounding (how quickly people come to a common understanding of the target of deixis), can be used as a success metric (Kirk et al., 2007).

Surface-based deictic gestures are different than the more general case because the target is often within reach and the target space is often limited. Kirk *et al.* (2005) examined hand movements during mixed-ecology collaborative tasks and developed a coarse-grained analysis of their characteristics. A finer-grained analysis was performed by Kettebekov and Sharma (2000), who developed a semantic classification for deixis based on observations of weather narrations. Because the goal of the research was automated gesture recognition, their conclusions focused on the effectiveness of the system in recognizing gestures rather than characterizing gestures within the context of collaboration.

Representing Deixis

CSCW research has two primary approaches to embodying users who are interacting with remote physical spaces. Abstract techniques, such as telepointers, are designed with little or no regard to a true representation of the physical world, and instead represent relevant characteristics of users (Benford et al., 1995; Stach et al., 2007) or their actions (Greenberg et al., 1996). Conversely, realistic embodiments show users as accurate representations of their physical presence. Often, this takes the form of video superimposition of hands and arms into real workspaces. This technique takes a variety of forms, from the vertical surfaces and mirrored displays of VideoDraw and VideoWhiteBoard (J. Tang & Minneman, 1991a; 1991b) to DOVE's mixed-ecology system (Ou et al., 2003). Digital video of arms alone has also been used: in this approach, video of users' arms on the table surface is extracted and transmitted. VideoArms is an example of this technique (A. Tang et al., 2007), and was later enhanced to use temporal traces to show the previous positions of users' hands (A. Tang et al., 2010).

Research into abstract embodiments such as basic telepointers (Hayne et al., 1994) has examined which components of the users' movement and characteristics are important to visualize (Stach et al., 2007; Pinelle et al., 2008). Research has also demonstrated how telepointers can convey gestures, finding that the use of temporal traces can improve gesture recognition (Gutwin & Penner, 2002). Realistic embodiment research has concentrated less on the effectiveness of gesture representation than on the addition of additional channels of communication such as facial expression (Li et al., 2007). However, there is evidence that video-realistic embodiments still fail to express the full range of deixis, forcing users to adjust their gestures to accommodate the limitations of the representation (Ou et al., 2003).

With the exception of the work by Kettebekov and Sharma (2000), there is little work that classifies and explicates surface-based natural deixis from the perspective of designing embodiments to convey those gestures. Because of this lack, there are there are no systematic attempts to understand whether current embodiment techniques express the full richness of deixis to remote collaborators.

Examining Surface-Based Deixis

To further our understanding of how deixis is used over surfaces and whether embodiments capture this use, we performed three observational studies of deictic communication: two laboratory-based studies and one field study.

Laboratory Study Methods

In both laboratory studies, participants were asked to carry out a series of tasks using a top-projected tabletop that showed a Google Earth map of the local city. Participants were allowed to move around the table as needed. The map was a combination of street map and satellite image at a resolution sufficient for counting (but not identifying) houses in the image. We used maps for two reasons. First, map-based collaborations are common activities performed both by amateurs (e.g., tourism) and by professionals (e.g., emergency response, urban planning, land-use negotiation). Second, maps afford rich opportunities for deixis: for example, identification of individual or groups of artifacts, paths between or along artifacts, and areas that include multiple artifacts. In this way maps approximate many other cluttered workspaces used for planning or design tasks.

We recognize that maps do not provide a setting for all the collaborative tasks in which deixis is used, but maps do capture a large subset of this task space, particularly for two-dimensional displays.

In the first study, four pairs of participants answered questions about the spaces represented by the displayed map. Questionnaires were formulated using previous work by Kettebekov and Sharma (2000) as inspiration. Although the questions were asked by the researcher, participants were instructed to direct their answers to each other. The questions in the questionnaire were designed to elicit different kinds of deixis: some questions were designed to elicit path gestures, others to elicit indication of areas, and others to elicit pointing. These tasks simulate a variety of information-sharing collaborative activities seen in the real world. Participants (one female and seven male) were all staff or students at the local university, and ranged in age from 22 to 56.

Sessions were videotaped with a single camera at an angle oblique to the table's surface. The resulting recordings were reviewed several times to identify episodes involving deictic gesture (deixis was separated from other kinds of actions such as conversational gesture), and to determine a set of candidate classification categories for the observed deictic gestures. Although the recordings contained a wide variety of deixis, our analysis identified limitations in our ability to capture gesture data: in particular, we determined that a single camera is insufficient for capturing all of the detail of a gesture. For example, the height of a gesture above the table was often difficult to determine, and when the gesture was performed above the table, the x and y-axis coordinates could be difficult to identify. With a single camera, participants' arms, hands, and bodies also sometimes occluded their gestures from our view. To resolve this problem, our second study used two cameras at 90 degrees to each other. One camera was located at the table's surface and aimed so that each gesture's height was easily determined. The second camera provided a top-down view of the table's surface.

The tasks in the second study were similar to that of the first, but we made small alterations in order to explore the issue of people's confidence in the accuracy of their answers. The first study had suggested that people express these qualities by changing the height of their deictic gestures or hesitating during a gesture; the second study therefore asked participants to use new and unfamiliar information in some of their tasks. This study was performed by two pairs of male participants (from the local university community), aged 22 to 30.

We reviewed and analysed the recordings of the second study in a way similar to that of the first. We found that the types of deixis seen, and the categories generated, from the second study were very similar those of the first study. No significantly new types of deixis were apparent, nor did the association between atomic gestures and targets (i.e., paths, areas, or points) change in any substantive way. As expected, however, the two-camera setup of the second study did provide new information that allowed clearer delineation of gesture location.

Field Study Methods

We carried out a third study of a real-world collaboration, in order to gather additional observations and to compare the findings of the laboratory studies with those gathered from a more realistic setting with a larger group of collaborators. With this study, we also hoped to observe a variety of collaborative tasks different from those we had created in the laboratory studies. We observed and recorded a group of four veterinary science students, one graduate-level teaching assistant, and a park warden during a two-day workshop in which the students learned about how wardens effect the transfer of herds of wild ungulates between parks and preserves. The workshop took place in conference rooms, indoor and outdoor animal enclosures, and a variety of outdoor facilities in Elk Island National Park, Alberta, Canada. The students and wardens carried out numerous discussions over different types of maps including wall-mounted maps and hand-held paper maps, in several indoor and outdoor settings. In addition, there were two cases of ad-hoc map use, one involving a sketched map on a blackboard, and one involving a map drawn in snow. Because of the nature of the workshop, most gestures came from one of the park wardens who provided a great deal of information to the other participants. Other participants, however, did perform gestures, usually in short bursts, and often for the purpose of achieving conversational grounding.

Recordings and notes from the field study were analysed with methods similar to that used for the laboratory studies – we identified all episodes where gestures took place, and then categorized each instance, using the categories developed in the earlier studies. Overall, we found that the types of deictic gestures seen in the field were similar to what we observed in the laboratory, and that our existing categories were able to characterize all of the gestures of the field study. We did note, however, that many of the episodes we observed in the field were in a presentation style, with a vertical surface and a seated audience. We discuss the effects of this difference in our analysis below.

Analysis: four basic questions about deictic gesture

We analysed the video of the study sessions using four basic questions that help identify and characterize the ways in which deictic gestures can vary in real-world activity, and therefore imply the variations that remote embodiments should attempt to convey. The questions are: what parts of the body are used to produce a deictic gesture?; what atomic movements make up deictic gestures?; where does the gesture occur in the space above the table?; and what additional physical characteristics do gestures have in addition to pointing?

What Parts of the Body are Used for Deictic Gesture?

The body parts used in the production of a gesture (i.e., its *morphology*) can provide insight into what information is needed to correctly interpret the gesture. This analysis is vital for the design of remote embodiments, as it tells us what should be tracked at the local site and visualized at the remote location, and how to optimize information about the gesture. It can also show what spaces are available for command gestures without risking mis-interpretation.

Our observations suggest that variations in the morphology of deixis over maps come primarily from the fingers and hand. The lower and upper arm, the shoulder, and the rest of the body are unlikely to play a role in the meaning of a deictic gesture; the movement and orientation of these body parts is most often the result of intended movement of the hand, not the result of a communicative intention. In some cases, the overall posture of the body and arm (e.g., an extended arm or a leaning-over body posture) provides valuable awareness information about the hand's location (e.g., that the speaker is reaching to point to something far away), but the idea of drawing attention to the gesture is a separate issue from the interpretation of the gesture itself. This means that the most important body parts for understanding and representing deixis are the hand and fingers, and their movement, posture, and orientation.

The parts of the hand available for use in the production of a gesture are the five fingers and the palm or the back of the hand. In our observations, we considered a part of the hand to be engaged in the gesture if it is not de-emphasized in the gesture (e.g. a finger curled into the palm); and it is integral to the interpretation of the gesture. Fingers can also be grouped or spread: for example, a gesture can be morphologically described as engaging the thumb by itself, first and second together, and third and fourth together, but not engaging the palm. The engagement of the palm (i.e., its importance in the gesture's interpretation) may not always be easily determined, but in our studies was often apparent in the larger context of the gesture.

Hand orientation describes the relative position of the palm with respect to the map surface. Gestures can be described as palm-down (palm faces the surface), palm-up (palm faces away from the surface), or sideways. This category is independent of the morphology of finger and palm engagement.

Of the parts of the hand actually used in deictic gestures, the index (1st) finger is of prime importance. In our first study, only 15 (6.7%) of the 225 observed gestures did *not* engage the index finger. Of those, 11 used the palm of the hand to indicate an area on the map – and all of these were generated by two of the participants. The second study was very similar, with only 10 gestures of 146 that did not involve the index finger. Four of these engaged the palm, always in a sideways orientation (i.e., a 'cutting' or 'separation' gesture); the remainder engaged the middle (2nd) finger and had no palm engagement.

Figure 1. Examples of the two most common pointing gestures. Left, a double-finger point with the palm away from the surface. Right, a single-finger point with the palm down.

In contrast to the laboratory observations, during the field study 26 (31.7%) of the recorded gestures engaged the palm and only 41 (50.0%) of the gestures engaged the index finger. The engagement of the middle finger was used as an alternative to the index finger in 26 (31.7%) of the gestures. Additionally, 36 (43.9%) of the gestures were performed palm-up rather than palm-down to the surface, a position that was likely easier due to the positioning of the map (several maps in the field study were tacked to the wall). All of these non-index-finger gestures in the field study data are from a single participant, however, and further work is needed to determine whether these morphologies are common.

Use of two hands for gestures was rare, with only one episode of deictic gesture involving both hands simultaneously for the gesture itself (a palm-engaged gesture with both hands to indicate a large area on the map). Two hands were used on other occasions, but with the second hand (always the non-dominant hand) used as a placeholder. For example, if the participant was tracing a large contour on the map, he/she might place the non-dominant hand at the start position and leave it there until the pointing hand returned to the start.

Our observations of deixis morphology over maps can be summarized in two ways: first, a large majority of episodes we observed used one of two pointing fingers in classic pointing gestures (Figure 1); second, the remaining smaller set of gestures were highly varied in their morphology. Between the two laboratory studies, 94.8% of deictic gestures engaged the index finger, although often in conjunction with additional fingers. Finger-based pointing was also extremely frequent in the field study (81.7% of gestures).

The fact that pointing dominates deixis may not be surprising, but the degree to which we observed pointing-based gestures (even within other types of deixis) reinforces that this aspect must be considered as a primary component for remote embodiments. In current techniques, however, there are many situations where a remote embodiment may not make these gestures as clear as they need to be. For example, VideoArms suffers from inaccurate video-separation techniques and low-resolution video capture, which can create blocky and unclear boundaries in the arm visualizations, and can fail to correctly show an extended finger in the embodiment (Tang *et al.*, 2007). This guideline also helps explain why telepointer embodiments can be so effective – the telepointer clearly represents the tip of a pointing finger, and therefore expresses the most important morphology of deixis.

However, telepointers do not show any of the other more complex and varied morphologies we observed, and in these cases, higher-bandwidth representations of hands and arms (e.g., video or multiple-sensor setups) are likely the only solutions that can fully convey the subtleties of a gesture to remote collaborators. In terms of existing solutions, DOVE-like embodiments (Li *et al.*, 2007) have a clear advantage over more abstract representations. The challenge in finding a middle ground between realistic and abstract embodiments is that identifying the important aspects of gesture morphology is difficult. We noted that two of our fourteen laboratory participants were responsible for 11 of the 15 observed non-single-finger pointing gestures. This suggests that between-subjects variability in deixis morphology could be a significant factor in the design and evaluation of gesture embodiments. In addition, we found that vertical displays, especially when used for presentation, encourage inverted hands (palm-up) and non-single-finger pointing. Therefore, abstract embodiment techniques that may work well for horizontal surfaces may not be as effective for vertical surfaces.

Finally, our classification describes only what portions of the hand are engaged in the gesture, not how that engagement (or disengagement) was manifested. For example, for an index-finger pointing gesture, we could also characterize the posture of the remaining fingers (curled tightly into a fist, curled loosely, or in a rest position next to the index finger but not touching the surface). None of these differences are represented in the morphology characterization we have used, but there are clear differences in how much of this variation the different embodiment approaches would be able to convey. If these postures are important for a particular collaboration setting, designers must consider whether a realistic embodiment (e.g., DOVE) has enough video fidelity to accurately represent these aspects of the gesture, or whether an abstract representation can be augmented to increase its expressive power (e.g., with additional sensors).

What Atomic Movements Create Deictic Gestures?

Gestures have been previously characterized in terms of small, atomic blocks of movement, a scheme designed to assist with automated classification (Kettebekov & Sharma, 2000). In this scheme, atomic gestures are strung together (often in long chains) to create complete gestures. Using this idea, we identified seven distinct atomic blocks from our observations, and uncovered several substantial problems for gesture embodiment as a result of this classification. The seven gesture 'atoms' we observed are: preparations, strokes, points, contours, retractions, rests, and hesitations. These differ only slightly from those of

Kettebekov and Sharma: we identify strokes as a kind of primitive, rather than a set of gesture primitives, and as a substitute for their 'circle' gesture; we re-define 'contour' as a closed stroke (very similar to their 'circle' primitive; and we add the hesitation atom. We discuss these atomic gestures in greater detail, below.

Gestures begin with *preparation*, a gesture atom with no explicit meaning, designed to move the hand and arm into a position where a meaningful gesture can occur. A preparation atom can, but does not always, serve to attract attention (Gutwin & Greenberg, 1998) to subsequent atoms.

The next three atom types involve meaningful movement, and form the core of the deictic gesture. *Stroke* atoms are movements along a line or path in two or three dimensions, *point* atoms are meaningful pauses in the gesture movement; and *contour* atoms are path-like gestures that curve and close, returning to the point of origin (or near the point of origin, depending on the precision of the gesture). Examples of stroke and contour atoms can be seen in Figure 2. All three of these atoms can be used to indicate any artifact in the workspace, but there is a natural mapping between stroke atoms for showing paths in the workspace, point atoms for showing point locations and directions; and contour atoms for showing areas. Strokes, contours, and points are all indicative atoms, in that they can be used to indicate artifacts or locations on the working surface.

Retraction atoms occur at the end of a deictic gesture and before the start of another. Although not all gestures have retraction atoms, many do. Retraction atoms may lead to *rest* atoms, where the hand and arm are no longer engaged in deixis, but remain in the working space.

Figure 2. Contour atom (left) and stroke atom (right). Arrows indicate movement of the finger.

The seventh and final atom is *hesitation*. In the time between a preparation atom and an indicative atom, people often hesitate in mid-gesture, performing a visual search of target locations or otherwise pausing in the conversational flow. During this time, people also pause the deictic gesture, but they rarely stop moving – instead, they often carry out a series of aimless movements over the potential target space. This movement is visually distinct from any of the other atoms, but is difficult to characterize, other than that the movements appear interrupted, hesitating often, and, in the case of visual searches, often loosely follow head orientation and gaze direction. A similar atom (although not described as such) was identified by Kirk et al. (2005) as the "wavering hand."

In all of the studies, we counted the frequency of indicative atoms. In the first study, there were 225 distinct indicative atoms, of which 91 (40.4%) were points, 104 (46.3%) were strokes and 30 (13.3%) were contours. In the second study, there were 146 indicative atoms, of which 56 (38.4%) were points, 61 (41.7%) were strokes, and 29 (19.9%) were contours. Deixis in the field study was less frequent than in the laboratory studies, but three segments of over three minutes of almost continuous deixis were observed. During these segments, there were 43 (52.4%) pointing atoms, 35 (42.7%) stroke atoms, and 4 (4.9%) contour atoms.

Brief hesitation atoms were observed in almost every series of atomic gestures in every study, and when they were not present, the participant usually paused in a rest atom before answering the task's question. Statements such as "somewhere over here", "I'm not sure where, exactly", or stalling vocalizations (e.g., "um") frequently accompanied hesitation atoms.

Our observations of gesture atoms suggest two potential problems with existing embodiment techniques, one for abstract embodiments and one for realistic embodiments. First, abstract embodiments like telepointers may have difficulty conveying the difference between different atoms. In some of our episodes, we observed very little visual difference between stroke and preparation atoms, between hesitation atoms and combinations of stroke and point atoms, and between rest atoms and point atoms. Although coincident conversation sometimes disambiguates these categories, differences between them can also often be seen in the shape of the hand. For instance, a pointing finger is usually completely extended in a point atom, but may be partially curled under during a rest atom. This means that embodiments with higher fidelity and bandwidth (e.g., video-based representations) will be more effective in differentiating similar atoms.

Second, realistic embodiments may have difficulty representing certain types of stroke atoms – but these problems could be reduced by combining abstract visualizations with the realistic base representation. In our observations, although point and stroke atoms were seen with almost equal frequency, stroke atoms were the most flexible in their application. Strokes were used to identify paths, as might be expected, but were also used for points and for areas. Almost every participant performed gestures where multiple repeated strokes were used to emphasize points (similar to a rubbing gesture, as previously reported by (Kirk et al., 2005). Strokes were also used to identify areas by performing a series of strokes similar to shading in the area. However, the limited visual representation of a remote embodiment can fail to adequately convey the salience of these gestures – for example, a 'rubbing' emphasis gesture with a 2D video arm may be less obvious than the corresponding real-world original, due to lower sampling and display frequencies in remote capture and display technologies.

This is a situation where abstract embodiments, which can be arbitrarily augmented to show different types information, can be superior. There is evidence that using temporal traces on remote embodiments can improve collaborative communication (Gutwin & Penner, 2002); (A. Tang et al., 2010). The prevalence of stroke atoms, combined with their versatility, suggest that traces and similar techniques that enhance stroke atoms could be particularly valuable in improving the noticeability and interpretation of deictic gesture. A few previous embodiments have implemented such enhancements, often of contour atoms, and usually in conjunction with automated gesture recognition or gestures as commands (e.g., Ou et al., 2003). This space is largely unexplored, however, and there may be great value in combining realistic and abstract embodiments to convey stroke atoms. This approach could provide the clear indications of a telepointer, the ability to visualize temporal movement with visual traces, and the richness and expressivity of a video representation.

Where Does the Gesture Occur in the Space Above the Table?

The presence of a planar surface in a collaboration setting introduces the possibility of measuring the *height* of a gesture from the surface, a measurement not feasible in a more varied workspace. However, representing height (or distance, in the case of a vertical surface) is limited in prior work. For example, this quality was shown incidentally as the opacity of the shadow in VideoWhiteBoard (J. Tang & Minneman, 1991), but later digital systems did not display this effect (e.g., Apperley *et al.*, 2003). Other systems display a separation effect, such as a narrow space between touching and hovering, as in the C-Slate system (Izadi *et al.*, 2007). In a system for collaborative video review (Fraser et al. 2007), distance from the display was explicitly and intentionally represented, in order to draw the attention of remote collaborators to an upcoming pointing action; this visual information was shown to improve coordination and reduce conversational latency. In our terms, this system visualized preparation atoms in order to improve the interpretation of pointing atoms.

Our observations also suggest that height is an important characteristic of gestures over surfaces. It is clear that as the height of a gesture changes, the gesture can imply different meanings than if the height were to remain the same. Additionally, movements such as tapping on a point or bouncing a finger along a path are difficult to express without considering variations in height.

In our studies, height of a gesture, and variation in that height, was highly meaningful. We observed four main heights: gestures touching the surface, gestures moving back and forth from just above the surface to touching; gestures carried out entirely just above the surface, and gestures performed above about 5cm from the surface. First, deictic gestures that touched the table surface were common, and almost always occurred when speakers were being more specific, more confident, and more precise. Second, gestures that moved between touching and just off the surface (e.g., tapping or bouncing actions) were also common, and were used for emphasis and to indicate a series of locations along a path. Third, gestures that hovered just above the surface, in a layer approximately 2-5cm above the surface, indicated less confidence or familiarity, or, occasionally, indicated areas rather than points or paths. Gestures above about 5cm were used to indicate reduced confidence, larger areas of the map, out-of-reach locations, or locations that were off the map. In a few cases, stroke gestures used height variations to represent variations in height in the real world. For example, one participant moved his finger in an arc while going "over the river" on a bridge.

Although a few embodiment solutions express some component of gesture height (e.g., VideoArms with traces (A. Tang et al., 2010)), no current technique expresses the full range of height seen in our studies. Some evaluations of remote embodiments have also noted the limitations of current approaches – for example, an evaluation of DOVE and DOVE-like embodiments (Ou et al., 2003; Li et al., 2007) found that participants modify their behaviour to adapt to the lack of height information in the embodiment. Our results suggest that height is a significant component of the information conveyed by a deictic gesture. A failure to fully represent height means that modified gestures or speech patterns must be employed to make up for the lost information. At best, conversational grounding takes longer without height information; at worst, information is lost, requiring greater effort to maintain the communication.

The height of a deictic gesture is complex, however, and not always easily represented. As with other components of deixis, height has a wide range of context-sensitive semantics. For example, in the context of a hesitation atom, height above the surface means that the gesturer is uncertain and not ready to engage in specific deixis. However, a similar gesture presented as a series of strokes and points might be identifying paths, areas, and points on the surface. In this case, the height of the gesture above the table can indicate larger areas, wider paths, or large artifacts. Height is also used more frequently for secondary references, which often have cursory accuracy (Krauss & Fussell, 1990).

Height was also used in a few other ways: as a component of 'ray-casting' gestures that pointed to out-of-reach objects; to mirror variations in height of the objects represented on the map; as another way of emphasizing a location; or to show variation in the precision of a location. Given the wide range of semantics for height, it seems clear that some representation of height is an important requirement for remote embodiment techniques – particularly to show whether a deictic gesture is touching the surface or not.

What Additional Physical Characteristics do Gestures Have?

In previous studies, a wide range of behaviours and subtleties have been observed in deixis (e.g., McNeill, 1992). Much of the variation in behaviour occurs once the gesture has reached its target, rather than during the approach or retraction, which generally involve standard movements. Therefore, deixis on surfaces can also be characterized by the possible movements that can be made on the target. Understanding what kinds of gestures are available and when they are used (e.g. in conjunction with certain kinds of targets, or certain modes of speech) can assist in filtering or augmenting this component of gestures in distributed environments.

From our observations, we present three additional characteristics that were seen several times during the studies. This is by no means an exhaustive set, but will serve to indicate the range of additional possible behaviours that can be observed in a deictic gesture. In each of our example characteristics, a range of meaning is provided by small movements of the arm and hand, or changes in pressure on the surface after a deictic target is reached. These variations in movement or pressure do not change the target of the deixis, but rather provide emphasis or convey qualities that can only be determined through the verbal record. The three characteristics we observed are width variation in strokes, wiggle motions in pointing, and pressure in pointing.

(1)   *Width variation* is variation in the movement along the plane of the surface that does not otherwise interfere with the target of the gesture. For example, width variation on a stroke atom could be sinusoidal movements that range along the axis perpendicular to the movement vector (i.e., a snake-like gesture, rather than a straight line).

(2)   *Wiggles* are movements of the hand or arm that do not change the target pointed to by a finger or hand. A wiggle variation during a point atom that touches the surface would leave the pointing finger in place while moving the hand or arm.

(3)   *Pressure variation* is a change in the pressure applied by a finger or hand on the table surface (presses occur only when the pointing hand is touching the surface). Pressure changes can be visually detected by the observer through subtle differences in the posture and appearance of the hand and finger (e.g., bending or colouration of the pointing finger).

The use of width variation and wiggling can occur on any of the indicative deixis atoms in the air or on the surface, but pressure variations are limited to deixis atoms that rest (at least briefly) on the surface. All three variations were found during both laboratory studies and in the field. In general, wiggle and pressure variations, although present, were noticeably less common than width variations, with some participants using neither. We note however that visual indications of pressure are subtle, and our video recordings may have been insufficient to permit the correct identification of all instances of pressure variation. Where it was possible to view wiggle and pressure variations, they were used for emphasizing a gesture, or accompanied verbal attention-drawing. In a few cases, wiggles and pressure changes were used in the same way as hesitation atoms – that is, as a 'stalling tactic' while the next location was identified. In a few other situations, wiggle variations were performed when the pointing finger or hand partially occluded an area of the surface that the speaker needed to see. The occlusion avoidance that resulted involved a wiggle as the participant moved his/her hand from side to side while peering at the surface.

Width variations were less homogeneous in usage: they were used to emphasize, to cover vague boundaries, to suggest areas rather than paths, to express lower levels of confidence, or as secondary referents to already-described locations. Width variations were more frequently accompanied with verbal utterances, which often clarified the reason for the width variation.

While both realistic and abstract embodiments already do a good job of representing width variations in atomic gestures, wiggle and pressure variations are more complex. Wiggle variations are expressed through changes in the angle and/or position of the hand without a major change to the primary point of contact with the surface; this means that representations showing more of the hand and arm will naturally represent these kinds of motions, but single-point representations such as telepointers will not.

Pressure shows few external signs other than a change in the posture or colour of the hand at the point of contact (and only if enough pressure is being applied). Even with sufficiently high video fidelity, realistic embodiments are unlikely to do well conveying information about pressure, and abstract embodiments do not represent pressure at all. However, the fact that pressure variations only occur on the surface suggest that sensing technology in the surface itself could be used to improve the expressiveness of an abstract embodiment. Some digital tables naturally sense pressure (e.g., FTIR technologies), and a visualization of this sensed value could easily be added to the embodiment of a remote participant.

Design Recommendations and New Designs

Our observations indicate that neither realistic nor abstract embodiments are entirely capable of representing the complex space of deixis over surfaces. In the next section we summarize the assessment of how each embodiment approach supports the representation of deictic gesture, and state a set of design principles that can be identified from our studies. We then consider the question of designing the best possible embodiment for showing deixis. We present one possibility – a hybrid design that combines the fidelity of realistic embodiments with an abstract embodiment's ability to selectively emphasize or de-emphasize components of the gesture. This approach can offer an effective solution to the problems seen in traditional approaches, and can substantially improve the expressiveness of embodiments on tables and surfaces.

Assessment of Realistic and Abstract Embodiments

Both extremes of the abstract-to-realistic embodiment spectrum facilitate the visualization of some of the important components of deixis over a collaborative surface. However, as shown in Figure 3, neither abstract nor realistic embodiments adequately represent the full range of possible behaviours and subtleties in deictic gesture. Although telepointers and other abstract embodiments are able to convey point and stroke atoms extremely well, and can in some implementations represent variations such as height, they cannot represent the full range of gesture morphology we observed, nor are they effective in differentiating between similar gesture atoms, such as rest and point atoms. The main advantage to abstract representations is that additional information such as height, pressure, or past locations can be shown by enhancing the visualization.

Component of Deictic Gesture	Abstract Embodiments	Realistic Embodiments
Show differences between similar atoms	No	Possible
Represent stroke atoms	Yes	No
Express one or two finger pointing	Yes	Yes
Express full range of possible morphology	No	Possible
Represent height	Possible	No
Represent wiggle variation	Possible	Yes
Represent pressure variation	Possible	No
Represent width variation	Yes	Yes

Figure 3. Gesture visualization capabilities of embodiments

Realistic embodiments such as video-based solutions can express a greater range of gesture morphology than abstract representations, although with the substantial caveat that the source images must be effectively separated and transmitted at a high enough resolution for those morphologies to be identifiable. Realistic embodiments generally fail to represent height effectively (due to the 2D projection of the image), do not show characteristics such as pressure, and are less noticeable than real arms in co-located settings, so may not adequately convey temporal aspects of stroke atoms.

Between these two extremes, however, lies a largely unexplored design space that combines the best parts of the two main approaches. The hybrid approach would use video-fidelity representations of hands and arms as the base representation for the embodiment, and enhance the image with abstract visualizations to represent components of the gesture that are not easily represented in two-dimensional video. An early example of this approach is the enhancement of VideoArms to show temporal traces whenever a user's fingers touched the surface (A. Tang et al., 2010). This change provided some emphasis of stroke atoms (but only on the surface) and an indirect representation of height (by separating the touching layer from the other layers). This idea could be taken much further, however: a hybrid embodiment could show a definite focus point, temporal traces both above and on the surface, as well as visualizations of height, pressure, and other qualities. We present one possible hybrid visualization below.

Design Recommendations

Our observations and evaluation of existing approaches suggest five main recommendations for designers of embodiments for surface groupware:

(1) Embody the hand and some portion of the arm with a high-fidelity image. This representation provides a near-complete coverage of the different gesture morphologies, assists with the differentiation of similar atoms, and helps identify wiggle variations.

(2) Add an abstract visualization of the point of the index finger (i.e., a telepointer). This addition will clearly indicate point and stroke atoms, regardless of problems in the separation and resolution of the video image, and can serve as the basis for other abstract visualizations.

(3) Enhance the representation of movement with visual traces or other visual effects. This will assist in emphasizing stroke gestures and in representing width variations.

(4) Use an abstract representation for height. An abstract height representation as an addition to a realistic embodiment will assist in differentiating similar atoms and provide a clear mechanism for showing height variations. Particular attention should be paid to representing the difference between touching, just off the surface, and above the surface.

(5) Use an abstract representation for pressure variations (if these values can be gathered from other sensors). Since pressure is a subtle communication channel, the abstract representation should be equally subtle. Since we noted little use of pressure, compared to other variations, this is a low priority design recommendation.

Finally, we stress that both the task and the display/collaborative environment can have a profound impact on design. For example, we found that vertical displays tended to influence palm orientation, which could influence the selection of sensor suites and display techniques.

An Example Hybrid Embodiment

The five design recommendations above can be used to create a hybrid visualization that is able to represent all of the important components of deictic gesture. One example embodiment that includes some of this information (shown in Figure 4) uses the fidelity of realistic techniques and the flexibility of abstract techniques to create an expressive hybrid visualization. We assume that 3-D sensing techniques are available and that we can therefore gather the actual location of the hand and arm.

The embodiment contains the following components:

(1)   High-fidelity top-down video image of the remote participant's hand and arm, reduced in opacity to avoid completely occluding the artifacts that are beneath the arm's representation.

(2)   Telepointer spot that shows the position of the index finger.

(3)   Temporal traces implemented as a motion blur to emphasize stroke atoms.

(4)   Height representation as a shadow, offset slightly with respect to the seating position of the user to permit a parallax 'raycasting' effect that can improve interpretation of pointing direction for more distant targets.

(5)   Nominal and binary representation of the touching/hovering height state is represented by a small ripple effect (as in Wigdor *et al.*, 2009) on contact (note that this also helps to emphasize strokes on the surface by acting as an implicit temporal trace).

(6)   Pressure variations represented as a heat map on contact points that change colour from blue for a light touch to red for heavy pressure.

This example embodiment addresses each of the design principles introduced above. The methods we used to address these design recommendations are arbitrary, although future work could determine whether, for instance, stroke atoms are best enhanced through trace-like effects (Gutwin and Penner, 2002), motion blur (as used here), or continuous fading lines as in the enhanced VideoArms technique (A. Tang et al., 2010).

Figure 4. A mock-up of elements of a hybrid visualization. Left, a coloured ripple effect enhances the contact point and provides pressure information. Right, temporal traces emphasize a stroke atom and a ray-cast shadow at the pointing target provides height information.

Conclusion

Deictic gestures are ubiquitous in tabletop collaboration, but the embodiments used in distributed tabletop groupware do not adequately express the range and subtlety of real-world deixis. To provide design information about what components and behaviours are important in deictic gesture, we carried out three observational studies. Our observations of collocated tasks provide new understanding of how deictic gesture works, and helps to explain why both abstract and realistic user embodiments fail to express the full range of deixis over surfaces. In particular, abstract embodiments fail to represent a small but significant portion of gesture morphology and can make it difficult to differentiate between similar gestures; realistic embodiments do not effectively represent the height or pressure of gestures, and have no mechanism for emphasizing movement. We identified five design recommendations to improve the expression of deixis through remote embodiments, and proposed a new embodiment approach that combines the best features of both realistic and abstract techniques.

Our studies suggest numerous avenues for further research. The most obvious next step is to implement the new embodiments for remote deictic gesture, and refine and test visualizations that combine the realistic and abstract approaches. We will then evaluate these designs to determine whether they can, as expected, improve the richness of gestural communication in tabletop groupware. Finally, we plan to expand and refine our characterization of deictic gestures through additional studies and further real-world observations.

References

Apperly, M., McLeod, L., Masoodian, M., Paine, L., Phillips, M., Rogers, B., and Thomson, K (2003): 'Use of video shadow for small group interaction awareness on a large interactive display surface', *Proceedings of the 4th Australasian user interface conference*, vol. 18, 81-90.

Bekker, M. M., Olson, J. S., & Olson, G. M. (1995): 'Analysis of gestures in face-to-face design teams provides guidance for how to use groupware in design', *Proceedings of the 1st conference on Designing Interactive Systems*, 157-166.

Benford, S., Bowers, J., Fahlén, L.E., Greenhalgh, C., and Snowdon, D. (1995): 'User embodiment in collaborative virtual environments', *Proceedings of the SIGCHI conference on Human Factors in Computing Systems* , 242-249.

Clark, H.H. (2003): 'Pointing and placing', in S. Kita (eds): *Pointing: Where language, culture, and cognition meet*, Erlbaum, Hillsdale, NJ, 2003, 243-268.

Fraser, M., McCarthy, M.R., Shaukat, M, and Smith, P. (2007): 'Seconds Matter: Improving Distributed Coordination by Tracking and Visualizing Display Trajectories', *Proceedings of the SIGCHI conference on Human Factors in Computing Systems*, 1303-1312.

Greenberg, S., Gutwin, C., and Roseman, M. (1996): 'Semantic telepointers for groupware', *Proceedings of the 6th Australian conference on Computer-Human Interaction*, 54-61.

Gutwin, C., & Greenberg, S. (1998): 'Effects of awareness support on groupware usability', *Proceedings of the SIGCHI conference on Human Factors in Computing Systems*, 511-518.

Gutwin, C., & Greenberg, S. (2000): 'The mechanics of collaboration: Developing low cost usability evaluation methods for shared workspaces', *Proceedings of the 9th IEEE workshop on Enabling Technologies: Infrastructure for Collaborative Enterprises*, 98-103.

Gutwin, C., & Penner, R. (2002): 'Improving interpretation of remote gestures with telepointer traces', *Proceedings of the ACM conference on Computer Supported Cooperative Work*, 49-57.

Hayne, S. , Pendergast, M., and Greenberg, S. (1994): 'Implementing Gesturing with Cursors in Group Support Systems', *Journal of Management Information Systems*, 10, 3, 1994 , 43-62.

Hindmarsh, J., Fraser, M., Heath, C., Benford, S., and Greenhalgh, C. (2000): 'Object-focused interaction in collaborative virtual environments', *ACM Transactions on Computer-Human Interaction*, vol. 7, no. 4, 477-509.

Hindmarsh, J., & Heath, C. (2000): 'Embodied reference: A study of deixis in workplace interaction', *Journal of Pragmatics*, vol. 32, no. 12, 1855–1878.

Izadi, S., Agarwal, A., Criminisi, A., Winn, J., Blake, A., Fitzgibbon, A. (2007): 'C-Slate: A Multi-Touch and Object Recognition System for Remote Collaboration using Horizontal Surfaces', *2nd Workshop on Horizontal Interactive Human-Computer Systems*, 3-10.

Kettebekov, S., & Sharma, R. (2000): 'Understanding gestures in multimodal human computer interaction', *International Journal on Artificial Intelligence Tools*, vol. 9, no. 2, 205–223.

Kirk, D., Crabtree, A., & Rodden, T. (2005): 'Ways of the hands', *Proceedings of the European conference on Computer Supported Cooperative Work*, 1–21.

Kirk, D., Rodden, T., & Fraser, D. S. (2007): 'Turn it this way: grounding collaborative action with remote gestures', *Proceedings of the SIGCHI conference on Human Factors in Computing Systems*, 1039-1048.

Krauss, R.M. and Fussell, S. R. (1990): 'Mutual Knowledge and Communicative Effectiveness', in J. Galegher, R. E. Kraut, and C. Egido (eds.) *Intellectual Teamwork: Social and Technological Foundations of Cooperative Work*, Erlbaum, Hillsdale, NJ, 111-145.

Li, J., Wessels, A., Alem, L., & Stitzlein, C. (2007): 'Exploring interface with representation of gesture for remote collaboration', *Proceedings of the 19th Australasian conference on Computer-Human Interaction: Entertaining User Interfaces*, 179-182.

McNeill, D. (1992): *Hand and mind*, University of Chicago Press, Chicago.

Ou, J., Chen, X., Fussell, S. R., & Yang, J. (2003): 'DOVE: Drawing over video environment', *Proceedings of the 11th ACM international conference on Multimedia*, 100–101.

Ou, J., Fussell, S. R., Chen, X., Setlock, L. D., & Yang, J. (2003): 'Gestural communication over video stream: supporting multimodal interaction for remote collaborative physical tasks', *Proc. of the 5th conference on Multimodal Interfaces*, 242–249.

Pinelle, D., Nacenta, M., Gutwin, C., & Stach, T. (2008): 'The effects of co-present embodiments on awareness and collaboration in tabletop groupware', *Proceedings of Graphics Interface*, 1–8.

Stach, T., Gutwin, C., Pinelle, D., & Irani, P. (2007): 'Improving recognition and characterization in groupware with rich embodiments', *Proceedings of the SIGCHI conference on Human Factors in Computing Systems*, 11-20.

Tang, A., Neustaedter, C., & Greenberg, S. (2007): 'Videoarms: embodiments for mixed presence groupware', in N. Bryan-Kinns, A. Blanford, P. Curzon and L. Niggy (eds.): *People and Computers XX*, Springer, London, 2007, 85-102.

Tang, A., Pahud, M., Inkpen, K., Benko, H., Tang, J. C., & Buxton, B. (2010): 'Three's company: understanding communication channels in three-way distributed collaboration', *Proceedings of ACM conference on Computer Supported Cooperative Work*, 271–280.

Tang, J. C., & Minneman, S. (1991a): 'VideoWhiteboard: video shadows to support remote collaboration', *Proceedings of the SIGCHI conference on Human Factors in Computer Systems*, 315–322.

Tang, J., and Minneman, S. (1991b): Videodraw: a video interface for collaborative drawing. *Transansactions on Information Systems* 9, 2 (April 1991), 170-184.

Wigdor, D., Williams, S., Cronin, M., Levy, R., White, K. (2009): 'Ripples: utilizing per-contact visualizations to improve user interaction with touch displays,' *Proceedings of the ACM symposium on User Interface Software and Technology*, 3-12.

VideoPal: Exploring Asynchronous Video-Messaging to Enable Cross-Cultural Friendships

Honglu Du[1], Kori Inkpen[2], Konstantinos Chorianopoulos[3], Mary Czerwinski[2], Paul Johns[2], Aaron Hoff[2], Asta Roseway[2], Sarah Morlidge[4], John Tang[2] and Tom Gross[5]

[1]Pennsylvania State University, [2]Microsoft Research, [3]Ionian University, [4]Chestnut Hill Academy, [5] University of Bamberg

[1]hzd106@ist.psu.edu,

[2]{kori, marycz, pauljoh, aaronho, astar, johntang}@microsoft.com

[3] choko@ionio.gr, [4]smorlidge@chestnuthillacademy.com, [5]email@tomgross.net

Abstract. Pen pal programs for connecting students from around the world through letter writing have been popular for generations. However, traditional technologies have several limitations in supporting pen pal activities. In this study, we explored the potential of video-based asynchronous messaging in supporting the development of children's cross-cultural friendships. This paper presents the results of a 2-month study of 30 children from the USA and Greece, exploring their uses of, and experiences with, email and an asynchronous video-based messaging tool we developed called VideoPal. The results from this work highlight the important benefits video provides compared to its text counterpart - email. We conclude with a discussion of the key factors that video enables to benefit the development of children's long-distance friendships.

Introduction

Pen pal programs for connecting students from around the world through letter writing have been popular for generations. Often, they are arranged informally through friendship networks in schools or churches (Bragg, 1989). Pen pal activities have been documented as supporting cross-curricular learning (Lemkuhl, 2002), developing cross-cultural understanding (Barksdale, Watson, and Park, 2007), and serving the need for a close and intimate friend for young children (Shulman, Seiffge-Krenke & Dimitrovsky, 1994). While traditional pen pal activities involve students exchanging postal mail to communicate with each other, advancements in communication technologies have transformed the way people keep in touch with each other. As a result, use of email is becoming more common for pen pal activities.

The work in this paper focuses on studying the use of asynchronous video messages to extend pen pal activities. We developed a video-based asynchronous tool called VideoPal. Similar to the notion of a pen pal, instead of writing letters or emails, children can send short videos or screen recordings to each other. We were particularly interested in asynchronous video because: a) the primarily text-based nature of email is a limited symbolic representation system (Keil, 2002); b) video may be more effective for young children who have not mastered text-based technologies (Yarosh, Inkpen & Brush, 2009; Hayes-Roth and Gent, 1997); c) video can support non-verbal communication which is often missing or attenuated in text-based communication; and d) the asynchronous nature makes it an ideal tool to support communication between people from different parts of the world spanning many time-zones.

While recent technical and infrastructure developments make the potential of using asynchronous video to support pen pal activities ripe for exploration, there has been little investigation into this type of communication for children. In this study, we explored the benefits of asynchronous video-mediated communication to support pen pal conversations for elementary school students from Washington State, USA and Corfu, Greece. We seek to answer the following two questions:

- What benefits does asynchronous video provide for communication compared to text-based email?
- What are opportunities and challenges for children's use of video-mediated asynchronous communication?

We start with situating our work in the context of previous research on pen pal activities and computer-mediated communication (CMC). We then describe the VideoPal system and present results from a study of 30 children from USA and Greece using this tool for two months. Finally, we discuss key features of VideoPal that were important to support observed usage practices.

Related Work

We draw upon a rich history of previous work on technology mediated pen pal activities, non-verbal communication and video-mediated communication.

Pen Pals

Pen pals are people who write to each other regularly, particularly through postal mail. Writing letters to pen pals has been a popular practice for generations (Barksdale, Watson & Park, 2007) and is especially popular among young children. Further, children's fascination with other cultures, travel, and names of foreign places promotes their eagerness to learn about the daily lives of someone their own age living on the other side of the world (Bragg & McWilliams, 1989).

Pen pal activities have been shown to be beneficial for children. According to Vygotsky (1978), children learn things more effectively through experiences that are meaningful and relevant to them. In addition, pen pal activities give children an authentic opportunity to learn about others and studies have shown that pen pal activities are effective in helping children develop cross cultural understanding (Barksdale, Watson, & Park, 2007; Kern, 1996; Hare, 1999; Charron, 2007). However, traditional technologies have several limitations in supporting pen pal activities. Exchanging postal mail is costly and can have lengthy delivery lags, which can be major obstacles to the development of pen pal friendships (Kern, 1996). Recently, text-based asynchronous communication tools, such as email, have been increasingly adopted to support pen pal activities because the cost of sending email is low and messages are delivered immediately (Kern, 1996).

In spite of the advantages email offers, the primarily text-based nature of email is a limited symbolic representation system (Keil & Johnson, 2002). To overcome this, some pen pal projects have explored the use of multimedia. For example, in one pen pal project between students from Singapore and Canada, the Canadian students used the fax machine to send local maps to Singapore to aid their communication (Soh & Soon, 1991). In 1989, Bragg and McWilliams organized a Video Pal program between two classes of middle school students from North Carolina and Alabama to learn about each other's state geography information. Students filmed videos about their local areas and sent the video by postal mail to each other. The video exchange program allowed students to see the geographical differences between these two places. Although it was successful, it was a cumbersome for the students to film the videos, sometimes requiring several months to produce one video. With current advances in the Internet and computing technologies, it is worth revisiting the idea that video could be an effective medium to support children's communication and collaboration.

Nonverbal Communication for Children

Nonverbal communication includes the use of gestures, body languages, postures, facial expressions, eye contact, and variations in the pitch and tone of voices, etc. to convey information (Mehrabian, 1972). The role of nonverbal communication in human interaction has been well researched. Studies have shown that nonverbal behavior can be used to regulate conversations and express emotions (Ekman, 1999). Appropriate use of nonverbal communication can lead to productive communication because facial cues can convey effective emotional signals to eliminate conversational confusions (Ekman & Friesen, 1968; Littlejohn, 2002). Further, Mehrabian demonstrated that nonverbal communication is particularly important for communicating feelings and attitude when nonverbal behaviors are incongruent with words (Mehrabian, 1972).

Nonverbal behaviors are also common and important in children's communication. Various studies have shown that children are usually ineffective communicators because they have not mastered the necessary linguistic or cognitive competencies (Piaget, 1926; Krauss & Glucksberg, 1969). Bruner asserted that all knowledge begins with action, progresses towards iconic representations, and then can be expressed with language. His theory suggested that a language-based medium like email would be more complex for children than a medium that leveraged actions, bodily movement, or imagery because children generally have an easier time expressing their knowledge and ideas through action rather than words. Furthermore, Mundy et al., (1995) demonstrated that nonverbal communication skills provide an important foundation for children's language development. Among various computer-mediated communication (CMC) technologies, video-mediated communication is perhaps the most desirable to support nonverbal communication among children (Ballagas, Kaye, Ames, Go & Raffle, 2009).

Video-Mediated Communication

Synchronous video-mediated communication, like videoconferencing, has been well studied in the workplace, and recently video conferencing has been increasingly adopted in homes to connect extended family members, allowing us to draw on relevant findings from this field (Bly, Harrison, & Irwin, 1993). Two CMC theories suggest that video has several distinctive advantages over text-based emails and thus could be more effective in supporting communications. According to media richness theory, video as a medium allows the simultaneous observation of multiple cues, including body language, facial expression and tone of voice. It is of a personal nature and utilizes natural language, which is high in variety (Daft & Lengel, 1984). Social presence theory suggests that communicating partners can have more awareness about each other's states using videos than using other media, like email or on the telephone (Short, Williams & Christie, 1976), and thus, video could be good for supporting communication among children. Ames et al. (2010) compared children's use of phones and synchronous video conferencing system and suggested that the benefits of video for children include that a) the visual aspects keep children engaged in synchronous video chat, b) less help from parents is needed for children to participate in video chat rather than in phone conversations because children can participate by simply sitting in front of the camera, but c) parents need to provide some scaffolding, namely conversation support, to keep children talking. However, since the context in that study was connecting children with adults, it is not clear whether this kind of conversation support is still needed when children talk with their peers of similar ages.

While previous research has examined the advantages and disadvatanges of video (Issacs & Tang, 1994), there is significantly less theoretical grounding as to what computer-mediated asynchronous video can and cannot do for communication. Several ethnographic studies of video conferencing systems in domestic settings have pointed to a strong need for using asynchronous video based communication to connect family members from different time zones (Kirk, Sellen & Cao, 2010; Cao, Sellen, Brush, Kirk, Edge & Ding, 2010; Modlitba, Schmandt & Globetoddler, 2008). Modlitba et al., (2008) found that children prefer using video chat to using telephones to talk to their travelling parents, but their parents' busy schedules makes it hard to coordinate synchronous video chat. Thus asynchronous video could be particularly rewarding. In another study, Cao et al., (2010) suggested that asynchronous video would be a more flexible means of communication because it only requires that one party be available and could be "initiated outside the communication window dictated by the time difference".

There has been some previous research on using asynchronous video to connect family members. Zuckerman and Maes (2005) proposed the Contextual Asynchronous System (CASY), which enables family members to send 'good morning' and 'good night' asynchronous video snippets into a shared family database. The recipient views the snippet in the context of going to sleep or waking up. While they did not actually build the system, they asked participants to use email to send videos as attachments and found that asynchronous video communication increased participants' feeling of connectedness. This work suggests that asynchronous video-mediated communication has great potential for connecting children with other family members, but an empirical study is needed to understand the specific opportunities and challenges of computer-mediated asynchronous video based communication tools with children.

VideoPal System

VideoPal is a computer-mediated, video based asynchronous communication system. It enables users to capture videos, record their screen, upload an existing video, and send, receive, and reply to a video message. Video messages are threaded by topic and each conversation is visually represented. The VideoPal user interface is primarily composed of four windows: the main window (Figure 1), the message play window (Figure 2.a), the create new message window (Figure 2.b), and the screen recording frame (Figure 3).

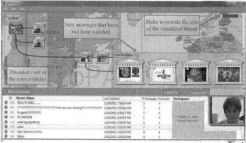

Figure 1. The main window of VideoPal.

The main window allows users to quickly see which conversation threads are available, the properties of each thread (e.g., number of messages, number of unread messages in the thread), a visual presentation of one conversation, the new messages which are shown at bottom of the visualization panel, and the current users' profile photo. From this main window, users can create a new video or play an existing video message. The visualization panel in the main window displays a topically threaded sequence of messages which shows the flow of a conversation – seeing who responded to whom and when, based on the way messages branch. Each video thumbnail is visually decorated to indicate where the video is from. Videos sent from Greece are surrounded by a Parthenon and videos sent from Washington (The Evergreen State) are surrounded by a forest. At the bottom right corner is the new message panel, which shows the thumbnails of the new videos that have been sent to the user but have not been watched yet.

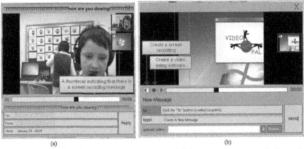

(a)   (b)

Figure 2. (a) the window for watch a video message; (b) the new message window, children can create a new video using webcam, or create a screen recording or upload a video.

Clicking on a video thumbnail in the main window will open the message play window (Figure 2.a). Children can easily create a reply message by clicking the reply button. Clicking on the New Conversation button in the main window or clicking the reply button in the "message play" window will bring up the new message window (Figure 2.b). Here the children have three different options: 1) they can choose to create a new video using the webcam by clicking the red record button, or 2) create a screen recording by clicking the camera icon, or 3) send an existing video by uploading a video from the computer. The screen recording feature enables users to share parts of their screen while simultaneously narrating if desired. The screen recording frame (Figure 3) outlines the area of the screen that will be recorded. Users can drag to resize the frame to choose the area of the screen they wish to record.

The Field Study

This section describes a two month field study we conducted using VideoPal and email to connect children from the USA and Greece.

The Children and Contexts

The VideoPal project started with a project in a private school in Washington State, USA (WA). One tradition in the WA school is that every year, each grade selects a country to study, and learns about that country's culture and lifestyles. In the final week of the fall semester, the children give presentations about what they have learned about that country to all the teachers, students and their parents. In previous years, the students learned about their chosen country by reading books and looking for information on the Internet. This year, the fourth grade students were studying Greece.

In the fourth grade at WA, there are 2 classes. Class1 has 13 students (6 boys and 7 girls), and Class 2 has 12 students (6 boys and 6 girls). All of the students from WA are 9 to 10 years old. Both Class1 and Class2 have a technology lesson every week which is taught by a specialist teacher in a technology lab. The technology lab contains 17 desktop computers.

We explored potential partner schools in Corfu Greece, but because of infrastructure challenges in the public school system, as well as difficulty getting permissions in place in time, the Greek side of the VideoPal project was administered through Ionian University. In the end, five students (3 boys and 2 girls, ages 11 to 12 years old in fifth and sixth grades) volunteered to participate

Figure 3. The screen recording frame

in this project. Instead of the project being a part of their school day, all of the students from Corfu took part in the study during their spare time. These students came to Ionian University every Friday evening to use VideoPal and correspond with their pen pals. One teacher also volunteered to come participate in the project and facilitate the interactions. The key motivations for these children and their parents was that it was regarded as a good opportunity for them to practice their English and it also enabled them to learn more about computers.

Study Procedure

Because the number of students in WA was asymmetric to that of Corfu, we divided the 25 children from WA into 5 groups. Each group communicated with one child from Corfu during the study. Since we paired boys to boys and girls to girls, one girl from Corfu communicated with 7 girls from WA, and the other girl from Corfu communicated with the other 6 WA girls. Each of the Corfu boys communicated with 4 WA boys.

The study consisted of three phases. The first phase was a training session, lasting one week. In this phase, the children were taught how to use VideoPal to send videos and how to use email. Each of the students from WA was given an email account assigned by their school, which ran on a Microsoft Outlook Exchange Server. Each of the Corfu children was given a hotmail account. During this phase each child had the opportunity to practice composing and sending email and they also sent an introduction video about themselves to their pen pal.

During the second phase, which lasted three weeks, the children discussed 2 pre-selected topics every week, one using email and one using VideoPal. Topics were provided to the children to scaffold their use for the first three weeks since they did not know each other. The topics were selected by the teachers from WA, along with a list of suggested questions for the WA children to ask. The topics were counter-balanced to ensure that all the children used both email and VideoPal to communicate with their pen pal, and that each topic was covered using both media. Each week, children from Class1 used VideoPal to discuss one topic and used email to discuss the other topic, and Class2 swapped the method they used for each topic. The children from Corfu typically sent one reply video message and one email to their pen pals each week. The topics covered included school, hobbies/sports, food, holidays, music, family and pets.

The third phase was the freeform use portion, lasting four weeks. The children were no longer required to use both email and VideoPal, but instead could choose whatever medium they desired. They were also allowed to opt out if they no longer wanted to correspond with their pen pal. Additionally, the children were free to talk about whatever they wanted, and did not need to discuss pre-defined topics. Because other material was being covered in the WA school during technology class, the children were given a 30 minute period when they could use the technology lab and send a message to their pen pal. The children from Corfu continued coming to Ionian University on Friday evenings to participate.

Data Collection

A wide range of data was collected to address our research questions including: surveys, interviews, and analysis of the videos and emails the students sent to each other.

During most of the sessions, a researcher was present to assist and observe the children when they were sending their pen pal messages. All of the videos and emails the children sent to each other were recorded and transcribed for later analysis. The students also completed three paper based surveys: one at the beginning of Phase 1 (pre), one at the end of Phase 2 (mid), and one at the end of Phase 3 (final). The pre-survey collected students' background information, including how interested they were in learning about the other country, their prior pen pal experiences, computer experience and experience using email, video chat, and IM. The mid survey and final survey gathered feedback on their use of VideoPal and explored the differences between VideoPal and email. At the end of Phase 2 and Phase 3 we also conducted semi-structured interviews with the students to get a better understanding about what they liked and disliked about VideoPal and email.

Results

We report on the children's previous experiences with pen pal activities and communication tools. We then report on the children's use of VideoPal and email during the study and their perceptions of the benefits of each.

Background Data

In the pre survey, both the WA and Corfu children were asked to rate, on a 5-point scale (from very boring to very interested), how interested they were in learning about the other country and meeting new friends from the other country. Almost all the students (97%) rated themselves as being interested or very interested.

Prior Pen Pal Experience: Most of the students from WA (92%) had some pen pal experience. Nineteen participated in a pen pal project organized by their school the previous year where they sent letters to children from Ghana, but at relatively low rate (i.e., once every few months); however, none of these children currently have a pen pal. For the children from Corfu, one of the girls used to have a pen pal and she used email to communicate with her pen pal for 2 years.

Experiences with email, IM and Video chat: Many of the children had never used Video chat before but they were relatively familiar with email. See Table I for a detailed report on the children's prior experiences.

Tools	Never Used	Some Experience	Use Every Day
Email	40%	50%	10%
IM	67%	30%	3%
Video Chat	60%	33%	7%

Table I. Students' prior experiences with email, IM and Video chat.

Overall Experience

Overall, the children from both Corfu and WA were extremely excited about the opportunity to exchange messages with children from the other country. When we asked the children what the best thing about the project was, many commented on the opportunity to meet someone from another country. Some of the comments included: *"Sending videos and emails and having the chance to be able to know someone from Greece is just amazing"*, *"I can meet friends in the US"*, *"Seeing somebody in Greece and talking with them and seeing what life was like in Greece"*, *"making a new friend"*, and *"communication with people that I will probably never meet"*.

Phase		WA	Corfu	Mean Length(SD)
2	Video	77	22	28.66s (sd=1.64)
	Email	69	16	41 words (sd=23)
3	Video	97	41	14.20s (sd=10.0[1])
	Email	18	12	21 words (sd=3)

Table II. Summary of # of emails and videos sent in Phase 2 and Phase 3.

VideoPal vs Email: A Peek at the Messages Exchanged

Usage data for both email and VideoPal are shown in Table II. In Phase 2, on average every student sent 1 video message and 1 email each week (which was the suggested use given the study protocol). The length of both the videos and emails were relatively short. In Phase 3 the children were free to choose whatever medium they wanted to use to communicate with their pen pal. We saw that video was strongly preferred with the children sending more than three times the numbers of videos compared to email. Additionally, the length of the videos and emails decreased during this phase. Further analysis showed that it was because in this phase instead of reciting a list of questions or answers, the messages were less scripted and more conversational.

During Phase 3, participation was optional and the children could choose to not participate if desired. All of the Corfu children continued to participate each week, while some weeks a small handful of students (2-4) from WA choose not to send messages to their pen pal. During the final interview we asked these students why they sometimes chose not to participate, and most replied that it was because they had a lot of homework, or because they had an after-school activity requiring preparation time. Even though some of the WA students did not participate some weeks, all participated at some point during Phase 3.

---

[1] In the final 2 weeks of the study, 13 screen capture messages of boys playing a video game were sent. All of these were significantly longer in duration than the average video message and did not contribute to a conversation. These were coded as outliers and are not included in the median length calculation.

Below is an exemplary video conversation (using pseudonyms) from Phase 2. In this conversation, the child from WA asked questions about family and pets and the child from Corfu responded. In addition, Figure 4 shows screenshots of videos children sent to each other during the project.

John (40''): Hi Achilles, I do not play soccer. I am really bad at it. I have a question for you. Do you have any pets? If you have any pet, what kind? Is it common or unusual for Greek families to have pets? What kinds of pets do people have if they do? Do Greek people have any special traditions related to pets? Just wondering. How many people are in your family? How many brothers and sisters do you have? Do you see your grandparents, aunts, uncles, and cousins very often? What kinds of things do you like to do with your family? Are you named after someone in your family? If yes, who? Bye.

Achilles (34''): Hi, my favorite pets are dogs. My dogs! They are beautiful, smart, and cute and they are hunter dogs. We don't have a special custom in Greece with our pets. We will just take them at the mountains to hunt and bring something birds to eat or rabbit. I love my dogs!

Figure 4. Screenshots showing example videos the children sent to each other.

The children used email in similar ways. Children from WA asked questions on a specific topic and the Corfu children responded. Below is an exemplary email conversation:

Jessica: Hi, I have a dog named Daisy. I have a few more questions to ask u. What kind of music do u listen 2? Do u play any instruments? Do u listen 2 any American music?

Aalisha: Hi...I want to tell you about my favorite music. I play piano six years and also I am in a choir. I like music too. I am interested in pop and classic music. On the other hand Greek music is very good. I have a question for you. Have you ever listened Greek music? If yes, what song do you know? Many Kisses. Eleni.

VideoPal vs Email: Children's Perceptions of Use

In the mid and final surveys students were asked to rate their experience using VideoPal and email, from very happy (5) to very unhappy (1) (e.g., "Please show us how you feel about using VideoPal to communicate with your friend over the past several weeks"). We used emoticons as visual aids for the choices (see Figure 5). Although both email and VideoPal were rated highly, the mid-survey

Very Happy   Happy   Neutral   Not Happy   Very Unhappy

Figure 5. Emoticons used in the survey to measure children's experience using VideoPal and Email

	Happiness		Easier to use		More useful		
	VideoPal	Email	VideoPal	Email	VideoPal	Email	Equally the same
Phase 2	4.48	4.07	76%	24%	48%	11%	41%
Phase 3	4.59	3.97	82%	18%	66%	3%	31%

Table III. Results from the mid and final surveys regarding children's experience using VideoPal

and the final survey revealed that the children were happier with their experience using VideoPal than email (Marginal Homogeneity Test $p<.05$) (see Table III).

We also asked children which tool they felt was easier to use (see Table III). Results from both the mid-survey and the final survey revealed that most of the children (76%) felt that VideoPal was easier to use than email (mid: $\chi^2(1, 29) = 7.76$, $p<.05$, final: $\chi^2(1, 27) = 10.70$, $p<.05$). The children were also asked which they felt was more useful for them to learn about their friend. Most of the children felt that VideoPal was either more useful, or equally useful. A one-sample chi-square test of children's perception of usefulness showed significant differences in proportions, (mid survey: $\chi^2(2, 29) = 7.10$, $p<.05$, final survey: $\chi^2(2, 29) = 16.83$, $p<.001$. Post-hoc tests showed that more children felt that video was more useful than email ($p<.05$). The perceived difference in usefulness actually grew in Phase 3 with more children stating that VideoPal was more useful, and only one child stating that email was more useful.

"VideoPal is more fun!"

Data from both the mid and final surveys and interviews indicated that the children generally liked using both email and VideoPal, however, when asked which medium (email or VideoPal) they would use if they could only have one, all of the children except two chose VideoPal. The children were also much more enthusiastic about their use of VideoPal. Some comments included: *"VideoPal is more fun"*, *"(I like) the awesome movies from Corfu"*, *"I like sending videos to my friends and my video pals."*, *"I have enjoyed making the videos and sending them to people"* and *"I like to talk with my friends, and I want to see them every Friday because I love to have communication with them"*.

Several distinctive features of video emerged that explained why the children preferred video to email. This included: being able to see and hear their friends, enabling them to know their friend better, enabling a feeling of being there, showing things easily, and avoiding typing. The following sections elaborate on each of these findings and also discuss the benefits of email.

"You Get to See the Person"

The children found it beneficial to be able to see their pen pal friends and hear their voices. The most common reason the children gave for wanting to use VideoPal was that they could *"see the person"*. As Aalisha explained, *"I like to see them on the Video. It is better than email.*" Jane commented that "*you can see who you are talking to and listen to their voice and everything. For the email, you might in a million years, never even see the person*". Kim mentioned that "*I like VideoPal better because you can see the person and see what they talk like*" and "*you can actually hear how they speak, what they look like and see what other kids are doing*". Monica said "*You get to see their personality, what they look like. It is cool because you get to see them from a far off place*", and Achilles explained that he could "*talk face-to-face*".

The children also felt that being able to see their friends gave them the opportunity to interact with them in a personal way and get to know their personality. Matt said, "*(I like VideoPal because) it is easy to goof off with video and you can see their expressions in the video.*" Emily said "*I like VideoPal because you can do more in person*" and Karen said "*I really like that you can see the person and tell their personality*". Amy emphasized that "*I think one good thing about VideoPal is that ... if they really get excited about something, you can see their motions like I am so excited about this. I can explode.*" Maggie also commented that "*you can actually see their emotions in VideoPal*".

"*You Get to Know Them Better*"

In the final interview many of the children commented that they felt they were able to get to know their pen pal friend better because they used video. Jane commented that "*You get to really know your pen pal a lot better. You get to see what they look like. You get to know their personality and how they talk.*" John remarked that "*I know him better because of video. You can see what they look like*" and Emily explained that "*you could recognize them*".

As mentioned above most of the children from WA had traditional pen pals from Ghana the previous year. They exchanged 3-4 letters with these pen pals over the year. When asked to compare how well they knew their Corfu pen pals as compared to their Ghanaian pen pals, almost all of the children felt that they knew their Corfu pen pals better. As Maggie explained, "*It seems like we have known our Greek VideoPals for more than a year ... and like Ghana, it feels like we've only met them for a day.*" The two students who did feel like they knew more about their friend from Ghana explained that her letters were quite long and gave a lot of detail about her family. However, despite knowing a lot of facts about their pen pals from Ghana, they felt that they knew the personality of their Corfu friend better.

"*It Feels Like You Are With Them*"

During the final interview, some of children commented that a benefit of VideoPal was that it helped them feel like they were "with" their friends. As John explained, "*it is kind of like they are right in front of you*", Katrina commented,

"Because it feels like you are there", and Jason remarked *"you can have a conversation with them"*. These feelings of being there were never expressed for email. Feeling like they were with their friends also made it easier for the children to feel like they were having a conversation with their pen pals. As Eleni mentioned, "I like VideoPal because I like to have a conversation with them, which is more important than email."

"You Can Show Them Things"

Another benefit the children expressed for VideoPal was that it enabled them to "show" their friends things. As Adam commented, *"if they are trying to show you something ....you can just show them"*. Given that the children used VideoPal in computer labs, this limited their ability to share somewhat, although there were some opportunities where the children did show each other things (Figure 6). For example, Aalisha plays the piano and loves music so she showed her music books in one of her VideoPal messages. Aalisha also took the opportunity to show her WA friends how to tie a knot in one of her VideoPal messages. In another message, Eleni explained to her WA friends that it was her birthday and showed them the shirt she received for her birthday.

(a)   (b)   (c)   (d)

Figure 6. (a) showing a watch he got for Christmas; (b) showing the shirt she got for her birthday; (c) showing her music book; (d) showing how to make a knot.

"I Don't Like to Type"

One practical reason why many of the children preferred VideoPal was that they were not good at typing. For example, Kim mentioned *"(I didn't like emails because) you have to type... (Typing) is just boring!"* John: *"I am really a slow typer, and it is easier for me to say what I want to say"*. Debbie: *"I am not a good typer and I don't want to type"*. We also noticed during our observations that many of the children type using one finger.

Benefits of Email

While VideoPal was generally preferred by the children, email was still desired and many children wanted access to both. One key benefit was that email helped overcome problems with accents, or audio problems. For instance, Amy commented *"You can get more information in email because in VideoPal sometimes it is hard to hear them or they have some accents. But in email, you can just see the words on the screen."* Adam also commented *"Email is better because you can always understand them."*

A second benefit to email was that the children did not need to worry about their appearance when using email and felt that it could hide emotions, if desired. For instance, Rose commented that *"If you had a bad hair day and you don't want anyone else to see it. You want to use email"*. Amy also commented *"if you don't want to see the person's feelings, email is better"*.

Another benefit of using email to communicate with their pen pals was that email sometimes made it easier to manage the exchange of facts in a more relaxed way. For example, Achilles commented that *"you cannot manage video message when there are many questions asked."* Eleni explained that *"(I can) take time to write details, comment on photos"*. Aalisha also mentioned that *"(email) is easier to focus on things and it is slower and relaxed"*. This was also an issue because editing and search facilities were not provided in VideoPal. For example Matt mentioned that *"You have to, like think before you do it. If I say something wrong, you have to redo the whole video. (For email), you can just (use) backspace"* and Maggie complained that *"If you can't remember the questions that they asked you, you can't really go back, you have to restart the whole video."*

As noted earlier, being expressive was clearly important to the children. Email does provide some forms of expression. In our study, 20% of the emails included text that was meant to express emotion such as a series of exclamation marks or emoticons. For example:

Jane: HEEEEEEEEEEEEEEEEEEEEELLLLLLLLLLLLLLLLLLLLLOOOOOOOOOOOOOOOOOOOO Eliza!!!!!!!!!!!!!!!!!!!!!!!!!!!!!!!!!!! I am very excited. We are going to have a snowstorm!!!!!!!!!!!!!!!

Aalisha: Hello. I am Eliza and I'm eleven years old. I live in Corfu. I go to the 5th class of Primary Shcool. My favourite hobby is dancing, volleyball,basketball and my favourite subject is History. What is your favourite hobby???

Information Density

We were interested in whether the amount of information exchanged using VideoPal and email was different. All the videos and emails were transcribed and coded for the number of questions asked in each video and email, and the number of words in each video and email. Since all the questions asked in the videos or emails were questions suggested by the teachers, the number of questions asked was further normalized based on the number of questions suggested for each topic. Two 2 (media) x 3 (weeks) within-subject ANOVAs were performed. One was performed on the normalized questions asked and the other was done on the number of words in each message (see Figure 7).

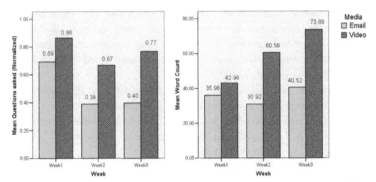

Figure 7. Results of the 2 x 3 ANOVAs: left, the normalized # of questions asked; right: the word counts.

The 2 x 3 within-subject ANOVA on the normalized # of questions asked revealed a significant effect of media, $F_{1,11}$=7.31, p<.021 (p<.001); namely, a higher percentage of the suggested questions were asked in videos than in email; the effect of time (from week 1 to week 3) was also significant, $F_{2,22}$=4.25, p<.028. The interaction was not significant, $F_{2,22}$=2.48, p =.107.

The 2 x 3 within-subject ANOVA on the number of words revealed a significant effect of medium, $F_{1,11}$=10.42, p<.009 (p<.001), namely, more words were spoken in the videos; the effect of time (from week 1 to week 3) was also significant, $F_{2,22}$=3.84, p<.04. Finally, the interaction was also significant, $F_{2,22}$=5.36, p < .02.

It was not surprising that the children felt that they could get more information from the videos (as reported earlier) given that video provides nonverbal information, such as gestures, eye gaze, emotions and expression information. However, it was interesting to find that video also provided more verbal information than email. The children asked more questions and spoke more when using video as opposed to email.

Scaffolding Use

According to Bruner (1975), scaffolding represents the support provided by adults to help children do something beyond their independent efforts. In this study, the WA teachers provide scaffolding for the first three weeks in the form of suggested discussion topics and questions. The scaffolding was provided because it was felt that the children would find it difficult to come up with questions to ask or things to talk about since they did not know anything about their pen pal at the beginning of the study. The suggested questions were given to every child with a reminder that they were just suggestions, and they should feel free to rephrase them if desired. All of the children used the suggested questions, and often placed the list near the computer so that they could easily refer to it while composing a message to their pen pal.

Free Choice

In Phase 3 the children were allowed to use whatever medium they desired, and were free to send messages about any topic. As reported before, VideoPal was used significantly more than email during this phase. Additionally, VideoPal tended to be one that the children used first. For example, at the beginning of the sessions, most of the children would first start up VideoPal, check for new video messages, and then send a VideoPal message to their pen pal. About half of the children would then choose to return to class, while the remainder checked their email and sometimes sent a reply.

Given that the children were free to talk about anything, the topics were quite varied. This included recent events, presents they got for Christmas, their upcoming birthday parties, new clothing, things they have learned recently, events that they have been to, their common interests (music, sports) and things happening in their everyday life (losing a tooth, a van on fire near the school). Additionally, the conversations seemed to be much more natural in this phase. Instead of reciting a list of questions or answers, the messages were more conversational. For example, during one VideoPal conversation, two children discussed their favorite songs, while in another two children discussed birthdays and a tooth that one of them lost recently (which she showed in the video).

Jackie (11''): Hi, Achilles. My friend told me that you are a huge Lady Gaga fan. So am I. I just want to say hi. I also like Lady Gaga. Bye.

Achilles (12''): So you like Lady Gaga. Who is your favorite song? Alejandro?

Jackie (13''): Hi Achilles, my favorite singer is Lady Gaga. It is Alejandro, Paparazzi and Bad Romance. What's yours? Bye.

Aalisha (11''): hello, tomorrow I will have my birthday party. My present for my birthday is this shirt. When is your birthday? Bye

Jane (14''): Hi Aalisha. My birthday is Feb14th, Valentine's Day. But my birthday party will be on Feb.13th. And I lost my tooth today.

Aalisha (7''): So! really! I lost the same tooth this day. Bye.

The children also used email to talk about similar topics, like presents they got for Christmas, their favorite books or favorite songs.

Aalisha: Happy new year!!!! How did you spend your Christmas Holidays?? What present did you get?? My present was a karaoke set. What about you??? AALISHA

Rose: Oh my goodness!!!!!!!!!! That's so funny because I wanted a karaoke set for Christmas and I didn't get one but you got one! Ha ha ha! I got nail polish, a wii game, and some candy. I spend my Christmas with my family at home. Happy New Year to you too! Rose

Discussion & Conclusion

This cross-cultural VideoPal project has been very successful. Most importantly, the children from WA and Corfu developed friendships and have loved using VideoPal (none of the children want the experience to end). The project offered children an authentic experience to talk to children from the other side of the world and learn about each other's cultures and lifestyles. Given our global economy, this kind of cross culture dialog can be very beneficial for children.

In terms of research goals, the results from this study have highlighted the potential of video to support rich conversations for children, compared to email. The children generally preferred VideoPal to email because they felt that it was more fun to use and they liked being able to see each other. The children also felt that the use of video was more personal, that it enabled them get to know each other better, and made them feel like their pen pals were closer to them. The use of video also enabled the children to communicate in a natural way, utilizing natural language, body language and facial expressions. These results are consistent with media richness and social presence theories and demonstrate that these benefits can be realized using asynchronous video messaging with children.

Besides the richness of video, we also believe that the asynchronous nature of VideoPal was critical to its success. For cross-cultural pen pal activities where the children are located many time-zones apart, synchronous communication is not possible. Additionally, even if the children are in the same time zone, synchronous interactions require that both parties be available at the same time. Given the busy schedules in most schools, trying to coordinate exact meeting times would be problematic. Finally, current networking infrastructure in most schools would inhibit real-time video communication, especially with many children trying to interact simultaneously. Our use of asynchronous video enabled messages to be delivered off-line, and therefore the children's exchanges were not impacted by network latency.

One key design goal for the VideoPal system was that it should be easy for the children to send and receive videos, and follow a conversation comprised of several messages. The children in our study found VideoPal easy to use, and even easier to use than email. This, combined with the fact that children often find it easy and natural to talk and express themselves using video, led to more frequent use of video and higher information density in the videos compare to email.

Although this study uncovered many benefits of video, the children also enjoyed using email and we observed several benefits of email. For example, email can help overcome accent issues, audio problems, or feelings of self-consciousness. It was also felt that email could make it easier to manage the exchange of facts in a more relaxed way.

The VideoPal project has been an invaluable learning experience for the children. Although the VideoPal system was designed as a generic video messaging system and has not been adapted to the particular needs of schools and learning, the teachers have reported that the students who are participating have increased both their technical and personal skills. In particular, the Corfu teachers have reported that the students have improved their English and computer skills, as well as gained increased self-confidence in talking with others. Since learning is a social process, besides the immediate social context, students are benefited by socializing with remote students from the same or different cultures where they can discuss common topics of shared interest. A potential area for future work is to examine the use of VideoPal for a particular course or learning activity, such as a common school project that takes place over distance.

Some of the limitations with this study included the fact that we had an imbalanced number of children from WA and Corfu. As a result, the children from WA usually received emails and videos that had been sent to a group, and may have felt less personal. Additionally, the sending and receiving of messages was done as a structured activity once a week. It would be interesting to see how the communication would differ, as well as the resulting relationships, if the children could correspond more frequently, whenever they desired.

The results of this work clearly demonstrate the power of asynchronous-video to connect children in cross-cultural exchanges; however, there are many other interesting research questions in this space that have yet to be explored. For example, what happens when the children get to know each other better, would this reduce the need for video and increase their use of email? What if the children do not speak a common language, are there ways they can utilize video and machine translation to communicate despite not being able to understand each other's language? Also, can VideoPal be used to structure peer learning over distance? These questions remain fodder for future work in this area.

References

Ames, M. Go, J. Kaye, J. and Spasojevic M. (2010): 'Making love in the network closet: the benefits and work of family videochat', *CSCW 2010*, pp. 145 -154.

Ballagas, R., Kaye, J., Ames M., Go, J., and Raffle H. (2009): 'Family communication: phone conversations with children', *Interaction Design for Children 2009*, pp. 321-324.

Barksdale, M.A., Watson, C., Park, E.S. (2007): 'Pen pal letter exchanges: taking first steps toward developing cultural understandings', *The Reading Teacher*, 61(1), 2007, pp.58-68.

Bly, S.A., Harrison, S.R., and Irwin, S. (1993): 'Media spaces: bring people together in a video, audio, and computing environment', *Commun. of the ACM*, 36(1), 1993, pp.28-46.

Bragg, R.R. and McWilliams. ((1989): 'Cultural exchange: a video pen pal program', *Journal of Geography*, 88(4), 1989.

Bruner, J.S. (1975): 'The ontogenesis of speech acts', *Journal of Children Language*, vol.2, 1975, pp. 1-40.

Cao, X., Sellen, A., Brush, A.J., Kirk, D. Edge, D., and Ding, X. (2010): 'Understanding family communication across time zones', *CSCW 2010*, pp. 155-158.

Charron, N.N. (2007): "I learned that that's a state called Victoria and he has six blue-tongued lizards!" *The Reading Teacher*, 60(8), 2007, pp. 762-769.

Daft, R., Lengel, R. (1984): 'Information richness: A New Approach to Managerial Behavior and Organization Design', In B.M. Staw & L.L. Cummings (Eds.): *Research in organizational behavior*, JAI Press, Greenwich, CT, pp. 191-233

Ekman, P. & Friesen, W. (1968): 'Nonverbal behavior in psychotherapy research', *Research in psychotherapy: proceeding of the third conference*, vol. 3, 1968, pp. 179-183.

Ekman, P. (1999): Emotional and Conversational Nonverbal Signals. In L.Messing & R. Campbell (eds.): *Gesture, Speech and Sign*, London: Oxford University Press, pp. 45-55.

Hare, S.C. (1999): 'Using E-mail to promote to promote cross-cultural understanding of families', *Teaching sociology*, 27(1), 1999, 67-73.

Hayes-Roth, B. and Gent, R.V. (1997): 'Story-making with improvisational puppets', *Conf. on Autonomous Agents*, 1997, pp. 1-7.

Isaacs, E.A. and Tang, J.C. (1994). What video can and cannot do for collaboration: a case study. *Multimedia Systems 2*(2), 1994, 63-73.

Keil, M., Johnson, R. (2002): 'Feedback channels: using social presence theory to compare voice mail to e-mail'. *Journal of Information Systems Education*, 13(4), 2002, pp.295- 302.

Kern, R. 'Computer-mediated communication: using e-mail exchanges to explore personal histories in two cultures', in M. Warschauer (eds.): *Telecollaboration in foreign language learning*, University of Hawaii Press, 1996, pp. 106-120.

Kirk, D., Sellen, A. and Cao.X. (2010): 'Home video communication: mediating 'closeness'', *CSCW 2010*, pp.135-144.

Krauss, R. M., & Glucksberg, S. (1969) 'Some characteristics of children's messages', *The meeting of the Society for Research in Child Development*, Santa Monica, Calif., March 1969.

Lemkuhl, M. (2002): 'Pen pal letter: the cross-curricular experience', *The Reading Teacher*, 55(8), 2002, pp.720-722.

Littlejohn, S. (2002): *Theories of Human Communication*, Wadsworth (2002)

Mehrabian, A. (1972): *Nonverbal communication*, Aldine-Atherton, Chicago, Illinois.

Modlitba, P., Schmandt, C. Globetoddler. (2008): 'Designing for Remote Interaction between Preschoolers and Their Traveling Parents', *CHI 2008 Extend Abstracts*, pp. 3057-3062.

Mundy P., Kasari C., Sigman M. and Ruskin E. (1995): 'Nonverbal communication and early language acquisition in children with down syndrome and in normally developing children', *Journal of Speech and Hearing Research*, vol.38, February 1995, pp. 157-167.

Piaget, J. (1926): *The language and thought of the child*, Harcourt, Brace & Company, Inc., NY.

Short, J., Williams, E., & Christie, B. (1976): *The social psychology of telecommunications*, John Wiley, London, England.

Shulman, S., Seiffge-Krenke, I. & Dimitrovsky, L. (1994) 'The functions of Pen pals for adolescents', *The Journal of Psychology*, 128(1), pp. 89-100.

Soh, B., Soon, Y. (1991): 'English by e-mail: creating a global classroom via the medium of computer technology', *ELT Journal*, 45(4), 1991, pp. 287-292.

Vygotsky, L.S. (1978): 'Mind in Society: The development of higher psychological processes', (M.Cole, V. John-Steiner, S. Scribner & E. Souberman, Eds. & Trans.) Cambridge, MA: Harvard University Press.

Yarosh, S., Inkpen, K.M, & Brush A.J. 'Video playdate: toward free play across distance', *CHI 2010*, pp. 1251-1260.

Zuckerman, O., Maes, P. (2005): 'Awareness system for children in distributed families', Paper presented at *Interaction Design for Children 2005*.

Mixed-Initiative Friend-List Creation

Kelli Bacon and Prasun Dewan

The Boeing Company and The University of North Carolina at Chapel Hill

gu.kitkat@gmail.com and dewan@cs.unc.edu

Abstract. Friend lists group contacts in a social networking site that are to be treated equally in some respect. We have developed a new approach for recommending friend lists, which can then be manually edited and merged by the user to create the final lists. Our approach finds both large networks of friends and smaller friend groups within this network by merging virtual friend cliques. We have identified new metrics for evaluating the user-effort required to process friend-list recommendations, and conducted user studies to evaluate our approach and determine if and how the recommended lists would be used. Our results show that (a) our approach identifies a large fraction of the friend lists of a user, and seeds these lists with hundreds of members, few of which are spurious, and (b) users say they would use the lists for access control, messaging, filling in friend details, and understanding the social structures to which they belong.

Introduction

A variety of collaborative systems group users who are to be treated equally in some respect. Perhaps the earliest reason for grouping users was to define access lists – groups of users who have the same access rights to some set of objects. These are supported by traditional file systems, and the more recent wide-area repositories (e.g. SharePoint) and collaborative editing systems (e.g. Google Docs). A complementary reason is to define message lists – groups of users who are to be sent the same set of messages – which are supported by mail and SMS systems. In some sense, they are also access lists, as they determine the recipients who are able to read the message. It is not surprising, then, that the popular social networking site, Facebook, combines these two uses, allowing first a grouping of all users into friends and non-friends, and then, a division of friends into smaller lists.

Allowing a coarse division of friends is one of the (many) reasons for the growth of Facebook. It was originally only open to students at select universities. As it added features to its interface and its users' world grew, it introduced the limited profile list. This list provided its users the opportunity to restrict parts of their profiles to people to whom it would be socially unacceptable to deny a "friend request" but with whom users did not want to share everything. Today, Facebook users can create and manage multiple personally-named finer-grained lists, called friend lists, which provide a variety of forms of access control, and in addition, support group messaging. The designers of Facebook now consider them so fundamental that when users add new friends, they are prompted to add them to one or more friend lists. Moreover, it has expanded the role of (personally-named) friend lists to recently include posting of status updates to such lists. The importance of these lists is underscored by the numerous reports of employees being fired over their updates and posts.

Despite their potential uses, a study shows that relatively few number of Facebook users understand and use the notion of friend lists (Skeels and Grudin, 2009). Moreover, this study and our own work show that it takes time and effort to organize friend lists, which many users are not willing to put forth. This is consistent with the high effort of creating access control lists in general (Dewan, Horvitz, Grudin, 2007). These two problems seem related: If users have not seen concrete friend lists, then it is likely they do not understand or appreciate them.

Therefore, it is attractive to automate this process by supporting mixed-initiative access control, which allows agents and humans to cooperate in enforcing access control (Dewan, Horvitz, Grudin, 2007). Here we propose the idea of using such cooperation for friend-list creation.

Any research effort along these lines is bound to be iterative. Like other difficult predictions made by mining data, friend-list recommendations can be expected to have room for improvement for a long time. We have performed an initial iteration of such an effort in a 5-page workshop paper (Bacon and Dewan, 2009). Here we describe a subsequent, larger iteration, which presents substantial additions to the algorithms, metrics, and evaluations given in the previous paper.

As we will see in detail below, there are several other approaches to (semi) automatically cluster friends, but all except one of them – implemented in Facebook - have not been targeted at the domain of friend grouping. This does not, of course, mean they would not be suitable for this domain. However, it does make it almost impossible for us to find an optimal approach for this domain. As the inventors of these schemes, or others, have not evaluated how well these schemes work for friend grouping, it means we must do so, which, in turn, implies implementing and performing (user) studies of each of these schemes. As there are scores of such schemes, this effort is far beyond the scope of a conference paper.

Fortunately there are three ways to make partial progress towards the goal of an optimal solution: Identify a scheme that is better than (1) manual composition of friend lists, or (2) the previous best scheme used for grouping friends, which in our domain is the Facebook approach. (3) Identify a set of requirements that distinguishes the domain of friend lists from other domains, and rule out some of the alternatives based on a low-cost evaluation based on these requirements.

Our work uses a combination of these three approaches. In our workshop paper, we used (2) by comparing two new mechanisms with the Facebook approach. The subjects of this study rated the goodness of the lists found by our mechanisms far higher than those found by Facebook. In this paper, we present an extension of these mechanisms, which, by transitivity, can also be expected to be better than the Facebook approach. In addition, we use both (1) and (3). While our implementation, examples, and evaluation are all targeted at Facebook, our approach can be applied to any social networking site that allows an external tool to determine the friends of a user, and the friends of these friends.

Our work assumes that creation of a friend list is an independent task, which is consistent with the approach used in Facebook of prompting a user to add a new friend to one or more friend lists. It can be argued that friend-list creation is a portion of a more primary task, such as sending a party invitation or protecting the receipt and sending of a status update. Friend lists are expected to be used repeatedly in multiple tasks – otherwise it is not cost effective to create them. Thus, their creation can be considered a first-class independent task.

Requirements

Our overall goal, of course, is to develop a mixed-initiative user-interface that reduces the user-effort required to create friend lists. This goal can be decomposed into a smaller number of sub-goals or requirements.

Compatibility with non mixed-initiative user interface: As mentioned above, other research (Skeels and Grudin, 2009) and our own studies show that few users take the trouble to create friend lists. A mixed-initiative user-interface reduces this effort, but adds the overhead of learning a new user interface. Therefore, it should reuse concepts from its non mixed-initiative counterpart.

High coverage and accuracy: The amount of user effort is a function of (a) coverage: how may friend lists are missed by the recommender, and (b) accuracy: how close the recommended lists are to corresponding actual friend lists. Therefore, ideally the mixed-initiative user interface should use a recommender algorithm that provides both high coverage and accuracy. The coverage requirement can be further decomposed into the following sub-requirements.

Small and large groups: Our studies show that the size of friend lists can vary. For instance, currently, the second author's family friend list consists of less than ten members, while his CSCW friend list consists of more than fifty members. Both small and large friend lists are important. For instance, one may wish to give family members (CSCW researchers) access to pictures taken at a Thanksgiving dinner (CSCW conference banquet). Therefore, another requirement is to find friend-lists of varying size.

Overlapping groups: Our previous work also shows that friend lists overlap – for example, there is a high overlap between the second author's CSCW and Microsoft friends, and the high school and college friends of many of our subjects. Thus, another requirement is support for overlapping groups.

Hierarchical groups and preference to leaf-level nodes: We also found that several friend lists are hierarchical. For instance, our subjects' dormitory friends were subsets of their college friends. Thus, it is useful to identify a tree of friend lists.

Preference to leaf-level nodes: Because the number of nodes grows exponentially as we go down a tree, if there is a choice between identifying leaf-level and internal nodes of the friend-list tree, preference should be given to the former. The reason is that merging two friend lists into a higher-level node has $O(1)$ cost, while splitting a friend list of size N into sub-lists has $O(N)$ cost.

Survey and Analysis of Previous Work

Friend list recommendation is a special case of the problem of automatically creating subsets of a set, where members of a subset are more "connected" to each other than those of other subsets. There is a rich literature of related work addressing this general problem, which is so large that there is not enough space to reference each published paper on this topic. Therefore we present it as a new design space, and evaluate points in this space with respect to our requirements. This design space and analysis is, thus, a contribution in its own right.

Explicit Tags vs. Implicit Relationships

Recognizing the problems of creating manual friend lists, Facebook started automatically creating friend lists for their users based on friend details explicitly entered by users when they formed friendships. Friends sharing some friend detail were put in an automatically created friend list named by the common friend detail. We refer to this approach as tag-centric recommendation as it uses keywords entered by users to derive semantics. The tag centric approach of Facebook works in several situations. For example, the automated family list generated for the second author included several of his family members. On the other hand, it has two major problems. First, multiple tags can imply the same semantics, and vice versa. The first author experienced this problem when Facebook automatically created three friend lists (GSBA, GSBA-Senate, and Senate) for the same student-government group because different friend details conveyed the same relationship. Second, and more important, the tag-centric method works only for those friends for whom friend details have been filled out. Our previous work shows that such information is not available for the vast majority of users.

The work on SOYLENT (Fisher and Dourish, 2004) has suggested that it is possible to overcome the second problem of the Facebook tag-based approach by grouping users based on implicit relationships among them. Specifically, the email conversations of users provide a basis for grouping them (to different degrees) based on how many emails were sent to a group and when these emails were sent. It is possible to extend this approach to a social network by looking at not only asynchronous messages but also other interactions among users in the network, such as Facebook wall postings, synchronous chat messages, and comments on various kinds of postings.

Multiple vs. Single Relationships

However, the SOYLENT approach has the following problem when applied to the specific case of Facebook (the system used in our study): Facebook applications are not supplied this information. Although much of this information about users is "publically" available to other users, Facebook policies prevent the collection of this information by external tools. Thus, at least in the short term, this approach may not be implementable by software that is not deployed by Facebook. It is possible that other social networking sites provide this information; we have not investigated them, focusing instead of on the more challenging problem of living with this constraint.

One piece of information that is available to Facebook applications is the public friendship relationships among the friends of the users running the applications. Our work, therefore, focuses on this relationship.

Network-Centric vs. Ego-Centric Relationships

As we consider friendship relationships among the friends of the user for whom the friend lists are to be recommended, we take a *network-centric* recommendation approach. This is in contrast to the *ego-centric* approach taken in SOYLENT, where the relations between the contacts of the user for whom the groups are identified are not considered. In SOYLENT, if user A sends the same message to users B, C, and D, then B, C, and D are grouped together regardless of whether they send messages to each other. Taking an ego-centric view in our project would result in a single friend list that has all the friends of a user, as we do not have information about the activities of a user.

Network-Centric vs. Ego-Centric Groups

While we do use network-centric relationships, the groups we find are ego-centric, that is, are subsets of the group of friends of the user for whom friend lists are being computed. This goal contrasts our work from that of community-detection systems, which try to find all possible groups, called communities, in the set of all nodes among whom the relationship on which they focus can hold. When the relationship is the friend relationship in a social network, a community detection system would divide the set of all users of the social network to create social communities. While we know of no work that is targeted at finding ego-centric groups from network-centric relationships, there are numerous schemes for finding social communities from these relationships, many of which are surveyed in (Hanneman and Riddle, 2005).

Community-Detection Dimensions

Most of the community detection algorithms such as (Clauset, Newman et al., 2004) (Girvan and Newman, 2002) find non-overlapping groups, though a few explicitly target overlapping communities (Li, Tan et al., 2005; Palla, Der'enyi et al., 2005). Some of these work top-down, starting from the complete network, and dividing it into smaller groups; while other work bottom-up, greedily merging smaller sets into larger ones. By keeping track of the divide/merged nodes, these algorithms can find hierarchical nodes(Li, Tan et al., 2005).

These algorithms do not focus on a single application such as friend lists in our project, but instead, attempt to discover fundamental algorithms and constants for finding a variety of communities. Example communities include groupings of (a) proteins based on known interactions between them (Li, Tan et al., 2005; Palla, Der'enyi et al., 2005; Wakita and Tsurumi, 2007) (b) authors based on co-author relationships among them (Palla, Der'enyi et al., 2005), (c) words based on whether they are (frequently) associated with each other (Palla, Der'enyi et al., 2005), and (d) products based on whether they are (frequently) bought together (Clauset, Newman et al., 2004).

If these algorithms are indeed fundamental, they may be able to find friend lists. Hogan (2010) used one of these (Wakita and Tsurumi, 2007) to group his friends and create a new scheme for visualizing the groups. As the main goal of his work was the visualization, he did not evaluate the coverage or accuracy of the lists found. In personal communication with the second author, he reported that small groups were merged into large ones – for example a family is merged into high school because siblings tend to go to the same high school. In addition, the algorithm he used did not support hierarchical or overlapping groups.

Low-Cost Evaluation of Previous Work

None of previous schemes, including our own previous work, explicitly considers a mixed-initiative user-interface for recommending friend lists, though the simple interface we present below could accommodate any of these approaches. Thus, the inability to meet this requirement is not fundamental.

Several of the well-known community-detection algorithms do not support the more fundamental requirements of overlapping and hierarchical groups. The only algorithm known to us that does so is LCMA (Li, Tan et al., 2005), which was developed for identifying protein groups, and requires its users to specify a threshold value. Like our approach, described below, it repeatedly merges an initial set of sets until no more merges are possible.

We implemented LCMA and used it to merge cliques for eleven users. For all of the experiments reported here, we acquired mutual friendship data using a Facebook application, which each participant had to run. The mutual friendship data allowed us to create a social network. We used the Facebook unique identifiers in order to avoid a situation in which a user had two friends with the same name. This mutual friendship data was transformed into a JGraphT (Naveh) simple undirected graph. We chose an undirected graph because in Facebook, friendships are commutative, and only one connection exists between each pair of users. All of the algorithms presented here were implemented in Eclipse using JDK compiler 1.6. None of them performed merges of sets whose size was less than 3.

For the majority of the participants, all threshold values we tried yielded hundreds and sometimes thousands of friend lists. These were the final sets generated by the algorithm, and thus, formed the second level of the group tree identified by it, with the top level mode being the set of all friends. LCMA supports hierarchical lists by keeping track of the merged sets – the result of a merge is the parent, in the group tree, of the merged sets. Thus, the number of lists at lower levels was even higher. In fact, this tree took so much space that the Java Virtual Machines on our test computers had to be reconfigured to accommodate it. Based on the number of lists generated, it did not seem worthwhile to perform a user study determining the accuracy and coverage of these lists.

It is possible that there are other community-detection algorithms that support hierarchical and non overlapping groups; we did not perform an exhaustive survey because of the effort involved in implementing these approaches, choosing appropriate threshold values, and performing an evaluation.

Consider now schemes not designed to detect communities: the Facebook approach based on tags, the SOYLENT approach based on multiple relationships, and our previous work. They support overlapping but not hierarchical groups. As SOYLENT was not designed or used for friend lists, and cannot be implemented in Facebook, we did not perform user studies to evaluate it. In our previous work, we compared the friend lists generated by the Facebook tag-based approach and our own mechanisms. The participants in this study noted that although the Facebook lists had accurate descriptions (which is to be expected as these are based on friend details explicitly entered), these lists were incomplete to the extent of being useless. In contrast, in the case of our two mechanisms, about 80% and 60%, respectively, of their friends were put in recommended lists, and about 90% and 80%, respectively, of these lists were considered by them to be close to corresponding ideal lists. They also pointed out the need for hierarchical groups and better accuracy. Thus, our previous work is the most promising of those used for recommending friend lists. Below, we focus on how we extended it to remove its limitations.

Approach

User Interface

There are several possible approaches for mixed-initiative composition of friend lists. We propose a two-phase process in which the system recommends a set of friend lists, which the user edits and merges to create actual friend lists, as illustrated in our prototype desktop user-interface shown in Figure 1. In Figure 1(left), the system suggests a set of lists, each of which is given a tentative name based on the members and size of the list. In Figure 1(right), the user edits one of these lists, using a desktop interface that mimics the Facebook web interface for performing this task.

Figure 1.(left) Recommended Lists (right) Facebook-like interface to edit a recommended list

This two-phase process is different in one important aspect from the one Facebook uses to automate friend lists. In Facebook, the computed list is automatically added to a user's set of friend lists. In our approach, a recommended list is not committed until the user edits its name and saves it. This approach corresponds to a friend recommendation in Facebook, which does not take effect until the user accepts it. It is motivated by the fact that (a) unlike Facebook, we do not use details about friends to create lists – we have no information other than friend lists. Thus, it is not possible to give a recommended friend list a usable name, which, in turn, means the list is not usable until the user changes its name and commits to it; (b) some of our subjects in our previous work were annoyed by Facebook automatically creating friend lists for them, and deleted these lists once they noticed them; (c) it is difficult to predict friend lists perfectly, given that users show a high degree of variability in their privacy preferences (Olson, Grudin et al. 2005) and there is a variety of uses of friend lists. Any friend-list prediction is bound to have inaccuracies; thus, users should be involved in a mixed-initiative process before the recommended list is committed.

This interface concretely demonstrates the nature of mixed-initiative friend list composition. It meets our user-interface requirement by making a small change to its existing non mixed-initiative counterpart. Our main innovation, however, is identification and evaluation of a new mechanism for friend-list recommendation.

Virtual vs. Actual Friend Clique

Unlike the community detection algorithms, our project is directly targeted at finding only one kind of groups – friend lists. Thus, we are able to formulate a domain-specific intuition as to why it should be possible to recommend friend lists using friend relationships, and develop an algorithm that directly reflects this intuition.

Our intuition and algorithm are based on the notion of friend cliques. In graph theory, a clique is a set of vertices in a graph that are all connected to each other by edges of the graph. By this definition, every subset of a clique is also a clique. A *maximal clique* is a clique that is not a subset of a larger clique. Graph cliques are *human cliques* when the vertices of a graph represent users. When the nodes of such a graph represent friendship relationships, the human cliques are *friend cliques*. Depending on whether these are actual or virtual friendship relationships, the cliques represent *actual* or *virtual friend cliques*. In the rest of the paper, we assume that an actual friend link exists between two users if they have some degree of friendship between them, that is, if they are acquainted with each other.

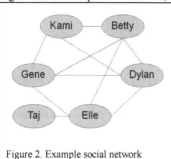

Figure 2. Example social network

Moreover, we will use the term clique to refer to a maximal friend clique.

Deriving actual cliques from virtual cliques requires identification of the missing links. These missing links result in actual cliques being split into multiple virtual cliques, leading to the clique explosion problem. Given the set of virtual cliques, we must combine virtual cliques with a high degree of commonality to approximate a smaller set of actual cliques.

To illustrate this approach, consider the social network in Figure 2, where the edges represent virtual friend relationships. It contains three maximal cliques: (1) Kami, Betty, Dylan, Gene; (2) Betty, Dylan, Gene, Elle; (3) Taj, Elle.

These three cliques are a subset of the virtual cliques of one of our participants - the names have been changed to preserve anonymity. In this example, Kami and Elle do know each other, but are not friends on the social network. Thus, virtual cliques (1) and (2) should be merged with each other. Based on how strong the actual friend relationship is between Kami and Elle, the merged group would either be part of a network or a subgroup within a network.

Hybrid Finder

As mentioned before, algorithms created for other applications also merge sets. However, the reasons for merging are different in our application.

In our work, we assume that some links between nodes are missing because one or more of the users (a) is new to the social network, or (b) requires a virtual friend to be more than an acquaintance. As long as there is a "small" percentage of such friends of a user that is independent of the user, we can write a user-independent algorithm that merges virtual friend cliques to create the missing actual friend links, and hence, the friend lists of the user. Put another way, our reason for merging is that we are trying to derive one kind of link (actual friend) from another kind of link (virtual friend), and how closely one link reflects the other depends on the node (friend). This is not the case in some of the other applications. For example, the "co-author" and "bought-together" links used to cluster authors (Palla, Der'enyi et al.) and purchased items (Clauset, Newman et al.), respectively, have unambiguous, node-independent, semantics, and the data are not assumed to have any noise. The only application that seems close to ours is protein merging, as the link between two proteins reflects known interaction between the proteins, and the clustering algorithm tries to find unknown interactions. However, our experiments with LCMA seem to imply that even this domain is not close enough to ours.

Thus, it made sense to start from first principles and use domain-dependent semantics to (iteratively) create our own algorithm, described by the pseudo-code shown in Figure 3. The algorithm continues to merge cliques until no more merges are possible. After each pass through the top-level loop, the merged smaller cliques are removed from the set of cliques. However, during a pass, as the top-level algorithm shows, an assimilated clique does not disappear – it is compared with other cliques, thereby promoting the creation of overlapping groups. It merges cliques based on two factors that capture the commonality between two cliques: the similarity and dissimilarity between the two sets considered for merging, determined by computing the sizes of the intersection and difference, respectively, between the smaller and larger of the two sets. The algorithm has two parameters, S and D, which reflect the minimum similarity and the maximum dissimilarity the two sets must have if they are to be merged. The similarity and dissimilarity values are normalized by the size of the smaller set. Thus, percentSame, percentDiff, S and D are fractions rather than absolute numbers.

```
cliques <- getAllMaximalCliques()
loop
   merged = false;
   mergedCliques = {};
   for each outerC in cliques
      for each innerC in cliques
         larger, smaller = compareCliques(outerC, innerC);
         if (Merge(larger, smaller))
            mergedCliques += smaller;
            merged = true;
   if (!merged) exit;
   cliques -= mergedCliques;
end

boolean Merge(A, B)
  AIntersectB = A ∩ B
  BMinusA = B - A
  percentSame = |AIntersectB| /|B|
  percentDiff = |BMinusA|/|B|
  if (percentSame ≥ S || percentDiff ≤ D)
     A += BMinusA
     return true;
  return false;
```

Figure 3.Non Hierarchical Recommendation Algorithm

There are several approaches possible for finding hierarchical groups. As mentioned before, one approach, used in LCMA, is to use each merge pass to create the next level in the group tree, which, in the case of LCMA, resulted in a large number of groups at all levels. Even in the case of our algorithm, we could not find appropriate values of S and D to make this approach work on our training data. Therefore, we limited ourselves to two-level friend-list identification, in which we found networks, and sub-groups within these networks. The two-level approach is consistent with the requirement of giving preference to leaf level groups, and is motivated by the fact that manually combining a small number of networks takes few user operations.

Both the network and subgroup finder use the algorithm described above. The difference is in the values of parameters, S and D, and whether cliques that are not merged are recommended as friend lists. In the subgroup finder, the thresholds, S and D, are 1 and 0.15, respectively, and non merged cliques are not recommended, as many of them tend to be spurious. In the network finder, the parameters are 0.9 and 0.35, respectively, and both merged and non merged cliques are recommended, as spurious cliques tend to get merged into larger networks.

Thus, subgroup merge looks only for a maximum dissimilarity, while network merge look for maximum dissimilarity *or* minimum similarity, and uses a larger threshold for maximum dissimilarity. As a result, it is more aggressive in merging sets. To illustrate the difference between the two merges, if A = {Alice, Bob, Carol, David} and B = {Alice, Bob, Carol, Eva}, then BMinusA = {Eva}, AIntersectB = {Alice, Bob, Carol}, precentDiff = 0.25, and percentSame = 0.75. In the case of the subgroup finder, as percentDiff is higher than 0.15, the two sets are not merged. In the case of the network finder, as percentDiff < .35, A and B are merged. This example and our user data show the social groups returned by the subgroup finder are sometimes subgroups within larger social groups returned by the network finder.

It is possible to run the network and subgroup finder independently, as we did in our previous work, but this approach would not explicitly identify subgroups of a network. To support hierarchical groups, we created a hybrid finder that decomposes groups found by the network finder into subgroups using the subgroup finder. We found that not all groups found by the network finder were actually networks, that is, groups that could be further divided. After piloting, we found that networks tended to have at least 50 members. Therefore, the hybrid finder runs the subgroup finder only on groups greater than 50. For each such group, N, returned by the network finder, it computes all the cliques involving members of N, and feeds these cliques to the subgroup finder, whose output is recommended as subgroups within the network. The recommended lists, thus, are the union of the groups returned by the network and subgroup finder.

The hybrid finder has three potential benefits over the independent finders: First, users are able to create both coarse-grained and fine-grained friend lists. Running the two finders independently also gives them both networks and subgroups, but in this case, they have to remove duplicate groups, because, as mentioned above, network merge does find groups that cannot be divided further. Second, as mentioned above, it explicitly identifies subgroups of a network. Third, it increases the quality of the subgroups. Given the goal of finding subgroups in a network N, it is better to ask subgroup merge to consider nodes only in N, rather than all friends, as otherwise, it is possible and even likely (given that it is heuristic-based), that it would add nodes to these subgroups that are not in N. A potential disadvantage of hybrid merge is that, unlike all of the other group-finding algorithms, it involves finding (maximal) cliques twice, once to find networks, and once to find subgroups. There are at least two ways to find all cliques involving members of a network N: (a) Compute all the cliques in N. (b) Select from all cliques computed for network merge those that involve only members of N. Both re-computing cliques and searching in a large clique space are computationally expensive operations. We chose the first approach as it was easier to implement - we could just reuse existing code for finding cliques.

Our hybrid finder is similar to several other group-finding mechanisms. In particular, like LCMA, it continues to make merge passes until no more merges are possible, like K-plexes and K-Cores (Hanneman and Riddle, 2005), it uses the abstract notions of maximum dissimilarity and minimum similarity, respectively, to unite cliques, and (c) like (Palla, Der'enyi et al., 2005), it identifies thresholds based on experimentation. However none of the previous works have any of the following features of our scheme: (a) use of both minimum similarity and maximum dissimilarity thresholds in a single algorithm, which is important for finding networks, (b) computation of percentages rather than absolute numbers for similarity and dissimilarity, which is important for identifying friend lists of varying size, (c) not keeping track of links between members of the two merged sets, because each member of the union is considered to have actual or missing links to each of the other members of the set, (d) use of similarity/dissimilarity thresholds without bounding the number of merge passes, which is important for avoiding the friend-list explosion problem, and (e) identification of thresholds specific to friend lists.

Comparison with Manual Composition

In general, a group finding scheme can be evaluated for both performance and correctness. Because of space limitations, we do not present performance results, focusing only on correctness, which is inversely related to the user-effort required in a mixed-initiative process for creating friend lists. We performed a user study involving 21 students from our university, consisting of twelve males and nine females, ten undergraduates and eleven graduates. Some of the subjects in the earlier study reported in the workshop paper were also participants in this study – so we were able to get subjective comments comparing the flat independent schemes used in the previous study and the hierarchical hybrid one used here.

Interestingly, none of the previous works on automatic group detection have identified quantitative correctness metrics. In fact, all of the domain-independent papers use only one data point in each domain (for instance, one co-author/word/protein network (Palla, Der'enyi et al., 2005)) and show a visualization of the data point to demonstrate the goodness of the scheme. Our previous work used multiple data points, and explicitly defined quantitative metrics, but it was coarse-grained as it asked users to divide lists into good and bad, without giving any measure of the degree of goodness. Therefore, for this project, we defined new, finer-grained metrics, which computed the difference between the set of lists recommended by them and the set of "ideal friend lists." The quotes indicate that there is some subjectivity involved in identifying such lists, as friends can be grouped in several ways. Therefore, we used the following process to identify such lists, which essentially asked users to morph the recommended lists into ideal lists.

We asked each participant to give each recommended list a name that describes the social group (e.g. Family, Research Group, High School, Grad School, Internship) to which several members of the list belong. If a list represented multiple social groups (e.g. High School and Science Geeks), we asked them choose the one that contained the largest number of members. We asked them to give the same name to multiple lists representing the same social group (e.g. High School) to help us identify lists that should be merged. The names could be coded for privacy purposes.

Each of the named lists was expected to contain certain members who belong to a different list. Against each of these members, we asked the participant to put the name of a different friend list or the word "other". For instance, if our system put Alice in a list a participant had labeled as High School Science Club, and she really belongs to a list named High School Soccer, we asked the participant to put High School Soccer next to Alice's name in the High School Science Club List.

Thus, at the end of this process, users would have both redistributed members among the recommended lists and created new lists. These morphed recommended lists and the new lists, together, formed the set of ideal lists. As it was likely that users would not take the effort to create new lists, we also asked them names of missing lists without asking them to fill them.

There are several ways to measure the cost of morphing recommended lists, and it depends on the exact user interface for performing this task. We discuss below some metrics useful for comparing this cost with the cost of manual composition of friend lists.

We associate each recommended list, R, with a goodness degree, computed by the following algorithm:

```
float goodness (R)
   degree = 0;
   for each ideal list, I
      degree = max (degree, |R ∩ I| / |R|)
   return degree
```

Figure 3.Goodness Algorithm

This algorithm assumes that the user goes through each recommended list and morphs it into the "closest" ideal list, where the closest ideal list is the one that has the highest number of elements of R. It determines the number of common elements in the recommended and (closest) ideal list, and normalizes this number by the size of the recommended list. The higher this fraction, the fewer the spurious members in the recommendation. It does not measure the cost of adding missing elements in R to create the closest ideal list. A problem with considering both insertions and deletions is that they have unequal costs, and insertions have variable costs – a user might type the name of the missing friend or browse the database to find the friend. Thus, it is not clear how these costs should be integrated into one per-list metric, and we don't have space to consider multiple per-list metrics in any depth. In addition, insertion costs are not necessary to compare our approach with manual composition of lists, and comparison with an ideal recommender is beyond the scope of our evaluation. Moreover, friend lists and other user groups, even those generated manually, can be expected to be incomplete as users might not remember or take the effort to add missing elements. Furthermore, in many uses of friend lists, the cost of missing a valid member (e.g. a happy hour buddy) can be expected to be much lower than the cost of including an invalid member (e.g. parent or (prospective) employer). Thus, incomplete lists can be useful (e.g. post a status update for happy hour buddies, identify a social group), as long as they do not have spurious members. The goodness metric we report measures the cost of removing these members. The subjective comments we report below give an idea of the overall quality of the lists, which goes beyond this one metric.

Only 10 of the 21 participants turned in the morphed lists. This could be attributed to their (a) not finding time to participate in the time-consuming task of identifying the ideal lists , or (b) feeling the recommended lists were so bad that they were unsalvageable. As we mention later, all 21 participants answered the subjective questions on the quality of the lists, and almost all of them were effusive. Thus the likely reason is (a). In Table 1, we give the results from the 10 participants who morphed the lists. For each participant, we indicate the id, goodness degrees of the recommended lists, average goodness degree of each list, the number of recommended, missing, and ideal lists, the number of merges required, and the sum of the sizes of the recommended lists, given in parenthesis next to the number of these lists. The sizes of the lists varied tremendously; for example, for participant 25, they were 22, 7, 4, 4, 7, 21, 4, 5, 24, 150, 37, 354, 3, 3, 4, 3, 3, 4, 4 (networks), and 10, 8, 9, 10, 9, 12, 21, 135, 18, 207 (subgroups).

As the number of lists was both large and variable, and we have limited space, we present the goodness degrees of lists of a participant using the cryptic syntax:

degree1(# of lists of degree 1), degree2 (# of lists of degree 2), ...

Omitting the number of lists implies 1 list. Thus the text

1(17), 0.8, 0(2)

indicates 17 lists with (goodness) degree of 1, one list of degree 0.8, and two lists of degree 0. We report the goodness degrees of the lists returned by the subgroup and network finder separately.

The number of missing lists was the sum of the number of new lists created and named by the participants. The number of merges was computed by looking at the names of the ideal lists – if two ideal lists had the same name, they had to be merged. The number of ideal lists was computed by subtracting the number of merged lists from the sum of the number of recommended and missing lists.

What is truly remarkable about these results is that the vast majority of lists had goodness degree of 1, that is, had no spurious members. Moreover, for all but one of the 10 participants, the number of missing/merged lists was less than 20% of the number of ideal lists, and for half of them, there were no missing or merged lists. Our scheme essentially found needles in haystacks consisting of thousands of cliques with information only about friendship relationships. It is a significant improvement over manual composition of friend lists, as it (a) helps users determine a large fraction of the social groups to which they belong, and (b) seeds corresponding friend lists with hundreds of members, few of which are spurious. To help interpret these data, we gave the participants a questionnaire that required them to comment on various aspects of the lists. It was filled by all of the 21 participants. Thus, the comments provide a much broader evaluation in comparison to the quantitative data. They are in italics, as many of them contain quotation characters. To ensure anonymity of the subjects and their friends, we have replaced some specific names (e.g. UNC) with their abstract descriptions (e.g. <univ>) in angle brackets. The comments indicate that almost all of the respondents were impressed by the results. One of our questions was:

Did our system help you identify social groups that you did not expect to see amongst your friends? If so, which groups surprised you? Why?

Table 1. Goodness Degrees

Id	Goodness Degree			Rec (Tot Size)	Miss	Merg	Ideal
	Network	Subgroup	Av.				
11	1(5), 0.7	1(3)	.97	9(185)	2		11
12	1(3), 0	1(5), 0.8	.88	10(260)			10
13	1(4), 0.9, 0.8, 0.6, 0	1(7), 0.6(2)	.86	17(324)	5	11	11
14	1(3), 0.6	1(2)	.93	6(248)			6
17	1(14), 0.9(2), 0.7, 0.6,	1	.91	20(430)			20
18	1(4)	1(8)	1	13(592)	3		16
19	1(3)	1(2), 0.8,	.89	7(544)			7
20	1(11)	1(7), 0.9	.99	19(799)			19
22	1(5), .9(2), 0(2)	1, 0	.71	11(591)	1		12
25	1(17), 0.8, 0(2)	1(9), 0.9	.92	30(1097)	1	3	28

We really wanted to know if they learned something about their friend set that they did know already. However, many of them answered by commenting on how surprisingly well the algorithms worked. We give below some of the answers that expressed surprise, identified by participant id: (1) *I was surprised that <person> was in the <univ> group. I know her from <previous school>, but she came to <univ> for undergrad, so she knew <univ> people too.* (8) *club football for each year. Was nice to see them split.* (9) *I was surprised that it was able to pick up on a lot of the informal groups that I have.* (10) *found my suitemates from freshman year. I forgot we were friends on facebook .* (16) *The <univ> + <high school> group surprised me. I tried to figure out which name to give it, like the instructions said, but due to a lot of overlap, significantly more than half of the list would be in each of the lists for <univ> and <high school>. I didn't expect so many of my high school (<high school>) friends to have a lot of the same (non-<high school>) <univ> friends, since <univ> is such a large school. It should probably be less surprising, though, because a large percentage of <high school> students end up going to <univ>* (21) *I was surprised to see a group* *based solely on fraternity members* (22) *The NATO groups were surprising. I'm impressed by some of the family groups too.*

In response to a question that asked them to express general comments and concerns, we got similarly positive remarks: (9) *This thing was really cool!* (10) *incredible work, borders on scary good.* (11) *very good job, efficient and accurate.* (12) *This is really cool! I was surprised by how well it grouped my friends. There weren't any people it put in an incorrect list, although some lists were very broad.* (15) *I find this version of your application very improved with respect to its last version. It captured everything it had to capture, all the substructures of the graph of my friends, including overlapping between these substructures (communities).* This remark, of course, was made by a person who also participated in the earlier study. (16) *This seems like a very useful tool. I'm considering making some of these suggested friend lists manually.* (20) *The lists are not quite what I expected but overall it worked really well. The s groups broke down some of the larger groups a bit better.* The lists were identified to the participants using numbers, and the suffix 's' was put against a number to indicate it was a subgroup of a larger list.

This is not to say that the results were always good and unanimously liked. As we see in Table 1, there are some lists with low degree of goodness, including a few with degree 0. Some of the comments pointed out this problem. (19) *I think if I was making lists, I would not have made clique 3s. It just seems like a random subset of the people I know around here.* (9) *There were a lot of groupings that were just a compilation of friends I had from <univ> that didn't really fit together in any specific social circle.*

One person (14) said they would not use these lists: *I would not use any of the groups except maybe the Macc alumni grouping (if it in fact included all members). The groupings are too large for my preferences or uses. I would probably like to form my own groupings of those that can see my information and those that cannot.*

Another issue, shown in Table 1, is the need to merge some of the lists. One person (who did not morph the lists) explicitly commented on this problem. (24) *Some of the groups seemed too narrow and could have been merged into one group instead of many (ex: There are few CGS groups, with no real connection other than CGS).* As mentioned before, we believe merging is a minor problem as each merge should ideally require a single user command, and few merges were needed.

The last issue had to do with missing lists. As Table 1 shows only a few reported missing lists, which means the list coverage was good. The following answers to a question asking them if there were any missing lists indicate the kind of lists we missed: (1) *I don't know... 'People I know from [city] through [person]'?* (9) *There were lots of sub-cliques from high school that weren't captured, largely because I didn't become 'facebook friends' with those people until after I graduated.* (11) *Friends from my high school in <city> (actually, it is a subgroup of clique 1 <city> Friends)...others are 'Friends of friends of friends* (16) *I had one 'other' that was not in another list. He is my sister's boyfriend. I could create a list for my sister's friends and* *include him in it, but I probably wouldn't use it for anything. Maybe I could make an 'Acquaintances' list that includes people like him that I don't know very well. That would be useful for privacy settings. (18) Yes. The group of Chinese friends I have from <city>, and my old soccer team, which wasn't associated with any high school, and overlaps a lot with the previous group. Also the group of everyone over 40, who are parents and parents of friends who are connected through facebook. (25) missed group: Friday Happy Hour.*

The remark by (6), (11), and (18) shows some fundamental limitations of the clique-merging approach – it groups people based on the existence rather than non existence of relationships among them, or other attributes. Hence it did not automatically create acquaintance, friends of friends of friends, and "people over 40" groups. It may be useful to put everyone not on any recommended list in an others group.

Potential Friend-List Uses

The discussion above gives a good idea of the extent to which we captured the social groups of a user. To determine some of the specific uses to which these groups could be put, one of our questions asked them to indicate whether they would use one or more of the ideal lists they created (by morphing the recommended lists) for some specific choices given to them. In addition, we asked them to indicate other purposes, not in the set of predefined choices. All 21 subjects answered this question. For each of the specific choices, we give, in parentheses, the number of users and the fraction of the total number of subjects who would take each choice. For the "others" choice, we indicate some of the uses suggested by the subject.

1. Gain an understanding of the social structures to which I belong. **(9, 0.42)**
2. Use name of the friend list as publically-available friend details (assuming, of course, that a friend detail about a friend is published only if the friend agrees to the detail being publically available). **(9, 0.42)**
3. Publish status updates to the list. **(15, 0.71)**
4. Publish videos to the list. **(12, 0.71)**
5. Publish pictures to the list. **(20, 0.95)**
6. Publish links to the list. **(17, 0.81)**
7. Publish application-related posts to the list **(9, 0.42)**
8. Send messages to the list. **(20, 0.95)**
9. Look at newsfeed for the list. **(19, 0.9)**
10. Use the list as an organization of Facebook "Chat" **(11, 0.52)**
11. Block the list on Facebook "Chat" (members of that list cannot see that you are online) **(12, 0.57)**
12. Use the list in some other privacy settings to give or exclude access to its members. **(17, 0.80)**

13. Other: **(generate events for specific lists, hide wall posts posted from one friend list member from members of another friend list, address book)**

Use 2 is the dual of the approach taken in Facebook, which creates friend list from friend details. Here we are suggesting that friend details be created from (automatically or manually) created friend lists. This approach can violate the privacy of the users and their friends. Interestingly, about half the number of respondents thought they would use this (unimplemented by Facebook) application of friend lists. As we see above, the other applications received at least this much support, with ability to send status updates to, post videos to, and look at the newsfeed from a friend list receiving almost unanimous support.

Conclusions and Future Work

The main contribution of our work, as highlighted by its title, is motivation for a new line of research addressing mixed-initiative composition of a special form access-control lists: friend lists. The novel aspects of our work include: (a) a set of requirements in this domain, (b) identification and analysis of a design space of schemes for meeting various subsets of these requirements, (c) metrics for quantitatively evaluating the user-effort required in these schemes, (d) an approach for identifying ideal lists from recommended lists, (e) a domain-specific recommendation mechanism and its evaluation, and (f) identification of the potential uses of friend lists. Our evaluation results show that the lists recommended by our approach have few false positives, the number of missed/merged lists is small, commands for manually-merging recommended lists would be useful, and users say they would use the morphed recommendations for a variety of purposes.

As this is the first full-length paper on this line of research, we have had to, out of necessity, broadly, rather than in-depth, address aspects of such research, ignoring several issues raised by it. Further work is needed to (a) develop a user-interface for conveniently merging and splitting friend lists, (b) using a broader and larger list of subjects to get more representative results, (c) incorporating insertion costs in the metrics, (d) using email communication in clustering by mapping social network identifiers to email addresses, when possible, (e) develop collaborative filtering algorithms wherein the friend lists of a user are merged with those of members of these lists, (f) allow users to seed initial friend lists, and recommend additional users based on the seeds, possibly using one algorithm such as ours to identify and seed the lists and another to expand these lists, (g) use more sophisticated schemes such as (Chang, Boyd-Graber et al., 2009) for reducing human errors in identifying correct lists, (h) recommend general access lists and rights in traditional repositories such as file systems, and (i) identify the ways in which users actually use friend lists as opposed to how they say they will use them. Facebook has recently started supporting (f) and it would be useful to do studies of their (unpublished) algorithm and others that are developed.

Our work has provided motivation for and basis for further and larger industrial and research efforts to pursue these and other future directions.

Acknowledgments

This research was funded in part by NSF grant IIS-0810861.

References

Bacon, K and Dewan, P. (2009). Towards Automatic Recommendation of Friend Lists. TrustCol Workshop, IEEE.

Chang, J., J. Boyd-Graber, et al. (2009). Reading Tea Leaves: How Humans Interpret Topic Models. Proc. NIPS.

Clauset, A., M. E. J. Newman, et al. (2004). "Finding community structure in very large networks." Physical Review E. **70**(066111).

Dewan, P., E. Horvitz, J. Grudin. (2007). A "Thought Experiment" to Illustrate and Motivate Mixed-Initiative Access Control,. TustCol Workshop, IEEE.

Fisher, D. and P. Dourish (2004). Social and Temporal Structures in Everyday Collaboration. Proc. CHI.

Girvan, M. and M. E. Newman (2002). "Community structure in social and biological networks." Proc. Natl. Acad. Sci.(99).

Hanneman, R. A. and M. Riddle (2005). Introduction to social network methods, http://faculty.ucr.edu/~hanneman/nettext/.

Hogan, B. (2010). "Pinwheel layout to highlight community structure." Journal of Social Structure.

Li, X., S. Tan, et al. (2005). "Interaction graph mining for protein complexes using local clique merging." Genome Inform **16**(2).

Naveh, B. Jgrapht, http://jgrapht.sourceforge.net.

Olson, J. S., J. Grudin, et al. (2005). Toward Understanding Preferences for Sharing and Privacy. Proc. CHI.

Palla, G., I. Der'enyi, et al. (2005). "Uncovering the overlapping community structure of complex networks in nature and society." Nature **435**: 814–818.

Skeels, M. and J. Grudin (2009). When Social Networks Cross Boundaries: A Case Study of Workplace Use of Facebook and LinkedIn. Proc. Group.

Wakita, K. and T. Tsurumi (2007). Finding Community Structure in Mega-scale Social Networks. Proc. ACM WWW.

What Are You Working On? Status Message Q&A in an Enterprise SNS

Jennifer Thom[1], Sandra Yuen Helsley[2], Tara L. Matthews[2]
Elizabeth M. Daly[1], David R. Millen[1]

IBM Research - Cambridge[1], Cambridge, MA USA 02140
IBM Research - Almaden[2], San Jose, CA USA 095120
{jthomsa, syuen, tlmatth, dalyeliz, david_r_millen@us.ibm.com}

Abstract. Social networking services (SNS) have been deployed within enterprises to encourage informal social interactions and information sharing. As such, users have turned to the status message functionality in a SNS for social information seeking by employing it as a medium for question asking. In this paper, we present the results of a qualitative study observing emergent question and answer (Q&A) behaviors in an enterprise SNS and then describe user motivations in employing this medium for social information seeking. We report data describing the types and topics of questions asked within the workplace and the prevalence of questions and responses within this system. Results suggest that users choose status message Q&A for non-urgent information seeking needs and perceive question asking as a way to elicit social support from their professional networks.

Introduction

Business workers encounter a variety of information seeking needs each day. For instance, one might have to find the appropriate market research to help determine the best strategy to win a major account. Another scenario might involve looking for the right person to move across the world to fill a newly created leadership position. Everyday concerns can also arise, such as finding the right lunch spot or how to properly file travel expenses.

Professional networks, whether through face-to-face peer support or online forums, have long played a critical role in helping employees get answers to questions (Nardi et al., 2002; Preece, 2000; Wenger, 1998). With an increasingly distributed and matrixed workforce, companies are increasingly turning to social networking services (SNS) to continue enabling questioning and answering (Q&A) via these peer support networks (Matthews et. al., 2011). The advent of social software in the workplace provides business users with new ways of interacting with their professional social networks for question-asking (DiMicco, Geyer, Millen, Dugan, & Brownholtz, 2009).

In this changing landscape, it is important to understand whether and what aspects of employee Q&A behavior are supported via SNS, so companies can make informed decisions about which to deploy and designers can understand what design decisions lead to specific workplace usage practices. Prior studies have shown that SNS users outside the enterprise have appropriated microblogging and status message functionality to broadcast questions to their networks (Morris, Teevan, & Panovich, 2010). Benefits of such an approach include additional personal context possessed by one's social ties and the ability to ask a natural language question with the possibility of various responses, particularly when a question is subjective in nature.

Questions directed towards one's professional social network in an internal enterprise system, however, may serve a different purpose than those asked to one's personal network. First, a worker's job role likely affects the information seeking needs, resulting in different topics of inquiry. In addition, managing one's workplace reputation may influence what types of questions are asked to one's professional social network, since such interactions to anyone in the company who visits the SNS. Finally, within a large enterprise, a multitude of tools already exists for social information seeking, such as user-generated knowledge repositories, online communities, and expertise location systems (Ackerman & Malone, 1990; Millen et al., 2007). However, initial evidence suggests that employees do turn to an organizational microblogging tools for social information seeking (Zhang et al., 2010; Zhao, 2011) and to ask work-related questions (Ehrlich & Shami, 2010).

In this paper, we answer the following research questions through a qualitative study of question-askers and questions-asked in the context of status messages in an enterprise SNS.

RQ1: *What types of questions and question topics are being asked within an organizational SNS?*

RQ2: *What motivates users to appropriate status message functionality for question asking within an enterprise?*

We observe that users within an enterprise turn to status message Q&A for both information seeking and social support for a wide range of non-urgent, primarily work-related topics. We discuss the importance of Q&A via a SNS as a means for employees to garner peer support, as evidenced by the prevalence of rhetorical or discussion-oriented questions, including a significant number on social topics. Finally, we describe user motivations for choosing other tools for question and answers, namely a desire for structured interactions and searchable content.

RELATED WORK

Organizational Q&A

We characterize question asking within the workplace as an instance of social information seeking, which can include the activities of social search and expertise finding. Beyond meeting information seeking needs, social information seeking in the workplace provides social support, increased rapport, and visibility to one's coworkers (Morrison, 2002). Question asking, as a social information seeking strategy, can help to reduce uncertainty regarding job-related tasks and processes. These questions can be overt in nature, when a question-asker feels comfortable with asking someone in a direct manner (Miller & Jablin, 1991). Non-interrogative questions (e.g. one employed primarily to establish rapport) can be used when the question-asker is uncomfortable in seeking information or hopes to avoid seeming unknowledgeable (Miller & Jablin, 1991). This suggests that question-askers make judgments regarding the content of questions, depending on the potential answerer.

Question asking can be costly and time consuming for the seeker and requester. As a result, technologically mediated solutions to reduce the burden have emerged within workplaces. One example, Answer Garden 2, provides a collaborative help system through a series of question dialogues routed to local employees and intelligently escalates requests for help to organization-level experts (Ackerman & McDonald, 1996). In addition, the social information seeking process can be supported by tools that support people-finding within the enterprise (Farrell et al., 2007) and expertise location systems (Ackerman et al., 2002). Microblogging has been used by workplace project teams for social information seeking among other uses, such as sharing information and status udpates (Zhao et al., 2011). These systems may be especially useful within an enterprise, as perceived safety within a corporate intranet may influence employees' perceptions of information quality provided by fellow co-workers (DiMicco et al., 2008). Additionally, because reputation as an expert can be beneficial to one's career, certain employees may actively seek out attention as an answerer to bolster's one standing as an expert, and contribute valuable and relevant information (Thom-Santelli et al., 2008).

We propose that organizational SNS may also be particularly well-suited to supporting social information seeking, as an employee may feel comfortable asking work-related questions of their professional network. In addition, if these requests for help emerge in the forms of questions, identifying and classifying these behaviors in an organizational SNS can help designers better support social search and help-seeking within the enterprise.

Online Q&A Outside the Workplace

Online requests for information are not a new phenomenon, with Internet users turning to e-mail (Camino et al., 1998), and online forums such as Usenet (Welser et al., 2007), for answers. More recently, Q&A sites, such as Yahoo! Answers, Mahalo Answers or Quora, offer explicit support for such activity. Research has investigated the topical content of questions on these sites, ranging from technology-related questions to entertainment-related ones (Adamic et al., 2008; Nam et al., 2009).

However, these sites do not specifically leverage one's social network. Recently, Facebook has also introduced a separate question and answer feature on their site where users can pose questions and Facebook users, regardless of network connection, can provide an answer. For questions that require context or when seeking the advice or opinions of one's connections, users have appropriated microblogging to ask questions of their social network. Categorization of Twitter messages revealed that a proportion of tweets contained a question, suggesting that users appropriate these systems to find information (Ehrlich & Shami, 2010; Naaman et al., 2010). Morris et. al. (2010) provide an initial categorization of the types and topics of questions posted on Facebook profiles and observe that these particular questions may be more subjective and opinion-based in nature.

The context of one's personal social network can be different from one's professional network, which may lead to different types of question asked. For instance, one may feel comfortable asking one's Facebook network about dating relationships, but this is less likely to happen in one's work network. In this paper, we extend Morris et. al. (2010) to describe how the different information seeking needs inherent in an enterprise affect the types and topics of questions asked of one's professional network as opposed to one's personal network.

The ecology of workplace tools

The particular organization under study is a global enterprise that encourages social software use by their employees. As a result, there is a diverse ecology of tools available for use that leverage employee expertise and user-generated content for information seeking and collaboration. Despite the availability of a wide selection of systems, prior research suggests that users' choice of collaboration tool is influenced by characteristics of their work task and the tool's design (Balakrishnan, Matthews, & Moran, 2010). We suggest that employees meet social information seeking needs within the enterprise by making similar judgments about the search task and the affordances of available tools.

For example, employees have used a social bookmarking system as an exploratory information-seeking tool to browse and re-find online personal and community resources (Millen et al., 2007). Along with traditional e-mail and instant messaging tools, other systems supporting social information search include shared repositories of automated web search processes (Leshed et al., 2008) and expertise location (Shami et al., 2009). However, the type of information seeking supported by each of these systems has its limits (e.g. only web pages, processes or people returned respectively). Q&A has also been supported by a number of systems within this particular enterprise, such as through peer-support interfaces to initiate chat with targeted communities (Ribak, Jacovi, & Soroka, 2002). There are also online forums for technical help and online communities for users of similar interests, which offer threaded, asynchronous conversations. However, the forums and communities do not leverage a user's articulated social network but instead solely the members of that particular online environment.

SNS and status messages have a number of design characteristics that may influence how questions are asked. Status message functionality possess character limits to encourage brevity and cross-platform posting and possess a post form that encourages natural language statements. The asynchronous responses to questions are public and visible to those who have access to a profile. Taken together, these factors can shape how social information seeking occurs through status message Q&A in the enterprise.

Method

Since 2009, LOTUS CONNECTIONS has been the primary SNS of a large global technology firm with approximately 400,000 employees. LOTUS CONNECTIONS offers a variety of social software features, such as blogging and wiki tools, but of particular interest is the personal profile. The profile page in LOTUS CONNECTIONS contains a personal photo, contact information, job title and manager/report to information, populated automatically from the corporate directory. The profile displays an articulated social network in the form of reciprocal friend connections (e.g. invitations to connect must be accepted.)

There is a microblogging/status message feature within the profile with a prompt on the post form that states, "What are you working on right now?" Users can view status messages in a number of ways. First, there is a homepage, which aggregates the recent messages of your connections, much like the Facebook NewsFeed. Second, the profile page displays one's own status messages and comments by other members of LOTUS CONNECTIONS on a Board, similar to Facebook's Wall feature. Status messages can be entered on one's profile page, on the homepage, or using various browser plug-ins and applications. Comments can be added on anyone's Board; that is, members can leave a comment regardless of whether he or she has an articulated friend connection. There is a 500-character limit on status messages in LOTUS CONNECTIONS, compared to Twitter's 140 characters and Facebook's 423-character limit.

The following analysis is based on a crawl of LOTUS CONNECTIONS, containing profile activity from April 2009 to September 2010, with 22647 distinct users contributing one or more status messages. We collected 309,925 status messages that formed 191,752 distinct threads. To determine what messages were questions, we looked for status messages with question marks at the ends of complete sentences and eliminated those messages with extraneous questions marks (e.g. embedded inside URLs), with 10.96% (17,508) of the threads originating with a question. Note that this has likely missed some questions where posters excluded the question mark.

In addition to understanding the types and topics of questions asked through the system, we wanted to understand why people asked questions of their professional social network and what value they derived from the exchanges. Hence, we conducted 14 (12 M, 2 F)1 semi-structured 60-minute interviews with question-askers from a selection of organizational units and work locations. Because it was important that participants have experience asking a variety of questions and receiving a variety of responses in order to reflect on question and answering behavior and value, we recruited from the most active question-askers.

From this log analysis, we determined an initial interview sample of the most active question-askers, and then narrowed down the potential participants by those who had last asked a question in the month prior to the interviews. Table 1 describes our participants' demographic characteristics in detail. Participants described their general social software usage activity both inside and outside the organization, including microblogging and SNS sites and whether or not they engaged in question asking in those systems. We selected three recent questions from each participant's board as probes to elicit descriptions of their motivations for question asking and to gauge their reactions to the answers they may or may not have received.

---

1   The gender distribution is consistent with past user studies of systems deployed within the enterprise.

	Job Role	Years at company	# of connections
J	Consultant	8	244
L	Social Software Expert	13	1618
A	Software Marketing	9	213
JB	Software Strategy	10	391
H	Online Learning	27	213
R	Software Strategy	14	211
K	Software Marketing	14	244
M	Hardware Planner	10	251
Y	Social Software Expert	2.5	319
RB	Software Engineer	13	133
S	Social Software Expert	3	260
P	Support Engineer	11	271
D	IT Specialist	20	58
G	Sales Engineer	14	260

Table 1. Interview Participants

Finally, we sampled the 306 most recently posted English-language questions and coded them according to categories drawn from prior research and from open-coding. Each question was coded for type and topic, with four researchers developing the codes and settling disagreement through discussion (kappa for type = 0.88, $p < 0.01$, kappa for topic = 0.80, $p < 0.01$). We chose recent questions to control for system novelty effects and to observe these behaviors in a stable production system. The interview participants also contributed 25% of the questions coded.

Results

Question types and topics

Overall, the questions (n=17,508) in the dataset were a mean length of 25.83 words (SD=22.41) with a median response time of 55.37 minutes (a minimum of 0.41 minutes and a maximum of 11,275 minutes). Threads beginning with a question (n=17,508) received a mean of 2.4 (SD=3.35) responses while threads beginning with a non-question (n=174,244) received a mean of 1.54 (SD=1.97) responses. 18.7% of threads beginning with a non-question (n=141,611) received a response, while 42.1% of question threads (n=17,508) received a response.

Table 2 describes the coding scheme we applied to the 306 most recent questions, exemplars of each category, and the frequency distribution of the question types. We defined information seeking questions, drawing from Morrison's (2002) model, where questions were in search of factual knowledge to reduce uncertainty. Rhetorical questions were consistent with Morris et al. (2010) and Harper et al.'s (2009) definition of conversational questions, with the question's intent to elicit discussion or social support. Solution-type questions consisted of "how do I"-type inquiries in search of specific answer to a problem (Cross et al., 2001).

People-seeking questions can be likened to expertise-location, where users are in search of a specific person who may be able to provide help or further information (Cross et al., 2001). Opinion-gathering questions, drawn from Morris et. al. (2010), deal with requests for subjective information that provides judgment on a topic. Favor questions were defined as requests for services while offers gauge interest in available items or services (Morris et al., 2010). Coordination questions are those that are meant to organize a desired action (e.g. scheduling a room reservation). Invitation questions advertise or request attendance at an event (Morris et al., 2010).

Type	Example	Frequency
Information Seeking	Is there a Windows 7 image I can use on my dual-boot system? I d prefer something that didn't require me to wipe the MBR and current XP partition (i.e an upgrade path).	121 (39.54%)
Rhetorical	Wow, I just *personally* qualified for 150 million dollars in stimulus funds! (spam filters have a tough job, don't they?)	82 (26.79%)
Solution	new laptop - Windows 7 - how to get Notes 8.5.2?	32 (10.45%)
Invitation	Did you miss the Practitioner Portal demo last week on the Blue IQ session? The replay has been posted here: http://xyz.com/1BTP - Check it out!	20 (9,71%)
People-seeking	Recruiting an engagement manager to help deploy InfoSphere at major accounts in the MidAtlantic...do you have any candidates to refer?	15 (4.90%)
Favor	Hi Matthew - I am sure you can save me some time :-) I am searching for the plugin/feature that syncronizes Sametime status with this in Lotus Connections - I think I have seen a discussion about it on your Board some time ago. Can you please post a link to the project/download page?	16 (5.23%)
Opinion Gathering	So what s your opinion on posting duplicate blog entries on different blogs? I see it as reaching different folks via different channels. Just like posting the same information on Twitter, Facebook, and LinkedIn (even Connections - myDeveloperworks or xyz.com/communities). What say you?	14 (4.58%)

Table 2. Question types.

Table 3 describes the topics of the questions observed in the sample. Internal products referenced systems and technologies that are deployed or sold by the technology company under study, while the technology category referred to external systems or competitive products. Internal knowledge described processes employees may need to do for their job (e.g. filing expenses, booking travel). Conceptual questions included abstract or philosophical questions meant to guide one's behavior, similar to Morris et al.'s (2010) category of ethics & philosophy. The social category described questions that were related to social support or interaction (e.g. jokes or congratulations). People/connections described questions with topics dealing with finding a specific person or connection. General professional topics dealt with questions that were related to broad issues relating to career development.

Topic	Example	Frequency
Internal Products	What is the best "Intro to [our product]" file that you have seen or used? Looking for suggestions, so point me to the [our product] Files based file that you feel is best! Thanks :-)	94 (30.72%)
Technology	Anyone tried greasemonkey enabling dojo? dojo.require not working	60 (19.61%)
Internal Knowledge	Hi C - is there any list that says what [our company]'s discount program includes at Staples?	47 (15.36%)
Status	Back in Ottawa, trying to figure out the next few weeks. CIDA, Talisman?, Mobility Strategy gigs? Marketing events on Collab and virtual workspace, kick-off on United Way.	31 (10.13%)
Social	TL M, how are you? take care	28 (9.15%)
Personal	trying to read through mountain of mail. Busy day made busier by a pediatrician appointment AND a mortgage refinance closing today. It never rains, right?	15 (4.90%)
People/connection	Recruiting an engagement manager to help deploy InfoSphere at major accounts in the MidAtlantic...do you have any candidates to refer?	12 (5.83%)
Conceptual	now that it is "legal", would you / have you jailbreak your iPhone ?	11 (3.59%)
General Professional	are you attending or chairing? could i have a short session with you the next time we are in the same location? I am still at mediocre level and would like to (in *company* language) raise the bar :)	4 (0.03%)

Table 3. Question topics.

As shown by Table 2, the most popular type of question-asked in the sample was information seeking, followed by rhetorical and solution. Question topics, as befitting a global IT enterprise, focused on internal products technology, internal processes, and status, but also interestingly included 'social' in the top five topics (Table 3). Aside from the social questions, these results are consistent with prior research on enterprise microblogging: questions are focused on work-related topics, regardless of whether they are information-seeking or rhetorical in nature (Ehrlich & Shami, 2010). The prevalence of social questions in an enterprise SNS is unique to our results.

Table 4 reports the frequency of question type by topic, for the most popular question types. Of the questions regarding social topics, the two predominant question types were information-seeking and rhetorical. Information-seeking questions regarding social topics are consistent with the notion of people sensemaking, where SNSs support impression formation and informal communication of one's fellow co-workers (DiMicco et al., 2009). Rhetorical-type questions regarding social topics and internal products tended to evoke commiseration about general workplace frustration with the workplace in an informal, non-confrontational way, similar to the playful expressions of dissent observed in other types of media sharing in an enterprise SNS (Thom-Santelli & Millen, 2009).

Motivations for asking questions at work

From our analysis of the most recent questions and the interview data, we observed three themes that describe the motivations of employees to turn to microblogging Q&A in the workplace. First, urgency plays a role in the decision to turn to one's social network. Second, status message Q&A encourages easy posting and broadcast but retrieving the answers for later use proves difficult for users. Third, the questions asked within status messages, consistent with the relative popularity of the rhetorical questions, are also posed because of the broadcast nature of microblogging.

Urgency and timeliness

Participants noted that they tended to turn to microblogging Q&A in LOTUS CONNECTIONS when the question in mind was not urgent or critical to one's work.

| | Topic | | |
Type	Internal Products	Technology	Social
Information-seeking	41	25	17
Rhetorical	16	9	10
Solution	14	16	0

Table 4. Frequency of question type by topic.

From our analysis of response times, we observed a median time of 44.21 minutes to first response for information seeking-type questions and a median response time of 66.75 minutes for solution-type questions. This suggests that users' perceptions of a non-immediate response time are not necessarily unfounded. Eight of the participants expressed this motivation in their interviews.

> What I'm asking about is not really really urgent. It's not urgent enough to say that I really really have to know right now. I either am just curious or just something that I am comfortable with lagging for at least 15 minutes.....It wasn't that big of a deal. (H, online learning)

Below, we show an example of a non-urgent information-seeking question about an internal process cited by a participant during his interview. In this case, the participant's question related to an upcoming trip to another location within the organization and the possibility of finding drop-in workspace there.

Q: Are there any drop-in desk in Meguro office? I've never been there.... Sep 30

(Y, social software expert)

A1: Respondent A Sep 30

I'm afraid I don't think there are. But it's directly connect to the Meguro
Sta. so that really convient (sic) and looks very modern which looks unlikely a
Company office....

A2: Respondent B Sep 30

have used a meeting room there when I couldn't find the place to work.
So, it might be possible if you can find the meeting room and work there.

A3: Respondent C Sep 30

I now work near Meguro office, so I knew there isn't. Meeting rooms are
for Company-ers who registered for the office only. And recently, they even
change the reservation system with ACL check so that you can't even check
whether the rooms are available or not. I'd say there are not friendly for
visitor use.

The participant did receive satisfactory answers to his question, but this matter was one in which he possessed adequate lead time in planning his tasks. As a result, this particular information seeking need did not require immediate turnaround and the response time satisfied the participant.

One possible reason for participants to reserve the microblogging channel for less urgent questions is a low expectation for a response from others. Participants attributed this sense to a variety of factors such as the nature of the SNS, an overload of items in social awareness streams, or the size of their social network.

> No, I did consider posting it elsewhere; I was looking at a short timeline, but not so short that I needed a response right away. If it was really customer urgent, I would take the trouble of posting it in multiple places. In Lotus Connections it's ok if nobody answers. (S, social software expert)

At the same time, all participants noted that they accessed LOTUS CONNECTIONS in between tasks, time permitting, contributing to fragmented usage patterns. Such interstitial activity, if common among users, likely contributes to the response rate and time to response.

In addition, the likelihood of response in a global enterprise also depends on the time of day of posting and the availability of online readers. We observed one instance where an interview participant re-posted his question in a status message at two points in time to gather responses from both Europe and the United States.

> There's a specific reason [for posting the question again]. The specific reason was reaching out to different audiences based on geography. [...]
>
> I think the first time I posted, it was actually posted more for a European audience, and since that didn't get much of a European response, that's why I went and posted it a second time to reach out to the US audience. That's one of the things about having a global network, like we all do at Company, is that we're working on projects [...], sometimes we need to be conscious that the people we need to reach out to, we need to fine tune to get them at their best time zone.
>
> So typically if I'm looking for a European audience, I wouldn't post a question, for instance, right as we speak, because right now it's 7pm on a Friday afternoon (in Spain). I would go and rely on my US audience. But something like Monday morning, 9am my time, would be the best time to post that question for a European audience. (L, social software expert)

This participant, as an EU resident, has had to adjust his posting style in order to maximize the chances of eliciting responses from a globally distributed network. However, for the participants with more geographically homogenous networks, such adjustments were not as common.

Participants also reported choosing other channels for social information seeking when the matter at hand is urgent. In these situations, the channel chosen is usually synchronous in nature, such as finding colleagues face-to-face if working in a traditional office setting. When working remotely, participants turned to instant messaging to meet immediate needs, but this choice is likely to be more successful if a potential answer can be found within one's immediate contact list.

Structure and Future Search

Prior research studying the usage of available systems in the collaboration environment within this enterprise suggests that employees assess the characteristics of their tasks to make an appropriate choice from the ecology of tools (Balakrishnan et al., 2010). As the previous theme suggests, the time sensitivity of the information seeking need is one factor that influences whether or not users will turn to microblogging for Q&A. In this section, we observe two socio-technical characteristics of systems employed for Q&A that are salient in the decision-making process – whether the community supports general or specific requests and the manner in which a system archives Q&A interactions.

Seven of the interview participants reported they turned to question asking within status messages for less-technical work-related questions intended for a general audience with a wide range of expertise. The rationale for this choice related to a sense that reaching out to one's social network would likely garner a helpful answer, particularly if this were a question where a number of possible answers. Related to the likelihood of finding an answer through one's social network, five of the interview participants noted that they felt their social networks were large and varied enough to provide enough of a chance to receive a response.

Below is a question from one of the interview participants regarding references and examples that she needs for an upcoming presentation.

Q: Any references / case studies for [our company] regarding social networks and retail? (S, social software expert) Oct 25 6:09 AM

A: **Respondent A** Oct 25 6:13 AM

I believe [company M] is our reference. Do a search in connections for "Lotus Connections customer references" . LMK if you can't find it.

A: **Respondent B** Oct 25 6:14 AM

Hi S., not sure whether there would be plenty of them, but under my Bookmarks I have got a bunch of reference links on case studies under the tag "case-studies" and / or "business-value"; you may want to have a quick look through and scan through some of them... Hope that helps...

A: **S (question-asker)** Oct 25 7:24 AM

Working on deck about social networking and retail: (html link provided) - looking into beefing up "Next steps" section.

A: **Respondent C** Oct 25 8:47 AM

Take a look at Company B from Company C They are an [Our Company] Global Entrepreneur. So far they have not adopted any [of our company's] platforms - however, their intention is to do so. If you wish, I can put you in touch with their CEO.

A: **Respondent D** Oct. 25 8:47 AM

CompanyM is not a reference for [our company]. it is only a reference for Commerce.

In this case, the participant received answers from a diverse set of respondents from different sub-organizations within the Company, and none with whom she works with directly. This example also illustrates the conversational nature of the information seeking questions that received more than one response. The conversational turns, however, are brief, and participants reported that long posts and long threads on a Profile Board could be hard to follow and track, as noted by this participant.

For information seeking needs that are detailed or technically complex, participants reported choosing more structured systems for Q&A. Five of the participants turned to online forums in a traditional online bulletin board set-up, with topic-specific areas, for such questions. For these participants, complex technical questions that are central to one's day-to-day work tasks were more appropriate for the forum, particularly as they were designed to aggregate people with common expertise and interests and providing topic-based support, as noticed by the following participant.

Forums are where I go when I'm stuck and need an answer before I can proceed on a problem. If I really need help and I need the attention of multiple people who know about that area, I'll go to that forum. It's like a directed questions (area) and it's things where it's pretty urgent for me to get some help here. (D, IT engineer)

In addition, there are subject-matter experts whose job roles include forum participation to specifically address any technical concerns and questions. Four of the participants used Answers, a traditional Q&A site, because they felt that the responses they received there were longer and more detailed. We observed that three of the participants cross-posted between status message Q&A, forums and Answers by either posting a link in a status message to the other site to re-direct responses to those channels so that they could these sites for future reference. The four participants noted that the cross-posting was an attempt to elicit responses from their general social network in another system and inform readers of a potential answer elsewhere.

Participants noted that both Answers and the forums were better suited for search and refindability of content. The current design of the Lotus Connections board is a social awareness stream displayed in chronological order, from most recent updates at the top of the page, with older messages collapsed and hidden from view. Forum and Answers content is searchable, with both systems surfacing older content in search results according to relevance.

> There's a little bit of a different focus in there as to why I would use one or the other, and it's also a little bit of a focus from the perspective of how permanent I want that answer to be. If I want to have an answer to a question that stays there forever, and can be retrieved easily, probably I won't go to Connections Profiles, since right now there's no easy way to find older information. [For something 6-12 months later] I would probably go to a blog or more to a discussion forum, or whatever else. (A, software marketing)

There is the danger, as observed by two participants, that archived technical content in the Forums, in particular, can be outdated so questions must be repeated, which introduces additional noise into the search results. However, overall participants expressed greater satisfaction with the ways that structured question tools archive information.

Commiseration and Requests for Social Support

The relatively unstructured nature of the status messages, however, encourages discussion and conversation, which is consistent with the higher number of rhetorical-type and social-topic questions we observed in our coding. Four of our participants indicated that they posed questions to specifically encourage debate about open-ended issues.

> I post for several reasons. One is to provoke discussion. So, sometimes I ask questions to do that. Or I'll make a statement and ask for feedback. Sometimes, I'll take a weird position to get people to think about it. Othertimes, I'm working on a problem. So, I'll take a position on a problem and see if I can get some interaction. Usually, it's something fairly work-related. And sometimes, it's where I'm trying to be the conscience for people who are all going into one direction. And I think that might not be as healthy as people think about things more carefully. And debating. (B, software strategy)

However, these four participants, in particular, have garnered professional reputations as thought-leaders within the organization, such that responses are likely more forthcoming than others who are less visible.

Even when responses are unlikely, ten participants reported that rhetorical questions served as a way to air frustrations encountered in everyday tasks at the workplace, such as in the question below.

Q: I'm starting to wonder if all these reply to all is a way for people to have fun? I don't necessarily mind the emails, I can delete them. What I mind is that every time a message comes in, it kicks my Pavlovian instincts to unholster my blackberry. Getting a good workout.. :) (G, sales engineer) Sep 23

A: Respondent A. Sep 23

I am on the same list and its scary that these folks do not understand a simple concept - hit the delete key!!!!

A: Respondent B Sep 23

I had to turn that incoming message alert off on my blackberry. I couldn't fight the urge to check everytime a message came in.

A. Respondent C Sep 23

LOL

The participant notes his motivation for asking such a question below.

Maybe it was a rough day. I may have gotten conservatively 150 emails in the span of a day and a half. Um, with all of these reply to all, stop replying to all comments. It's kind of funny. I used to see this a lot. Maybe 5-6 years ago. And, it hasn't happened in the last 5 or 6 years, This is the first time in 5-6 years that this thing is still going. So I was thinking, is this thing for real? Are people actually doing this? (Laughs) It kind of surprised me. It was more a surprise than anything. I suppose..it was also a post to gauge who else was getting these emails and who else was on the distribution list, you know, indirectly.

We observed that participants intended these types of questions to elicit commiseration from their social network, consistent with prior research that suggests that comments on social media content can help users discuss sensitive workplace topics (Thom-Santelli & Millen, 2009). However, whether or not these questions are effective in gathering responses is uncertain. Rhetorical questions had a median time to first response of 85.23 minutes as compared to information seeking questions (44.21 minutes), with both receiving a median of 2 responses. Posters of these types of questions also had a low expectation of response, as we observed with respect to information-seeking questions. However, our data suggests that simply broadcasting the information was the main intent, as opposed to receiving a direct response.

Besides seeking social support through rhetorical questions, seven of the participants reported using question-asking as a way to request assistance or attendance, such as in the quote below.

No, I didn't get any responses but essentially it wasn't much of a question, it was more of a reminder and an announcement, [...] basically what I wanted to do was to broadcast the message out that if people wanted to submit an abstract for the conference [they could still do it]. I wasn't expecting an answer on that one, more than anything else, because I knew if people would answer, they would tell me, "Yes I'm interested," "No, I'm not interested" [...] [but it wouldn't necessarily fulfill the answer itself,] it was more meant from a broadcasting perspective more than getting an answer to it. And I didn't get any other responses through IM or email or whatever else. I wasn't expecting them. (L, social software expert)

In the categorization of question-types, however, we did observe relatively fewer examples of favor questions and invitation questions, and it is possible that users may modulate these behaviors to reduce the appearance of freeloading on their social network. Participants noted that wording requests or announcements as questions was a conversational strategy to make such statements more engaging or encouraging, as in the quote below informing others of a job post.

It wasn't information seeking, but posting it as a question makes it more conversational. I wasn't expecting responses, they might be just to go to the job post.] It was a fake question. [It was to make the job posting more engaging. I could have said something more direct, which was fine, but it was more interesting this way. (S, social software expert)

This suggests that users are aware that burdening their network with impolite requests or too many invitations may affect their audience's impression of their activity on the SNS.

Discussion and Implications

This is the first study focused on social Q&A behavior in the workplace. Comparing to social Q&A behavior outside the workplace (Morris et al. 2010), we see that the types and topics of questions asked are quite different. Topics asked to a general social network included entertainment, home and family, shopping and so on (Morris et al., 2010). Topics such as these were completely missing from workplace social Q&A, which instead focused on the company's products, technology, company-internal knowledge, and work status. While this difference is not surprising, we were intrigued to find that social and personal topics made up a substantial 14% of question topics, showing that a social Q&A system in the workplace will not be exclusively work-related. This departs from prior research on enterprise microblogging behaviors, which has characterized it as primarily work-related (Ehrlich & Shami, 2010; Zhao et al. 2011). Our data suggests that professional networks provide workers with peer support of a personal and social nature. The top question types found in a general social network were recommendations and opinions (Morris et al., 2010), compared to information seeking and rhetorical in the workplace. Again, the need for peer support in a work context guides these results.

The desire to connect with peers is indicated by the prevalence of rhetorical questions (27% of questions). Our interview data reveals that our participants used these types of questions as a form of self-expression regarding their opinions of work issues or to elicit commiseration about work matters. Our participants saw rhetorical-type and social-topic question *asking* as increasing their social capital in a workplace context, whereas prior studies of general social Q&A behavior have focused on question *answering* as a way to build social capital (Morris et al., 2010). The resulting responses to these rhetorical questions, if any, may help to maintain ties by serving as a signal to the asker that the answerer valued the social relationship enough to reply (Donath, 2008). However, we did observe that users were not necessarily expecting a response to rhetorical questions, but using the question format to express an opinion in an interactive manner.

While our data suggests that workplace users find it relatively easy to ask a question for information seeking via microblogging, re-finding the responses received at a later date was more difficult. As a result, participants turned to workplace systems, such as forums or Q&A sites within the intranet, with more structure when they needed answers to complex technical problems, as they found the social awareness stream difficult to follow or that search capabilities were greater for systems that were intended to be archival. However, the potential audience available through one's professional social network on LOTUS CONNECTIONS is still a valuable resource, and we observed a few instances of a workaround where users cross-posted links between the systems to gain the benefits of both. On the other hand, the lack of structure also contributed to the openness necessary for users to post questions to stimulate conversations or gather opinions.

Finally, we observe that workers chose microblogging functionality for Q&A when the need for responses is not time-critical, consistent with earlier analysis of Q&A outside the workplace (Morris et al., 2010). Our analysis of site activity suggests that status messages phrased as questions do elicit responses more often than non-questions; however, there are relatively few responses and they do not arrive immediately. This may be partially influenced by general usage of the site, as participants reported visiting LOTUS CONNECTIONS interstitially and as a break from other tasks during the workday. For non-work SNS usage, Morris et. al. (2010) report that users find the lag acceptable for non-urgent queries that may be difficult to compose in a search engine. In a work context however, our participants report that the longer response cycle leads them to turn to other media for questions when the need for an answer is urgent.

From these results, we suggest the general choice to employ microblogging Q&A within the ecology of workplace tools occurs because of two key design affordances: the ease of posting a question and the potential social and broadcast nature of the medium. The nature of the information seeking need, however, also influences how users make the decision to favor a particular social information seeking system over another. In addition, we observed that users seek social support through their peers by eliciting interactions on a publicly visible networked online space.

A possible explanation for an employee's motivation to turn to an enterprise SNS for Q&A may lie in changes in team structure. Modern companies are moving away from work focused on stable teams to a more matrixed way of working that involves teams where membership is constantly in-flux (Chudoba et al. 2005; Mortensen and Hinds 2002; Nardi et al. 2002; O'Leary et al. 2011). With this change, workers can no longer rely on a stable set of teammates to provide peer support functions, which are critical to individual and group success (Kraut 2003; McGrath 1984). These peer support functions center around Q&A, with workers asking their peers for information, feedback, social support, and so on. The result is that professional networks have become increasingly important at providing these peer support functions for individual workers (Nardi et al., 2002, Matthews et al., 2011). Workers participating in teams with dynamic membership also turn to their professional networks to find people with specific expertise to join their teams (Matthews et al., 2011). Based on this prior research, we propose that employees may be appropriating status message Q&A as one possible source of stable peer support.

Finally, we address the limitations of the current study. The behaviors observed may be influenced by the particular culture of this organization and further comparison work should be conducted, if generalizability across organizations is the goal. An additional limitation is the focus on active lead users, which may not be representative of the total population. Nonetheless, they do shed light on the motivations of our active users whose contributions are central to the health of the system.

Conclusion and Future Work

The contribution of this paper is an in-depth qualitative study of user motivations and a characterization of status message Q&A behaviors within the workplace context. We describe user motivations for status message Q&A within the enterprise and the characteristics of the questions asked in the appropriation of this particular functionality. We also observe how users integrate microblogging Q&A into the ecology of workplace tools available for social information seeking, and will now propose a categorization of information seeking needs that are suited to these kinds of interactions. However, we also note that question asking, depending on type, in this environment provides social support for employees within a large distributed organization.

Future work to build upon these findings includes a systematic evaluation of how team characteristics (e.g. stability, collocation) affect how employees obtain peer support and the circumstances under which they use an enterprise SNS for such activity. We also plan to conduct additional analysis of the non-English status messages to investigate geographic differences in user appropriation. While we provided an initial high-level analysis of the responses, a deeper understanding of the answers and the factors influencing responses is necessary to improve the utility of microblogging as a medium for Q&A. Finally, prior work has suggested that the members of one's workplace network can play multiple relationship roles depending on the context (Wu et al., 2010). Our future research will investigate whether these roles influence whether or not responses are elicited and the types of response that are likely to occur depending on the relationship between the asker and answerer.

References

Ackerman, M. S., & Malone, T. W. (1990): 'Answer Garden: A tool for growing organizational memory', *Proceedings of COCS 1990*, pp. 31-39.

Ackerman, M. S., & McDonald, D. (1996): 'Answer Garden 2: Merging organizational memory and collective help', *Proceedings of CSCW 1996*.

Adamic, L. A., Zhang, J., Bakshy, E., & Ackerman, M. S. (2008): 'Knowledge sharing and yahoo answers: everyone knows something', *Proc.WWW2008*, pp. 665-674.

Balakrishnan, A. D., Matthews, T., & Moran, T. P. (2010): 'Fitting an activity-centric system into an ecology of workplace tools', *Proc.CHI2010*, pp. 787–790.

Bernstein, M., Tan, D., Smith, G., Czerwinski, M., & Horvitz, E. (2009): 'Collabio: A game for annotating people within social networks', *Proc.UIST2009*, pp. 97-100.

Camino, B. M., Milewski, A. E., Millen, D. R., & Smith, T. M. (1998): 'Replying to email with structured responses', *International Journal of Human Computer Studies*, *48*(6), 763-776.

Chudoba, K.M., Wynn, E., Lu, M., Watson-Manheim, B. (2005): 'How virtual are we? Measuring virtuality and understanding its impact in a global organization,' *Information Systems Journal*, 15, pp. 279-306.

Cross, R., Rice, R. E., & Parker, A. (2001): 'Information seeking in social context: Structural influences and receipt of information benefits,' *IEEE Transactions on Systems, Man, and Cybernetics, Part C*, *31*(4), 438-448.

DiMicco, J., Geyer, W., Millen, D. R., Dugan, C., & Brownholtz, B. (2009): 'People Sensemaking and Relationship Building on an Enterprise Social Network Site', *Proc.HICSS2009*, pp. 1–10.

DiMicco, J., Millen, D. R., Geyer, W., Dugan, C., Brownholtz, B., & Muller, M. (2008): 'Motivations for social networking at work', *Proc.CSCW2008*, pp. 711-720.

Donath, J. (2008): 'Signals in social supernets', *Journal of Computer-Mediated Communication*, *13*(1), 231-251.

Dunbar, P. R. (1998): *Grooming, Gossip, and the Evolution of Language*. Harvard University Press, Cambridge, MA.

Ehrlich, K., & Shami, N. S. (2010): 'Microblogging Inside and Outside the Workplace', *Proc.ICWSM2010*.

Farrell, S., Lau, T., Nusser, S., Wilcox, E., & Muller, M. (2007): 'Socially augmenting employee profiles with people-tagging', *Proc.UIST2007*.

Harper, F. M., Moy, D., & Konstan, J. A. (2009): 'Facts or friends?: distinguishing informational and conversational questions in social Q&A sites', *Proc.CHI2009*, pp. 759-768.

Kraut, R. E. (2003): 'Applying social psychological theory to the problems of group work', in J. Carroll (eds.): *HCI Models, Theories and Frameworks*, Morgan Kaufman, New York, 2003, pp. 325-356.

Leshed, G., Haber, E. M., Matthews, T., & Lau, T. (2008): 'CoScripter: automating & sharing how-to knowledge in the enterprise,' *Proc.CHI2008*.

Matthews. T., Matthews, T., Whittaker, S., Moran, T., Yuen, S. 'The New Organizational Ecology: Symbiotic Relationships Between Collaborations', *IBM Technical Paper*.

McGrath, J. E. (1984): *Groups: Interaction and Performance*. Prentice Hall, Englewood Cliffs.

Millen, D., Yang, M., Whittaker, S., & Feinberg, J. (2007): 'Social bookmarking and exploratory search', *Proc.ECSCW 2007*.

Morris, M. R., Teevan, J., & Panovich, K. (2010): 'What do people ask their social networks, and why?: a survey study of status message q&a behavior', *Proc.CHI2010*.

Morris, M. R., & Horvitz, E. (2007): 'SearchTogether: an interface for collaborative web search', *Proc.UIST2007*.

Morrison, E. W. (2002): 'Information Seeking Within Organizations', *Human Communication Research*, *28*(2), pp. 229-242.

Mortensen, M. and Hinds, P. (2002). 'Fuzzy teams: Boundary disagreement in distributed and collocated teams', in P. Hinds and S. Kiesler (eds), *Distributed Work*, MIT Press, Cambridge, MA, 2002, pp. 283-308.

Naaman, M., Boase, J., & Lai, C. H. (2010): 'Is it really about me?: message content in social awareness streams', *Proc.CHI2010*.

Nam, K. K., Ackerman, M. S., & Adamic, L. A. (2009): 'Questions in, knowledge in?: a study of naver's question answering community,' *Proc.WWW2009*.

Nardi, B. A., Whittaker, S., and Schwarz, H. (2002): 'Networkers and their Activity in Intensional Networks', *Computer Supported Cooperative Work*, 11, 1-2, pp. 205-242.

O'Leary, M., Mortensen, M., and Woolley, A. (2011): 'Multiple Team Membership: A Theoretical Model of Its Effects on Productivity and Learning for Individuals, Teams, and Organizations', *Academy of Management Review*. To appear.

Ribak, A., Jacovi, M., & Soroka, V. (2002): '"Ask before you search": peer support and community building with reachout', *Proc.CSCW2002*.

Shami, N. S., Ehrlich, K., Gay, G., & Hancock, J. T. (2009): 'Making sense of strangers' expertise from signals in digital artifacts,' *Proc.CHI2009*.

Thom-Santelli, J., & Millen, D. R. (2009): 'Learning by seeing: photo viewing in the workplace', *Proc.CHI2009*.

Thom-Santelli, J., Muller, M. J., & Millen, D. R. (2008): 'Social tagging roles: publishers, evangelists, leaders,' *Proc.CHI2008*.

Welser, H. T., Gleave, E., Fisher, D., & Smith, M. (2007): 'Visualizing the signatures of social roles in online discussion groups', *The Journal of Social Structure*, *8*(2).

Wu, A., DiMicco, J. M., & Millen, D. R. (2010): 'Detecting professional versus personal closeness using an enterprise social network site,' *Proc.CHI2010*.

Zhang, J., Qu, Y., Cody, J. and Wu, Y. (2011): 'A case study of microblogging in the enterprise: use, value and related issues', *Proc.CHI2010*.

Zhao, D., Matthews, T., Moran, T., Rosson, M.B. (2011): 'Microblogging's Potential Impact on Team Collaboration Awareness', *Proceedings of the International Conference on Collaboration Technologies and Systems 2011*.

The Hugging Team: The Role of Technology in Business Networking Practices

Anne Thorsø Sørensen and Irina Shklovski
IT University of Copenhagen
annethorsoe@gmail.com, irsh@itu.dk

Abstract. Technological devices for social networking are produced in droves and networking through media seems to be the way of getting ahead in business. We examine what role technology plays in the creation, development and maintenance of business relationships among entrepreneurs in Copenhagen. We find that mediated communication is useful in all stages of relational maintenance but only in a supportive role in relational development where co-presence and shared personal experiences take center-stage, generating trust necessary for business relationships to work. These trust-developing experiences take effort and hard work and although they can be successfully supported and even facilitated through the use of communication technologies, they need not be replaced or made simpler. The difficulties of creating these experiences make working business relationships viable in the uncertain and risky world of entrepreneurship.

Introduction

See you on Facebook, let's chat over Messenger or connect on Xing or LinkedIn and "land jobs and close deals"[1]. Requests of connection fill the air of business meetings, Friday bars and corporate dinners. These are networking practices, often lauded as a way of getting ahead in business today (2010). Communication devices that synchronise with LinkedIn that then synchronise with Twitter that in turn synchronise with status updates on Facebook make for something that looks like a well-lubricated machine for networking. The ever burgeoning range of

---

[1] About Linkedin - http://press.linkedin.com/about/

technologies that capitalize on human sociability and the benefits of connecting have been of special interest to scholars of collaboration. Being able to connect anywhere, anytime and to anyone has become simpler with the advent of social networking sites (SNS) such as Facebook and LinkedIn. The use of these commercially available sites has gained significant momentum in the business world although the benefits of such use are still debated by scholars and managers alike (Wu, DiMicco, & Millen, 2010).

In this paper we present a nuanced study of the role SNSs play in how professionals initiate, develop and maintain business relationships. After all, it is relationships that make business happen (Seibert, Kraimer, & Liden, 2001). We focus on independent entrepreneurs as potential power users of technology and as people for whom extreme connectedness would be especially important. Entrepreneurs tend to work independently and their professional success is highly dependent on meeting new contacts and maintaining existing relationships as they "rely on networks for business information, advice, and problem solving, with some contacts providing multiple resources" (Hoang & Antoncic, 2003). Being successful in business is largely related to having the right connections. In order to move forward with their businesses entrepreneurs must depend on many developed professional relationships and a steady influx of new contacts and ideas.

Social network sites (SNS) enable easy upkeep of weak ties and the creation of broad networks (Barkhuus & Tashiro, 2010; DiMicco, et al., 2008; Skeels & Grudin, 2009). These broad networks can provide access to information that could be valuable both professionally and socially (Ellison, Steinfield, & Lampe, 2007; Steinfield, DiMicco, Ellison, & Lampe, 2009). People who have never physically met sometimes establish relationships using communication technologies (Boase & Wellman, 2006). The same technologies can help maintain these relationships (Barkhuus & Tashiro, 2010; Shklovski, Kraut, & Cummings, 2008) making it possible to not only collect, but also keep accessible a large number of contacts. This kind of use of communication technology can translate into the creation of certain kinds of social capital making it especially useful for "those whose roles naturally involve networking" (Jack, Moult, Anderson, & Dodd, 2010; Skeels & Grudin, 2009) such as entrepreneurs.

The Hugging Team

Our research questions are best illustrated by an evocative story that one entrepreneur told us in the course of our fieldwork. He was trying to win the title as head of an Inner Circle of external partners for a large company but initially did not succeed. When the winners of the title were announced he noticed that the winning CEOs of small partner-businesses and the CEOs of the large company were hugging in celebration. He then decided, that the goal of his own company for the coming year should be getting on what he called "*The Hugging Team*" of the Inner Circle. After a year of developing closer personal relationships with the relevant

CEOs of the large company and hugging them, he advanced to the head of the Inner Circle of small-business partners, thus advancing his companies' standing and winning more beneficial contracts.

This story is striking for two reasons. First, no technology – no cell phones, no social networking sites – seemed to be party to the hugging success. Second, the story underscores the ambiguous nature of professional relationships. On the one hand it is calculating and strategic in the way this respondent carefully planned to move his business forward. On the other hand, the road to success was paved with something as intimate and personal as hugging. Although hugging someone could not be done over the phone or online, we noted that phones and the Internet were constant companions in the everyday practices of entrepreneurs. In this case merely establishing a connection was not enough. It was important to deepen the relationship making hugging a natural aspect of it. In the telling of this story, the practice of hugging stood out, while the constant use of communication technology to manage relationships that enabled this practice remained in the background.

In this paper we ask what role communication technology plays in managing professional relationships? We are especially interested in how currently available as well as future communication technologies may be involved in the creation of hugging teams. Specifically, given the nature of entrepreneurial business relationships, what might these power users and the way they use technologies for social networking suggest for future business technology design and development?

Background

Relationships, whether they are friendships or business ties, do not appear out of thin air, but start with an initial meeting, be it due to strategic networking or happenstance. Communication technologies certainly play a role in expanding the playing field and making more people accessible to others by removing such barriers as distance, scheduling conflicts and time differences. Regardless of how people may have met, relationships require effort and investments of time and attention to continue (Parks, 2007). There are many theories of how relationships develop and grow, from basic notions of investment, exchange and equity (Sprecher, 1988; Thibaut & Kelley, 1986) to requirements of self-disclosure and interdependence (Berscheid, 1994; Perlman & Fehr, 1986). There is a pattern to relational development, starting with an initial meeting, subsequent investments and self-disclosure to achieve growth, and continuing maintenance to keep the relationship from fading away (Parks, 2007; Perlman & Fehr, 1986). Arguably, communication technologies have not made relational work unnecessary, but perhaps they have enabled people to accomplish such relational work more efficiently and effectively, especially in a business context.

Much research has documented the role of communication technologies such as email, instant messaging and social networks sites in how, where and when people establish relationships, deepen and grow nascent connections and maintain them. While mediated communication is heavily implicated in all of these processes, face-to-face interaction remains an important and often surprisingly necessary component of developing and maintaining successful business relationships and collaborations (Rocco, 1998). We summarize the disparate relevant research on relationship initiation, development and maintenance below.

Establishing new relationships

The SNS' promise of meeting people that one would like to meet without the constraints of physical proximity is as old as the ability to communicate over distances. Although the original purpose envisioned by SNS designers was to foster a safe and productive space for meeting new people and extending social networks, the majority of SNS users maintain their existing contacts rather than find new ones (boyd & Ellison, 2007). Nevertheless, some users do initiate relationships via SNSs, especially in the context of work and business activities (Steinfield, et al., 2009). For example, employees of one large multinational corporation successfully used what Lampe and colleagues have called "social browsing" (Lampe, Ellison, & Steinfield, 2006) to find colleagues they did not know, but who they thought may be interesting or useful to meet (DiMicco, et al., 2008). SNSs provided not only a convenient way to locate and contact relevant people, but also became a resource that offered the opportunity of vetting someone by giving insight into personal life of this person (Skeels & Grudin, 2009). The ability to quickly learn the relevant details about a person could be especially helpful when preparing to meet someone new. In fact, this very access to a broader range of expertise was one of the main drivers for employees using SNSs in companies (Steinfield, et al., 2009).

Prior research shows that connecting with individuals you do not know well is made easier by SNS because of the practical support SNSs provide for such connections (Barkhuus & Tashiro, 2010). Instead of facing the possibility of rejection by stepping too far into someone's personal sphere by initiating a phone call or showing up in person, SNSs offer an easy way to "send an invitation to connect which you can accept with a couple clicks, no imposition" (Barkhuus & Tashiro, 2010). These so-called "low-key" (Skeels & Grudin, 2009) connections are useful making this kind of connecting more of a symbolic thing, "a promise to consider a further request" (Skeels & Grudin, 2009). Although contemporary communication technologies offer myriad opportunities to meet new people, meeting people is only one part of the process. The effort of initial contact indicates an interest in future interaction and potential for a relationship, but does not guarantee that a productive relationship would be the result.

Developing relationships:

In order to become productive relationships, social connections need to be developed through expressions of commitment and self-disclosure (Perlman & Fehr, 1986). Nascent relationships require communication in any form in order to deepen (Shklovski, et al., 2008). Although we know that people use SNSs and other technologies for developing and deepening relationships, research differs on whether these technologies are successful. Self-disclosure can happen via any medium and SNSs have been implicated in the process of certain kinds of relational growth (Burke, Marlow, & Lento, 2010). For example, DiMicco and colleagues (DiMicco, et al., 2008) found that the use of the company-internal SNS at IBM built stronger bonds as a result of users "connecting on a personal level," while Steinfeld and colleagues (Steinfield, et al., 2009) reported that "bonding social capital is predicted by intensity of use and using the site". However, these studies were focused on an internal site, safely cocooned in a closed organizational space. Outside the organizational fence, sites like Facebook at times fall short of people's expectations, primarily enabling lightweight relational maintenance (Lee, 2010). We ask whether entrepreneurs who do not have access to such "safer" spaces can utilise publicly available SNSs to support relational growth and if so, how.

Trust in relationships:

Despite the proliferation of mediated communication technologies, issues of trust remain problematic in distance work and relational development (Rocco, 1998; Wilson, Straus, & McEvily, 2006). Although people do develop trust in mediated settings, the process is often slower, more fragile and vulnerable to opportunistic behaviour (Bos, Olson, Gergle, Olson, & Wright, 2002). Trust is a crucial component of successful distance work and productive mediated communication (Jarvenpaa, 1999) and is especially important in developing workable business relationships for entrepreneurs. Yet mediated communication continues to cede ground to face-to-face interaction for developing trust in nascent relationships (Rocco, 1998; Zheng, Veinott, Bos, Olson, & Olson, 2002).

In this study, we define trust as the willingness to be vulnerable, following Mayer and colleagues (Mayer, Davis, & Schoorman, 1995). This vulnerability is derived from a lack of insight into the intentions or prospective actions of a potential partner or a collaborator (Lewis & Weigert, 1985). For entrepreneurs this notion of vulnerability is especially apt because for them relational development and self-disclosure involve sharing ideas and information that are vital for business. Here a strong sense of trustworthiness is important because it influences the quality of the resources and the information that flows between parties and because it reduces transaction costs (Hoang & Antoncic, 2003; Jack, et al., 2010). We investigate what role SNSs and other communication technologies play in how and whether entrepreneurs develop trust in business relationships.

Maintaining relationships:

Once relationships are developed to a desired level, communication technology can be extremely useful for maintenance activities (Shklovski, et al., 2008). Relational maintenance behaviours can take on the form of comments, photo sharing, email exchanges, and a myriad of other small actions on SNSs that can function as behavioural infusions into established relationships at a distance in order to maintain them in a desired state (Shklovski, et al., 2008; Sigman, 1991). These actions do not necessarily substitute for other forms of contact, such as phone calls or in-person interaction, but can be thought of as additions to or compensations for its rarity. The use of lightweight interaction such as comments or other small gestures can become unobtrusive reminders of a shared past and of the intention to maintain a connection without investing too much time or effort (Skeels & Grudin, 2009). While SNSs can be useful for relational maintenance, people tend to maintain weaker ties of a lighter character through this channel (Barkhuus & Tashiro, 2010). Given these findings, we asked what role might SNSs play in how entrepreneurs manage a variety of their business relationships?

Despite the proliferation of communication technology, face-to-face interaction and the demand for physical proximity stubbornly refuse to disappear. In fact, some research suggests that SNS may eliminate too many emotional risks making it difficult to become vulnerable enough to deepen relationships (Lee, 2010). Although frequent face-to-face meetings may not be necessary for adequately supporting distance work, occasional infusions of such interactions are crucial for making things function well (Nardi, 2005; Nardi & Whittaker, 2002). In fact, these face-to-face meetings are not as important for technical work-related discussions as they are important to actually manage the human aspects of work relationships. This line of research suggests that communication technology may have to be relegated to a secondary and supportive function in the way entrepreneurs would establish, develop and maintain their relationships. Given the demands placed on entrepreneurs in the course of selecting business partners and developing relationships, we wondered just how much of an aid would communication technology become when it came to literally getting down to business? Would social network sites and other forms of staying connected through technology provide the right kind of flexibility, information and scaffolding to help entrepreneurs locate and eventually transform weak ties into hugging teams?

Method

We present results from a qualitative study based on a series of in-depth interviews and extensive observations conducted in the spring of 2010 in Copenhagen, Denmark. Data collection and analysis were iterative processes of repeated analysis and contrasting of hypotheses and ideas, going between the research field and data assessment. The data is based on repeated informal and semi-structured interviews with seven independent Danish entrepreneurs who network as part of their professional life. The first author also performed in-depth extensive observations of these entrepreneurs' day-to-day activities at their places of business, at formal networking events and at informal gatherings.

In the course of our study, we used the method of theoretical sampling as a way of selecting participants for observation and interview. This sampling approach is described in detail by Corbin and Strauss (2008). We continually intermingled data collection with data analysis resulting in a hermeneutic process where we created, explored and altered concepts during our fieldwork. This practice helped us to define a tight focus of our study early on and to narrow down our selection of subjects. Because of a research process that in this way fed on itself we reached saturation surprisingly quickly. Our research focus originated from an informal conversation in the course of initial observations during a networking meeting of entrepreneurs with the story of the hugging team. An important criterion in our selection of informants was that they were already successful entrepreneurs and that their businesses were flourishing. We carefully selected our respondents to cover a wide spectrum of types of businesses, some reliant on technology and others dependent on physical places. Regardless of business type, however, all of the respondents depended on having numerous contacts to ensure that their businesses were successful. Additionally, all but one had connections abroad, such as suppliers, employees, mentors or costumers.

We recruited entrepreneurs using a snowball sampling technique initially seeded from personal contacts. The criteria for participation was to have started at least one business, to have achieved success by attaining financial solvency and to have serious intentions for continuing entrepreneurial activities in the near future. All participants except one were native to Denmark. These were young entrepreneurs, ages ranging from 25 to 45, who conducted business in a variety of areas from IT and finance, to small restaurant ownership. All participants used mobile phones and email extensively and all but one maintained profiles on Facebook and LinkedIn.

The first author, who is a native Danish speaker, observed and interviewed six male entrepreneurs and one female entrepreneur. Although we intended to achieve a gender-balanced sample, this proved difficult. This may be partly related to the fact that in Denmark men are nearly three times as likely as women to be self-employed[2]. The first author spent 15 hours observing participants and collected an additional 8 hours of interviews over multiple occasions in the course of a month. The interviews were focused on past and current business relationships, elicited examples of using such relationships to promote business, discussed how they would solve hypothetical problems and how they were solving real problems they currently faced. We deliberately did not focus interviews on discussions of technology use, letting the kinds of technologies used for managing relationships

---

[2] Statistics Denmark

emerge organically, without external prompting (Kvale, 1996). All mentions of technology use were followed up with requests for specific examples and further explanations.

All observations were summarized in field notes and memos and translated in summaries for the second author who does not speak Danish. We developed a coding scheme based on an initial open coding of transcripts and field notes (Emerson, Fretz, & Shaw, 1995). We then combined open codes into themes distinguished by the type of relational process (initiation, growth or maintenance of business relationships), technology-use orientation (SNS, mobile phones, email) and insistence on in-person interaction. Relevant quotes, notes and references were combined and summarized to form a coherent narrative for each theme. These summaries then allowed a look at the bigger picture. All representative quotes presented here were translated by the first author, who is a native Danish speaker. Names were changed to preserve confidentiality.

Findings

Connecting online

All but one of the entrepreneurs in our study were avid users of communication technologies for social networking and for relational maintenance. We found two distinct patterns of behaviour. Half of the respondents used SNSs almost exclusively to connect with people they already knew and to maintain connections previously established through face-to-face interaction:

"I need to know them. Most of the people that I have on my list [on Facebook], 85 percent of them, I know personally." (DN)

Another participants added:

"If it is someone I haven't met before I won't accept them as contacts [on LinkedIn]." (JB)

This kind of technology use had the character of "extra communication." Connecting via an SNS became something that could take place after a first impression had been formed elsewhere – similar to exchanging business cards.

While the other half of the entrepreneurs reported using SNSs as business card repositories as well, they also actively searched for and often made connections *before* a face-to-face meeting took place using the sites. SNSs provided a way to search for people with certain qualifications or interests, to vet them by checking out their profiles, and to establish initial connections. They then decided whether they wanted to meet these new contacts in-person. As one participant explained:

"Often we are 'friends' from Facebook and therefore there is also a recognition factor that can potentially help set up an arrangement to cooperate" (NS).

Making use of an SNS to establish initial contact with someone became a way of finding out that they shared something in common. Another participant explained how he used LinkedIn to locate new contacts through friends of friends:

"I don't use it that much but if there is a certain person I want to get in touch with I might check if I know someone who knows the person in question and can introduce us" (NSE).

One of the most common reasons our respondents decided to establish initial contact through an SNS was to overcome physical distance and a lack of existing personal contacts in a location that was new to them. For example, an entrepreneur shared how he used LinkedIn to find and vet potential business contacts in Poland:

"I knew one person and he [my partner] knew no one (...). So he went on Linked-In and found 10 profiles (...) And then he wrote to them saying, 'Hi, we are going to Poland would you like to meet us about a new project we are doing'. And in that way we booked six meetings" (JB).

While this approach was successful for establishing necessary connections the same respondent quickly pointed out that this way of connecting was not optimal:

"If this was in Denmark I would have gone to someone who knew someone instead" (JB).

Even though SNSs could function as efficient channels to meet people online and some respondents used this approach often, the need to eventually meet face-to-face remained paramount. In fact, we heard stories of respondents going to great lengths to establish initial contact with potential business connections in person. In a somewhat extreme example, one participant confronted the challenge of distance by frequently travelling between Denmark and the United States:

"In LA there are lots of conventions and a lot of businesses, retailers, buyers and guitar builders meet there (...). It's a mix of people and therefore it is really important to be there. (...) Then you talk about how you think you might help each other. (...) And therefore a negotiation situation has already been furnished and that's a really sensitive situation because you offer yourself (...) then hopefully in 20-30 minutes you have created a comfortable situation where you find out if you can help each other" (NS).

The above quote provides an important insight into why our respondents travelled long distances to meet in-person even though LinkedIn or Facebook were merely a click away. Even when they used SNSs, and especially Facebook for business-related activities daily, meeting in-person remained important because when initiating a potential business relationship *"you offer yourself"*. Recalling the definition of trust as a willingness to be vulnerable (Mayer, et al., 1995), our participants clearly indicated that one of the biggest issues they needed to resolve in the course of meeting new contacts was determining their trustworthiness.

Deciding who to trust

There is no sure way to assess someone's trustworthiness, especially in a nascent relationship, and entrepreneurs in our study tended to rely on a complex combination of logic and gut feeling for this process:

"I met a guy in a bar once and I knew he earned a lot of money (...). But I didn't find him very likeable. We were just standing there, hanging out and listening to some music. It was just some small talk and touching glasses. But I just sensed that it didn't feel right. For the short moment we talked I just felt it" (NS).

There are volumes of information available via Google search and on various SNS profiles, yet developing trust online is often more difficult and can take a longer time than through face-to-face interaction (Bos, et al., 2002; Wilson, et al., 2006). In spite of the efficiency technology offered our participants, it was the impressions that could not be summarized in an address book or an SNS profile that influenced decisions on trustworthiness. As one participant reflected:

> *"Yeah, sure I use Facebook and Linkedin, but what works best is actually the stuff you remember"* (JB).

The things that they remembered were not necessarily pieces of factual information and in some cases these difficult to articulate impressions seemed almost irrational in a business sense. As one entrepreneur, who heavily used Facebook to promote his business and to keep in contact with business prospects, explained:

> *"If I'm in front of a person and my body sensation is not good – off path immediately! If I'm uncomfortable with it, it doesn't really matter what they say, I don't care. I watch the people a lot …. And for me …. the whole thing needs to be … I need to feel the vibes"* (DN).

Another participant referred to something similar when he described what it was like to meet a potentially good business connection:

> *"It is like when you meet a new person that you like being close to and where you feel that you need each other"* (NS)

Apart from whatever facts may have been available about a potential business contact prior to the meeting, emotional impressions as social linkages necessary for the exchange of information (Nardi & Whittaker, 2002), had to be positive in order to assess initial trustworthiness.

Business relationship growth

After the initial stages of meeting and vetting, actually making use of a newly established business relationship demanded further relational growth and development of trust. Here too the resources offered by SNSs were important, but they played a unique supportive role in the process where emotional connections, co-presence and personal experience took centre stage.

Trust and business

Business relationships involve exchanges of resources and services, built on notions of reciprocity and expectations of gain. As one participant explained:

> *"The work related stuff is probably more so the kind of thing where you are conscious of the exchange. What can I get from you, what can you get from me and what can we give each other?"* (MG).

This exchange was more of a sensitive issue to entrepreneurs because they worked independently and were not backed by large organizations, as one participant explained when talking about involving a powerful collaborator in his business:

> *"How sympathetic is he to my input? How attentive is he to the fact that I'm the little guy in this game?"* (CW).

Finding people that were trustworthy was vital for business relationships. This transition was important in order to move forward and actually make business happen. In this phase entrepreneurs tended to establish if the relationships they had initiated would actually work. Merely being a match structurally and competence-wise was not enough for a beneficial business relationship.

Entrepreneurial relationships that have survived for a long period of time evidence that trust indeed binds them together. Over time these kinds of relationships shift from initially being of a calculative character to being affective relationships built on reciprocity, resembling something more akin to friendship rather than business (Jack, et al., 2010). The process of establishing this level of trust is delicate. Our participants relied extensively on face-to-face interaction and spoke of this need in ways that were reminiscent of the media richness hypothesis (Daft & Lengel, 1984). For example, one participant explained how this lack of a good gut feeling influenced his business choices:

"He made enough of money so that part of the respect was there, but I just felt that the way he presented himself wasn't very (...) appealing to me" (CW).

This thick and sometimes intangible flow of information affected the choices entrepreneurs made. Even if all formal matters of doing business seemed fulfilled, some business relationships never developed because the little cues of trust in face-to-face interaction revealed an intuitive dissonance.

Connecting through commonalities

To build trust in their business relationships our respondents sought common ground, often expressing a sense of community or sympathy towards the other party: *"We are kind of in the same club"* (MG). One of the formal networking events that we attended was called a "club" and this definition of the event was something that many of the attendees referred to when meeting someone new. Another participant who was originally from Argentina explained: *"We fix all things the Argentinean way"* (DN), when describing his relationship to good business contacts. As in previous research, lasting relationships meant high levels of trust and shared values.

"It wasn't like 'now you get that and then I'll get that in return'. It was more like, 'now we help each other" (JB).

Shared values, in fact, were not strictly business related, but meant a kind of sharing of personal preferences and attaining a deeper closeness, as one participant confided: *"Common values (...) make us get closer personally"* (MG).

SNSs facilitate learning personal information that can enhance the process of getting to know and ease finding commonalities. In fact our respondents used vetting prior to meeting and additional looking up in the course of relational development specifically to help them get "under the skin" of potential business partners. These commonalities suggest commonly held beliefs, cultural norms and expectations that had to be assessed in the course of interaction through a combination of technological "social browsing" (Lampe, et al., 2006) and in-person testing out of "vibes." Our observations suggested that SNS use allows an unobtrusive way of sharing these commonalities prior to meeting. Yet these commonalities remained conceptual until they were "tested" and the "testing" was best done in person. One participant gave an evocative example that led to some of his business relationships taking off and becoming beneficial:

"...on this trip over Easter with some partners. Six days in Turkey, all out. Some of my limits were really crossed at that trip and I thought about if we could do this together with the business relationship we have" (VA).

Strikingly, the level of involvement in these business relationships was in fact very personal. All future business partners in this instance had to cross boundaries of formal conduct and make themselves vulnerable to each other by sharing decidedly co-present non-business related experiences.

Technological support for relational development

As our participants sought commonalities to develop their relationships and to build stronger bonds, they did so in-person and through technology use. This was most evident in their SNS use. For example, one participant explained how he maintained many of his US contacts via Facebook:

"We comment on each others pictures and that makes the relationship a bit softer. Introduces a friendly side that is quite interesting. (...) I use Facebook for strengthening my relations" (NS).

SNSs provided a space for discovering commonalities and moving relationships forward for the participants in a casual way that could remove some of the attention from the more calculative side of business:

"Facebook is a softer medium where talking business doesn't seem so business-like" (NS).

While some relationships were well suited for development on Facebook, more than half of the entrepreneurs noted that serious business relationships belonged on LinkedIn. Where Facebook was of a lighter character, LinkedIn sent a more serious signal. *"[Facebook] is more of a friend thing..."*, a participant expressed and concluded: *"LinkedIn is more for professional relations"* (NSE). We investigated what constituted managing serious relationships on LinkedIn through observations and further probing interview questions. All six users of LinkeIn utilized it as an online address book or for vetting contacts. Very little direct interaction took place through the site despite recent innovations on the part of the site. The development of serious relationships took place mostly face-to-face, but the information that supported some of this interaction was gleaned from the SNS. Although technologies helped span distance, where serious business contacts were concerned, the need for co-presence trumped convenience:

"Then we just decided to go and visit [the US] *every three months. That was the only way it would be possible"* (JB).

When asked why travelling to see someone can sometimes be the "the only way" another participant explained:

"It is nicer to discuss things [in person] *instead of e-mailing. It becomes so formal"* (CW).

Clearly, our participants preferred not just any kind of co-presence, but in-person meetings of a specific character. Many times the nature of in-person interactions of these serious relationships did not seem very serious at all:

> *"It was someone from* [the US], *who was in Denmark and we had invited him out to eat. It* [dinner] *was very formal in some way. We talked about Denmark and he asked if there wasn't something called Christiania[3]? And I said that it was right near by ... And then we took a walk and had a beer there ... and then my colleague and him got completely stoned ... And then he said, 'do you ski?'... and three months later we went skiing together in the US. And after that trip we just had a completely different relation and we could talk together in a deeper way and we could use each other a lot better"* (JB).

A formal dinner or a regular meeting was not enough to develop the level of trust needed to make relationships mature for future business ventures. Trust in serious business relationships of entrepreneurs was paradoxically created by occasionally loosing control. A participant who owns a wine bar commented on this:

> *"Normally people, after 2-3 glasses of wine, get far more friendly. That is why I can really build powerful networks. Because people are far more... I wouldn't say vulnerable... but they speak far more freely"* (DN).

The encounters that resulted in a loss of a controlled presentation of self put our respondents on the spot, but also lubricated business ties, built stronger bonds, created trust and in the end brought benefits. Yet despite the need for intimacy and the requirement of vulnerability for trust building, too much vulnerability could cross the thin line of business relationship into too much friendship. Our respondents struggled to strike the right balance between business and friendship, since close friends often do not make good business partners (Maldonado, Klemmer, & Pea, 2009).

Co-presence is no panacea

Co-presence is not a perfect answer to managing the risks of meeting new business partners. It is fraught with dangers because people lie, first impressions may be misconstrued and crossing too many boundaries can end in hurt feelings. Entrepreneurs were aware of these issues when meeting a possible collaborator:

> *"Will he lead you up the garden path? Will he buy you for peanuts and then throw you out afterwards? What is his ulterior motive really?"* (CW).

Even though the participants expressed a definite fondness of co-presence, they were well aware that the intimate qualities of co-presence were an effective and at times calculative tool for creating an engaging atmosphere that would make an object of business courtship more cooperative:

> *"Next time we meet up: Out for dinner, eat, drink him under the table, become best friends and swing and dance and stuff like that... I do it to make him think that I'm really cool and so that we can get more things through"* (JB).

Almost all of the participants had experienced getting seduced by such a *"business flirt,"* as one entrepreneur called it, because the business relationship came to resemble a friendship. A respondent noticed this when getting to know the person with whom he later formed a rather problematic business partnership:

---

3 A self-proclaimed autonomous neighborhood in Copenhagen that is, among other things, known for its cannabis trade.

"It was strange to get that kind of compliments, and I didn't really know what to do with them (...) It was like an exchange that belonged in another kind of relationship" (NES).

Some respondents deliberately tried to limit "connectedness" both online and offline to avoid forming too many demanding and obligating relationships. For example, one entrepreneur only rarely gave out their email-address, stayed off social media and did not pick up their phone after hours in order to keep a clear separation between private and professional life, thus managing relational distance with colleagues and customers both digitally and physically:

"With some costumers you have to keep two steps away, so they don't get a hug" (MG).

In another example, a respondent who owned a bar used the actual bar as marker of a personal boundary. Through observations of his interacting with potential business contacts it became apparent that he would sometimes cross this boundary by leaning across the bar or actually walking to the other side of the bar as a special means of getting closer to a potential business contact – and thereby closer to a deal – making physical distance both a means of protection and calculation.

Neither technology nor in-person interaction were foolproof for identifying the right business contacts to trust. Even when trying to limit the exposure that is part of establishing new relationships and sharing ideas by using a range of technological and in-person tools for communication and vetting, our participants were aware that they would remain vulnerable. Ultimately entrepreneurs had to rely on something inexplicably intuitive when deciding whether to trust people and to let a relationship take off. As another participant concluded:

"I like to think that what goes around comes around" (NSE).

Maintenance

Having developed their relationships to a desired level, entrepreneurs needed to maintain them through occasional infusions of attention and contact. Our participants used technology extensively for relationship maintenance. Several participants used Facebook for spreading titbits of information through status updates that they felt kept the interest of their contacts alive:

"I just posted a bit of fun and some headlines and then some of them caught on to that" (JL).

In this way SNSs provided an efficient channel for lightly engaging existing contacts by presenting them with information in an unobtrusive manner.

"I use Facebook to maintain relations and remain in peoples' consciousness" (NSE).

This made it acceptable to initiate contact even though the occasion may not have been pressing. Spreading information and promoting themselves this way was done both to attract costumers and to remind their contacts of their existence:

"...if you don't cultivate [the relationships] you don't know what is going on in your process. (...). It is more fun to keep up to date on a regular basis. Then you get a much better sparring and dialogue" (CW).

A regular stream of information not only kept the memory of what had been developed alive, but also offered occasions for activating the relationships again and developing them further if necessary.

However, as our participants gained a larger list of contacts, they became conscious of the fact that their posts on SNSs reached everyone at once, regardless of who they were. While this was useful for certain kinds of promotion activities, this also naturally limited just how personal a profile could be, once again carefully treading between the informalities of friendship and the seriousness of business relationships. A participant pointed out this challenge:

> *"Earlier, if I had a bad day, I might post some quote that expressed negativity. I'm a bit more aware of that now. Even though it irritates me that I think like that. I just wouldn't like my dealers to get that impression"* (NS).

This instance of what Meyrowitz called "collapsed contexts" (Meyrowitz, 1985) represented a blessing and a curse, making it difficult to aim communication at specific contacts. To manage risk, some participants chose to use more synchronous ways of communication for specific instances of maintenance:

> *"I prefer calling. Then it is easier for me to sense if this is the time to say everything or only half of it"* (JB).

Reactivating relationships

Despite the opportunities SNSs and other communication technologies offered, our participants managed to keep only so many relationships active at a time. They found SNSs especially useful for re-activating ties in the event those were needed. A participant described how he had used the chat function on Facebook for reactivating a relationship:

> *"One of my dealers had been to Montreal skiing with his wife and I could see that and asked if he had had a good trip and maybe using it as an opening. You know, that we should talk and I'll call you next week"* (NS).

When an occasion came for reactivation of a relationship the participants would move interaction to more synchronous platforms of communication. They also expressed that mediated communication often functioned as a temporary pit stop before moving on to seeing each other face-to-face. A participant described this when describing the thoughts that came to mind when receiving a phone call from an old business contact:

> *"It is like then I become conscious of the fact that I have some people that I can always call and say, 'you wanna grab a cup of coffee?'"* (JB).

When considering business ties our participants employed a full ecology of communication modalities, where seeing a Facebook update from a contact would lead to a conversation on Facebook chat, then to a phone call, and maybe eventually a shared cup of coffee.

It's all about connecting

Relational maintenance via technological means is efficient and timesaving and our respondents demonstrated as much. The more people you know, the more information is available and the more possible business ventures lie ahead. For our entrepreneurs SNSs and other communication technologies were crucial for keeping their business relationships from deteriorating. They used SNSs, email and phone to get customers, promote their business, maintain connections and seek new contacts. Yet the ease with which SNSs, electronic address books and contact lists allowed them to catalogue the people they met in the course of business could be overwhelming. For some, the possibilities of indexing endless amounts of names, numbers and faces often turned laptops into trophy cupboards of contacts:

> "I have more than 2.000 contacts in my file on the computer. They are all people that I have met (...). Some of them I don't even remember anymore, but I've got them all here" (NSE).

The very notion of being connected was problematic for many of our respondents. The majority used Facebook and LinkedIn to literally store contacts, archiving them for some abstract potential future use. Another participant underlined this perspective when discussing his rather impressive contact list:

> "Can you imagine how many numbers I've got? (...) I don't even know who they are..." (DN).

Having connections – access to contact information – was quite easy for our respondents. In order to actually make use of these contacts, however, they invested substantially more effort to develop them into and maintain them as usable connections. Ultimately content and the catalogue of shared experiences, both business and otherwise, defined the relationships. Technology provided a way to store contacts, created scaffolding for the initial vetting and was crucial for ongoing maintenance. Yet to make a business relationship work it was necessary to do the hard work of relational development. Our participants insisted that some of that work was still best done face-to-face.

Discussion and conclusions

We began this study with the goal of exploring how entrepreneurs use available communication technologies and social networking tools to broaden their business connections and to manage their business relationships. We chose young entrepreneurs because they represented a group of people whose use of technology for networking would best illustrate networking practices in this digitally connected world. Since many small business entrepreneurs work independently, they tend to network outside the confines of a shared organizational space, seeking potential customers and business partners in a variety of situations.

In the course of our fieldwork we found that, as we had expected, SNSs, phones and email were heavily implicated in the way entrepreneurs established, developed and maintained their business relationships. In the process of establishing relationships, communication technologies in general and SNSs specifically were useful tools for narrowing down the search for business prospects, for overcoming barriers of distance and for vetting prospective partners prior to engaging in negotiations. Social browsing on SNSs could speed up the process of getting to know one another when meeting face-to-face by providing the background information necessary for connecting over existing commonalities and establishing rapport. SNSs, email and phones were even more integral to the way entrepreneurs engaged in maintaining existing relationships. SNSs allowed users to easily and conveniently ply large numbers of contacts with a regular stream of unobtrusive information and attention that could serve as reminders and that kept the relationships alive and ready for reactivation. In this context the lighter character of SNS-based interaction shined, confirming prior research on how and why people might use these technologies (Skeels & Grudin, 2009; Steinfield, et al., 2009).

It was when we considered how entrepreneurs might move from meeting potential business partners to actually making deals that the role of communication technology became far less straightforward. Despite the connectivity and opportunities gleaned from technology use, the biggest reason for a relationship to move from a potential contact to a productive business partnership was development of trust – a tortuous and uncertain process for our participants. For want of something resembling the comfort zone of an organizational context (Wu, et al., 2010), entrepreneurs looked for, tested and created a comfort zone of equal amounts of vulnerability, commonly held values, co-present experiences and sympathies that could provide the safety needed to make a business relationship take off. SNSs provided initial information of shared context and values on which entrepreneurs could base this development of relationships. The format of Facebook, for example, made it possible to intermingle business talk with other topics of a lighter non-business character, making conversation flow easier. LinkedIn, on the other hand, showcased recommendations of friends or co-workers and clearly communicated relevant background information.

At the same time, SNSs perhaps offered too much mediation and made the work required for relational growth too convenient and controlled, a finding similar to recent research on friendships (Lee, 2010). This was where meeting face-to-face became important because factual information gleaned via SNSs was not adequate when deciding if someone was trustworthy. The high level of trust that entrepreneurs required for a relationship to grow into a partnership was formed as a result of impressions from face-to-face interactions that were irrational, difficult to articulate and paradoxically had little to do with the notion of business. For our participants, raw co-present shared experience forced the kind of self-disclosure that helped create conditions for a successful business relationship. Despite the access and efficiency technology provided, it did not allow the user to skip the hard work of relationship development. No matter the kind of business our entrepreneurs engaged in, they preferred at least rare instances of co-presence to accomplish the tricky and delicate kinds of relational work. In the words of Nardi (2005) they were looking to establish "feelings of affinity, commitment and attention." The social linkages created in moments of vulnerability to each other allowed the exchange of information that was really essential for creation of trust: information that was not censured by the social expectations of the business world.

Yet in-person interaction was no panacea. The very experiences necessary to create trust could be staged by a contact that was calculating and insincere. Vulnerability and shared informal experience could also result in a relationship that was too much friendship and not enough business. Where to meet on the continuum of private and professional, of intimate and interactive was a tricky balancing act determined for each individual relationship. We found entrepreneurs alternating between extensive use of SNSs and other communication technologies for vetting and checking their contacts and limiting the use of the same technologies to keep business relationships from slipping into too much friendship.

Finally, our respondents pointed out that connections could be overwhelming and hollow at the same time. New technological devices and social media tools for networking flood the markets and their value is often touted in terms of storage space, speed, ability to synchronize with other media and the ability to reach out to any contact around the world. For the more technically savvy of our participants, connecting using these tools was easy, seductive and initially seemed enduring, similar to the kind of behavior observed in college students (Ellison, et al., 2007) . Yet our findings also illustrated that although the kinds of connectedness social media offered could be useful and exciting, the expectation of being always available and always presentable could be overwhelming. Just how many names on your contact list are more than simply names anymore?

Our findings then question what being connected means for entrepreneurs in the digital world. SNS use allowed entrepreneurs to maintain a wide range of contacts and provided opportunities to locate potential partners more broadly, softening and lubricating the process of meeting new people and maintaining relationships. Yet it was clear that when it came to really connecting, shared co-present experience trumped everything else, demanding real investments of time, effort and emotion. Here use of technologies shifted into the background, giving space to the "gut feeling", We are not certain that technological advance should aim to somehow replace the deep and raw connection of physical experiences with conveniently technologically mediated ones. At times, barriers and difficulties that had to be overcome were what made new business ties that much more valuable when they finally worked. Showing up was what made entrepreneurs believe the other person really meant what they said, especially if the effort to meet was substantial. Once these decisions were made, however, SNSs offered exciting new ways to help manage, maintain and advance the businesses of these entrepreneurs.

Limitations

Despite careful sample selection, we readily acknowledge the limitation of our small sample size, focused as it was on Danish entrepreneurs in the city of Copenhagen. Such narrow geographical focus made it impossible to observe potential differences of how entrepreneurs go about business and networking in places less centrally located. A larger sample size and a comparative cross-cultural study would have undoubtedly provided greater detail and insight into the phenomena under study. Our future work is aimed at remedying these limitations and focusing deeper on the curious distinction between friendship and business partnership as it might be managed via social media.

Acknowledgments

We are indebted to all of our respondents for their generous participation in our study. We thank anonymous reviewers for helping us improve this paper with constructive criticism.

References

Barkhuus, L., & Tashiro, J. (2010). Student socialization in the age of facebook. *Proceedings of CHI 2010*

Berscheid, E. (1994). Interpersonal relationships. *Annual Review of Psychology, 45*, 79-129.

Boase, J., & Wellman, B. (2006). Personal relationships: On and off the Internet. In D. Perlman & A. L. Vangelisti (Eds.), *Handbook of Personal Relations*. Cambridge: University Press.

Bos, N., Olson, J., Gergle, D., Olson, G., & Wright, Z. (2002). Effects of four computer-mediated communications channels on trust development. *Proceedings of CHI 2002*

boyd, d., & Ellison, N. (2007). Social Network Sites: Definition, History, and Scholarship. *Journal of Computer-Mediated Communication, 13*(1), 210-230.

Burke, M., Marlow, C., & Lento, T. (2010). Social network activity and social well-being. *Proceedings of CHI 2010*.

Corbin, J. M., & Strauss, A. L. (2008). *Basics of qualitative research : techniques and procedures for developing grounded theory* (3rd ed.). Los Angeles, CA: Sage

Daft, R., & Lengel, R. (1984). Information richness: A new approach to managerial behavior and organizational design. *Research in Organizational Behavior, 6*, 191-233.

DiMicco, J., Millen, D. R., Geyer, W., Dugan, C., Brownholtz, B., & Muller, M. (2008). Motivations for social networking at work. *Proceedings of CSCW 2008*.

Ellison, N., Steinfield, C., & Lampe, C. (2007). The benefits of Facebook "friends:" Social capital and college students' use of online social network sites. *Journal of Computer-Mediated Communication, 12*(4), 1143-1168.

Emerson, R. M., Fretz, R. I., & Shaw, L. L. (1995). *Writing ethnographic fieldnotes*. Chicago: University of Chicago Press.

Hoang, H., & Antoncic, B. (2003). Network-based research in entrepreneurship: A critical review. *Journal of Business Venturing, 18*(2), 165-187.

Jack, S., Moult, S., Anderson, A. R., & Dodd, S. (2010). An entrepreneurial network evolving: Patterns of change. *International Small Business Journal, 28*(4), 315-337.

Jarvenpaa, S., & Leidner, D. (1999). Communication and trust in global virtual teams. *Organization Science, 10*(6), 791-815.

Kvale, S. (1996). *Interviews: An introduction to qualitative research interviewing.* Thousand Oaks, CA: Sage.

Lampe, C., Ellison, N., & Steinfield, C. (2006). A face(book) in the crowd: Social searching vs. social browsing. *In proceedings of CSCW 2006.*

Lee, J. (2010). 500 Friends and No One to Call: Insights on the Reality of Social Networking. Copenhagen, DK: ReD. Retrieved 1/23/2011, http://www.redassociates.com/redpapers/social-media/

Lewis, J. D., & Weigert, A. (1985). Trust as social reality. *Social Forces, 63*(4), 967-985.

Maldonado, H., Klemmer, S. R., & Pea, R. D. (2009). When is collaborating with friends a good idea? insights from design education. *Proceedings of CSCL 2009 - Volume 1.*

Manjoo, F. (2010, August 26, 2010). Social Networking Your Way to a New Job. *The New York Times.*

Mayer, R., Davis, J. H., & Schoorman, F. D. (1995). An integrative model of organizational trust. *Academy of Management Review, 20*(3), 709-734.

Meyrowitz, J. (1985). *No sense of place: The impact of electronic media on social behavior.* New York: Oxford University Press.

Nardi, B. (2005). Beyond Bandwidth: Dimensions of Connection in Interpersonal Communication. *Computer Supported Cooperative Work, 14*(2), 91-130.

Nardi, B., & Whittaker, S. (2002). The place of face to face communication in distributed work. In P. Hinds & S. Kiesler (Eds.), *Distributed work* (pp. 83-112). Cambridge, MA: MIT Press.

Parks, M. R. (2007). *Personal relationships and personal networks.* Mahwah, N.J.: Erlbaum.

Perlman, D., & Fehr, B. (1986). Theories of friendship: The analysis of interpersonal attraction. In V. Derlega & B. Winstead (Eds.), *Friendship and social interaction* (pp. 9-40). NY: Springer.

Rocco, E. (1998). Trust breaks down in electronic contexts but can be repaired by some initial face-to-face contact. *Proceedings of CHI 1998,* 496-502.

Seibert, S. E., Kraimer, M. L., & Liden, R. C. (2001). A Social Capital Theory of Career Success. *The Academy of Management Journal, 44*(2), 219-237.

Shklovski, I., Kraut, R., & Cummings, J. (2008). Keeping in touch by technology: Maintaining relationships after a residential move. *In proceedings of CHI 2008.*

Sigman, S. J. (1991). Handling discontinuous aspects of continuing social relationships: Toward research on the persistence of social forms. *Communication Theory, 1,* 106-127.

Skeels, M. M., & Grudin, J. (2009). When social networks cross boundaries: a case study of workplace use of facebook and linkedin. *Proceedings of GROUP 2009.*

Sprecher, S. (1988). Investment Model, Equity, and Social Support Determinants of Relationship Commitment. *Social Psychology Quarterly, 51*(4), 318-328.

Steinfield, C., DiMicco, J. M., Ellison, N. B., & Lampe, C. (2009). Bowling online: social networking and social capital within the organization. *Proceedings of C&T 2009.*

Thibaut, J. W., & Kelley, H. H. (1986). *The social psychology of groups.* New Brunswick: Transaction Books.

Wilson, J. M., Straus, S. G., & McEvily, B. (2006). All in due time: The development of trust in computer-mediated and face-to-face teams. *Organizational Behavior and Human Decision Processes, 99*(1), 16-33.

Wu, A., DiMicco, J. M., & Millen, D. R. (2010). Detecting professional versus personal closeness using an enterprise social network site. *Proceedings of CHI 2010.*

Zheng, J., Veinott, E., Bos, N., Olson, J. S., & Olson, G. M. (2002). Trust without touch: jumpstarting long-distance trust with initial social activities. *Proceedings of CHI 2002.*

Group Crumb: Sharing Web Navigation by Visualizing Group Traces on the Web

Qing Wang[1], Gaoqiang Zheng[2], Ya Li[3], Huiyou Chang[1], Hongyang Chao[1]

School of Software, Sun Yat-sen University

[1](wangq79, isschy, isschhy)@mail.sysu.edu.cn, [2]kenkofox@qq.com,
[3]gzhu_liya@gzhu.edu.cn

Abstract. Although the sharing of Web navigation experiences can be useful, it is not supported by contemporary browsers. The Web has been constructed along the lines of a spatial metaphor, but with a flaw of not being able to share navigation experiences, that is, group traces, as is possible in a physical space. This paper shows that from the viewpoint of Information Foraging Theory, sharing Web navigation experiences among group members can increase their information foraging performance. To verify this, a simple prototype, the Group Crumb Prototype (GCP), has been designed. The GCP visualizes *group Web traces* by altering the appearance of links on a Web page according to their Group Crumb Scents, which are calculated from the recentness and times of group navigations to corresponding links. A longitudinal user study has been conducted to compare user performance and experience when surfing the Web with and without the aid of the GCP. Results show that making group navigation traces available on Web pages to group members increases their Web information foraging performance, promotes group collaboration, and enhances their Web browsing user experience as well.

Introduction

Web browsing was originally envisioned as a solitary activity, and most contemporary browsers were designed for that purpose, as were Web sites in the era before Web 2.0. However, the Web has evolved into the era of Web 2.0, which is more concerned with collaboration between Web users than solitary Web activities. Many Web sites and applications have been designed to facilitate various kinds of sharing and cooperation, but ironically the browser itself has not. Almost everything is shared on the Web, except for the most basic activity, Web navigation or browsing path.

The Web navigation system, including Web page links and browser navigation functions, is built along the lines of a spatial metaphor and provides an important foundation for the Web (Bertel, 2001; Marshall & Shipman, 1993; Stanton & Baber, 1994). Unfortunately, its imitation of the spatial metaphor is incomplete due to the absence of a trace-sharing function (Wexelblat & Maes, 1999). In other words, in a physical space, before making a navigation choice, a user can observe other user traces, both current and past; on the current Web, however, this is not possible.

In fact, as stated in Vannevar Bush's famous 1939 article "As We May Think," which is often cited as an early source of hypertext ideas, proposed not only the idea of links between information, but that people might share the "trails" they create through information space. Group traces can be useful in making navigation choices, irrespective of where we are, either in a physical or the artificial Web space. Previous studies have shown that collaborative Web navigation is an integral part of users' information retrieval practices in many domains, particularly education (Amershi & Morris, 2008; Large et al., 2002; Twidale, Nichols, & Paice, 1997) and knowledge acquisition (Fidel et al., 2000; Hansen & Järvelin, 2005; Morris, 2008). For example, school children work together to find information for group homework assignments (Amershi & Morris, 2008), and academics collaborate on literature searches for jointly-authored publications (Morris, 2008).

HCI (Human-Computer Interaction) and IR (Information Retrieval) researchers have designed several tools aimed at facilitating collaborative Web browsing and navigation, specifically collaborative Web search tools (Amershi & Morris, 2008; Diamadis & Polyzos, 2004; Freyne & Smyth, 2006; Morris & Horvitz, 2007; Pickens et al., 2008) and collaborative Web browsing tools (Anupam et al., 2000; Brandenburg et al., 1998; Graham, 1997; Greenberg & Roseman, 1996; Yeh et al., 1996). These tools provide support for activities such as group query histories, shared views of searching result lists, identical browsing experience, and collaboration on Web activity awareness. Nevertheless, each of these tools either only focuses on a particular specific domain of Web usage or only provides pieces of navigation information in a particular scenario for group collaboration. They seldom address the flaw in current Web navigation systems of a lack of trace-sharing. Consequently, all these tools and approaches have limited usage in terms of common group information foraging on the Web.

Here, we define a group Web trace as the accumulated group visitations on a particular Web page (URL), and we believe that if we make the current Web navigation system more consistent with the spatial metaphor by visualizing group Web traces properly, it can promote Web users' information foraging performance, user experience and group awareness at the same time. Our study attempts to answer two research questions:

- Theoretically, how will information about group Web traces affect a Web user's information foraging performance?
- In practice, how will the presentation of group Web traces impact Web users' information foraging performance and their user experience and group awareness?

In the rest of this paper, we first review related works on navigation, collaboration, and information foraging on the Web. We then analyze the impact of sharing group Web traces from the viewpoint of Information Foraging Theory (Pirolli, 2007). Thereafter, we introduce the design concerns of visualization of group Web traces on a Web page. Next, we describe the design and implementation details of our prototype, the Group Crumb. We report on a longitudinal user study conducted to test the impact of sharing group Web traces by comparing users' Web information foraging performance and experience with and without the assistance of the Group Crumb. We analyze the data collected to ascertain research results. Finally, we conclude by discussing the contributions of this paper and suggesting possible future work.

Related work

Flaws in the current spatial metaphor have been discussed in several previous studies. Stanton and Baber (1994) have already criticized the absence of group traces and the unquestioned assignment of the spatial metaphor, further elaborated by Bertel (2001). According to the latter, the lack of signs of other users' visiting traces and too many unwanted and unsuitable properties of the physical space, such as direction and distance, are motivated by spatial representations of the Web. These issues can potentially lead to incorrect conclusions. Of all the flaws, the absence of group traces is critical now that the Web has evolved into the Web 2.0 era, which focuses more and more on collaboration among Web users, requiring Web space or hyperspace to be a social or group space rather than a solitary space.

Web navigation is an ongoing topic in Web research literature. According to previous studies, following links is the most important navigation action, accounting for 45.7% (Catledge & Pitkow, 1995), 43.4% (Cockburn & Mckenzie, 2001), and 43.5% (Weinreich et al., 2006) of all navigation actions. Hence an improvement in link following, which may be realized by sharing group traces, could substantially increase the efficiency of navigation on the Web.

Social navigation is a stream of research that explores the ways of organizing users' explicit and implicit feedback to support information navigation (Dieberger et al., 2000). In this research domain, several approaches have been developed. Knowledge Sea II is an E-Learning system which proposes a social adaptive navigation support by summing group traffic/traces of Web pages in the corpus, and then visualizing these traces by multiple shades of blue on a dedicated navigation map/index (Brusilovsky et al., 2004). Juggle is a tool of recognizing URLs in text and then automatically opening them in a browser (Georgia & Dieberger, 1997). By this means it simplifies and facilitates explicit social navigation via communication tools, such as email and instant messengers. Compared with these approaches, the approach proposed here is more implicit, generic and supporting multiple groups.

In the research domain of Collaborative Web Browsing, many approaches have been proposed to provide a synchronous browser for tightly coupled group collaboration. Some approaches use a special browser that allows users to control each other's browsers, to know what they are doing, and to know at which page they are looking. Examples include GroupWeb (Greenberg & Roseman, 1996), Albatross (Weinreich et al., 2006) and GroupScape (Graham, 1997). Other approaches use a common browser, but in different ways. The WebVCR system (Anupam et al., 2000) and Artefact framework (Brandenburg et al., 1998) use client side technology, such as a Java applet, to synchronize or share Web page browsing and to set up an additional communication channel for users. These Collaborative Web Browsing methods provide a totally synchronous browser experience between group members. This is the opposite of what we are proposing here, that is, only sharing group traces, the navigation experiences, among group members to promote their information foraging performance and enhance their group awareness.

Utilization of group traces has been observed in many Web research domains. In collaborative Web searches, both the approach of Morris et al. (2008) and that of Sun et al. (2006) use group traces to filter and rank search results. Another interesting tool is WCSA (Diamadis & Polyzos, 2004), in which group traces, called group member URL traversal awareness (GMUTA), are used to help filter search results. In the semantic Web approach of GroupWeb (Grcar et al., 2005), user profiles are mined from group traces. In personal Web searches, the group traces are used to build better queries (Tan et al., 2006), as well as to filter and rank search results (Teevan et al., 2005). Our research differs from the above approaches in that its utilization of group traces is for a different purpose - as a visual heuristic to promote information foraging performance and enhance group awareness.

Mining Web users' navigation patterns is a popular research topic in Web mining. Several studies (AlMurtadha et al., 2010, Ting et al. 2009, Borges and Leven, 2008) have been undertaken in recent years. All these studies mined Web users' navigation patterns and then made predictions to improve users' Web navigation efficiency. Compared with what we are proposing here, these studies are complex and seldom take into account the similarity of group members, whereas, fellow Web users or group members working in the same context can be better predictors than a computer or a complicated algorithm. Meanwhile, these studies predict on patterns mined, without any reasonable explanation of these patterns, which is also different to what we do in this study. We show group navigation traces based on Information Foraging Theory, and explain the effectiveness thereof from a cognitive science viewpoint.

In fact, the sharing of group traces is also an interesting research topic out of the Web studies. Hill et al. (1992) shared the history of interactions between author and reader within documents. Deline et al. (2005) found sharing source code navigation among programmers can improve their comprehension on code. These studies showed sharing group traces promoted users' work performance and enhanced their group awareness. In this paper we extended these studies and found similar results in the information foraging on the Web.

Information foraging

Information Foraging Theory has been used to explain and predict Web users' information foraging actions, especially their navigation choices, on the Web. It models the Web as a space with many information patches, from which Web users can forage information and between which they can travel. It also recognizes that a forager's information gain within a patch is a diminishing function of her within-patch time. Then according to Charnov's Marginal Value Theorem (Charnov, 1976), the within-patch time t_W, between-patch time t_B, user's information gain function g, and average information foraging rate R satisfy,

$$R = g'(t_w) \qquad (1)$$

Furthermore, Information Foraging Theory shows that there are two effects of *between-patch enrichment,* in which a Web user's traveling cost (time) decreases. First, the *within-patch time* also decreases; and second, the *overall information foraging performance* increases (Figure 1).

From an Information Foraging Theory's viewpoint, sharing *group Web traces* among members on the Web is a *between-patch enrichment.* For a Web user with a certain information foraging goal, a Web page may serve her in two ways, either as an *information patch/destination,* from which she forages information, or as a *navigation spot* which is merely by-passed as she finds a path to her destination. Obviously, the *between-path time* of her information foraging on the Web depends on the probability of choosing the right path; in other words, clicking on the correct links on *navigation spots.* If a user has a higher *correct choice probability,* she will have a smaller expected *between-patch time,* which eventually leads to *between-patch enrichment.*

The SNIF-ACT (Fu & Pirolli, 2007) model of Information Foraging Theory predicts a user's navigation choice with a goal G and candidate links C, as a probability function of a given link L's utility $U_{L|G}$,

$$\Pr(L \mid G, C) = \Pr(U_{L|G} > U_{K|G}, \forall K \in C) \qquad (2)$$

According to the Random Utility Model (McFadden, 1974; McFadden et al., 1978), L's utility $U_{L|G}$ in the context of goal G is defined as the sum of all activations received by cognitive chunks representing a user's goal from proximal cues associated with a link, plus some stochastic noise ε.

$$U_{L|G} = \sum_{i \in G} (B_i + \sum_{j \in L} W_j S_{ji}) + \varepsilon \qquad (3)$$

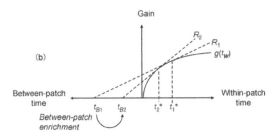

Figure 1. A between-patch enrichment of information patch model. The average rate of information gain, R, increases with a decrease in between-patch time, while simultaneously decreasing the within-patch time (Pirolli, 2007).

Here B_i is the base-level activation of chunk i, and S_{ji} is the association strength between an associated cue j and chunk i. Each proximal cue j emits a source activation W_j, which reflects the Web user's attention at the beginning. These source activations spread across cognitive Spreading Activation (Anderson & Pirolli, 1984) to feature i that is part of the information goal G.

In the *group Web traces* sharing scenario, we assume that there is a *group navigation similarity*, which means that typically group members trust each other and they may have a greater probability of choosing the same navigation link(s) on a Web page. This assumption has been verified in our study described in the *User Study* section.

Therefore, links with *group Web traces* are more likely to be links a Web user may choose to follow, and showing *group Web traces* on a Web page both provides additional heuristics and attracts more attention to these links, which in turn increases the source activation W_j for each proximal cue j of these links. Moreover, these additional cues and increased source activations then spread through cognitive Spreading Activation and hence, lead to a higher *correct choice possibility*, which eventually decreases the *between-patch time*, and as a final result, *between-patch enrichment* occurs.

At this point, it is clear that sharing *group Web traces* among group members realizes *between-path enrichment* of Web information foraging. According to Information Foraging Theory, we therefore, predict that this sharing will lead to a smaller *within-patch time* and higher *overall information foraging performance* for each group member on the Web.

Visualization of group Web traces

Although according to Information Foraging Theory, sharing *group Web traces* increases group members' information foraging performance, given here is actually an implied premise that while sharing group trace information, this sharing will not sabotage Web users' normal cognitive processes on other information within corresponding Web pages. In other words, we must visualize *group Web traces* with little disruption and proper informativeness to a user's cognitive process. Hence, from a cognitive science viewpoint, it is better to show *group Web traces* as some visual hint(s) on links, such as font color, font weight, background color, text decorations, etc., and any explicit additional elements, such as a direct text description or icon, is not an option.

In fact, there is already a similar visual hint, the Bread Crumb (Bernstein et al., 1991), in all contemporary browsers. The BC alters the color of the text and underscore of recently visited links, discriminating them from unvisited links. This visualization has a long history, since about 1991, and is an indispensable part of the spatial metaphor by providing signs of where we have been. Actually, regarding *group Web traces*, the BC is a kind of personal trace on the Web. So, it is reasonable to design the visualization of *group Web traces* in the same way as the BC, which has already been accepted by Web users. Hence we called the group trace visual hint, Group Crumb (GC). Like the Bread Crumb, the GC shows *group Web traces* by altering the appearance of links. Specifically, it alters the font weight and font size of links and adds group visitation information to the tooltips. Here the design decision is based on the principle of no additional elements deduced from cognitive science in the previous paragraph. It does not consider image links, since the visualization here is only for a research prototype verifying our prediction on sharing group Web traces, and this omission does not affect the result.

System design and implementation

We have designed a simple research prototype, called the Group Crumb Prototype (GCP) to evaluate the impact of sharing group Web traces on the information foraging performance and user experience of group members. It consist of two parts, a Firefox extension, called the Group Crumb Extension (GCE), which visualizes Group Crumbs by altering the font size and font weight of links on a Web page, and a server on Django, called the Group Crumb Django (GCD), which stores group members' visitation data in a MySQL database and answers queries from the GCEs (Figure 2).

In practice, when a user opens/enters[1] a Web page, the GCE sends the Web page's URL to the GCD, and queries the GCD about Group Crumb Scents (GCS) of links on that Web page. The GCE then alters the font size and font weight of links on the Web page according to the query result, and adds group visitation information on tooltips (Figure 4). Generally speaking, a link visited recently by more group members will be shown in a bigger font size and a stronger font weight (Figure 4).

---

[1] In contemporary multi-window and multi-tab browsers, a user can either open/close a Web page, or enter/leave a Web page in another window or tab.

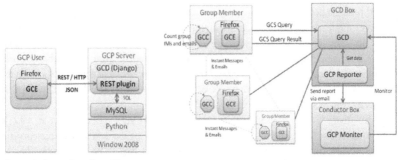

Figure 2. Group Crumb architecture   Figure 3. GCP study environment

(a) An ordinary Web page

(b) A GCP-altered Web page

Figure 4. A partial Web page rendering

Group Crumb Scent

The GCP calculates and then uses the GCS of a link as the dominant factor determining its font size and font-weight. In practice the GCS is calculated in the following way.

The *group visitation scent* on a certain link is an imitation of human memory, which follows the rough formula of a *forgetting curve* (Ebbinghaus, 1913), where t is the number of days since the visitation and λ is the relative strength of memory, which is set to 7 here according to the study of Obendorf et al. on Web page revisitation patterns (Obendorf et al., 2007). In this study, Web users' revisitations older than 7 days (one week) are categorized as 'long-term' revisitations, which despite being valuable, are not well supported in contemporary browsers.

$$s = e^{-\frac{t}{\lambda}} \tag{4}$$

For a particular link l, we sum all the *group visitation scents* S_v as the *group link scent* S_l.

$$S_l = \sum_{v \in V_l} S_v = \sum_{v \in V_l} e^{-\frac{t_v}{\lambda}} \tag{5}$$

Then, the GCS of a certain link is calculated by normalizing its *group link scent* S_l in the range [-1, 1], with regard to the *group link scents* S of all links on the same Web page.

$$G_l = \frac{2 \times S_l - \max(S) - \min(S)}{\max(S) - \min(S)} \tag{6}$$

Finally, GCS is used to alter the font size and font weight of links. In equations (7) and (8), f_s and f_w represent the original values of the link's font size and font-weight, respectively, and f'_s and f'_w are the respective GCP-altered values.

$$f'_s = (1 + \mu \times G_l) \times f_s \tag{7}$$

$$f'_w = \begin{cases} \min(100 \times [\mu \times G_l \times 4] + f_w, 900), G_l > 0 \\ \max(100 \times [\mu \times G_l \times 4] + f_w, 100), G_l < 0 \end{cases} \tag{8}$$

In the above formulas, μ is a configurable parameter used to control the strength of GCS, and f_w is restricted to integer multiples of 100, no greater than 900 according to CSS 2[2].

Foraging vs. Passing

As stated in the *Information Foraging* section, the Group Crumb should separate group members' foraging visitations on information patches from their passing visitations on navigation spots, and only calculate GCS from these foraging visitations.

However, this separation can hardly be done precisely without direct identification of the user, which is obviously impossible in the GCP's implementation. Therefore, we have to find an approximate solution. Fortunately, according to the study of Cockburn et al. (Cockburn & Mckenzie, 2001), Web pages viewed by web users for less than 10 seconds are often passing-through pages, and not pages they are really interested in. Hence we use this heuristic in the GCP to filter these *passing visitations*; that is, the GCE sends all the user's visitation data to the GCD, and the GCD tracks the current viewed Web page of the user, and only considers pages viewed for more than 10 seconds when calculating the GCS.

---

[2] CSS 2 Fonts, http://www.w3.org/TR/CSS21/fonts.html#font-boldness.

GCS Query

The GCP stores group foraging visitations and calculates GCSs on its server, the GCD. When a user opens/enters a Web page, the GCE sends a *GCS query* with GCE_ID, GROUP_ID, URL, ACTION_TYPE[3], and VISIT_TIME to the GCD. The GCD then calculates the GCSs of all links on the Web page according to the URL and GROUP_ID and wraps them all in a corresponding *GCD answer*. Moreover, the GCD caches the URL and VISIT_TIME, and will add a visitation to the former URL if the interval between the two VISIT_TIMEs is more than 10 seconds[4].

According to (8), before altering a Web page, a GCE must know all the GCSs of the links on it. This means that a GCE cannot render *group Web traces* on a Web page properly before the *GCD answer* arrives. Obviously, this delay may cause a user's browser to freeze and thus, have a negative effect on the user's experience. To resolve this issue, the GCP adopts two strategies. First, a *GCE query* is sent asynchronously without blocking the normal page rendering and the GCE visualizes GCs by means of animated changes on the link appearance when the *GCD answer* arrives. Second, instead of sending all links of a Web page in a *GCS query*, only the URL of the queried Web page is sent, and then the GCD figures out all the other links on its own. This is more efficient than sending all links of a Web page since the GCD caches/stores the links of queried Web pages, thus reducing the retrieval time of links in follow-up queries.

Group Crumb Server

We implemented the GCD as a simple Django application deployed in an Apache HTTP server using the mod_python module. We chose Python and Django for their simplicity, easy and rapid development, and maintainability. The GCD stores all group visitation data in a MySQL database, and answers GCE queries via REST Web Services with data in JSON format.

Although scalability and performance issues were not our primary concern, in practice, the scalability of the GCP is good enough for our research purposes. A GCD can handle at least 200 GCEs concurrently, while each GCE issues a GCS query every 10 seconds on average, and without any data loss at the server or frozen browsers at the client.

Privacy

Another important issue we have to consider here is how to protect user privacy when sharing *group Web traces*. We made two decisions about privacy. First, the GCE only shares *group Web traces* among group members; and second, these *group Web*

---

[3] A Web page can be opened by following a link, typing a URL, reloading a bookmark/history, and these actions are distinguished by the ACTION_TYPE parameter.

[4] In the current GCD, other visitations are also stored for research purposes.

traces are only shown in the containing Web page as a Group Crumb without details of group visitations, that is, a user only knows that a link has been visited by some of the group members, but has no idea exactly who. According to our user study results (see *Privacy* section of *Results and Discussion*), these decisions effectively solved the privacy issues.

Initialization and configuration

The GCE_ID, GCD_URL, and GROUP_ID of a GCE must be set or configured properly before executing the GCE. In the current GCE, for the purpose of our research, the GCD_URL is preconfigured to our GCD server, and GROUP_ID can be set via a prompt window when the GCE is first executed, and later changed in the Firefox preferences. A GCE also issues an INITIAL request to the GCD when executed initially. It retrieves Web page visitations longer than 10 seconds during the past 7 days[5] from Firefox's history records, and wraps these in the INITIAL request to the GCD. The GCD stores and allots these visitations to the group identified by the GROUP_ID in the request, and answers the request with a unique GCE_ID generated. In this way, each GCE receives a unique GCE_ID when initially executed and uses it in the subsequent communications with the GCD.

For the purpose of our user study, the GCD was configured as a 'dummy' server to a certain group(s). This means that the GCD did not answer *GCS queries* from GCEs of the configured group(s), and hence these GCEs did not alert Web pages. However, all visitations of the group(s) were still stored for our study.

Table I. Details of groups

Group in Exp.	Team in Comp.	Members	Project
G1	T1	5	**Campus Map**, a mashup Web application
	T2	6	**QReader**, an E-book reader on Android
G2	T3	6	**AnswerIt**, an answering machine on Android
	T4	5	**Happy Hospital**, an SNS game

Table II. Groups' GCD configuration

	Phase 1	Phase 2
G1	active	dummy
G2	dummy	active

User study

We conducted a 2-month longitudinal user study on the GCP to test our prediction, based on Information Foraging Theory, that sharing group Web traces leads to a smaller *within-patch time* and higher *overall information foraging performance*. Hence the study was designed to capture changes in participants' information foraging

---

[5] According to (4), visitations older than 7 days have little *scent.*

before, during and after exposure to their Group Crumbs. The study lasted two months from November 10th, 2010 to January 9th, 2011 with two phases each lasted one month (30 days). Participants are grouped into two groups, namely Group 1 (G1), and group 2 (G2). During the experiment participants' browsers were configured either with or without showing Group Crumbs on Web pages they visited, and their performance data were collected to verify our prediction.

Participants, apparatus and environment

We recruited 22 participants (15 male, 7 female), aged between 19 and 21, from the sophomore class of the Software School of Sun Yat-sen University. All the participants had majored in Software Engineering, and were taking part in a one-year software development competition conducted by the Software School (beginning Oct. 1st, 2009). This made these participants perfect study subjects, since they were already grouped and were working collaboratively on the Web in foraging useful information for their competition projects. The number of members and project for each team are shown in Table I.

We separated the four teams into two groups, G1 and G2. All participants were required to use Firefox, with the GCE Extension installed, as their only browser during the study. In the 1st phase of the experiment, the GCD was configured active for G1' GCEs while dummy for G2's, and vice versa in the 2nd phase (Table II).

All participant groups used agile methods in their software process. They all made use of 2-week iterations, and therefore released their software four times during our study.

Because the duration of the study was long, we developed tools to guarantee it ran effectively and smoothly. The first tool was the GCP Monitor, a long-running process that monitored the GCD. It sent a warning email to experimenters when the GCD's service was unavailable. The second was the GCP Reporter, which was deployed as a scheduled task, executed daily, to report on data collected (Figure 3).

To analyze the GCP's impact on group collaboration, all participants were also required to install a tool called the Group Conversation Counter (GCC), which was only run at the end of each phase. This tool counted the group instant messenger dialogs and email conversations of each participant by retrieving them from configured email addresses and instant messenger accounts of her teammates. The group email conversations of a participant were retrieved directly from the POP server(s) of her email box(es), and the instant messenger dialogs were retrieved from the local message cache file of Tencent QQ[6], which is a popular instant messenger and independently chosen by all participant groups as their primary daily conversation tool. Then the GCC generated a GCC result by counting the numbers of email conversations and instant messenger dialogs each day during the longitudinal user study. A GCC result is a plain

---

[6] http://www.qq.com/

text file containing only the numbers of email conversations and instant messenger dialogs. It did not include anything about the content of the conversations, thereby protecting the participants' privacy.

Surveys and data collected

During the longitudinal study, we collected Web information foraging activities for all participants based on the following fields: GCE_ID, GROUP_ID, VISIT_TIME, URL of the Web page, and ACTION_TYPE (Open, Close, Enter, Leave). At the end of the study, participants were required to submit their GCC results and complete an online survey designed to collect free form comments about users' positive and negative experiences with the GCP and to ascertain the GCP's impact on their group awareness and collaboration. The survey also provided information about which situations participants found the Group Crumb most useful (Table III).

Results and discussion

During the longitudinal study, the participants visited a total of 30,691 Web pages, about 22 pages per day per participant ($\mu=22.3$, $\sigma=9.7$), and dwelled more than 10 seconds on 18,722 (61%) of these, about 14 pages per day per participant ($\mu=14.2$, $\sigma=10.2$). The latter pages were regarded as *information patches,* and the others *navigation spots* (39%). 82% of all Web visitations (20,582) were from following links, but the figure drops to 73% if considering only *information patch* visitations. Among all visitations, each participant spent on average 72.3 sec ($\sigma=8.7$) on a Web page, with the figure increasing to 102.3 sec ($\sigma=8.7$) when excluding visitations to *navigation spots*. Participants conducted a total of 2,798 email conversations and 5,766 instant messenger dialogs during the study. All 22 participants completed the online survey, and some provided addition comments on the usability and their experiences with the GCP.

In the following sections, we compare the data in two collections, Collection Active (CA) and Collection Dummy (CD). CA summarizes participants' performance with Group Crumb's help (GCD active), that is, the data of G1 in phase 1 and G2 in phase 2; and CD summarizes participants' performance without Group Crumb's help (GCD in dummy), that is the data of G2 in phase 1 and G1 in phase 2 (Table II). By this cross summing-up, the biases of time and group were very likely been swept off. We also cite survey results to analyze the GCP's impact on group Web information foraging and collaboration. Significance is reported using one-tailed paired *t*-tests.

Group navigation similarity

The *group navigation similarity* assumption in the *Information Foraging* section was supported by the user study. Either with or without the GCP's help, participants tended to choose those links also visited by their group mates. In the CD, participants selected a total of 6,670 links to follow, about 1% ($\mu =.9\%$, $\sigma =.2\%$) of all 717,423 links presented on all the visited Web pages. However, regarding in *group navigation similarity*, they selected significantly more links, 21% ($\mu =19.7\%$, $\sigma =4.3\%$), to follow from the 6,670 links visited by the group ($p<.01$). The same trend was seen in the CA where participants selected 1% ($\mu =.9\%$, $\sigma =.2\%$), 8,124 links in total, to follow from all 876,852 links presented, and selected significantly more links, 37% ($\mu =37.3\%$, $\sigma =4.4\%$), to follow from the 8,124 links visited by the group ($p<.01$).

GCP effectiveness

We found that the use of the GCP influenced participants' navigation decisions. As shown in the previous section, with the aid of the GCP participants followed significantly more group visited links in the CA ($\mu_1=19.7\%$, $\sigma_1=4.3\%$, $\mu_2=37.3\%$, $\sigma_2=4.4\%$, $p<.01$). Furthermore, in the CD, participants clicked on average 1.2 times ($\mu =1.18$, $\sigma =.13$) on a group visited link; but in the CA, this figure increased significantly to 1.3 ($\mu =1.33$, $\sigma =.12$, $p<.03$). Moreover, the survey results also confirmed that the GCP effectively influenced participants' link following as they preferred to click on a link with a Group Crumb (see 1 in Table II). One participant reported her feelings on the GCP's influence:

> "The GCP gives me great hints about what might be interesting. I prefer to select a GCP link rather than others since my buddies have already polled it."

Between-patch time

We predicted sharing group traces using the GCP as a kind of between-patch enrichment from the viewpoint of Information Foraging Theory. This is consistent with the user study, where both the proportion and dwell time of *navigation spots* dropped after participants were exposed to Group Crumbs. In the CD, without the GCP, 43% ($\mu =42.5\%$, $\sigma =3.7\%$) of the entire visited Web pages were *passing pages* or *navigation spots*; but in the CA, this figure dropped significantly to 36% ($\mu =35.7$, $\sigma =3.6\%$, $p<.03$). Moreover, in the CD, participants spent on average 8 sec ($\mu =8.3$, $\sigma =.7$) on a navigation page; yet in the CA, they only spent 6 sec ($\mu =6.7$, $\sigma =1.1$, $p<.02$). Combining these two facts, it is clear that participants' between-patch time in their information foraging activities on the Web decreased using the GCP, and this confirms the proposition that using the GCP is a *between-patch enrichment*.

Within-patch time

In the CD, participants spent on average 80 sec ($\mu =79.5$, $\sigma =4.2$) on a Web page; but in the CA, they only spent on average 65 sec on a Web page ($\mu =65.1$, $\sigma =4.7$, $p<.01$). Taking only these information patches into account (*within-patch time*), participants spent on average 113 sec per page in the CD ($\mu =112.7$, $\sigma =4.2$), and

92 sec per page in the CA (μ =92.3, σ =5.2, p<.01). This is consistent with the indication from Information Foraging Theory that a decrease in *within-patch time* is a consequence of *between-patch enrichment*.

It is also worth mentioning here, that in the CD the average dwell time on group-shared Web pages, visited by more than one group member, was 84 sec (μ =84.4, σ =4.1), about 8 sec longer than that for other visited Web pages, 77 sec (μ =76.8, σ =3.8, p<.04). In the CA, although the average *within-patch time* decreased, the difference between the dwell-time on group-shared Web pages and others increased significantly to about 14 sec (μ_g=72.7, σ_g=5.2; μ_o=59.2, σ_o=4.8; p<.01).

Information Foraging Theory predicts that an information forager will leave an information patch when its diminished gains drop to the average information foraging rate, and hence dwell time on a rich information patch with higher diminished gains is longer than on a poor one (see Figure 5). According to this, the longer dwell time on group-shared Web pages suggests that these group-shared Web pages had higher diminished gains than the others, and the increase in the difference in dwell time between group-shared Web pages and others can be interpreted as participants choosing to find more valuable information patches with GCP's help.

Overall information foraging performance

In the CD, participants visited 3,811 information patches (μ =173.2, σ =18.6) and spent 429,217 sec on them (μ =19,509, σ =2,030). The average information foraging rate was 0.53 patches per minute (σ =.04). In the CA, participants visited 5,443 information patches (μ =247.4, σ =28.5) and spent 502,607 sec on them (μ =22,846, σ =2,577). The average information foraging rate increased to 0.64 patches per minute (σ =.05, p<.02). This result supported that sharing group traces using the Group Crumb significantly increased participants' *overall information foraging performance*.

GCP users' comments in the survey also confirmed this finding. Participants said:

"I really like the GCP, It makes me more efficient in finding things I am looking for..."

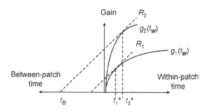

Figure 5. Dwell time difference (time spent in a poor patch t1*, and in a rich patch t2*)

"GCP is a good link filter and recommendation engine for me. It filters those irrelevant links and recommends other interesting links. With its help, I can get information from the Web with less time and errors."

Group awareness and collaboration

Another interesting observation is that the GCP enhanced participants' group awareness and collaboration. In the CA, participants' Web visitations showed a greater group tendency, indicated by a significantly higher proportion of *group-shared* Web pages in *all visited* Web pages than in the CD ($\mu_1=57.5$, $\sigma_1=3.5$, $\mu_2=64.3$, $\sigma_2=3.7$, $p<.02$). This occurred without a significantly longer dwell time on group-shared Web pages than other Web pages ($\mu_1=7.61$, $\sigma_1=3.9$, $\mu_2=13.5$, $\sigma_2=5.1$, $p=.06$).

The same trend was also found in both email conversations and instant messenger dialogs. Together the participants conducted 1244 email conversations in the CD ($\mu=56.5$, $\sigma=4.9$), which increased significantly to 1554 in the CA ($\mu=70.6$, $\sigma=7.3$, $p<.01$). At the same time, they conducted 2365 instant messenger dialogs in the CD ($\mu=107.5$, $\sigma=8.9$), which also increased significantly to 3401 in the CA ($\mu=154.6$, $\sigma=12.3$, $p<.01$). Participants' comments also confirmed this enrichment. One of them said:

"The GCP shows me a group vision of the Web. Knowing your buddy has been somewhere is definitely cool. As you known, following your buddies makes you feel safe and somehow protected in your incoming findings."

Usefulness and usability

Despite the fact that the GCP is only a simple research prototype, our survey results confirmed that it is useful and usable in assisting participants in their information foraging on the Web (Table III).

Table III. Survey Results (Likert-Scale, 1=strongly disagree, ..., 5=strongly agree)

Question	$\bar{x}$
I prefer to click on a link with a Group Crumb.	4.0
The Group Crumb is useful for navigation on the Web.	4.0
The Group Crumb is useful for highlighting useful links.	4.5
The Group Crumb is useful for filtering irrelevant links.	4.0
I experienced less navigation cost/time with Group Crumb's help.	4.0
My Web information foraging efficiency increased with Group Crumb's help.	3.5
I felt better group awareness with Group Crumb's help.	4.5
The Group Crumb clutters original Web pages.	2.5
The Group Crumb is annoying to me.	1.5
The Group Crumb should be more conspicuous.	3.5
I do not mind showing my entire browsing history to my group mates.	1.5
The Group Crumb compromises my privacy.	1.5

Privacy

Recent research (Brush et al., 2009) shows that only about 20% of Web users are comfortable sharing the URLs of Web pages they recently visited. This applies in our experiments as well, but we also found some more specific results. Participants were not happy to show all URLs they visited to their teammates, but they did not mind showing their group Web traces/visitations using the Group Crumb. According to our survey, only 3 of the 22 participants were happy to show a list of all URLs they visited to their teammates, but none of them thought that the GCP compromised their privacy or that sharing *group Web traces* through GCP was dangerous (Table III).

Limitations of the study

There are some limitations to this study. First, we used a selected, small sample population consisting of university students who were working on a specific collaborative task, programming and developing software. This means that this study is limited in educational arena now and we cannot expect our results to generalize to a larger, less homogeneous population on other tasks. Instead, the results of this study provide insight into how GC impacts a skilled Web user's information foraging on the Web for his/her software developing tasks. Second, we applied the factor found by Cockburn to label visitations shorter than 10 seconds as passing visitations, and this approach might be too simple. Further studies with other sophisticated methods are needed. Third, due to previous teammates' biases or mistakes on their information forging, GC may augments links wrongly and then leads the user missing useful links. How to resolve this problem is still an open problem now. Finally, the small sample size in this study may not provide sufficient statistical significance to draw strong conclusions and a longitudinal study using a larger sample size is required to verify our results.

Conclusions and future work

We found that group Web traces complement the current spatial metaphor in contemporary browsers. We predicted that sharing group Web traces would increase Web users' information foraging performance from the viewpoint of Information Foraging Theory.

We presented the design of the Group Crumb, which follows the Bread Crumb's convention and shows group Web traces by altering the appearance of corresponding links on Web pages. We also presented the Group Crumb Prototype, a novel tool for showing Group Crumbs on the Web. With its help, users can see their group Web traces with little effort.

We presented a user study on the impact of showing group Web traces on users' information foraging performance and their group awareness and collaboration. This evaluation is based on the GCP. We found that with the GCP's help, the information foraging performance improved and the group awareness and collaboration was significantly enhanced. These results confirm our prediction of sharing group Web traces, and provide answers to the research questions posed in the introduction. Showing group Web traces consequently improves group members' information foraging performance and also enhances their group awareness and collaboration.

Future work includes extending this study to ascertain the impact of showing group Web traces to users neglected in this work, and a broader deployment of the GCP to explore its impact over longer periods of time and within a larger user population. Future development of the GCP will focus on a better visualization method, a more sophisticated algorithm for identifying passing pages, and perhaps more group collaboration information on the Group Crumb, such as a list of visitors and the time and dwell time of visitations, so long as privacy can be properly protected.

References

AlMurtadha, Y. M., Sulaiman, M. N., Mustapha, N., & Udzir, N. I. (2010): 'Mining Web Navigation Profiles For Recommendation System', *Information Technology Journal*, *9*(4), 790–796.

Amershi, S., & Morris, M. R. (2008) : 'CoSearch: a system for co-located collaborative web search', In *Proceeding of the twenty-sixth annual SIGCHI conference on Human factors in computing systems* (pp. 1647–1656).

Anderson, J. R., & Pirolli, P. L. (1984) : 'Spread of activation', *Journal of Experimental Psychology: Learning, Memory, and Cognition*, *10*(4), 791–798.

Anupam, V., Freire, J., Kumar, B., & Lieuwen, D. (2000): 'Automating Web navigation with the WebVCR', *Computer Networks*, *33*(1-6), 503-517.

Bernstein, M., Bolter, J. D., Joyce, M., & Mylonas, E. (1991): 'Architectures for volatile hypertext', In *Proceedings of the third annual ACM conference on Hypertext* (pp. 243-260). San Antonio, Texas, United States: ACM. doi:10.1145/122974.122999

Bertel, S. (2001): *Benutzerunterst\ützung im World Wide Web mit Hilfe r\äumlicher Konzepte*, Hamburg, Department for Informatics, Universit \ät Hamburg.

Borges, J., & Levene, M. (2008): 'Mining Users' Web Navigation Patterns and Predicting Their Next Step', *nato security through science series d-information and communication security*, *15*, 45.

Brandenburg, J., Byerly, B., Dobridge, T., Lin, J., Rajan, D., & Roscoe, T. (1998): 'Artefact: a framework for low-overhead Web-based collaborative systems', In *Proceedings of the 1998 ACM conference on Computer supported cooperative work* (pp. 189-196). ACM New York, NY, USA.

Brush, A. B., Meyers, B. R., Scott, J., & Venolia, G. (2009): 'Exploring awareness needs and information display preferences between coworkers', In *Proceedings of the 27th international conference on Human factors in computing systems* (pp. 2091-2094). Boston, MA, USA: ACM. doi:10.1145/1518701.1519018

Brusilovsky, P., Chavan, G., & Farzan, R. (2004) : ' Social adaptive navigation support for open corpus electronic textbooks', In *Adaptive Hypermedia and Adaptive Web-Based Systems* (pp. 176–189).

Catledge, L. D., & Pitkow, J. E. (1995): 'Characterizing browsing strategies in the World-Wide web', *Computer Networks and ISDN Systems*, *27*(6), 1065-1073. doi:10.1016/0169-7552(95)00043-7

Charnov, E. L. (1976): 'Optimal foraging, the marginal value theorem', *Theoretical population biology, 9*(2), 129–136.

Cockburn A., & Mckenzie B. (2001): 'What do web users do? An empirical analysis of web use', *International Journal of Human-Computer Studies, 54*, 903-922.

Deline, R., Czerwinski, M., & Robertson, G. (2005): 'Easing Program Comprehension by Sharing Navigation Data', *Visual Languages and Human-Centric Computing, IEEE Symposium on* (Vol. 0, pp 241-248). Los Alamitos, CA, USA: IEEE Computer Society. doi:http://doi.ieeecomputersociety.org/10.1109/VLHCC.2005.32

Diamadis, E. T., & Polyzos, G. C. (2004): 'Efficient cooperative searching on the Web: system design and evaluation', *International journal of human-computer studies, 61*(5), 699–724.

Dieberger, A., Dourish, P., Höök, K., Resnick, P., & Wexelblat, A. (2000, November): 'Social navigation: techniques for building more usable systems', *interactions, 7*, 36–45.

Ebbinghaus, H. (1913): *Memory: A contribution to experimental psychology.* Teachers College, Columbia University.

Fidel, R., Bruce, H., Pejtersen, A. M., Dumais, S., Grudin, J., & Poltrock, S. (2000): 'Collaborative information retrieval', *The New Review of Information Behaviour Research, 1*(1), 235–247.

Freyne, J., & Smyth, B. (2006): 'Cooperating search communities', In *Adaptive Hypermedia and Adaptive Web-Based Systems* (pp. 101–110).

Fu, W., & Pirolli, P. (2007): 'SNIF-ACT: a cognitive model of user navigation on the world wide web', *Hum.-Comput. Interact., 22*(4), 355-412.

Georgia, A. D., & Dieberger, A. (1997): 'Supporting Social Navigation on the World Wide Web', Retrieved from http://citeseerx.ist.psu.edu/viewdoc/summary?doi=10.1.1.25.8360

Graham, T. C. N. (1997): 'Groupscape: Integrating synchronous groupware and the world wide web', In *Proceedings of the IFIP TC13 Interantional Conference on Human-Computer Interaction* (pp. 547-554). Chapman & Hall, Ltd. London, UK, UK.

Grcar, M., Mladenic, D., & Grobelnik, M. (2005): 'User profiling for interest-focused browsing history', In *Workshop on End User Aspects of the Semantic Web, ESWC-2005, Heraklion.*

Greenberg, S., & Roseman, M. (1996): 'GroupWeb: a WWW browser as real time groupware', In *Conference companion on Human factors in computing systems: common ground* (pp. 271-272). Vancouver, British Columbia, Canada: ACM. doi:10.1145/257089.257317

Hansen, P., & Järvelin, K. (2005): 'Collaborative information retrieval in an information-intensive domain', *Information Processing and Management, 41*(5), 1101–1119.

Hill, W. C., Hollan, J. D., Wroblewski, D., & McCandless, T. (1992): 'Edit wear and read wear', *Proceedings of the SIGCHI conference on Human factors in computing systems*, CHI '92 (p 3–9). New York, NY, USA: ACM. doi:10.1145/142750.142751

Large, A., Beheshti, J., & Rahman, T. (2002): 'Gender differences in collaborative web searching behavior: an elementary school study', *Information Processing & Management, 38*(3), 427–443.

Marshall, C. C., & Shipman III, F. M. (1993): 'Searching for the missing link: discovering implicit structure in spatial hypertext', In *Proceedings of the fifth ACM conference on Hypertext* (p. 230).

McFadden, D. (1974): 'Conditional logit analysis of qualitative choice behavior', *Frontiers in econometrics, 8*, 105–142.

McFadden, D. et al. (1978): 'Modelling the choice of residential location', *Spatial interaction theory and planning models, 25*, 75–96.

Morris, M. R., & Horvitz, E. (2007): 'SearchTogether: an interface for collaborative web search', In *Proceedings of the 20th annual ACM symposium on User interface software and technology* (p. 12).

Morris, M. R. (2008): 'A survey of collaborative web search practices', In *Proceeding of the twenty-sixth annual SIGCHI conference on Human factors in computing systems* (pp. 1657-1660). Florence, Italy: ACM. doi:10.1145/1357054.1357312

Morris, M. R., Teevan, J., & Bush, S. (2008): 'Enhancing collaborative web search with personalization: groupization, smart splitting, and group hit-highlighting', In *Proceedings of the ACM 2008 conference on Computer supported cooperative work* (pp. 481-484). San Diego, CA, USA: ACM. doi:10.1145/1460563.1460640

Obendorf, H., Weinreich, H., Herder, E., & Mayer, M. (2007): 'Web page revisitation revisited: implications of a long-term click-stream study of browser usage', In *Proceedings of the SIGCHI conference on Human factors in computing systems* (pp. 597-606). San Jose, California, USA: ACM. doi:10.1145/1240624.1240719

Pickens, J., Golovchinsky, G., Shah, C., Qvarfordt, P., & Back, M. (2008): 'Algorithmic mediation for collaborative exploratory search', In *Proceedings of the 31st annual international ACM SIGIR conference on Research and development in information retrieval* (pp. 315–322).

Pirolli, P. L. T. (2007): *Information Foraging Theory: Adaptive Interaction with Information* (1st ed.). Oxford University Press, USA.

Stanton, N. A., & Baber, C. (1994): 'The Myth of Navigating in Hypertext: How a" Bandwagon" Has Lost Its Course!', *Journal of educational multimedia and hypermedia*.

Sun, J., Wang, X., Shen, D., Zeng, H., & Chen, Z. (2006): 'Mining clickthrough data for collaborative web search', In *Proceedings of the 15th international conference on World Wide Web* (pp. 947-948). Edinburgh, Scotland: ACM. doi:10.1145/1135777.1135958

Tan, B., Shen, X., & Zhai, C. (2006): 'Mining long-term search history to improve search accuracy', In *Proceedings of the 12th ACM SIGKDD international conference on Knowledge discovery and data mining* (pp. 718-723). Philadelphia, PA, USA: ACM. doi:10.1145/1150402.1150493

Teevan, J., Dumais, S. T., & Horvitz, E. (2005): 'Personalizing search via automated analysis of interests and activities', In *Proceedings of the 28th annual international ACM SIGIR conference on Research and development in information retrieval* (p. 456).

Ting, I. H., Clark, L., & Kimble, C. (2009): 'Identifying web navigation behaviour and patterns automatically from clickstream data', *International Journal of Web Engineering and Technology*, 5(4), 398–426.

Twidale, M. B., Nichols, D. M., & Paice, C. D. (1997): 'Browsing is a collaborative process', *Information Processing & Management*, 33(6), 761–783.

Weinreich, H., Obendorf, H., Herder, E., & Mayer, M. (2006): 'Off the beaten tracks: exploring three aspects of web navigation', In *Proceedings of the 15th international conference on World Wide Web* (pp. 133-142). Edinburgh, Scotland: ACM. doi:10.1145/1135777.1135802

Wexelblat, A., & Maes, P. (1999): 'Footprints: history-rich tools for information foraging', In *Proceedings of the SIGCHI conference on Human factors in computing systems: the CHI is the limit*, CHI '99 (pp. 270–277). New York, NY, USA: ACM. doi:10.1145/302979.303060

Yeh, P. J., Chen, B. H., Lai, M. C., & Yuan, S. M. (1996): 'Synchronous navigation control for distance learning on the Web', *Computer Networks and ISDN Systems*, 28(7-11), 1207-1218.

SCHO: An Ontology Based Model for Computing Divergence Awareness in Distributed Collaborative Systems

Khaled Aslan, Nagham Alhadad, Hala Skaf-Molli, Pascal Molli
LINA, Université de Nantes, France
*khaled.aslan-almoubayed@univ-nantes.fr, nagham.alhadad@univ-nantes.fr,
hala.skaf@uni-nantes.fr, pascal.molli@univ-nantes.fr*

Abstract. Multi-synchronous collaboration allows people to work concurrently on copies of a shared document which generates divergence. Divergence awareness allows to localize where divergence is located and estimate how much divergence exists among the copies. Existing divergence awareness metrics are highly coupled to their original applications and can not be used outside their original scope. In this paper, we propose the SCHO ontology: a unified formal ontology for constructing and sharing the causal history in a distributed collaborative system. Then we define the existing divergence metrics in a declarative way based on this model. We validate our work using real data extracted from software engineering development projects.

Introduction

Web 2.0 applications showed the importance of collaborative systems. These systems changed the internet users into web writers. Many collaboration tools are currently available like: Wikis, blogs, video-conferencing systems, version control systems. These collaboration tools are classified using Ellis matrix (Ellis and Gibbs, 1989). This matrix is based on two dimensions; time and space. Users can be distributed in time and space. But there is another dimension which is working on different copies. This collaboration mode is called multi-synchronous (Dourish, 1995). In this mode users replicate shared objects and they converge or diverge among each other. This divergence can be observed, measured and visualized. This is called divergence awareness.

Many previous work have addressed the measurement and the visualization of the divergence. Divergence awareness is provided in different systems with ad-hoc visualizations, such as State Treemap (Molli et al., 2001), Palantir (Sarma et al., 2003), Edit Profile (Papadopoulou et al., 2006), Wooki (Weiss et al., 2007), etc.

Existing systems define their own divergence metrics without a common formal definition. Metrics are coupled with the application and cannot be used outside their original scope. There is no previous work that tried to build a unified formal model for divergence awareness. Unified model for computing divergence opens the opportunity to build a middleware for distributed collaborative systems.

Multi-synchronous collaborative systems rely on optimistic replication models (Rahhal et al., 2009). Optimistic replication models are based on history sharing which are application independent. We propose to conceptualize and formalize the sharing of causal history in distributed collaborative system. This allows to compute divergence metrics in a declarative way independently of the application.

In this paper, we use semantic web technology to define an ontology for constructing and sharing the causal history in a distributed collaborative system. Then we define the existing divergence metrics in a declarative way based on this model. We validate our work using real data extracted from software engineering development projects.

The paper is structured as follows. First section presents divergence metrics in distributed collaborative systems. The second section details the SCHO ontology. The third section presents the formal definition of divergence awareness metrics based on this ontology. The fourth section presents the validation of the proposed model using real data. The last section concludes the paper.

Divergence Metrics in Distributed Collaborative Systems

Divergence occurs when there are more than one copy of a shared document and participants can modify their copies in parallel. A cooperative work is a cycle of divergence and convergence. Divergence occurs when two activities have different views of a shared document. After divergence participants synchronize their activities to reestablish a common view of the document; further individual activities will cause divergence again, necessitating further synchronization and so on (Dourish, 1995). State Treemap (Molli et al., 2001), Palantir (Sarma et al., 2003), Edit Profile (Papadopoulou et al., 2006), Wooki (Weiss et al., 2007) are examples of tools that provide the user with divergence awareness.

State Treemap

State Treemap(Molli et al., 2001) is a divergence awareness mechanism, it enables the participant to be aware of the differences among her documents and the others' documents by using the different document states:

- *Locally Modified* enables the participant to know that her own copy was modified where the others are not.

- *Remotely Modified* makes the participant aware of the changes that occur in the remote workspaces.

- *Need Update* means that a new version of the document is available.

- *Potential Conflict* means that more than one participant are updating the same document.

When a document has been modified by a participant, it will be marked as (Local Modified) in her own workspace, where in the others participants' workspaces it will be marked as (Remotely Modified).

Palantir

Palantir (Sarma et al., 2003) is another awareness tool that provides software developers with insight into others' workspaces. It gives awareness information about concurrent modifications performed in isolation in the context of configuration management systems. Palantir captures a number of events, for instance, *added, removed, changes in progress, changes committed,* etc. The effect of the changes is computed and presented to the users by means of two metrics: the severity and impact metrics. The severity metric measures how much a component in a user's workspace has changed when compared to its latest checked version in the repository, or its version on the collaborators workspaces. It can be binary, indicating that a change of any kind occurred, or a number indicating the percentage of lines of code that were modified in any way. The impact measure takes into consideration the code dependencies and computes how much a component in a local workspace is affected by changes to related components in remote workspaces. Table I summarizes the awareness states defined in Palantir proposal.

Edit Profile

Edit Profile (Papadopoulou et al., 2006) provides awareness at different levels: document, paragraph, sentence, word and character. The participant has the possibility to choose at which level she needs to be aware of the changes on a document. So the metrics are calculated based on the participant choice of details. The participant also has the possibility to choose which type of operations she is interested in. For example; insert or delete operations. The system assigns a different color for each participant to distinguish his/her contribution from the others.

Event	Meaning
Populated	Artifact has been placed in a workspace
Synchronized	Artifact has been Synchronized with repository
ChangesInProgress	Artifact has Changed in the workspace
ChangesReverted	Artifact has been returned to it's original state
ChangesCommitted	New Version of artifact has been stored in the repository
SeverityChanged	Amount of changes to an artifact has changed

Table I. Palantir divergence awareness states.

Wooki (Concurrent Modifications)

Wooki (Weiss et al., 2007) is a P2P wiki composed of a P2P network of autonomous wiki servers. Each wiki page is replicated over the whole set of server. A change performed on a wiki server is immediately applied to the local copy and then propagated to the other sites. A remote change when received by a server is merged with local changes and then applied to the local copy. To avoid the conflicts, the redundancy or even the unreliable information that result from the merge, a concurrency awareness mechanism is used. This mechanism makes users aware of the status of the pages they access regarding concurrency: Has this page been merged automatically? In this case show me where concurrent changes occur since the last reviewed state?

Existing systems such as State Treemap, Palantir, Edit Profile and Wooki; define their own divergence metrics without a common formal definition. Metrics are coupled with the application and cannot be used outside their original scope. In the next section, we propose a unified formal model for divergence awareness. This model allows to compute all existing divergence metrics.

SCHO: Shared Causal History Ontology

Divergence occurs when there are more than one copy of a shared document. Optimistic replication model (Saito and Shapiro, 2005) considers (N) sites sharing copies of shared document. A document is modified by executing an operation on it. Any operation has the following life cycle:

1. Generated on one site and executed locally immediately,

2. broadcasted to the other sites,

3. received by other sites and re-executed.

The causality property is essential in a collaborative system to avoid users' confusion (Sun et al., 1998). Causality ensures that all operations are ordered by a precedence relation in the sense of the Lamport's happened-before relation (Lamport, 1978). Therefore they will be executed in same order on every site. Broadcasting operations is not fully determined in the general optimistic replication framework. But it is assumed that all operations should be eventually delivered to all sites. The causality and broadcasting are application independent.

We observed that divergence metrics on a document can be computed relying on the state of its operations according to the operation life cycle in the optimistic replication model. Our approach is to define an ontology to formalize concepts and relations that allow to build and to share causal histories. This ontology allows the formal definition of existing divergence metrics and to calculate them as semantic queries.

The broadcast is represented using the general approach of publish/subscribe that can be used by any distributed collaborative system (Rahhal et al., 2009). The model is not application dependent. Consequently, we have to determine the underlying concepts required to exchange change sets i.e. set of operations. The publish/subscribe model works as follows:

- When a document is modified on a site, patches are generated. A patch is a set of operations related to one document.

- Several patches can be combined in one changeset that can be published into one or several channels called PushFeeds.

- An authorized site can create a PullFeed corresponding to an existing Push-Feed and pull changesets. Then the patches contained in the changesets can be re-executed locally. If needed, the integration process merges this modification with concurrent ones, generated either locally or received from a remote site.

Unified Shared Causal History Model (SCHO)

The Shared Causal History Ontology (SCHO) shown in Figure 1 represents all the concepts of SCHO: changesets, patches, push and pull feeds. This ontology enables the SCHO users to query the current state of the document and its complete history using semantic queries. This ontology is populated through the user interaction with the system using five basic operations: *createPatch*, *createPush*, *push*, *createPull* and *pull*. These operations are inspired by the Push/Pull/Clone model used in distributed version control systems such as Git, Mercurial and Bazaar (Allen et al., 1995). These operations create instances of the SCHO ontology. The details and the algorithms of each operation are presented in the following section.

Each site can perform five operations:

- createPatch: Generates operations

- createPush: Creates a topic (or feed) in the publish/subscribe model

- push: Publishes local operations on the feed

- createPull: Subscribes to a remote feed

- pull: Consumes remote operations.

These five operations enable the building and sharing of causal history.

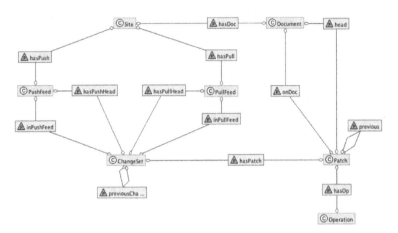

Figure 1. Shared Causal History Ontology.

The OWL file for the Shared Causal History Ontology (SCHO) is provided in Appendix A.

The ontology defines basic concepts common to distributed version control systems such as ChangeSet, Patch, Previous, Operation, etc. It also defines more precise concepts such as PullFeed and PushFeed. These concepts allow the distinction between published/unpublished operations and consumed/unconsumed operations which is essential for computing divergence awareness.

- *Site*: a site has the following properties:

    - siteID: This attribute contains the identifier of the site.

    - hasPush, hasPull and hasDoc : The range of these properties are respectively a *PushFeed*, a *PullFeed* and a *Document*. A site has several PushFeeds, several PullFeeds and several Documents.

- *Document*: a document has the following properties:

    - docID: This attribute contains the identifier of the document.

    - head: This property points to the last *Patch* applied to the document.

- *Operation*: This concept represents a change in a document. An operation has the following property:

    - operationID: This attribute contains the unique identifier of the operation.

378

- *Patch*: A set of operations. A patch is calculated during the save of document. A patch has the following properties:

  - patchID: A unique identifier of the patch.
  - onDoc: The range of this property is the *Document* where the patch was applied.
  - hasOp: This property points to the *Operations* generated when the document was saved.
  - previous: Points to the precedent executed *Patch* on the local site.

- *ChangeSet*: A set of patches. This concept is important to support transactional changes. It allows to group patches generated on multiple documents. Therefore, it is possible to push modifications on multiple documents. it has the following properties:

  - changSetID: A unique identifier of a *ChangeSet*.
  - hasPatch: Points to the *Patches* generated since the last push.
  - previousChangeSet: Points to the precedent *ChangeSet*.
  - inPushFeed: The range of this property is a *PushFeed*. This property indicates the *PushFeed* that publishes the *ChangeSet*.
  - inPullFeed: The range of this property is a *PullFeed*. This property indicates the *PullFeed* that pulls a *ChangeSet*.

- *PushFeed*: This concept is used to publish changes made on a site. It has the following properties:

  - pushID: A unique identifier of the *PushFeed*.
  - hasPushHead: This property points to the last published *ChangeSet*.

- *PullFeed*: This concept is used to receive the changes made on a remote Site. It has the following properties:

  - pullID: A unique identifier of the *PullFeed*.
  - hasPullHead: This property points to the last pulled *ChangeSet*.

The ontology is managed by the five operations mentioned earlier. The algorithms for these operations are presented in the following. These algorithms ensure that each site implements a causal reception (Rahhal et al., 2009). Consequently, the proposed framework ensures causality.

Unified Shared Causal History Algorithms

The *createPatch* operation is called when a document is modified. It calls a *diff* function that computes the operations related to a particular type of document. The *diff* function is an application dependent function.

```
createPatch(doc : String, docMod : String) :
 Patch(pid = concat(site.siteID, site.logicalClock++))
 foreach op ∈ diff(doc, docMod) do
   Operation(opid = concat(site.siteID, site.logicalClock++))
   hasOp(pid, opid)
 endfor
 previous(pid, doc.head)
 head(doc, pid)
 onDoc(pid, doc)
```

The communication between sites is made through feeds. The *createPush* operation creates a PushFeed. A PushFeed is used to publish the changes.

```
createPush(name : String, docs : set of Document ) :
 PushFeed(name)
 hasPush(site, name)
 call Push(name)
```

The *push* operation creates a ChangeSet corresponding to the documents and adds it to the PushFeed.

```
push(name : String) :
 ChangeSet(csid=concat(site.siteID, site.logicalClock++))
 inPushFeed(csid, name)
 published = {∃x∃y(Patch(x)∧Changeset(y)∧inPushFeed(y,name)∧hasPatch(y,x))}
 patches = { ∃x∃p (Patch(P)∧Document(x)∧onDoc(x,p))}
 foreach patch ∈ patches / published
   hasPatch(csid, patch)
 endfor
 previousChangeSet(csid, name.hasPushHead)
 hasPushHead(name, csid)
```

PullFeeds are created to pull changes from PushFeeds on remote sites to the local site. A PullFeed is related to a PushFeed. In the sense that it is impossible to pull unpublished data. The *createPull* operation perform this task.

```
createPull(name : String, pushID : int) :
 PullFeed(name);
 call Pull(name);
```

The *pull* operation fetches the published ChangeSets that have not been pulled yet. It adds these ChangeSets to the PullFeed and integrate them to the documents on the pulled site.

```
pull(name : String) :
  cs = get(name.headPullFeed)
  while (cs ≠ null)
  CS' = {∃x(ChangeSet(x)∧inPushFeed(x,name))}
  if cs ∉ CS' then
    inPullFeed(cs, name)
    call Integrate(cs)
  endif
  cs = cs.previousChangeSet
  endwhile
```

The "Integrate" function in the *pull* algorithm is an Commutative Replicated Data Type (CRDT) algorithm (Weiss et al., 2010) (Weiss et al., 2009) (Preguica et al., 2009)

Divergence Metrics in SCHO

This section details the formal definition of existing divergence awareness metrics based on SCHO model. Divergence awareness metrics are calculated on a site for a given document. We use the following notations: *LS* to denote a local site on which divergence metrics are calculated. *RS*: to denote a remote site. We define the following formula:

- *onSite(P,D,S):* This means that a patch P belongs to a document D was generated on a site S.

$$onSite(P, D, S) \equiv \exists P \exists D \exists S : Patch(P) \wedge Document(D) \wedge Site(S) \wedge onDoc(P, D) \wedge hasDoc(S, D)$$

- *inPushFeed(P,S):* This means that a patch P is published by the site S.

$$inPushFeed(P, S) \equiv \exists P \exists PF \exists S : Patch(P) \wedge PushFeed(PF) \wedge Site(S) \wedge hasPush(S, PF) \wedge inPushFeed(P, PF)$$

- *inPullFeed(P,S) :* This means that a patch P is consumed by the site S.

$$inPullFeed(P, S) \equiv \exists P \exists PF \exists S : Patch(P) \wedge PullFeed(PF) \wedge Site(S) \wedge hasPull(S, PF) \wedge inPullFeed(P, PF)$$

State Treemap Divergence Awareness

To calculate the State Treemap metrics using the SCHO model, we made the following interpretations and defined the corresponding formula.

- *Locally Modified(LM):* There are new patches in a local site which are not published in its PushFeeds.

$LM(D, LS) \equiv \exists P \exists D \exists LS : Patch(P) \wedge Document(D) \wedge Site(LS) \wedge onSite(P, D, LS) \wedge \neg inPushFeed(P, LS)$

- *Remotely Modified(RM):* There are new patches in remote sites which are not in the PullFeeds of the current site.

$RM(D, LS) \equiv \exists P \exists D \exists LS \exists RS : Patch(P) \wedge Document(D) \wedge Site(LS) \wedge Site(RS) \wedge (LS \neq RS) \wedge onSite(P, D, RS) \wedge \neg inPullFeed(P, LS)$

- *Potential Conflict (PC):* It is the state where the document is Locally Modified and Remotely Modified. This is the intersection of the two previous states.

$PC(D, LS) \equiv \exists D \exists LS \exists RS : Document(D) \wedge Site(LS) \wedge Site(RS) \wedge (LS \neq RS) \wedge LM(D, LS) \wedge RM(D, LS)$

- *Need Update(LNU):* There are PushFeed(s) in remote sites that were not pulled locally.

$LNU(D, LS) \equiv \exists P \exists D \exists LS \exists RS : Patch(P) \wedge Document(D) \wedge Site(LS) \wedge Site(RS) \wedge (LS \neq RS) \wedge inPushFeed(P, RS) \wedge \neg inPullFeed(P, LS)$

- *Will Conflict (WC):*

$WC(D, LS) \equiv \exists D \exists LS : Document(D) \wedge Site(LS) \wedge LNU(D, LS) \wedge LM(D, LS)$

- *Locally Up To Date (UTD)*

$UTD \equiv \forall D \forall S : Document(D) \wedge Site(S) \wedge \neg LM(D, S) \wedge \neg RM(D, S)$

Palantir Divergence Awareness

We define the divergence awareness of Palantir detailled in the table I using SCHO ontology.

- *Populated (Pop):* A document has been created on a site.

$$Pop \equiv \exists D \exists LS \forall RS : Document(D) \wedge Site(LS) \wedge Site(RS) \wedge (LS \neq RS) \wedge$$
$$hasDoc(LS, D) \wedge \neg hasDoc(RS, D)$$

- **Change in progress (CP):**

  This state is similar to the Locally-Modified or Remotely-Modified states already mentioned in State Treemap.

$$CP \equiv \exists D \exists S : Document(D) \wedge Site(S) \wedge (LM(D, S) \vee RM(D, S))$$

- **Change Reverted:** The document has returned to its original state.

$$ChangeReverted \equiv \exists UndoOperation(LS)$$

- **Severity Changed:**

  The number of patches has been done on a document.

$$\sum P : P \in \{LM(D, S)\}$$
$$\sum P : P \in \{RM(D, S)\}$$

It is interesting to notice that the SCHO model allows to use State Treemap metrics to calculate Palantir metrics. This was not possible without the formal ontology.

Concurrent modification Divergence Awareness

The patches which were made locally in parallel with the patches which were made remotely. If we know the causal relation between patches on a document we could know the concurrent patches. The multi-synchronous environment satisfies the causality which ensures that all the operations are ordered by a previous relation. This means that the operations will be executed in same order on every site. The history in this approach will be causal graph.

$$CM \equiv \exists D \exists S \exists P1 \exists P2 : Document(D) \wedge Site(S) \wedge hasDoc(S, D) \wedge$$
$$onDoc(P1, D) \wedge onDoc(P2, D) \wedge \neg previous(P1, P2)$$

Validation

In order to validate our approach we populated the SCHO ontology with the causal history data. We used *git* (Git, 2005) repositories. *git* is a distributed version control system that supports a multi-synchronous collaboration. *git* repositories have rich sets of data with different size that can be used to compute divergence metrics.

To use *git* data, First we had to inject the *git* history data into a triple store to populate our ontology. We used the Jena TDB (Jena, 2009) triple store, then we implemented a parser code which is responsible for the mapping between the concepts defined in *git* history and SCHO ontology. Figure 2 shows the history log of a sample *git* project.

We made the following assumptions when we parsed the *git* history:

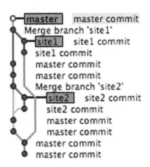

Figure 2. A sample project *git* history.

- We considered the project as one shared object, so any changeset we find is a modification to this object.

- Whenever we find a branch in the history we create a PushFeed and the corresponding Site.

- Whenever we find a merge changeset we create a PullFeed and the corresponding Site.

- Each site represents one user.

So for the sample project we will have: three Sites, two PullFeeds, two Push-Feeds and thirteen ChangeSets. Figure 3 shows the populated ontology resulting from parsing the *git* history. Figure 4 shows the same RDF graph but without the concepts for the sake of clarity.

Based on the assumptions mentioned above we were able to find the different sites and the push/pull interactions between the sites as it is shown in Figure 4.

Then we used the metrics described earlier to calculate the divergence between the sites using SPARQL (SPARQL, 2008) queries. For example the following query returns the state *Remotely Modified* for a ChangeSet *$CSid*.

```
SELECT ?pf   WHERE {
        MS2W: $CSid MS2W: inPullFeed ?pf .
        MS2W: $CSid MS2W: date  ?date  .
        ?pf MS2W: hasPullHead ?CSHead
        MS2W:?CSHead MS2W: date  ?headDate .
        NOT EXISTS { MS2W: $CSid MS2W: published  "true".}
        FILTER (xsd : dateTime (?headDate)  <= xsd : dateTime (?date))
        }
```

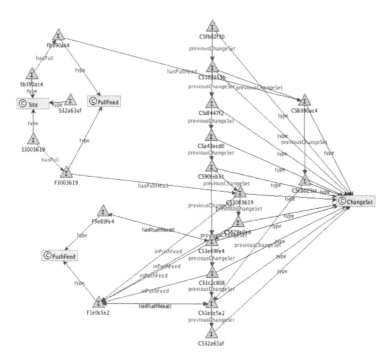

Figure 3. A sample project equivalent RDF graph.

The following query returns the state *Published* for a ChangeSet *$CSid*.

```
SELECT ?pf  ?date WHERE {
      MS2W: $CSid MS2W: inPushFeed ?pf  .
      MS2W: $CSid MS2W: date ?date  .
      FILTER ( xsd: dateTime (?date) <= \ $date ^^xsd: dateTime )
      }
```

If a ChangeSet is not in one of these states i.e. not *Published* and not *Remotely Modified* then it will be in the state *Locally Modified* Table II shows the resulted states for State Treemap and Palantir for our sample project.

We plotted the corresponding divergence graph. Figure 5 shows the results we found for the sample *git* project. We can observe clearly the divergence and convergence phases.

Figure 4. A sample project equivalent RDF graph without the concepts.

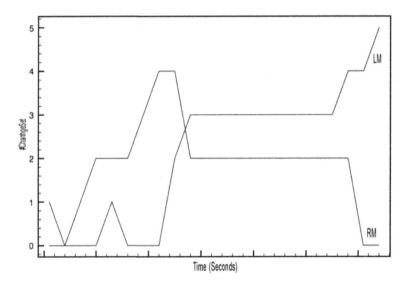

Figure 5. Divergence awareness for sample project.

ChangeSet No.	State Treemap	Palantir
1	Locally Modified	Populated
2	Up to Date	Changes Committed
3	Remotely Modified	Change in Progress
4	Remotely Modified	Change in Progress
5	Potential Conflict	Change in Progress
6	Remotely Modified	Changes Committed
7	Remotely Modified	Change in Progress
8	Remotely Modified	Change in Progress
9	Potential Conflict	Change in Progress
10	Potential Conflict	Change in Progress
11	Potential Conflict	Change in Progress
12	Locally Modified	Synchronized
13	Locally Modified	Change in Progress

Table II. Divergence awareness results for the sample project.

Then we used real *git* projects to validate the approach, such as reddit (Reddit, 2008), gollum (Gollum, 2010), CakePHP (CakePHP, 2005) and MongoDB (MongoDB, 2009). The reddit project has 424 changesets in its *git* history over 26 months. The gollum project has 554 changesets over 10 months. The CakePHP project has 7508 changesets over 64 months. The mongoDB has 11086 changesets over 38 months.

Table III shows the details of each project and the execution time for populating the ontology with the causal history of these projects that we used to validate our approach.

Project name	#ChangeSets	Project Lifespan (month)	Execution time (ms)
Sample project	13	-	2079
Reddit	424	26	3549
Gollum	554	10	7976
CakePHP	7508	64	384409
MongoDB	11086	38	783560

Table III. Execution time for populating the SCHO ontology.

Figures 6, 7 and 8 show the results obtained after calculating the divergence awareness metrics on the reddit, gollum and mongoDB projects respectively. The *Y-axis* represents the number of changesets, while the *X-axis* represents the time.

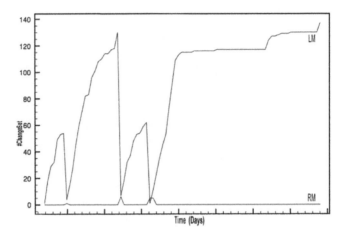

Figure 6. Divergence awareness for reddit project.

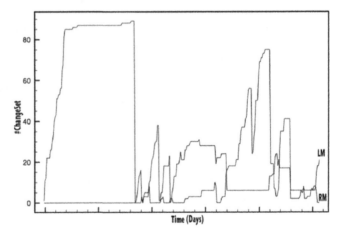

Figure 7. Divergence awareness for gollum project.

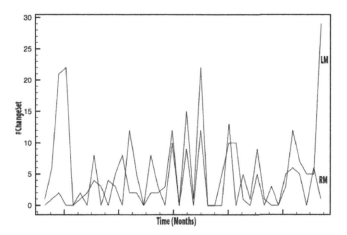

Figure 8. Divergence awareness for mongoDB project.

Conclusion

Building a system that computes divergence awareness can be a very challenging task. Different propositions have been made to compute divergence awareness, like StateTreemap, Palantir, etc. Such divergence metrics are highly dependent on applications and cannot be reused outside of their original scope. In this work, we proposed a general framework that allow to capture and to share causal histories. We expressed this model using semantic technologies. Next, we demonstrated how it is possible to compute all existing divergence metrics on this framework using semantic queries. Thus, divergence metrics are no more dependent of application models. We validated this result by transforming the distributed version control systems history into this ontology and computing the divergence metrics on them.

In the future we plan to embed SCHO ontology inside distributed version control systems in order to allow users and developers to take advantage of divergence awareness and semantic technologies. We also plan to analyze more systems to characterize divergence evolution in time.

References

Allen, L., G. Fernandez, K. Kane, D. Leblang, D. Minard, and J. Posner (1995): 'ClearCase MultiSite: Supporting Geographically-Distributed Software Development'. *Software Configuration Management: Scm-4 and Scm-5 Workshops: Selected Papers.*

CakePHP (2005): 'PHP framework'. http://www.cakephp.org/.

Dourish, P. (1995): 'The Parting of the Ways: Divergence, Data Management and Collaborative Work'. In: *4th European Conference on Computer Supported Cooperative Work.*

Ellis, C. A. and S. J. Gibbs (1989): 'Concurrency Control in Groupware Systems'. In: *SIGMOD Conference*, Vol. 18. pp. 399–407.

Git (2005): 'Fast Version Control System'. http://git-scm.com/.

Gollum (2010): 'A wiki built on top of Git'. https://github.com/github/gollum.git.

Jena (2009): 'Open source Semantic Web framework for Java'. http://openjena.org/.

Lamport, L. (1978): 'Times, Clocks, and the Ordering of Events in a Distributed System'. *Communications of the ACM*, vol. 21, no. 7, pp. 558–565.

Molli, P., H. Skaf-Molli, and C. Bouthier (2001): 'State Treemap: an Awareness Widget for Multi-Synchronous Groupware'. In: *Seventh International Workshop on Groupware - CRIWG*. IEEE Computer Society.

MongoDB (2009): 'Document oriented database'. http://www.mongodb.org/.

Papadopoulou, S., C. Ignat, G. Oster, and M. Norrie (2006): 'Increasing Awareness in Collaborative Authoring through Edit Profiling'. In: *IEEE Conference on Collaborative Computing: Networking, Applications and Worksharing - CollaborateCom 2006*. Atlanta, Georgia, USA.

Preguica, N., J. M. Marques, M. Shapiro, and M. Letia (2009): 'A Commutative Replicated Data Type for Cooperative Editing'. *2009 29th IEEE International Conference on Distributed Computing Systems*, pp. 395–403.

Rahhal, C., H. Skaf-Molli, P. Molli, and S. Weiss (2009): 'Multi-synchronous Collaborative Semantic Wikis'. In: *10th International Conference on Web Information Systems Engineering - WISE '09*, Vol. 5802 of *LNCS*. pp. 115–129, Springer.

Reddit (2008): 'Reddi - the voice of the internet'. http://www.reddit.com/.

Saito, Y. and M. Shapiro (2005): 'Optimistic replication'. *ACM Computing Surveys*, vol. 37, no. 1, pp. 42–81.

Sarma, A., Z. Noroozi, and A. V. D. Hoek (2003): 'Palantr: Raising Awareness among Configuration Management Workspaces'. pp. 444–454.

SPARQL (2008): 'SPARQL Protocol and RDF Query Language'. http://www.w3.org/TR/rdf-sparql-query/.

Sun, C., X. Jia, Y. Zhang, Y. Yang, and D. Chen (1998): 'Achieving convergence, causality preservation, and intention preservation in real-time cooperative editing systems'. *ACM Transactions on Computer-Human Interaction (TOCHI)*, vol. 5, no. 1, pp. 63–108.

Weiss, S., P. Urso, and P. Molli (2007): 'Wooki: a P2P Wiki-based Collaborative Writing Tool'. In: *Web Information Systems Engineering*. Nancy, France.

Weiss, S., P. Urso, and P. Molli (2009): 'Logoot : a Scalable Optimistic Replication Algorithm for Collaborative Editing on P2P Networks'. In: *International Conference on Distributed Computing Systems (ICDCS)*. IEEE.

Weiss, S., P. Urso, and P. Molli (2010): 'Logoot-Undo: Distributed Collaborative Editing System on P2P Networks'. *IEEE Transactions on Parallel and Distributed Systems*, vol. 21, no. 8.

A   SCHO Ontology described in OWL

```
Namespace(rdf    = <http://www.w3.org/1999/02/22-rdf-syntax-ns#>)
Namespace(owl    = <http://www.w3.org/2002/07/owl#>)
Namespace(xsd    = <http://www.w3.org/2001/XMLSchema#>)
Namespace(rdfs   = <http://www.w3.org/2000/01/rdf-schema#>)
Namespace(a      = <http://www.semanticweb.org/ontologies/2009/4/scho.

Ontology( <http://www.semanticweb.org/ontologies/2009/4/scho.owl>


  Class(a:ChangeSet partial
   owl:Thing)
  Class(a:Document partial
   owl:Thing)
  Class(a:Operation partial
   owl:Thing)
  Class(a:Patch partial
   owl:Thing)
  Class(a:PullFeed partial
   owl:Thing)
  Class(a:PushFeed partial
   owl:Thing)
  Class(a:Site partial
   owl:Thing)
  Class(owl:Thing partial)

  ObjectProperty(a:hasDoc
   domain(a:Site)
   range(a:Document))
  ObjectProperty(a:hasOp
   domain(a:Patch)
   range(a:Operation))
```

```
ObjectProperty ( a : hasPatch
 domain ( a : ChangeSet )
 range ( a : Patch ) )
ObjectProperty ( a : hasPull
 domain ( a : Site )
 range ( a : PullFeed ) )
ObjectProperty ( a : hasPullHead
 domain ( a : PullFeed )
 range ( a : ChangeSet ) )
ObjectProperty ( a : hasPush
 domain ( a : Site )
 range ( a : PushFeed ) )
ObjectProperty ( a : hasPushHead
 domain ( a : PushFeed )
 range ( a : ChangeSet ) )
ObjectProperty ( a : head
 domain ( a : Document )
 range ( a : Patch ) )
ObjectProperty ( a : inPullFeed
 domain ( a : ChangeSet )
 range ( a : PullFeed ) )
ObjectProperty ( a : inPushFeed
 domain ( a : ChangeSet )
 range ( a : PushFeed ) )
ObjectProperty ( a : onDoc
 domain ( a : Patch )
 range ( a : Document ) )
ObjectProperty ( a : previous
 domain ( a : Patch )
 range ( a : Patch ) )
ObjectProperty ( a : previousChangeSet
 domain ( a : ChangeSet )
 range ( a : ChangeSet ) )

)
```

Common Ground and Small Group Interaction in Large Virtual World Gatherings

N. Sadat Shami, Thomas Erickson, Wendy A. Kellogg
IBM TJ Watson Research Center, United States of America
{sadat, snowfall, wkellogg} @ us.ibm.com

Abstract. Virtual worlds can allow conversational participants to achieve common ground in situations where the information volume and need for clarification is low. We argue in favor of this assertion through an examination of a semi-structured activity among hundreds of users held in a virtual world. Through the idea of implicit grounding, we argue that the affordances of contextualized space, knowledge of the social occasion, and creative self presentation allowed attendees to achieve common ground in a low information volume, low clarification need activity. We use the success of the event to re-examine and extend Clark and Brennan's work on grounding in communication.

Introduction

The term common ground refers to the mutual understanding among communicators about what is being discussed (Clark & Brennan, 1991). The interactive process through which communicators exchange evidence in order to reach mutual understanding is referred to as grounding (Clark & Wilkes-Gibbs, 1986). Establishing common ground has been shown to be essential in the success of collaborative activity (e.g., Kraut et al., 2002).

According to Clark and Brennan's framework of key attributes that constrain grounding in conversation (Clark & Brennan, 1991), virtual worlds should have significant liabilities. For example, even though user avatars are co-present in a virtual world, a user may step away from puppeting her avatar, causing her to 'be there without really being there.' Or multi-tasking may achieve the same result. Also, adjacent users in virtual worlds may see different people or objects depending on their camera settings. Technical difficulties aside, these are some of the reasons virtual worlds have not been more successful as a collaboration platform (Erickson et al., 2011).

In keeping with this, we would expect users of virtual world technology to suffer from a lack of common ground and from the extra effort required to achieve it. However, as the results reported in this paper will show, and consistent with the most recent work on grounding constraints in computer mediated communication (CMC), the ability of virtual worlds to support grounding may be less constrained than theory would predict. The affordances of contextualized space, and situational characteristics such as knowledge of the occasion and self-presentation in virtual worlds may facilitate grounding, particularly if the amount and type of information to be communicated and the need for clarification is low.

In this paper, we draw on the concept of 'grounding needs' (Birnholtz et al., 2005) – the amount of ambiguity that must be resolved in the negotiation of common ground – and show how grounding was achieved in a semi-structured event held in a virtual world. Understanding the situations and processes that facilitated grounding can assist designers of virtual worlds and virtual events, and improve interactions in virtual worlds.

The rest of the paper is organized as follows. We review related work on common ground in CMC. We then argue how grounding and small group interaction can be achieved in certain situations in virtual worlds and demonstrate this empirically. Finally, we conclude with a discussion and a set of implications.

Related Work

There has been considerable work on how grounding is achieved through various CMC technologies. Research has shown that visual information can reduce the verbal communication needed to achieve grounding by offloading it to non-verbal channels (e.g., Gergle, Kraut & Fussell, 2004; Kraut, Fussell & Siegel, 2003). Veinott and colleagues (1999) found that video helped non-native speakers achieve common ground through non-verbal gestures. Birnholtz and colleagues (2005) show how grounding was achieved through chat in a large, geographically distributed ad hoc group. It seems the only CMC technology left to study in relation to its effect on grounding is virtual world technology.

To the best of our knowledge, there has been little work exploring how the affordances of virtual worlds may help or hinder grounding. Bowers and colleagues (1996) looked at the nature of turn-taking and how user embodiments are used in the MASSIVE system (Greenhalgh & Benford, 1995), but did not investigate the process of grounding. Kelly and colleagues (2004) describe an experiment comparing the process of establishing common ground in shared visual spaces for real and virtual environments. Traum and Rickel (2002) describe the design of an embodied agent and its dialog model for successfully engaging in conversations, including establishing common ground. Without specifically investigating grounding, several researchers have discussed the issues that arise when virtual worlds are used for collaboration (e.g. Fraser et al., 1999; Heldal et al., 2005; Hindmarsh et al., 1998). We contribute to this literature by identifying situations and processes through which virtual worlds may allow grounding.

There have been various uses of spatial metaphors in structuring interaction among collaborators (see Dourish, 2006 for a review). Examples of such work include media spaces (e.g., Bly, Harrison & Irwin, 1993) and spatial video conferencing (e.g., Sellen, Buxton & Arnott, 1992). Within collaborative virtual environments (CVEs), spatial structures provide a context for reference (Benford et al., 1995) and allow partitioning of the environment into rooms, buildings and zones that may facilitate social interaction (Benford & Greenhalgh, 1997). We draw on these concepts of the use of space and place as a resource for structuring small group interaction in large virtual gatherings.

Extending Clark and Brennan's Common Ground Framework to Virtual Worlds

Grounding in conversation can be achieved through language, as well as physical space (Clark & Marshall, 1981). Linguistic co-presence allows grounding because participants in the conversation are privy to the same utterances. Physical co-presence allows grounding because participants inhabit the same physical setting (Clark & Marshall, 1981). Additionally, participants possess prior knowledge and beliefs, and while those may not be uttered, they nonetheless influence grounding. We will use these ideas of grounding through the physical environment and personal knowledge to develop our argument.

Clark and Brennan present eight properties of media that act as constraints on the grounding process: copresence, visibility, audibility, cotemporality, simultaneity, sequentiality, reviewability, and revisability (Clark & Brennan, 1991). They consider common ground to have been established when "The contributor and his or her partners mutually believe that the partners have understood what the contributor meant to a criterion sufficient for current purposes" (Clark & Brennan, 1991). Birnholtz and colleagues correctly identify that the key phrase here is "sufficient for current purposes" (Birnholtz et al., 2005). They develop the argument that situational characteristics (e.g., asymmetries in access to information by conversational participants), not just media properties, affect *grounding needs*. In particular, they state that the amount and complexity of information needed to be exchanged, and the amount of clarification necessary, define appropriate communication strategies. In situations where the information to be exchanged is low or uncomplicated and the need for clarification is low, the grounding needs are also low.

We argue that the affordances of contextualized 'places in spaces' combined with participants' understanding of the interaction occasion, and their creative self-presentation in the virtual world provide implicit grounding. We use implicit grounding to refer to the situation where at the *beginning* of a conversation, interlocutors draw on their physical environment, the social situation at hand, and the affordances of the virtual world to create common ground. Participants obviously need to update their common ground moment by moment through questions or clarifications as conversations progress. Nonetheless, grounding can be achieved even when interlocutors do not know each other.

According to the principle of 'least collaborative effort' (Clark & Wilkes-Gibbs, 1986), speakers and listeners will strive to use the least amount of joint effort required to achieve their conversational goals. Thus when location in a particular place or participation in a particular event provides evidence of others' understanding, both speakers and listeners will make use of this evidence to the extent possible to reduce their collaborative effort. For example, if a speaker can see that addressee(s) have gathered in a place reserved for a particular purpose, such as a poster booth, they may rely on that visual evidence instead of producing spoken evidence. If the goal of the interaction is to create new connections and renew existing ones in addition to information exchange, interlocutors will try to make each other feel welcome, to be helpful, and to show interest in each other's work. Therefore, the use of place and situation not only makes language more efficient, but it may also eliminate the need for some language or actions.

Implicit Grounding in Virtual Worlds

Clark and Brennan (1991) mention two types of coordination required for collective action: content and process. Coordination of content depends on a shared understanding of the subject (know that). Coordination of process depends on a shared understanding of the rules, procedures, timing, and manner in which the interaction will be conducted (know how). Convertino and colleagues (2009) studied content common ground and process common ground in the context of teamwork. Here we use it as a lens to understand interactions in virtual worlds.

Implicit grounding in virtual worlds relies on both content and process common ground. An important type of content common ground is identity information which can by conveyed through a user's name and avatar appearance. Identity can also include position, background, role and expertise. In social situations where newcomers are involved, identity information is particularly crucial in knowing with whom to connect and in creating a positive impression. For example, the use of real names conveys identity, and can be used for looking someone up in a corporate directory, providing an implicit source of content common ground. Process common ground can be created through situational information available in a virtual world environment. For instance, in a poster session, it is understood that every poster has a *presenter* whose role is to stand in the vicinity of a poster display and wait for *visitors*. It is understood that a poster's presenter *gives a brief explanation* of the poster to visitors who signal interest by moving into the vicinity of the poster, and that visitors may *interrupt with questions*. It is understood that visitors may *arrive* at any point, and *depart* at any point, and that they will generally move through the posters area looking at different posters. This is important because it enables participants to enter the situation knowing how to act, rather than having to figure it out as the situation unfolds. In such a manner, process common ground enables more efficient communication by drawing on people's pre-existing notions of interaction.

Case Study

Through the case study presented here, we will show how a semi-structured activity requiring low information / low clarification – a poster session – provided conversational grounding for a large number of users and interactions.

Setting

This research was part of a larger evaluation of a distributed conference that used web conferencing and virtual world technologies. The conference brought together the technical leadership of IBM at the annual meeting of an organization known as the Academy of Technology. All 800 members of the Academy, and some guests, were invited to the conference; 502 attended. The conference consisted of plenary sessions conducted through a web conferencing tool; keynotes, poster sessions and socials in Second Life[1]; and online text-based discussions. For this study, we focus on the use of Second Life for the poster sessions, as that was considered to be the most successful activity of the conference (Erickson et al., 2011). Our goal is to unpack how participants of a semi-structured activity such as a poster session achieved grounding.

Poster Sessions in Second Life

The Second Life virtual world we studied differed from the public version in two important ways. First, it was accessible only from behind IBM's firewall, limiting participation to authorized employees. Second, avatars were identified with real names taken from the corporate directory.

---

[1] Second Life is a Registered Trademark of Linden Lab, Inc.

Figure 1. Birds' eye view of the poster halls with the directory in the middle and individual posters along boulevards.

Figure 2. The poster directory displaying thumbnails of posters.

The poster sessions were set along an island on Second Life. Figures 1 and 2 show the setup for poster sessions. As can be seen, the poster area had a central directory with a wall of abstracts that could teleport users to particular posters.

Users could also walk along a boulevard and browse posters at will. This promoted social and unplanned interaction through the introduction of a public and socially neutral area through which people could move en route to their destinations. Poster booths were voice isolated, meaning that conversation in a poster booth did not carry outside the booth. This enabled focused interaction between the poster presenter and attendees. Users walking the boulevard could see who was present in a booth, but could not hear them. This is shown in Figure 3. The boulevard design supported the kinds of conversation that occur in hallways, coffee rooms and lounges in the physical world without interfering with the poster presentations. In total, there were 9 poster sessions held across 11 time zones throughout the 3 days of the conference. Poster presenters were required to present twice; once in their own time zone and once in another. The vast majority of presenters were either newly elected members of the Academy or invited guests. A total of 103 attendees presented posters.

Figure 3. Navigating a poster session. Users could see where activity is occurring (but not hear) and decide to join or not.

Method

We used participant observation and semi-structured interviews. All authors observed the poster sessions, taking field notes and screenshots. We interviewed 30 randomly selected informants using a semi-structured protocol. Interviewees were from 6 countries; 24 were male, 6 female. Interviews lasted 30 to 45 minutes, and all were recorded and transcribed. Data were analyzed by repeatedly listening to recordings and working over transcripts to extract emergent themes.

Results

We use the CoFIRe model (Erickson et al., 2011) to analyze how implicit grounding was created in the poster session. CoFIRe (Coalescence, Focused Interaction, Remixing) begins with Goffman's observations of "accessible encounters" (Goffman, 1963). Here Goffman considers the case of a very large gathering that lacks a common focus (such as a party) within which smaller focused interactions occur (e.g., groups of people chatting). Whereas Goffman is primarily concerned with individual groups, and problems such as how groups maintain focused interaction via processes such as shielding, CoFIRe takes a macro view of the gathering as a whole.

CoFIRe views large gatherings as consisting of three processes that operate in parallel: the coalescence of small groups from the larger gathering; focused interaction among members of a small group; and remixing, where one or more members of a small group disengage and 'browse' the larger gathering, seeking a new group to join. All three of these processes are important because in conjunction they have the potential to expose one person to a steady stream of people. As one attendee said *"Posters are better than a conference call or even a video conference because you can get more people in"* [P22, Male, USA].

Coalescence

One interaction problem that large unfocused gatherings must resolve is how to support the coalescence of groups that are small enough to engage in a focused interaction. The concept of a poster session is, in essence, a solution to this problem. A poster session provides a series of spaces and nuclei for small group interactions, and a set of roles and rules for conducting such interactions. The designers of the posters area went to great lengths to evoke real world poster sessions, and the expectations that accompany them. In the context of the Academy poster sessions, the main interaction problem individuals needed to solve was deciding which poster to attend. While the poster directory – a wall with a series of poster thumbnails (Figure 2) and teleportation provided one approach, many participants choose to stroll along the boulevard between posters (Figure 1). Some paid attention to where the 'crowds' were:

"I could actually see a lot of people hanging out in one poster area which again makes you curious... so you also go to spend time there." [P15, Male, India]

Others reported being drawn in when they saw people they knew:

"If I saw a person I knew who was looking at a poster that was a natural magnet ... because I knew who this person was and what their interests were." [P12, Male, USA]

A few said they went in when they saw presenters with no one to talk to because they felt sorry for them. Some participants took extra measures to project their real identity by attaching photos to their avatars or name bubbles (Figure 4).

Figure 4. User appropriation of avatar faces. Users replaced avatar faces with real pictures (left) or let them float on top of their heads (right).

One participant even designed "body armor" out of his slides so that he could present his poster anywhere:

"I attached a large transparent box to my body and put [in] some illustrative slides. Afterwards I bumped into [person's name]. And I whipped [out] my presentation body armor and showed her some of the slides." [P17, Male, USA]

Focused Interaction

A second interaction problem that must be solved is how a small group can carry out a focused interaction in the context of a larger gathering. One approach that Goffman refers to is shielding – a way to protect an interaction from the relative chaos of the larger interaction in which it is embedded. In the poster sessions this was achieved by the creation of 'sonic shields' around each poster booth so that visitors outside could see what was going on but not hear the discussion. Respondents remarked that this interaction worked really well:

"And I loved that when you left you couldn't hear, and when you came in you could hear. That was fabulously done." [P2, Male, USA]

This feature was particularly appreciated because the social gatherings – another activity in the same conference – lacked such shielding (because they lacked demarcated spaces for small groups) and had too much overlapping talk to allow effective small group conversation (Erickson et al., 2011).

Once one or more visitors were present, the shared understanding of how to conduct a poster session dictated what happened. Presenters took the lead, and often relied on tactics from their real world experience:

"As they came in I'd say hello and ask how they're doing. So I used the same social techniques that I'd use in the real world to draw people in. ... The only limitation is that you can't see their expression or read their body language, so that was a little harder." [P25, Female, USA]

Even so, presenters did what they could to interact 'naturally' with their visitors. This is evident from the most common complaint of poster presenters, who reported being annoyed by the awkwardness of having to turn their avatar one way to look at slides and another way to look at the visitors. In face to face situations this is simple to do, but in the virtual environment with its narrower field of view and more cumbersome avatar control, it is not so easy.

One presentation tactic that did work reasonably well was trying to understand to whom a presenter was speaking. This was facilitated by the fact that the Academy conference was designed to display visitors' real names, and many informants reported looking up the names of their visitors in the corporate directory while they were interacting in the virtual world. As one said:

"I present my poster differently depending on who I am talking to – an engineer I might use more technical information; if I know they're a top executive in sales I'll talk very differently to them about how this technical idea might affect their sales. So I felt it was better – I wanted to focus more on the names, and I was writing down names, and matching them with [the corporate directory]" [P25, Female, USA]

To facilitate this sort of behavior, some attendees even wore a floating badge that linked to an online profile.

Remixing

The final interaction problem that must be solved is how a member of a focused interaction can first break off the focused engagement, and second 'browse' the gathering to find a new group to join. While the concept of a poster session eases many interaction problems associated with large gatherings, it does little to provide support for breaking off an engagement, other than the shared understanding that interactions around posters are generally brief ones. While visitors might take advantage of the arrival of new visitors to depart, the poster sessions often weren't that crowded. In the absence of new arrivals, often departure would be mediated by a closing comment like:

"Okay that was nice (presenter name)! So I will leave you to it. Thanks for that and I'll definitely get in touch with you."

After leaving, visitors were back in the aisles between posters. Many reported that they moved along the aisles, browsing the posters as they went:

"I walked down the hall and I looked at what the poster topic was and who the presenter was." [P9, Female, USA]

This was also a chance to have serendipitous encounters with other visitors:

"I really liked that – I ran into people, and that's the one thing that makes the virtual world stand out to me. ... You're not asking them to make time for you, it's not like scheduling a call... They were there and you were there at the same time: it's accidental, a serendipity kind of thing." [P9, Female, USA]

Respondents reported that bumping into people one knew happened most during the poster sessions. It was an informal way of getting to meet colleagues from different countries across the world. Interacting with strangers also occurred the most during these sessions. The informal setting of the poster session and the fact that people were there to mix and talk facilitated conversation. According to one interviewee:

"What makes it different is if there are people there I don't know, if it's not a poster session I'm probably not as apt to reach out and say 'hey, I'm here, talk to me'. I have to have a reason for talking to someone, right?" [P11, Female, USA]

Discussion and Conclusion

In the wake of a study of a large virtual conference (Erickson et al., 2011) we were struck by the participants' nearly unanimous appreciation of the conference's poster sessions. Many informants expressed surprise at how well the posters worked, and how similar it felt to a face to face poster session. One said:

"I seriously almost felt like I was there – it was amazing! I've done a lot of posters in real life, and you almost got that same feeling because you could see people walking by. When I first got there, someone I knew flew down to say hello and it was just so cool bumping into them. And then when I gave my poster, I could see people walking by, and you got the same feeling: are they gonna stop to see it, are they going to come in? [P25, Female, USA]

Yet this comment, and others like it, were made despite widespread infelicities ranging from technical problems to the cumbersome nature of gesturing and moving about. Why did posters work so well, in spite of many obvious problems?

This question lead to the current study, in which we examined the poster sessions of the conference using the theoretical construct of grounding developed by Clark and his colleagues. In particular, we drew on work by Birnholtz and colleagues (2005) that develops the notion of grounding needs, and argues that in certain situations – when the need for information and clarification is low – quite restricted communications channels can suffice to achieve grounding. This suggested looking at poster sessions with particular attention to their grounding needs.

The paper argues that the success of the poster session is due to implicit grounding – common ground that is established before conversation actually begins. Implicit grounding is achieved in different ways for different types of information. Content common ground was achieved by personal information such as participants' avatars, and by the ability of other participants' to use the names displayed by the avatars as an index into an associated corporate directory. This information was critical because a basic aim of the conference was to create connections between participants. Content common ground also existed due to Academy members' understanding of the structure and purpose of the annual meeting – for example, the tradition of newly elected members and invited guests giving poster presentations. Process common ground was achieved through the design and collective use of the environment. The virtual environments mimicry of features from face to face poster sessions (slides, booths, aisles), and their use by participants (formally dressed presenters, crowds of visitors in booths, visitors wandering the aisles) helped invoke appropriate behavioral norms. Both types of implicit grounding, by making it clear who was present and what was going on, reduced the need for verbal communication.

An important lesson of this work is that virtual world design is more than window dressing or eye candy. Done properly, it can provide implicit grounding, and thus provide some compensation for the technical and interactional problems of today's virtual world technology.

However, to achieve this and provide implicit grounding, the design must be done strategically. First, designers must be clear on the fundamental goals of the event they are designing. Is the aim to create persistent connections between participants? Is it to enable one to present information to others? Is it meant to foster equal exchange between different participants? Is it meant to entertain? The basic goals, whatever they are, will shape the design. Second, designers must understand their audience, that is, the likely participants in the event and the expectations they may bring to it. The key question is what knowledge are participants likely to have in common? It is this pre-existing mutual knowledge that has the potential to act as common ground. In this case study, poster sessions worked well not because there is something magical about poster sessions, but because participants already knew what poster sessions were and how to behave in them. Finally, designers must create artifacts and environments that evoke their audience's common knowledge and that draw their participants into recognizable patterns of interaction.

References

Benford, S., Bowers, J., Fahl, L. E., Greenhalgh, C., and Snowdon, D. (1995): 'User embodiment in collaborative virtual environments', in Proc. CHI 1995, ACM Press, pp. 242-249.

Benford, S., and Greenhalgh, C. (1997): 'Introducing Third Party Objects into the Spatial Model of Interaction', in Proc. ECSCW 1997, Kluwer Academic Publishers, pp. 189-204.

Birnholtz, J. P., Finholt, T. A., Horn, D. B., and Bae, S. J. (2005): 'Grounding needs: achieving common ground via lightweight chat in large, distributed, ad-hoc groups', in Proc. CHI 2005, ACM Press, pp. 21-30.

Bly, S. A., Harrison, S. R., and Irwin, S. (1993): 'Media spaces: bringing people together in a video, audio, and computing environment', *Commun. ACM*, vol. 36, no. 1, pp. 28-46.

Bowers, J., Pycock, J., and O'Brien, J. (1996): *'Talk and embodiment in collaborative virtual environments'*, in *Proc. CHI 1996*, ACM Press, pp. 58-65.

Clark, H. H., and Brennan, S. E. (1991): 'Grounding in communication', in L. B. Resnick, J. M. Levine & S. Teasley (eds.): *Perspectives on socially shared cognition* (APA, Washington, 1991, pp. 127-149.

Clark, H. H., and Marshall, C. E. (1981): 'Definite reference and mutual knowledge.', in A. K. Joshi, B. L. Webber & I. A. Sag (eds.): *Elements of discourse understanding* (Cambridge University Press, Cambridge, 1981, pp. 10-63.

Clark, H. H., and Wilkes-Gibbs, D. (1986): 'Referring as a collaborative process', *Cognition*, vol. 22, pp. 1-39.

Convertino, G., Mentis, H. M., Rosson, M. B., Slavkovic, A., and Carroll, J. M. (2009): *'Supporting content and process common ground in computer-supported teamwork'*, in *Proc. CHI 2009*, ACM Press, pp. 2339-2348.

Dourish, P. (2006): *'Re-space-ing place: "place" and "space" ten years on'*, in *Proc. CSCW 2006*, ACM Press, pp. 299-308.

Erickson, T., Shami, N. S., Kellogg, W. A., and Levine, D. (2011): *'Synchronous Interaction Among Hundreds: An Evaluation of a Conference in an Avatar-based Virtual Environment'*, in *Proc. CHI 2011*, ACM Press.

Fraser, M., Benford, S., Hindmarsh, J., and Heath, C. (1999): *'Supporting awareness and interaction through collaborative virtual interfaces'*, in *Proc. UIST 1999*, ACM Press, pp. 27-36.

Gergle, D., Kraut, R. E., and Fussell, S. R. (2004): *'Action as language in a shared visual space'*, in *Proc. CSCW 2004*, ACM Press, pp. 487-496.

Greenhalgh, C., and Benford, S. (1995): 'MASSIVE: a collaborative virtual environment for teleconferencing', *ACM Trans. Comput.-Hum. Interact.*, vol. 2, no. 3, pp. 239-261.

Heldal, I., Steed, A., Spante, M., Schroeder, R., Bengtsson, S., and Partanen, M. (2005): 'Successes and Failures in Co-Present Situations', *Presence: Teleoperators & Virtual Environments*, vol. 14, no. 5, pp. 563-579.

Hindmarsh, J., Fraser, M., Heath, C., Benford, S., and Greenhalgh, C. (1998): *'Fragmented interaction: establishing mutual orientation in virtual environments'*, in *Proc. CSCW 1998*, ACM Press, pp. 217-226.

Kelly, J. W., Beall, A. C., and Loomis, J. M. (2004): 'Perception of Shared Visual Space: Establishing Common Ground in Real and Virtual Environments', *Presence: Teleoperators & Virtual Environments*, vol. 13, no. 4, pp. 442-450.

Kraut, R., Fussell, S. R., Brennan, S. E., and Siegel, J. (2002): 'Understanding the effects of proximity on collaboration: Implications for technologies to support remote collaborative work', in P. Hinds & S. Kiesler (eds.): *Distributed Work* (MIT Press, Cambridge, MA, 2002, pp. 137-162.

Kraut, R., Fussell, S. R., and Siegel, J. (2003): 'Visual information as a conversational resource in collaborative physical tasks', *Hum.-Comput. Interact.*, vol. 18, pp. 13-49.

Sellen, A., Buxton, B., and Arnott, J. (1992): *'Using spatial cues to improve videoconferencing'*, in *Proc. CHI 1992*, ACM Press, pp. 651-652.

Traum, D., and Rickel, J. (2002): *'Embodied agents for multi-party dialogue in immersive virtual worlds'*, in *Proc. AAMAS 2002*, ACM Press, pp. 766-773.

Veinott, E. S., Olson, J., Olson, G. M., and Fu, X. (1999): *'Video helps remote work: speakers who need to negotiate common ground benefit from seeing each other'*, in *Proc. CHI 1999*, ACM Press, pp. 302-309.

Collaboration in Augmented Reality: How to establish coordination and joint attention?

Christian Schnier, Karola Pitsch, Angelika Dierker, Thomas Hermann
Faculty of Technology, Applied Informatics, Bielefeld University, Germany
{cschnier}{kpitsch}{adierker}{thermann}@techfak.uni-bielefeld.de

Abstract. We present an initial investigation from a semi-experimental setting, in which an HMD-based AR-system has been used for real-time collaboration in a task-oriented scenario (design of a museum exhibition). Analysis points out the specific conditions of interacting in an AR environment and focuses on one particular practical problem for the participants in coordinating their interaction: how to establish joint attention towards the same object or referent. Analysis allows insights into how the pair of users begins to familarize with the environment, the limitations and opportunities of the setting and how they establish new routines for e.g. solving the 'joint attention'-problem.

Introduction

Over the last 15 years a range of initiatives has emerged that develop and explore Augmented Reality (AR) systems, in which the user's perception of the world is overlayed with additional, digital information (Caudell & Mizell 1992; Azuma 1997). Most commonly, these systems focus on augmenting the user's visual perception by video taping in real-time the user's environment and displaying this image together with overlayed additional information on a screen. To achieve this effect, existing AR-systems either (i) exploit the cameras/displays of recent mobile phone technlogies or (ii) equip the user with specialized glasses, so-called headmounted displays (HMD). The first approach benefits from using an already available technology and easy integration into the user's everyday practices, which is reflected in the current boom of applications for navigation, interactive tourist guides etc. The second approach allows to support richer and more complex activities, during which the user could freely use his hands to manipulate objects, which is relevant e.g. in aircraft maintainance where 3D construction plans are made available, in situ, to the engineer. Whilst existing research predominantly focuses on individual users, little is known about AR-technologies in collaborative settings.

If we want to explore AR-systems using HMDs supporting real-time collaboration of physically co-present interaction partners, this creates particular conditions for the interaction: In comparison to natural face-to-face interaction, to wear HMDs and see the world through its lenses, results in limited access to usually available communicational resources: reduced field of view (Arthur 2000), lower resolution (Azuma 1997) and problems in determining the co-participant's focus of attention (Brennan et al. 2008). Additionally, looking through HMDs results in significantly less eye rotation and increased head orientation when attempting to focus on a given point or object (Kollenberg et al. 2008). It seems that a new prototype of mediated co-present face-to-face interaction emerges that places particular demands on the ways in which users can collaborate and organize their joint actions. A range of empirical questions and technical challenges arises: How can co-participants, under these conditions, organize their interaction and coordinate their activities? How can they establish joint attention? How could we design such collaborative AR-systems in a way as to substitute for the technological constraints and support the users' collaboration?

In this paper, we will present some initial findings from a quasi-naturalistic AR-experiment, in which we have equipped pairs of users with HMDs and asked them to jointly design a museum exhibition while arranging a set of objects (the exhibits) on a given floor plan. Our analysis will address the questions raised above and – using sequential micro-analysis stemming from Conversation Analysis – focus (1) on the specific interactional conditions that arise from this setting, (2) the ways in which users organize their (inter-)action and (3) how they start to establish new collaborative orientation routines. Finally, we will discuss the analytic results with regard to insights into communicational procedures and implications for the design of collaborative AR-systems.

Background

Endeavours to support realtime remote collaboration in the workplace have seen the development of a wide range of novel technologies, such as video-conferencing systems, media spaces or collaborative virtual environments. Empirical investigation of such systems has revealed the limitations of such technologies in comparison to unmediated face-to-face interaction: "gaze, gesture and other body movements are generally not as effective as in normal face-to-face communication" (Yamashita et al. 1999). When designing such systems, particular challenges consist in dealing with time delays caused by the technical transmission and the interdependencies of action and the physical environment. Participants in social interaction orient themselves and others in the local environment, refer to objects and its specific features, and attempt to animate and transform these for their practical purposes at hand – aspects which have shown to be highly problematic in technically mediated interaction: "the system fractures the environments of action and inadvertently undermines the participants' ability to produce, interpret, and coordinate their actions in collaboration with each other" (Luff et al. 2003: 53). For a collaborative virtual environment – which shows a range of parallels with the setup used in this paper – Fraser et al. (2000) show that differences between the experience of virtual environment and physical reality occur, e.g. reduced field of view, no haptic feedback, and technical network delays in VR setups. They suggest to render the limitations of the technology visible to the user, e.g. by artificially providing – similar to our system – information about the co-participant's field of view via an additional object projection or by giving haptic feedback in other media. Thus, comparison between the ways in which users deal with such augmentations in AR- vs. VR-setups will be interesting to investigate (Milgram & Kishino 1994).

While a few collaborative AR-setups have been proposed (Schmalstieg et al. 1996, Billinghurst et al. 2002, Dierker et al. 2009), little is known yet as to how participants can deal with the conditions implied by the technical constraints when attempting to fulfill a joint task. In fact, with the collaborative HMD-based AR-scenario, a new prototype of face-to-face communication seems to arise: On the one hand it encompasses aspects typical of face-to-face interaction: physical co-presence, shared interaction space, participants can touch, smell and hear each other and they can jointly manipulate the same objects. On the other hand, participants see the world through the eyes of a videocamera with a reduced field of view and – due to cost and computing power – mostly monoscopic vision, and virtual augmentations are not necessarily similar for both co-participants; these features are comparable to technologically mediated settings. In such co-present, but technologically mediated setting, the co-participants are faced with the task of organization their multimodal interaction (Goodwin 2000): to coordinate their actions (Deppermann & Schmidt 2006), to monitor and take into account the co-participant's current state of action (Goodwin 1980) and to establish joint attention (Kaplan & Hafner 2006). From this, the empirical questions arise as to how users can interact with each other under these specific conditions, and to which extent they might adapt or develop new procedures and interactional strategies.

AR-System for collaborative task-oriented interaction

Over the last years, we have developed an AR-system, that allows for real-time collaboration of two users and to record, intercept and manipulate the users' natural communication channels. The system encompasses the following components: HMDs with an integrated camera that captures the view from the user's perspective and passes it on as a video frame that is projected on the screen of the corresponding HMD. Similarly, audio signals can be captured with microphones and relayed via in-ear headphones. This paradigm allows to precisely record the relevant sensory information available to interacting users. This enables us to reconstruct the user's audio-visual perceptions and to gain a better understanding of their respective member's perspective in co-present interaction. We furthermore record the detailed head movements by inertial sensors worn on the head. This allows us to measure accurately amplitude, timing of head gestures such as nodding and head shaking.

Secondly, we can manipulate (modify or augment) the information streams and thus study effects of disturbances, ranging from enduced color-blindness to completely different scenes the users perceive when looking at one at the same physical object. Beyond this basic *Interception & Manipulation* functionality, we augment virtual objects on top of physical objects in the interaction space using ARToolkit (Kato & Billinghurst 1999). Specifically, for the museum planning scenario, these virtual objects are exhibit pictures shown on wedge-shaped 3D objects. As novel contribution we introduced a coupling of users by a joint-attention-support channel: each user sees by coloring of the exhibit objects whether and how much they are in the view field of their interaction partner. More precisely, the object's frame color changes from yellow (peripheral) to red (in the center of the partner's field of view). Details on this augmentation are explained in Dierker et al. (2009).

Experiment: Collaborative museum exhibition design

To investigate collaboration under the specific conditions of AR-technology, an experiment has been conducted (08/2010), in which pairs of users were asked to jointly plan a museum exhibition while arranging a set of objects (the exhibits) on a given floor plan (Pitsch & Krafft 2010, Luff et al. 2009, Dierker et al. 2011). The participants were seated face-to-face at a table, equipped with AR-glasses, microphone headsets and an inertial sensor on top of their heads. The participants were asked to carry out three subsequent tasks: (1) In a *familiarization phase* (5 minutes) the participants were asked to chat with their partner about a self-chosen topic in order to familiarize with being videotaped and wearing the devices. (2) In the following *individual phase* (with vision obstructing barrier) they were asked to individually plan a museum exhibition using a set of 8 different exhibits each (wooden blocks as material 'handles' for augmented objects sitting on top of the blocks), and arrange them on a given floor plan. (3) In the subsequent *dyadic phase*, the participants were asked to discuss their arrangement of the exhibits with their partner (without barrier) and to develop a joint solution for all 16 exhibits in one of the two identical floor plans.

The specific conditions of interacting in an AR-setting

The specific conditions of an AR-system place particular demands on collaborative action. Analysis will enable us to gain a first understanding of the extent to which the participants have to deal with a new situation, and, at the same time, build the basis for subsequent analysis in the following parts.

(1) *Dual ecology and the world's instability*: AR-settings present a dual ecology for the participants: On the one hand, they have physical access to the real world such as the table with wooden blocks and floor plan, and are in physical co-presence with the interaction partner. On the other hand, on the level of visual perception, this world is mediated through the display of the real-time video-stream and the added virtual augmentations.[1] During the interaction, this dual ecology is a mixture of stability and instability, e.g. the wooden block actually forms a stable reference point, but this is not the case in the augmented content. Consider now the short fragment F1 (Figure 1) showing the respective participants' view.

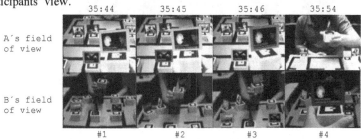

Figure 1. Participants' view

When A lifts the wooden block and presents it to B, it is visually augmented as the exhibit 'Plasmascheibe (plasma dial)' (fig. 1, #1). For participant B, however, it appears firstly as having no augmenteation, then secondly as being positioned sideways (fig. 1, #2) and thirdly, it appears as the exhibit 'Dreieck im Hause (triangles in the house)' (fig. 1, #3). Thus, at this moment of the interaction, both

---

[1] We borrow the term "dual ecology" from Kuzuoka et al. (2004), but re-define it. Kuzuoka et al. use the term for a remote collaboration setting to denote the ecology of the local site vs. that of the remote site.

participants are faced with *different* exhibits in the augmented world although referring to the same object in terms of the real world. Only after the object has been handed over from A to B, the object also appears as exhibit 'Plasmascheibe (plasma dial)' to him, while – now – being displayed sideways for A (fig. 1, #4). Thus, the participants cannot be sure to share the same representation of their interactional world, which will have consequences for the way in which they are able to refer to objects and establish joint attention. In this particular case, the observed instabilities are caused by irritations in the marker tracking due to obstruction and rotation of the objects as they occur in social interaction, and improvements in an iteration of the system are under way. However, in more subtle ways similar effects occur also in other AR-settings, so that participants generally have to deal with them to some extent.

(2) *(Dis-)Embodiment*: The dual ecology between real and virtual world and the lack of a stereoscopic view also influence the ways in which participants can deal with their own and the co-participant's bodily existence in the world. This becomes evident e.g. when they attempt to handle objects or exchange them with their co-participant. In the following fragment F2 (fig. 2), participant A presents an object to B, which he, in turn, attempts to grasp (cf. #1). Pic 2 and 3 show the orientation of his open, ready-to-grasp-hand, however, slightly disoriented to the side. In pic 4, he has repaired this action and orientation of the hand, so that in (#5) he can indeed grasp it (#6). Thus, the participants' interact under the condition of unusual tactile senses and awareness of the environment.

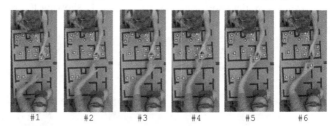

Figure 2. Grasping

(3) *Orientation and interactional coordination*: The participants have available – due to the AR-glasses – only a highly reduced field of view with a masked periphery, so that they can only either look at their co-participant or inspect (parts of) the museum plan and/or objects. Thus, focusing on the task, they are hardly aware of the partner's physical representation, body movements, head orientation etc. – aspects, which are known from face-to-face interaction, to be important resources for coordination and organizing social interaction. This places a particular demand on coordinating their actions and establishing joint attention to some object or area on the plan as shown in Fragment F3 (fig. 3). This sequence

of video-stills, i.e. #1-4, shows a point in time where participant B is looking forward to have the floor but does not have chosen a specific object group yet.

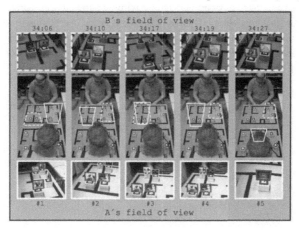

Figure 3. Participants' difficulties in coordinating their foci of attention

However, this choice has been made in #5 but participant A is not aware of it just at that moment. Because of the impossibility to coordinate their gaze direction, both interlocutors are focused on different parts of the map, except for a random gaze overlap in image #3. The physical projections of participant B are outside of participant A's field of view, and vice versa. Moreover, it is obvious that the technical highlighting support is not used here. The mutual orientation is indicated by the red highlighted object frame (#3). However, picture #4 and #5 show that the attention shift of subject B is not retraced by interlocuter A.

This demonstrates that the users' head movements cannot be used as an indicator of the co-participant's visual orientation, e.g. they are not available as communicational resources. Additionally this example suggests that orientational cues, such as leaning forward to a specific object, have only restricted interactive relevance. Similarly, the participants don't have access to facial expressions as the HMDs hide important parts of the user's face.

Organizing (inter-)action: Establishing joint attention

Fragment F4 occurs early in the third interaction phase (32s after beginning) and reveals the practical problems in establishing mutual orientation on some object. At the beginning participant B tries to orient his interlocuter A to the object 'lasershow', which he attempts to do exclusively by verbal means: "euh-well this LASERshow here;" (01). However, this verbal deictic reference turns out to not be sufficient for a precise reorientation of the co-participant. A does indeed not change her orientation, and answers with an elongated "hm:=hm", which participant B treats as only 'claiming', but not 'showing' understanding. B correctly treats her answer as not having followed his orientation and reformulates his suggestion. He adds "you see it here," (02). This time, he adds a gestural pointing to the object (#1) and designs his turn as a question, which projects the co-participant's confirmation. A indeed reacts to this second attempt by leaning forward and commenting on the indicated object.

Fragment F4 (32:53-33:00)

```
01 B:        |äh=also diese LASERshow hier;|  (0.2)
             euh=well this LASERshow here;

02 A:        |hm:=hm:-|
   B: -->    |und die |(0.2)|siehste hier,|(0.5)
             and the        you see it here,
                                 #1

03 B:        |in diesem RAUM hab ich den extra reingestellt,|
             I put it in this ROOM for a good reason,

04 B:        |<<p>mh=weil>|
             mh=because
   A:        |warte,       |
             please wait,
```

A second fragment (fragment F5) allows us to investigate the procedures of orienting attention in greater detail. It follows directly on fragment F3 (fig. 3), for which we have shown that the participants are oriented to different parts of the floorplan without being aware of the other's orientation.

Fragment F5 (34:28- 34:35)

```
01 B: -->  |<<all>.h |zum Beispiel HIER in der=in der> (.)
                #1    for example HERE in the=in the

02 B: -->  also von dir aus| OBEREN rechten ecke-|
           that is to say from your perspective in the UPPER right corner-
   A:                                             |hm?|
                                                   #2

03 B:      |da sind äh: einmal diese pfeile-|
           there are er: once this arrows-
                 #3
```

#1, 34:30 | #2, 34:33 | #3, 34:34

A's field of view | A's field of view | A's field of view

When participant B now attempts to orient B to a particular object using a combined verbal and gestural procedure – "for example HERE in the=in the" and pointing to the object – participant A is oriented to a different part of the floorplan (#1). B then repairs his action and adds a precise verbal localization: "that is to say from your perspective in the UPPER right corner" (02). It is only as a reaction to this explicit localization that A begins to re-orient. Interestingly, she looks to B's face (rarely done in our setup), sees him being oriented to his left side (#2) and then follows his gesture to the indicated location on the plan (#3). The participants thus are faced with the problem of formulating places in a way that they can be subject to a locus of shared visual focus with the co-participant. While interacting, they experience that they cannot rely on well-established procedures from their daily life, but have to be attentive to the lack of their co-participant's reaction and repair their actions to provide more information than usual. At the same time, they don't appear to repair at each stage, which means that they have to interact under the assumption that – if not otherwise signaled – their co-participant is following their actions.

Experimenting procedures and establishing routines

While the participants at the beginning of the collaborative part have to familiarize themselves with the specific conditions of the setting, during the interaction they can be seen to adapt to the specific needs and how to best collaborate with their interaction partner. In this vein, the AR-setting proposes to be a valuable setting for investigating how participants exploit the constraints of the technology and how these may lead to emerging new interactional routines. We will explore this issue by presenting the following fragment F6, in which we continue our focus on the participants' practices around establishing joint attention.

Two minutes after fragment F4, the pair of users comes to a decisive turning point in the ways in which they attempt to orient the co-participant's visual focus of attention: They give up the exclusive use of verbal deixis or verbal-plus-gestural-deixis (which have turned out to be problematic and in need of repair if no explicit point of common reference has been established before, see previous section). Instead, participant A introduces a new procedure: She lifts the object from the floor plan and presents it slightly elevated for a longer stretch of time (4 seconds), and detects that her co-participant is able to follow her orientation easily, so that – differently from the procedures shown in the previous section – no repair is required.

Fragment F6	Fragment F7

A´s field of view	B´s field of view		
#1, 35:02	#2, 35:02	#1, 36:45	#2, 36:47

In subsequent fragments, we find her re-using this procedure several times, while the previously deployed strategies diminuish. In re-using this procedure, she experiments with different ways of perfoming it until a new orientational routine has emerged that is well-functionning 'for all practical purposes' for these participants: lifting the object with more pronounced hand movements.

Thus, the participants' first attempts of establishing a joint focus of attention have provided them with a practical experience that enables them to gain a conception of the actual possibilities and limitations imposed by the technology and the ensuing specific interactional conditions.

The following fragment F7 shows this new orientation method in a distinct form as it emerges for the first time. Participant A lifts the object out of the original context, shows it to participant B, and verbally specifies it by denominating the corresponding exhibit 'triangle in the house' (#1). This enables participant B to respond adequatly by selecting the appropriate object from his plan, which he, then, places in the emerging common perceptual space (#2).

While being highly functional in orienting the co-particpant's visual focus of attention to a given object/point of reference, it also helps to solve a further problem: In this case, the exhibit, which has been pointed out by A, did not appear at first in its augmented form in participant B's field of view. By slightly turning the wooden handle this problem – caused by marker orientation and obstruction – can easily be dealt with.

Discussion

We have presented an initial investigation from an experiment, in which we have used our HMD-based AR-system for real-time collaboration in a task-oriented scenario (collaborative design of a museum exhibition). We have pointed out the specific conditions, under which the participants interact with each other, namely: (i) dual ecology and the world's instability, (ii) (dis-)embodiment, and (iii) limited access to the co-participants conduct and thus lacking information for organizing the interaction. We have then focused on one particular practical problem for the participants in coordinating their interaction, namely how to establish joint attention towards the same object or referent. Analysis has revealed two procedures and the co-participants' reactions to it. A chronological investigation of the participants' procedures and methods has lead to first observations on how the pair of users begins to familarize with the environment, the limitations and opportunities of the setting and how they can use it to establish new routines for e.g. solving the 'joint attention'-problem.

This experiment presents an important practice-based trial for our technology under new interactional conditions. It performed well, robust and stable and constitutes a solid basis for further interaction experiments. However, minor technical aspects have come to light that need addressing, in particular the stability of marker tracking in an environment where users are likely to obstruct parts of the patterns.

From our analyses some general implications for the design of HMD-based AR-settings arise: We have to exploit novel ways for dealing with the limited availability of communicational resources. Most prominently, we have to provide support for allowing a participant to access the co-participant's visual orientation in space. In the current setting the implemented method has only rarely been used for orientation by the participants. Further investigation is required into the conditions, under which such orientational cues might become relevant and usable for the participants, and to think of other forms of augmentation.

Another novel aspect emerges: the AR-setup as a tool for investigating social interaction. Our AR setup enables us to systematically intercept and manipulate a range of interactional features in real-time (vision, audio). This opens the innovative possibility to modify both auditory and visual perceptual signals as controlled variables, e.g. by introducing delays, changing frequencies or specific characteristics. This allows us to address questions such as: Up to which differences do interacting users tolerate specific disturbances? Which multimodal features of the complex holistic phenomenon 'multimodal interaction' are relevant for which kind of interactional effect? How do interacting users attempt to repair or compensate such effects? How might they change their communicative procedures and develop new interactional routines?

With our combined approach which fuses (i) a technology-driven modification of the interactional situation, (ii) semi-natural social interaction, and (iii) technical measurement of some signal streams in real-time, we gain the possibility to link qualitative micro-analysis stemming from Conversation Analysis with quantitative approaches on a larger corpus.

Acknowledgments

This work has been supported by the Collaborative Research Centre 673 *Alignment in Communication*, funded by the German Research Foundation (DFG). We are indebted to Ulrich Dausendschön-Gay for invaluable discussions.

References

Arthur, K. (2000): *Effects of field of view on performance with head-mounted displays.* Dissertation, University of North Carolina.

Azuma, R. (1997): 'A Survey of Augmented Reality', *Presence: Teleoperators and Virtual Environments*, vol. 6, no. 4, August 1997, pp. 355-385.

Billinghurst, M. and Kato, H. (2002): 'Collaborative Augmented Reality', *Communication of the ACM*, vol. 45, no. 7, 2002, pp. 64-70.

Brennan, S., Chena, X., Dickinsona, C., Neidera, M. and Zelinsky, G. (2008): 'Coordinating cognition: The costs and benefits of shared gaze during collaborative search', *Cognition*, vol. 106, no. 3, March 2008, pp. 1465-1477.

Caudell, T. and Mizell, D. (1992): *Augmented Reality: An Application of Head-Up Display Technology to Manual Manufacturing Processes*, Proceedings of the Twenty-Fifth Hawaii International Conference on System Sciences, vol. 2, January 1992, pp. 659-669.

Deppermann, A. and Schmitt, R. (2006): 'Koordination. Zur Begründung eines neues Forschungsgegenstands', in: R. Schmitt (ed.): *Koordination*. Gunter Narr Verlag Tübingen.

Dierker, A., Pitsch, K. and Hermann, T. (2011): *An augmented-reality-based scenario for the collaborative construction of an interactive museum*. Bielefeld: Bielefeld University.

Dierker, A., Bovermann, T., Hanheide, M., Hermann, T. and Sagerer, G. (2009): *A multimodal augmented reality system for alignment research*, Proceedings of the 13th International Conference on Human-Computer Interaction, pp. 422–426, San Diego, USA.

Fraser, M., Glover, T., Vaghi, I., Benford, S., Greenhalgh, C., Hindmarsh, J. and Heath, C. (2000): *Revealing the Realities of Collaborative Virtual Reality*.

Goodwin, C. (2000): 'Action and embodiment within situated human interaction', *Journal of Pragmatics*, vol. 32, no. 10, September 2000, pp. 1489- 1522.

Goodwin, Marjorie H. (1980): 'Processes of mutual monitoring implicated in the production of description sequences', *Sociological Inquiry*, vol. 50, no. 3, July 1980, pp. 303-317.

Kaplan, F. and Hafner, V. (2006): 'The challanges of joint attention', *Interaction Studies*, vol 7, no. 2, pp. 135-169.

Kato, H. and Billinghurst, M. (1999): *Marker tracking and hmd calibration for a video-based augmented reality conferencing system*, Proceedings of the 2nd IEEE and ACM International Workshop on Augmented Reality, pp. 85-94.

Kollenberg, T. et al. (2008). *Visual Search in the (Un)Real World: How Head Mounted Displays Affect Eye Movements, Head Movements and Target Detection*. ACM SIGGRAPH conference proceedings.

Kuzuoka, H., Yamazaki, K., Yamazaki, A., Kosaka, J., Suga, Y. and Heath, C. (2004): *Dual Ecologies of Robot as Communication Media: Thoughts on Coordinating Orientations and Projectability*. SIGHCI conference on Human factors in computing systems.

Luff, P. et al. (2003): 'Fractured ecologies', *Human-Computer Interaction*, vol. 18, 1, pp. 51-84.

Luff, P., Heath, C., and Pitsch, K. (2009): 'Indefinite precision: the use of artefacts-in-interaction in design work', in C. Jewitt: *The Routledge Handbook of Multimodal Analysis*, 213-224.

Milgram, P. and Kishino, F. (1994): *A Taxonomy of Mixed Reality Virtual Displays*. IEICE Transactions on Information and Systems E77-D, 9 (September 1994), pp. 1321-1329.

Pitsch, K. & Krafft, U. (2010): 'Von der emergenten Erfindung zu konventionalisiert darstellbarem Wissen. Zur Herstellung visueller Vorstellungen bei Museums-Designern', in U. Dausendschön-Gay, Ch. Domke & S. Ohlhus (eds.): *Wissen in (Inter-)Aktion*. Berlin: de Gruyter, pp. 189-222.

Schmalstieg, D., Fuhrmann, A., Szalavari, Z. and Gervautz, M. (1996). *Studierstube – An Environment for Collaboration in Augmented Reality*, in CVE '96 Workshop Proceedings, 19-20th September 1996, Nottingham, Great Britain.

Yamashita, J., Kuzuoka, H., Yamazaki, K., Miki, H., Yamazaki, A., Kato, H. and Suzuky, H. (1999): *Agora: Supporting Multi-participant Telecollaboration*, Proc. of HCI, pp. 543-547.

Index of Authors